Chris Burden

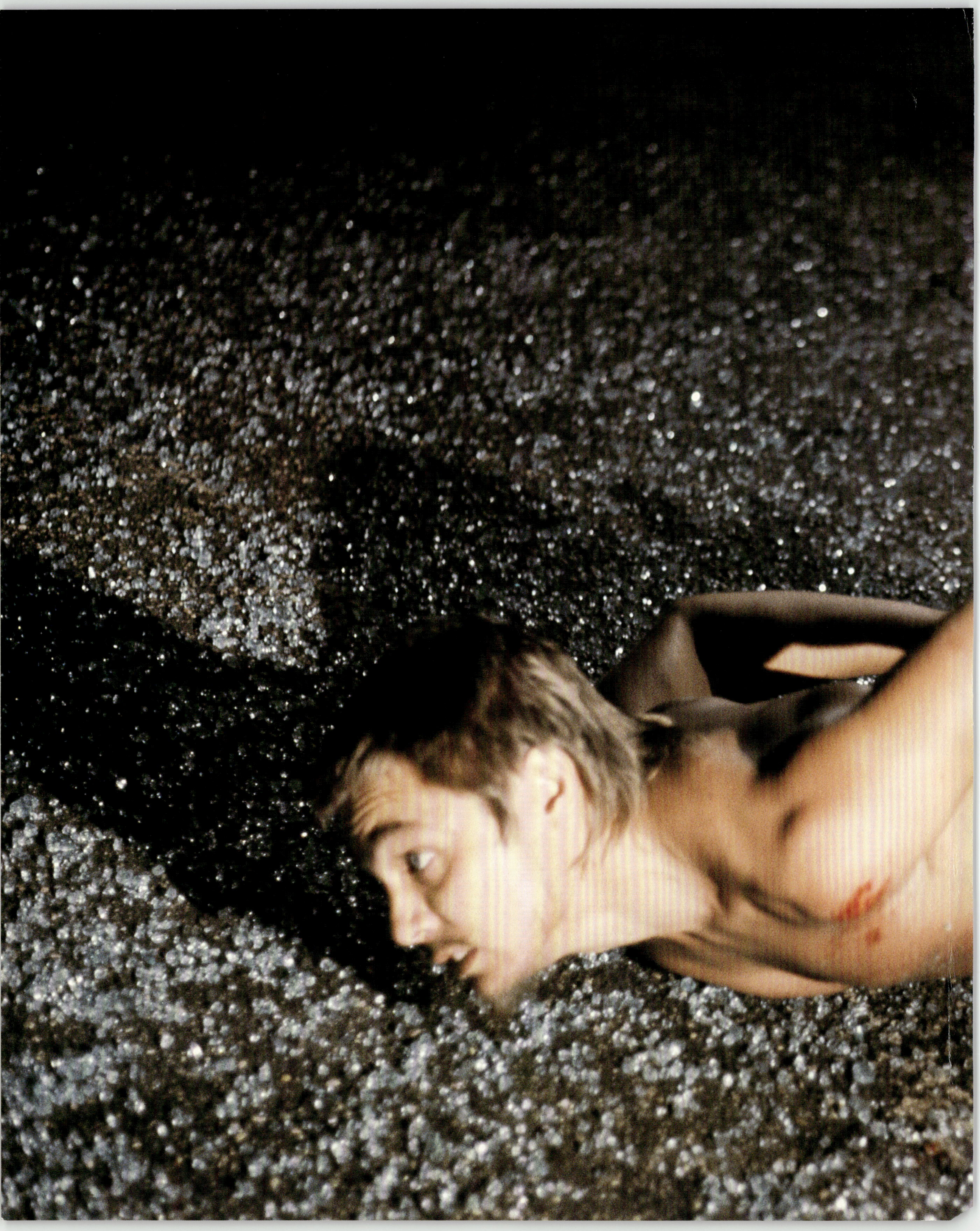

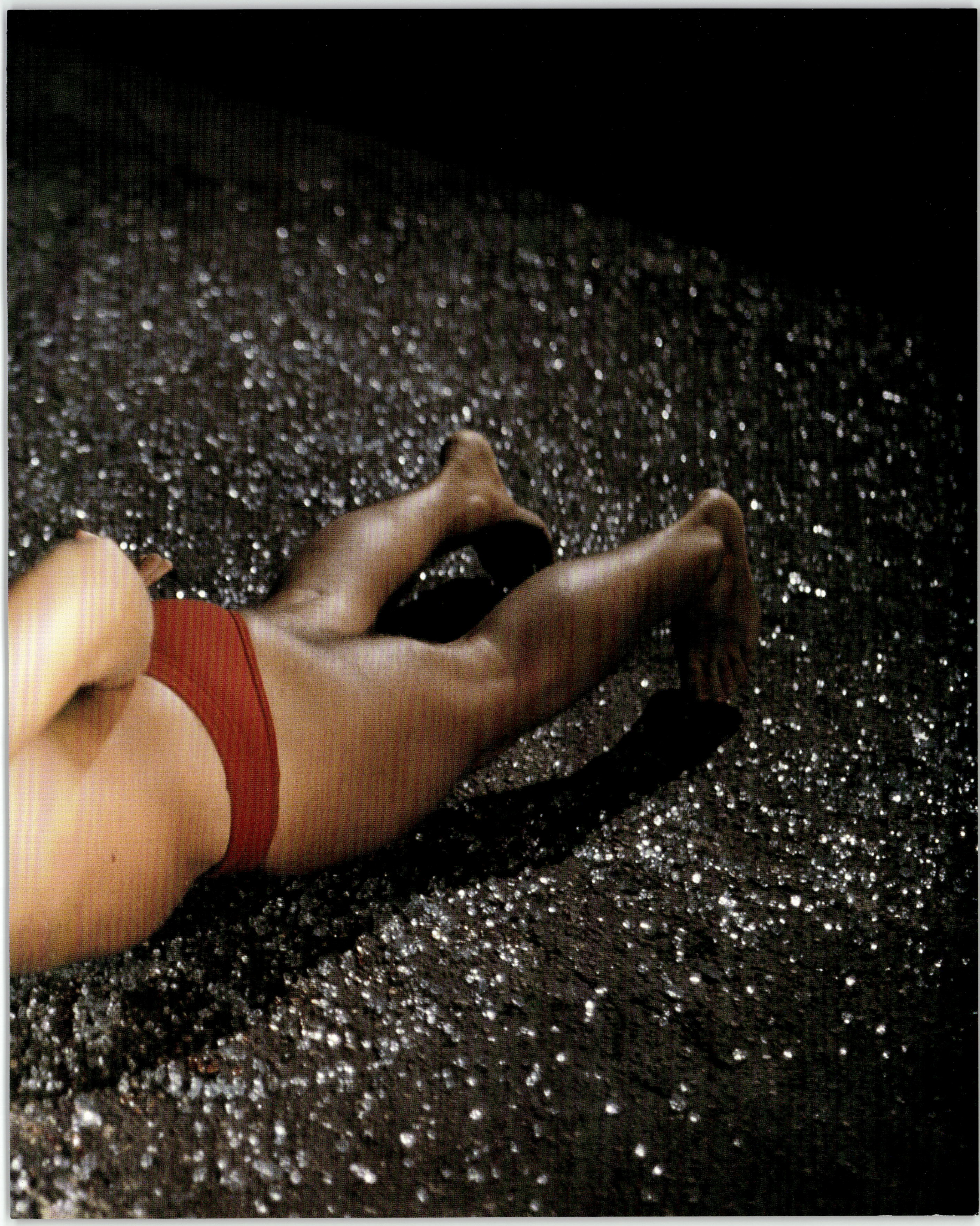

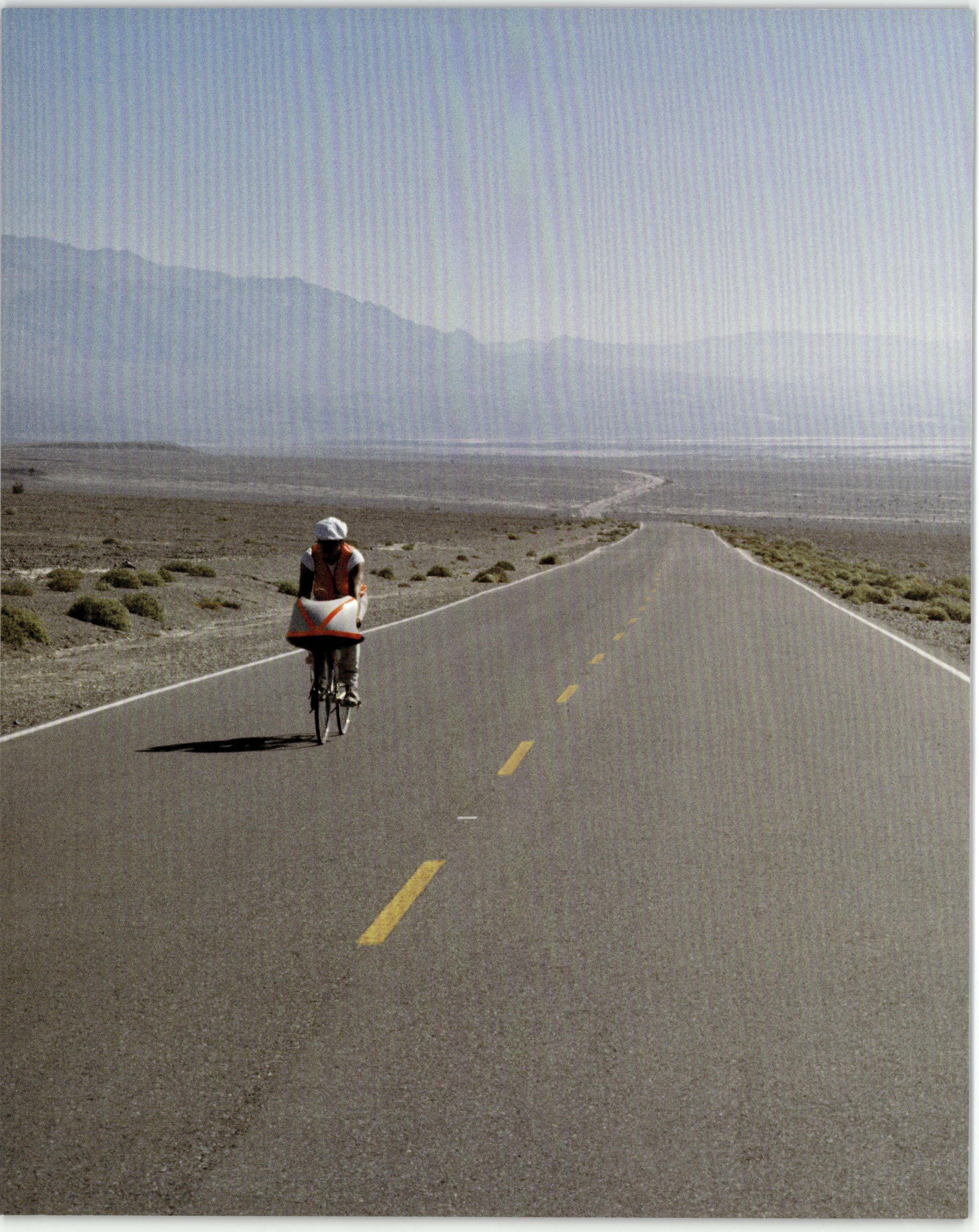

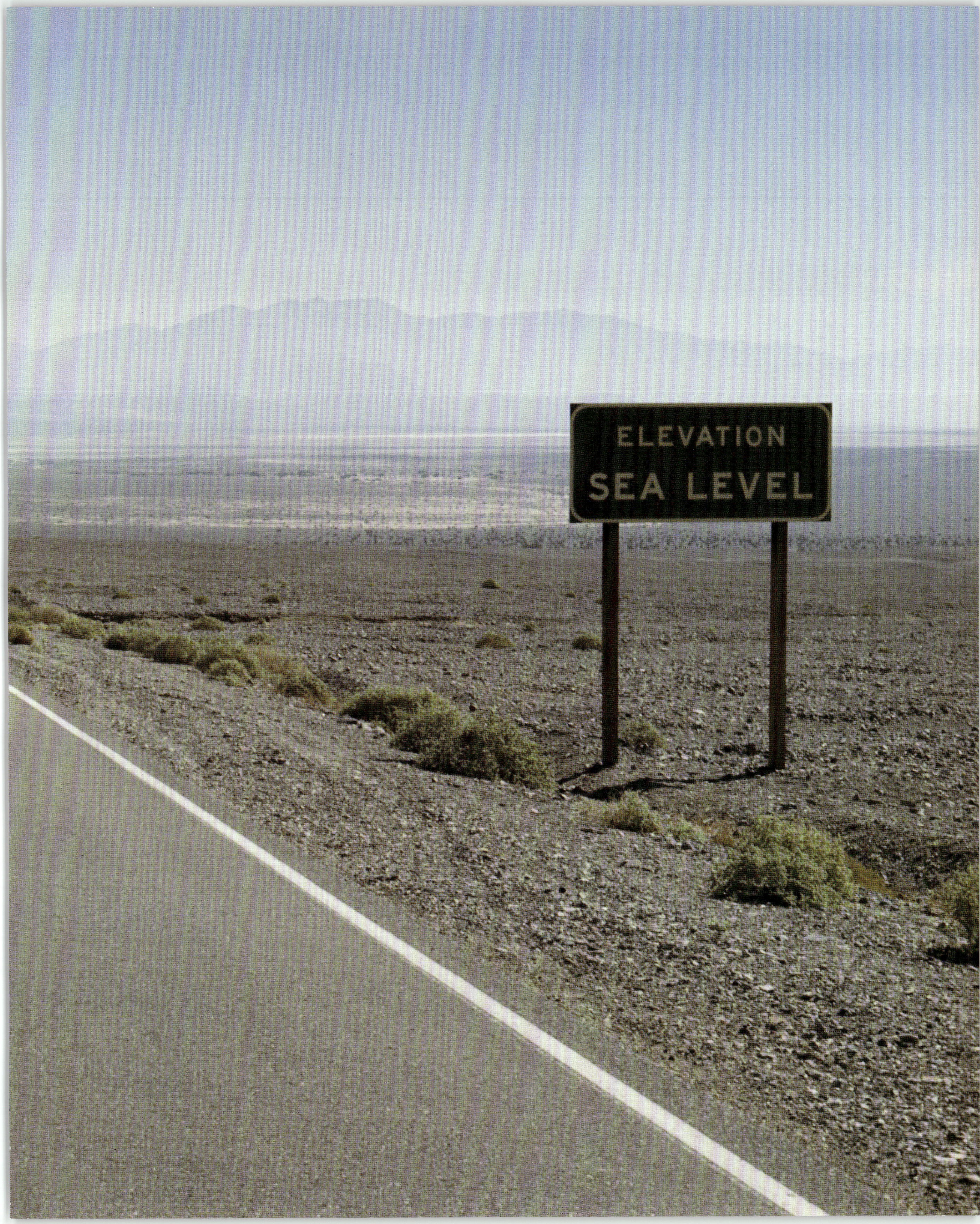
ELEVATION
SEA LEVEL

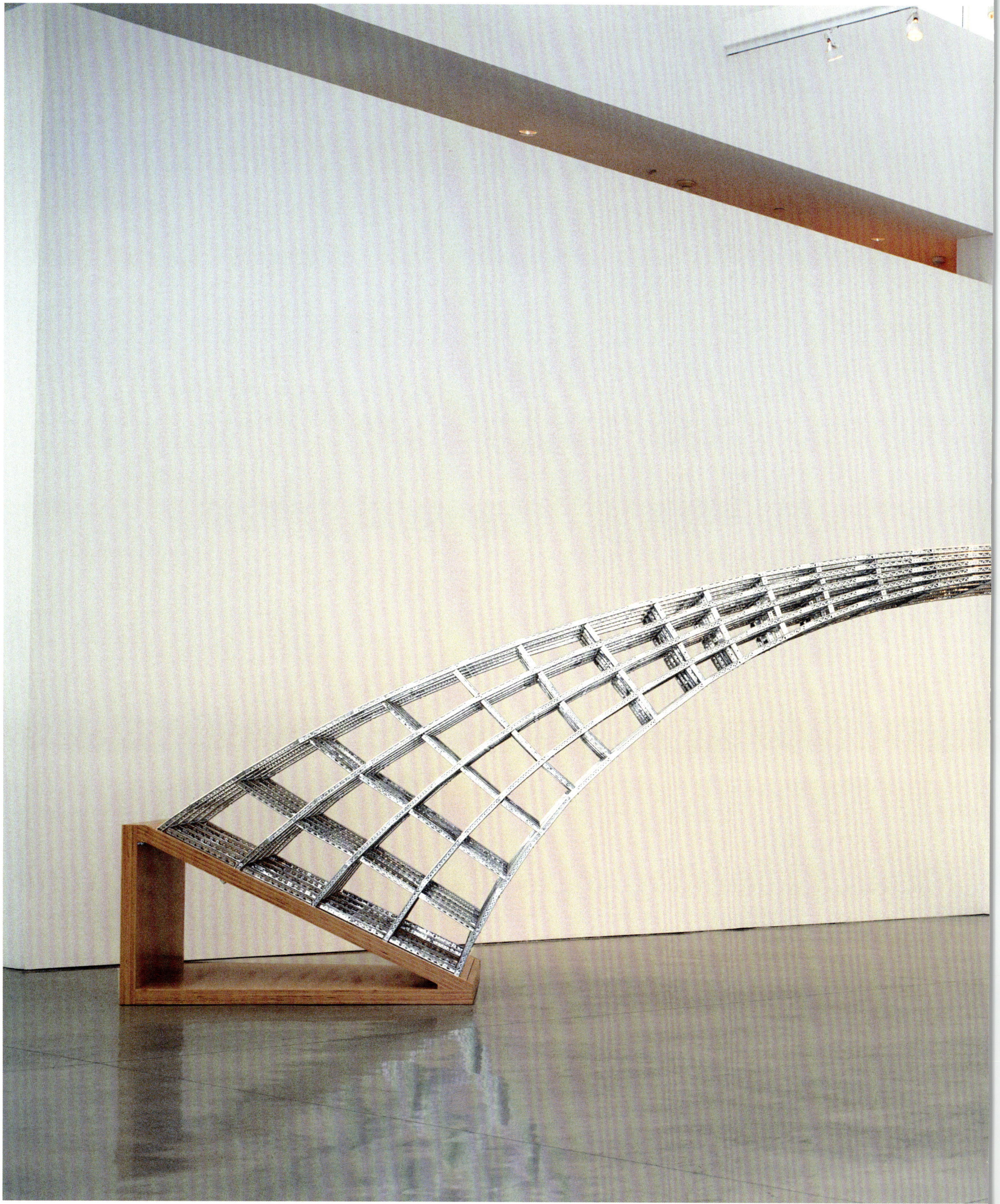

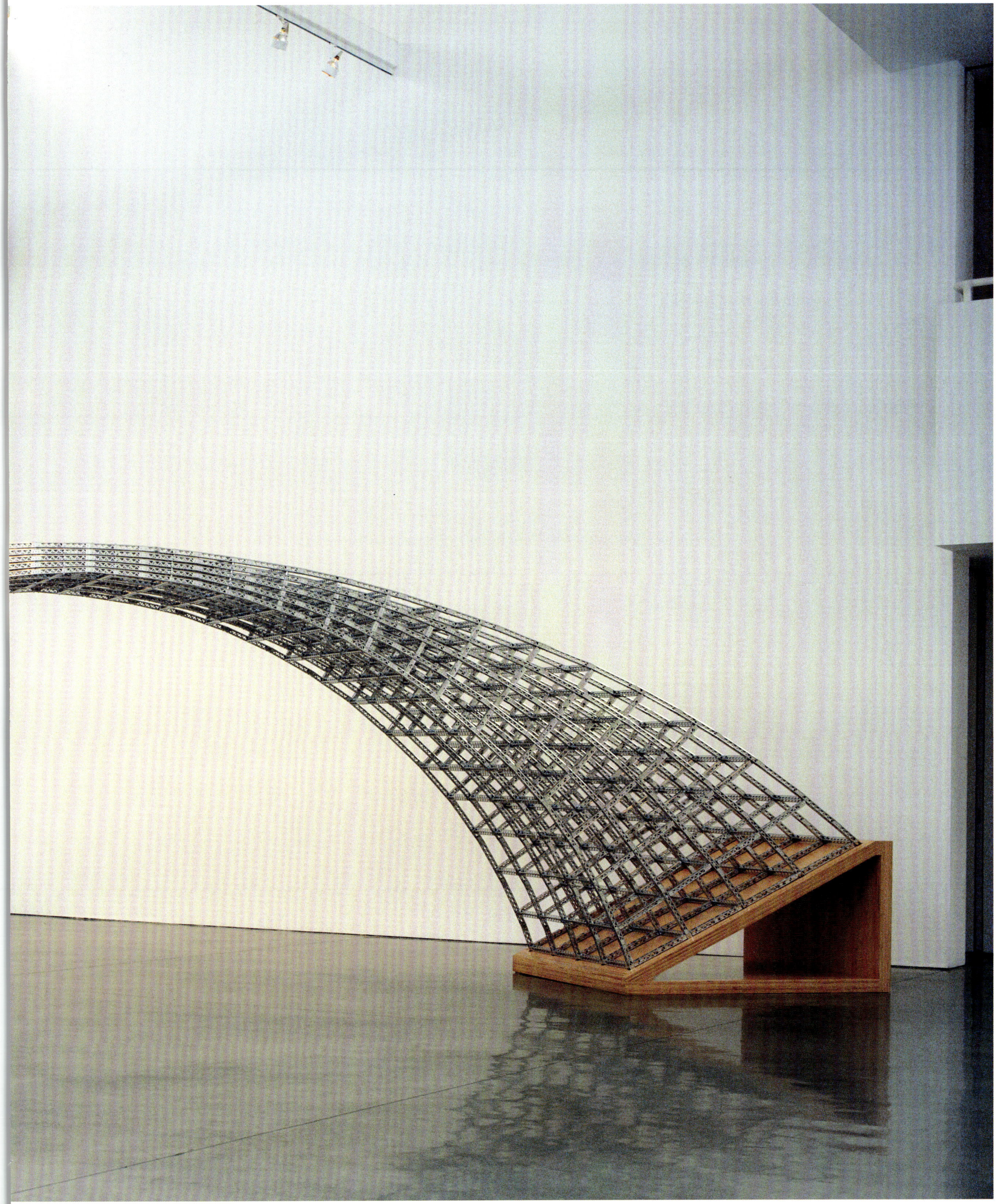

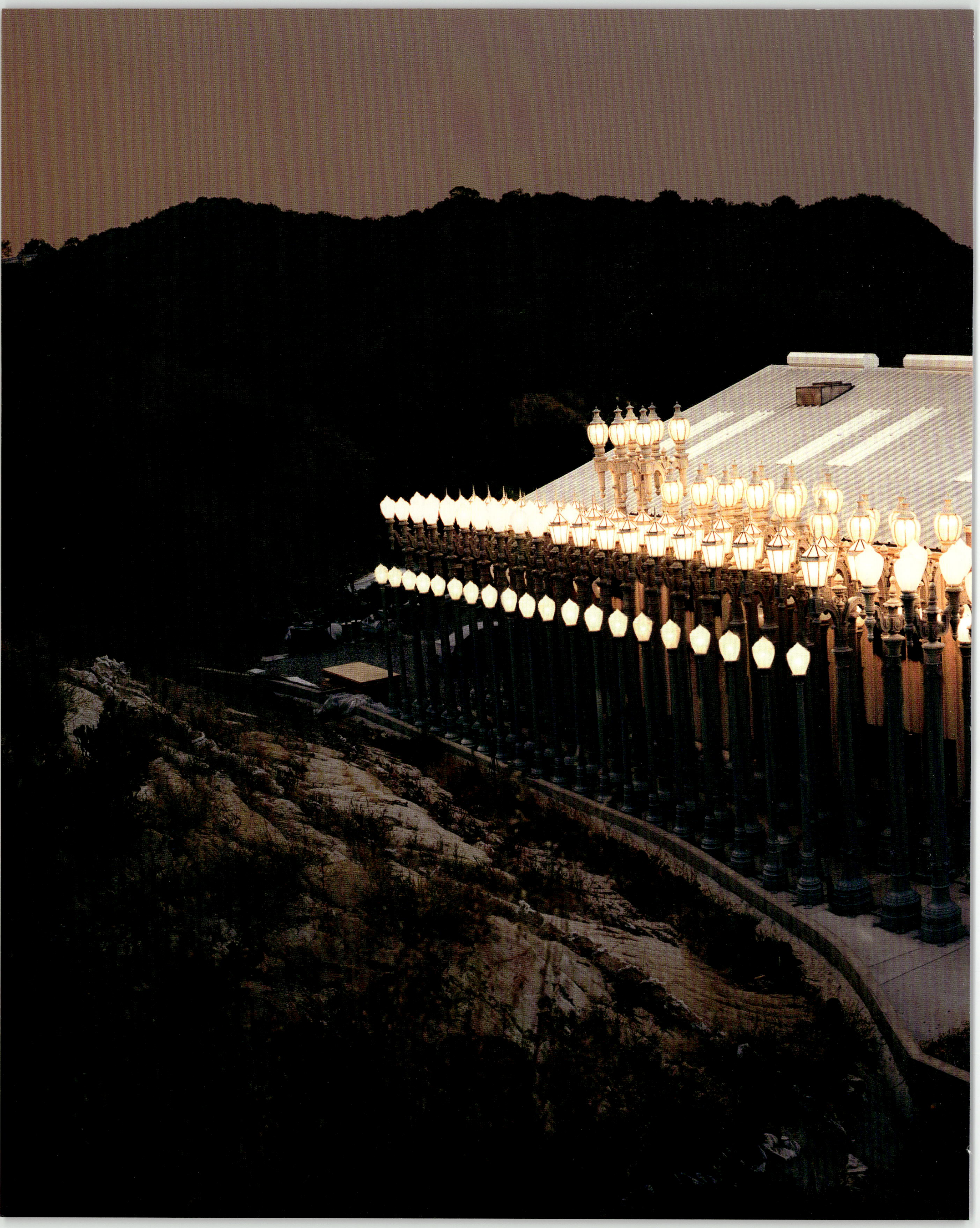

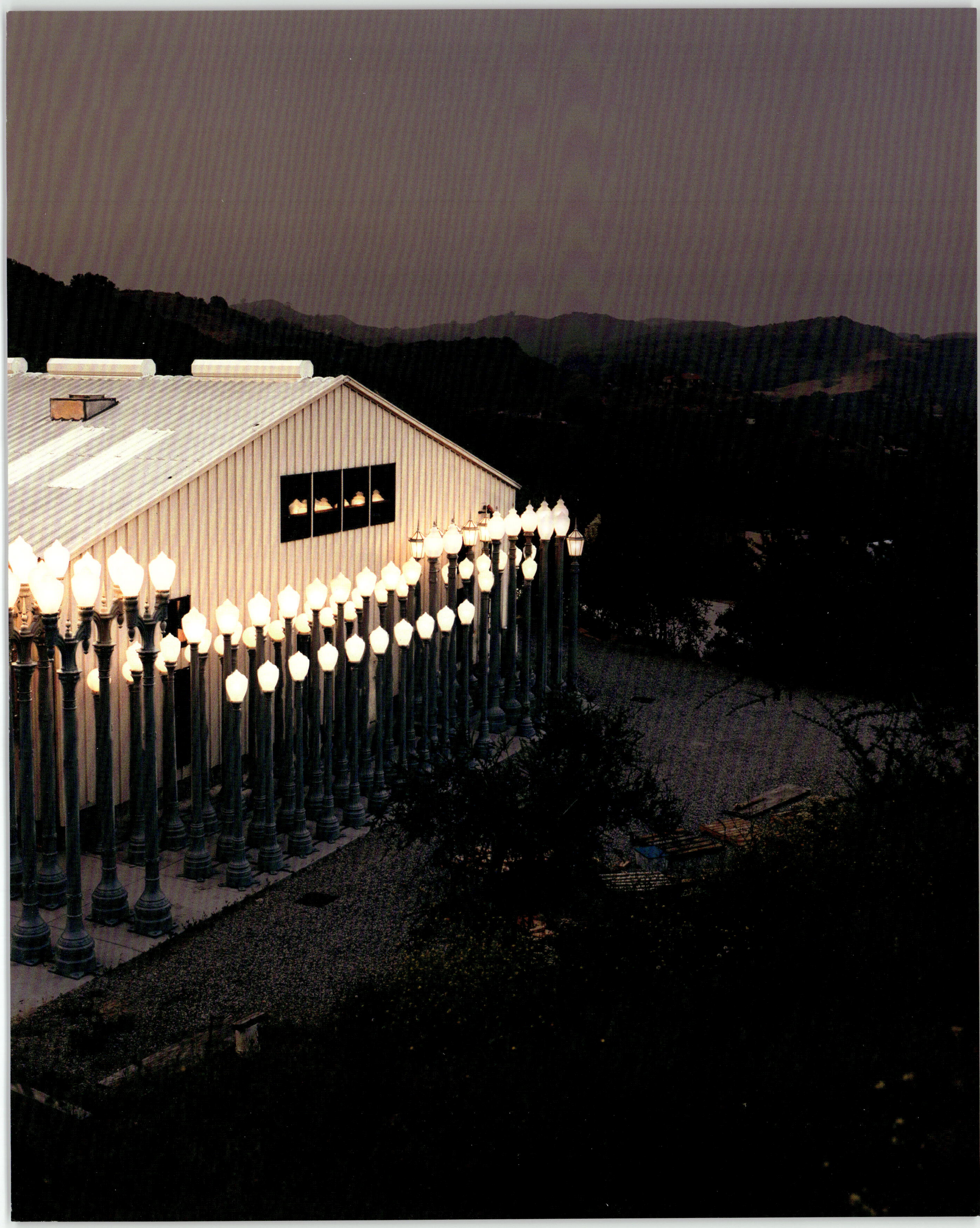

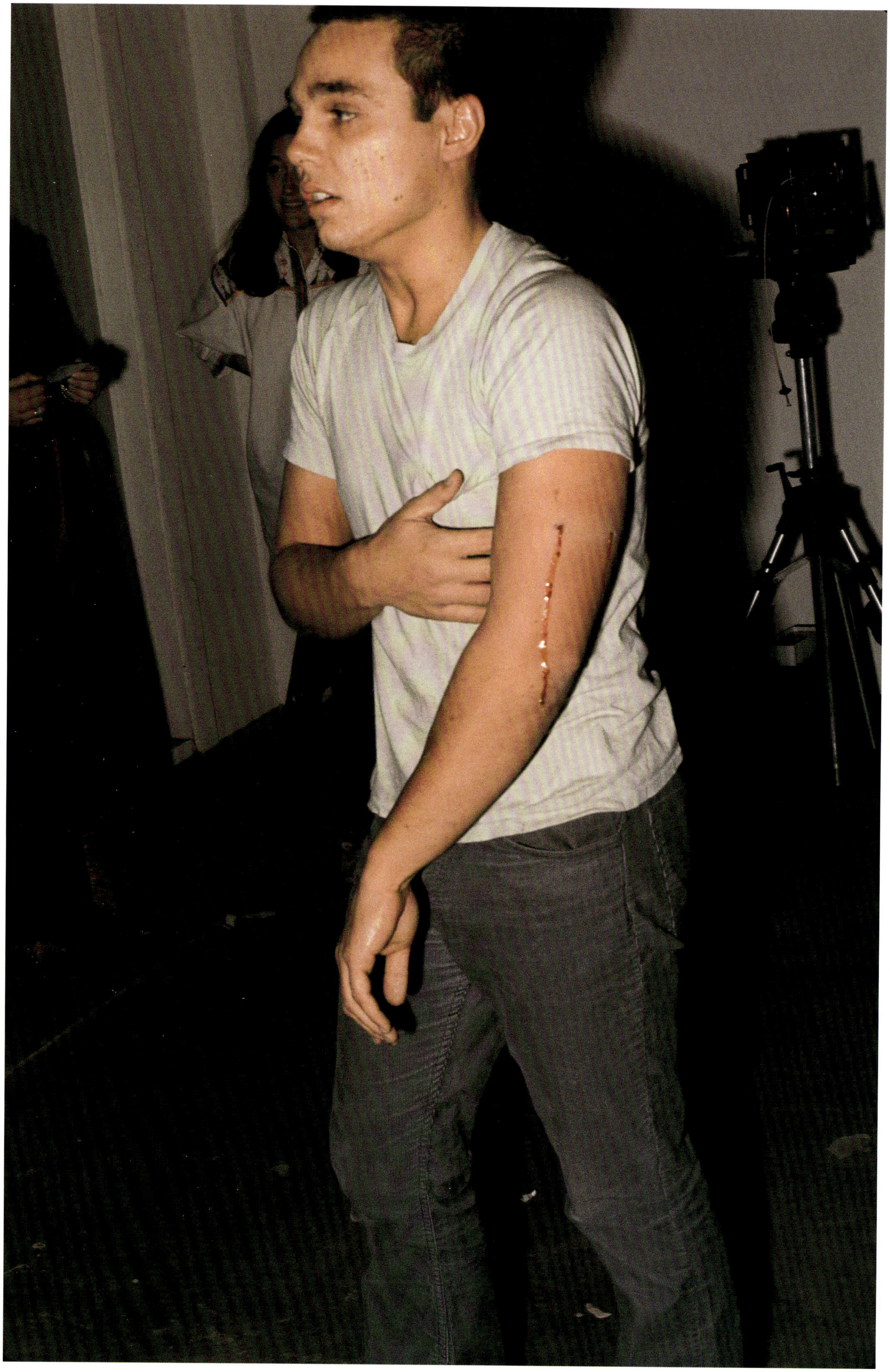

A Locus+ book
coordinated by Fred Hoffman
in association with Gagosian Gallery

texts by
Fred Hoffman
Lisa Le Feuvre
Paul Schimmel
Kristine Stiles
Robert Storr

Chris Burden

Chris Burden

First published in 2007 by Locus+ Publishing Ltd
Wards Building, 31–39 High Bridge
Newcastle upon Tyne NE1 1EW, UK

Coordinated by Fred Hoffman
Edited by Jon Bewley and Jonty Tarbuck
Designed by Mark Thomson

www.locusplus.org.uk

ISBN: 978-1-899377-18-3

Contents

previous pages:

pp 2–3
Through the Night Softly 1973

pp 4–5
Death Valley Run 1976

pp 6–7
Curved Bridge 2003

pp 8–9
Urban Light 2005

p 10
Shoot 1971

Fred Hoffman

Preface

Approximately three years ago, Locus+ approached Chris Burden with the proposal to undertake a new project. This ambitious not-for-profit organization based in Newcastle upon Tyne, England, had previously commissioned and produced The Sailing Destroyer *in 1990. Now their goal was much more complicated, requiring an even greater commitment. They desired to produce a major monographic study of the artist.*

Artists are rightfully dubious when they consider participating in a monographic study of their life and work. The idea of reviewing thirty-plus years of activity, with the daunting task of evaluating the relative importance and intent of each work, can easily become an intrusion into one's life and current art production.

In part fueled by the energetic drive of Locus+, Burden agreed to proceed with the project. I think he was especially attracted to their commitment to provide the time and reflection necessary for such a large scale undertaking to unfold. In this regard, he was especially taken by their belief that dialogue should precede decision-making. While they came to the artist with many ideas about his work, they approached him with an eagerness to learn how he considered his own activities and processes.

Having worked together on various projects since the early 1980s, Chris Burden suggested that I act as the project facilitator. It would be my job to consult with the artist and Locus+ on a regular basis in the review of all extant material, as well as to choose particular projects and images for the publication.

What became especially interesting to us was the idea that many now-famous early works, especially the legendary early performances, could be reconsidered from a more complex, retrospective viewpoint. We acknowledged that the artist is primarily known through a small number of iconic images. This stems from a decision Burden made fairly early on his career to release only a few, specific images taken from

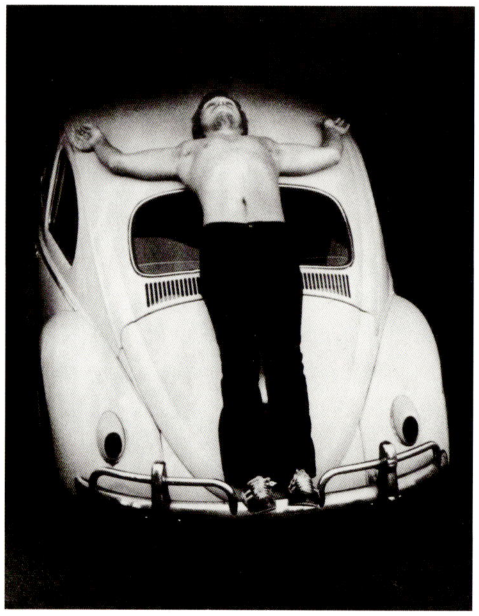

Trans-fixed 1974

only a handful of the early performances. One of the results has been the mythologizing of the performance work. For instance, the image most commonly associated with Trans-fixed *(1974) is a striking high-contrast black and white image, which is actually a detail taken from one of several photographs shot at the time of the performance. The supplementation of this well-known documentary image with a color version, as used on the front cover of this publication, provides a more coherent contextualization of the work insofar as it includes greater information about the circumstances and setting of the action as well as restoring a sense of immediacy to the scene. This image presents a fuller record of the cultural paradox of Chris Burden's art: a sometimes violent confrontation of the banal and the extreme, enacted here through the eruption of a radical experience of physical threat into an environment of repressive suburban domesticity. This publication includes many such new archival materials – both images and explanations by the artist – in a direct attempt to broaden the critical understanding of Burden's practice.*

This publication also aims to illustrate the conceptual lineage that structures the artist's oeuvre from the highly controversial and influential performance works of the early 1970s to the more recent installations and large-scale sculptures, which are of fundamental importance to contemporary art history both for their complex modes of political engagement and for their unique features of construction and process. The themes of Burden's work are of particular relevance to current art world issues of institutional critique, collaborative and public experience, and the analysis of social and national power relations. This recognition that many Burden works from the last four decades present questions relevant to both art history and a broader cultural discourse today, led us to consider whether there might be an alternative method of organizing the material from the traditional historical sequencing of the artist's career. Rather than focusing purely on chronology, this book therefore addresses the artist's critical engagement with systems of institutional, political and social authority as well as his ongoing fascination with engineering in the broadest sense, from architectural structures and technological systems to the programmed nature of our behaviors and values in a culture dominated by repressive normativity.

In light of our goal of unveiling new insights into his career, it is exciting to announce the discovery of a work not previously considered in the literature and exhibition history on the artist. It is commonly believed that Chris Burden's first performance was his graduate thesis presentation of Five Day Locker Piece *(1971). My research has uncovered an important performance that predates* Five Day Locker Piece *by several months. This project, recently titled by the artist* Being Photographed: Looking Out, Looking In, *was presented at F Space, a modest-sized industrial alternative exhibition venue in Santa Ana, California, very early in 1971.*

The work consisted of three elements. Stationed at the front door, a photographer with a Polaroid camera photographed every person that entered the space (including the artist) each day the performance was open to the public. For this publication, Burden retrieved from his archive the 140 Polaroid photographs that constitute the record of the performance/installation. A selection of these images, along with the accompanying drawing that documents the project, are made public for the first time here.

The second element of the work was a wooden platform suspended from the ceiling beams by chain link, approximately 12 to 14 feet above the concrete floor. Positioned next to this platform was an A-frame ladder, an apparent invitation to climb to the hanging platform. The gallery visitor would ascend the ladder and crawl onto the platform. There he or she would have immediately become aware of their fear in now being suspended on top of this precarious construction. Beyond the anxiety of sensing their distance from the floor, the viewer would then also discover that a hole had been opened in the ceiling directly above the platform, encouraging them to lie on their back and stare out into the sky above through a small rubber eyepiece suspended from the ceiling (from descriptions of the platform, there was only a small amount of space, a couple of feet, between the platform and the ceiling).

In so doing, the participant was confronted by two seemingly conflicting feelings and responses: fear of the precarious nature of the physical setting and attraction to the transporting, otherworldly experience of gazing up into the sky above. From accounts I have recently been able to obtain from individuals who actually witnessed or participated in this performance/installation, the psychological response created by the ascent onto this viewing platform was very powerful, creating a lasting sense of both disorientation and freedom.

The third element of this piece consisted of a small bathroom located in one corner of the space. The door to the bathroom was locked and the viewer was invited to peer into this small interior space through a fish-eye lens inserted into the existing door. What confronted the viewer was the artist sitting on top of the toilet seat. Having played on the participants' emotions through the situation created on the platform, he in turn allowed them to have the feeling that they were able to 'invade' his physical and psychological space. This work demonstrates that from the outset, Chris Burden engaged with issues concerning the fragility and preservation of one's psychological state within the context of real, lived experience.

Pre-dating Five Day Locker Piece *by several months, this was Burden's first performance and the first project in which an action involving his own body was a central part of the work. While* Being Photographed: Looking Out, Looking In *has heretofore been overlooked or not considered, it clearly evidences the artist's development of a fully realized artistic practice as a graduate student many months prior to receiving his graduate MFA degree.*

I would like to comment briefly on certain aspects of the editorial process used in the organization of the material presented in this publication. Most significantly, the artist played a central role in the selection of the works included, as well as in the selection of each photograph reproduced. What was especially interesting about this process was how forthcoming Chris Burden was about his past, his own history. The more questions presented to him, the more comfortable he was in sharing his insights into the intent and motivation for undertaking each particular performance and object. The extent of the artist's input is registered in the unprecedented documentary depth and rich historical detail of this book.

Secondly, regarding the structuring of the material presented, we resisted the practice of organizing the material according to chronology. While this method tells one story, it does not necessarily reveal important nuances about the artist's intent, about the ideas and issues that motivate a creative individual to undertake a particular body of work. We therefore spent a considerable period of time attempting to develop an alternative method of organization. Stemming from a significant period of discussion and reflection, Chris Burden and I devised a group of concept/subject categories into which we felt that his artworks could be placed. We hoped that this method of organization would stimulate discussion and reveal fresh insights into the work. Having now presented the career according to our set of categories, we are all excited by the new associations and relationships that this choice has afforded. We expect that it will lead to a reopening of previously closed accounts of certain works and allow for a much deeper evaluation of Burden's art historical legacy.

I would also like to acknowledge the writers who have contributed to this publication. Each of these distinguished scholars provides a clear and distinct voice, a different perspective from which to approach the work of Chris Burden. I believe that these essays demonstrate not only the range of issues and subjects of concern to the artist, but the ongoing significance of his practice. I would like to thank personally Lisa Le Feuvre, Paul Schimmel, Kristine Stiles and Robert Storr for giving their time and labor to this project.

I would like to acknowledge the work of Katy Lucas and Mark Thomson. Katy has worked with Chris Burden for a great number of years as his administrative assistant, colleague and close friend. Her understanding of the artist's work is complete and her insight into his intent and vision is equally clear. Simply, without her participation this book could not have been realized. Moreover, her patience and willingness to handle the countless requests for images, dates and texts was simply beyond any of our expectations. I would like to thank her on behalf of all of us who worked on this project. I would also like to acknowledge the participation of Mark Thomson. Mark joined our team several months after we had initially culled through the material. He quickly became familiar with even the most minute facts about Burden and his work. Mark not only showed us the way as we attempted to map out this book, but also provided the skills and knowledge that have turned it into a work of both beauty and subtlety. It has been a great pleasure to work with him. Many thanks are due to those who initiated this project: Jon Bewley and Jonty Tarbuck of Locus+. Their ongoing partnership with Chris Burden has created a new phase of scholarship on the artist's career. The gratitude of all involved in this project goes out to our friends and partners who supported the long process of publication with their insights and patience. And lastly I would like to thank my wife, Winter, for her constant support of my efforts and for her special contribution to this project in making me aware of Chris Burden's previously unknown first performance/installation.

Santa Monica, California. November 16, 2006.

▷▷
Being Photographed:
Looking Out, Looking In 1971
18 of 140 Polaroid photographs
Each photograph 4¼ × 3¼ inches

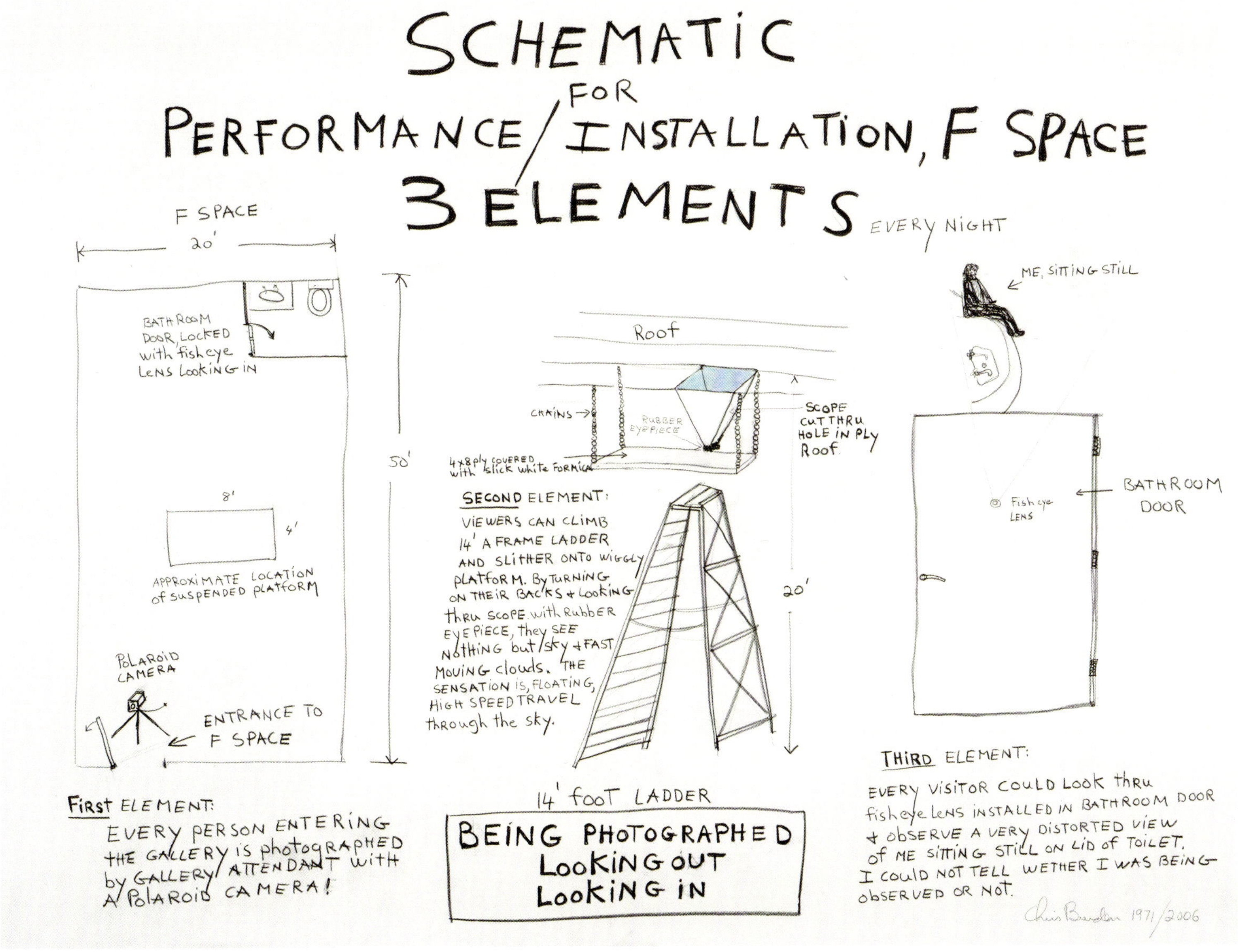

Being Photographed:
Looking Out, Looking In (1971/2006) 2006
Ink, pencil and colored pencil on paper
22½ × 30 inches

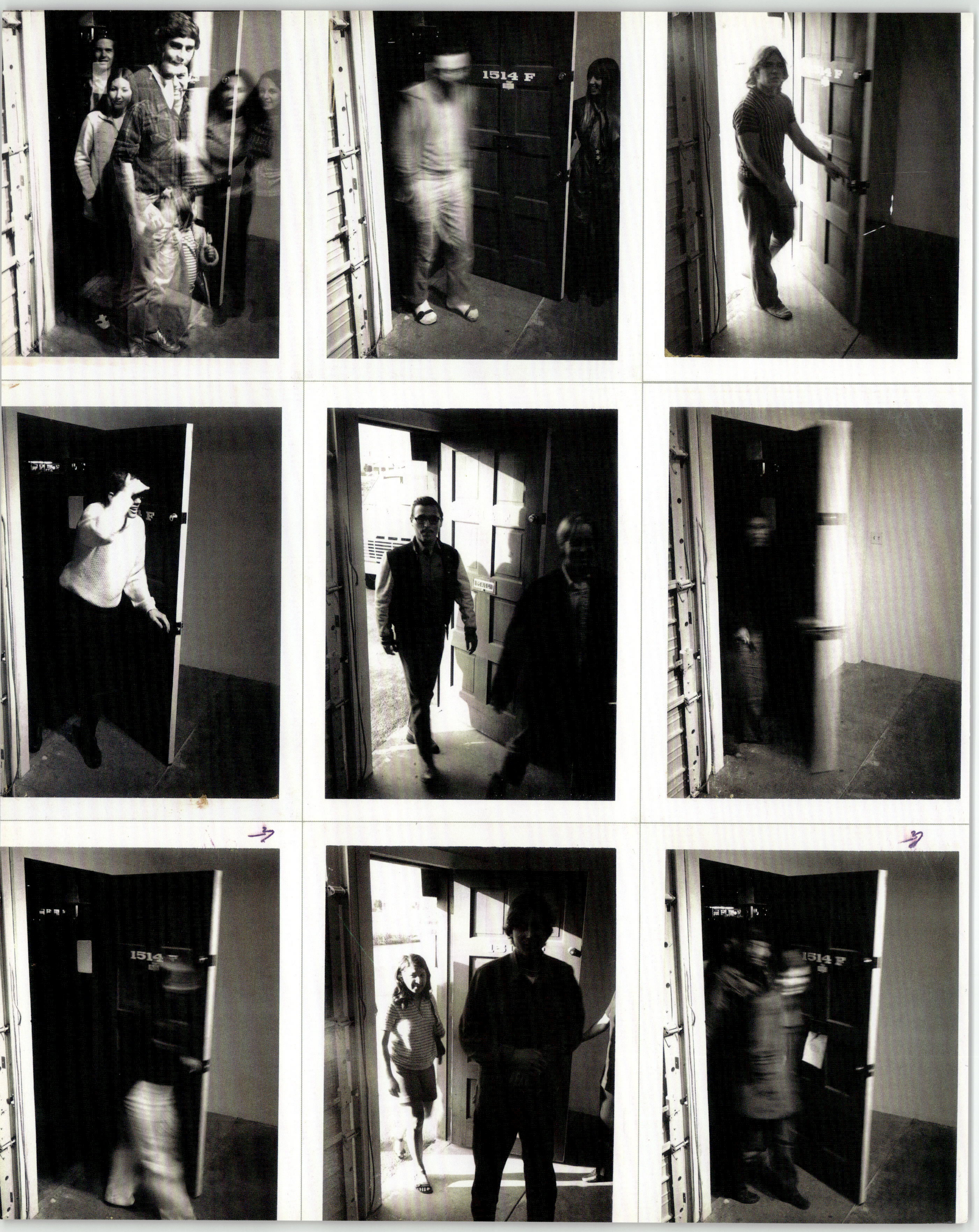
1514 F

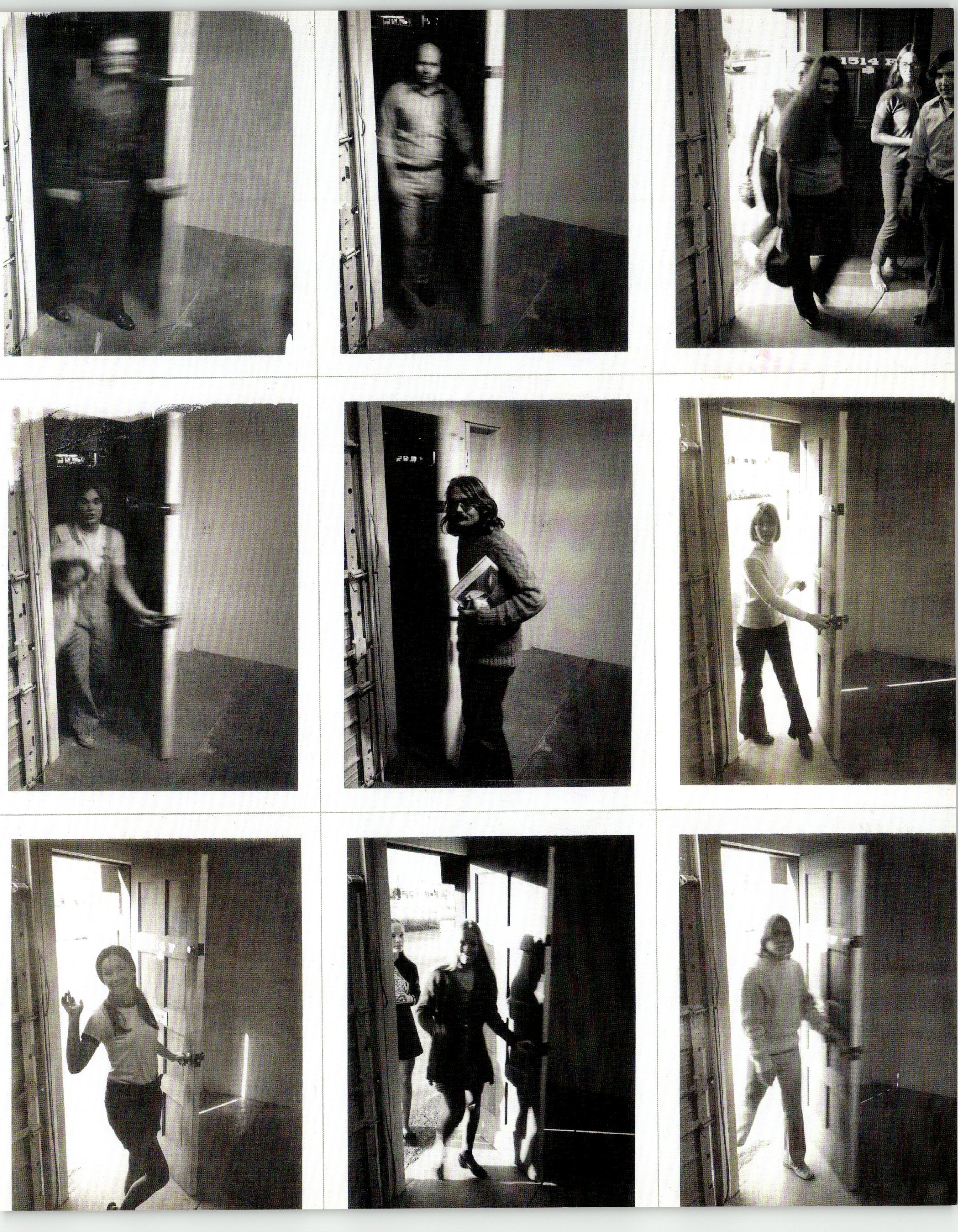
1514

Kristine Stiles

Burden of Light

'Swear on your eyes ... to the truth.'
José Saramago, *Blindness*

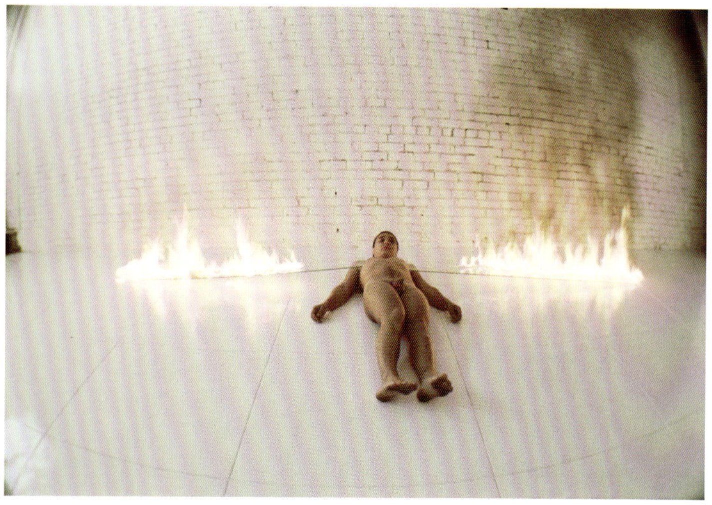

Icarus 1973

Light pervades Chris Burden's work from the glint of a bullet to that light emitted by solar rays, fire, electricity and the refracted luminosity of materials like glass, nickel, water, gold and diamonds. Titles such as *Icarus*, *The Speed of Light Machine*, *The Fist of Light* and *Urban Light* attest to four decades of Burden's fascination with the capacity of light to elucidate aspects of human experience and consciousness. Rather than using light as a medium in and of itself, light becomes a multifaceted signifier for a wide range of meanings and subjects in his work, including myths and metaphors for knowledge; the authority of institutional practices, especially those of science and technology; the politics of social space and war; the mysterious energies of natural forces; and questions of morality, ethics and the obverse, as darkness partners equally with light in Burden's art. It can be sinister and foreboding, plunge viewers into pitch-blackness, expose the lethal and life-giving potentialities of light and juxtapose visibility and invisibility. I shall suggest that light bears a singular task in his art to manifest and communicate the ancient concepts and qualities of *lux* (symbolizing 'the light of ideas, speculations, inference, revelation and divine illumination') and *lumen* (related to knowledge gained from empirical evidence in the observable dimensions of light).[1]

Light figures in over 50 works in Burden's art in a range of media. Yet despite its physical, physiological and psychological centrality to his practice, art historians and critics have uniformly neglected light as a crucial dimension of Burden's oeuvre. This is due in no small measure to the critical hyperbole that has plagued his reception and interfered with an appropriately scholarly consideration of his work's semiotics. An example of this sort of criticism is a 1974 review by James Collins, who charged Burden with 'game-playing' and 'tokenly dangerous' acts, as well as 'raging for chaos'.[2] Erroneously claiming that Burden shot 'himself in the arm' in his performance *Shoot* (1971), Collins then linked this inaccurate account to the equally erroneous story that Austrian artist Rudolf Schwarzkogler had 'sequentially mutilated his own penis'.[3] Such criticism unfairly discredited performance art and justifiably dismayed Burden. 'I didn't do performances for that many years [because] the press was too distorting' he said. 'I would read what they had written and [think], "My God! Who are they talking about?!"'[4] In contrast, more thoughtful criticism has noted a range of significant conceptual and historical themes in Burden's work, including a 'will to power',[5] the pursuit of 'self- and situational control',[6] 'danger, risk, and unexpected survival in the cosmos of technology',[7] masochistic extremes,[8] and 'pure renunciation'.[9] These subjects are qualities and conditions of Burden's art, but such descriptions miss a quintessential philosophical dimension of his work: the sculptural role that light plays as it shapes Burden's viewers' psychological and psychophysical experiences and both transmits and sustains Burden's own unique aesthetic vision and the principled concepts represented in his art.

Nevertheless, it is true that danger distinguishes the material conditions of many of Burden's works. Burden calculates unleashing violence as a means to oblige himself and his viewers to act with mutual responsibility and trust. So that while one may justifiably point to unprecedented fearsome aspects of his work, at the same time no other artist has so consistently trusted the public to react to dangerous and challenging situations and to treat the artist and his artworks with such responsibility. In short, Burden trusted viewers not to electrocute him in *Prelude to 220, or 110* (1971) and *220* (1971); not to kill him in *Shoot*; not to starve him in *Bed Piece* (1972) and *Doomed* (1975); not to abandon him in *Deadman* (1972); not to permit him to be severely burned in *Icarus* (1973); not to let him drown in *Velvet Water* (1974); not to permanently damage his body in *Trans-fixed* (1974) and *Back to You* (1974); not to destroy buildings in *Samson* (1985) and *Exposing the Foundation of the Museum* (1986–88); not to let technology overpower reason in *Big Wheel* (1979); not to neglect cultural heritage in *Urban Light* (2005); not to forget the transgressions of power in *The Other Vietnam Memorial* (1991), *America's Darker Moments* (1994), *Hidden Force* (1995), *Mexican Bridge* (1998), and *L.A.P.D. Uniforms* (1993); and not to forget the possibility of nuclear holocaust in *A Tale of Two Cities* (1981). Given this litany of ways in which Burden has activated the conscience and ethics of viewers, the time has come to shift the discourse about his art away from its more spectacular aspects to its experiential depth where together *lux* and *lumen* unite in trust.

Blind Truth

In *White Light/White Heat* (February 8–March 1, 1975), Burden remained invisible on an elevated platform in the Ronald Feldman Gallery in New York for 22 days, neither seeing nor speaking to anyone and not coming down. Burden based his title on John Cale's 1967 song about heroin addiction, sung by The Velvet Underground.[10] In part, the endurance of his performance obliquely referred to the physical effects of heroin, including the ways in which heroin slows respiration and heart rhythms, lowers the body's temperature, constricts the pupils, and also makes one indifferent to pain, grief, fear, hunger and cold, all of which result in feelings of sensory deprivation and physical isolation. Burden achieved a similar, although non-narcotic state, reproducing some of these effects by remaining isolated, fasting, and drinking one six-ounce glass of celery juice a day (a liquid known for its utility in lowering and maintaining blood pressure and for its calming effects) during the entire three-week period.[11]

Read through the normative conditions for seeing art, *White Light/White Heat* offered viewers nothing to look at but a stark minimalist structure in an architectural and institutional setting saturated with light. With nothing to see in *White Light/White Heat* visitors' perceptions were submitted to the contemplation of that which could not be witnessed, yet with the pledge that Burden inhabited the space. Burden's inaccessibility in visual terms required viewers to experience the art through other means than mere looking, and conceptually to connect visibility to invisibility.[12] By restricting what spectators could witness and validate as truth, Burden expanded the necessity for viewers to attend to other corporeal perceptions and heightened their senses to discern his presence in the gallery and 'feel that something was wrong.'[13]

The fact that Burden used his body to enhance feelings over seeing emphasized physiological over visual methods of knowing, thereby activating viewer proprioception, or what neurobiologist Paul Grobstein has referred to as the 'I-function.'[14] Proprioception is a mechanism of the central nervous system that governs one's awareness of self most significantly through determining which senses identify environmental stimuli and enable decision-making that is necessary for wellbeing. Grobstein coined the term 'I-function' in order 'to refer to those aspects of brain function that support/create "consciousness" (as opposed to the much larger sphere of brain function that supports behaviour without consciousness).'[15] 'In this regard', Grobstein maintained, 'proprioception ... represents an enormous and continual barrage of incoming information that greatly influences our behaviour but that we have little or no direct access to.'[16] Moreover, as Alain Berthoz writes in *The Brain's Sense of Movement*, proprioception is about kinesthesia, a characteristic feature of which 'is that it makes use of many receptors, but remarkably it has been forgotten in the count of the senses.' Berthoz adds that one 'plausible explanation' for the neglect of proprioception 'is that it is not identified by consciousness, and its receptors are concealed.'[17] To make this point even more clear, a familiar example of the operations of proprioception is how the mind produces the sensation of pain in an absent limb.[18]

What I am suggesting is that in *White Light/White Heat* Burden produced an experience akin to that of the phantom limb by making himself visually unavailable and leaving viewers to sense that something was amiss in the gallery. One critic described the mild psychological disturbance that this sensation induced as the room feeling 'haunted ... by the vacuum of [Burden's] withheld presence.'[19] Such sensations put the body on alert. In this way, Burden's work illustrated how proprioception is a key survival mechanism of the body.[20] Few researchers have considered the role of survival as an aspect of proprioception in discussing the central nervous system's commands for movement to the muscles. But in a truncated comment, Berthoz posed a provocative point, explaining that while muscles are slow to contract, '80 milliseconds is a very long time if you are trying to get away from a predator.'[21] What is clear from this point is that one of the roles of proprioception in the central nervous system is to alert the body to danger.[22] In this regard, Burden's use of the body as an aesthetic medium in *White Light/White Heat*, as in many of his performances, presented the public with a subtle, but vital, discourse on, and experience of, the conditions of survival.

Comments by Noel Frackman, a critic who witnessed *White Light/White Heat*, reinforce the point that proprioception is a survival mechanism:

> The very air was molecularized by the unseen presence of Burden. The cool Minimal piece had living, breathing human content. There was never a question in my mind as to whether Burden was really there: he had to be there. Otherwise the piece would have no integrity.... Those who think of Burden as an exhibitionist in art are going to be disappointed when they see *White Light/White Heat*, [which] is full of astonishing implications.[23]

One of the most surprising implications of Burden's piece may be understood through an event that occurred two years before Burden performed this piece when he was featured in the May 1973 issue of *Esquire* magazine together with seven other individuals who were described as 'touchstones by which we know that ... something new is happening.'[24] One of these individuals, Neil E. Miller, a professor of physiological psychology at Rockefeller University, worked on experiments aimed at 'educating the autonomic nervous system ... to follow the instructions of the brain', and predicted that research in this area would 'enable us to lower our blood pressure by an act of will, just as today we ask our hands to scratch an itch.'[25]

What I am arguing is that Miller's experiments on the brain and nervous system paralleled Burden's aesthetic experiments in body art, insofar as both sought to harness the body/mind relationship for the enhancement of physiological experiences and that such research (whether scientific or aesthetic) informed the ways in which the body responds to survival needs through proprioception. Moreover, I want to suggest that *White Light/White Heat* supplanted viewers' knowledge-by-sight in order to awaken psychophysical felt relations to presence in place, space and time. Alerting visitors to unseen conditions in the gallery, Burden's work prepared them to be more attuned to the surrounding world, and in this way contributed to preparing the mind to assist the body's ability to become alert in extreme circumstances. Such a physiological operation recalls Claes Oldenburg's desire for art to function like 'the conversation between the sidewalk and a blind man's metal stick.'[26] Like Oldenburg's click of the stick, Burden's activation of human proprioception prepared consciousness to connect to social and environmental factors, at the same time as it offered viewers an experience akin to Burden's own while enduring the performance. I would argue that what one critic called the 'rarely equalled wholeness'[27] of Burden's art derives explicitly from its capacity to kindle proprioception as a localized response. *White Light/White Heat* achieved Burden's aim of interrupting the 'distance between me and the audience', as 'the audience was part of the work' due to physiological exchange.[28] In this way, Burden also assisted people in 'question[ing] what kinds of experiences are possible.'[29] This restrained action resoundingly rejected the aspect of spectacle with which Burden had become associated by 1975 in favor of the non-visual, perceptual, emotional and intellectual qualities of aesthetic experience that the light-drenched white gallery and proprioception evoked.

Galvanized by the combination of their uncomfortable proprioceptive perceptions, together with cynical disbelief and irrepressible curiosity about the artist, some viewers felt compelled to confirm what they could not see by jumping up and down to catch a glimpse of Burden. One visitor became so anxious that she succeeded in peeping in on and photographing Burden through an extended lens.[30] The media also responded to his provocation, and CBS television news attempted to film him descending from the platform at the end of his vigil.[31] But Burden's art dealer Ronald Feldman intervened, rejecting the idea as irrelevant to, and even destructive of, Burden's intention, which had less to do with the proof of presence than the experience itself. Others simply refused to believe that Burden had remained on the platform for 22 days.[32] Such incredulity is ironic given the fact that in *I Like America and America Likes Me* (May 23–25, 1974), Joseph Beuys tricked the public into thinking that he had lived with a wild coyote for three days in the René Block Gallery in New York. Few today still do not realize that Beuys did not remain in the gallery with the animal for 24 hours a day, but left after closing hours. In contrast, Burden did, indeed, live on the platform for 22 days, 24 hours a day, without eating or drinking anything but the small amount of celery juice.[33] Suppositions of Burden's putative duplicity fail to reckon with the fact that in order to dupe the public, he would have to deceive himself. Burden would not cheat himself of the wisdom he gains from the truths he discovers in his art, truths that provide the inner strength upon which the ethical foundation of his work is based and the bond of trust he creates with his viewers. Peter Clothier astutely identified these personal character traits when he observed that Burden's 'uncompromising … engagement with social reality' depends upon his ability 'to share in the common responsibility and his willing acceptance of that load.'[34] Thus, to suggest that Burden 'ignores conventions and obeys no moral or behavioral code', as a critic once proposed, is to fail to understand the moral purpose underlying Burden's belief in ethical action.[35] I would emphasize that Burden's aesthetic rests on such conviction and is an aesthetic of corporeal knowledge based on the truths of experiential insight.

There is something rather poignant about how Burden's sincerity translates into the production of knowledge. For example, what is seldom discussed in considerations of *White Light/White Heat* is that Burden encouraged his friends to come into the gallery and talk to him during the performance. He asked them to keep him company:

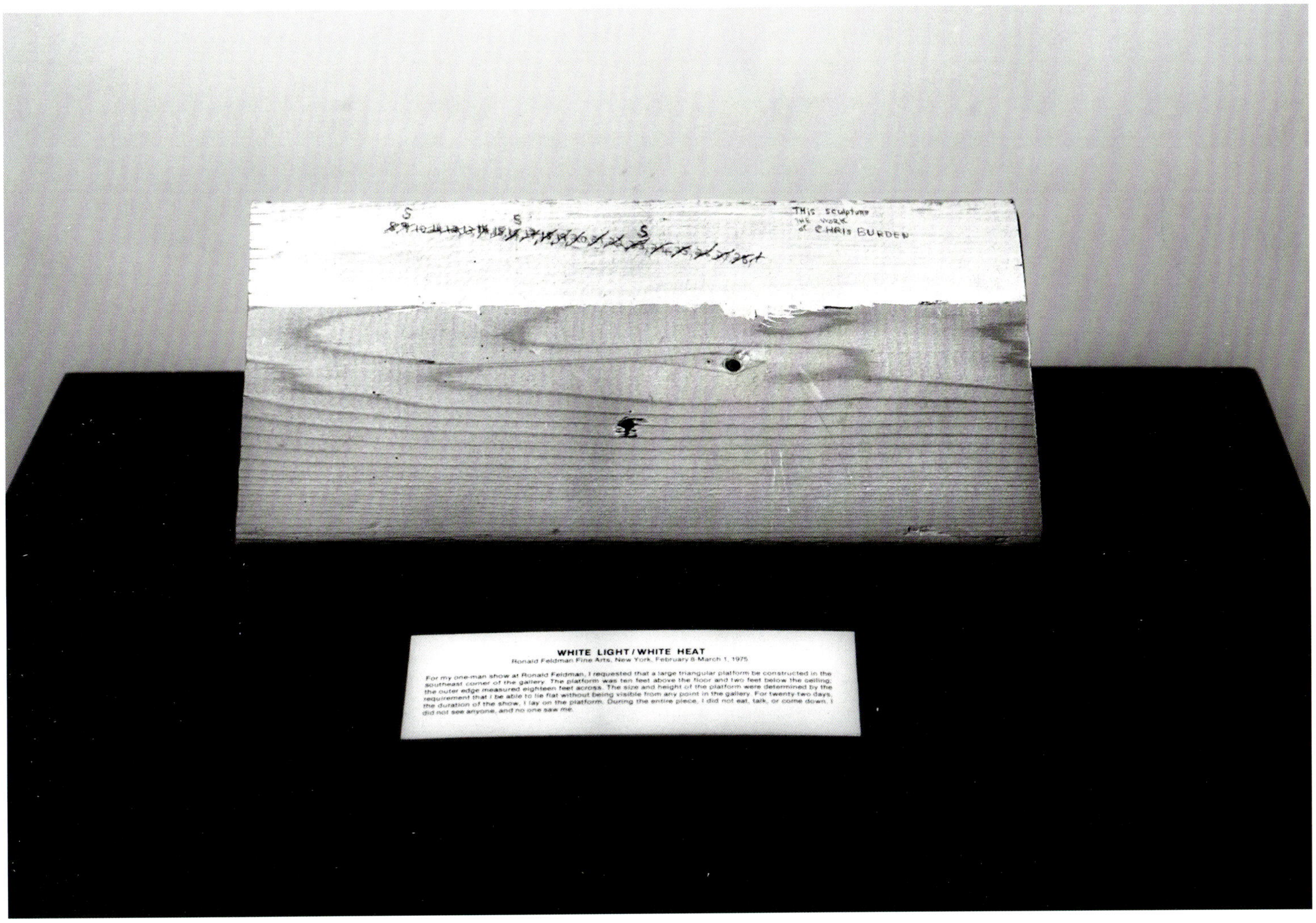

White Light/White Heat 1975
RELIC: Section of board

Even though I couldn't see, I could hear ... I would be really exhausted just from the activity down below. Ron was the only person who was really able to come in and talk to me. It's really hard to talk to somebody if they don't answer and you don't see them.... People would come in and would try to talk, stumble and leave. Ron Feldman would come in kind of like NBC News, yap away, and leave.[36]

Although Burden attempted to augment social engagement, he also isolated himself so successfully that he precluded the possibility of exchange, denying himself that which he most wanted. Howard Singerman believed that 'the more the audience needed Burden, the less Burden needed them.'[37] But while Burden did become increasingly psychologically removed as the work progressed,[38] it is equally true that what he reported learning from the action was that 'human beings really need other human beings.'[39]

Such interpersonal need relates to Burden's biography, which critics and art historians almost never consider and which he seldom discusses. But in understanding the psychological conditions out of which *White Light/White Heat* emerged, it is useful to know that at the age of 12 in 1958, Burden moved to the Isle of Elba in Italy where he lived off and on into the early 1960s with his mother, brother and sister while his father worked in the US. During this period, he spent some nine months in bed after a small Vespa truck in which he was riding flipped over and crushed his foot.[40] Kathy O'Dell is the only art historian to have theorized (even without knowing of this event) that Burden's bed pieces (she includes *White Light/White Heat* among them) feature what she perceptively called 'a home-sited mnemonic device and a manipulation of distance.'[41] *White Light/White Heat* may be described as just such a 'mnemonic device', which calls forth Burden's psychophysical memories of months of solitude and convalescence, and which contributes to the creation of art that reflects that distant experience on Elba. In this sense, *White Light/White Heat* is not only a key work in the history of performance art for activating viewers' visceral, proprioceptive survival responses but also reflects Burden's life and relates to the very foundations of why he decided to become an artist:

For me [the Vespa accident] was an isolation period and I actually attribute that to when I became an artist. I started taking pictures. My grandmother had given me a Brownie camera for my twelfth birthday [and] my mom let me use the Rolleiflex, this really fancy German camera ... so I started taking pictures. When my foot got crushed, I saw this big fancy book, *The Family of Man*, and I wanted to take pictures again.[42] I would go out with this camera when I was recovering with my limpy leg and I had this wicker basket – because I was a kid, I could kind of get away with carrying a fancy camera and taking pictures undercover, hiding my camera in the basket. It was about not wanting to invade people's privacy even though I was taking their picture. I wanted to be low-key and not annoy people. I would take bus trips and I was trying to take pictures like *The Family of Man*. I have a whole body of work that I took. I didn't have any friends. My brother and sister were real social because they were younger and going to local school. I was this freak that was lying in bed with, you know, a big crushed leg. Then the Spring came and I was taking all these pictures. That's how I kept myself entertained. I remember one time I went to the photo lab in the main town, which was about an hour and a half bus ride away. As the clerk was going through photos, I saw a couple of images. I did not immediately recognize them as being my own, as I took rolls and rolls of film. I initially thought that someone else was taking photos that were similar to mine.[43]

Rather than someone else, however, the person that Burden found was himself. He also discovered the will and the capacity to engage the world alone as an artist:

That was when I think I became an artist ... I wasn't conscious of it ... It was a turning point because that's what made my life have meaning. I got on a bus or my bicycle and went out into the country or I cruised the docks and took these pictures. That gave me reason to get up the next morning.[44]

This period served to exaggerate Burden's need to connect with others, and he answered that call by taking photographs that pictured humanity. Some 40 years later, as a continued response to his concern for social interaction, Burden would purchase and renovate over 100 stately 1920s Los Angeles cast-iron street lamps with art nouveau globes in an installation entitled *Urban Light*. These elegant street lamps cluster together as if to recuperate the human scale that Burden imagines made past nocturnal urban experience more congenial. In salvaging these artefacts of light, Burden thinks of himself 'as a preservationist', one who saves 'part of the infrastructure that makes a city a city' in order to provide 'some California light' wherever the work is exhibited.[45]

Burden has consistently harnessed sculpture to light the darkness with aesthetic objects that also provide inner revelation (*lux*). Burden's idealistic concept of social sculpture is also vivid in the installation *The Hidden Force* in which a large magnet, roughly the size of a human body, floats in each of three reflecting pools at McNeil Island Correction Center, a prison near Steilacoom, Washington. In Burden's words, the work constitutes 'a metaphor for the "right direction" or the "right way", and his 'hope [is] that the inmates might make the connection between this unseen, but internalized, force of nature and unseen human values ... that they must also internalize.'[46] *The Hidden Force*, with its concerns for universal moral law, and *Urban Light*, with its consideration of how scale and quality of light affect human behavior, both connect to *White Light/White Heat* in so far as Burden learned in this performance that rather than food or water, he missed human contact. He longed for the very sight of others:

> Actually seeing other people. Seeing them. Seeing other human faces ... [What] I've learned most, is that people need people.[47]

Mute Truth

The color white dominated the perceptual conditions of *White Light/White Heat*. It produced a visual vacuum of achromatic light like a blank sheet of paper on which an inscrutable event in the course of becoming was yet to be written. Burden considered *White Light/White Heat* to be a 'refinement' of *Bed Piece*, in which he similarly remained in a light-filled gallery for 22 days in a white-sheeted bed. But in this performance, he stayed under the watchful eyes of viewers with whom he had no verbal contact. Burden dressed all in white for three more unnerving performances, using white as a color to signify ritualized danger and/or isolation. In *TV Hijack* (February 9, 1972), he held a knife to the throat of the woman interviewing him on television; and in *Jaizu* (June 10–11, 1972) he wore dark sunglasses painted black on the inside. They rendered him virtually blind and confounded the very communal experience Burden appeared to have solicited, sitting silent in front of two pillows and a bowl of marijuana cigarettes that visitors who came to chat with him were invited to enjoy while he looked on mute and blind. The color white also dominated *Oh, Dracula* (October 7, 1974), which took place in the foyer of the Utah Museum of Art in Salt Lake City, in a room of Renaissance religious paintings. There Burden had himself suspended in a chrysalis-like white sheet and placed two lighted white candles on the floor, one under his head and the other under his feet, changing his envelope-like cocoon into an inverted altar.[48] Without narrative or pictorial content, his living presence presented the actual embodiment of the representational sacral subjects depicted in the paintings around him. While he hung silent in his shroud, Burden's title prepared the public to consider its own Draconian voyeuristic complicity in visually sucking the life-blood from the art 'object'.[49]

Burden revisited his implicit indictment of viewers' interactive responsibility to art in *Samson*, an installation with the capacity to split the architecture of display asunder when a 100-ton jack pushed two large timbers and steel plates against the weight-

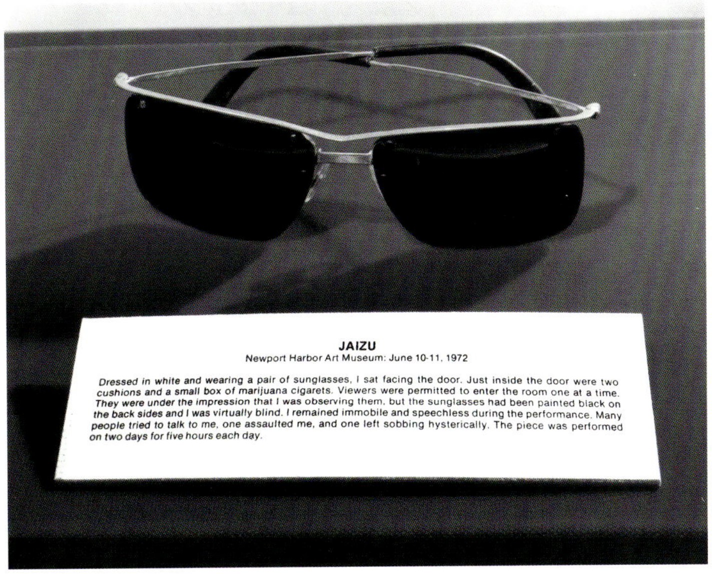

Jaizu 1972
RELIC: Sunglasses, painted black on the back

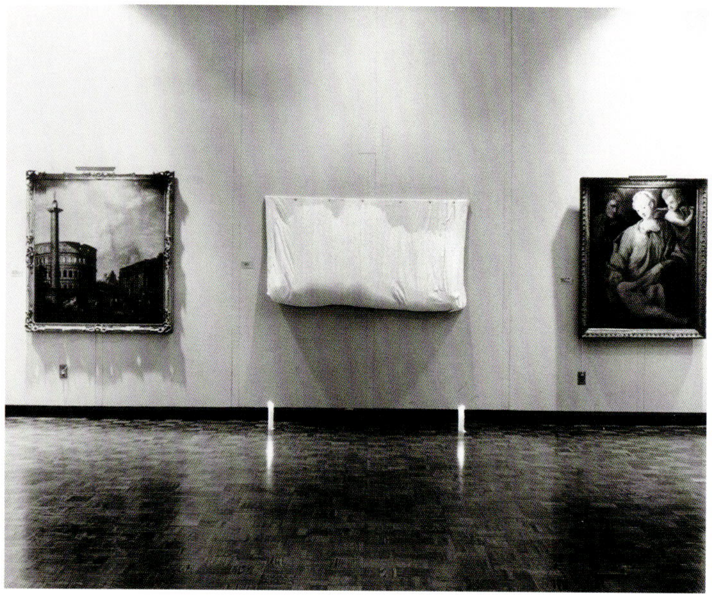

Oh, Dracula 1974

bearing walls of a building in response to the movement of visitors passing through the entrance turnstile. Burden's title linked *Samson*'s fatal flaw (his erotic attractions) to art lovers' search for visual pleasure (scopophilia). The installation examined the ways in which the interrelationship between the display of art and the compulsion to see (as sensual gratification) endangers the very capacity of art to exist.[50] Indeed, Burden's work is replete with the theme of viewer responsibility across the division of visibility and action. He addressed this topic again in *Velvet Water* when he positioned himself behind a wall in the same space as his audience and attempted to breathe in water. The audience could see Burden on a video monitor but actually hear him choking and gagging behind the wall. Confronting viewers with their complicity, Burden enabled them to watch and listen to what was taking place in the same space where they failed to intervene in a potentially life-threatening action. Again, in *Velvet Water*, as in other potentially lethal performances in which he staged suffocation and dehydration, Burden wore white clothing.

While white summons concepts of purity, awe and reverence, it also signifies death, as in snow and the end of life symbolized by the death of nature in winter. White is also the funerary color in Asian cultures, unlike black which is the more immediate symbol of death in the West. In a blacked-out room for audiences limited to four, Burden hung over 500 miniature metal spaceships and performed *The Citadel* (August 8–12, 1978), illuminating each tiny object one at a time with the light of a white candle. An audiotape accompanied his action of slowly lighting the elements of the scene; it played the sound of a rocket blast and a message about the end of the universe. *The Citadel* belongs to a number of works the artist has produced on the subjects of war, apocalypse and radiation.[51] Moreover, at least 75 works in his oeuvre juxtapose good and evil, life and death, and connect these concepts to aspects of light and dark, black and white.

The Fist of Light (1993) is an important and extreme example of Burden's ongoing interest in the physical effects of light on human physiology and emotion. The installation consisted of a rectilinear aluminum room covered on the inside with 112 metal halide high-intensity lamps that saturated the interior with direct and reflected light, generating enough heat to strip paint off the surface of the walls and, more significantly, to potentially blind an observer. From the exterior, the room resembled a metal cube with large cooling air ducts running over its surface, providing air conditioning that lowered the interior temperature and prevented the system from overheating. Burden imagined this piece 'like a clenched hand poised to strike at New York'.[52] In this way, *The Fist of Light* deployed light augmented by technology as an instrument of power to illuminate and destroy. Left out of control, the installation could have generated enough electrical energy to cause a blackout in lower Manhattan.[53] In part, *The Fist of Light* represented Burden's comment on the work of such artists as James Turrell and his teacher Robert Irwin, both of whom utilize light as a medium. 'By pushing to an extreme what is conventionally viewed as a benign and positive material', Burden explained, 'I altered light into an unconventional hazardous and powerful force.'[54] Disclosing the negative potential of a putatively benevolent medium, Burden joined the notion of *illuminati*, or enlightened souls, to the diabolical dimension of light as fire, as represented in the concept of Lucifer. Indeed, the signification of light as a representation of virtue is undermined to reveal the potential danger of energy and its connection to chaos, vice and destruction. Such a work summons the dazzling experience of light in Book X of Plato's *Republic* where a column of light stretches 'over the whole of heaven and earth' and in the middle 'hangs the spindle of Necessity, by means of which all the revolutions are turned.'[55]

Works of psychological and sensorial intensity such as *The Fist of Light*, *Samson*, *Oh, Dracula* and *White Light/White Heat* reveal how Burden's physical ordeals and sculptural installations critique both the institutions of art and the behaviours they reinforce. One of the more ingenious examples of such a critique is *Exposing the Foundation of the Museum*, a work in which Burden literally 'brought to light' the very foundations of the Temporary Contemporary building of the Museum of Contemporary Art in Los Angeles by removing a 52 × 16-foot section of concrete floor from the northeast wall and excavating a trench nine feet deep near columns supporting the structure. In exposing the foundation of the institution he revealed the site where art depends upon the meeting of nature and culture to sustain it. Burden performed similar exposés in *Full Financial Disclosure* (1977), in which he made his gross income public, in *Working Artist* (November 22–24, 1975), during which he worked in a gallery, treating visitors as guests, and in *Honest Labor* (March 26–30, 1979), for which he spent five days digging a deep ditch from 9 am to 5 pm in a Vancouver vacant lot.

Burden has also used light to contrast the spiritual with the dark side of human nature in the convergence of cultural and political affairs. One of his first youthful encounters with this dichotomy was on Elba where he recalled the vivid impression of opening his bedroom curtains on the first morning after his family's arrival on the island the night before:

> On one side of the brick building [next to his building], painted by hand with red paint, [was] a swastika four stories high. Four stories high in red paint! I knew what a swastika was. I'd seen them in France or in books. But I'd never seen one four stories high, graffiti-style, bright red. As a little kid, I remember looking at that and looking at that brand new Mayor's building painted all white and thinking, 'This is not an accident. This is an official statement of policy.'[56]

Burden's childhood awareness of the political intricacies of interpersonal relations (*lumen*) imprinted him with concepts of good and evil as primary forces of social life and led to his juxtaposition (in literal and metaphorical uses of light and dark) of moral principles of conduct (*lux*) with questions of individual and collective responsibility. The legacy of these critical moments of conscience is represented most profoundly in his infamous performance *Shoot*, which is particularly relevant in this context, in so far as for this event Burden 'found a friend ... willing to "graze"' his arm with a bullet from a distance of about 15 feet 'while others watched the "crime".'[57]

Burden had been thinking about what it would feel like to be shot ever since the Kent State Massacre took place some eighteen months earlier on May 4, 1970, when the US National Guard opened fire on students at the University in Ohio. Four students were killed, one permanently paralyzed, and eight wounded:

> Kent State was a bigger deal to me [than Paris, May 1968] because everybody was rioting [in those days] all the time. But all of a sudden US troops were shooting at protesting students. It's like: 'Uh ha, that never happened before!' They [the police] would beat them up, club them, and mace them, but they didn't actually whip out the guns and level a volley at people who were unarmed. All of a sudden it [the violence] ... took on another dimension.[58]

His new perspective on the immediacy of political violence took the form of a question that Burden posed himself. He wondered what would happen if, during a period when 'everybody's trying to avoid being shot, I flip it over and do it on purpose?' His answer: 'I'd be right there in that weird gray area.'[59] What Burden means by the 'weird gray area', I think, is that his actions would inhabit the ambiguous interstice between perpetrator and victim. As such, *Shoot* could exhibit the state's responsibility to care for and protect its citizens; the general accountability required of citizens in any social context; the interpersonal duty one person has to another and to the self; and the precarious balance amongst responsibilities.

The very values Burden examined and established for himself in *Shoot* would be challenged 33 years later in November 2004, when one of his own graduate students, in a class taught by visiting artist Ron Athey, staged a classroom performance. The incident has been reported as follows: 'The student withdrew a

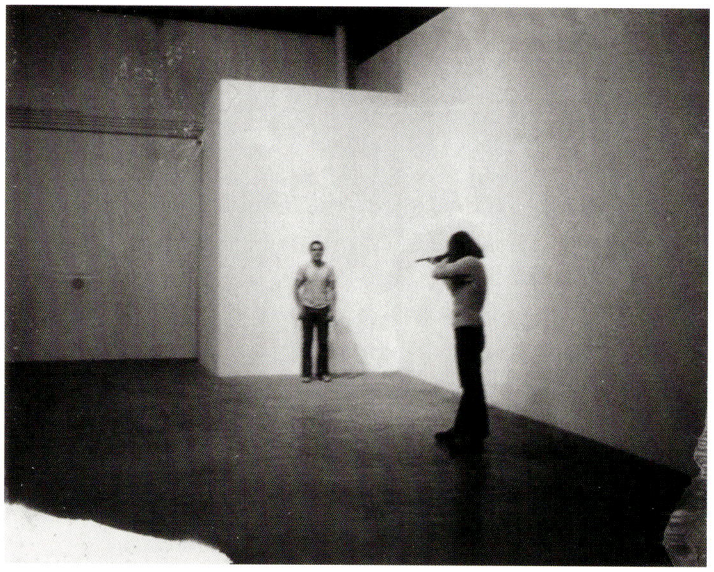

Shoot 1971

revolver from a paper bag, loaded one bullet into the chamber, and in a classic act of Russian Roulette, spun the chamber, held the gun to his head and pulled the trigger. The gun did not fire a bullet and the student abruptly fled the classroom into the night. Seconds later, the students in the classroom heard the gun being fired in the parking lot.' Burden was not present, and he resigned his 28-year teaching post after learning that the university refused to discipline the student. Significantly, in 2002, one year and several months before this incident took place at UCLA in 2004, Burden had explained why he had chosen not to perform *Shoot* on the campus of the University of California, Irvine, during a Duchamp symposium in 1971:

There was kind of a buzz. You knew there was a conference and people were going to do things. But then I started thinking about it and I thought: 'Guns on campus; that could be problematic.' It would have been a crisis with the Chancellor. It's not about testing the University or anything like that. I thought doing it in a university context could be problematic for the university. I'd already thought about shooting and being shot, and so I thought this would be a perfect place to do it and then I thought better of it. Which I think was a wise decision because the campus police would have been involved.[61]

Moreover, a letter Burden wrote the day he performed *Shoot* in 1971 explains how he came to the strategic decision not to perform such a work in a university context. To the editors of the avant-garde publication *Avalanche*, he wrote:

I was going to do a piece during the Duchamp Festival. I changed my mind and the piece is being done tonight at F Space. I will be shot with a rifle at 7:45 pm. I hope to have some good photos.[61]

Rather than highlight the sensational aspects of his deed, Burden focused on the aesthetic result of his act and its photographic documentation. This is not to say that Burden was not aware of the wider ramifications of his performance or that he did not do *Shoot* to draw attention to his work. He was and he did. But Burden limited his audience to a handful of close friends, performed the act in an obscure alternative space that he and fellow artists opened and managed, and ethically avoided any confrontation with police or the university. What must be understood is that the spectacular reception of *Shoot* went generally unnoticed until two years after it was performed when *Esquire* magazine featured Burden in the article I discussed above. It is important to put this history of *Shoot* in perspective, especially for younger artists (such as Burden's student) who may not grasp the ethical conditions under which Burden responsibly performed the piece. Moreover, in a period when the histories of performance art are increasingly distorted by critics lacking direct knowledge of its complexity and historical circumstances, by art historians inventing theories about it that are not based in the work, and by the media and Hollywood making a spectacle of performance to sell books and movies, careful examination of the origins of such renowned and controversial works as *Shoot* is even more pressing.[62]

Sensate Truth

In addition to explorations of personal responsibility, questions regarding the ethical practices of art institutions, and the moral responsibilities of viewers, Burden's work also contains overt Christian references, as in *Doorway to Heaven*, *Trans-fixed* and *The Visitation* (November 9, 1974). Not coincidentally, the impressive spectacle of salvation and damnation so often conjured in the liturgy and practices of the Catholic Church had an impact on Burden in his youth. 'My best friends were Catholics', he recalled, as were 'my brother and sister ... for a couple of years or so when they were going to a local school in [Elba] Italy.'[63] Burden remembered, for example, how his brother marched in church at the head of 'a [church] procession with the old banner swinging', and how he thought, 'Oh man they are going over; they are passing over to the Catholic side.'[64] Yet Burden's own performances, sculptures and installations rehearse a secular 'passing over' from transgression into a different order of consciousness, a transition often expressed through and/or experienced as light in a manner that recalls Christian liturgy. While Burden has never made such references himself, the symbolic and psychological use of illumination in his work evokes the figure of Christ as 'the light of the world' in the Gospel of John (8:12). Christians celebrate Easter, in particular, with fire and light rituals and 'the equation of God with the Absolute and the pure light essence finds expression also in the creed where the Son (Christi) is defined as "God of God, Light of Light, very God of very God".'[65] In Burden's art, such a view of light assumes an entirely different character, as in *Trans-fixed*, where, nailed Christ-like to a Volkswagen, Burden surged from a dark garage into the sunlight on a car that he described as 'screaming for me.'[66] While the title involves a wordplay with the term 'transportation' and the idea of being fixated on the local culture of Los Angeles with its cult of the car, it also implies the transfixing effect of Catholicism as a conveyor of meaning about life and death:

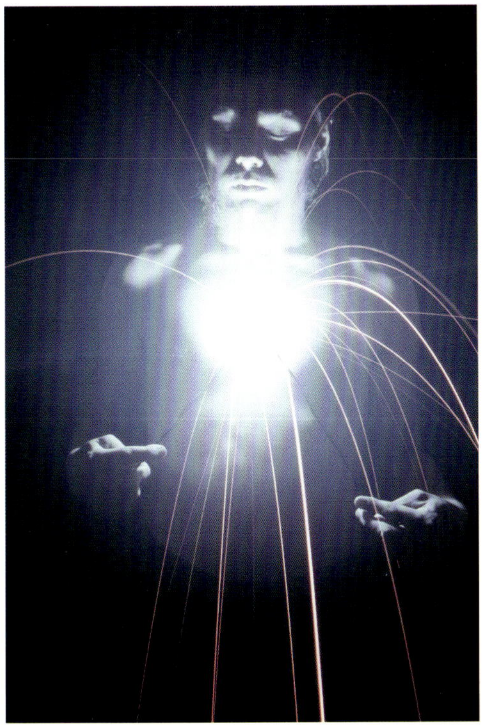

Doorway to Heaven 1973

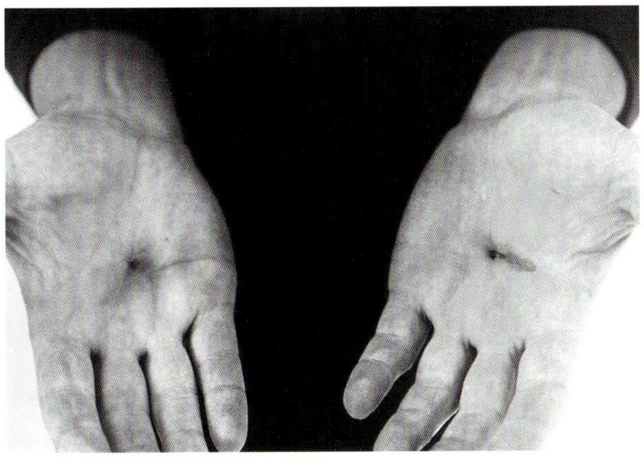

Trans-fixed 1974 (detail)

> I didn't grow up as a Catholic; I was aware of Catholic practices.... The darkness of those cathedrals is something you don't forget. They are dark and dank. Those things are spooky. It's the absence of light... Death. Those cathedrals are about nothing but death, aren't they? I think so – and how your life is transient and inconsequential in terms of the greater whole.... *Doorway to Heaven* was about doing this thing that should kill you but isn't going to because you figured out how to escape ... So the spark is a metaphor for life, if you want.... *White Light/White Heat* was a paradigm for life and for death. What seems infinite at the beginning towards the end seems transient and brief.[67]

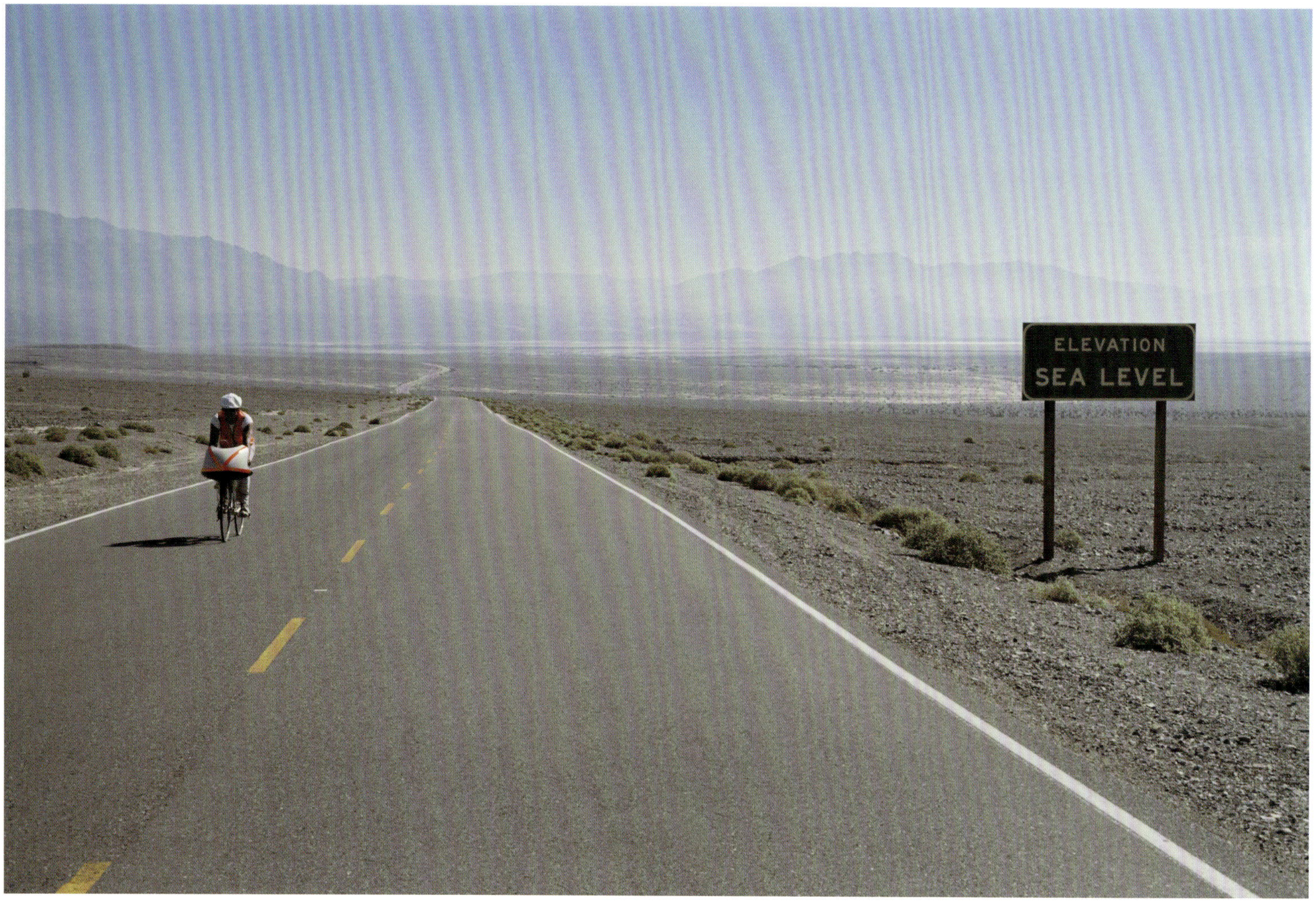

Death Valley Run 1976

Death Valley Run (October 14, 1976) also took life and death as its subject and cast the drama in the bright burning light of the desert, which also recalls the sites of Christ's torments. In this work, Burden rode a bicycle 84 miles for seven hours through the scorching heat of a mirage-filled desert in southern California, wearing all white (and an orange vest to alert motorists to his presence on the road). This action and its title suggest efforts to outrun death and to pass through the valley of death as conceived in the twenty-third Psalm, where one 'fears no evil.' As with *The Fist of Light*, riding through Death Valley exposed Burden to the dangerous aspects of light and heat that permeate his art. In another work, *B.C. Mexico* (May 25–June 10, 1973), Burden similarly exposed himself to the elements, especially the lethal aspects of light, by paddling in a small canvas kayak from San Felipe, Mexico, to a remote island beach in the Sea of Cortez. Again, in the white light and heat of sky and sea, Burden survived for 11 days with only water to sustain him in a daily average temperature of 120 degrees. The title – *B.C. Mexico* – inverts the artist's initials, drawing the subject of the work into the deep time of the earth itself as it stretches at least 4.5 billion years into the past. The reference to Mexico evokes a place of advanced civilizations, which thrived long before the Conquest with its decimating diseases and limited perspective that dates history to the birth of Christ.

Taking to the sea again in a canvas kayak in *Solaris* (October 23, 1980), Burden floated out several miles west into the Pacific into the glare of the setting sun, becoming progressively more invisible to viewers on shore who could only see him through a powerful telescope, which distorted his image and made him appear as though he had entered an otherworldly realm of light. This work recalls Russian filmmaker Andrei Tarkovsky's *Solyaris* (1972), a film suffused with a mood of foreboding, uncertainty, pain and grief that tells the story of a space station designed to study the ocean and that thematizes the failure of humanity to grasp the nature of creativity, the futility of technology to increase human understanding and human 'arrogance and faith in its own paucity of knowledge.'[68] Burden situated his own *Solaris* in the context of the Cold War space race, invoking the US space programme and using walkie-talkies to communicate with 'Mission Control'. Excerpts from the tape he presented during the performance suggest that he, once again, sought to enter the 'gray area': 'C.B. to Mission Control, Houston. / I am out here. / I am on the edge. / I am an Astronut. / Rotation 12 over 30, 39 over 52. / 14 over 23. / Vector .027. / Hull temperature 273. / Over and out.'[69]

A comment that Burden once made, in which he considered the function of his performances to be as 'sort of training for some sort of ... outer space program', is relevant to this performance as Burden's art prepared him to encounter the edges of known experience in a material universe of infinite possibility.[70] Another example of this aim might be his sculpture *The Speed of Light Machine* (1983), in which he studied the problem of light travel with the thought that he was preparing to 'travel to the distant stars.'[71] Devising original methods for the rigorous physical and mental training necessary to encounter, recognize and communicate about the unknown in itself, I theorize that Burden's art-making process and works of art represent a non-religiously based spirituality dependent upon light as a fundamental means of communication of moral concepts. While he does not purport to have religious beliefs attached to a particular doctrine, the values of Christianity appear to have determined his moral stance, even if his practices also suggest Eastern philosophy, especially Zen and Tao.[72]

Fire is another source of light in Burden's work important for its underlying secular spirituality and sensuality. Fire figures in *Match Piece* (March 20, 1972), *Dos Equis* (October 16, 1972) and *Oh, Dracula*, as well as in *Dreamy Nights* (October 15, 1974) and *The Visitation*, to name just a few performances. Additionally, many of the photographs Burden meticulously selects to represent his work often feature firelight, most notably *Deadman*, *Fire Roll* (1973), and *Icarus*.[73] Fire played a key role in Burden's installation *The Reason for the Neutron Bomb* (1979), which contained some 50,000 matchsticks, suggesting the potential for global conflagration when taken in conjunction with the work's title.[74] Among the four classic elements, fire is considered to represent a living force and is related to processes of transformation and purification. Moreover, fire is the light that signifies the active, masculine, Yang principle in Chinese symbolism and is often understood in the West as the symbol of emotion and sexual power. In *The Psychoanalysis of Fire* (1938), French philosopher Gaston Bachelard similarly linked fire with heart, love, hate and vengeance, drawing its semiotics into the domain of Eros and

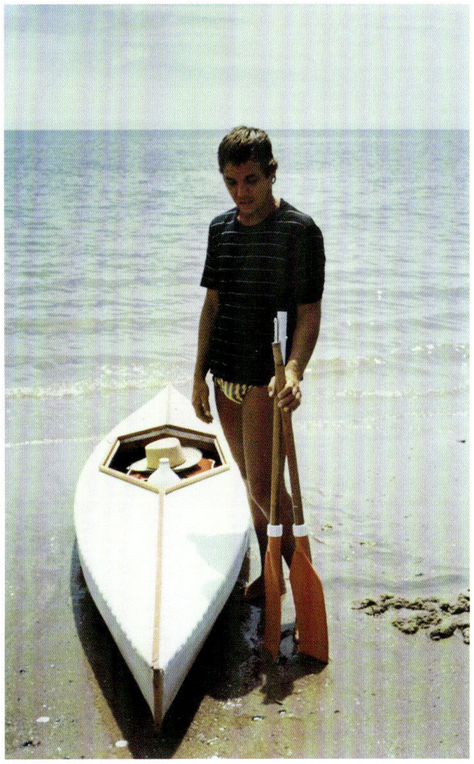

B.C. Mexico 1973

Thanatos, or the intertwining of sexuality and eroticism with mortality.[75]

I have already mentioned that many have written about Burden's masculinity, sometimes diminishing its artistic expression as the production of 'boys' toys.'[76] Such comments overlook the sexual magnetism that energizes Burden's art and its resulting hold on his viewers, trivializing the erotic attraction of his art in mere gender stereotypes. I would argue that the raw eroticism of Burden's art derives as much from his use and control of volatile materials (like fire) as it does from his personal fortitude, his fearless approach to danger, and his intrepid willingness to tolerate and survive peril. Moreover, Burden's ability to summon, endure and check intense experience, as well as to harness explosive and evocative materials and respond to and manage unpredictable audiences, unites his art with both mythic and actual powers of sexual energy and spiritual renewal. Burden imbues his objects and actions with an aloof poise that is simultaneously quiet and full of metaphorical fire. Fiercely autonomous, Burden's work is, nevertheless, connected to the viewer in ways that are simultaneously cool and hot, simple in form and dense in meaning, darkly dangerous and radiant, unyielding and forgiving, and wholly inculcated with the physiology of the muscular that is generally associated with the masculine. Finally, although personally charming and affable, Burden's trenchant refusal to court an audience – or at least to court it only on his own terms – creates a distance that neither requires approval nor is moved by censure. Such a position renders his work psychologically seductive for the ways in which it expresses his independence from the art world, at the same time as he makes his work available to the very institutions from which he remains aloof. Such qualities are the foundation of his work's sensual pull, an erotic dare that cannot be separated from the force of the ethical will behind and sustaining it.

Light Truth

While Burden does not deny the metaphysical or metaphorical implications of his art, he does not solicit such readings. Many critics support him in this effort, believing, as does Paul Schimmel, that Burden's works are 'uncluttered with religious, literary or historical references.'[77] For his part, Donald Kuspit has considered Burden's themes of transcendence only in relation to the artist's association with what he calls 'the 'mystical' character of the machine.'[78] Howard Singerman has identified Burden's 'quest for experience and knowledge', and quoted Robert Horvitz, who saw Burden's 'invitations to activity' and 'experience' as his work's key focus, rather than the 'metaphors [and] meaning' sought by the public.[79] Unquestionably, Burden is a skeptic, uninterested in 'dogma and propaganda' and wary of divulging his spiritual concerns, even though his work is saturated with characteristics that recall meditation, asceticism and mysticism. He prefers to refer to his position as that of 'free physics', which, given his educational background in science, I interpret as a manner of working that seeks to translate data from the interactions of matter and energy in both nature and culture into visual models.[80]

Burden channels his work through a rational analytic process grounded in a quality of conscience that includes principles of reason, ethics, morality and emotion. Decidedly not pious in any institutionally religious sense, Burden's vision expresses the fundamental principles of the energy that animates nature:

> When I got my new puppy, I would take her on long evening walks and try to photograph her. Invariably, by the time I had aimed the camera and pressed the button she was out of the picture frame. When I first saw this photo, I couldn't believe I had captured this nearly impossible and fleeting image of my exuberant little dog and the new moon rising. In this photograph I saw the incarnation of God.[81]

The reflection of light on the moon and the bursting life of a young animal constitute rich sources for Burden's imagination. Founded in active empirical investigations and pragmatic deliberations on material conditions, light – with all its multiple and far-ranging symbolic potentialities – carries the metaphysical weight of Burden's art. Rather than producing art that is dependent upon sight for truth, Burden unites the conceptual illumination of *lux* to the empirical understanding of *lumen*.

Attempting to capture such qualities of light, physicist Arthur Zajonc wrote in *Catching the Light* that 'the lights of nature and of mind entwine within the eye and call for vision.'[82] Indeed, light informs the theorist and the scientist, as well as 'the artist and the monk', Zajonc continues, as 'both know that through a disciplined practice they can internalize nature so that they can realize new capacities of mind.'[83] Burden has labored in light for over three decades.

Burden's art enables insight into hidden forces at the cusp of normative and mystical experience. At this nexus, Chris Burden's ineffable intelligence saturates his art with substance, integrity and peerless lucidity.

Notes

I am indebted to Rachel Leah Baum and Laurel Fredrickson for their exhaustive close readings and editorial suggestions on this manuscript, as well as to Susan Jarosi and Jay Bloom for their thoughtful commentary on the content and structure of my essay. Thanks to Katy Lucas for all her cheerful assistance in working in Burden's archive. My sincere appreciation goes to Nancy Rubins and Chris Burden for their hospitality, and to Burden for his willingness to engage in days of discussions, his openness, good will, and humor, and his fundamental insight into the nature of art, which changed my concept of art and life over the past 30 years.

1 Cathryn Vasseleu, *Textures of Light: Vision and Touch* in Irigaray, Levinas and Merleau-Ponty (London and New York: Routledge, 1998), 129. Between 1971 and 1980 Burden staged his own disappearance in the following performances: *Five Day Locker Piece* (April 26–30, 1971), *You'll Never See My Face in Kansas City* (November 6, 1971), *Disappearing* (December 22–24, 1971), *Bed Piece* (February 18–March 10, 1972), *Jaizu* (June 10–11, 1972), *Deadman* (November 12, 1972), *B.C. Mexico* (May 25–June 10, 1973), *Oh, Dracula* (October 7, 1974), *Dreamy Nights* (October 15, 1974), *The Visitation* (November 9, 1974), *White Light/White Heat* (February 8–March 1, 1975), *Oracle* (May 14, 1975), *The Citadel* (August 8–12, 1978), *Warning! Relax, Or You Will Be Nuked Again* (September 13, 1980), and *Hercules* (March 27, 1982). After 1980, Burden made a number of installations, sculptures, or visionary unrealized works that used light or its absence, including but not limited to, *A Tale of Two Cities* (1981), *Scale Model of the Solar System* (1983), *The Speed of Light Machine* (1983), *The Fist of Light* (1993), *The Hidden Force* (1995), and *Urban Light* (2005).

2 James Collins, 'Reviews', *Artforum* 11:9 (May 1973): 72.

3 In 1972, Robert Hughes authored an article that has had an enduringly negative impact on the reception of performance art and on the understanding of its cultural meaning and social purpose. Hughes wrote that Schwarzkogler 'proceeded, inch by inch, to amputate his own penis, while a photographer recorded the act as an art event... Successive acts of self-amputation finally did Schwarzkogler in.' See Robert Hughes, 'The Decline and Fall of the Avant-Garde', *Time* magazine (December 18, 1972): 111. In 1990, I published an article refuting this myth that was based on extensive research in Austrian archives (including Schwarzkogler's own library) and interviews with Schwarzkogler's common-law wife Edith Adam, as well as all of the artists associated with Vienna Action Art and Austrian art historians and art dealers. Six years later in 1996, Hughes publicly acknowledged my scholarship and his error in *The New Yorker* (November 11, 1996): 36. See Kristine Stiles, 'Notes on Rudolf Schwarzkogler's Images of Healing', *White Walls* 25 (Spring 1990): 13–26, reprinted in *Rudolf Schwarzkogler* (Vancouver: University of British Columbia, 1993), 29–39 and Stiles, 'Readings: Performance and Its Objects', *Arts* magazine 65:3 (November 1990): 35–47.

4 Mäns Wrange, 'A Conversation with Chris Burden', in *Chris Burden* (Stockholm: Magasin 3 Stockholm Konsthall, 1999), n.p.

5 Howard Singerman, 'Chris Burden's Pragmatism', in *Chris Burden: A Twenty-Year Survey* (Newport Beach: Newport Harbor Art Museum, 1988), 22.

6 Robert Horvitz quoted in Singerman, 22. See also Horvitz's 'Chris Burden', *Artforum* 14:9 (May 1976): 27.

7 Donald Kuspit, 'Man For and Against Machine', in Peter Noever, ed., *Chris Burden: Beyond the Limits* (Vienna and Ostifildern, Austria: MAK and Cantz Verlag, 1996), 83.

8 Kathy O'Dell, *Contract with the Skin: Masochism, Performance Art and the 1970s* (Minneapolis: University of Minnesota Press, 1998). O'Dell's study is an insightful psychoanalytic, sexual, and political theory of the masochistic artist that moves from Lacan's Law of the Father and the laws of the state to the failure of the social contract in the Vietnam War and the social and the politics of the sado-masochistic exchange. While I deeply admire O'Dell's work, I strongly depart from her description of Burden as a masochistic artist. His enactment of situations of danger and pain do, however, summon consideration of what I have called the 'social contract' between performance artists and their publics. I developed this concept in relation to performance practices during the seminar I taught at Berkeley in 1979, which O'Dell attended as a fellow graduate student. She later formulated a much deeper, richer, and broader concept of the 'social contract' for her doctoral dissertation, which became the basis for her book *Contract with the Skin*. My own notion of the 'social contract' in 1979 was limited to the role that interpersonal responsibility plays in Burden's and other performance artists' work. At my invitation, Burden, Tom Marioni, Linda Montano, and Laurie Anderson all came to my seminar to discuss their work in 1979.

9 See Kenneth Evett, 'Death Wish', *The New Republic* (May 17, 1975): 31.

10 The lyrics of the song include the following phrases: 'White light, white light goin' messin' up my mind/White light, and don't you know its gonna make me go blind'. See the Velvet Underground, *White Light/White Heat*. New York: Scepter Studios, 1967.

11 All of the documentation on *White Light/White Heat* neglects to mention that Burden drank this juice each day. Burden revealed this critical aspect of the work in our extended, unpublished conversations of September 11–14, 2003, in his Topanga Canyon studio in California. Hereafter this interview is cited as Burden/Stiles.

12 Moreover, by removing himself from view, Burden strategically refused to accede to what Frank Perrin has called 'the egotistical desires of artists and American society in general'. See Frank Perrin, 'An Administration of Extreme Urgency', in *Chris Burden: Un Livre de Survie* (Paris: Blocnotes éditions, 1995), 149.

13 Johannes Lothar Schröder, 'Science, Heat and Time', in Peter Noever, ed., *Chris Burden: Beyond the Limits*, 203.

14 See Paul Grobstein's commentary on October 16, 2005 in Kristine Stiles and Paul Grobstein, 'The Art Historian and the Neurobiologist: A Conversation About Proprioception, the "I-function", Body Art, and Story Telling?' in *Serendip*, Bryn Mawr University: http://serendip.brynmawr.edu/bb/artneuro/

15 *Ibid.*

16 *Ibid.*

17 Alain Berthoz, *The Brain's Sense of Movement* (Cambridge: Harvard University Press, 2000): 25.

18 See Grobstein's student, Shannon Lee's 'Proprioception: How and Why?' on *Serendip*, the Bryn Mawr College electronic journal: http://serendip.brynmawr.edu/bb/neuro/neuro02/web2/slee.html (accessed 5 June 2005). See also Nana Dawson-Andoh, 'Phantom Limbs, Phantom Pain, and The "I-Function"', http://serendip.brynmawr.edu/bb/neuro/neuro01/web1/Dawsonandoh.html (accessed 5 June 2005). For more on phantom limbs, see Rupert Sheldrake's 'Extended Mind' in his *Seven Experiments that could Change the World: A Do-It-Yourself Guide To Revolutionary Science* (London: Fourth Estate, 1995).

19 Robert Horvitz, 'Chris Burden', *Artforum* 14:9 (1976): 24.

20 Grobstein also uses the phrase 'story teller' for the 'I-function' 'in order to give increased emphasis to the point that there is an arbitrariness and potentially a creative/discretionary element, inherent in the process that produces what we are aware of. In addition, it has become clear to me that not all awarenesses are centered around 'I'... but can also be about communities or other less individualized, egocentric actors. Thirdly, the original I-function concept seemed to make the

process equivalent to verbal report/language usage, and it is clearly not. It is a process on which language depends but one that exists prior to language.' Paul Grobstein email to the author October 22, 2005. Having shared this essay and my work on Burden with Grobstein, he and I have agreed to collaborate on a publication concerned with the intersection between his concept of I-function (or 'story teller') and my theorizations of the survival functions of proprioception in art.

21 Berthoz: 28.

22 While this is not the place to expand on the central importance of proprioception to performance art and its viewers, this is a heretofore unexplored, foundational aspect of art that uses the body as its primary material. Moreover, it is no accident that such art should emerge in an historical period in which the body is under great threat from revolution, terrorism, wars, nuclear holocaust, environmental warming, disease and pandemics (such as HIV–AIDS and the Avian Flu), as well as genetic engineering and the post-human or post-biological age. I further explored my theory of proprioception in Burden's work in a lecture entitled 'The "I-Function" and Proprioception in Chris Burden's Performances and Installations', for the 19th annual meeting of the Society for Literature, Science, and the Arts (SLSA) in Chicago, 2005.

23 Noel Frackman, 'Chris Burden', *Arts* magazine 49:8 (April, 1975): 9.

24 Porn star Linda Lovelace was pictured on the cover of the issue. A photograph of Burden dazed and bandaged – immediately following *Shoot* – appeared on a two-page spread next to a picture of L. Patrick Gray III, J. Edgar Hoover's replacement as Director of the FBI. Other individuals featured in the issue included the flamboyant preacher Reverend Ike (aka Frederick J. Eikerenkoetter II), a card shark named Amarillo Slim, a former policewoman and novelist named Dorothy Uhnak, and the basketball legend Julius Erving. See *Esquire* 79:5 (May 1973): 159.

25 *Ibid.*

26 Claes Oldenberg, 'I Am for an Art...', *Environments, Situations, Spaces* (New York: Martha Jackson Gallery, 1961). See also Oldenburg and Emmett Williams, eds., *Store Days: Documents from The Store (1961) and Ray Gun Theater (1962)* (New York: Something Else Press, 1967), 39–42; reprinted in Kristine Stiles and Peter Selz, eds., *Theories and Documents of Contemporary Art: A Sourcebook of Artists' Writings* (Berkeley: University of California Press, 1996), 336.

27 Frank Perrin, 'An Administration of Extreme Urgency': 149.

28 Burden/Stiles.

29 Chris Burden quoted in Corina Ferrari, 'Interview with Chris Burden', *Domus* 549 (August 1975): 50.

30 Burden remembers the incident this way: 'During one of the last days, a young lady came in and she said she wanted to take pictures. People weren't allowed to take pictures. [She pulled] the old art student: 'Oh I'm just taking pictures for my art report.' All of a sudden she has this super long monopod and I am staring right at the lens of this camera. So the gallery people catch her. Ron [Feldman] and her tussle on the floor; he opens her camera and pulls the film out. She's screaming: "You manhandled me, I'm calling the cops. Give us back the film." There is this whole brouhaha. About two or three years later, she was going around Soho trying to sell these photos. She tricked them. She got to keep her real film and gave them a faux film. She outfoxed them. She was doing that, I'm convinced, because she was sure that nobody was up there [on the platform], and she was going to show the world with photographic proof that it was a fraud. She was surprised to see me there.' Burden/Stiles.

31 Larry Grobel, 'Chris Burden: Picasso used canvas, Michelangelo used marble. Chris Burden uses his body', *Playgirl* (April 1978): 48–51, 64–66.

32 Performance artist Marina Abramovic has questioned the truth of Burden's 22-day feat of endurance in *White Light/White Heat* while assuring the public of the veracity of her own perseverance in *The House with the Ocean View* (November 15–26, 2002), a 12-day action in which she lived on three platforms in the Sean Kelly Gallery in New York without eating or speaking. Rather than being invisible like Burden, she exposed all of her activities, living without privacy in rooms open to spectators who could also observe her close up with a high-powered telescope. Moreover, based on her questioning of its authenticity, Abramovic proposed to remake *White Light/White Heat* for a series of reenacted performances based on the work of artists of the 1970s at the Guggenheim Museum in New York, October 2005. Burden does not remake his own works and denied her permission to do so.

33 While it has often been rumored that Beuys left the gallery to enjoy an evening meal and a good night's rest after gallery hours, this fact is confirmed by Uwe M. Schneede in *Joseph Beuys Die Aktionen*, the most authoritative and comprehensive study of Beuys' performances. He wrote: 'On the three days, the Action lasted from 10 to 18 hours' (An den drei Tagen dauerte die Aktion jeweils von 10 bis 18 Uhr). See Schneede's *Joseph Beuys Die Aktionen: Kommentiertes Werkverzeichnis mit fotografischen Dokumentationen* (Ostfildern-Ruit bei Stuttgart: Verlag Gerd Haatje, 1994), 331.

34 Peter Clothier, 'Chris Burden: The Artist as Hero', *Flash Art* 94/95 (January/February 1980): 49.

35 Johannes Lothar Schröder, 'Science, Heat and Time': 207.

36 Burden/Stiles.

37 Howard Singerman, 'Chris Burden's Pragmatism': 22.

38 Burden remembered: 'After being up there three weeks, I really didn't want to come down. *White Light/White Heat* became really spooky for me because it became a microcosm for life, for one's life itself. It seems infinite when you start and as you get through it, 'Whoa, it's almost over: Jesus Christ!' Burden/Stiles.

39 Robin White, 'Interview with Chris Burden', *View* 1:8 (January 1978): 7.

40 Burden/Stiles.

41 Kathy O'Dell, *Contract with the Skin*: 66. O'Dell categorized the following performances as 'bed pieces': *Bed Piece*, *Oh, Dracula*, *White Light/White Heat*, *Doomed*, and *Oracle*. O'Dell deftly raised the psychological dimension of Burden's repetitive focus on the bed, referring to a bedroom œdipal drama. Again, she was correct: Burden spent his childhood in the midst of parental conflict.

42 In 1955, Edward Steichen organized the exhibition *The Family of Man* at the Museum of Modern Art in New York. It included Margaret Bourke-White, Matthew Brady, Robert Capa, Henri Cartier-Bresson, Jack Delano, Alfred Eisenstaedt, Dorothea Lange, Carl Mydans, Ben Shahn, and Edward Weston, among others. See, Edward Steichen, *The Family of Man: The greatest photographic exhibition of all time – 503 pictures from 68 countries* (New York: Museum of Modern Art and the Maco Magazine Corp., 1955).

43 Burden felt isolated even before the accident, as he 'was going to do correspondence school, this Quaker thing' and had not enrolled in public school. Burden/Stiles.

44 *Ibid.*

45 *Ibid.*

46 See Chris Burden's comments in Peter Noever, ed., *Chris Burden: Beyond the Limits*, 183.

47 Robin White, 'Interview with Chris Burden', *View*: 7.

48 For a discussion of dualisms related to light, see P.F.M. Fontaine, *The Light and The Dark: A Cultural History of Dualism*, Vol I, II, and III (Amsterdam: J.C. Gieben, 1986).

49 Discussing the necessity to feed himself and provide for his physical needs during *Bed Piece*, Burden noted that he 'was trying to confront Josh Young, who was the guy who ran [the gallery], that I was both an object and a human being. This was a special art show. He couldn't just lock the doors and

go home. The object had problems. If I had to get up and pee, I had to pee behind the desk on the floor or in the wastebasket or something. He had a problem on his hands, and he had to deal with it.' Burden/Stiles.

50 Kristine Stiles, 'Chris Burden's Free Physics', in *Chris Burden* (New York: Zwirner & Wirth Gallery, 2004), 4.

51 See also the following projects: *The Reason for the Neutron Bomb* (1979), *Pearl Harbor* (1979), *Atomic Alphabet* (1979), *Warning! Relax, Or You Will Be Nuked Again* (1980), and *A Tale of Two Cities* (1982).

52 Burden/Stiles.

53 *Ibid.*

54 Chris Burden in Frances Morris, Chris Burden: *When Robots Rule: The Two-Minute Airplane Factory* (London: Tate Gallery Publishing, 1999), 43.

55 Plato, *Republic*. Translated by G.M.A. Grube, revised by C.D.C. Reeve (Indianapolis and Cambridge: Hackett Publishing company, Inc, 1992): 287.

56 Burden/Stiles. With regard to the impact of Fascism on Burden's imagination, his sculpture/installation *Pizza City* (1996) bears a striking resemblance to the aerial view of Nuremberg in Leni Riefenstahl's film *Triumph of the Will* (1935) from the beginning sequence in which Hitler's plane flies over the city with its steeples and half-timber houses.

57 Paul Schimmel, 'Just the Facts', in *Chris Burden*: 16.

58 Burden/Stiles. On January 4, 1979, the state of Ohio agreed to pay $675,000 to families of the dead and injured victims of the Kent State University shootings.

59 Chris Burden quoted in Susan Freudenheim, 'The Artist as Canyon Jumper', *Los Angeles Times Magazine* (July 13, 2003): 23.

60 Burden/Stiles.

61 From an unpublished letter by Chris Burden, dated November 19, 1971 and addressed to Willoughby Sharp and Liza Béar; currently in Chris Burden's personal archive, Topanga, California. This terse statement parallels the infamous action, which took place in a fraction of a second when an assistant fired a .22 rifle and hit the artist in the arm. A photograph captures the image, recalling the relationship between photography and guns in the development of the history of photography from Etienne-Jules Marey's revolver-gun camera (*fusil photographique*) to the Austrian philosopher Ernst Mach's collaboration in 1886 with the Austrian photographer Peter Salcher (1848–1928) to photograph bullets in flight. Schlieren Photography is a technique that required casting a light source onto a knife edge where changes in the density of a transparent medium (such as glass or air) between the light source and the knife-edge altered the refractive index more or less, thereby diverting the light and causing light or dark areas in the picture.

62 Don DeLillo's novel *The Body Artist* (2001), which portrays a performance artist in the most arcane and unrealistic way, comes to mind, as does *Legal Eagles* (1986), the Hollywood film comedy starring Daryl Hannah as a 'crazy performance artist.' Moreover, in the December 11, 2005, issue of *The New York Times Book Review*, Barry Gewen, its editor, opened his essay 'State of the Art', with a comment meant to undermine contemporary art with a description of a work of art by Burden, presented without comment or context: 'In 1974, Chris Burden had himself crucified on the roof of a Volkswagen' (p. 28). Precisely such sensationalized representations of Burden's work (and performance art in general) detract from a rich and deep understanding of this medium of art, and fail to account for its appearance as a dominate global practice in the wake of the Holocaust and the atomic bomb when the body and survival of the planet itself became an abiding dilemma for humanity. Burden's performances, installations, and sculptures are resounding testimonies to the question of survival in the twentieth and twenty-first centuries.

63 Burden/Stiles.

64 *Ibid.*

65 R.J. Zwi Werblowsky, 'Light and Darkness', in *The Encyclopedia of Religion* (New York: MacMillan Publishing Company, 1987), 549.

66 Burden's documentation of this performance uses the phrase, 'Screaming for me, the engine was run at full speed for two minutes.' Any publication on this work contains these words. See, for example, Peter Noever, ed., *Chris Burden: Beyond the Limits*, 69.

67 Burden/Stiles.

68 Gerald Lucas, 'Tarkovsky's *Solaris*' http://litmuse.maconstate.edu/~glucas/archives/000359.shtml (accessed May 30, 2005).

69 Burden in *Chris Burden: Un Livre de Survie*, 141–142.

70 Robin White, 'Interview with Chris Burden', *View*: 1.

71 Burden in Peter Noever, ed., *Chris Burden: Beyond the Limits*, 174.

72 Thanks to Karen Gonzales for discussions on this formulation.

73 By igniting gasoline on six-foot sheets of glass resting on his shoulders, Burden created wings of flame in *Icarus*. By referring to the mythical boy intoxicated with flight whose wax wings burned when he got too near the sun and plunged to his death in the sea when the wings melted, *Icarus* raises more oedipal questions related to Kathy O'Dell's study of Burden. For Dædalus, an architect, sculptor, and inventor, as well as Icarus' father, constructed the wings. This parallels the relation of Burden and his diplomat, engineer father, and therefore suggest an intertwining between the violence and destruction in Burden's art and his relationship with his father. Georges Bataille compared Icarus to Prometheus and the Mithraic bull as examples of those who challenged the mythical alliance between the eagle and the sun, namely who challenged 'the unconstrained development of individual authoritarian power.' He also notes: 'The myth of Icarus is particularly expressive from this point of view: it clearly splits the sun in two – the one that was shining at the moment of Icarus's elevation, and the one that melted the wax, causing failure and screaming fall when Icarus got too close. This human tendency to distinguish two suns owes its particular importance ... to the fact that the psychological movements described are not ones that have been diverted, nor their urges attenuated, by secondary elements.' Georges Bataille, 'The "Old Mole" and the Prefix Sur', in *Visions of Excess: Selected Writings, 1927–1939*, ed. and trans. Allan Stoekly with Carl R. Lovitt and Donald M. Leslie, Jr. (Minnesota: University of Minnesota Press, 1985), 34, 58.

74 *Fire By Friction* (1982), *From Neanderthal to the 20th Century* (1983), and *The Frictionless Sled* (1983) all call for fire or friction, the prelude to fire.

75 Gaston Bachelard, *The Psychoanalysis of Fire*. Translated by Alan C.M. Ross. Boston, Beacon Press, 1964, published first in Paris by Gallimard, 1938.

76 Steve Mumford in a review of *The Fist of Light* (1993) associated Burden's work with 'boys' toys' and described his strength as an artist in inane terms as a 'mean streak of adolescent megalomania.' See Mumford's 'Art and Adolescent Megalomania: Boy Toys and Other Cool Stuff' (1997), in *Plexus Reviews* http://www.plexus.org/review/mumford/boytoys.html#mumford (accessed May 22, 2005).

77 Paul Schimmel, 'Just the Facts': 15.

78 Donald Kuspit, 'Man For and Against Machine': 79. In *Poem for L.A.* (1975), Burden stated 'SCIENCE HAS FAILED'. Nevertheless, Burden often consults scientific and technological manuals, subscribing to over 50 magazines ranging in subject matter from news, science, nature, and culture to popular mechanics.

79 Howard Singerman, 'Chris Burden's Pragmatism': 20.

80 K. Stiles, 'Chris Burden's Free Physics': 1.

81 Meg Cranston and John Baldessari, *100 Artists See God* (London, Institute of Contemporary Arts, 2004), n.p.

82 Arthur Zajonc, *Catching the Light: The Entwined History of Light and Mind* (New York: Bantam Books, 1993): 2.

83 *Ibid.*, 341.

Robert Storr

Immanent Domain

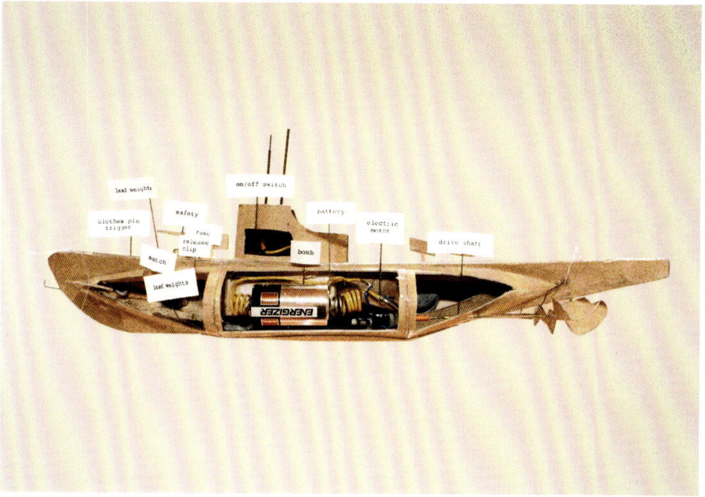

Exploding Subs 1983 (detail)

The gendering of art is a process well on its way. Too far along some would say. What happened, they protest, to the universal subject and the grandeur of classical art this fiction underwrote? And what of Kant's disinterested viewer whose ostensibly pure aesthetic judgments were unswayed by the contingencies of his – never her – own social status and context? 'Gone with the Gaze' is the shorthand answer.

The longer, more detailed and not always congruent answers regarding this shift in perspective can be found in the writings of Judith Butler, Laura Mulvey, Linda Nochlin, Craig Owens, Griselda Pollock and a host of others whose contributions to art history and theory have opened our eyes to the fact that we do not all 'see' the same things in the same manner. That is to say, we do not perceive reality in its manifold dimensions with identical fullness or intensity, much less assimilate or interpret it – if we in any way do so self-consciously – within the same conceptual framework. Of course, the notion that individual viewpoints are necessarily incomplete in relation to the complexity of observed phenomena and may be inherently skewed in relation to an ideal objectivity is hardly new to philosophical debate. What is of recent date are the overlapping patterns of analysis which map and correlate the structures of myopia or bias of a particular perspective in a particular time and place. Still, the fact that the seemingly unarguable contention that vision is partial and sexually inflected has met such resistance, merely proves that seeing is not exclusively, or even primarily, a sensory function – the 'innocent eye' is a myth – but rather a deeply ingrained and heavily filtered psycho-cultural one.

Yet inasmuch as this critique has been aimed at patriarchy by those who have suffered most from its assumption that the experience of men can be taken as an accurate measure of the diverse totality of experiences of the world, a reductive account of masculine sensibilities has often resulted from the need to create a monolithic male Other for the plurality of other 'Others' in rebellion. After a quarter century of challenges to such negative archetypes it is time to turn the tables several degrees and add some nuance to the discussion of what and how men actually think, and, more importantly given the focus of this essay, what and how they dream. Have no fear, I am not about to veer off into a sentimental plea for understanding of the victimized victimizer or an armpit-sniffing ode to manly virtues and values. You are in good hands so far as that goes. Not only does the author have scant interest in muscles or muscle cars, he can't even drive, though from some vantage points that might also disqualify him from writing about a Los Angeles artist of either gender. But after years of listening to polemical assessments of work by male artists of the postwar generations that automatically assume that bold brush work *ipso facto* constitutes some sort of ejaculatory performance and that a preference for steel or lead was *prima facie* evidence that a guy with a torch or a ladle was engaged in a sweat-soaked heroic action, I have become increasingly alert to how much of the messy business of masculine becoming gets lost in its translation into art critical discourse. I am thinking especially of the actual fantasies of boys-to-men and the quirky, often embarrassing, practices and pleasures they give rise to – pun intended.

I will continue with the first person for a bit longer but want to state flatly that the specific fantasies I am about to describe are, or were, my own. I have no intention of casually foisting them off on the artist, Chris Burden, about whom I will speak shortly. Nevertheless, operating on the hunch that collapsing the distance between us somewhat may serve a useful purpose for readers, especially those whose point of departure has little or nothing in common with his or mine, I would simply note that we both grew up in the 1950s in comfortable, well-educated, middle-class milieus. We both are white, straight, quick to react to emotional and intellectual impulses and disinclined to take other people's word for anything. Against this background I was probably more introverted than Burden and in subsequent phases of maturing less daring. That said, I was by no means timid or unsociable, nor, for all the time I spent in my own fanciful domain, was I a shut-in. There was no need to be since that alternative realm and its potential adventures accompanied me everywhere I went and I was safe so long as they remained vivid. Whether travelling down a highway or walking down the street, I opportunistically projected my portable universe onto the circumstances in which I found myself, like a movie onto the nearest available wall. Since much of its content came from movies and TV, this was easy.

However, the best of all oneiric theaters was live and interactive rather than remembered and replayed, and the vehicles for those imaginings were plastic soldiers – tellingly I called them 'little men' – augmented by horses, motorcycles, trucks and tanks that traveled with my own guttural sound effects over vast landscapes made up of bedspreads, rugs, bolsters, throw pillows and various pieces of less makeshift scenery that actually looked like the things I needed them to be. Of the latter, some were store-bought parts of model railroad sets, in various gauges from the big Lionel trains to the exquisite, small Swiss and German ones (disparities of scale did not impede suspension of disbelief). Some were period pieces like beautifully molded and polychromed catapults and castles produced by Britains Ltd. (expensive) and others were plain brown frontier fortresses built with Lincoln Logs (cheap). Some were made by my father, who was handy with tools, and some by myself, who wasn't but could do what was necessary with paint to make nailed together scraps of wood resemble a piece of field artillery. Toothpicks and matchsticks by the thousands were stuck with oozing white Elmer's Glue-All to make stockades, supplementary war machinery and a decent facsimile of the *Bridge Over the River Kwai*: cue a mental soundtrack of the Colonel Boogie March as visions of Alec Guinness and Sessue Hayakawa loom up. However, the basic substance of memory reclaimed here is not these tragic antagonists but the sight and sound of explosions sundering my construction.

Outside of this domain I was, or thought myself to be, helpless. Within it I held full command. Consequently I spent as much time there as I could, for as long as I could. The painful breakthrough into puberty and its shame-ridden aftermath came not when I was caught by an adult looking at the Playboy magazines passed on to me by my older sister's boyfriend but when, some time following my initiation into glossy erotica, this porn mentor interrupted me while I was in the midst of staging a Lilliputian Armageddon on my desk, complete with the sputtered noises of bombs going off which would have embarrassed me far less if they had been orgasmic grunts. He frowned at my childishness. I cringed at it and put away my 'little men' forever. Such are the rites of passage, American-style.

The male gaze so often spoken of in critical texts usually refers to the way men look at women in art and in the world, their motives presumably being both lustful and controlling. This by now standard interpretation in turn typecasts men as heterosexual and 'naturally' self-assertive, thereby obscuring latent vulnerabilities and competing, even divergent desires readily apparent to self-aware men looking at the same representations. It also tends to ignore or take for granted the complexities of that gaze when focused elsewhere. How little has been said of boys-with-their-toys is some indication of this tendency. Involuntarily triggered by my own hypersensitivity to the subject (the true 'subject' of course being my still humiliated former-self-in-transition), I have kept a mental catalogue of art in which elements of this play dynamic appear.

First in fantasy-driven sequence comes Eric Fischl's painting *Best Western* (1983), in which a boy wearing a white T-shirt and clutching oranges to his chest sits at the edge of an outdoor pool under the night sky. Scattered in front of him is a squad of tiny cowboys and Indians which he bowls over with a heavy round orange. Considering the developmentally staggered reveries of secret sex and secret violence – magazine masturbation eventually overtaking war games along this trajectory – the implicit companion piece to this picture by Fischl is his *Sleepwalker* (1979), in which an adolescent – this time entirely naked with his back to the viewer – jerks off in a plastic wading pool situated in the grassy middle of a well-lit back yard. The subtext of both is the awkward abandonment to fantasy in which the protagonist knows he will be seen; it is the exhibitionism of a man-child who can no longer endure the anxiety of a hidden compulsion, but most of all of his unmistakable in-betweenness.

Second comes Malcolm Morley, who omits the overt sexual component of this tension (its sublimation is nevertheless palpable in the oscillation between clean photographic illusionism and messy self-gratifying painterliness.), but uses lead French Legionnaires and comparable figurines as his stand-ins, along with model airplanes and ships, some of which he builds from scratch and attaches to his canvases. These 'action' surrogates tap into the same ambivalent reservoir of remembered play that Fischl's naturalist scenarios do. Moreover, Morley's work in this vein is incomprehensible as anything except a postmodern Mannerism (Formalists – dust off your references to readymades, assemblage and combines) if one fails to pay attention to the psycho-poetics of incorporating into painting an unsuppressed, innately surreal delight in the juvenile occupation of animating tabletop still lives of men and machines. Once again the minds of men will cue the appropriate sound effects 'Vroom, Vroom, Crash' – without in the least mocking Morley's self-declared 'fine art of painting'.

Next on this abbreviated version of my much lengthier roster is Kim Jones. His transposed reality consists of penciled maps and mazes nested with hieroglyphic shapes fractured here and there by gusts of erasure. The terrain is a battlefield, the labyrinths are roadways and fortifications, the signs represent everything from barracks full of bunk beds and warehouses full of munitions to machine-gun emplacements, tanks and super cannon, while the erasures simultaneously depict a 'hit' and remove the target from the scene. Jones started making these drawings when he was a boy, but then stopped as boys usually do. He resumed making them after returning from a rough tour of duty in Vietnam, and has continued ever since. That they are still a form of play is apparent from the rules he has devised and scrupulously follows. Each side has finite material resources and tactical reserves and strategic deployment of fire-power determines the outcome. In differing formats and sizes, Jones plays the role of both sides over a period of days or months – sometimes years – although the initially improvised disposition of forces in a given instance makes it impossible to predict the overall victor at the outset of the game. Far more of male culture in our country is organized around similar pursuits than many peace-loving souls would like to think, as platoons of armchair military buffs, weekend Civil War re-enactors, paintballers and enthusiasts of strategy board games prove. The war-tested but peace-loving inventor of his own strategy game, Jones has nevertheless created an intricately seductive model of conflict that recasts the pictorial narratives of Fischl and Morley as a series of semi-abstract zero-sum equations in which the physical evidence of struggle begins with a sharp pewter-gray incision and ends with the methodically annihilating smudge. Since the artist commands both of the antagonists, the winner is simultaneously the loser. It is an intimate diagram of assured mutual destruction. The hypnotic quality of these drawings will immediately exert its effects on anyone who has ever drawn the order of battle in the dirt or covered sheets of paper with graphic armies. The pathos that infuses them will strike anyone who has seen mechanized carnage or pondered documentation of it. Ultimately, they will mean most to those who can experience both responses, and the majority of that group will be men.

Then there is Chris Burden. I have taken the long way around to his work not because it comes last to mind – quite the contrary – but in order to make it truly central by first establishing the points of reference that bracket my sense of its logic and importance. Given the extent and variety of Burden's relevant production, those brackets must be widely placed, since they have to encompass pieces from early in his post-performance career up to the present – from the slightness of a wind-up airplane to a gnarled globe 14 feet in diameter. Common to all, and pronounced to varying degrees, is the simple formal operation of miniaturization and the complex phenomenological and metaphorical functions that reduction of scale and expansion of scope – microcosmic object, macrocosmic referent – set in motion. Enmeshed within this matrix are many of the conceptual and perceptual dynamics I have mentioned with regard to other artists as well as my own boyhood recreations, and all the emotional stresses and satisfactions that attend them.

Manipulating a thing smaller than oneself gives one a feeling of power. Seeing the whole of a situation as if from on high amplifies this sensation. Together they suggest total mastery over everything within reach, thus according one the role of an omnipotent and omniscient God. Run these last few sentences through the scanning devices of more Manichean gender theory, and Burden stands convicted of classic masculine hubris. When the specific iconography of some of his sculptures is taken into account – tanks and soldiers – bellicosity and destructiveness might be added to male delusions of grandeur. Granted, an extreme essentializing view such as that just sketched is something of a red herring. So far, no one has attacked Burden from this angle. But neither has there been much discussion of the thornier aspect of his consistent emphasis on fantasy formats which entail the power relations broadly spelled out. This silence has the quality of avoidance, as if it were easier not to notice how profound the maleness of his art is for fear of having to grapple with a readily recognizable but disturbing trait in a person otherwise embraced by critical consensus.

Nor has anyone taken a close look at the ways in which Burden's use of these tropes differs from that of his contemporaries. This may be the result of further parochial art world blind spots, since, as a performer, video artist and sculptor who came of age in the late 1960s, Burden belongs to generation now grandfathered into the neo-avant-garde. He is thus exempt from certain post-modern critiques, whereas Morley (older than Burden) and Fischl (younger) are painters whose prominence in the 1980s, when 'Neo-Expressionism' was all the rage in collecting circles (hence the target of rage among dissenters), leaves them outside of most post-modern discourse. Still, as an under-appreciated artist, Jones is a special case; he has the most in common with Burden, including a role in the inception of conceptually oriented body art in Southern California and he serves as a more useful referent overall. For the rest, though, it is plain to see that Burden's regression to the toy box does not have the exuberance of that grizzled and apocalyptic Peter Pan Morley, nor does his work have the Freudian narrative and nostalgic aura cultivated by Fischl. Burden is not reliving or portraying boyhood, but rather reviving its behaviors for coping with a world too big to be at home in so as to articulate an entirely adult skepticism about power and its follies.

For starters let's take *Coals to Newcastle* (1978) – one of Burden's last performances prior to his concentration on sculpture and one of the first works in which a model airplane appears – and consider the title. Employing a fragment of a nineteenth-century English expression signifying a gratuitous action that adds a useless increment to a pre-existing surplus of the same

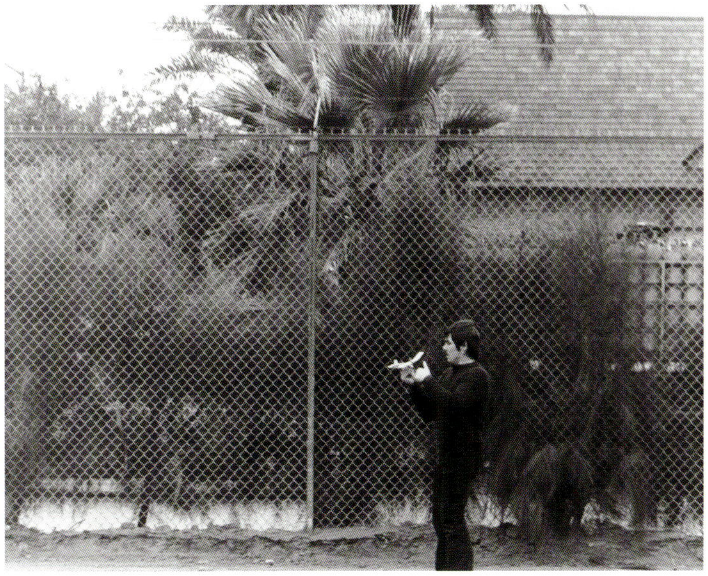

Coals to Newcastle 1978

thing, Burden labels this exercise in polemical foolishness with a phrase that only a fairly sophisticated twentieth-century American could catch. Californian kids don't talk that way. In this instance, the surplus substance was marijuana, and Burden's gratuitous gesture consisted of sending two joints attached to the wing of a rubber band powered, balsawood plane back across the border with Mexico whence most of the best dope came in those days. In short, the piece is an impudent gag directed at the pretense that the Southern frontier of the United States could be sealed by the vigilant forces of order, thereby protecting native youth from alien corruption. Burden simultaneously flew under government radar by absurdly primitive means (symbolically presaging the susceptibility of high-tech security to low-tech incursions that has since acquired far more ominous dimensions) and reversed the traffic, demonstrating that drugs are indigenous rather than foreign. *Coals to Newcastle* postdates another work, *C.B.T.V. to Einstein* (1977), that also uses a wind-up plane to satirize technology. While hurtling across the Atlantic at 1400 miles per hour in the Concorde, Burden flew his own hobby-kit aircraft down the length of the cabin, reasoning that his model traveled at the same rate as the Concorde plus its own velocity of 10 miles per hour, thus exceeding the speed of the larger plane.

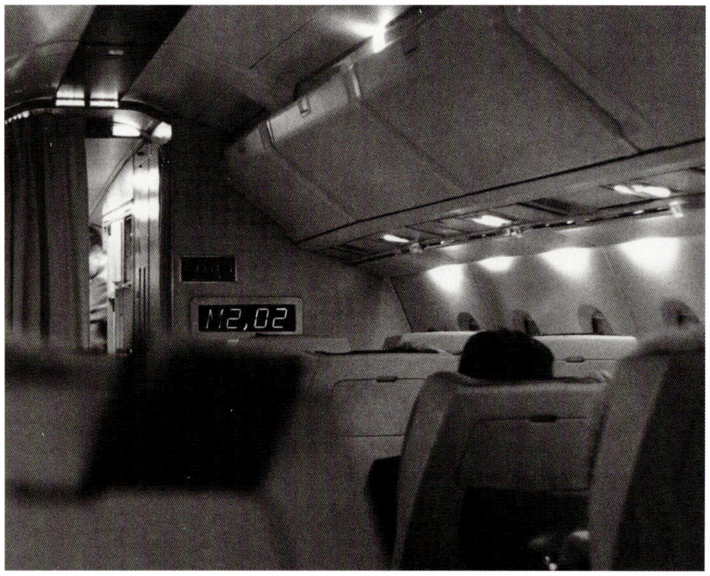

C.B.T.V. to Einstein 1977

Together, these early forays into screwball empiricism set the tone of much that was to follow, even as they methodologically connect the latter phases of Burden's art with his prior practice of experientially testing ideas of what it would be like to live under duress or at risk. These he performed by occupying spaces with different constraints for various periods of time, by exposing himself to the danger of falling, drowning, being run over, burned, lacerated by broken glass, electrocuted and shot and by channeling his aggression into staged assaults on others, for example holding a woman hostage at knifepoint on television, or firing a pistol at an airliner passing overhead. Such symbolic acts of self-jeopardy and terrorism literalized the violence latent in the American psyche of the 1960s and 1970s. Burden's subsequent works address related fears by objectifying them through other, equally matter of fact but more explicitly caricatural means.

Beginning in 1978 Burden mounted a series of temporary installation/performances employing model rockets, boats and toys of other kinds that referenced military institutions, history and planning. These include *The Citadel* (the name of a famously draconian military academy is lent to a piece requiring hundreds of lead spaceships), *Pearl Harbor* (commemorating that surprise attack on America's Pacific fleet with tiny ships, submarines and planes), *C.B. Airforce* (using more of the latter) and *Warship* (a model assembled from detritus of several varieties). Almost a decade of working in this mode produced *All the Submarines of the*

United States, a 3-D version of *Jane's Fighting Ships*, the almanac of Naval forces, recording every one of the 625 subsurface vessels launched by the American Navy since the end of the nineteenth century.

In 1979, Burden returned to themes relating to the United States' preparedness vis-à-vis its Cold War adversary, the Soviet Union. In a sly parody of Minimalism in general, and Carl Andre in particular, Burden arranged 50,000 matchsticks atop 50,000 nickels to concretize the disproportionate size of the Warsaw Pact tank threat to the combined US and NATO's forces of 30,000. By the same token, he ridicules in the most tangible way possible the exaggerated anxiety over Communist might that the Military Industrial Complex and its political spokesmen drummed up to justify huge budget increases for R&D and procurement of new weapons of mass destruction. The installation's laconic title – *The Reason for the Neutron Bomb* – caps the deadpan send-up of the Pentagon's customary fright-mongering. Whether this political critique gets under the skin of those predisposed to such anxieties depends in part on how visually mesmerizing the rank upon rank of quarters and matchsticks are. If one can conjure up, as the majority of boys-to-men can, what this steel-clad horde would look like on the march (or, more accurately, on the roll) then the spectacle becomes at once exhilarating – like a cinemascope version of Patton – and (taking heed of the Latin word for 'play' at the root of the adjective) ludicrous. Burden's gambit thus hinges on the double sense of 'belittling.' One kind of reduction in scale brings the object of his critical attention within the imaginative range of the very people most likely to fall for the alarmist ploys exploited by munitions salesmen and foreign policy 'experts', while a reductio ad absurdum of high-tech killing machines to small change makes the much hyped Red Menace laughable. He who registers the joke's sting most acutely is he who enters most spontaneously and completely into the fantasy world it summons from the depths of puerile blood lust. Such sadistic impulses are the precursors to generally less punitive desires in Freudian scenarios of the passage from anal to genital eroticism. For many – though by no means all – these drives remain a perpetual figment of the male gaze.

To what extent this kind of transferred involvement conditions responses to these or other works done in the same spirit and in similar materials is, of course, a matter of guesswork. Once again, though I will invoke heavily qualified 'male privilege' in order to italicize the strange mix of aggression and fun bound up in Burden's treatment of unsettling subjects, and simply assert that such involvement is, in some measure at least, an indispensable ingredient of his art insofar as it removes it from the category of blatant travesty and conditionally relocates it in the realm of hard-wired obsession. No matter how awake to complex meanings the man-child surveying one of Burden alternate realities is, some part of him is always thinking: if only this shrunken world were free of metaphor, if only it were just a game.

The specific proportion of seriousness to sandcastle-building upon which individual works are predicated ranges from the silly to the grim. On the silly side of the ledger sits *Tower of Power* (1985), a pyramid of ingots surrounded by miniscule armed guards that are cousins to paper dolls and bent pipe-cleaner figures. Made when currencies were still pegged to the price of precious metals (back when a million dollars – the value at that time of Burden's glittering minimalist stack – was greater than the cost of a mid-market New York condo), *Tower of Power* satirizes the Gold Standard and the macroeconomic hording of wealth. Add flashes of the assault by James Bond's nemesis Goldfinger on Fort Knox in the eponymous movie and the sculptural ensemble hotwires into the cerebral cortex of boy-brain and comes alive with swarming minions. As critique, it is obvious, effective and quickly absorbed; as a fetish it not only stimulates greed but film-fed dreams of the perfect heist. Jump cut to *Ocean's Eleven*; pick your version – vintage 1960 or 2001.

A Tale of Two Cities (1981) borrows Charles Dickens' title to lend extra ironic weight to a panorama of siege and counter-siege composed of several thousand 'little-men' with potted houseplants for verdant background wilderness and a fence of actual bullets. Depicting a stalemated war of attrition close in spirit to Kim Jones's allegorical charts, Burden puts his own patient assembly of the myriad parts and the viewer's slow delectation of their disparateness at the service of a meditation on futile, sanguinary chauvinism. Oh!, what I would have given, once upon a time, for the thrill of having genuine ammo provide the 'reality effect' for my mock combats. Evidently that thrill is not entirely gone for Burden either – he has continued to make sculptures of highly polished slugs – but in his case recollection of one piercing his arm must increase the morbid fascination of toying with violence, and the sense that such fascination courts trouble. Does one approve or disapprove of playing with fire-power in this way? It scarcely matters; the work is charged by the lethal objects it seems to take lightly and that charge throws an arc between juvenile caprice and the *Nightly News*.

America's Darker Moments (1994) is a reliquary of exactly what its name promises. Those moments include a massacre abroad (My Lai) and one at home (Kent State), the assassination of a president (Kennedy) and the killing of an ordinary man whose misfortune was to be black in a segregated society (Emmett Till) and finally the inaugural demonstration of nuclear terror America performed when it dropped Little Boy on Hiroshima. The fact that the vitrine is a pentagon is, of course, no accident. Moreover, when initially installed, the piece was surrounded by outsized uniforms of the LAPD, resulting in a composite representation of militarism and the police state that no one who remembers the Nixon and Reagan eras could fail to grasp. Just what those awakening to the present menace and horror, who are not otherwise intoxicated or intimidated by displays of force, will do with this knowledge remains to be seen, but suffice it to say that the deathly aura looming over us has deepened rather than dissipated in the Bush years. That said, the delicately cast low reliefs of Kennedy's limousine, of the National Guardsmen firing on students or the ascending vortex of the mushroom cloud are beautiful to behold. This is especially true of the latter, which, reflected by mirrors to the left and right, is multiplied, mise-en-abime, like a Doomsday chain reaction of explosions. The darkness of these historical moments thus scintillates in the light sensitive tracery of Burden's silvery figurines even as the hand is prompted to reach out and move them so as to whimsically re-enact the sinister events they embody.

Arguably, Burden is engaged in a genre of entrapment for which involuntary recall of childhood amusements is the bait. And arguably, those most likely to be tempted are men. If this is a fair assumption it should also be noted that it does not necessarily follow that the gender-advantage men may have as their point of departure into the work means that women face a comparable barrier and an *a priori* restriction in their capacity to understand. If this were the case, then Cindy Sherman's chameleon-like dress-up aesthetic or the doll's house photographic tableaus of Laurie Simmons would be partially or wholly off limits to male audiences. The issue here, though, is not the ultimate impact of art based on specific experiences of this sort, but the spontaneous auto-seduction upon which it operates and the recovered longing to 'make-believe' it taps into. These are thresholds of response, not insurmountable obstacles, and the instinctive or thoughtful translation of one kind of appeal or memory for another – Davey Crockett hats for Scarlett O'Hara pinafores, Barbies for GI Joes – can offer entry. (And, insofar as memory counts, do boys never play with their sister's toys or girls with their brother's?).

Meanwhile, the range of people Burden has targeted do not necessarily suffer from the same delusions or cherish the same things. Nor does all his work carry a clear cut message, much less a conventionally liberal one, as his affinity for cartridges attests. One example of the way in which Burden has gently teased liberal piety is his *The Sailing Destroyer* (1990), a modern warship retrofitted with full rigging and sails. At one level this nautical mutant renders the sleekest of the Navy vessels ungainly while at the same time divesting it of its killer profile. On another, it lampoons ecological utopianism by transferring the logic that has spawned wind-mill farms on undeveloped California hillsides to the least likely of sites, albeit one which has, looking to the curious combinations of steam and sail that lead up to modern ship design, historical precedents. Wilful anachronism thus challenges the absurd technological regression that underpins Green romanticism. At the same time, though, Burden's grafting of the old onto the new conflates the world of Horatio Hornblower or Joshua Slocum with newsreel footage of 'Victory at Sea'. And, in the blink of the eye, Burden's boat joins Malcolm Morley's regatta.

The biggest, most complicated, most monstrous of all Burden's exercises in microcosmic-macrocosmic inversions is *Medusa's Head* (1990). Modeled in concrete, gravel and grit over a massive wooden armature that divides in quarters like a Droste's chocolate apple every time the piece is taken down and put away for storage, the sculpture is, among all of Burden's preposterous empirical 'proofs' of dubious propositions, by far the most absurdly comic. Once again, the impetus came from a rhetorical inflation, and as with *The Sailing Destroyer* the focus is ecological hysteria. In the nineteenth century, so Burden learned, some observers who saw the advent of railroads as signaling the unrestricted penetration of industrialization into the naturally balanced realm of pastoral economies and small urban centers hypothesized that if their growth were to continue unchecked, they would turn the world into an outlandish labyrinth of track and tunnels. (Incidentally, those who welcomed trolleys and automobiles to big cities did similar calculations when they predicted that if the population of wagon and carriage horses expanded exponentially, the metropolises would have been smothered in manure.) In the same matter-of-fact manner with which he responded to extreme 'what if' questions in his performances and later in pieces like *The Reason for the Neutron Bomb*, Burden realized with a vengeance a sculptural equivalent of the worst case scenario that materially illustrates the implications of wildly abstract speculation. It is the use of visual – as well as tactile and kinetic – hyperbole as a retort to verbal hyperbole.

It is also a hallucinatory surrender to the pleasures – this time around lugubriously comic – of mapping imaginary worlds and then destroying them. For in boy-brain Thanatos leapfrogs Eros and the fixation on and fear of death dictates that it be ceaselessly, rapturously acted out. (When I played cap-gun World War II with friends, the person who could 'die best' – with the greatest surprise, fanciest fall and most twitches – won). Yards – perhaps actual miles – of track in multiple gauges snake the circumference of the crusty sphere, furrow the ground, plunge toward the core, erupt from craggy orifices – the anatomical allusions are quite deliberate and more scatological than maturely libidinal in this

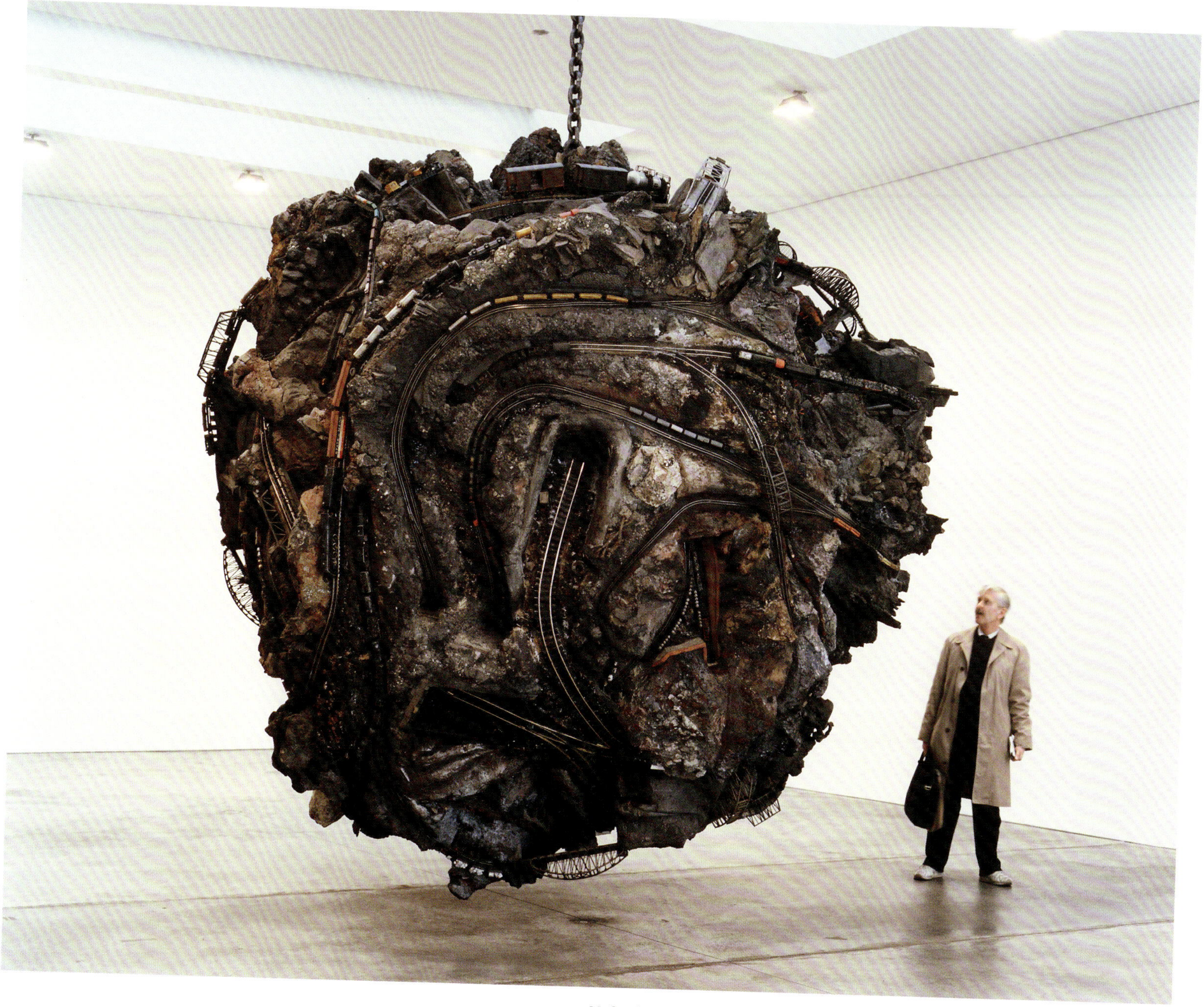

Medusa's Head 1990

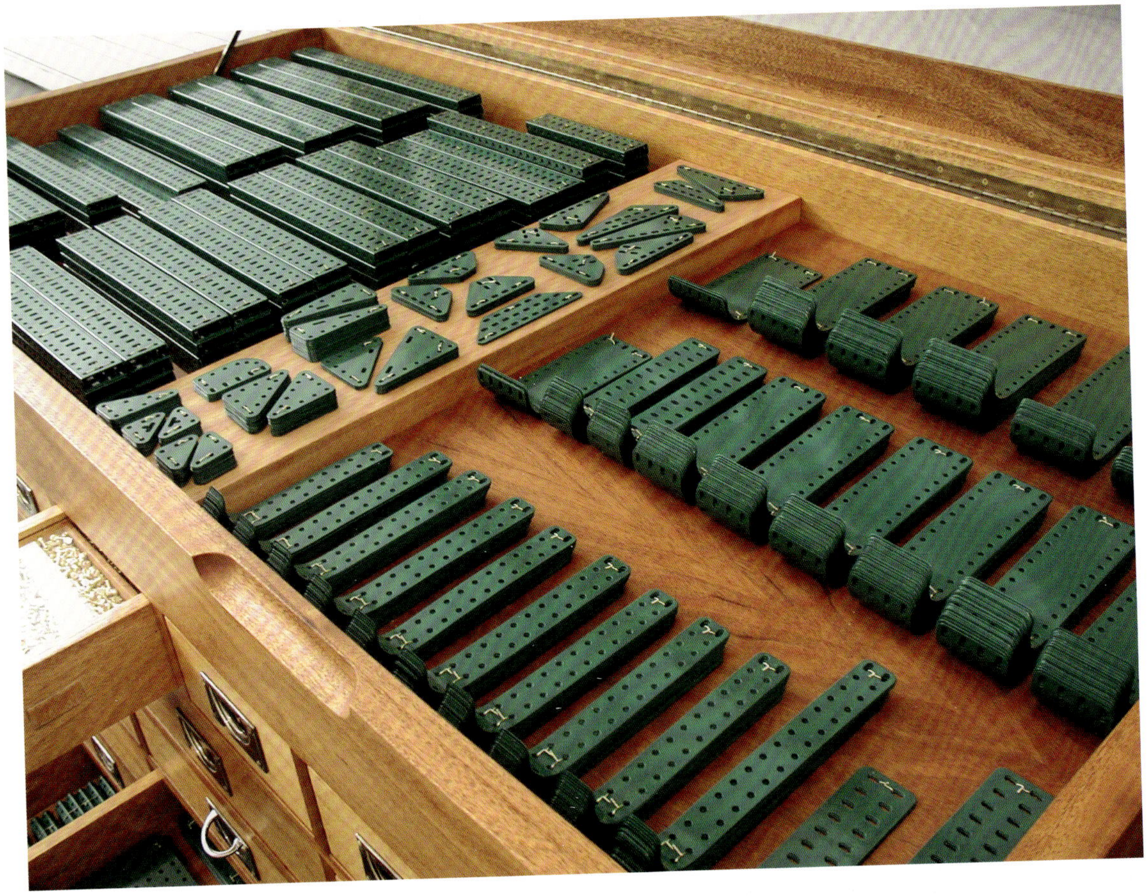

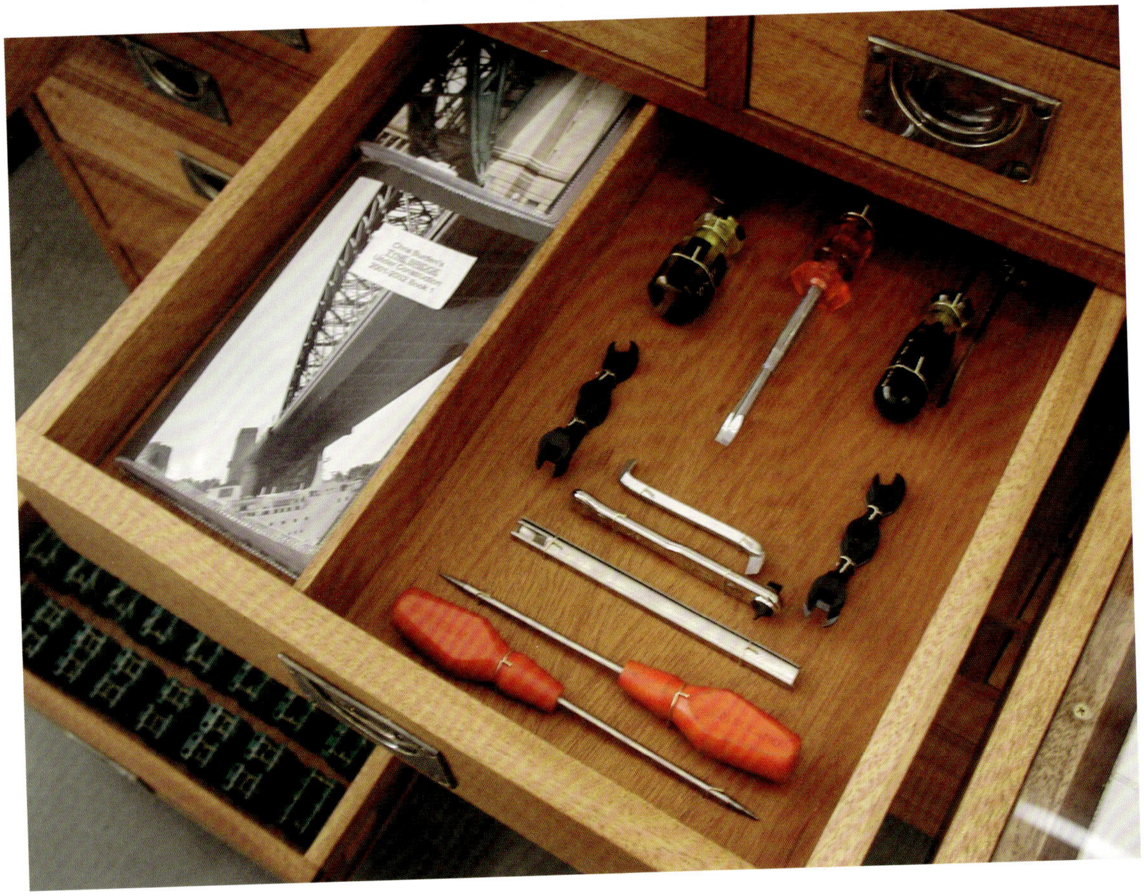

Tyne Bridge Kit 2004 (details)

context – traverse canyons on fretwork trestles and carry their load of engines, Pullmans, boxcars and flatbeds going nowhere special other than to Hell-on-Earth. On seeing *Medusa's Head* installed at the Museum of Modern Art in New York, where it now permanently resides, a former colleague said that it looked like a three-dimensional late twentieth-century equivalent of Pavel Tchelitchew's pre-war picture puzzle *Hide and Seek* (1940–42), a perennially popular painting also in MOMA's collection. This was said in elegantly hostile jest but there is some truth to it. Not because Burden traffics in coy optical illusions, as Tchelitchew did, but because both works capture a child-like vision of a threatening and impossibly confusing universe that mesmerizes even reluctant viewers. On first encounter, the pull is a little like that of watching the chase scenes in *Indiana Jones and the Temple of Doom* where the heroes go for a rollercoaster ride on a minirail through sulphurous mines. Only the stubbornly adult can resist being carried away into the knot of Spielberg's subterranean Coney Island and the same holds true for Burden, my waggish friend not withstanding.

But Burden's apocalyptic phantasmagoria is not gratuitously mystifying like Tchelitchew's confection, nor merely entertaining like Spielberg's retrograde romp. All crags and ominous plunging vistas, it is a simultaneously elephantine and crystalline grotesque of Edmund Burke's 'terrible sublime'. The hysterical fear of machinery it makes dismal fun of has its opposite – an infatuation with engineering and gadgetry – in many of Burden's other projects, including the ill-fated contraption *When Robots Rule: The Two-Minute Airplane Factory* (1999), which struggled mightily but with little success to launch model airplanes down the majestic Duveen hall of the old Tate Gallery in London. However, Burden the bridge builder – and late twentieth-century American descendent of English master bridge builder and all around genius of the Age of Steel, Isambard Kingdom Brunel – has realized the apogee of the exalted rather than infernal version of the technological sublime in a series of projects assembled out of huge quantities of hardware from old Erector and Meccano toy building sets.

To supply himself with the necessary parts, the artist was obliged to corner the market on this outmoded commodity, as if he were one of the Hunt brothers speculating on silver around the time Burden made *Tower of Power*. Silver was not 'as good as gold', so the Hunts went bust spectacularly. But there is more than a hint of go-for-broke extravagance in Burden's own hoarding as well. Thus real world economies enter into the game. Moreover, as a collective project executed with a team of collaborators, his bridges translate studio assistants into laborers, and the whole enterprise into a miniaturization of Industrial Revolution production. This reading is reinforced by the illustration from a vintage Erector Set manual in one of Burden's exhibition catalogues that shows boys in old-fashioned knee pants clambering over a partially finished bridge like pint-sized rivetors. It is impossible to look at this quaint advertisement and then turn the page to see pictures of the assemblage of the largest of Burden's constructions, *Hell's Gate* and *Mexican Bridge* (both 1998), without concluding that he and his squad are in truth playmates. The fact that one of the sculptures, *Tyne Bridge*, is sold as boxed kit, with drawers of tiny girders and all the required tools, is both a conceptual gambit to convey something of this dimension of the work and an open invitation to join in the fun. That I feel the lure is a consequence of who I was – and still am. Burden's majestic arches and supports will appeal to anyone with a modernist eye for grand elaborations of the principle of fitting form to function. But the poignancy of these works resides in the deep-seated psychological dynamics they materialize as well as the oblique critique of male fantasy they enact. In this regard one must not forget that Burden is of an age with the Minimalist artists for whom industry provided not only means but mystique, the former derived from heavy-duty processes and materials and later embodied in the stance of artist-as-worker. For instance, compare the literal monumentality of Richard Serra's work with the imaginary largeness of Burden's vision and a new dialogue of masculinities opens up. The differences between them that would arise from such an exchange do not concern aesthetic quality or conceptual seriousness, as each in his fashion represents the highest of both, but rather the harder to seize and still harder to assess question of precisely what types of boy-to-man-hood inhere in different types of art, and how. But that is for another time and place. Suffice it to say that Burden remains one of the most unpredictably audacious artists we have, not because he might still subject himself to the threat of actual harm, but because he has not repressed the part of himself that delights in childish pursuits, well-knowing that vulnerabilities, foolishness and all, they are the key to grown-up marvels and terrors.

Note: I have borrowed the 'boys-to-men' formulation from my friend and colleague Robert Lubar who, in turn, appropriated it from the eponymous hip-hop group. He is not to be blamed for my thoughts on gender theory.

Jaizu 1972

Newport Harbor Art Museum,
Newport Beach, California, USA;
June 10–11, 1972

Dressed in white and wearing a pair of sunglasses, I sat facing the door. Just inside the door were two cushions and a small box of marijuana cigarettes. Viewers were permitted to enter the room one at a time. They were under the impression that I was observing them, but the sunglasses had been painted black on the back and I was virtually blind. I remained immobile and speechless during the performance. Many people tried to talk to me, one assaulted me and one left sobbing hysterically. The piece was performed on two days for five hours each day.

RELIC: Sunglasses, painted black on the back

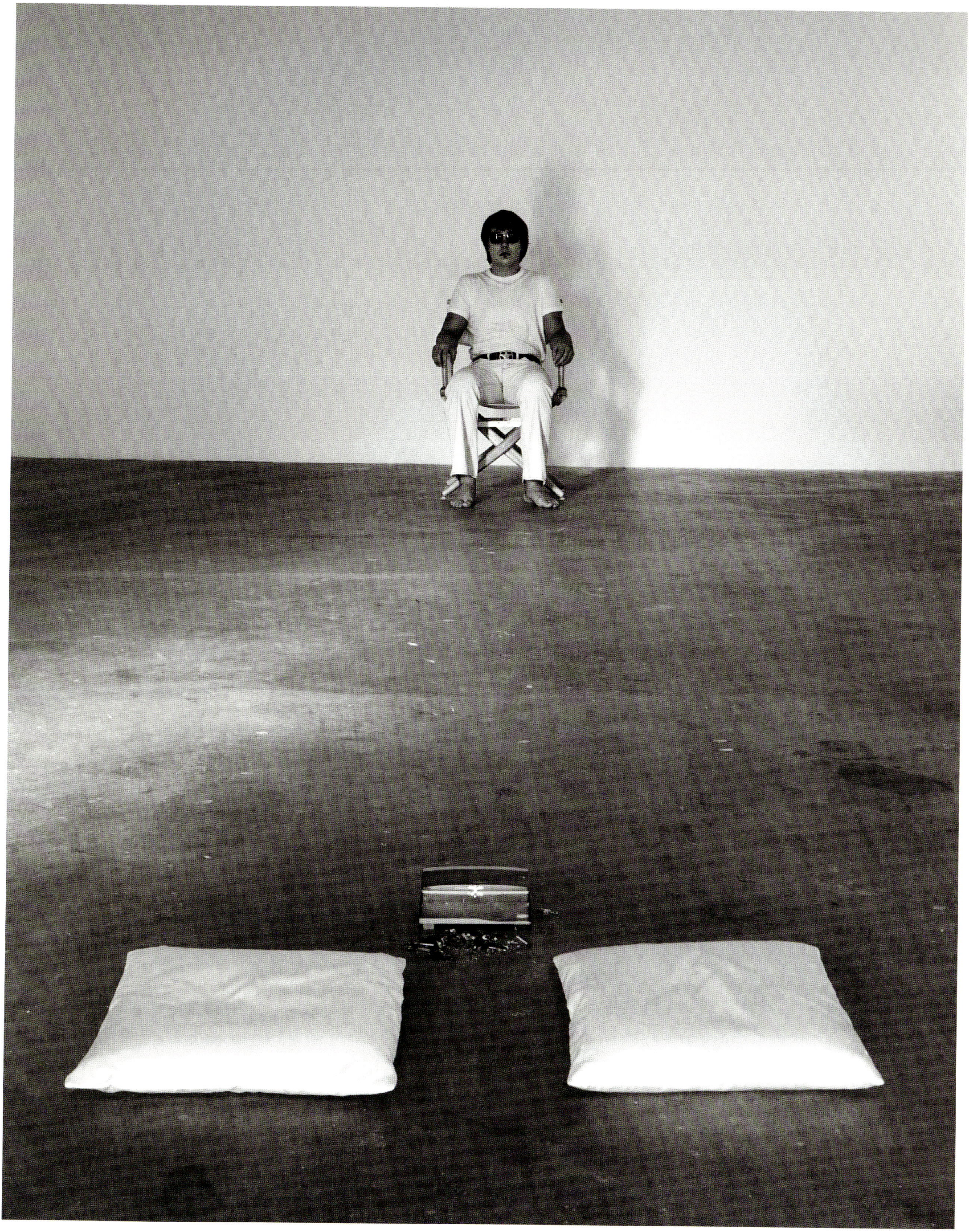

TV Ad 1973

KHJ-Channel 9, Los Angeles, California, USA; November 5–December 2, 1973

I purchased commercial advertising time on KHJ*-Channel 9 in Los Angeles. A ten-second clip of the movie documenting* Through the Night Softly *was shown nightly for one month.*

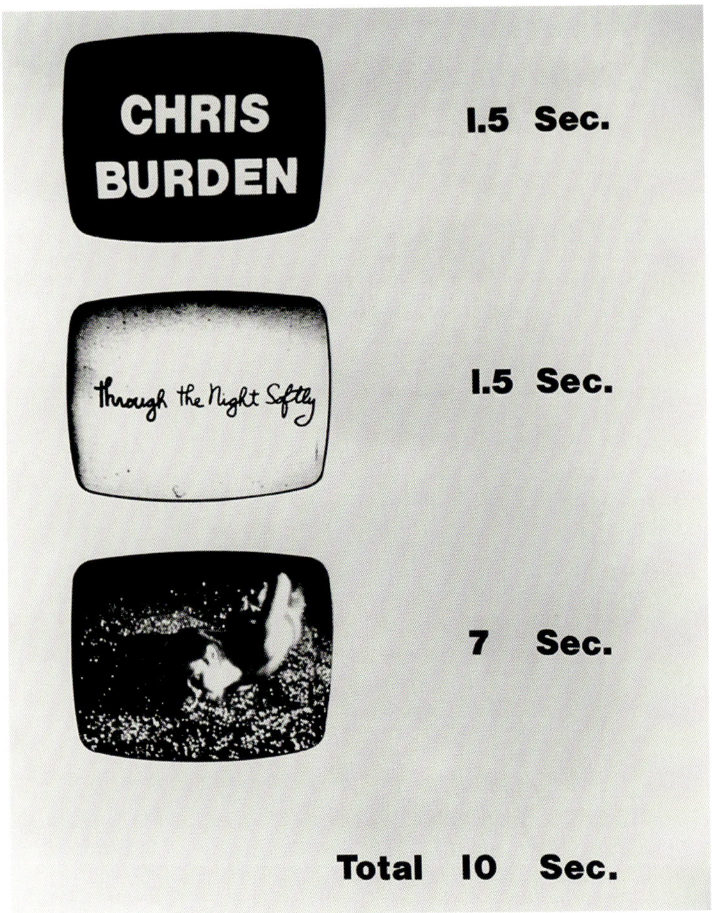

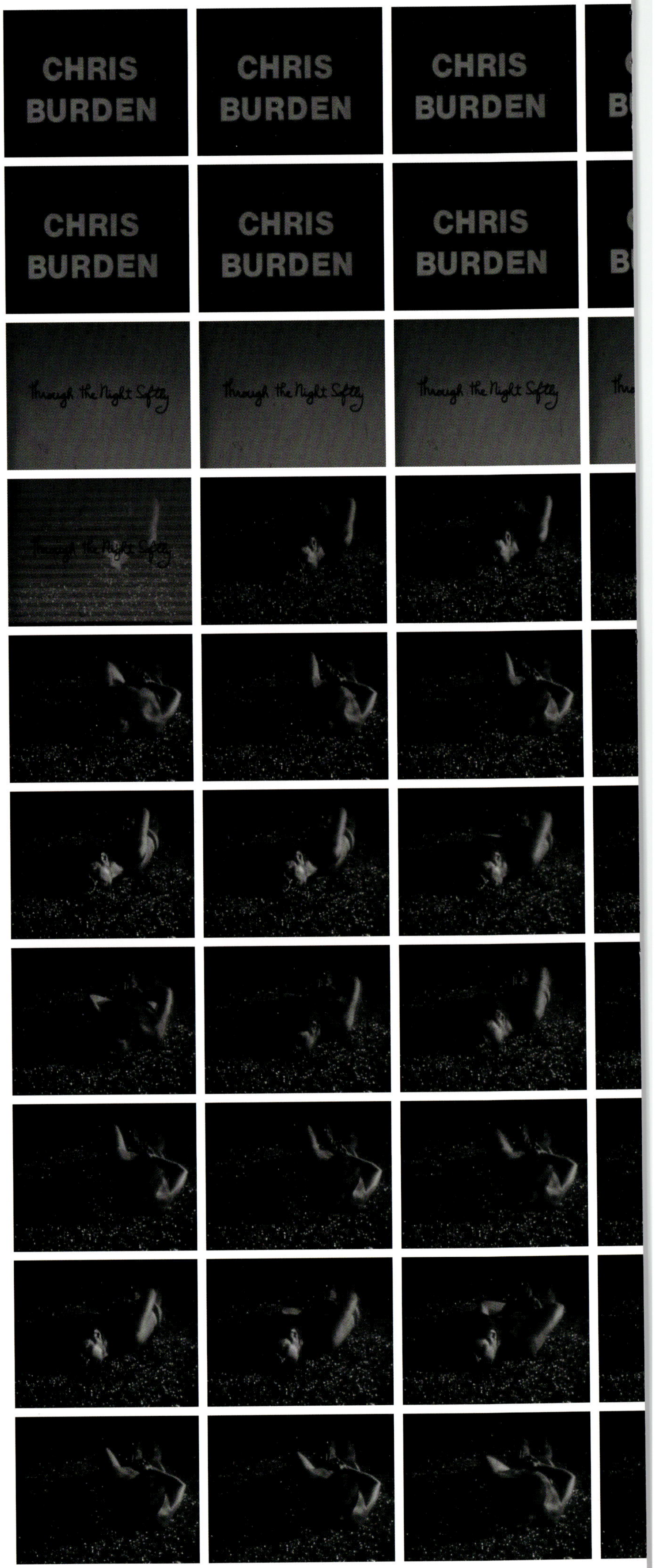

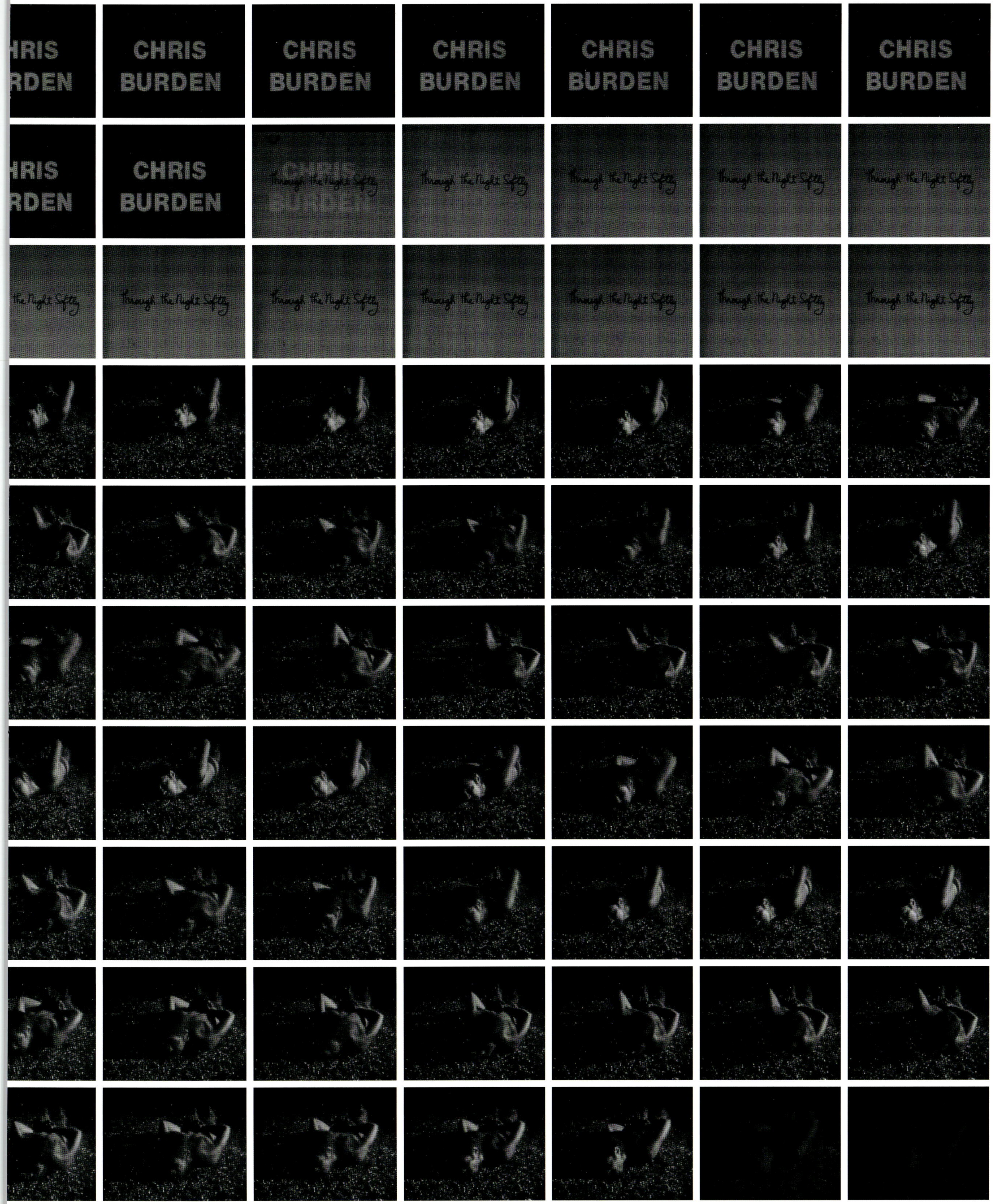
CHRIS
BURDEN
Through the Night Softly

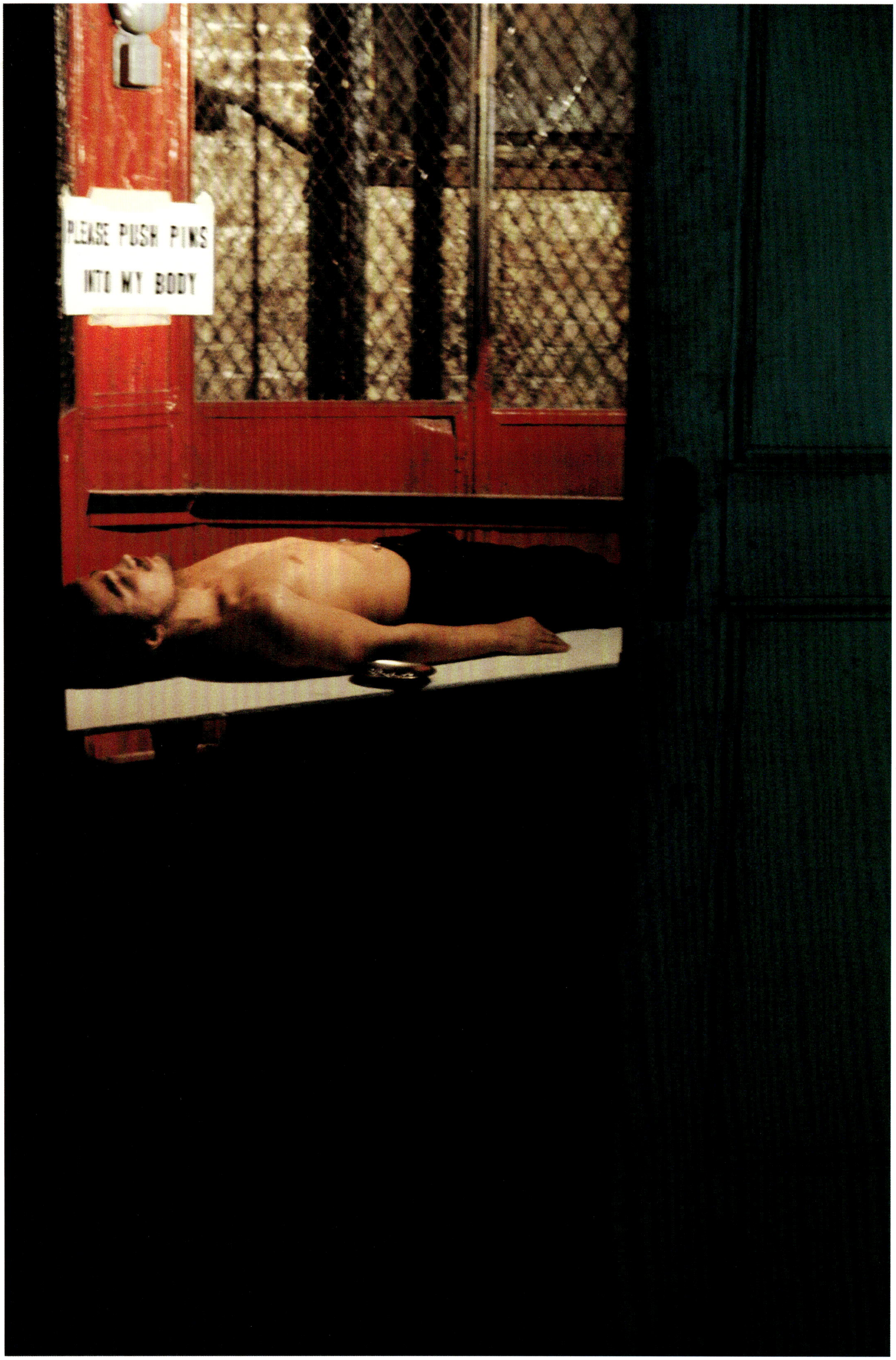
PLEASE PUSH PINS
INTO MY BODY

Back to You 1974

112 Greene St., New York, USA;
January 16, 1974

Dressed only in pants, I was lying on a table inside a freight elevator with the door closed. Next to me on the table was a small dish of ⅝ - inch steel push pins. Liza Béar requested a volunteer from the audience and he was escorted to the elevator. As the door opened, a camera framing me from the waist up was turned on and the audience viewed this scene on several monitors placed near the elevator. As the elevator went to the basement and returned, Liza told the audience that a sign in the elevator instructed the volunteer to 'Please push pins into my body.' The volunteer stuck four pins into my stomach and one pin into my foot during the elevator trip. When the elevator returned to the floor, the door opened, the volunteer stepped out and the camera was turned off. The elevator returned to the basement.

RELIC: Push pins, stainless steel bowl

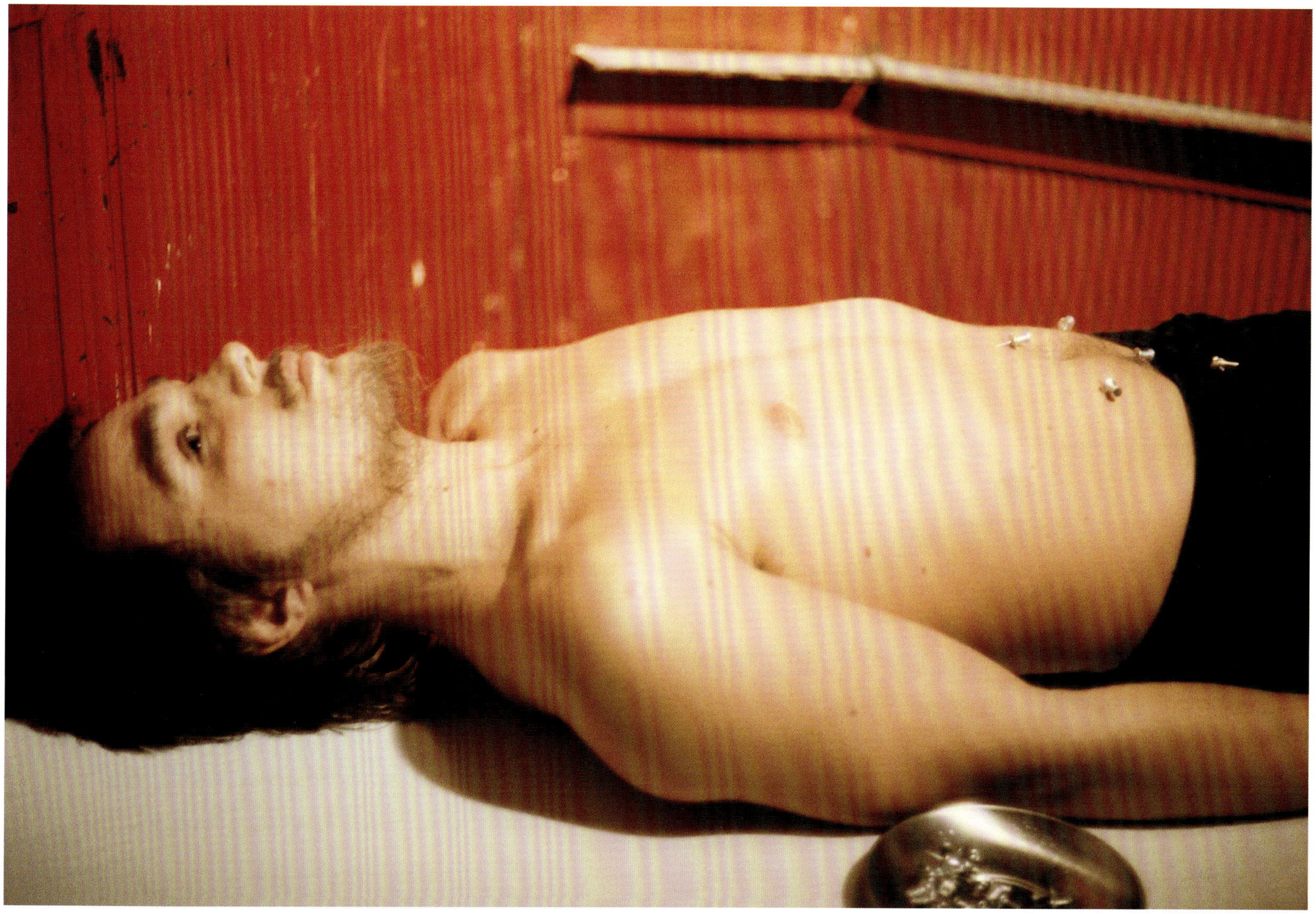

Velvet Water 1974

School of the Art Institute of Chicago,
Chicago, Illinois, USA; May 7, 1974

Separated from the audience by a wall of lockers, I sat next to a small sink filled with water. The audience sat facing a 19-inch monitor framed by four 9-inch monitors, two on each side. The large monitor showed an extreme close-up of my face and followed the movements of my head during the performance. The small monitors showed a fixed view of my head, shoulders and the sink. I started the performance looking directly into the cameras and saying, 'Today I am going to breathe water which is the opposite of drowning, because when you breathe water you believe water to be a richer, thicker oxygen capable of sustaining life.' I repeatedly submerged my face in the sink and attempted to breathe water. After about five minutes, I collapsed choking. The cameras were turned off.

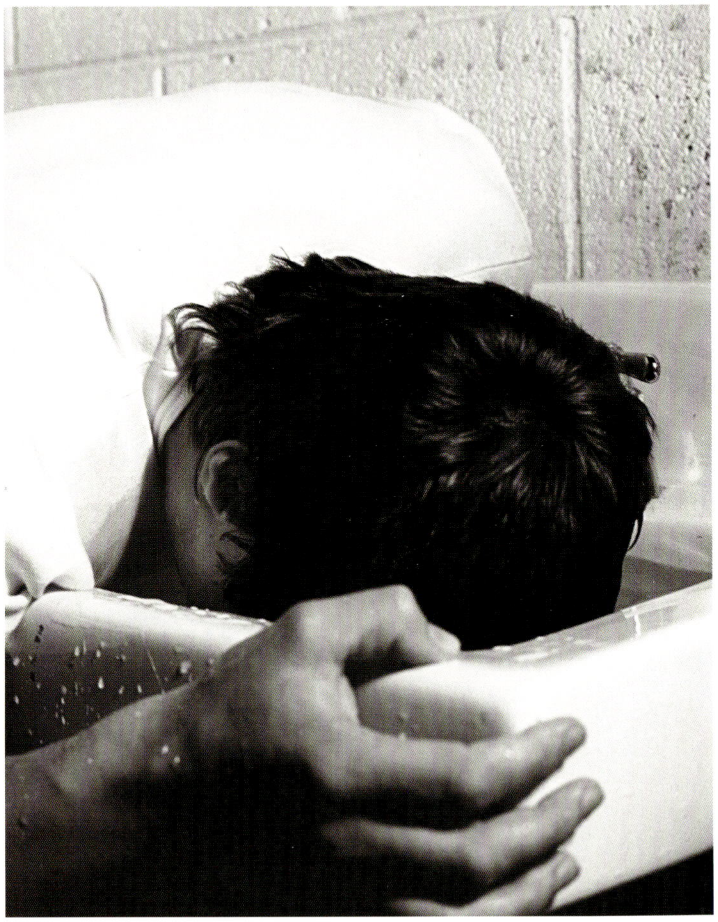

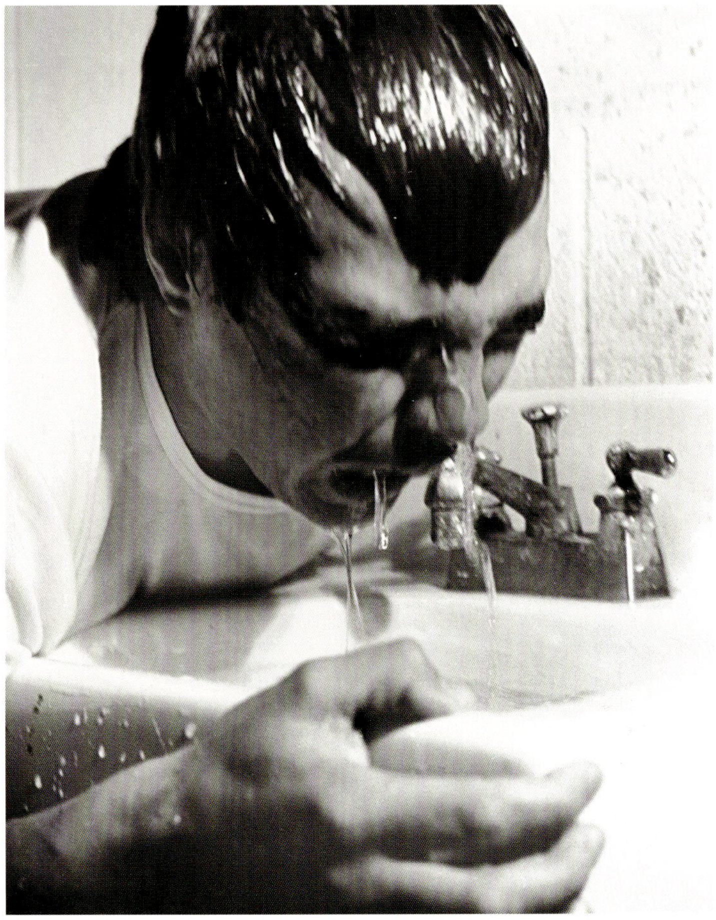

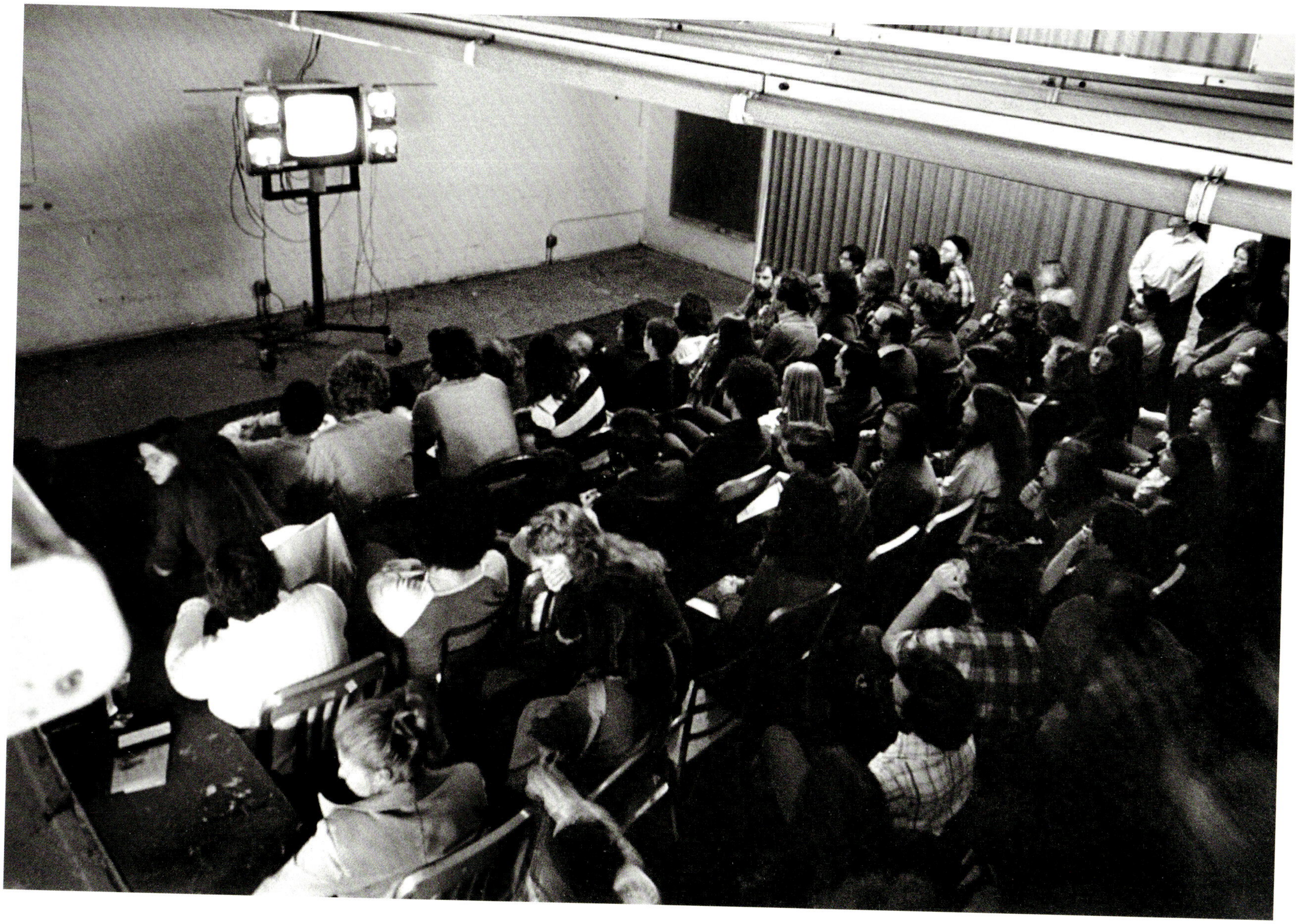

The Confession 1974

Contemporary Art Center, Cincinnati, Ohio, USA; December 12, 1974

A two-month show of documentary books and an interview videotape was installed at the Contemporary Art Center. I decided to use the monitor which regularly showed the interview tape. I invited only those people I had met and talked with since my arrival in Cincinnati, four days earlier. I called each of the 25 people and invited them to come to the Art Center on Thursday evening at 8:30. The guests were seated around the monitor when my face appeared on the screen. I began to talk about why I was very unhappy, confessing the most intimate details of my personal life. Faced with the need to make a decision concerning a love triangle, and being unable to act, I felt I had lost control of my life. The people watching had had an image of me created by the show and by personal contact since my arrival. They sat in complete silence as I exposed myself, imposing on them disturbing knowledge which had to be reconciled with my public image. I talked for about half an hour, until I was unable to continue. The audience left quickly without discussion among themselves.

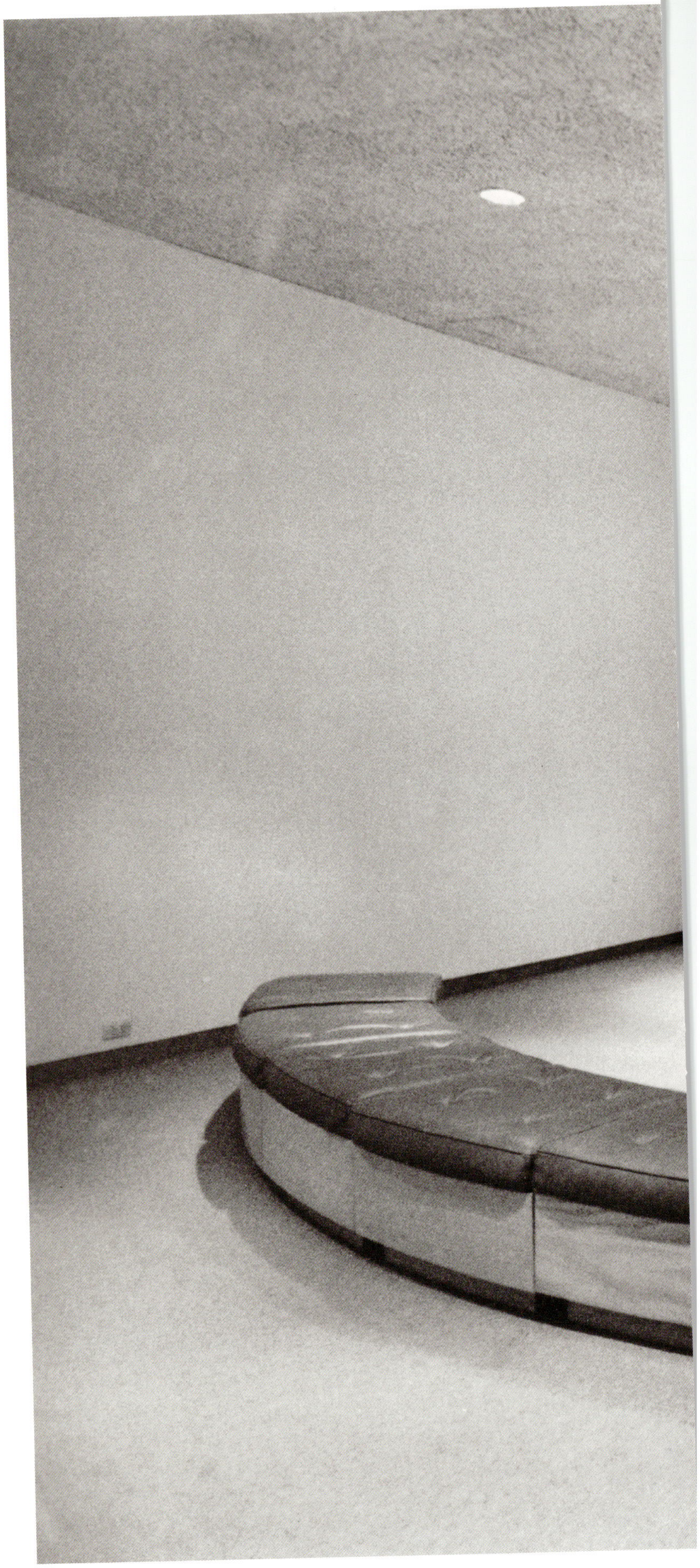

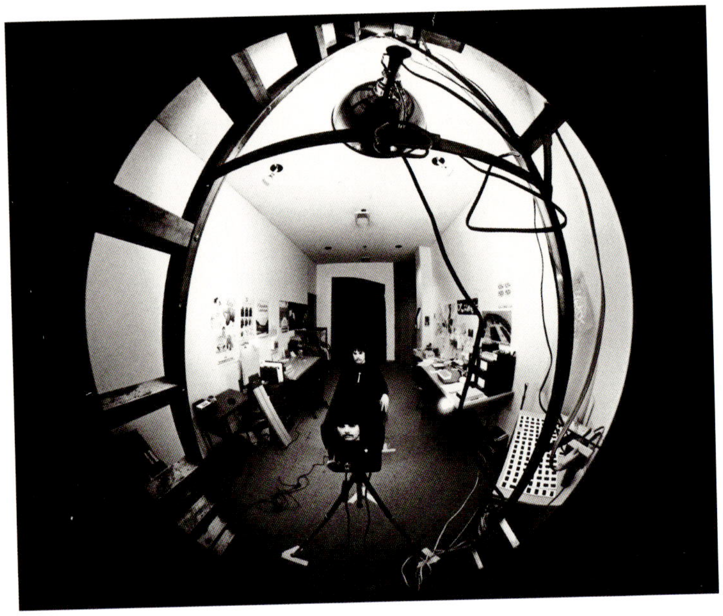

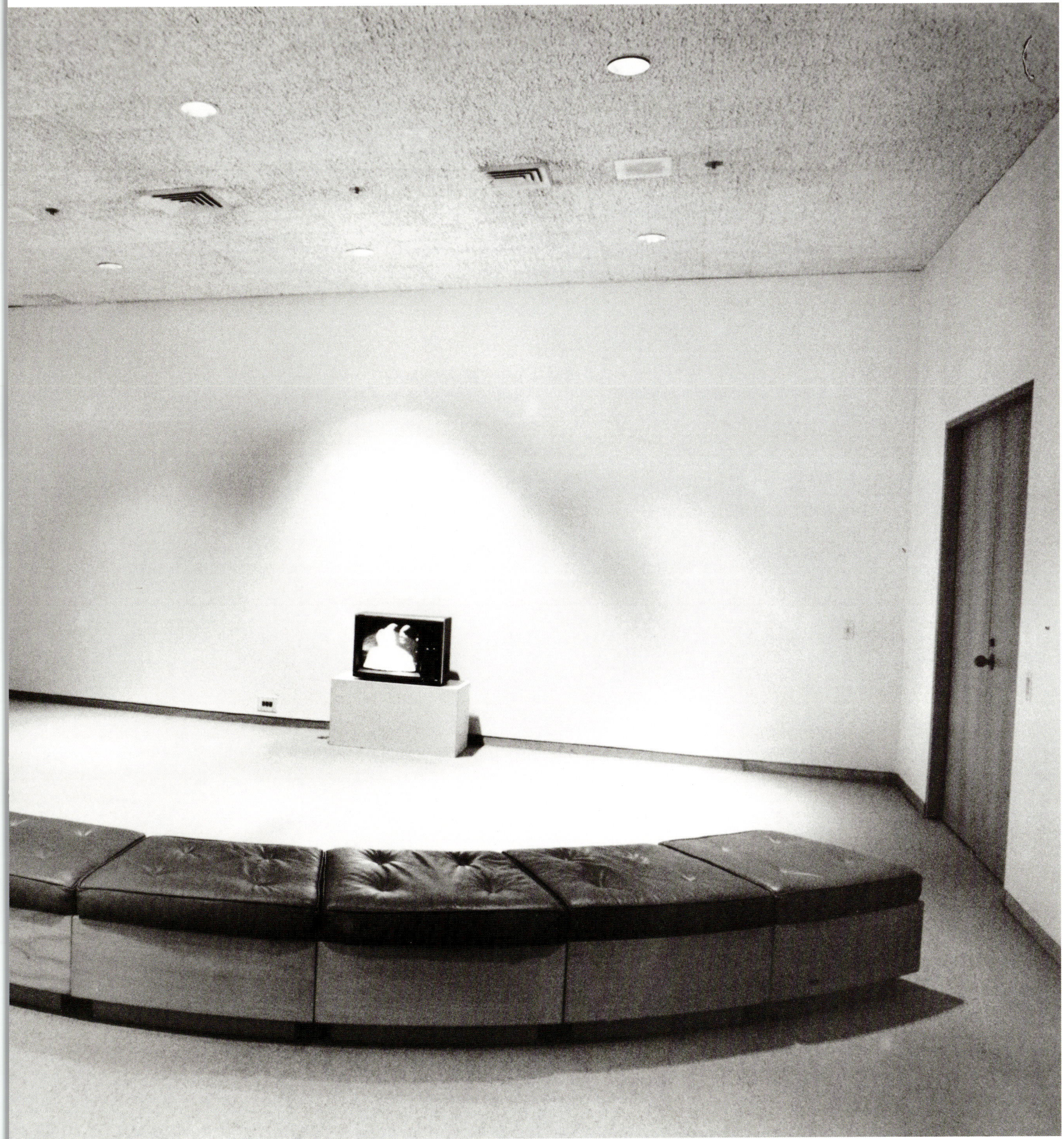

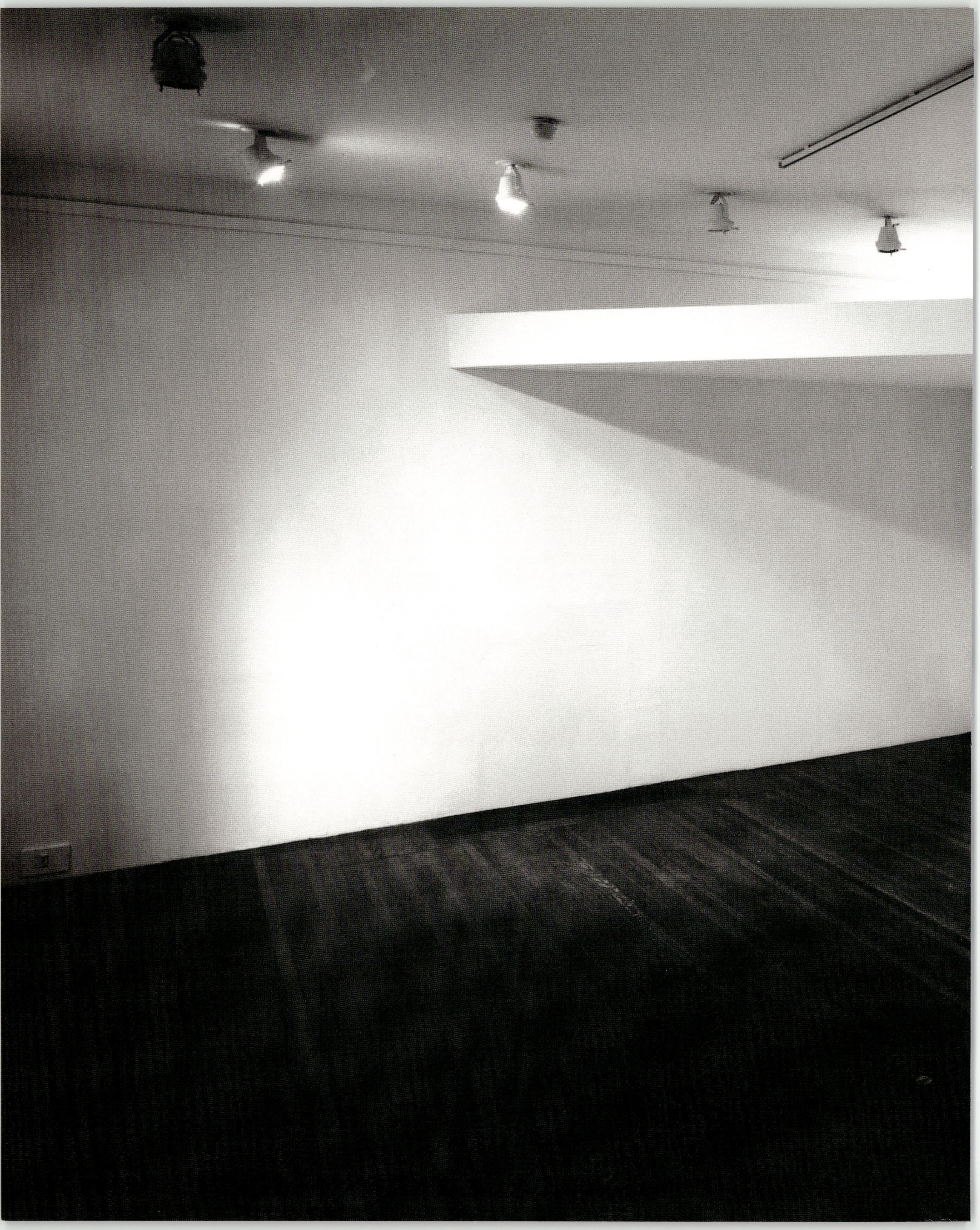

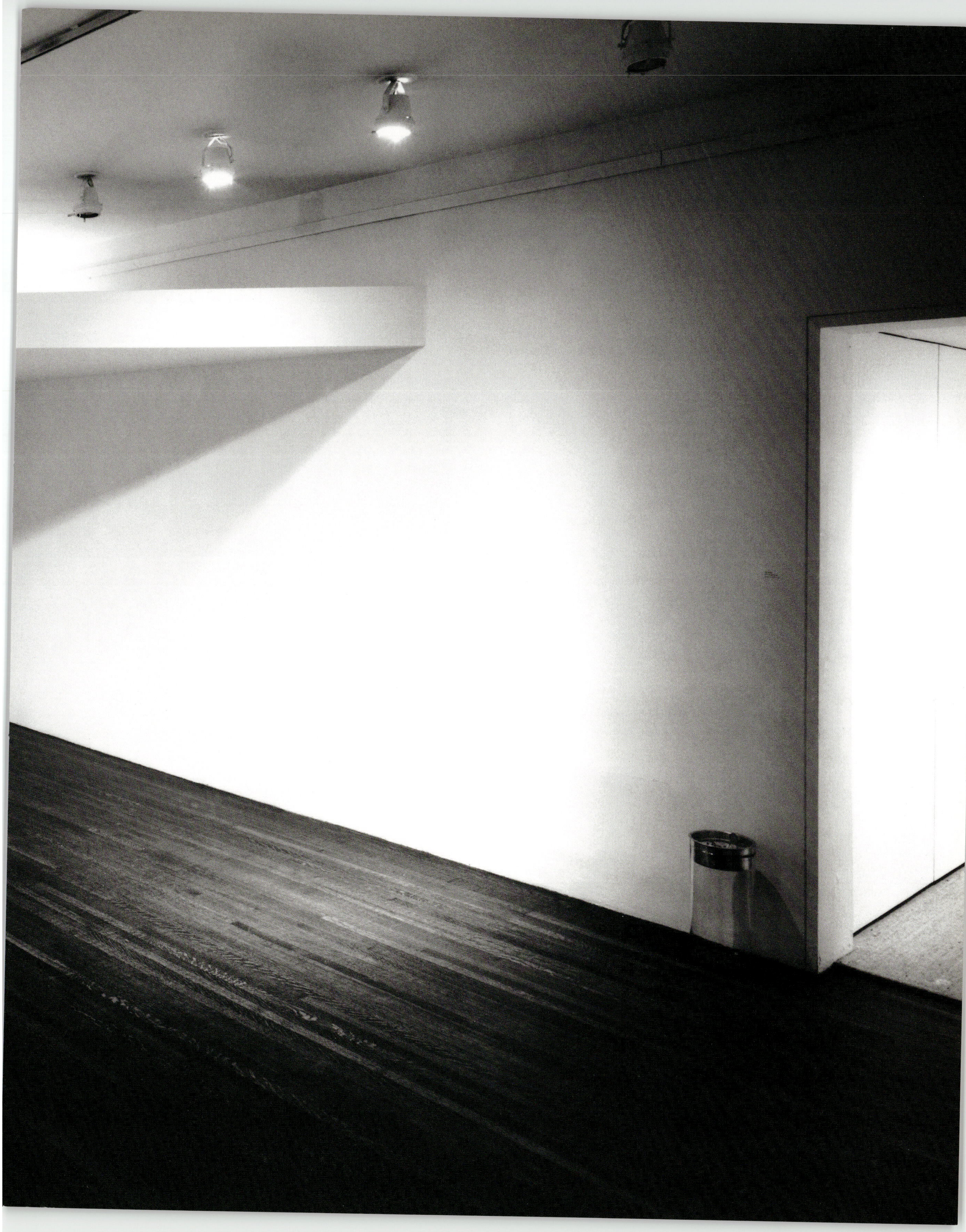

◁◁

White Light/White Heat 1975

Ronald Feldman Fine Arts, New York, USA;
February 8–March 1, 1975

For my one-man show at Ronald Feldman, I requested that a large triangular platform be constructed in the southeast corner of the gallery. The platform was ten feet above the floor and two feet below the ceiling; the outer edge measured 18 feet across. The size and height of the platform were determined by the requirement that I be able to lie flat without being visible from any point in the gallery. For 22 days, the duration of the show, I lay on the platform. During the entire piece, I did not eat, talk or come down. I did not see anyone and no one saw me.

RELIC: Section of board

Poem for L.A. 1975

KHJ-Channel 9 and KTLA-Channel 5, Los Angeles, California, USA; June 23–27, 1975

I produced a ten-second color TV commercial and purchased advertising time on two Los Angeles channels, KHJ (Channel 9) and KTLA (Channel 5). The commercial consisted of three statements: 'SCIENCE HAS FAILED', 'HEAT IS LIFE' and 'TIME KILLS'. An extreme close-up of my face against a blue background appeared on the screen and I spoke the first statement aloud. Then the same sentence written in bold graphics flashed on the screen. All three sentences were presented in this fashion, spoken first, then followed by silent graphics.
After the third statement, the words 'CHRIS BURDEN sponsored by CARP' appeared. For this piece, I purchased both 10-second spots and 30-second spots. The tape was played three times, back to back, during the 30-second spots. My commercial appeared a total of 72 times during the five-day period of June 23–27, 1975.

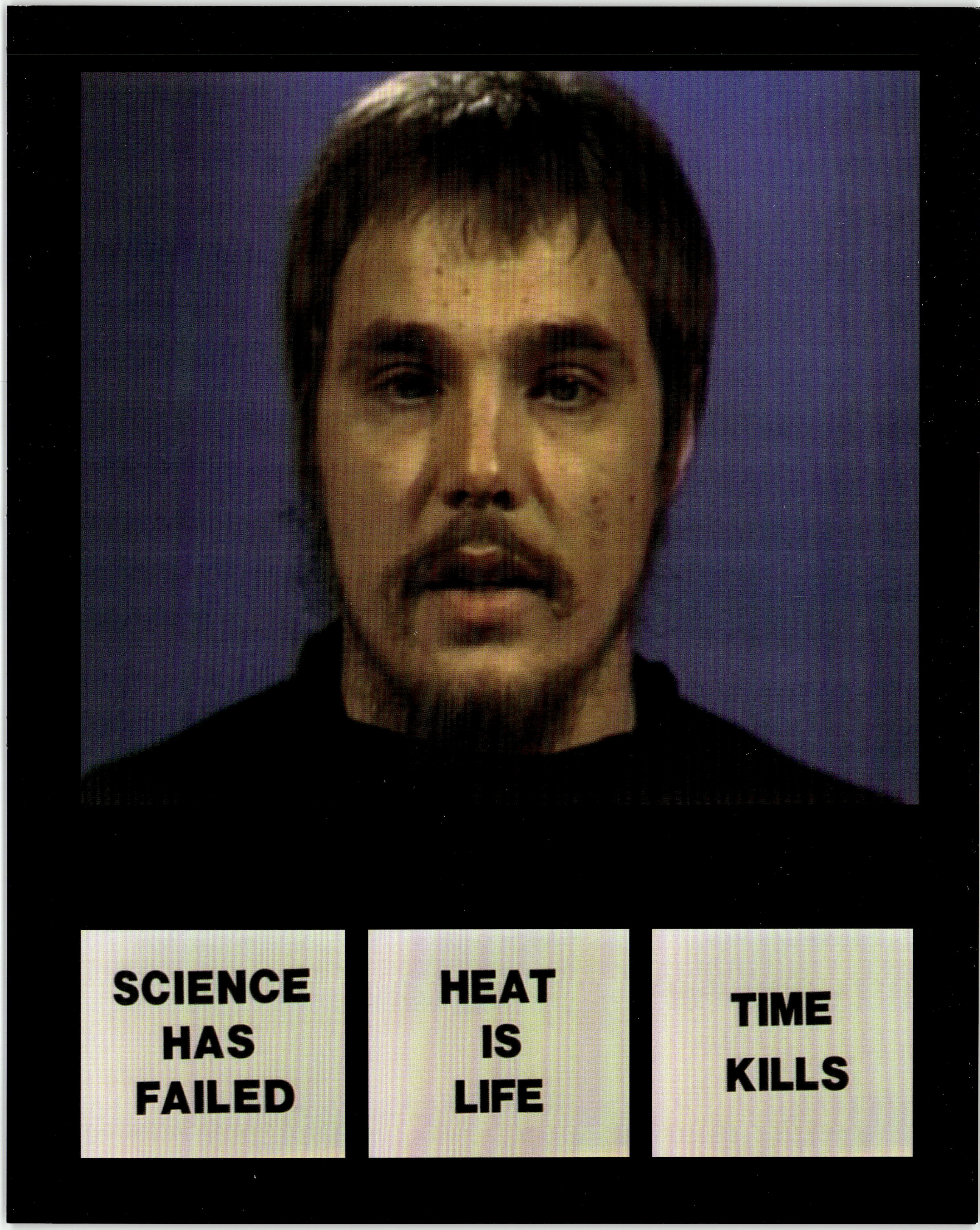
SCIENCE HAS FAILED
HEAT IS LIFE
TIME KILLS

The Rise and Fall of Western Industrialism as Seen Through the Automobile 1975

Hallwalls, Buffalo, New York, USA;
December 5, 1975

This performance took the form of a scientific lecture. The audience was seated in rows facing one end of a long room. I stood in front of a large blackboard with colored chalk and a pointer. I informed the audience of the nature of my lecture and suggested that anyone who was not interested in automobiles might want to leave. Then I outlined the problem – to design a four-wheeled vehicle to move a 150-pound human being from point A to point B as quickly and economically as possible. I followed this with a discussion of the different components of the automobile and their various historical solutions, which I illustrated with a series of simple chalk diagrams. My lecture lasted approximately two-and-a-half hours.

RELIC: Chalk

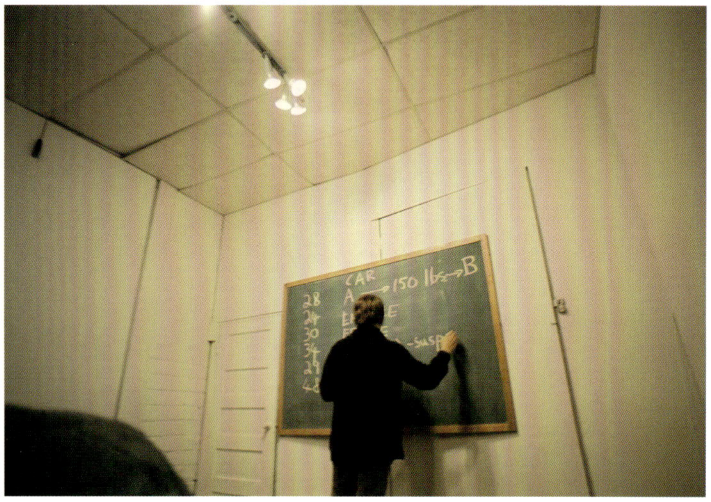

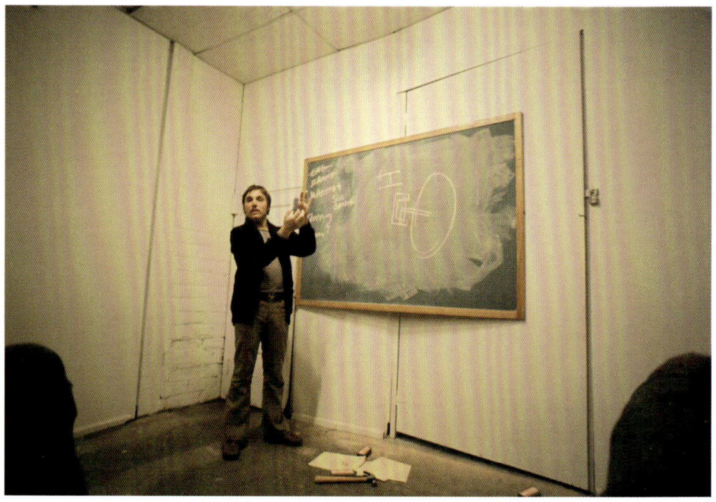

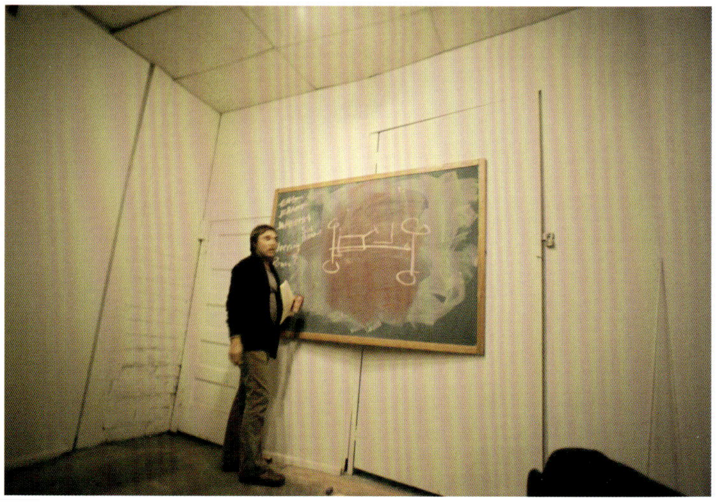

Do You Believe in Television? 1976

Alberta College of Art, Calgary, Canada;
February 26, 1976

The performance took place in a bare concrete stairwell within the underground parking structure. A trail of hay led from the bottom of the stairwell, spiraling three flights up to the outside. There was a large video monitor suspended above each landing. The spectators were let in and allowed to situate themselves around the monitors at the different levels, but were prevented from going below the first landing by a chain. All three monitors displayed the image of a black Swiss cross surrounded by hay. The image originated at the foot of the stairwell where the monitors were connected to a single, stationary camera. The real cross was not visible, however, from any point in the stairwell and could only be seen on the monitors. After the crowd had assembled and quietened down, a loud voice coming from the monitors asked 'Do you believe in television?' and a hand holding a lighted match appeared on the screen. The match which was centered over the cross was used to ignite the straw and flames and smoke began to work their way slowly up the staircase. The narrow path of straw burnt up to and past the first level before it was extinguished by spectators.

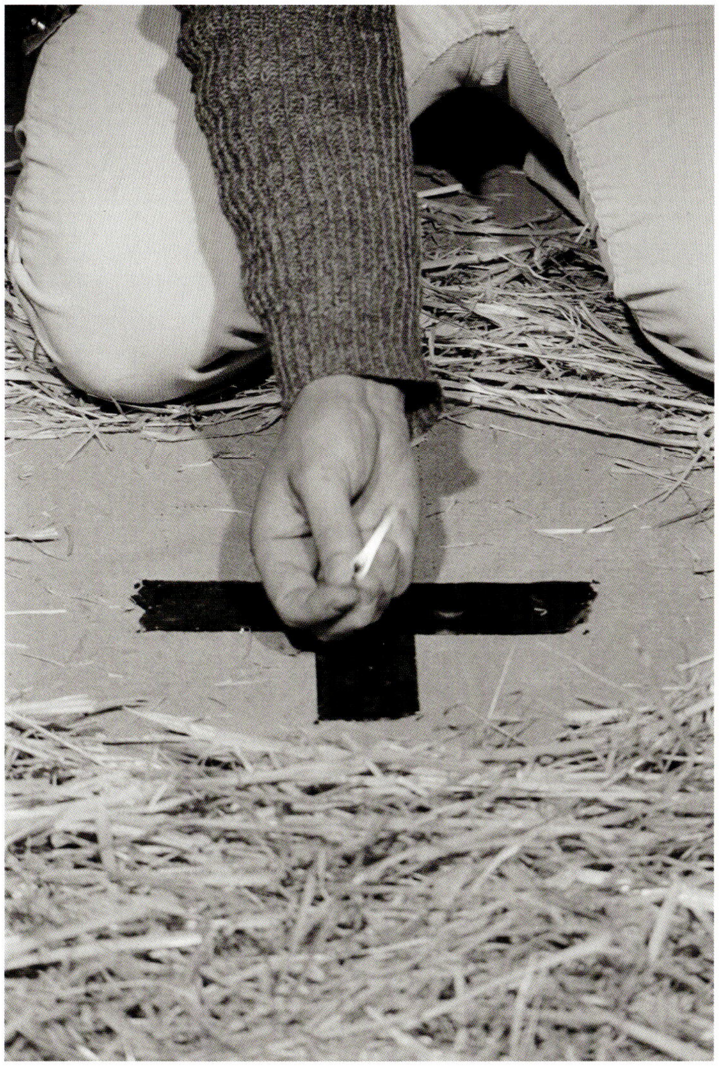

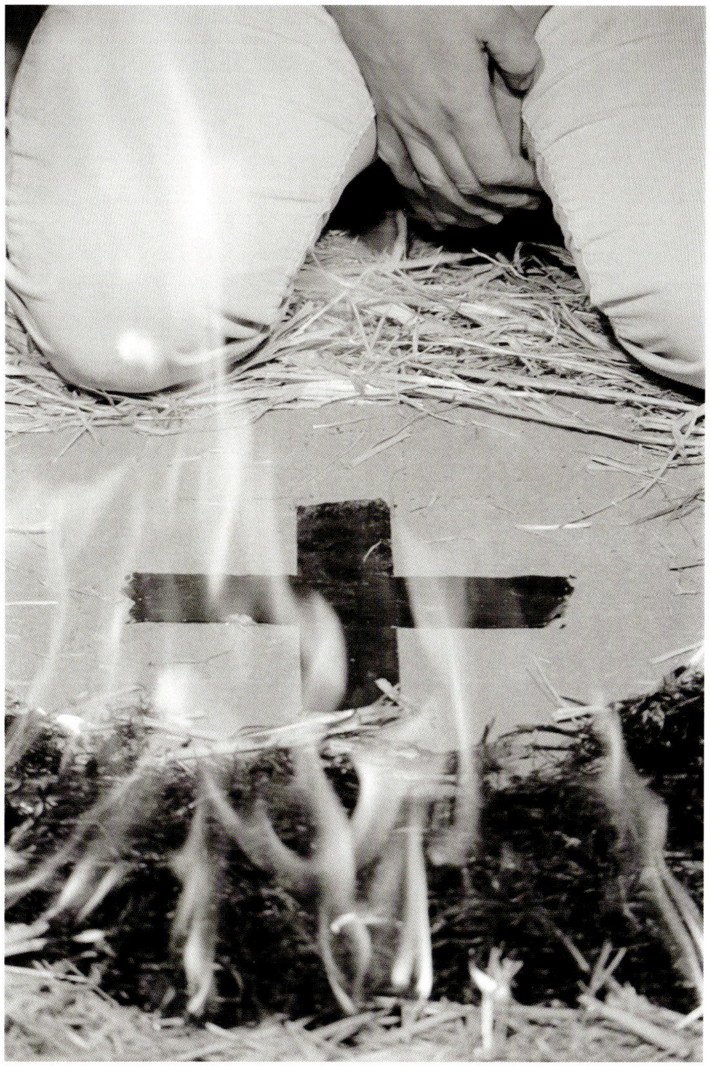

Merry Christmas from Chris Burden 1976

US Mail; December 14, 1976

One hundred new ten-dollar bills were sent to one hundred people that I was acquainted with in the art world. About half were personal friends and half business persons. The money arrived in a formal envelope, with a card which said 'Merry Christmas from Chris Burden'. An alphabetical list was kept, starting at Acconci and ending at Zlotnick, recording every person's serial number.

RELIC: Card, envelope, $10 bill

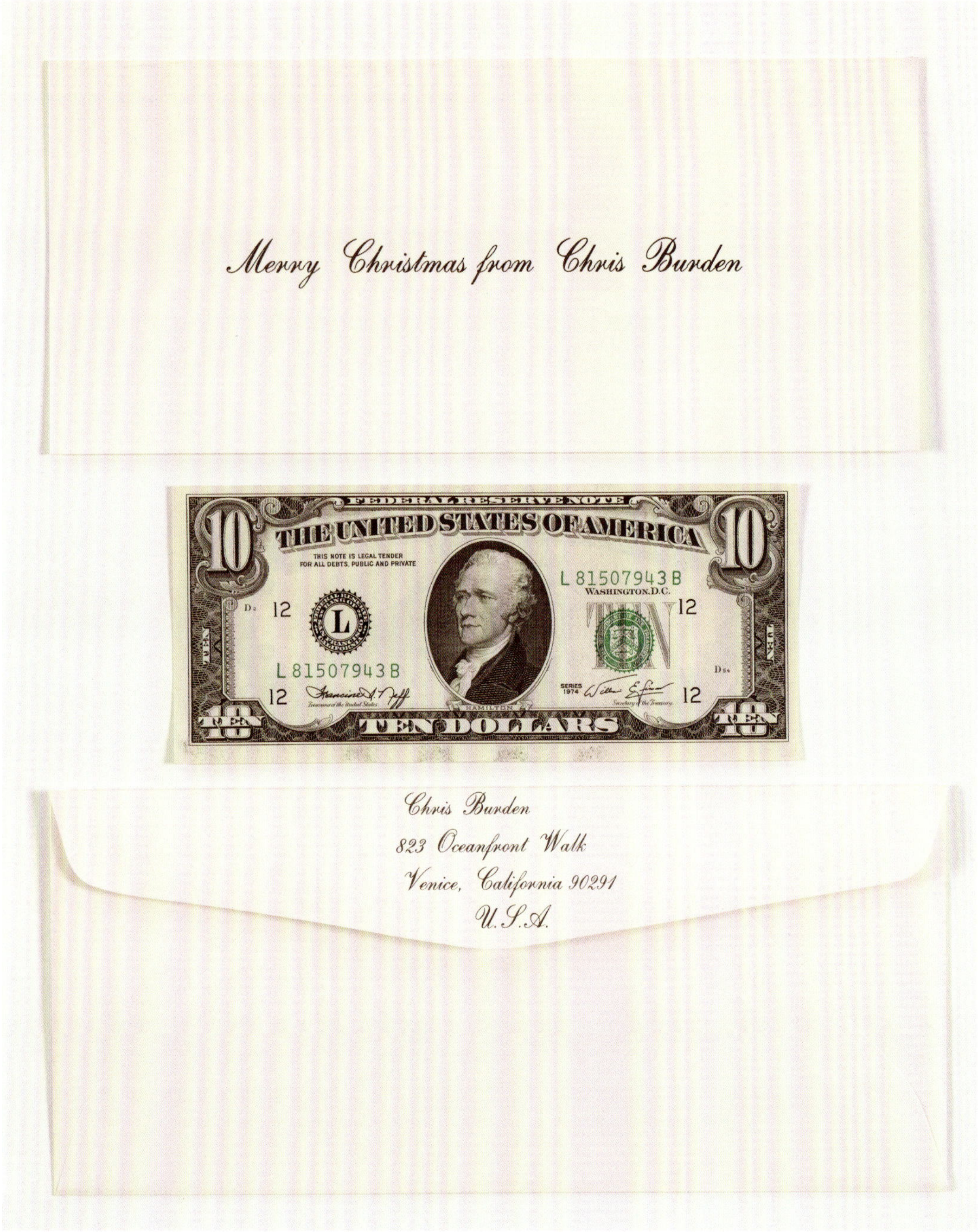

Wiretap 1977

Close Radio (KPFK-FM), Los Angeles, California, USA; January 17, 1977

I was asked to do a 14-minute audio piece for an FM radio station as part of a series of artists' audio pieces to be broadcast on a weekly basis over KPFK-FM Radio. During this period, Anna Canepa, a New York art promoter and organizer, was trying to convince me that she should represent my video work and that I should permit her to use my name in her advertisements. My regular art dealer in New York, Ronald Feldman, was opposed to the idea. The piece consisted of excerpts of two tape recorded telephone conversations, one between myself and Ronald Feldman and the other between myself and Anna Canepa. For seven minutes Ronald Feldman and I talked in generally disparaging terms about Anna Canepa and for seven minutes Anna Canepa talked negatively about Ronald Feldman. The piece was aired at 11:45 am January 17, 1977.

RELIC: Telephone, tape recorder, audiotape

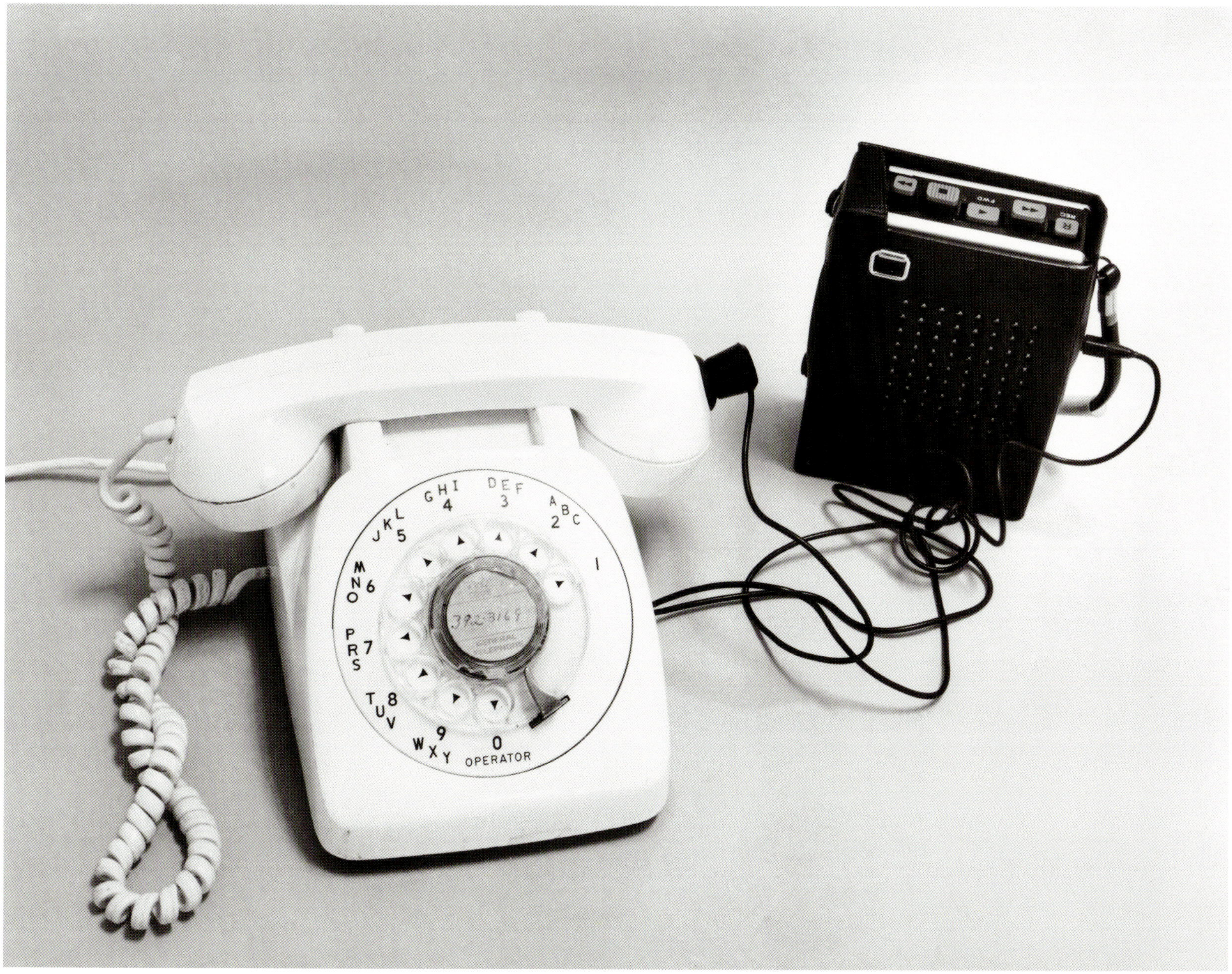

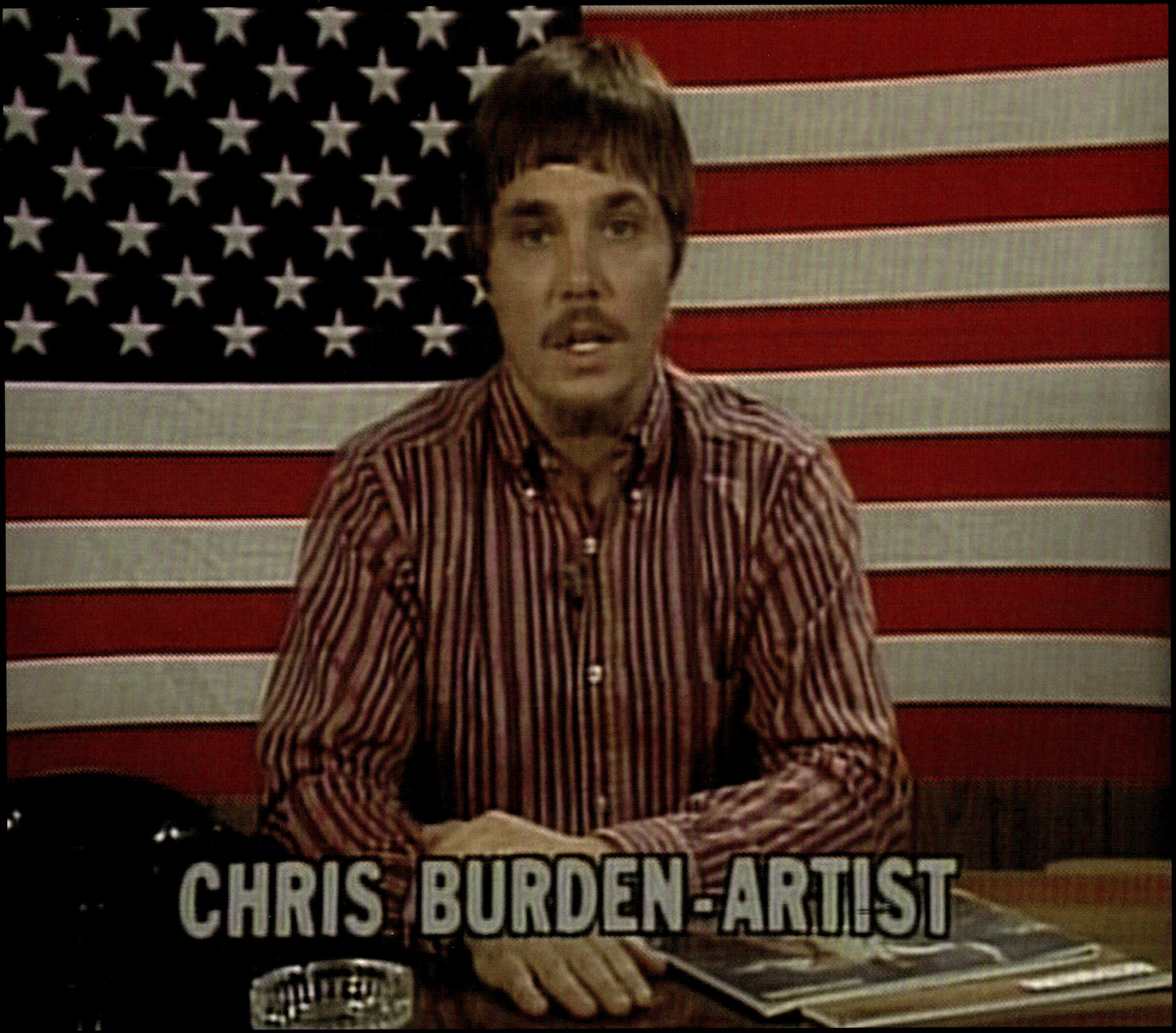
CHRIS BURDEN-ARTIST

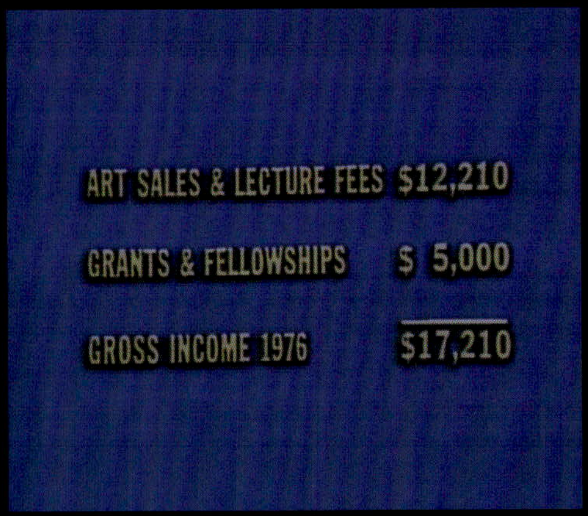
ART SALES & LECTURE FEES $12,210
GRANTS & FELLOWSHIPS $ 5,000
GROSS INCOME 1976 $17,210

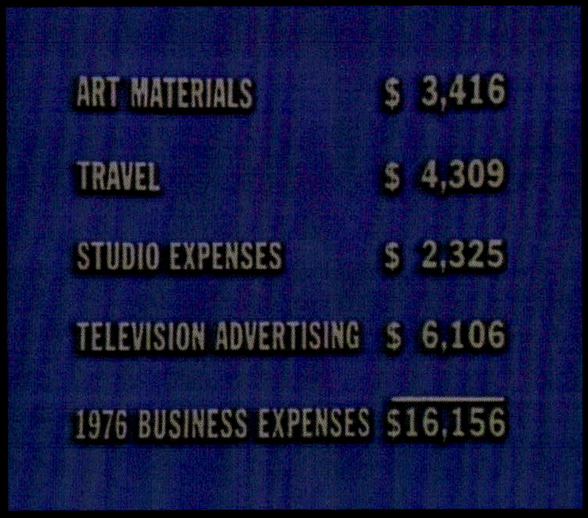
ART MATERIALS $ 3,416
TRAVEL $ 4,309
STUDIO EXPENSES $ 2,325
TELEVISION ADVERTISING $ 6,106
1976 BUSINESS EXPENSES $16,156

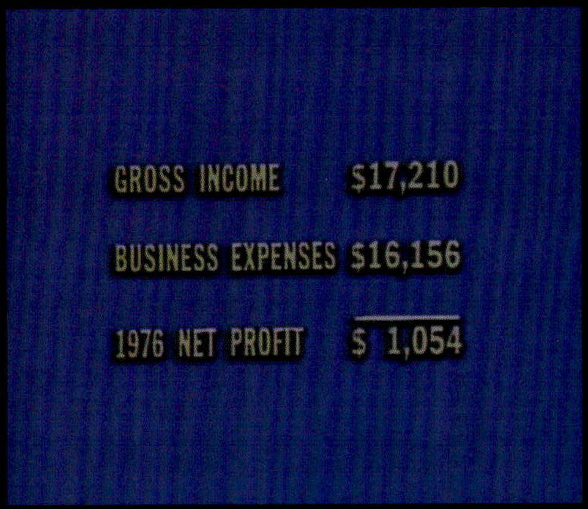
GROSS INCOME $17,210
BUSINESS EXPENSES $16,156
1976 NET PROFIT $ 1,054

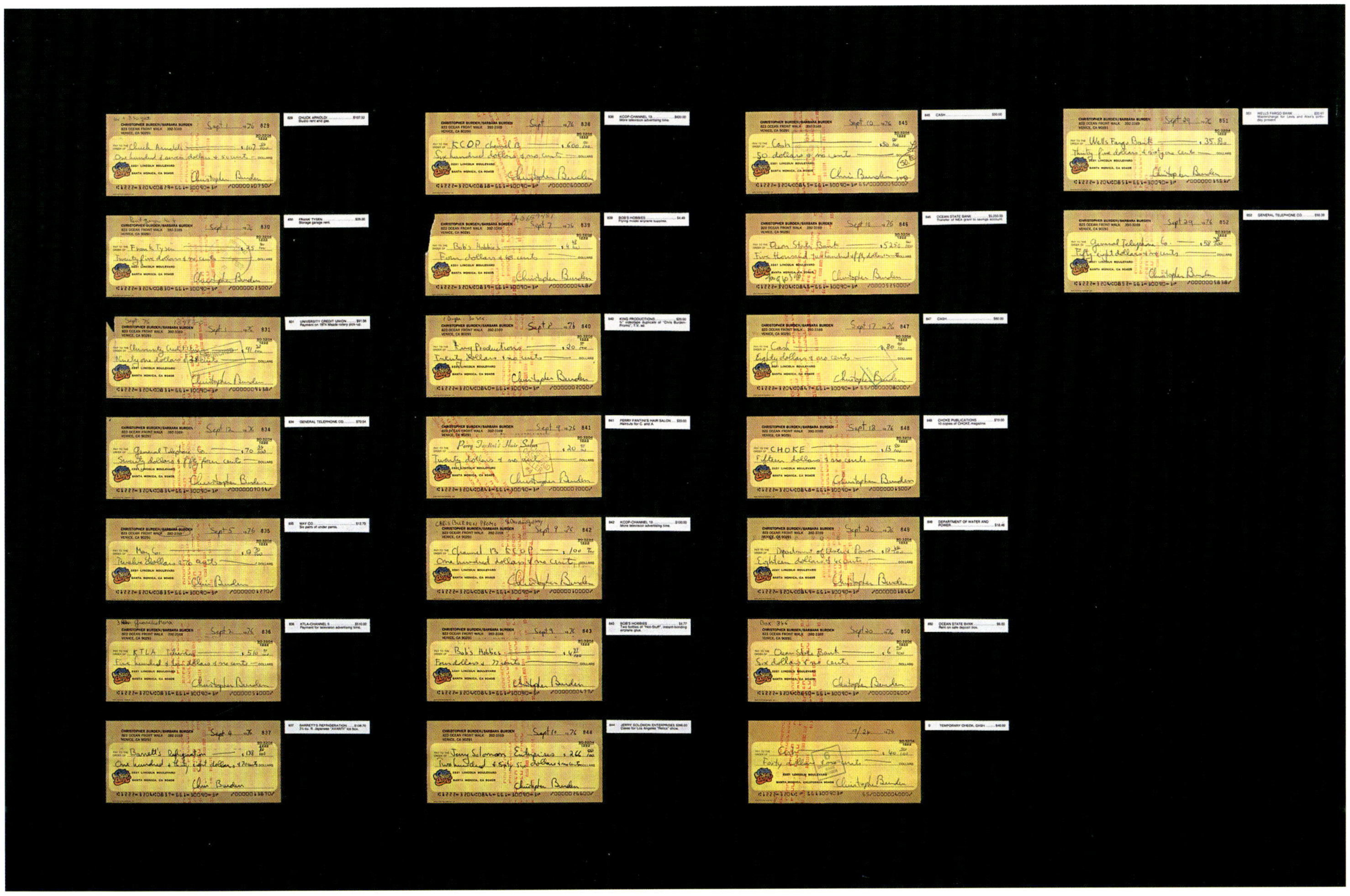

Full Financial Disclosure – April, 1977 1977
Collage – 18 checks and labels mounted on paper
30 × 36 inches

Full Financial Disclosure 1977

Baum-Silverman Gallery, Los Angeles,
California, USA; September 20, 1977

In September 1977, I became the first artist to make a full public financial disclosure. At the Baum-Silverman Gallery I displayed all my cancelled checks for the year 1976. A drawing was made of each month by mounting the cancelled checks on boards in vertical columns and framing them. Next to each check was a small typeset explanation. My bank statements and my 1976 Income Tax forms were also displayed as drawings.

In addition on Los Angeles television Channels 2, 4 and 7, I ran a 30-second commercial which showed me sitting behind a large desk in the manner of a sincere politician running for office. During this 'commercial' I announced that 'In keeping with the Bicentennial spirit, the post-Watergate mood and the new atmosphere on Capitol Hill, I wish to be the first artist to make a full public financial disclosure.' The television screen then displayed a series of graphics showing my 1976 gross income, a detailed list of my 1976 business expenses and finally my net income for 1976. This commercial was aired 30 times during a two-week period.

Send Me Your Money 1979

KPFK-FM Radio, Los Angeles, California, USA; March 21, 1979

For one hour, live on FM radio, I repeatedly asked the listeners to 'consider the possibility of sending money directly to me, to Chris Burden, 823 Oceanfront Walk, Venice, California 90291.' Interjected between my continuous appeals to send money directly to me at my address, I would explain that I was not selling anything and that I was not part of any charitable or religious organization. I emphasized that I was not asking for two or three big individual contributions, rather, I wanted everyone to send me a little, even as little as a quarter. I tried to emphasize that working together they could make me rich and that their loss would be invisible, whereas my gain would be substantial. I suggested that it would be as if they altogether just 'jogged one step to the left'. I did not pause or interrupt myself for a drink during this entire one-hour monologue. In addition to the radio listeners, a small audience of about 50 people witnessed the broadcast.

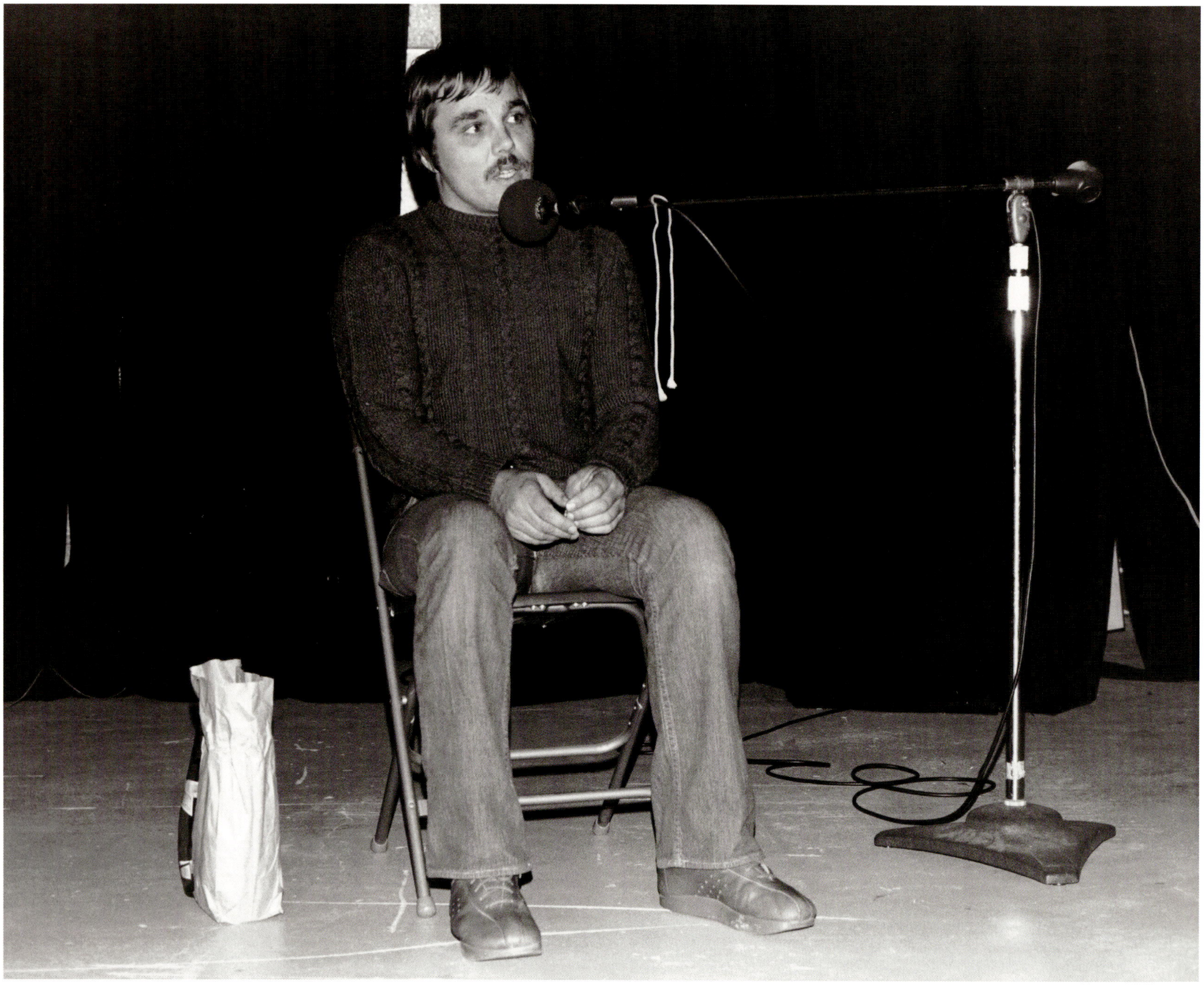

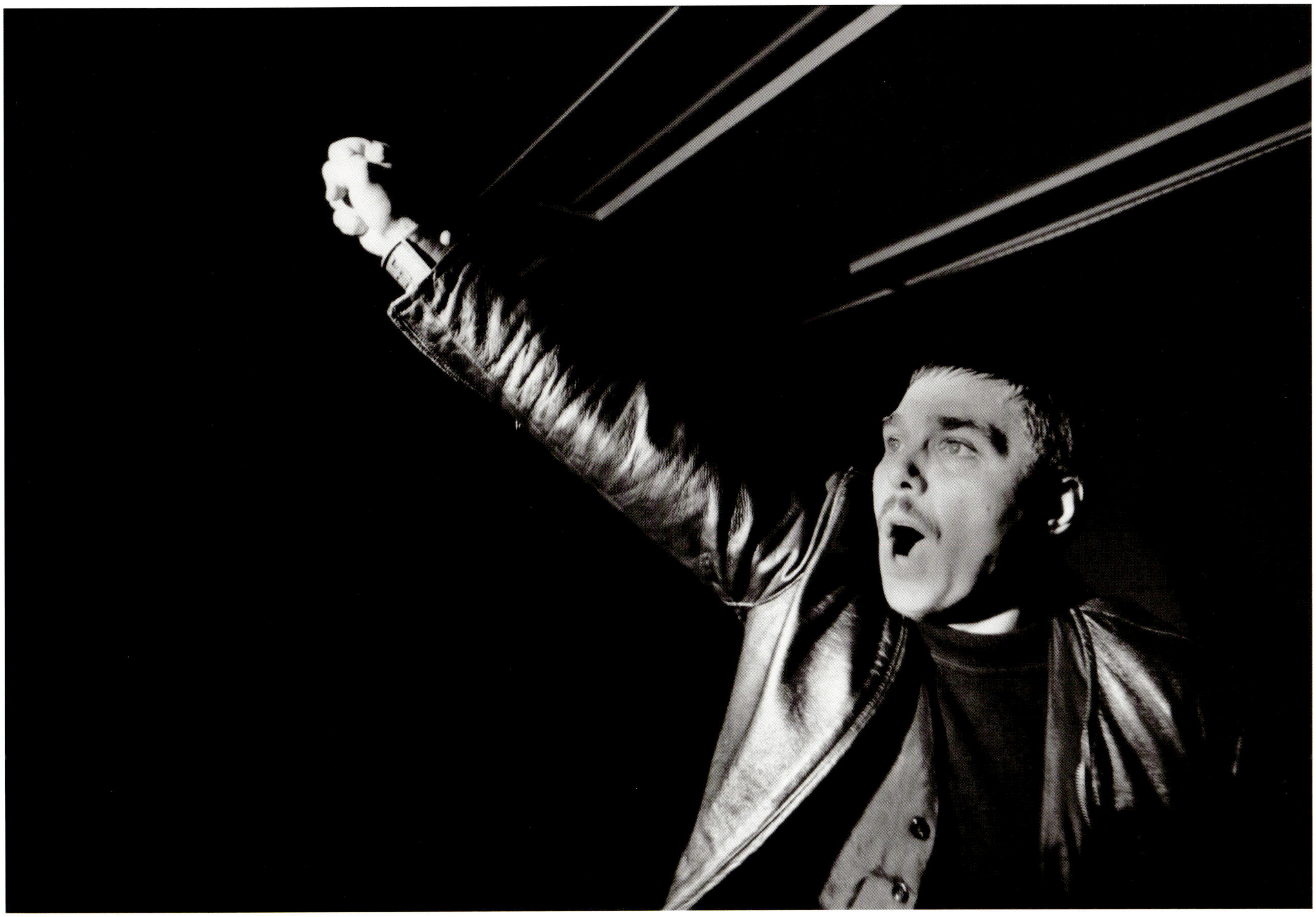

Atomic Alphabet 1979

San Francisco Art Institute,
San Francisco, California, USA;
November 17, 1979
Manitoba Theatre Workshop, Winnipeg,
Canada; November 20, 1979
Mudd Club, New York, USA;
June 8, 1980
Artists Union, Osaka, Japan;
September 9, 1980

Like a street tough, dressed all in black, with a black leather jacket and hat, I appeared spotlit in front of the audience. Raising my fist and stomping my foot to punctuate each word, I loudly and aggressively recited an alphabetical list of 26 words relating to atomic destruction: 'A for Atomic, B for Bomb, C for Combat', etc. The crazed chant ended with the terse cry, 'Yeh! Yeh! Yeh!' The performance lasted 30 seconds.

RELIC: Leather jacket

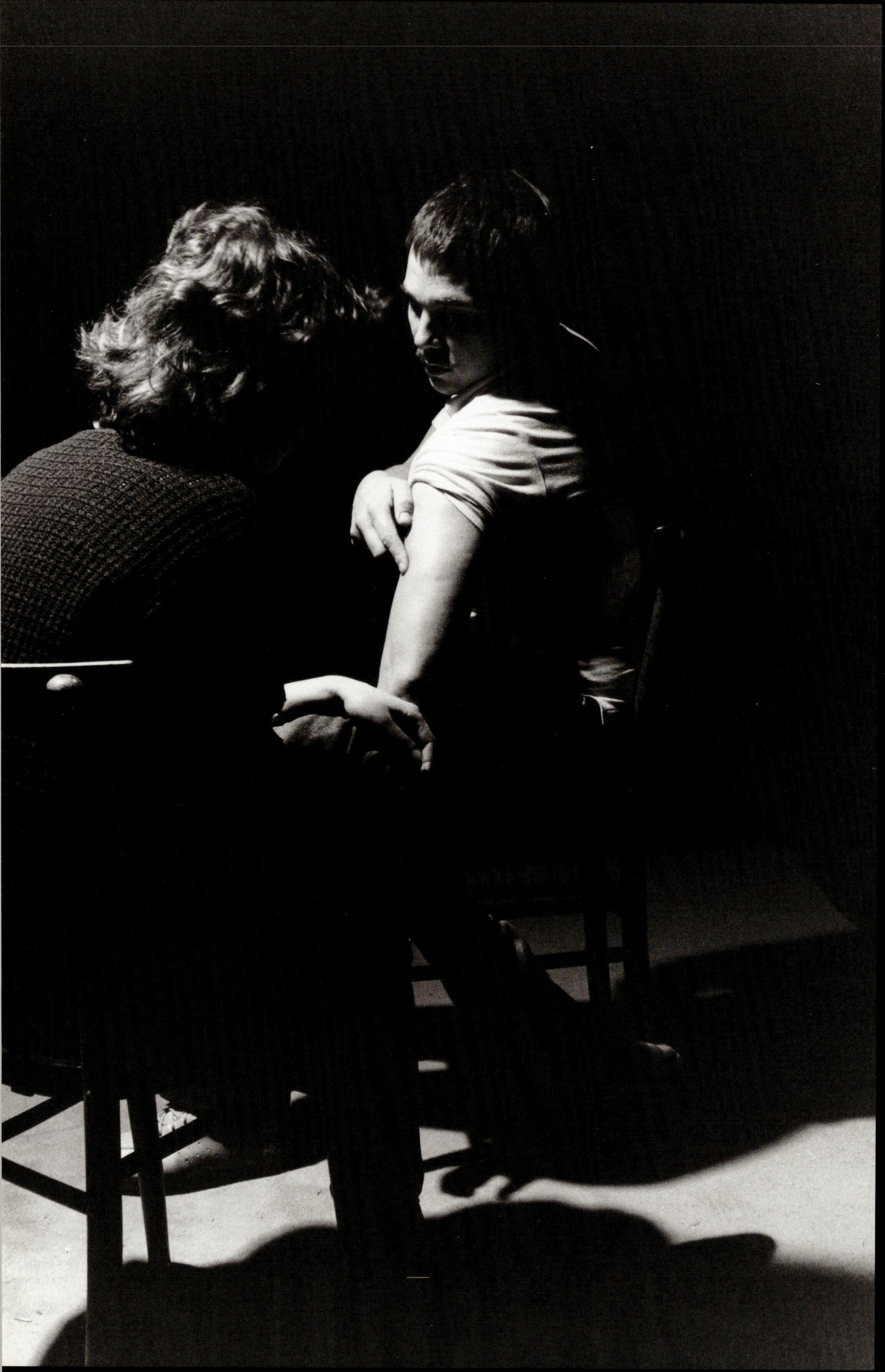

Show the Hole 1980

Italian Per/form/ance Festival, Florence,
Italy; March 4, 1980

Using black velvet curtains, I constructed a small private room in the entranceway of the theater that was being used to present the American performances. I sat in this small room with my name above me in white letters on the wall. One at a time, I received each person from the audience waiting outside. As each person entered, I addressed them in Italian and asked them in a cordial manner to 'Please sit down', then looking at them I said 'In 1971 I did a performance in which I was shot in the arm'. Finally, I would roll up my sleeve and as I pointed with my finger at the scar in my arm, I would say 'the bullet went in here and came out there'. Each spectator was alone with me and physically close to me. I received approximately 300 people, but because each person took about half a minute, some people had to wait in line up to three hours.

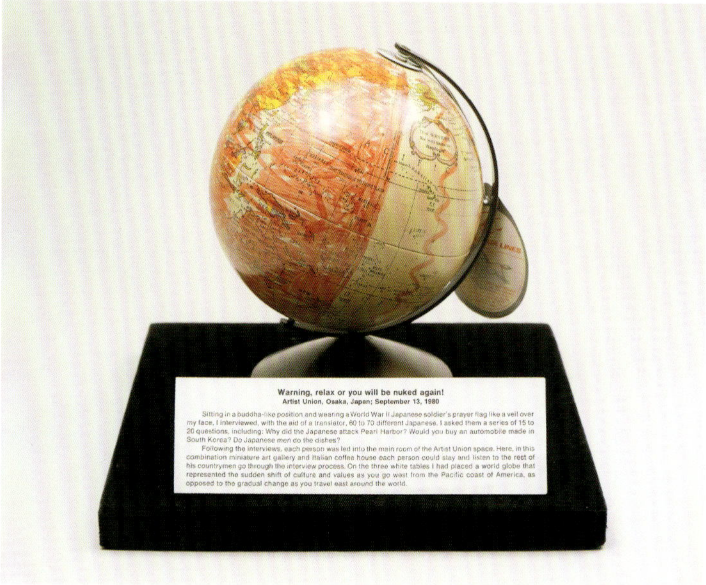

Warning! Relax, Or You Will Be Nuked Again 1980

Art House, Nishinomiya, Japan;
September 13, 1980

Sitting in a buddha-like position and wearing a World War II Japanese soldier's flag like a veil over my face, I interviewed, with the aid of a translator, 60 to 70 different Japanese. I asked them a series of 15 to 20 questions, including 'Why did the Japanese attack Pearl Harbor? Would you buy an automobile made in South Korea? Do Japanese men do the dishes?'

Following the interviews, each person was led into the main room of the Art House space. Here, in this combination miniature art gallery and Italian coffee house each person could stay and listen to the rest of his countrymen go through the interview process. On the three white tables I had placed a world globe that represented the sudden shift of cultures and values as you go west from the Pacific coast of America, as opposed to the gradual change as you travel east around the world.

RELICS: Three six-inch diameter globes, each with one hemisphere colored red; World War II Japanese prayer flag and formed wire hanger

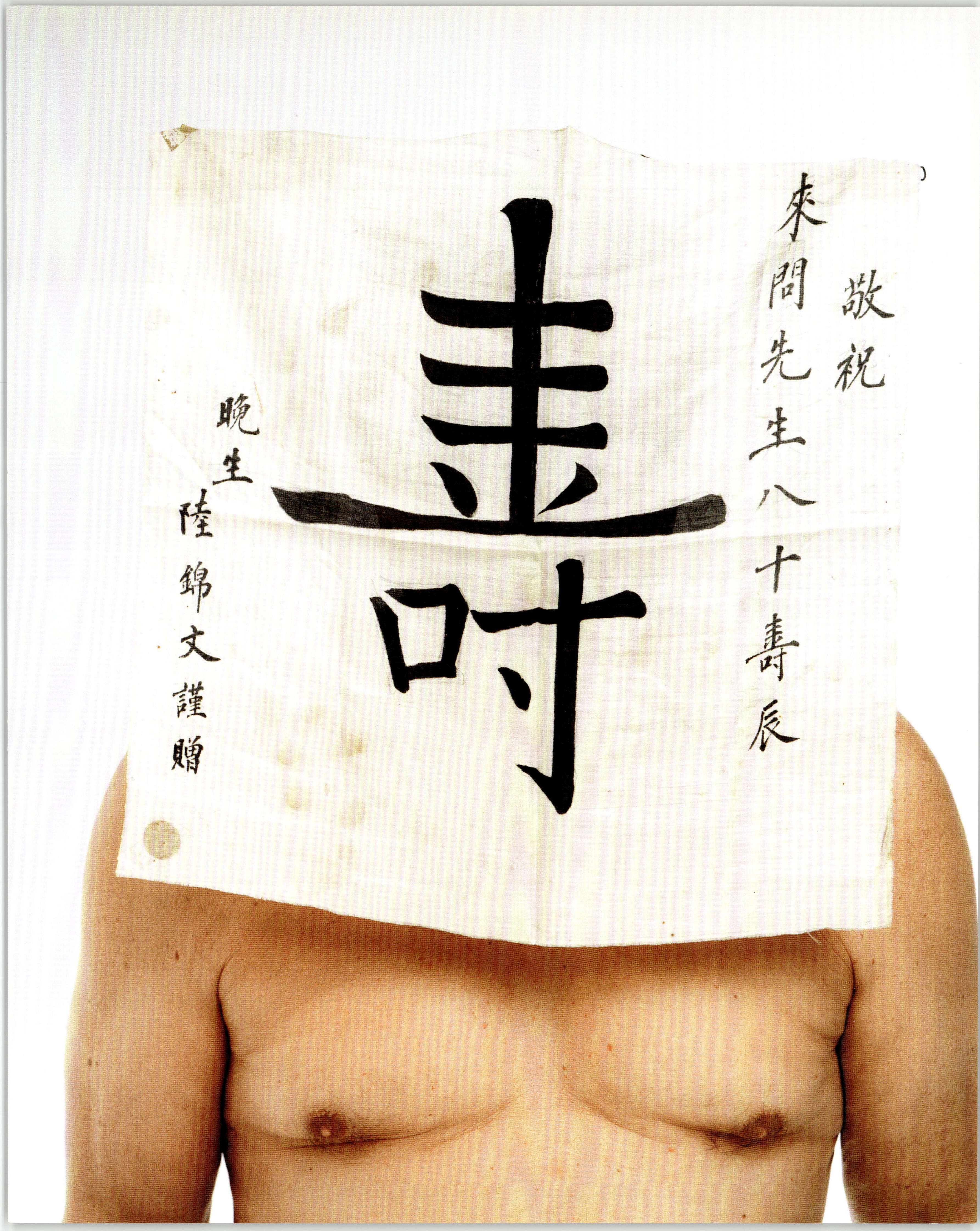
敬祝
來問先生八十壽辰
壽
晚生
陸錦文謹贈

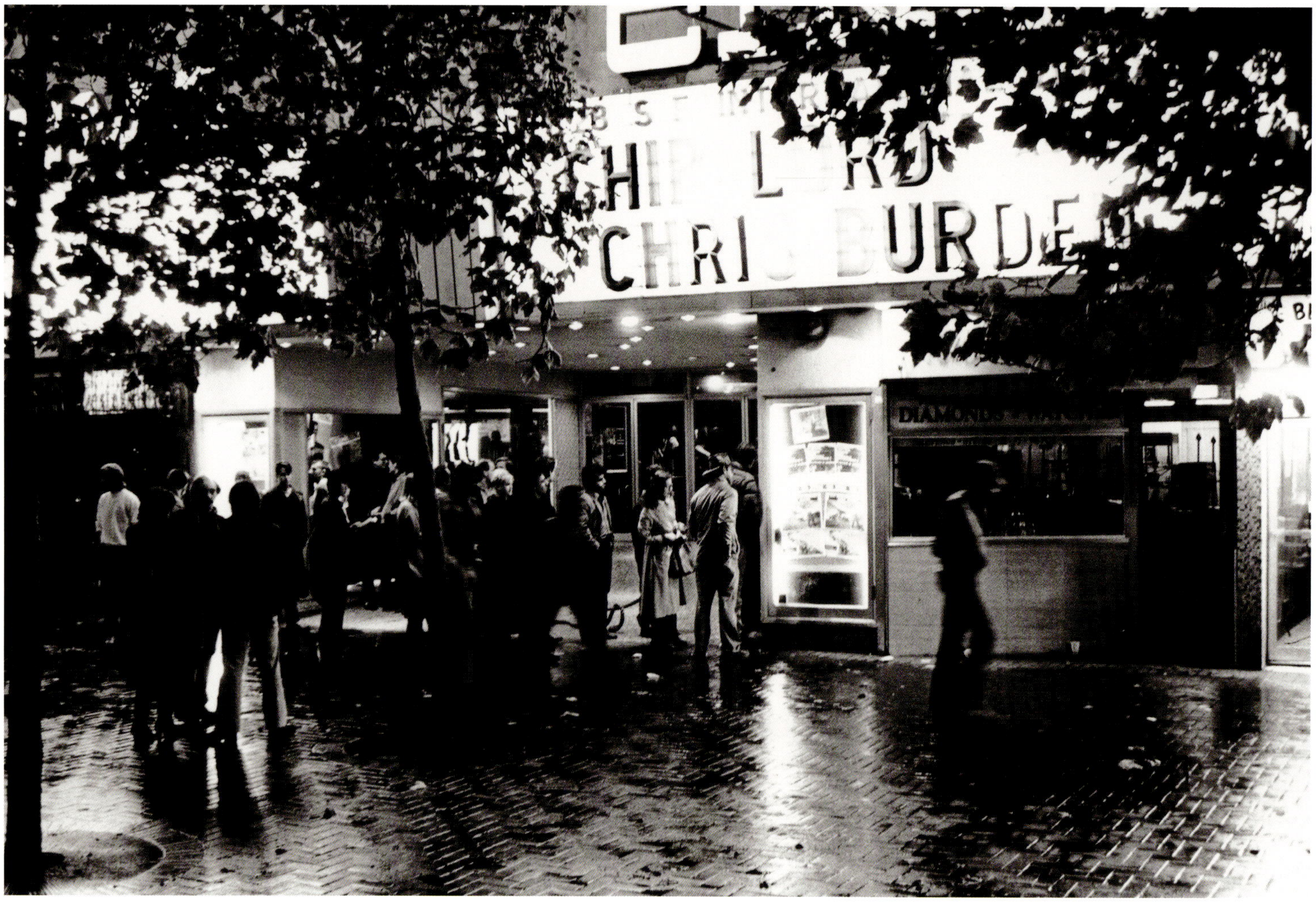

There Have Been Some Pretty Wild Rumors About Me Lately and I Just Want to Set the Record Straight 1981

San Francisco Video Festival, San Francisco, California, USA: October 28, 1981

This performance took the form of an oral narrative in which I revealed the truth of certain startling crisis events in my personal life which formed the basis of many wild rumors. Except for the one evening, no record, written or otherwise, of this oral narrative has ever been released publicly. Like a catholic confession, the content of what I revealed remains only in the memory of the audience.

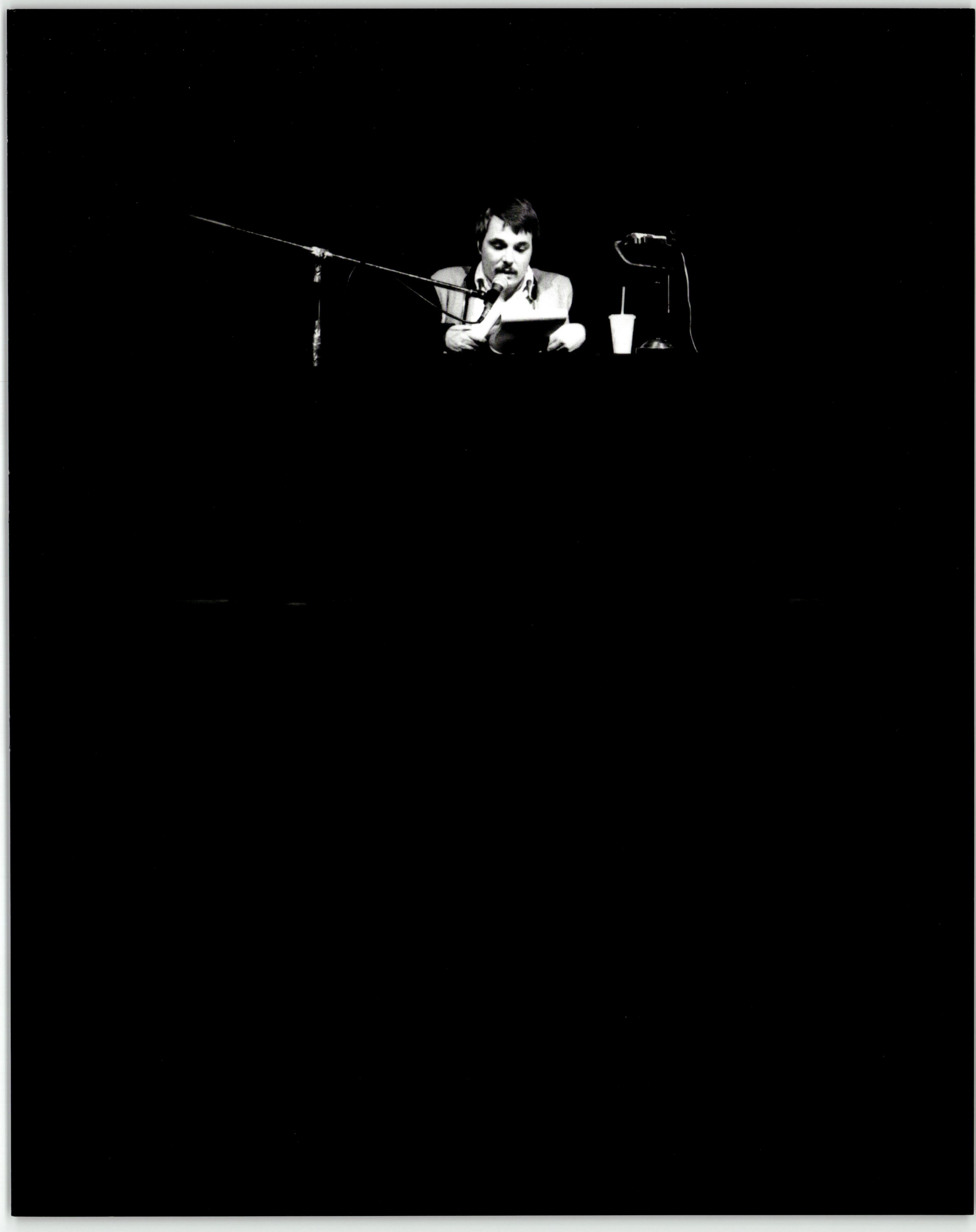

Work:

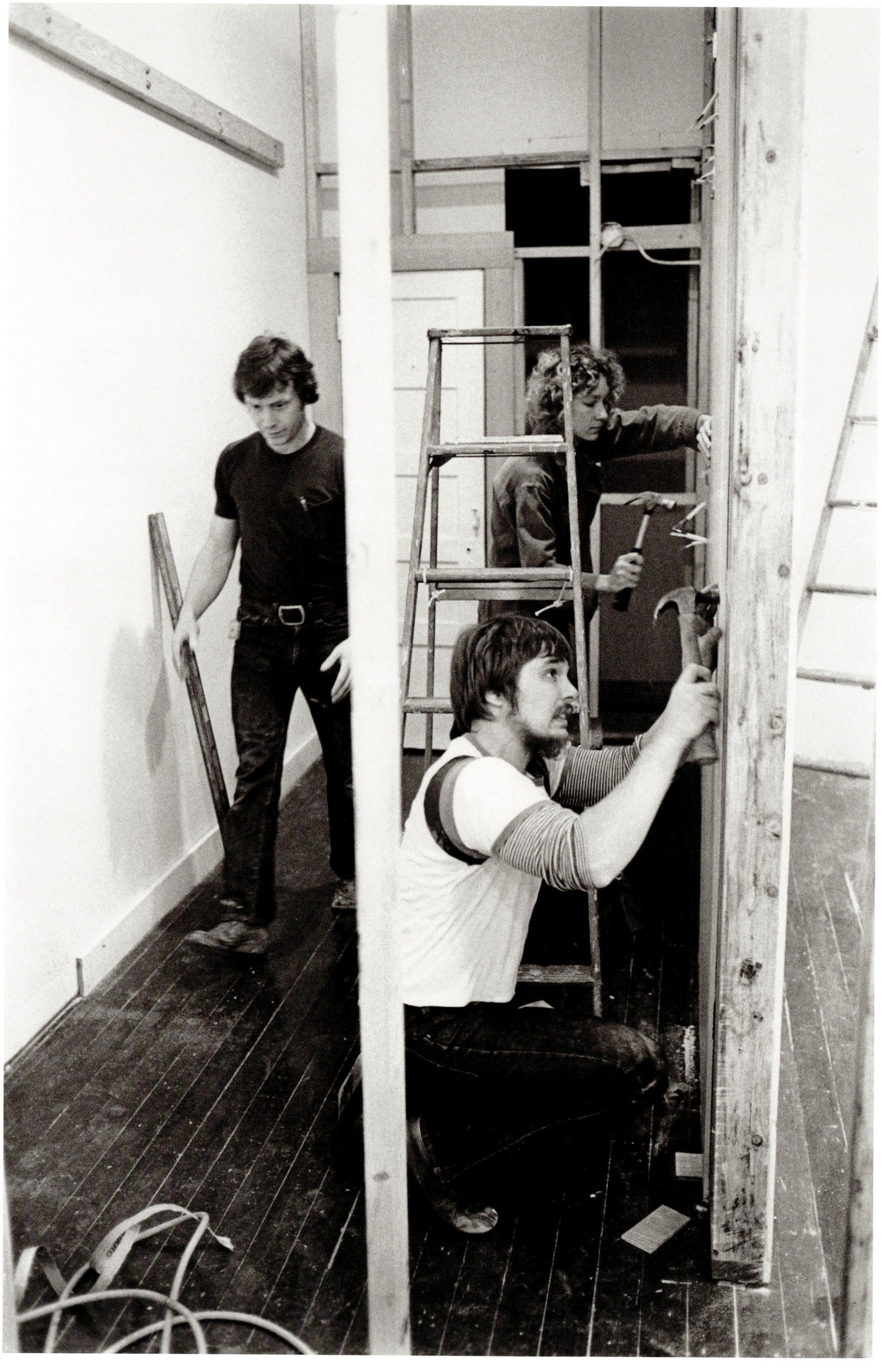

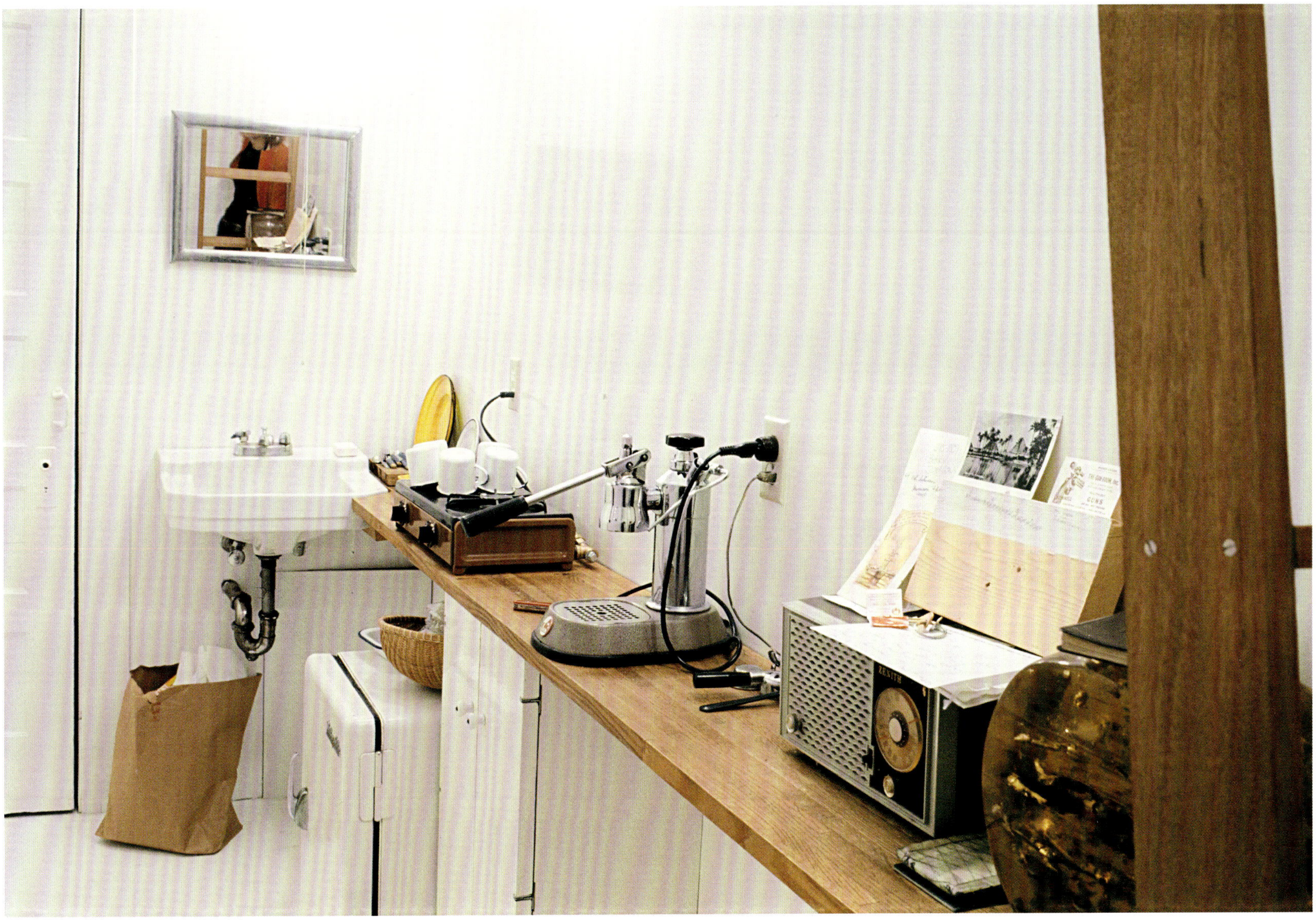

Natural Habitat 1976
(with Alexis Smith)

Portland Center for the Visual Arts, Portland, Oregon, USA; January 8–15, 1976

For my piece in a group show at the Center for the Visual Arts, we constructed a full-scale replica of the compact living quarters of my Venice, California studio (which I shared with Alexis Smith). The entire contents of our living quarters were shipped to Portland and installed in the duplicate space, which was perfect in almost every detail. During the first week of the exhibition we lived in the reconstructed studio. Visitors could observe us by looking through the open doorway, but a chain prevented them from actually entering our space. During the course of the performance we were free to come and go as we pleased, as we would have been at home.

Samson 1985

Turnstile, winch, worm gear, leather strap, jack, timbers, steel, steel plates
Dimensions variable

A museum installation consisting of a 100-ton jack connected to a gear box and a turnstile. The 100-ton jack pushes two large timbers against the bearing walls of the museum. Each visitor to the museum must pass through the turnstile in order to see the exhibition. Each input on the turnstile ever so slightly expands the jack, and ultimately if enough people visit the exhibition, Samson *could, theoretically, destroy the building. Like a glacier, its powerful movement is imperceptible to the naked eye. This sculptural installation subverts the notion of the sanctity of the Museum (the shed that houses the art).*

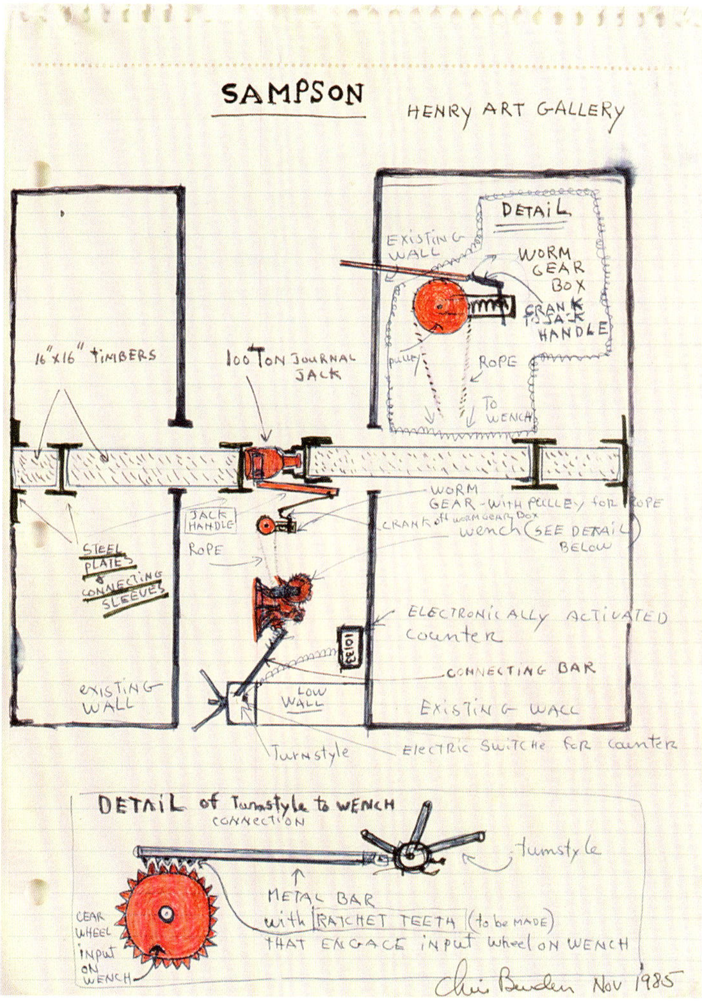

Samson 1985
Ink on paper, 11 × 8½ inches

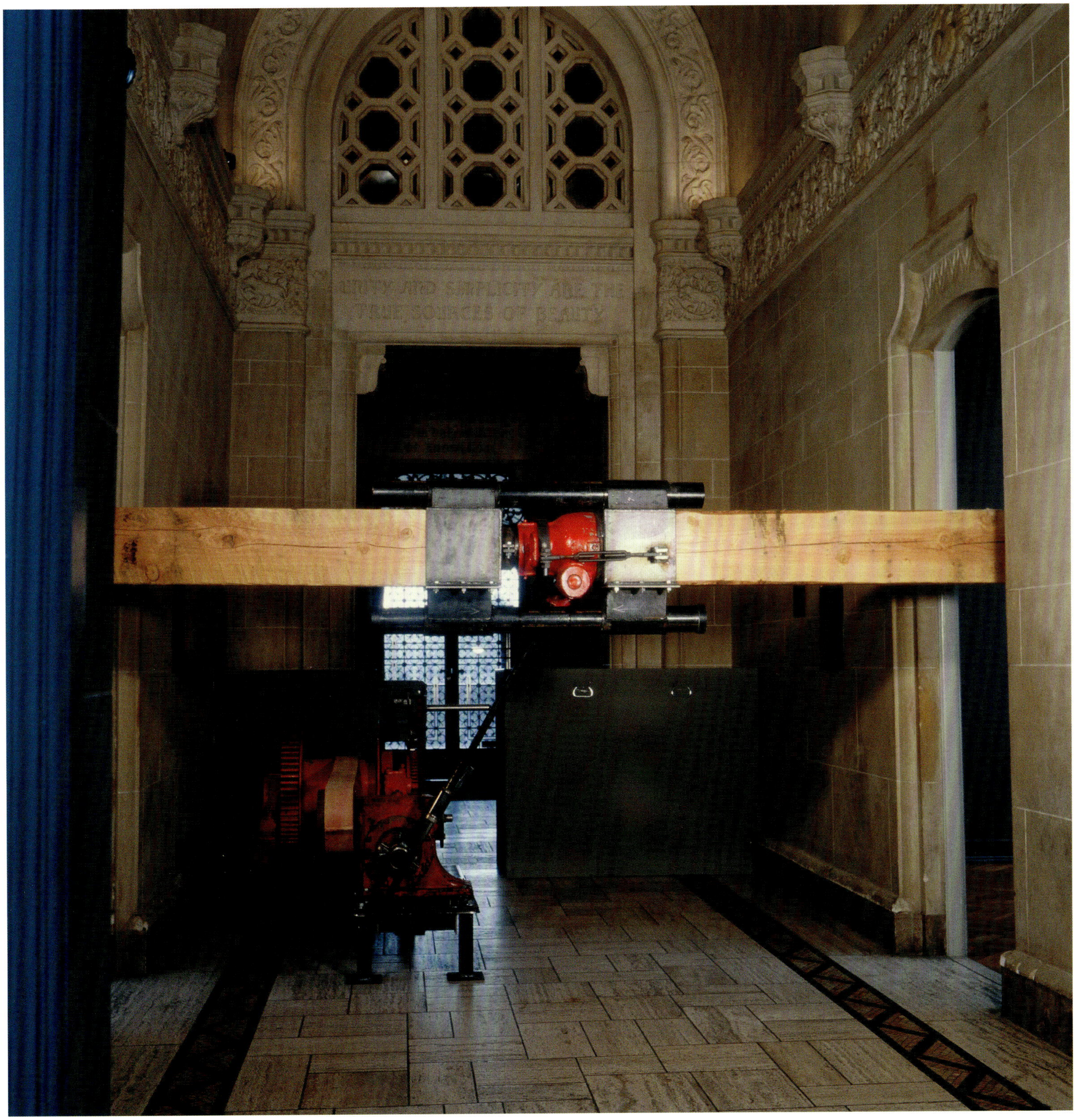
UNITY AND SIMPLICITY ARE THE
TRUE SOURCES OF BEAUTY

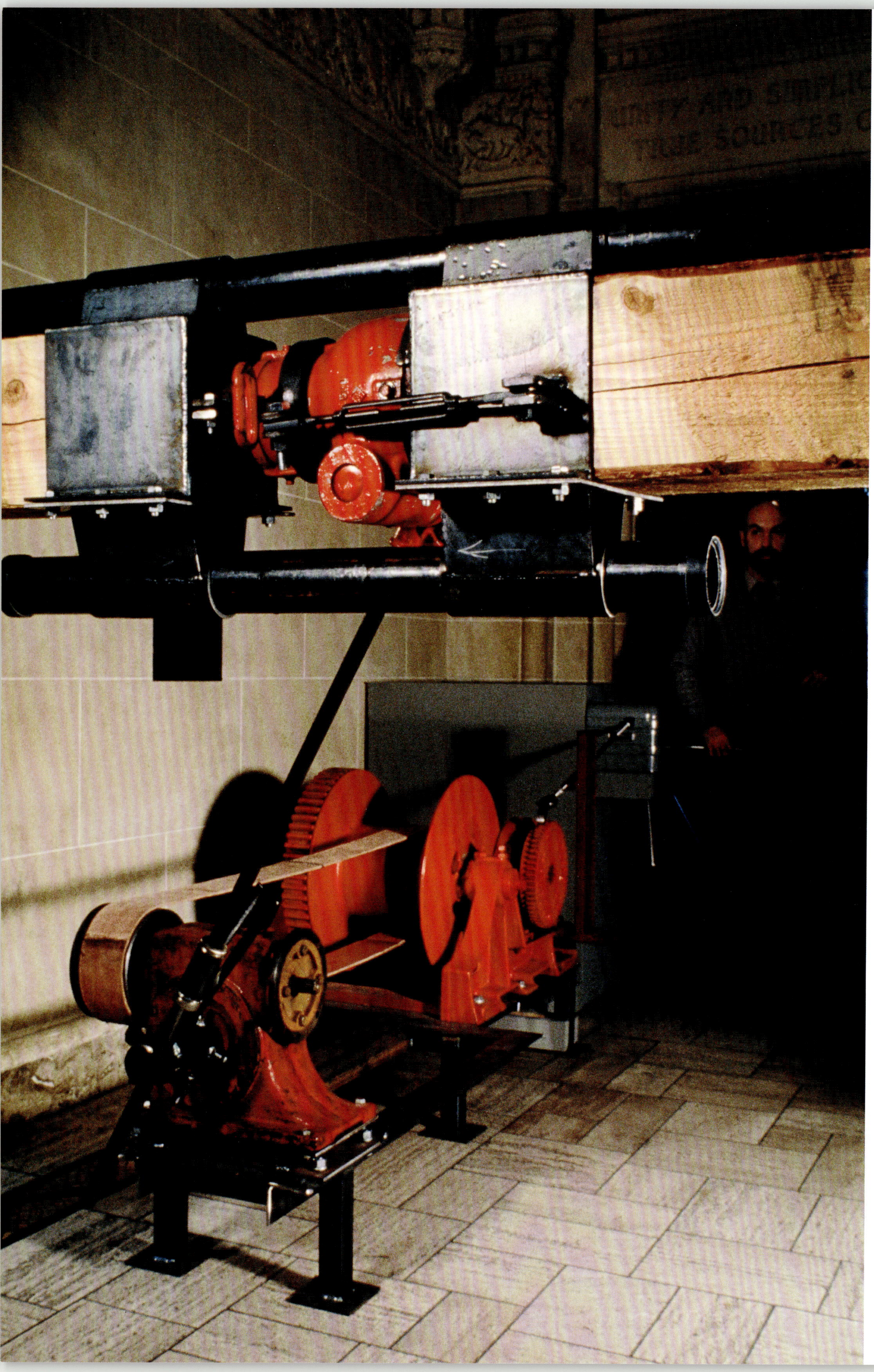
UNITY AND
TRUE SOURCES

▷▷

Exposing the Foundation of the Museum 1986

Excavation and removal of
52 × 16-foot section of concrete floor,
three excavations of earth, each
approximately 9 feet deep × 16 feet
wide, with three sets of wooden stairs
624 × 192 × 108 inches
Installation at the Museum of
Contemporary Art (MOCA),
Los Angeles, California, USA;
December 10 1986–June 19 1988

Three excavations, approximately nine feet deep by 16 feet wide, were made in the earth to reveal the concrete footings which supported three steel columns. Stairs enabled visitors to descend into the excavations to observe where the concrete met the earth. The concrete floor in the museum was removed before excavations.

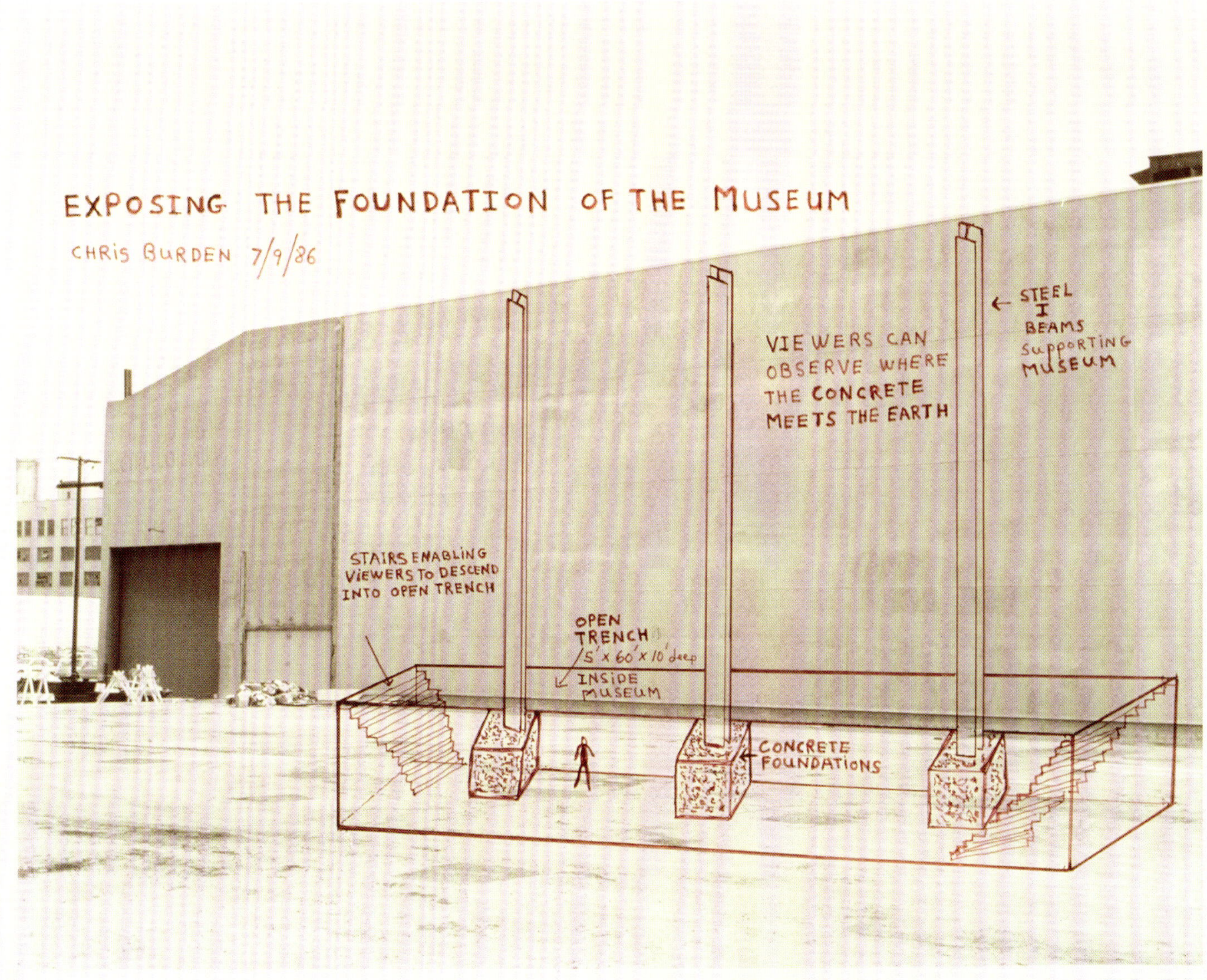

Exposing the Foundation of the Museum 1986
Black and whte photograph with ink
11 × 14 inches

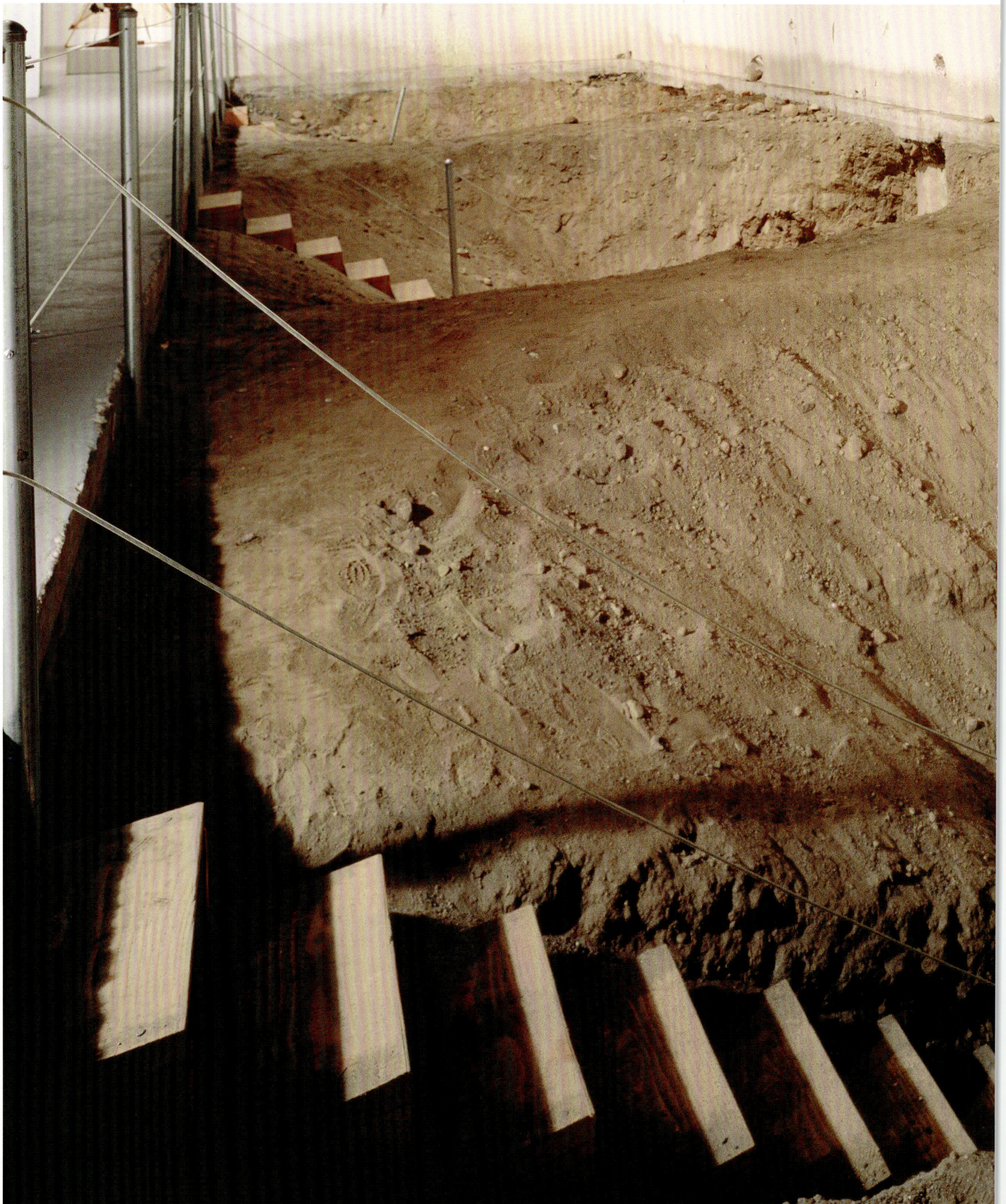

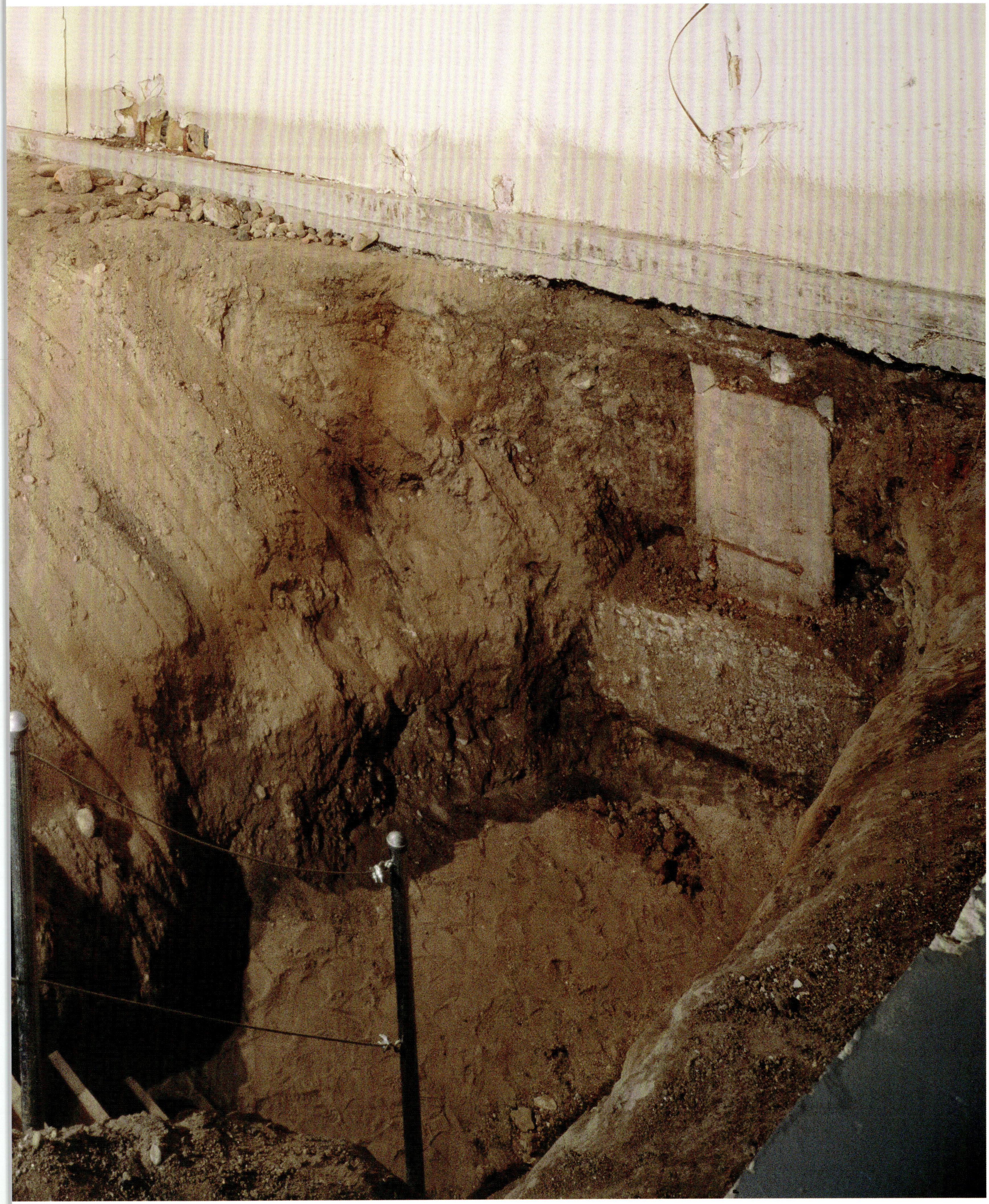

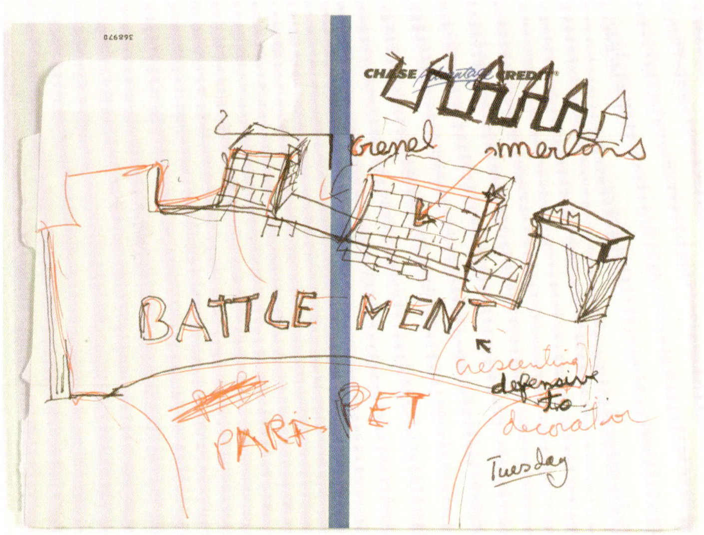

Wexner Castle II 1990
Ink on paper, 5½ × 8 inches

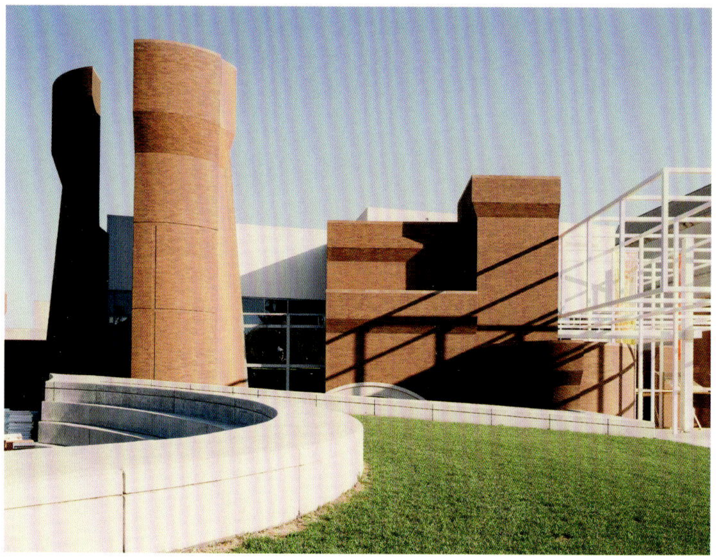

Wexner Center for the Visual Arts

Wexner Castle 1990

Addition of crenels and merlons to existing Peter Eisenman-designed museum building.
Installation at Wexner Center for the Visual Arts, Ohio State University, Columbus, Ohio, USA; October 6 1990–January 26 1991

The work of art for the exhibition: 'New Works for New Spaces', October 1990 to January 1991, at the Wexner Center for the Visual Arts consisted of modifying the brick towers by adding the classic saw-toothed brickwork, architecturally referred to as the crenels (the empty space) and the merlons (the teeth), to the top of the brick turrets as they existed on the original armory. The modifications were executed with the appropriate materials (i.e. matching masonry) and level of craftsmanship so that they appeared to be part of the original Eisenman/Trott construction.

Historically, crenellations were functional architectural features of fortifications, providing openings for soldiers to discharge and hurl their weapons at the enemy below. Gradually, over the centuries, their functional aspect waned and they became purely decorative. The fact that crenellations continued to be employed in such recent buildings as the armory itself, is an indication of their powerful and everlasting symbolism. By restoring the crenellations to the Eisenman/Trott brick towers I tried to create art strong enough to stand up to the architecture and at the same time I tried to strengthen one's understanding of the past, to evoke the presence of the vanished armory and to clarify the source of the brick towers.

My artistic response is an architectural one. By restoring the crenels and the merlons to the brick turrets as a sculptural work of art, the architecture becomes a pedestal for the art, the building becomes the basis for the interaction and the art is not swallowed up as so many critics of the building had feared. At the same time, restoring the crenellations as an art work also speaks about art being 'decorative' versus the 'functionalism' of architecture, while hopefully, concurrently contributing to the process that Eisenman refers to as 'a building forever coming into being'. The addition of the crenels reinforces the building's links to the past and thereby reinstates the decorative/functional aspects of the turrets and by extension the decorative/functional duality of all architecture.

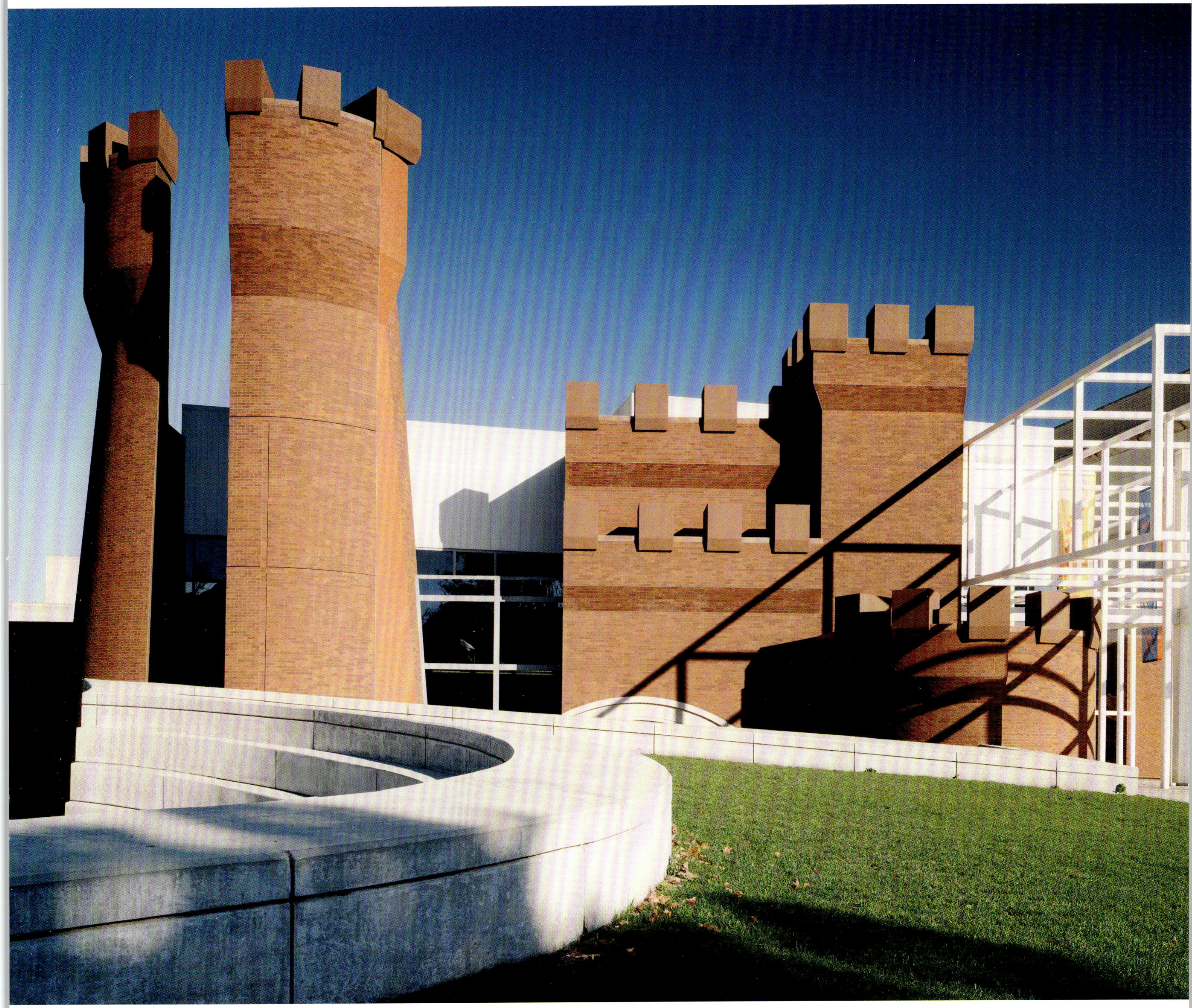

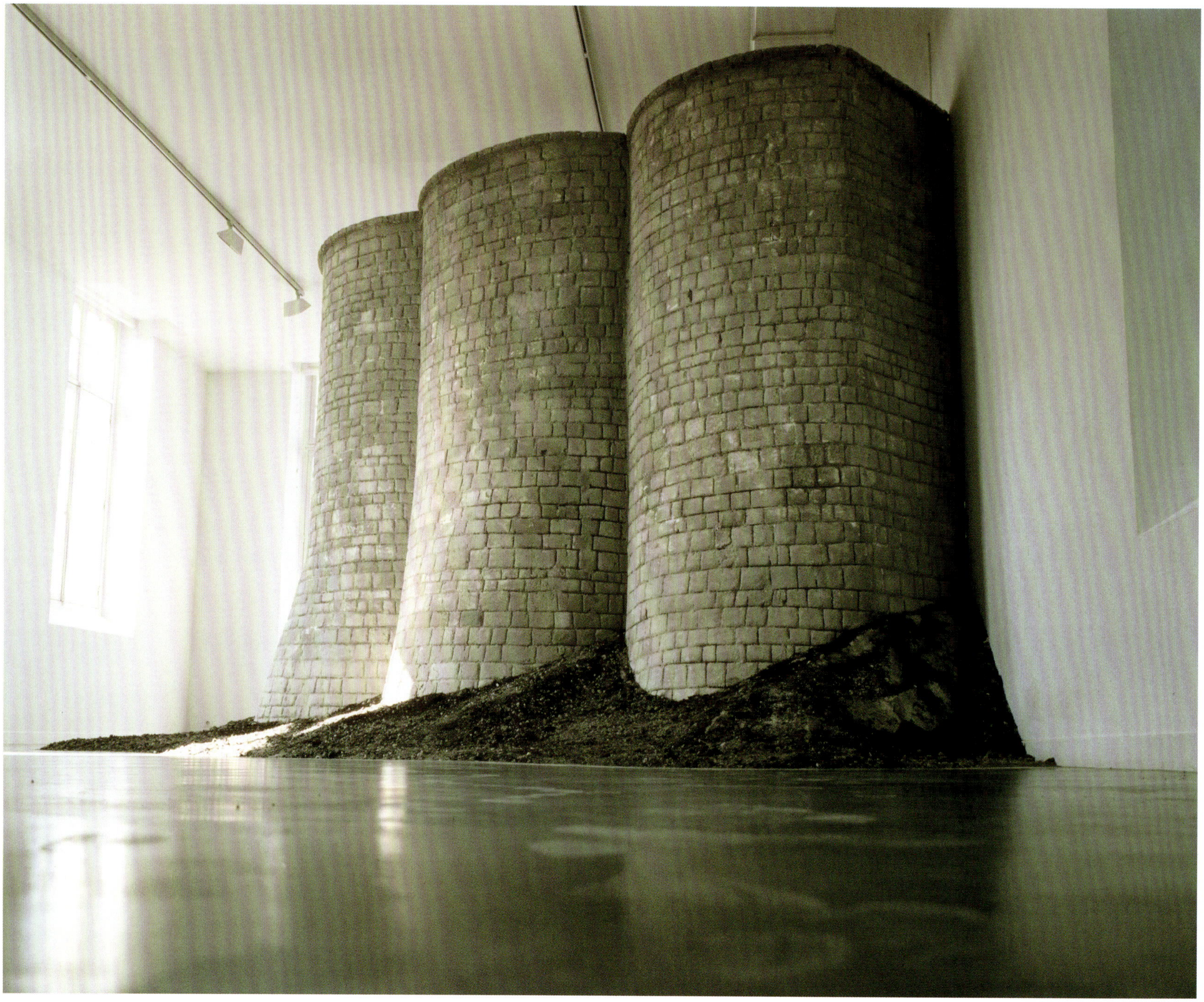

Tours des Trois Museaux 1994

Wood, foam, paint, rocks
126 × 177 × 98 inches

The Tours des Trois Museaux *is a model of a thirteenth-century fortification. During the Middle Ages, the city of Reims had a fortified wall around it. At some point one of the entrances to the city was blocked off by building a third tower between two existing gate towers. This triple tower has since been destroyed, but images of it are still depicted on postcards found in Reims today.*

The crude stonework and the three towers placed side by side results in a slouching structure that is both bizarre and primitive. The three towers are in sharp contrast to the much more dignified and

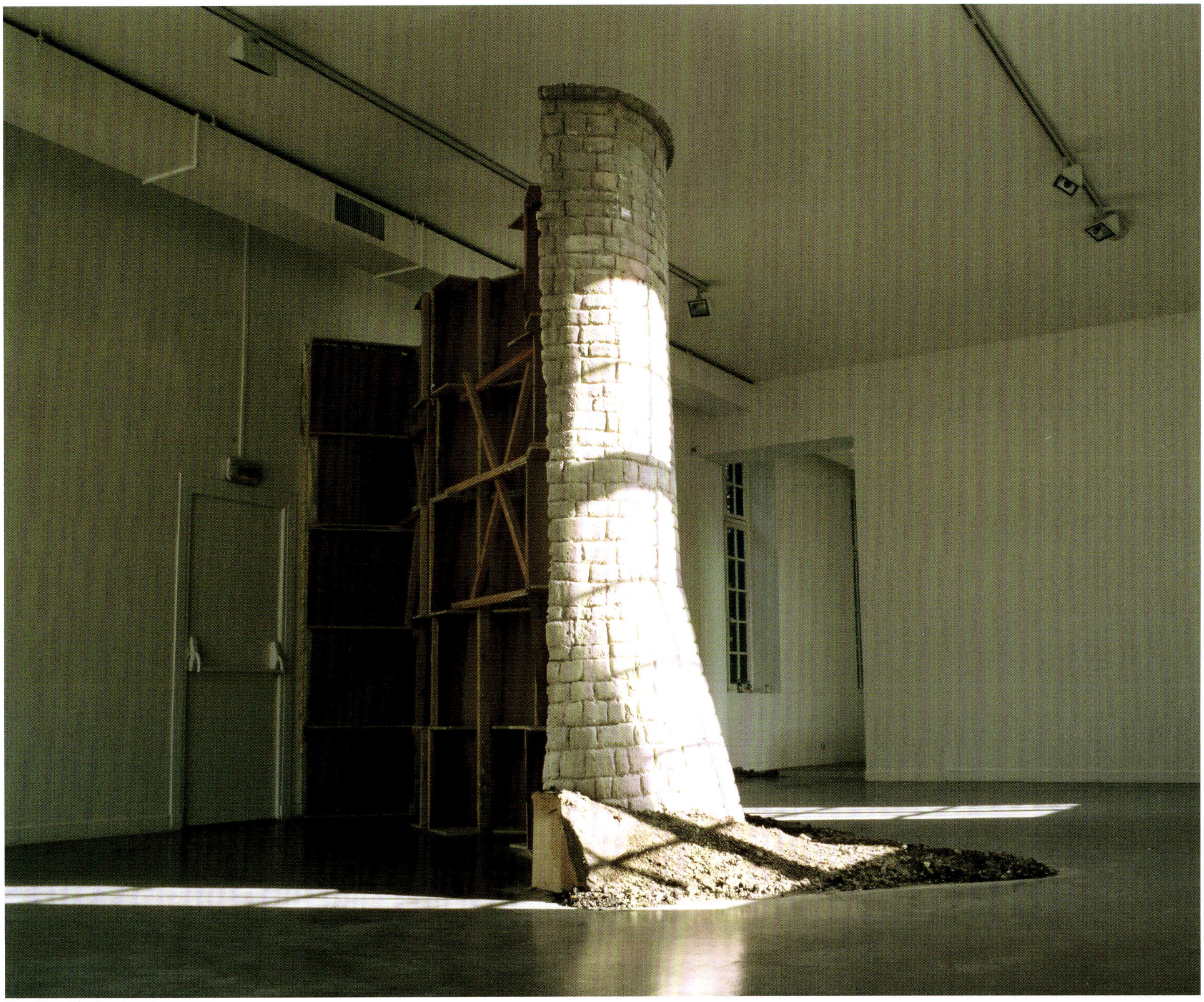

sophisticated buildings found throughout Europe. I was interested in modeling these three towers because I playfully fantasized them to have been the source and the basis for the later, more refined stonework and structures as seen through Europe in the cathedrals, the castles, the monasteries, the fortresses, etc.

My model of the three towers is built using carved foam, paint and wood. Though the towers look real, as one turns and comes around to the inside of the towers, one realizes the artifice of the whole structure.

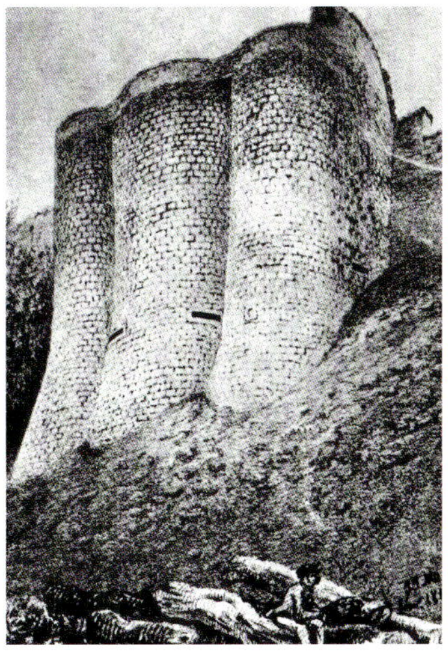

¼ Ton Bridge 1997

(Edition of three, with one artist's proof)
Metal toy construction parts
(Meccano and Erector). Each bridge
is accompanied by *Static Test* (2000),
a signed and dated color photograph
produced in an edition of 12.
Bridge: 12¾ × 33 × 6¾ inches

¼ Ton Bridge *is an engineered arched bridge constructed of Meccano and Erector parts. It is capable of supporting 500 pounds. The thin diagonal struts attaching the deck to the arch transfer the considerable load to the arch and prevent the span from collapsing.*

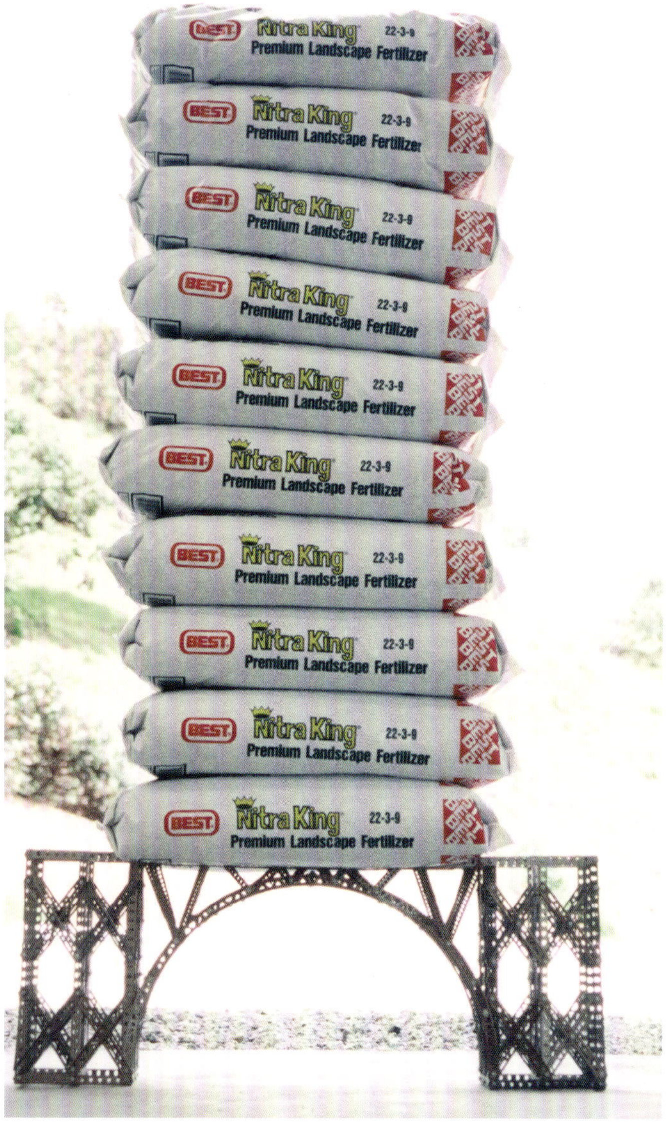

Static Test 2000
Colour photograph, 20 × 16 inches

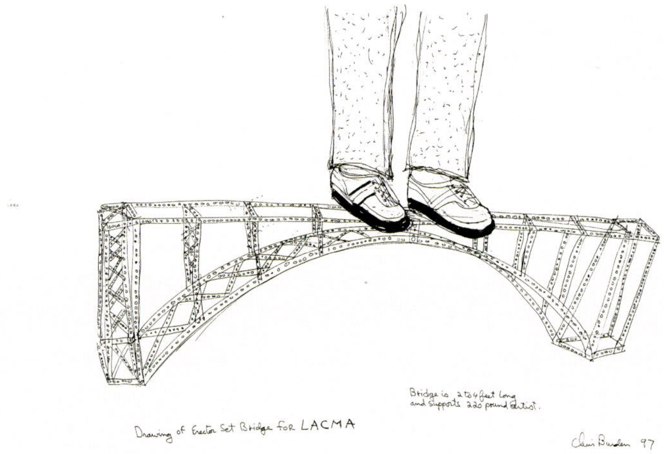

Erector Set Bridge for Los Angeles County Museum of Art 1997
Ink and pencil on paper, 17 × 22 inches

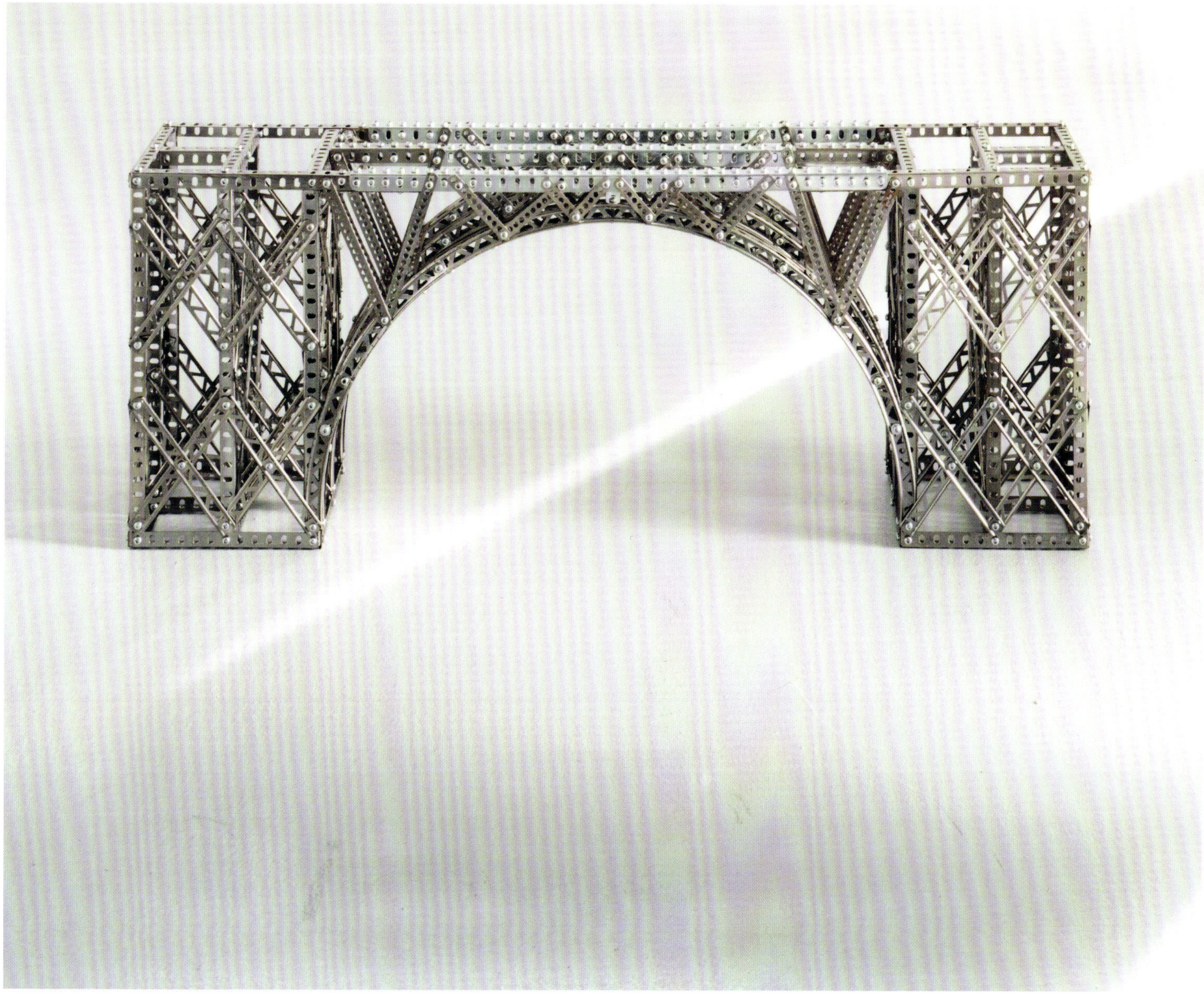

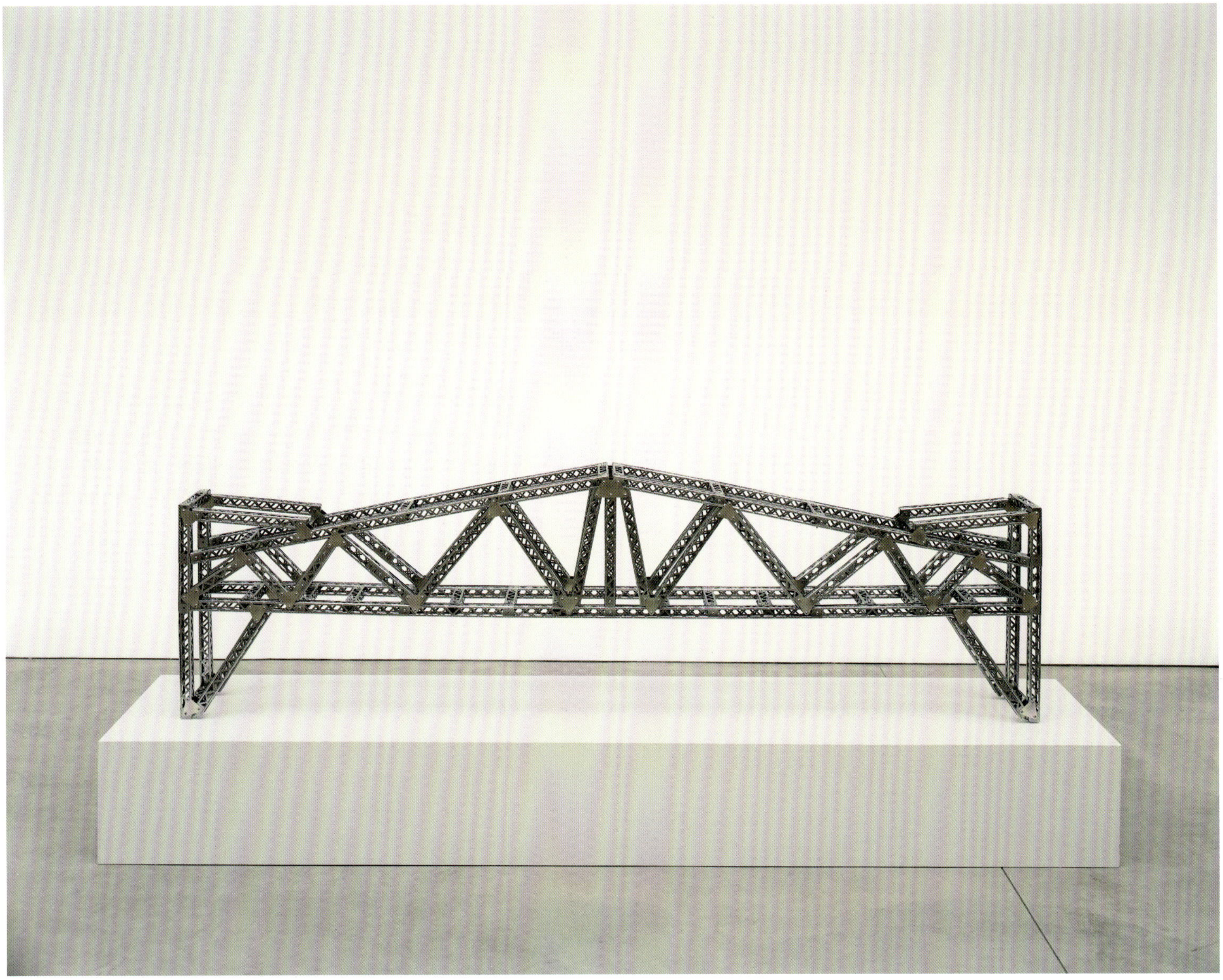

Antique Bridge 1998

(Edition of two, with one artist's proof)
Early 20th Century (1913) metal toy construction parts (Mysto Type I Erector)
23¾ × 91 × 8½ inches

The Antique Bridge *was built entirely of rare antique Mysto Type I Erector parts, dating from 1913 and based on an illustration advertising these early Erector sets. The ad shows three boys, two working at opposite ends of the bridge and the third sitting in the middle of the top of the bridge. An interesting feature of the Erector manuals published by A.C. Gilbert in the early part of the 1900s, was that the illustrations were not intended to be absolute blueprints or instructions on how to build the models. The illustrations were merely suggestions and were often purposely drawn incorrectly, so that the young builder had to struggle to find his own solution. The illustration of the* Antique Bridge *from 1919 appears to be accurate. However, if you carefully count the one-foot intervals along the bottom of the span, you will note the length from the center point of four-and-a-half feet on the left side and three-and-a-half feet from the right side. Due to the fact that the drawing of the* Antique Bridge *is inaccurate, there was some doubt among Erector and Meccano enthusiasts as to whether this bridge has ever been built or could be built. Like an M.C. Escher drawing, it might simply have been the artist's creation. It gave me great pleasure to discover this bridge was indeed buildable.*

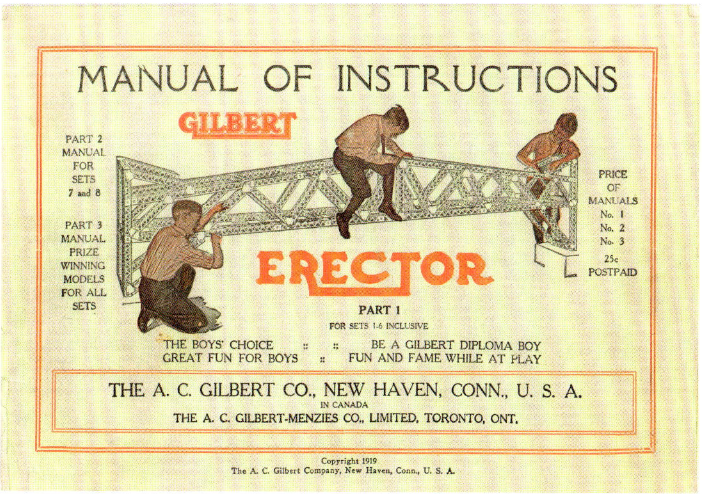

Cover of 1919 Erector Construction Set Manual

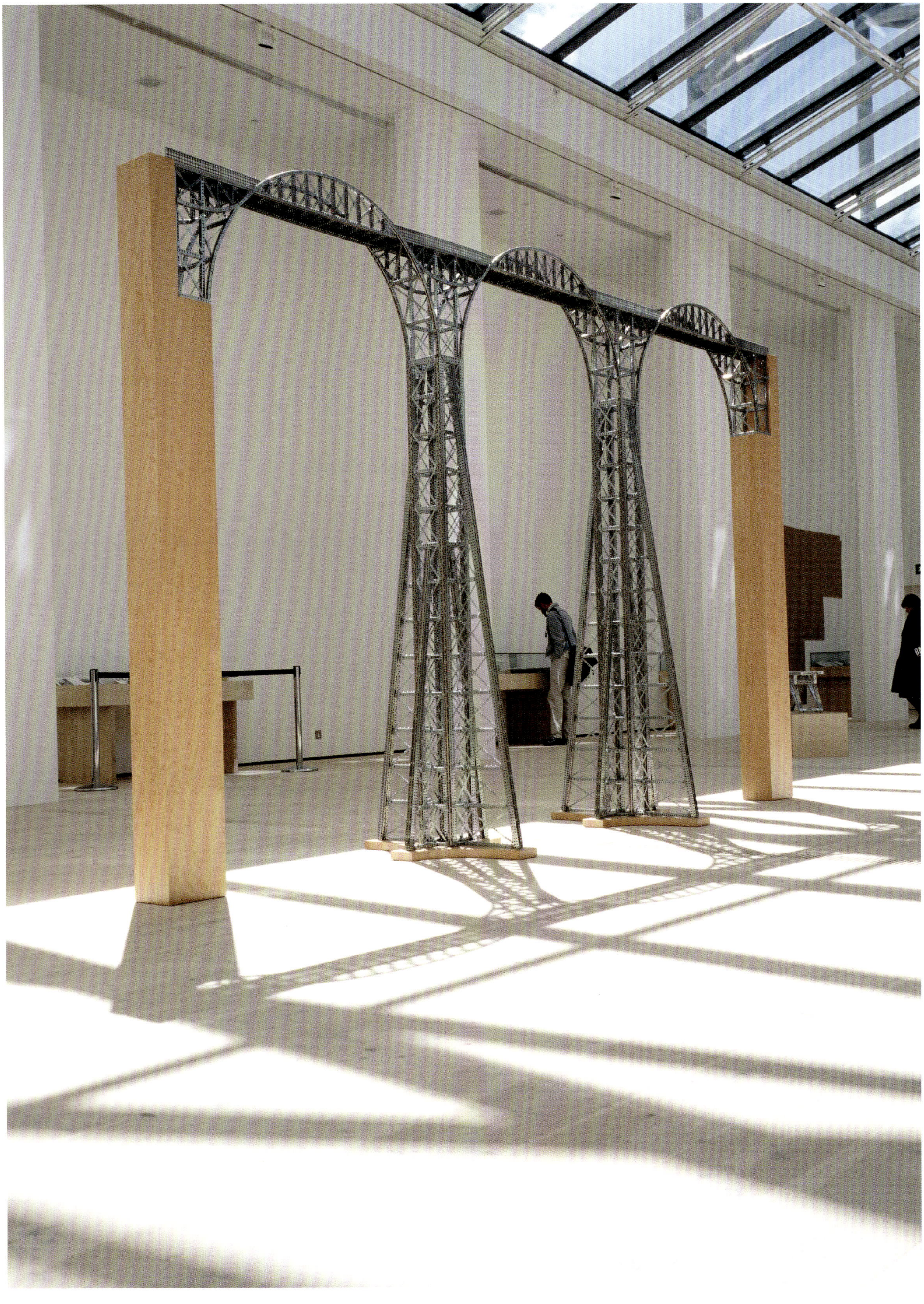

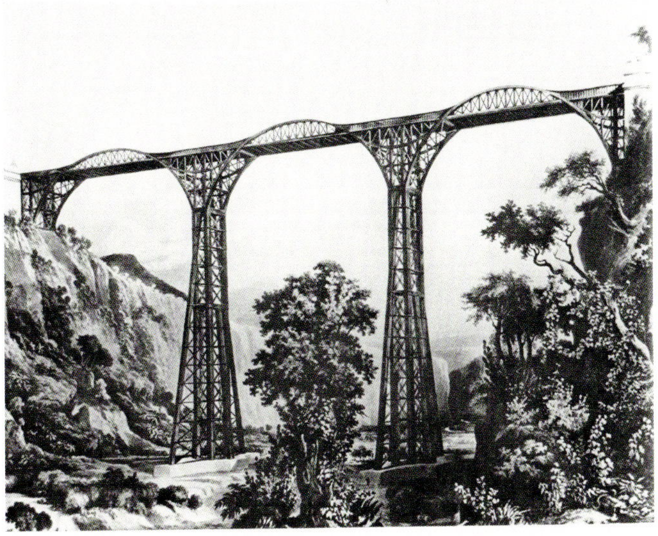

AUTHOR'S COLLECTION

AS ORIGINALLY PLANNED the Mexicano's track was to cross the Metlac River's gorge near its mouth, the present location of Highway 150. Fairbairn designed this bridge comprised of tubular iron members; but it was not built because the final location was farther upstream.

'Railroads in Mexico', p 34

Mexican Bridge 1998

Metal toy construction parts (Meccano
and Erector), wood
111¾ × 180 × 37 inches

The Mexican Bridge *consists of serpentine reverse arches. This bridge is a model of a cast iron bridge designed in the 1860s, but never built, for the fledgling Mexican railroad system to span the 1,000-foot-wide Metlac Gorge.*

For five years I periodically studied the drawing of the bridge, illustrated on page 34 of 'Railroads in Mexico'. The illustration of this elegant, sensuous bridge mesmerized me and I found great pleasure in entertaining the idea that it might be possible to build a giant scale reproduction of this bridge using Meccano and Erector parts.

Before I attempted the design and construction of this model, I designed and built the ¼ Ton Bridge *out of Meccano and Erector parts. The* ¼ Ton Bridge *was initially designed to simply hold my own body weight. But, upon completion, I discovered that this five-pound structure could in fact hold 500 pounds, or a quarter ton, hence its name. With the successful completion of the* ¼ Ton Bridge, *I had the confidence to undertake translating the drawing of the Metlac Gorge Bridge into a 15-foot-long, accurate Meccano/Erector model.*

Because the actual bridge was never built I would like to believe the English bridge designer, William Fairbairn, would be pleased to see his design finally realized in a three dimensional form.

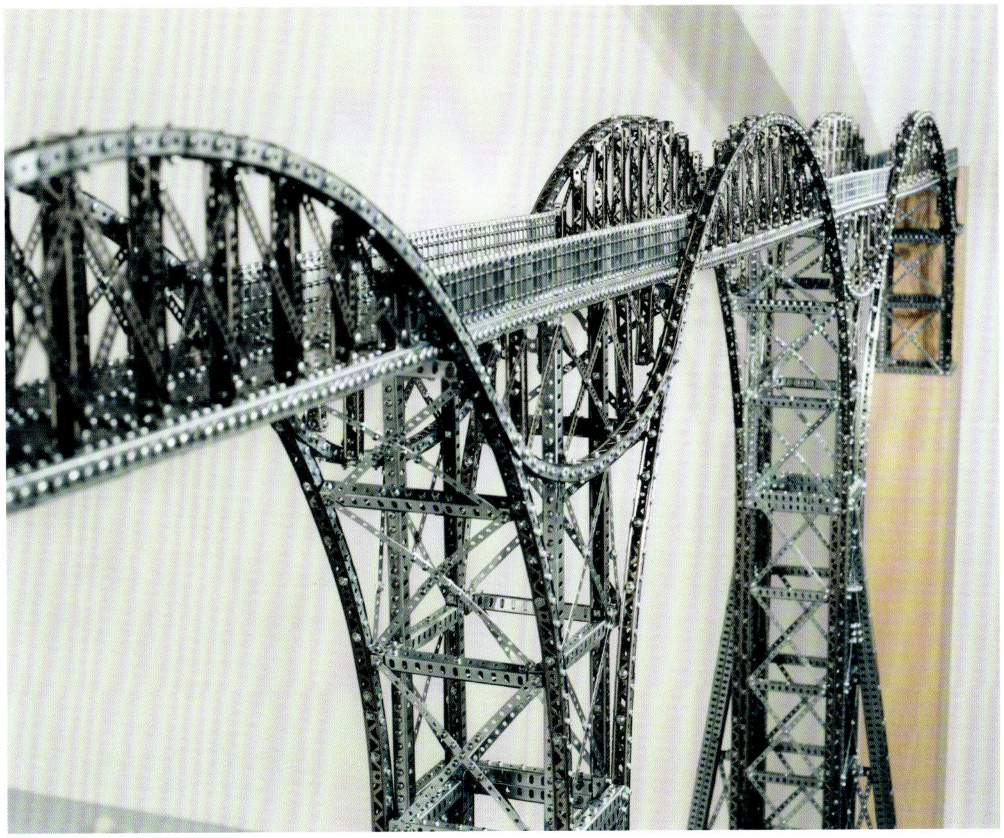

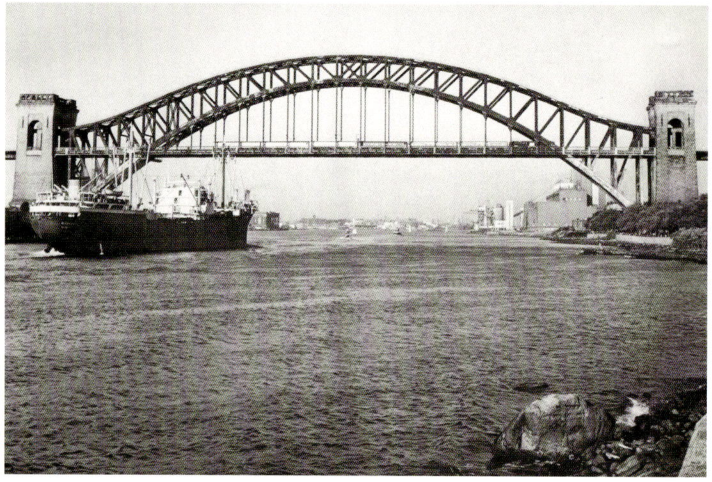

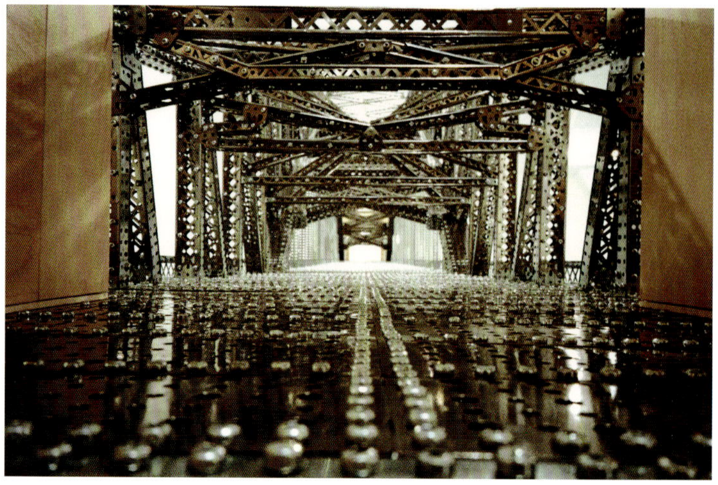

Hell Gate 1998

Metal toy construction parts (Meccano
and Erector), wooden towers
88½ × 339 × 40 inches

Hell Gate *is a model of New York's famous Hell Gate Bridge, which spans the East River. This bridge was constructed in the early 1900s and is still in use today. The model is approximately one-fortieth the size of the actual 1017-foot span of the bridge. By using thousands of current and obsolete Meccano and Erector parts, I was able to accurately duplicate the different types of steel girders and X-bracings of the actual bridge.*

I built the Hell Gate *model during the same period I built the Mexican Bridge. I chose to build a Meccano/Erector model of the Hell Gate Bridge for several reasons. When the actual bridge was completed in 1916, it was the longest arch bridge in the world and was considered an engineering marvel. Also, using a similar scale, I wanted to build a Meccano/Erector model that would be a counterpoint to the tall delicate Mexican Bridge. The Hell Gate Bridge, with its dense, massive form seemed like the personification of the masculine, whereas the Mexican Bridge, with its grace and delicacy, was the personification of the feminine.*

I did not have a set of blueprints or accurate drawings when I designed the Meccano/Erector model of the Hell Gate Bridge. Instead, I used the photograph on page 114 of the book, 'The Beauty of Railroad Bridges' and a small scale ruler to produce a large drawing on brown craft paper. This drawing served as a full scale pattern and was taped to the floor of my studio throughout the construction of the bridge.

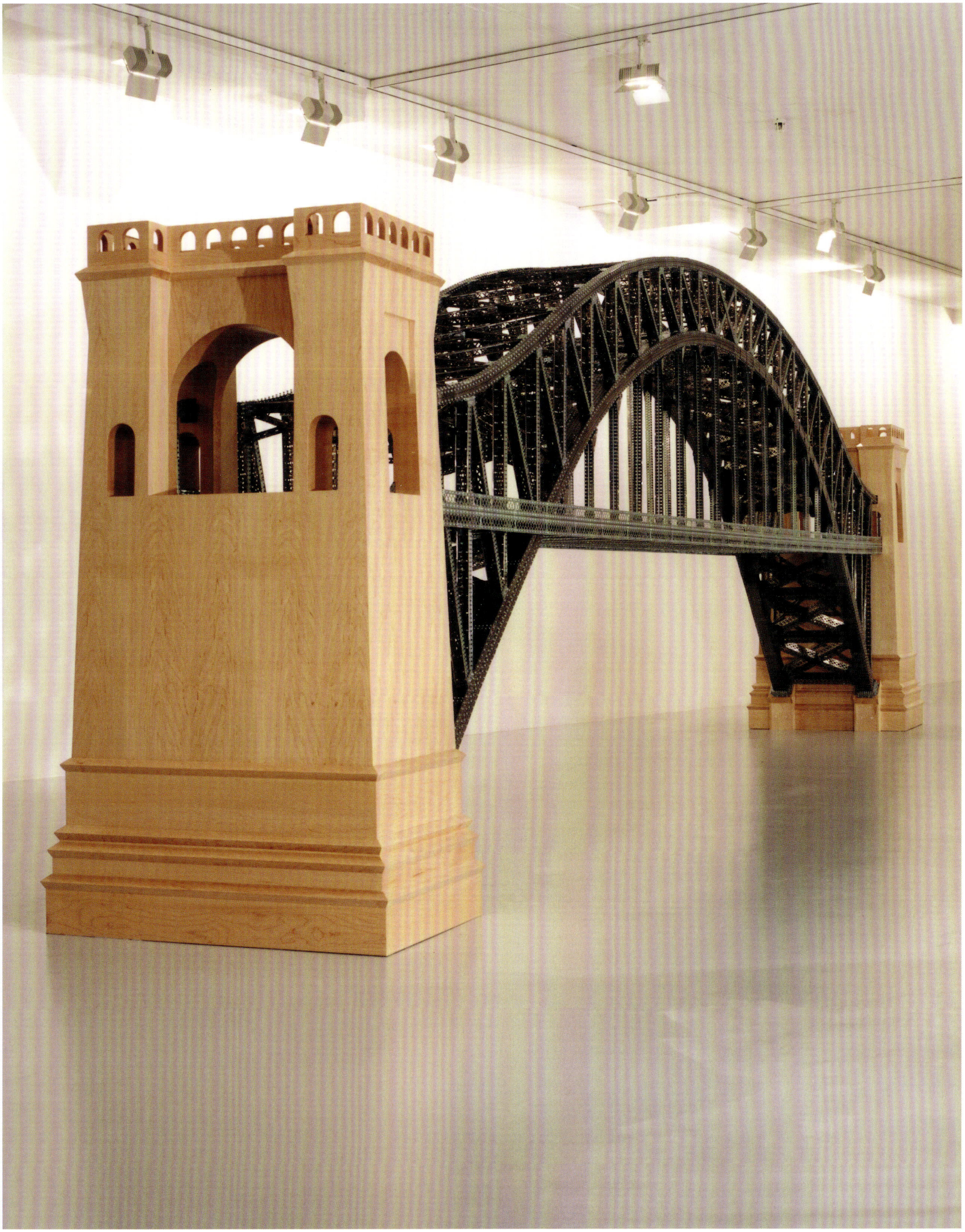

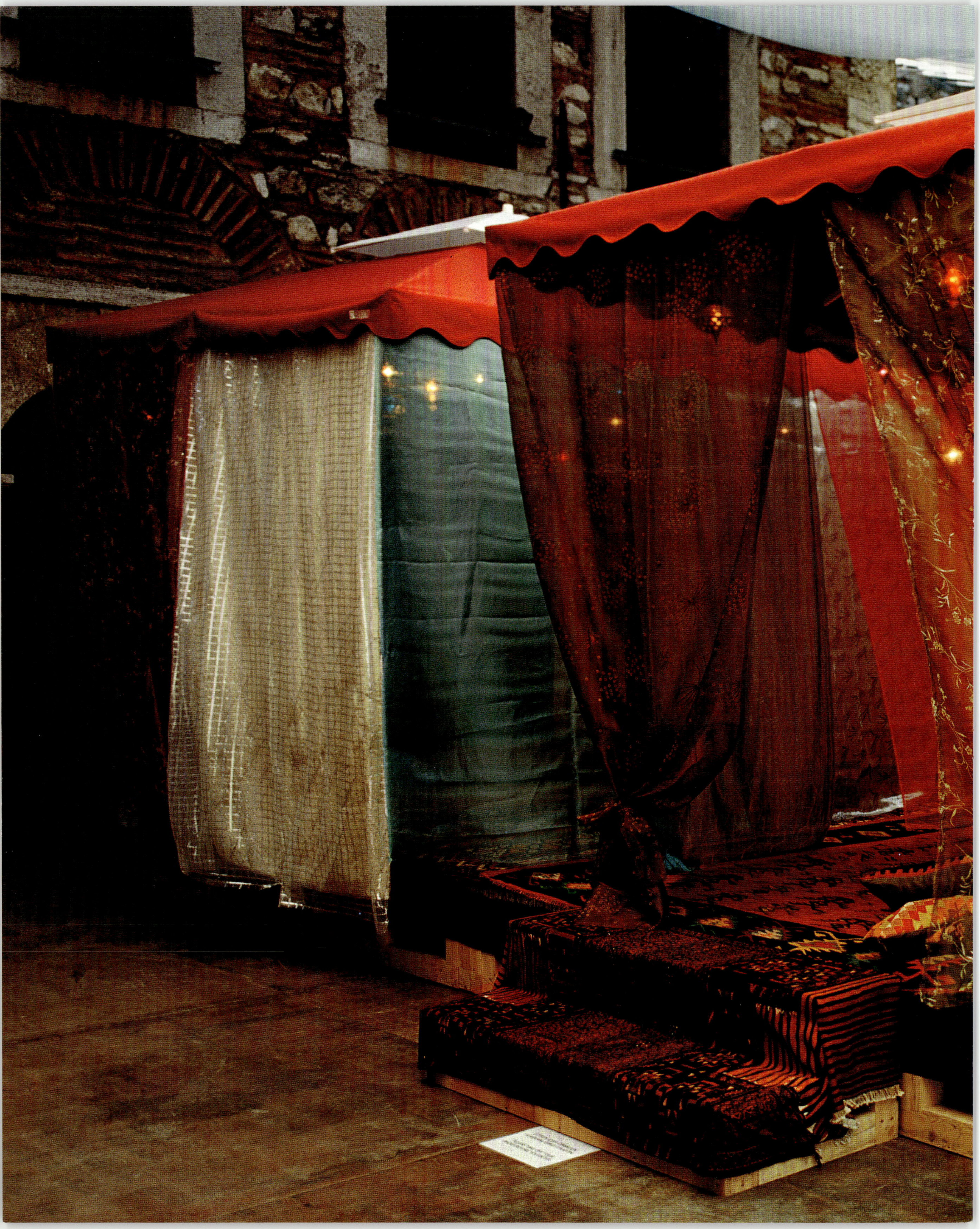

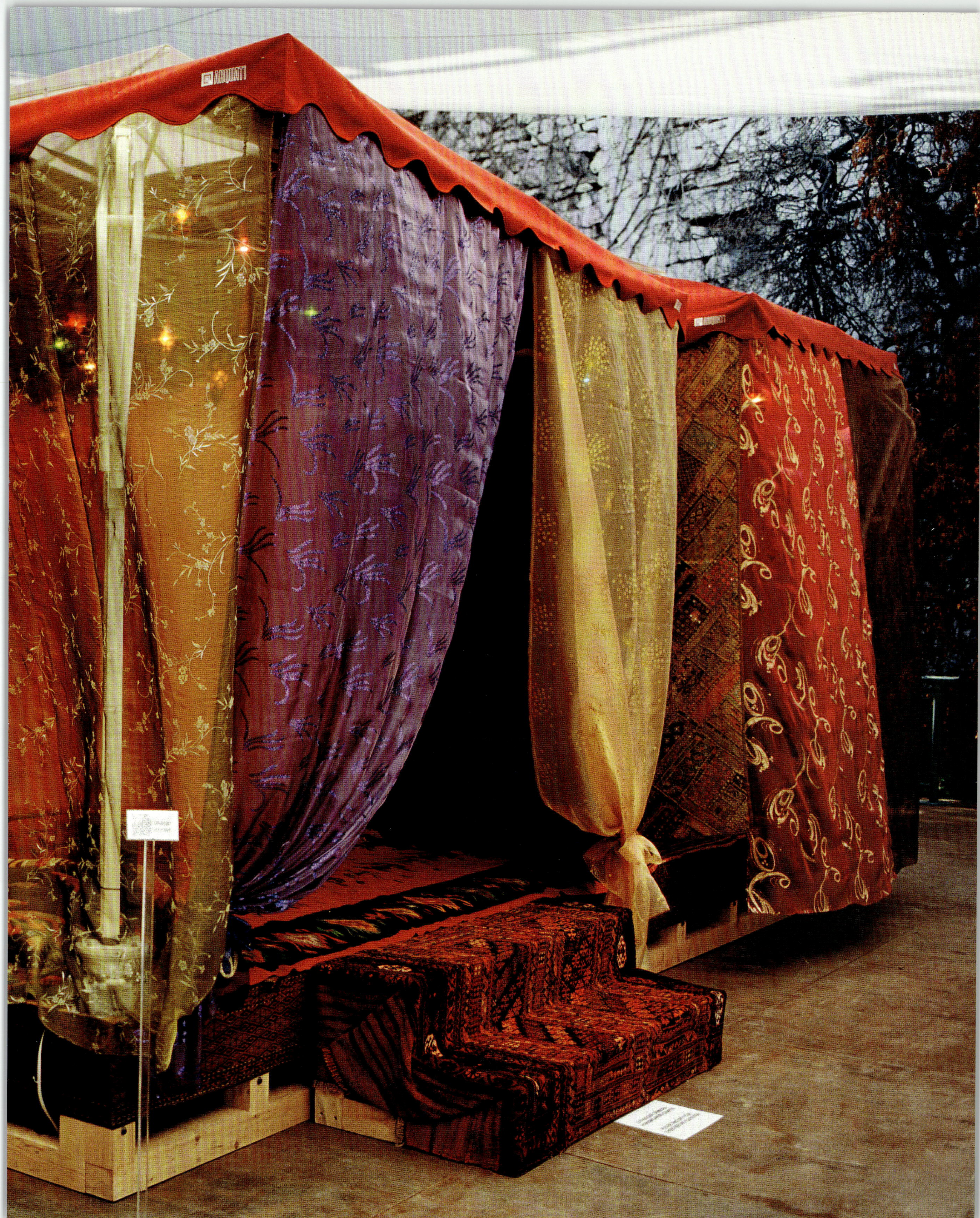

Nomadic Folly 2001

Wood platform, four cloth and metal umbrellas, woven carpets, braided ropes, pillows, silken fabrics, glass and metal lamps, CD player and speakers
138 × 240 × 240 inches

The Nomadic Folly *is a distillation and a concentration of a Middle Eastern aesthetic. This installation evokes the luxurious opulence befitting a Sultan. This jewel-like pavilion was originally set within the decaying and crumbling Imperial Mint Building in Istanbul, Turkey, for the seventh International Biennial in 2001. Visitors tend to linger and find respite in this oasis of beauty.*

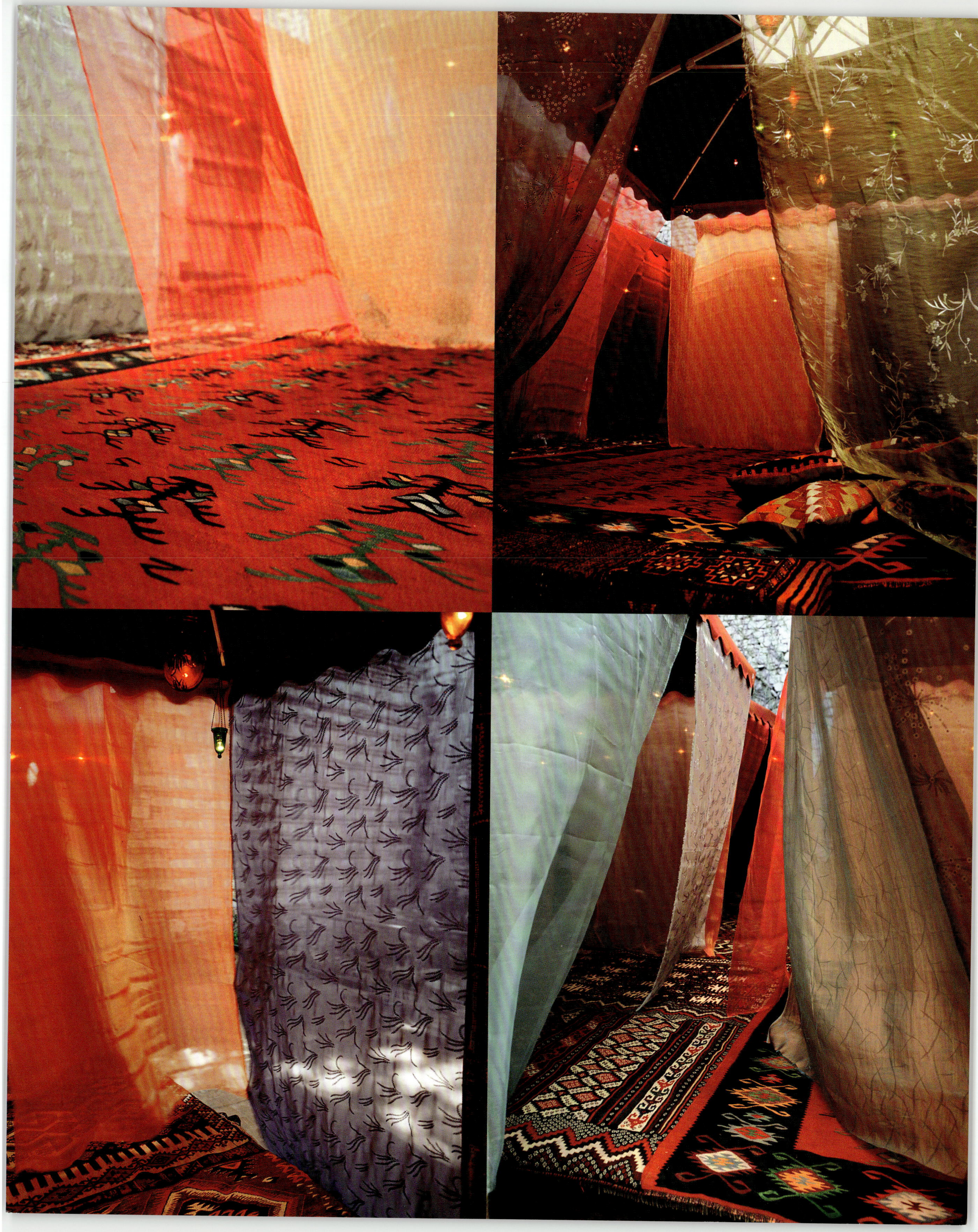

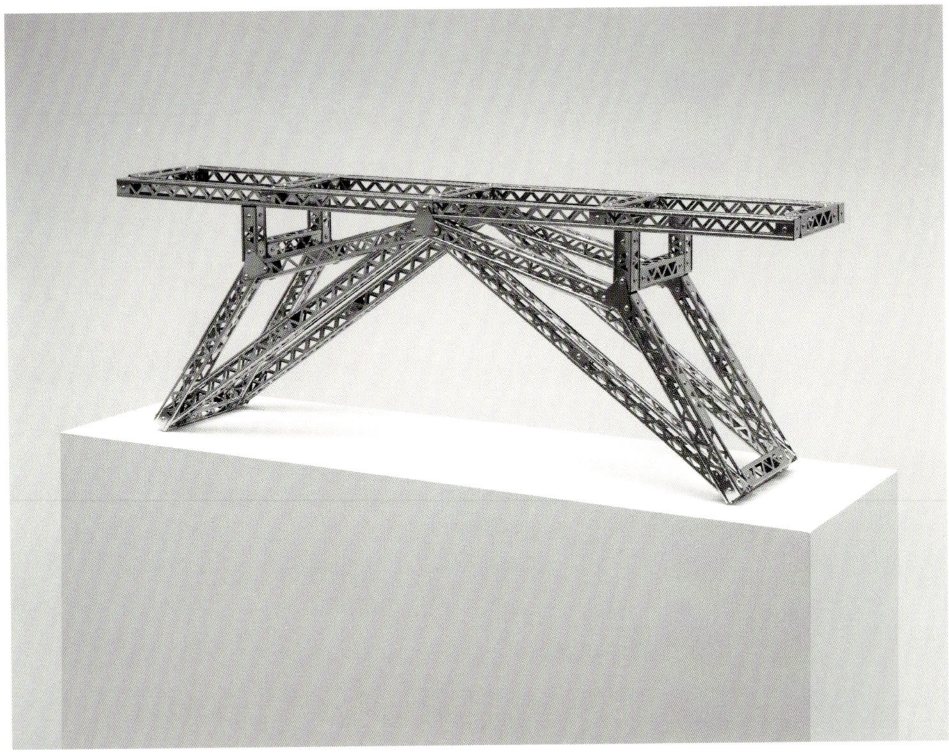

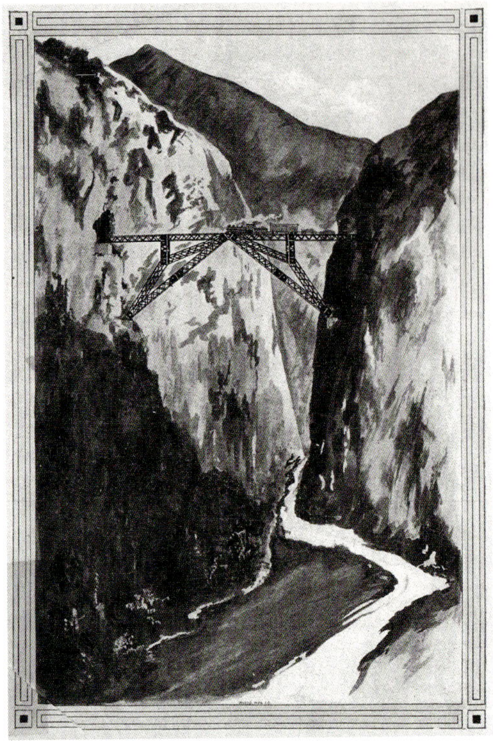

Illustration of original bridge from Erector manual

Indo-China Bridge 2002

(Edition of 12, with four artist's proofs)
Stainless steel reproduction
Mysto Type I Erector parts
15¼ × 45¼ × 8¾ inches

The Indo-China Bridge *is based on an actual bridge in Asia that spanned an extremely deep gorge. The peculiar geometry of this bridge was dictated by the extreme conditions that necessitated moving all the bridge beams through opposing tunnels and lowering them into position on the steep cliffs. The edition of the* Indo-China Bridge *is built using reproduction Mysto Erector parts, fabricated in stainless steel for greater strength and corrosion resistance.*

Mysto Erector parts are a 1913 American metal toy construction system. The Type I Mysto Erector system is based on a single girder, complete with rivet detailing. A box beam can be formed using four girders, two nuts and two bolts. This strong but light box beam is the basis for the entire building system. With just a few basic parts, it is much simpler, though less versatile, than the Meccano and Erector construction systems. I find the resulting simple linear form of the Indo-China Bridge *to be extremely attractive.*

Trapezoid Bridge 2003

(Edition of 20)
Stainless steel reproduction
Mysto Type 1 Erector parts
17¼ × 23½ × 8½ inches

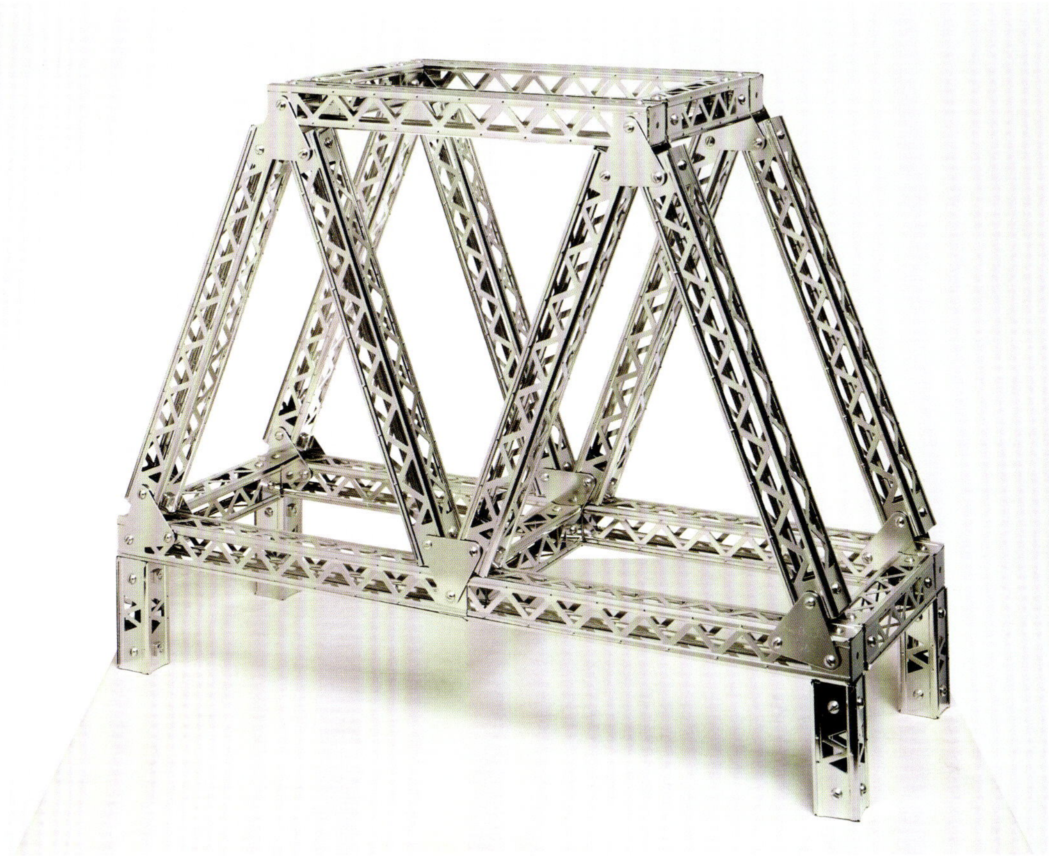

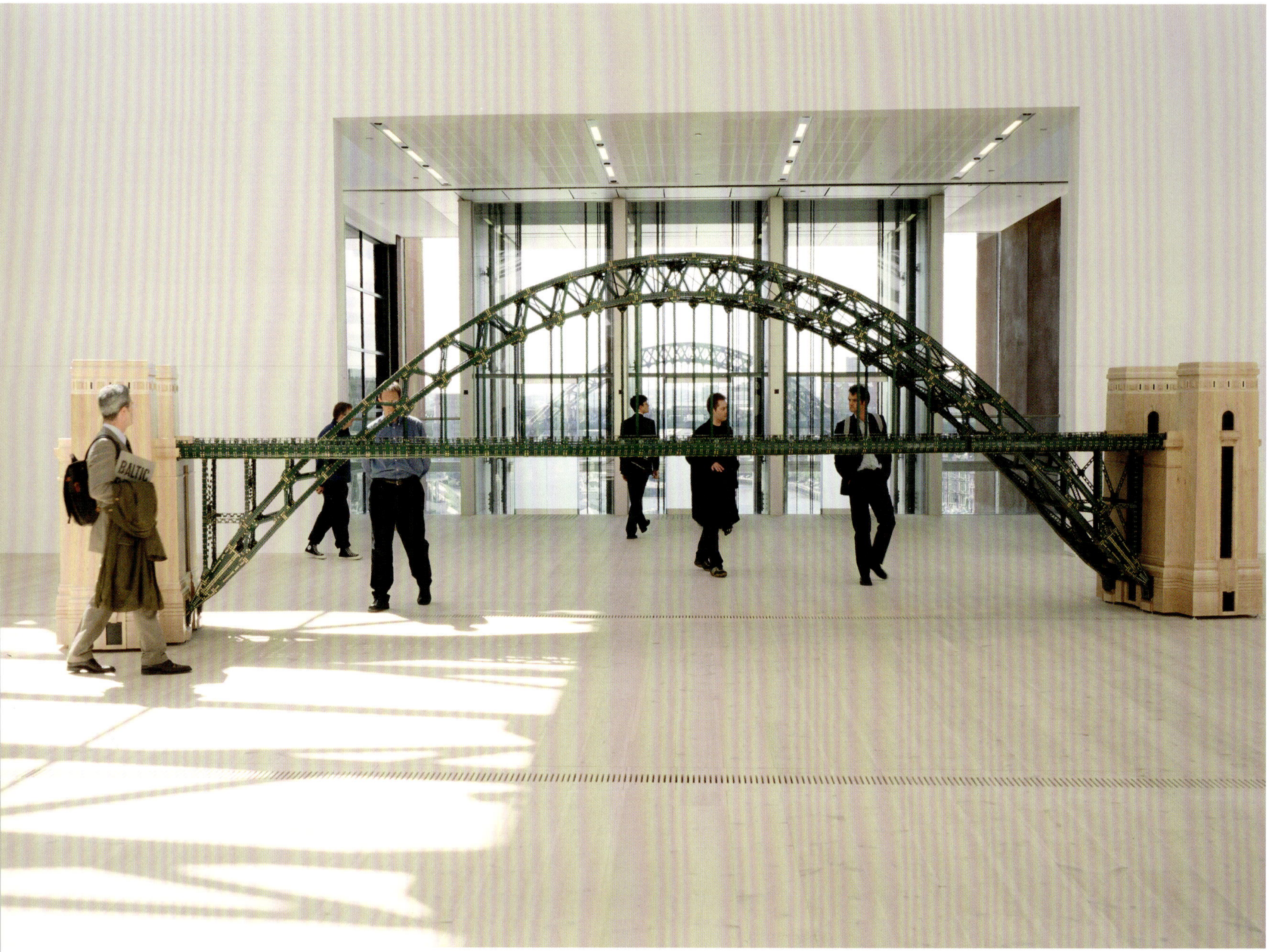

Installation in Newcastle upon Tyne, England;
actual bridge in background

Tyne Bridge 2002

Powder coated and made to order
Meccano metal toy construction parts,
wooden towers
111 × 372 × 60 inches

The inspiration for building a Meccano replica of the Tyne Bridge occurred to me in October 2000, when the then director of the Baltic Centre for Contemporary Art, took me on a tour of the building while it was still under construction. On the fourth floor, I was immediately struck by the fantastic view of the Tyne Bridge directly out of the west-facing windows. I realized that being able to build and exhibit a substantial Meccano model of a bridge, with the actual bridge in the background, was a unique and rare opportunity. I proposed that I build a Meccano model of the Tyne Bridge and that this sculpture would form the basis of an exhibition of all my bridges.

I obtained a copy of an engineering drawing of the bridge and a book about the construction of the bridge, 'Spanning the Tyne'. With these materials and with the numerous photos I had taken of the actual bridge, I was able to translate the bridge into an extremely accurate Meccano model.

The 200,000 parts used to construct the model are based on the Meccano system of half-inch hole spacing. At first glance they appear to be Meccano, but in fact, they are not. A majority of the parts were fabricated to my specifications. Because each part was specifically made, the parts did not have to be overlapped in order to create specific lengths of beams. It was this ability to produce specific parts that enabled me to so precisely model the Tyne Bridge. The parts were produced in the south of India and in Argentina. The new steel parts were powder coated with a custom green paint to match the actual Tyne Bridge. They were shipped to my studio in Los Angeles, where my crew of seven studio assistants and I worked approximately 5,000 hours to complete the bridge. Subsequently, the bridge was shipped from my studio in California, via the Panama Canal, to the Baltic Centre in Newcastle upon Tyne, England.

The Meccano model of the Tyne Bridge is an evolutionary step in the development of my Meccano/Erector bridge series. The fact that I was able to have the parts fabricated to my specifications enabled me to make not only a physically precise model of the Tyne Bridge, but also, a structurally accurate model of this most elegant of bridges in this city of many bridges.

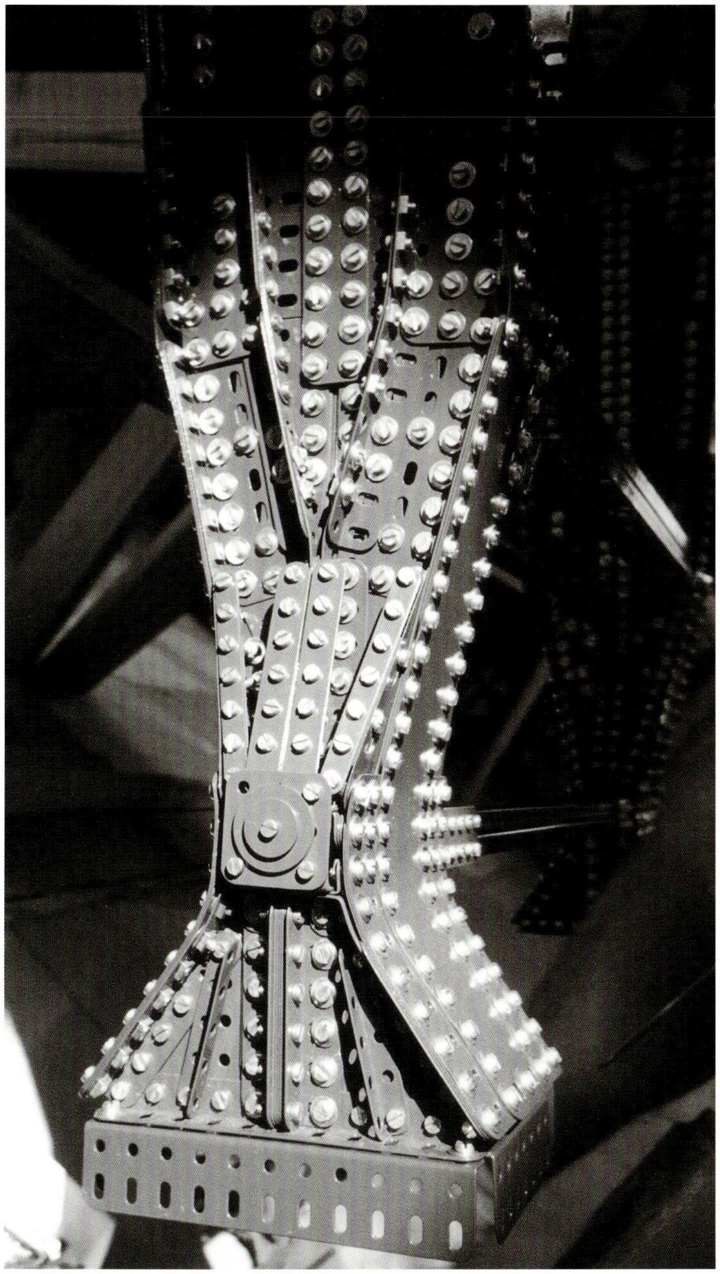

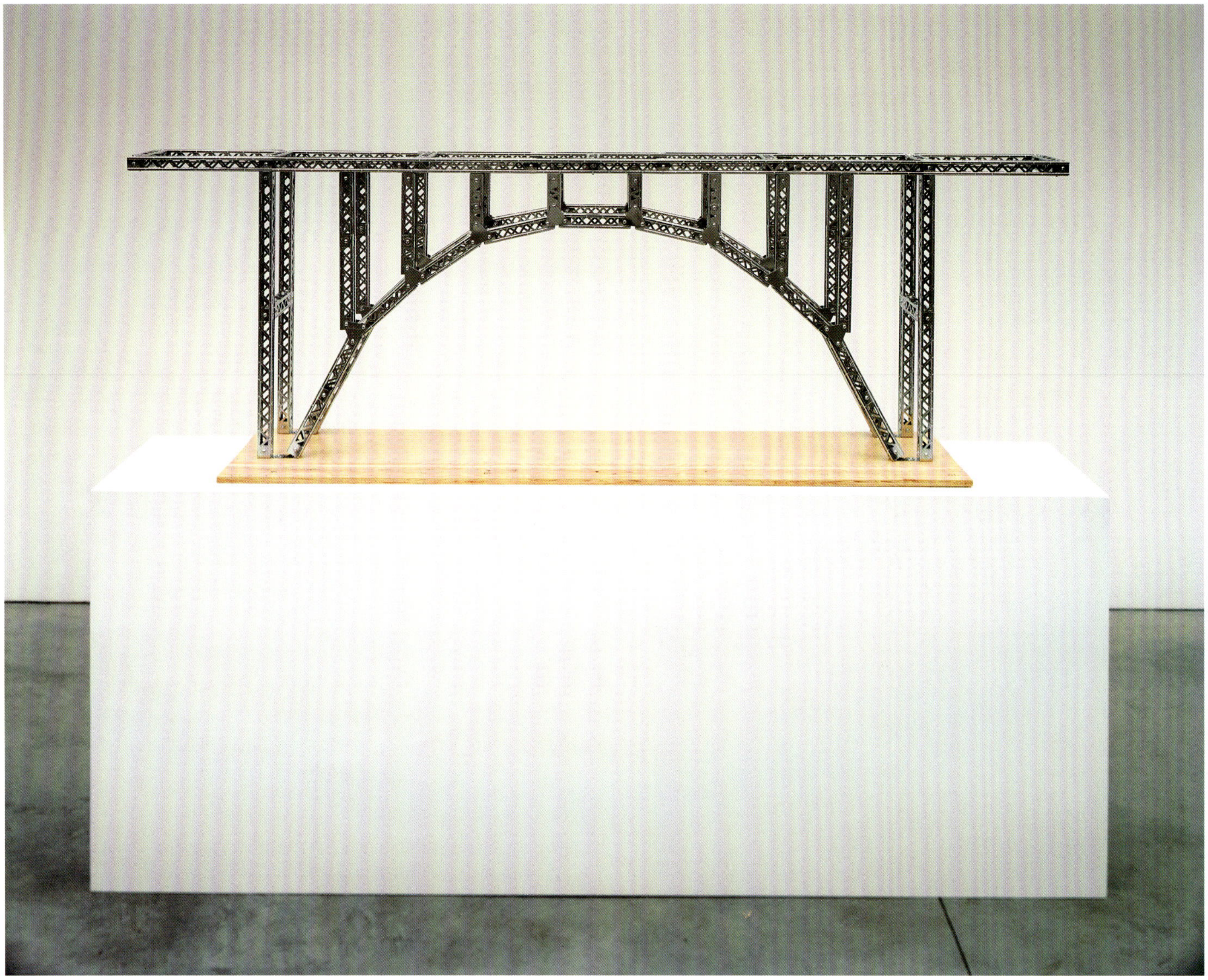

Victoria Falls Bridge 2003

(Edition of six, with four artist's proofs)
Stainless steel reproduction Mysto
Type I Erector parts, wooden base
Bridge: 24½ × 78 × 8¾ inches

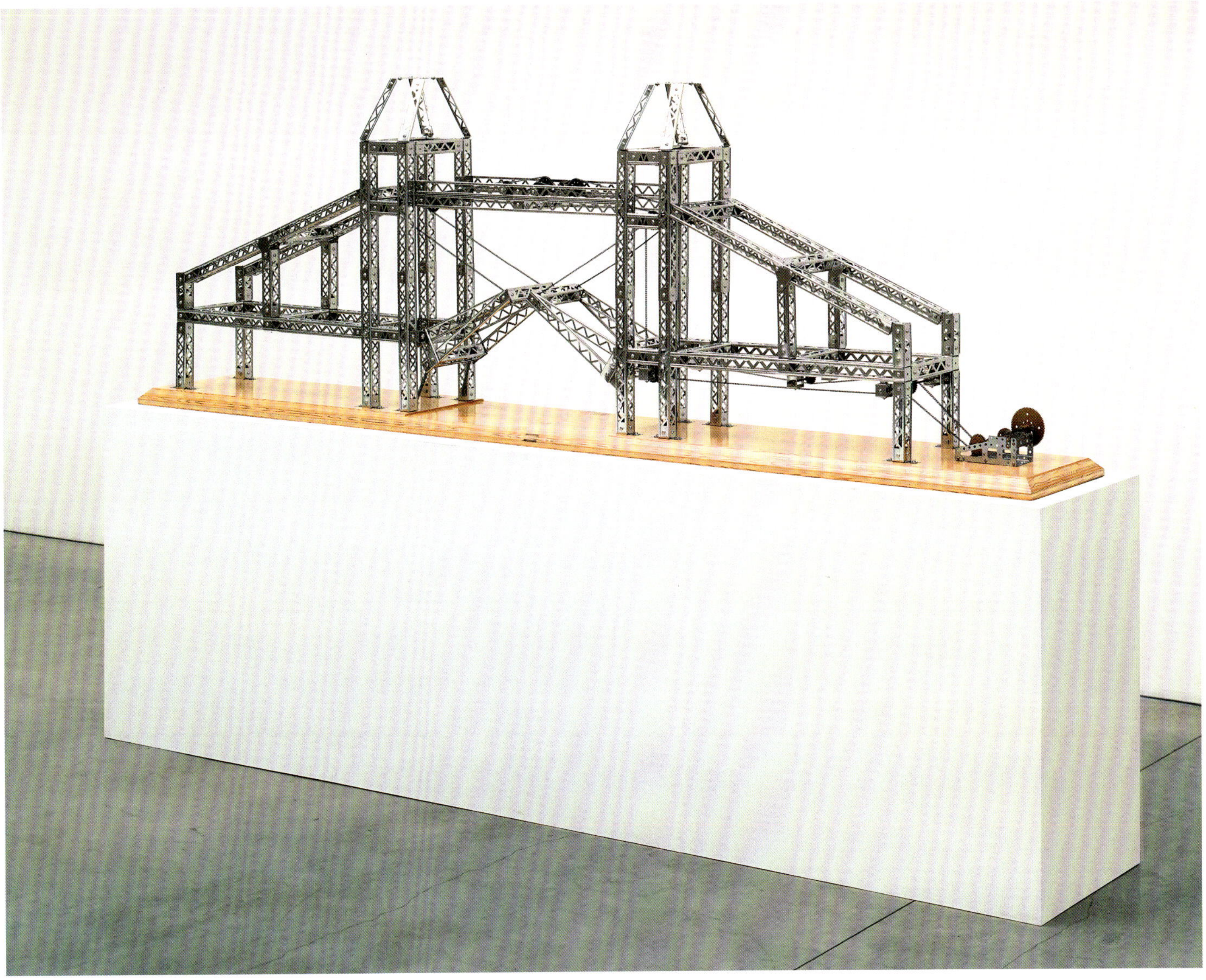

Tower of London Bridge 2003

(Edition of six, with three artist's proofs)
Stainless steel reproduction Mysto
Type I Erector parts, gearbox,
wooden base
Bridge: 28¼ × 80¼ × 8½ inches

21 Foot Truss Bridge 2003

(Edition of three)
Stainless steel reproduction
Mysto Type I Erector parts,
45¾ × 234 × 14¾ inches

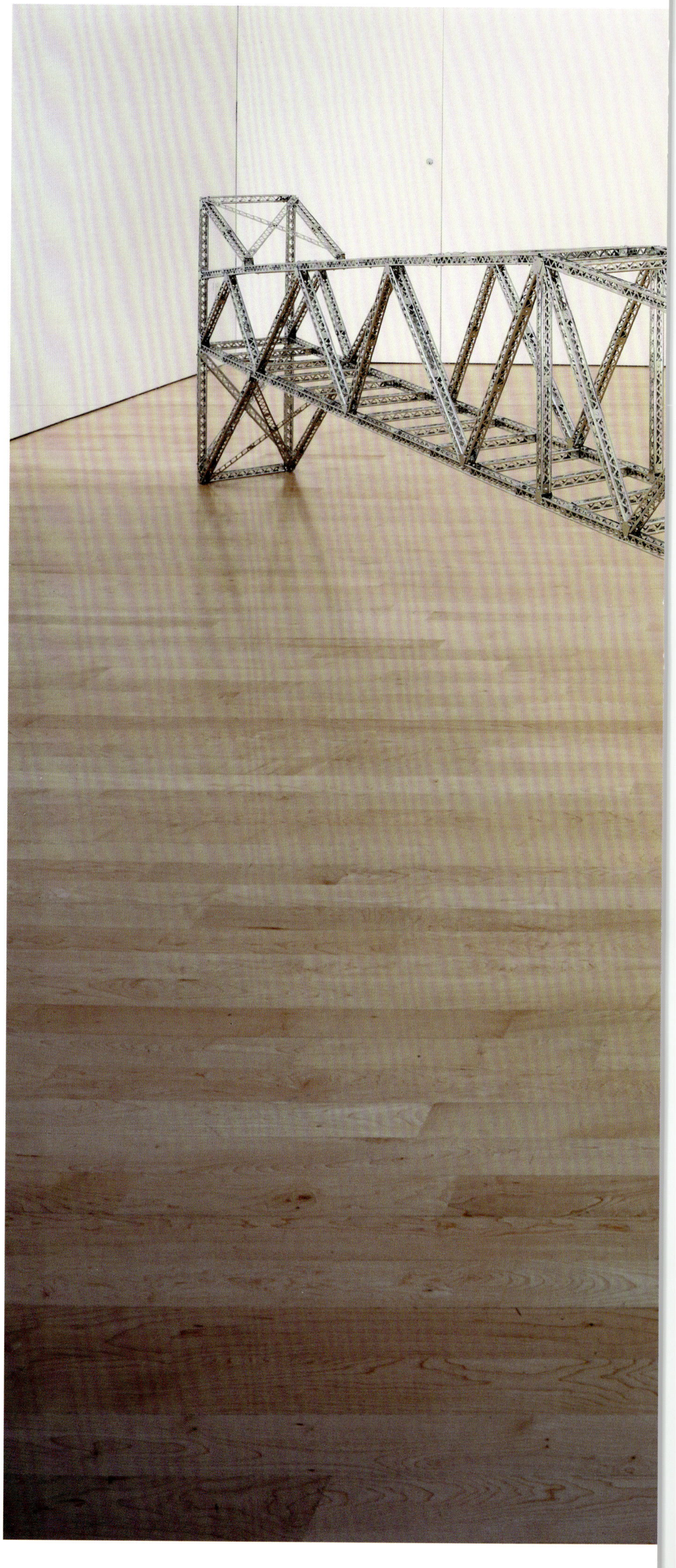

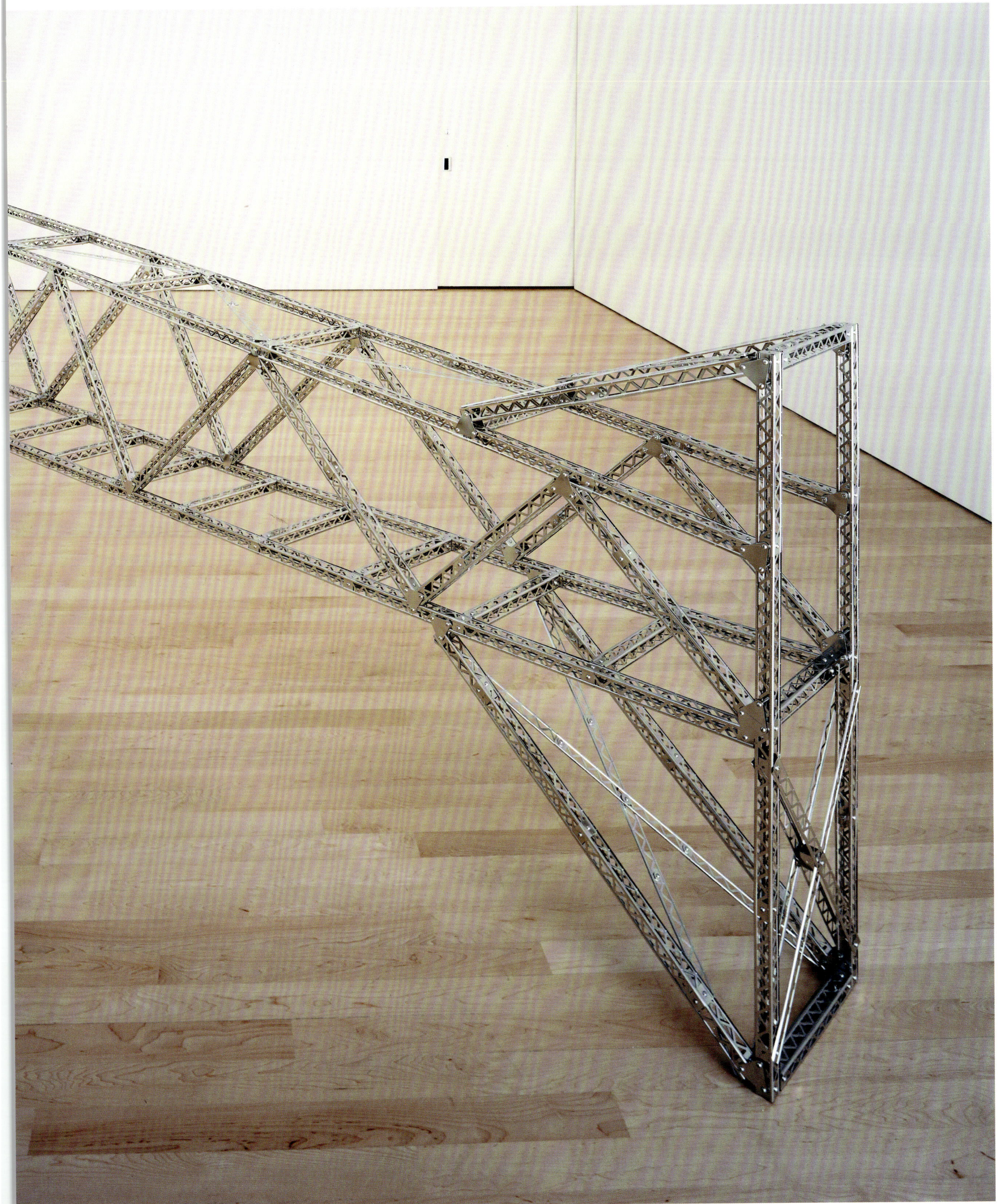

Curved Bridge 2003

(Edition of three)
Stainless steel reproduction
Mysto Type I Erector parts,
wood base
96 × 390 × 57 inches

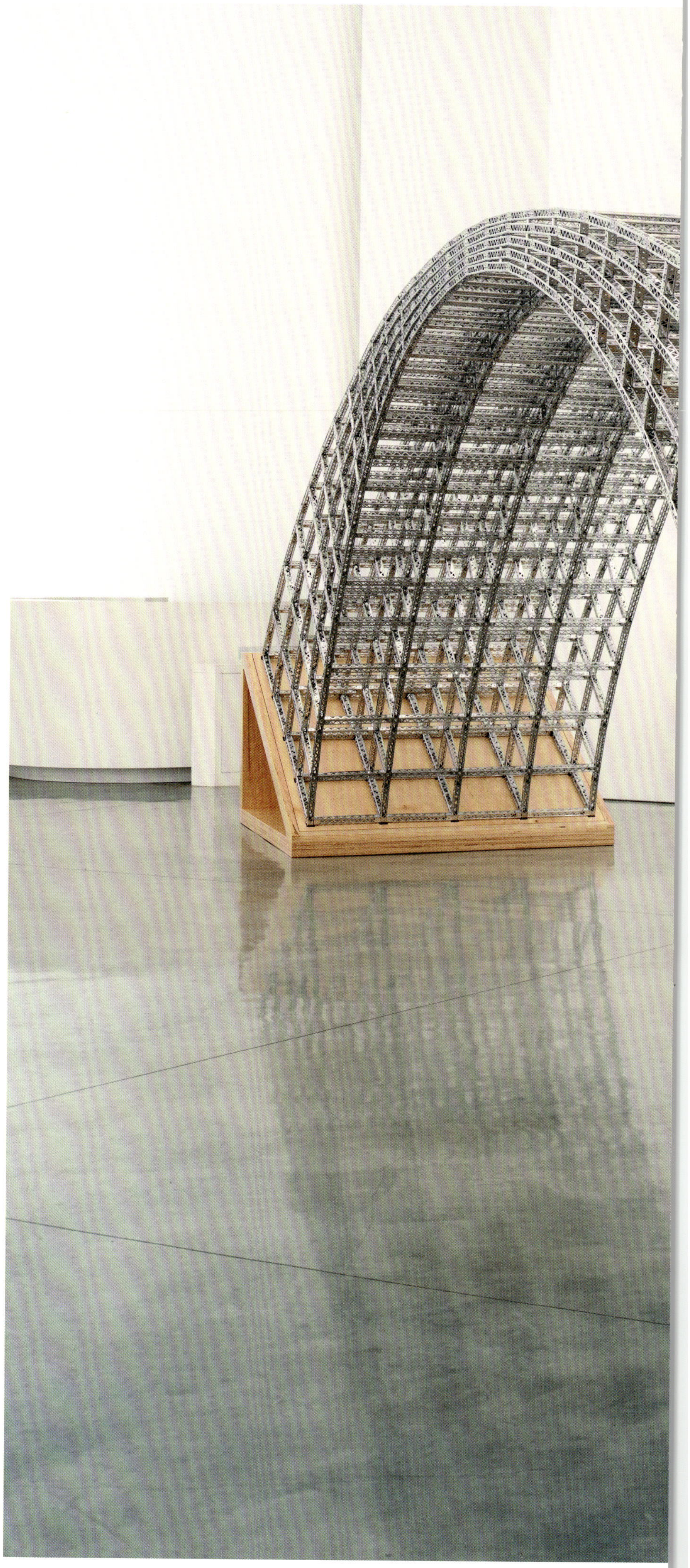

Small Skyscraper 2003

In collaboration with TK Architecture, Los Angeles, California, USA.
Structural aluminum framing, glass, wood 2 × 4s, steel hardware (stainless steel cables, turnbuckles, clips and angles, t-nuts, ½-inch bolts)
432 × 120 × 120 inches

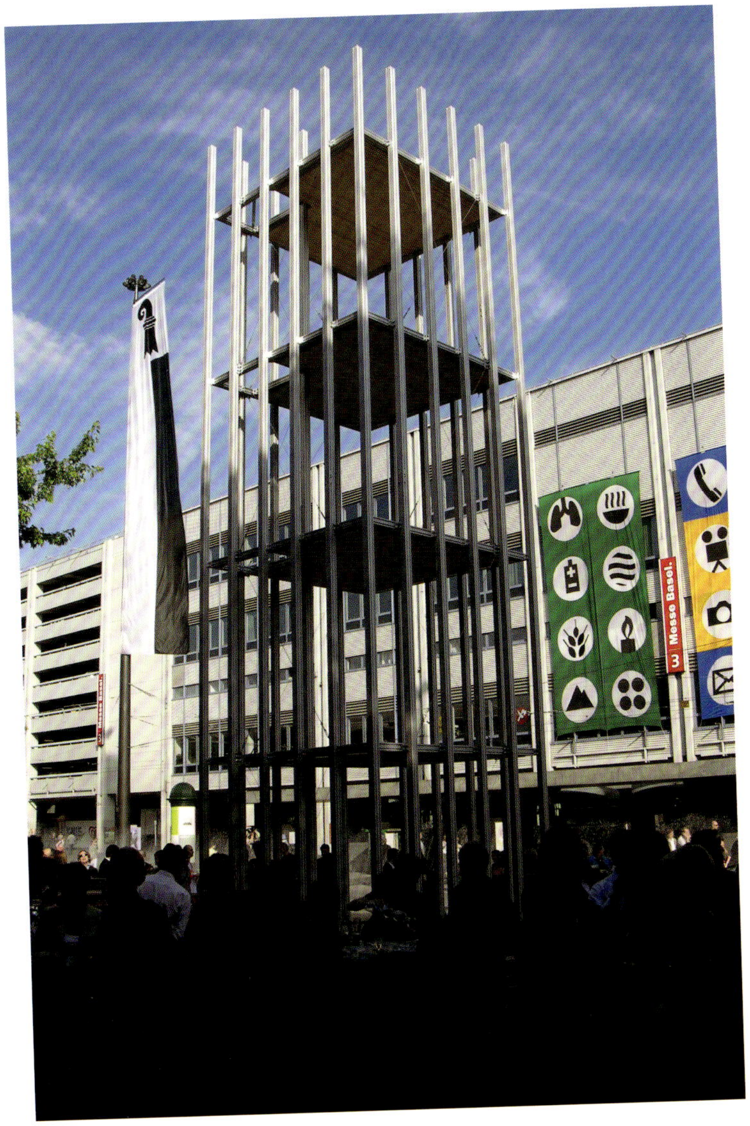

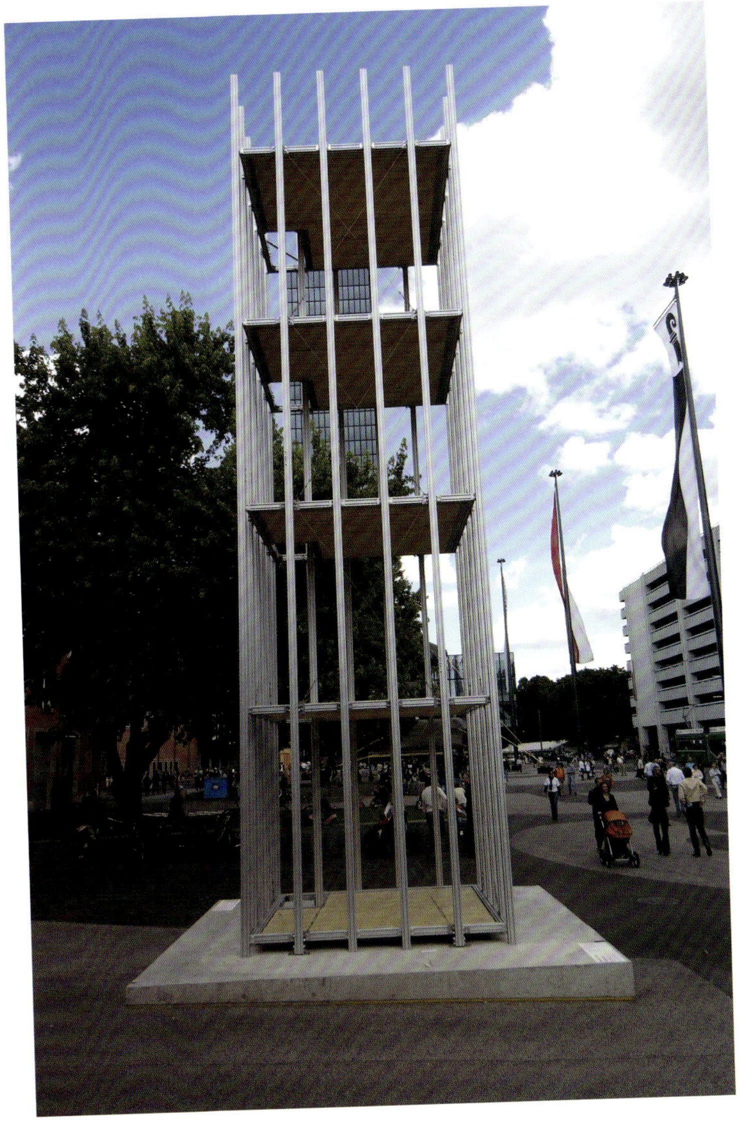

Tyne Bridge Kit 2004

(Edition of two)
Powder coated and made to order
Meccano metal toy construction parts,
wooden cabinet on casters.
Each kit: 42½ × 65½ × 32¼ inches

In 2002 I built a 31-foot-long replica of the Tyne Bridge, which is located between Newcastle upon Tyne and Gateshead, England. The replica was built entirely of Meccano (a metal toy construction system similar to Erector) type steel parts. Most of these parts were produced to my specifications in order that I could actually model every beam and strut in the actual bridge. The parts were painted the correct color of green and brass nuts and bolts were used throughout.

Because I had gone to considerable effort to calculate the specific metal parts to build this bridge, it seemed a waste to only to only produce one work, the Tyne Bridge*. Therefore, I conceived of the* Tyne Bridge Kit*, in the manner of traditional boxed Erector Sets. To that end, a large wooden chest with multiple drawers was constructed to hold all the metal parts. The chest also contains all the tools, a blueprint of the bridge and extensive photo documentation of the building process. The 200,000 parts in the one-ton* Tyne Bridge Kit *represents a potential, like water behind a dam. It was not my intention that these kits would be built, but rather would be seen as the* Tyne Bridge *in a condensed form.*

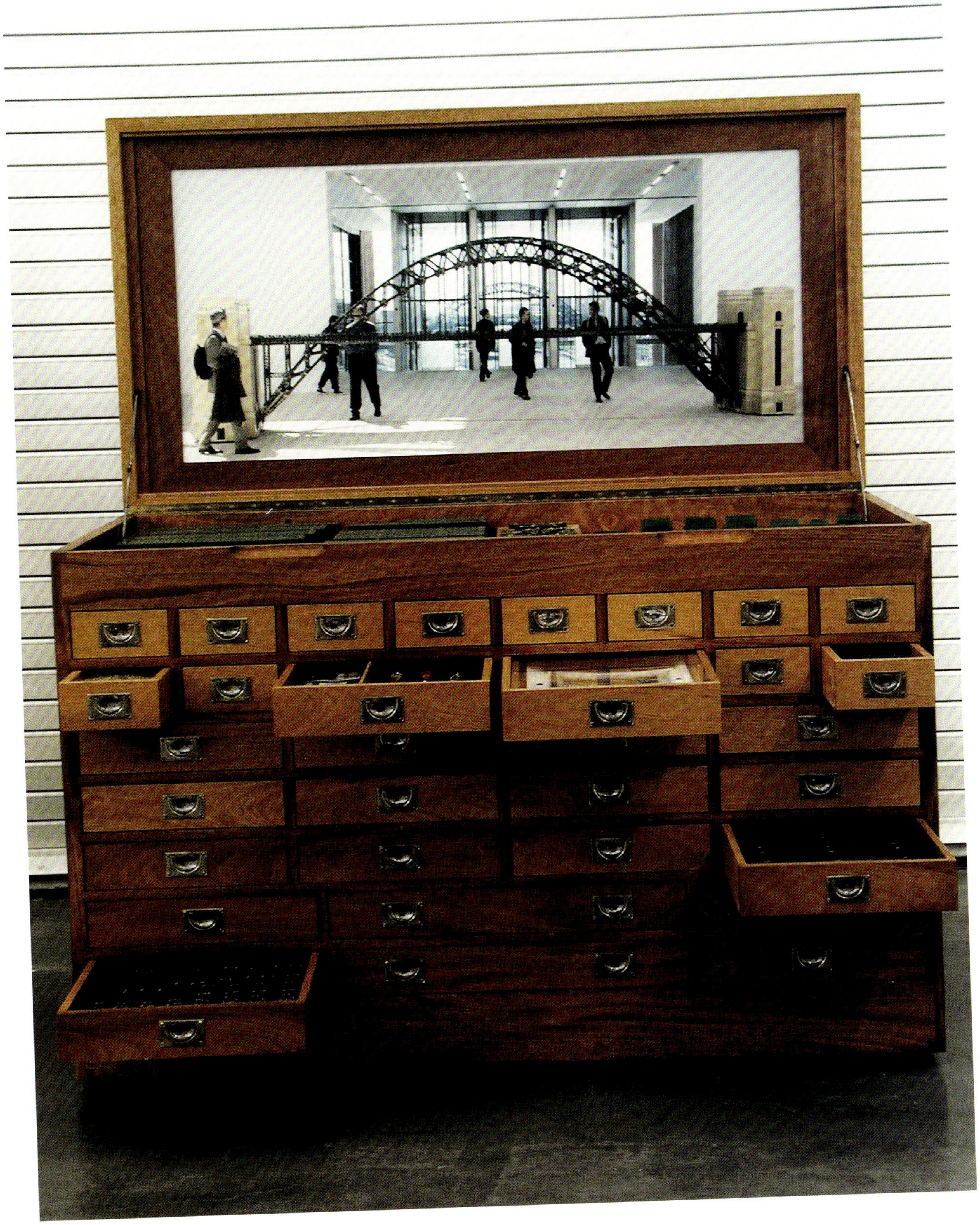

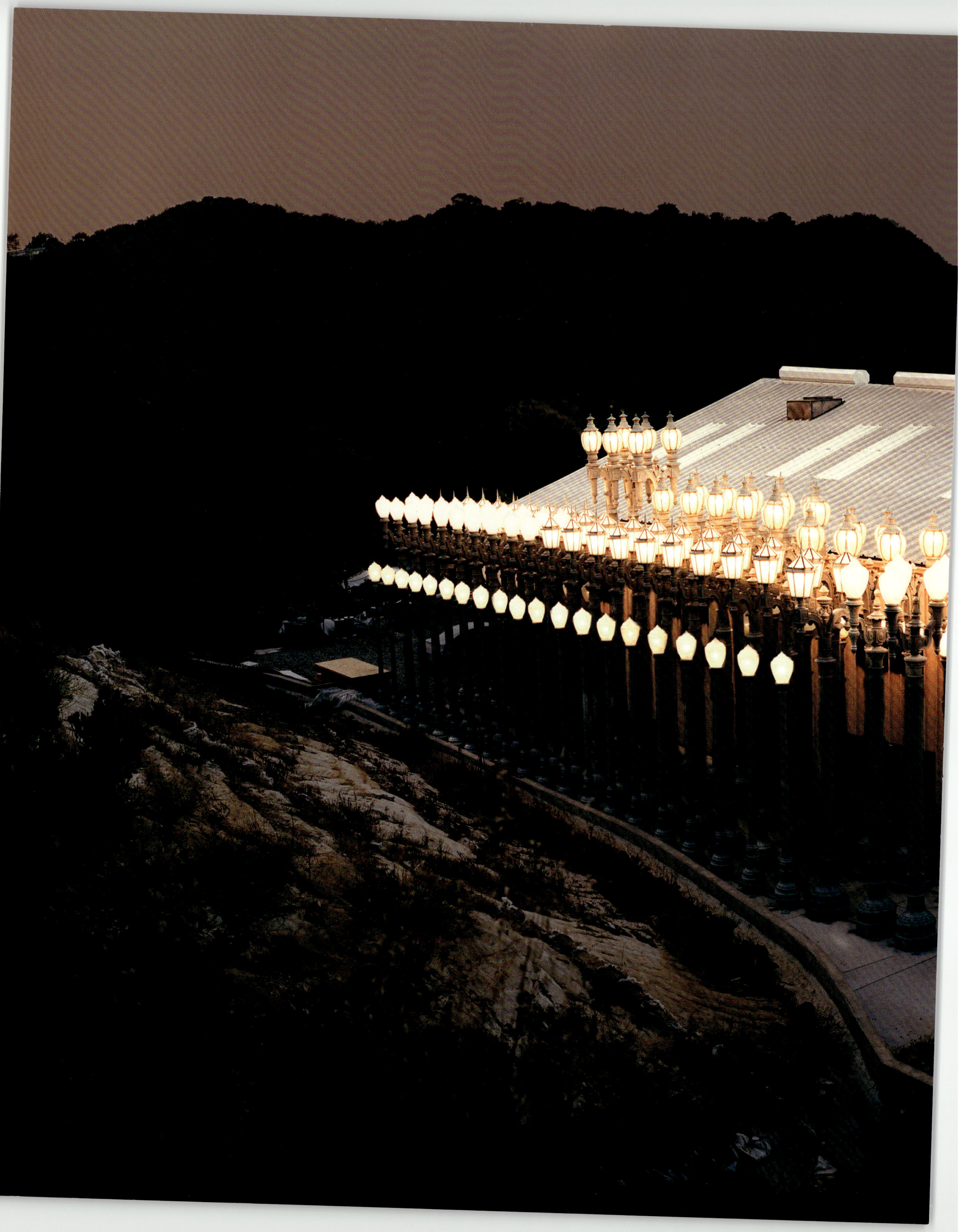

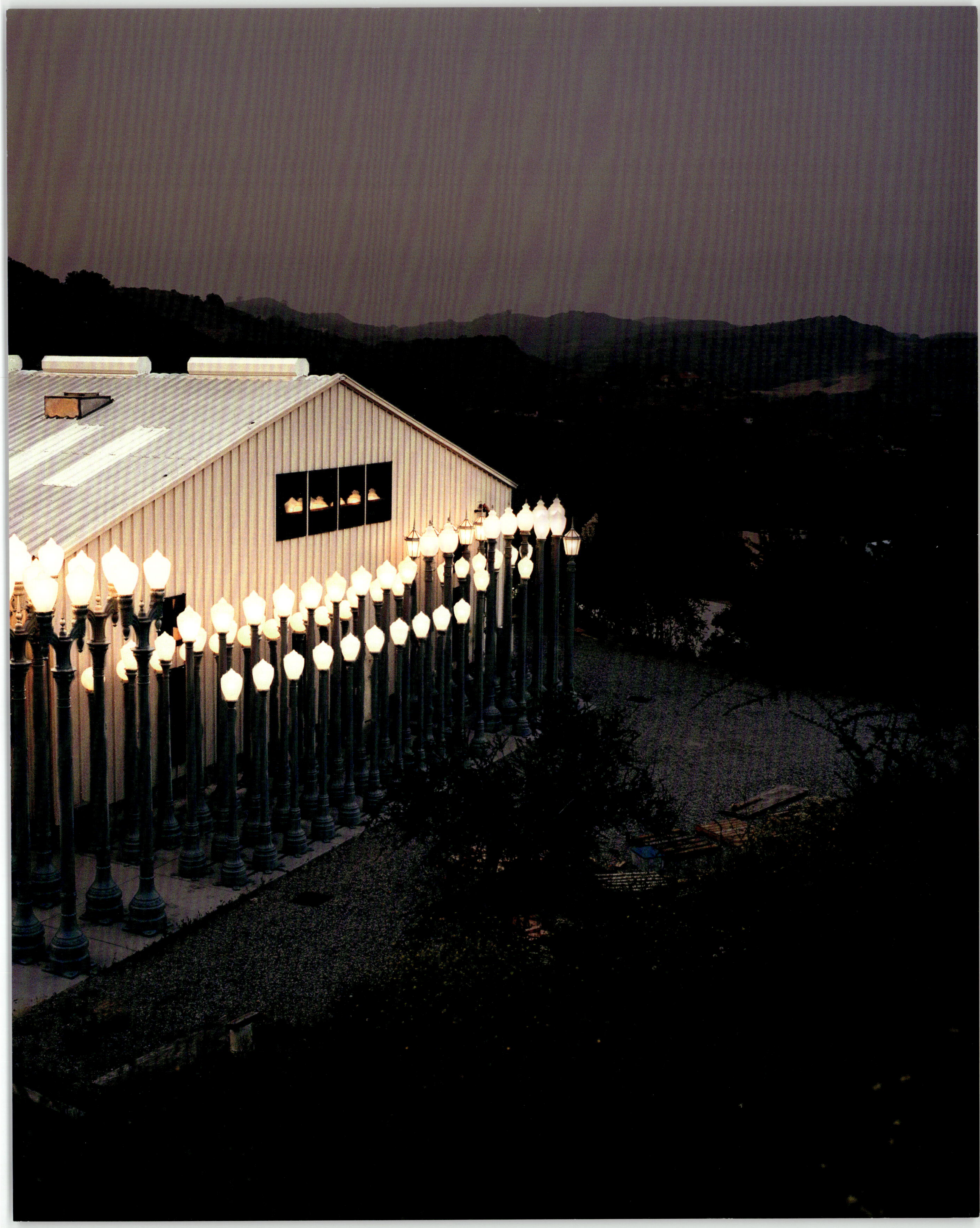

Urban Light 2005

150 fully restored Los Angeles street lamps from the 1920s (16 different styles that have been sandblasted, powder coated and electrified)
Dimensions variable

Urban Light *is an artwork that I have created by amassing and restoring a huge collection of 1920s cast iron street lamps from Los Angeles and its many adjacent cities. Street lamps are one of the fundamental building blocks of an urban metropolis. The richly detailed fluted lamps are an ornate totem to industrialism and represent a form of public art. My artwork,* Urban Light, *is ultimately a statement about what constitutes a civilized and sophisticated city, safe after dark and beautiful to behold.*

By placing the 150 human scale lamps very close together and in long colonnades, I have usurped the lamp's function as a street lamp. The viewer's experience of traversing through these tightly spaced fluted columns is an exalted one that recalls the marvel of seeing and walking through classic Greek and Roman architecture or a European cathedral. The feelings of recollection and wonder transform the street lamps, day or night, into the sculpture Urban Light.

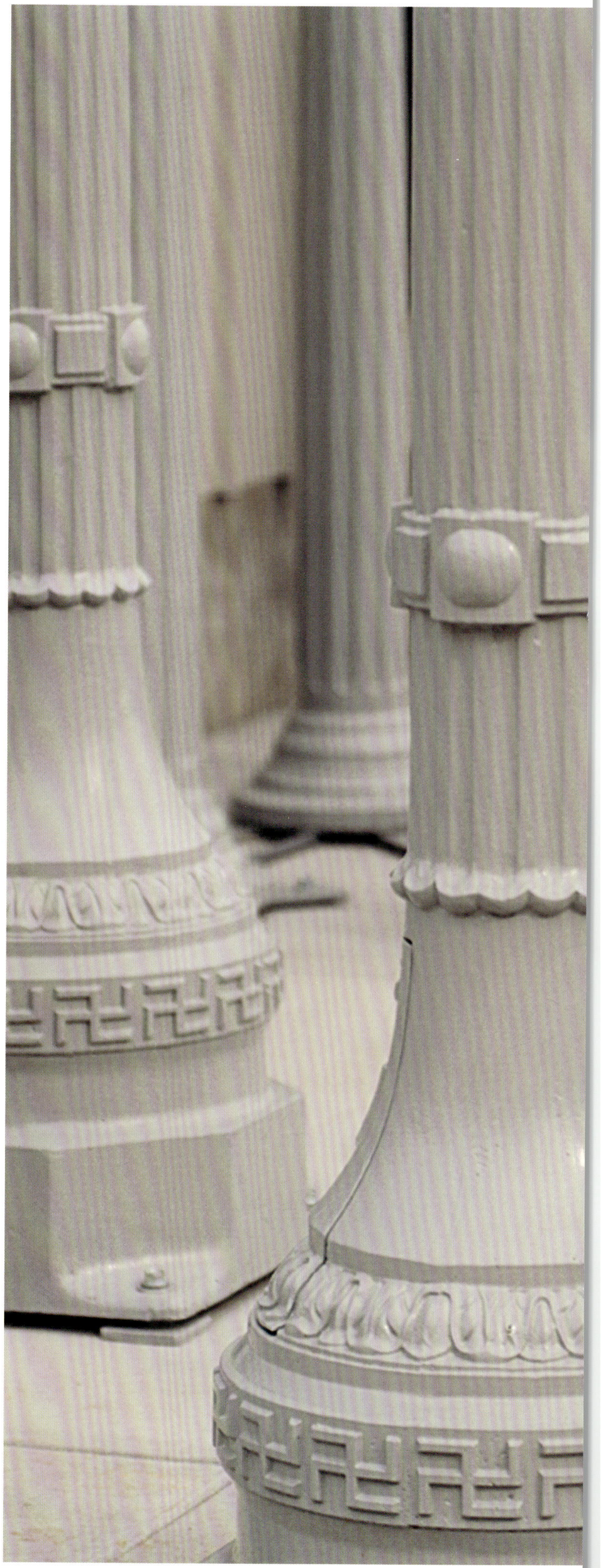

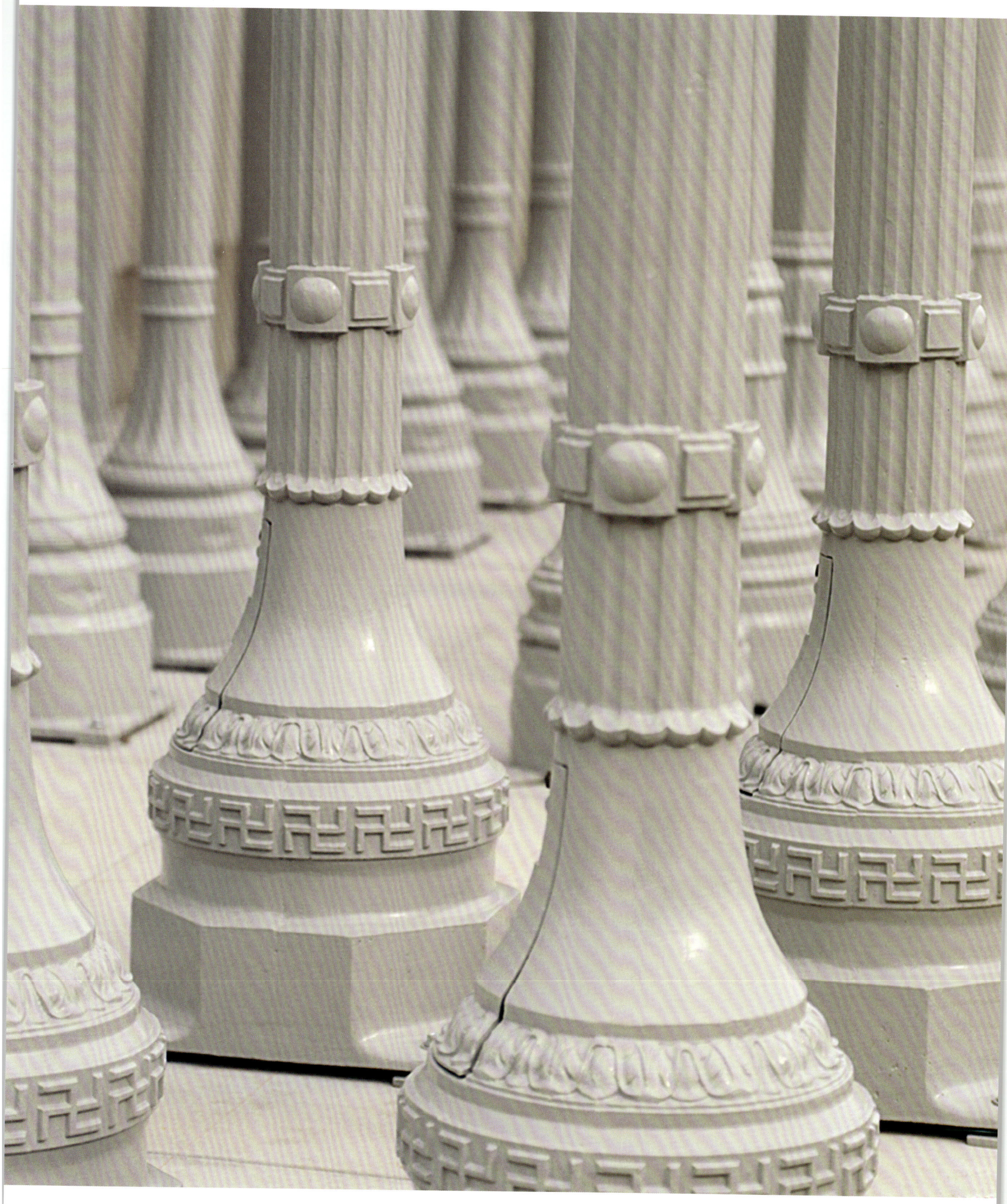

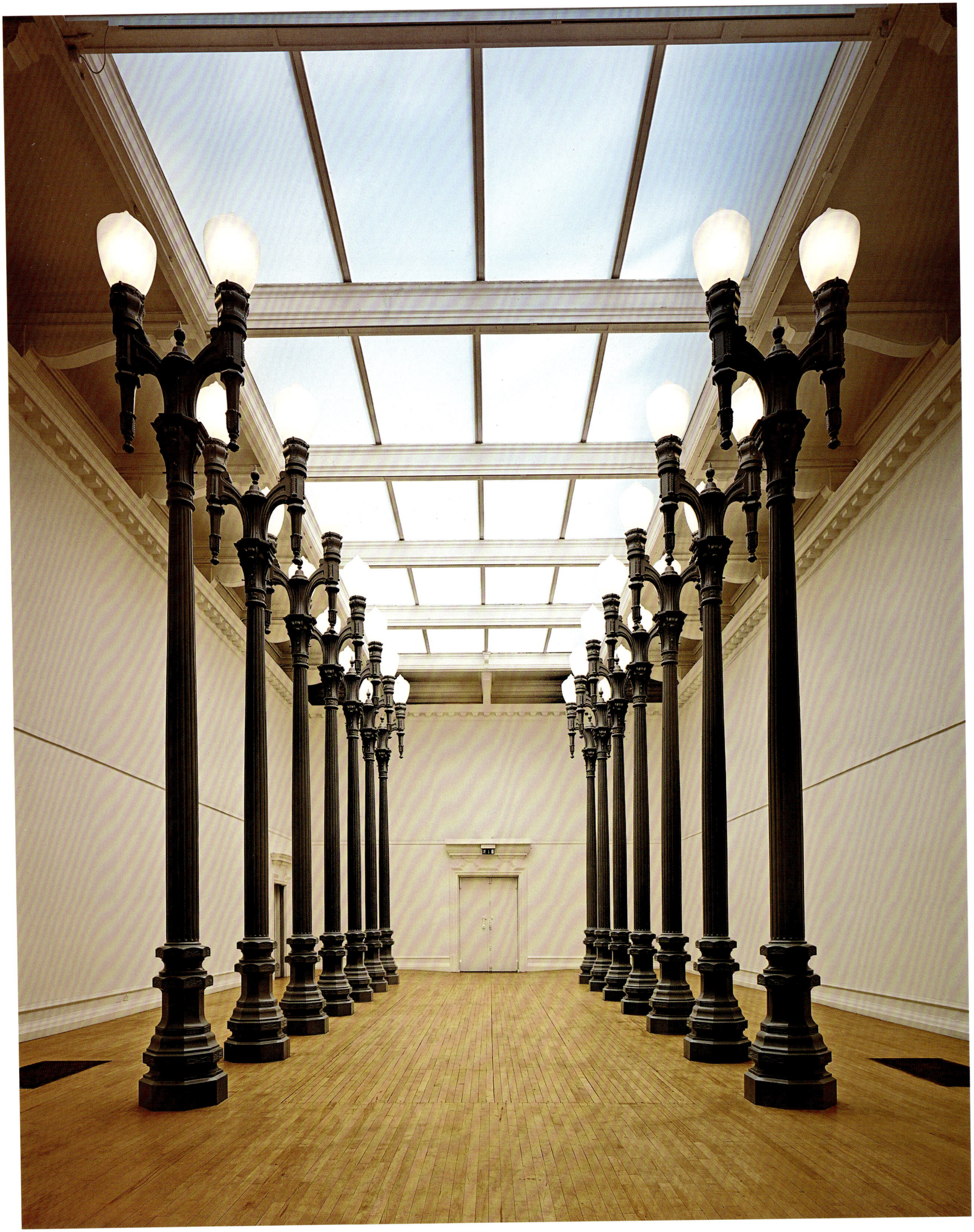

14 Magnolia Doubles 2006

14 fully restored Los Angeles street lamps from 1915–1921 (sandblasted, powder coated and electrified)
Each lamp 242½ × 47 × 22 inches

The 14 Magnolia Doubles *were originally cast and constructed by Westinghouse from 1915 through 1921, and installed along Magnolia Boulevard in North Hollywood. These elegant and highly decorative lamps are entirely constructed of cast iron and when fully assembled weigh close to 3,000 pounds each. Functioning Magnolia Double street lamps can still be found today in North Hollywood, near Lankershim Boulevard and Magnolia Boulevard.*

The 14 Magnolia Doubles *were first exhibited, installed inside the South London Gallery, in a beautiful 30 × 70 foot Victorian room with a parquet floor. Sections of the floor were removed and replaced so it appeared that the floor had been built around the lamps. The* 14 Magnolia Doubles *were fully electrified and the light from the lamps focused the viewer's attention upwards, towards the decorative, ornate capitals of the lamps and to the richly detailed and ornamental ceiling and moldings. During most exhibitions at the South London Gallery the decorative aspects of the ceiling, skylight and upper walls are generally unseen and ignored. The installation of the* 14 Magnolia Doubles *was a fortuitous meeting between lamps and building.*

Beehive Bunker 2006

An edition of three and one single artwork
consisting of three bunkers in a triangular
configuration
Concrete, steel rebar, steel wire,
cast iron manhole cover, plastic hoses
120 × 112 inches

The Beehive Bunker *is a conical structure that is made out of stacked bags of pre-mixed concrete, i.e. gravel, sand and cement. The structure is built using only manual labor and employs no cranes or other specialized tools or machinery. In situ, a team of three men hand stacks the 90-pound bags of concrete in a circle. The concrete bags are placed in layers and the concrete is hardened by garden soaker hoses that are placed between each layer during construction.*

The Beehive Bunker *was conceived as an extremely low cost defensive structure to be occupied by one to three persons. Those using the bunker can enter through an opening at the top of the structure and close a thick metal cover once inside. Like ancient castles, the* Beehive Bunker *is provided with six vertical slit windows through which the occupants can fire their weapons. The* Beehive Bunker *provides the combatants inside protection from substantial small arms fire. Because of its simple conical shape, the* Beehive Bunker *would be more difficult to destroy than a rectangular building. It is, in essence, always offering a deflective surface to the trajectory of incoming bullets. Complementing the structural function of this building is the aesthetically pleasing shape, which ironically, is the shape of a bullet.*

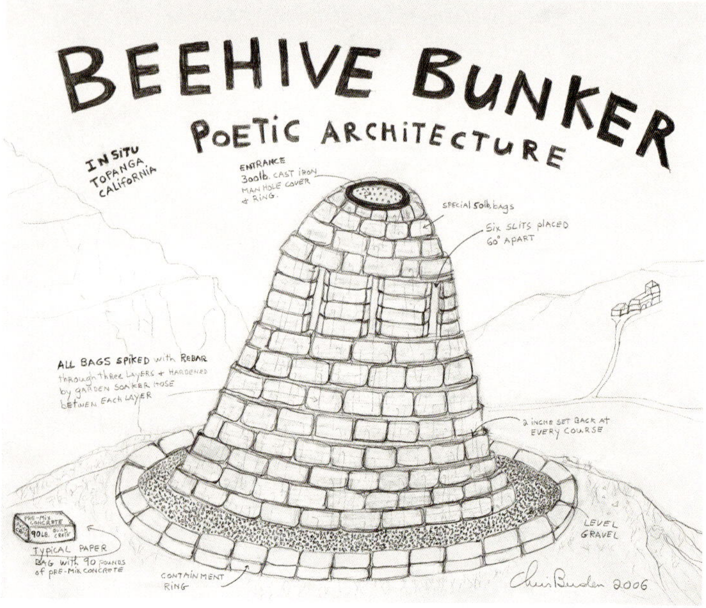

Beehive Bunker Poetic Architecture 2006
Ink on paper, 14 × 17 inches

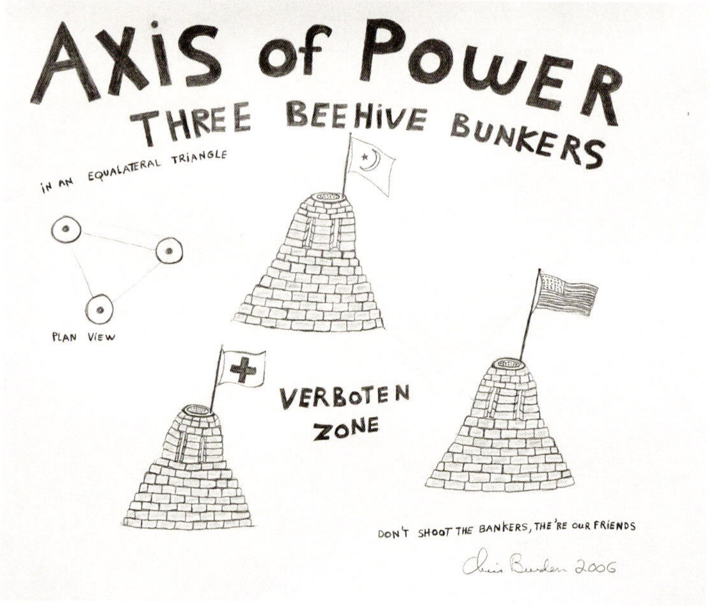

Axis of Power: Three Beehive Bunkers 2006
Ink on paper, 14 × 17 inches

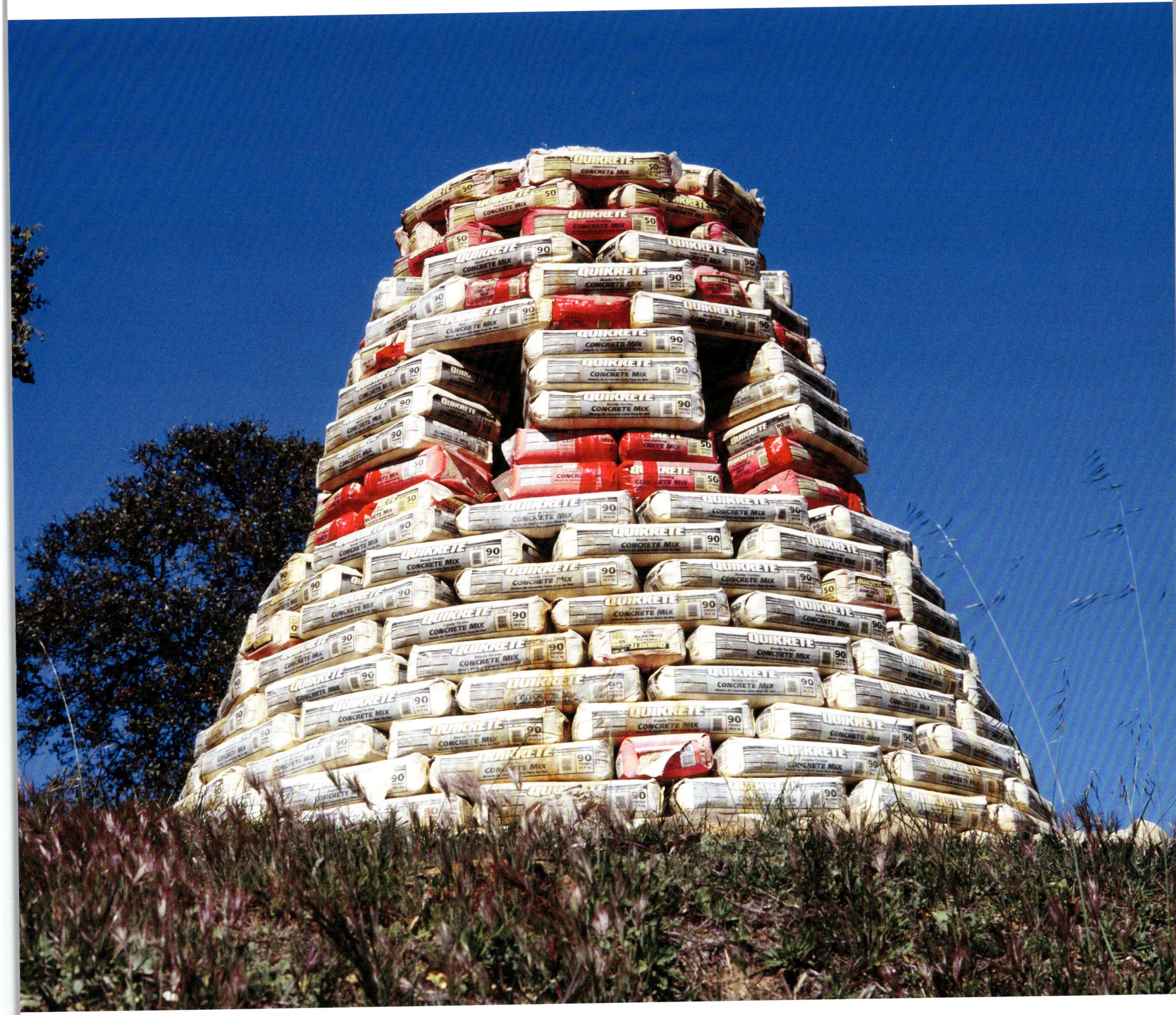
QUIKRETE
CONCRETE MIX
90
50

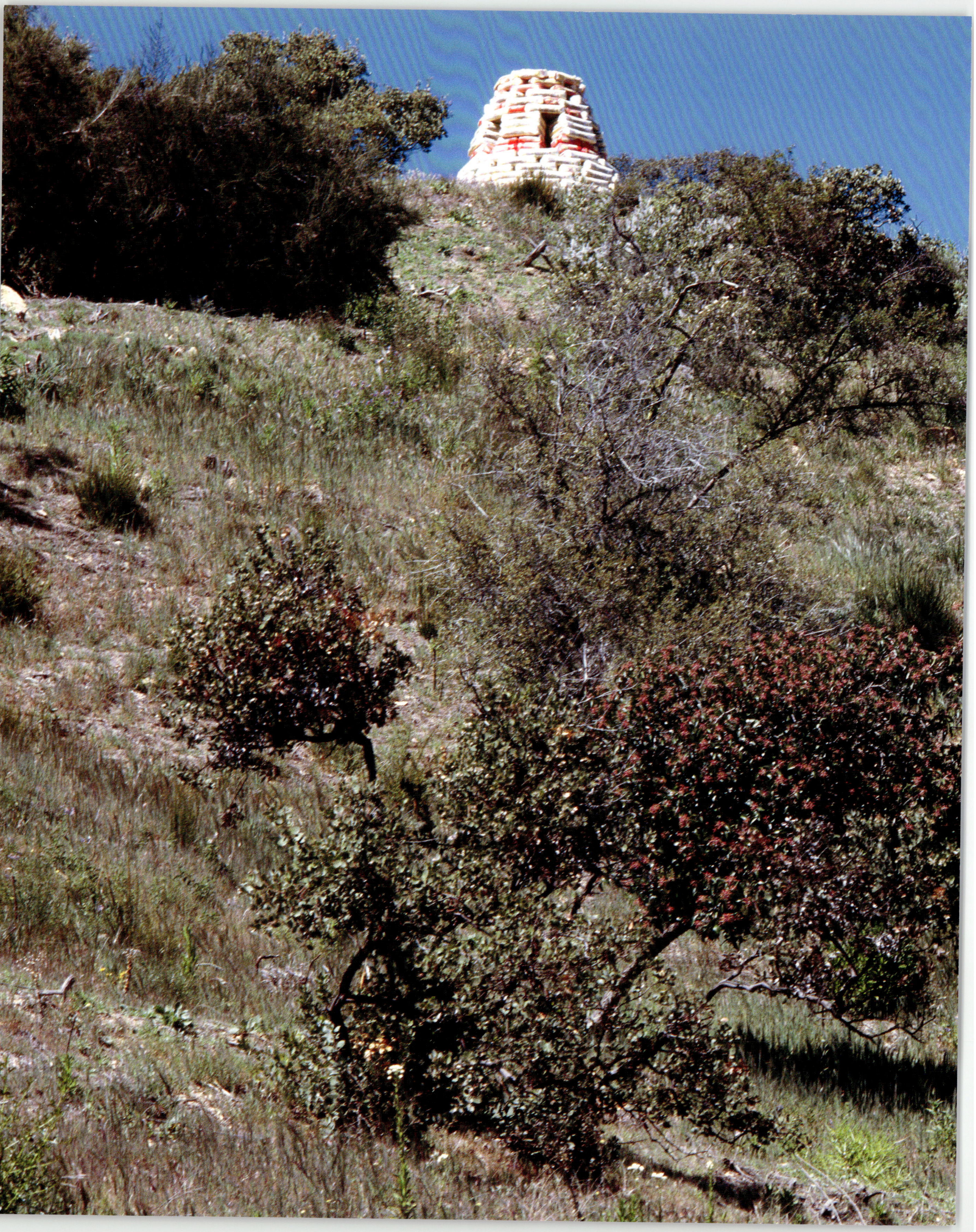

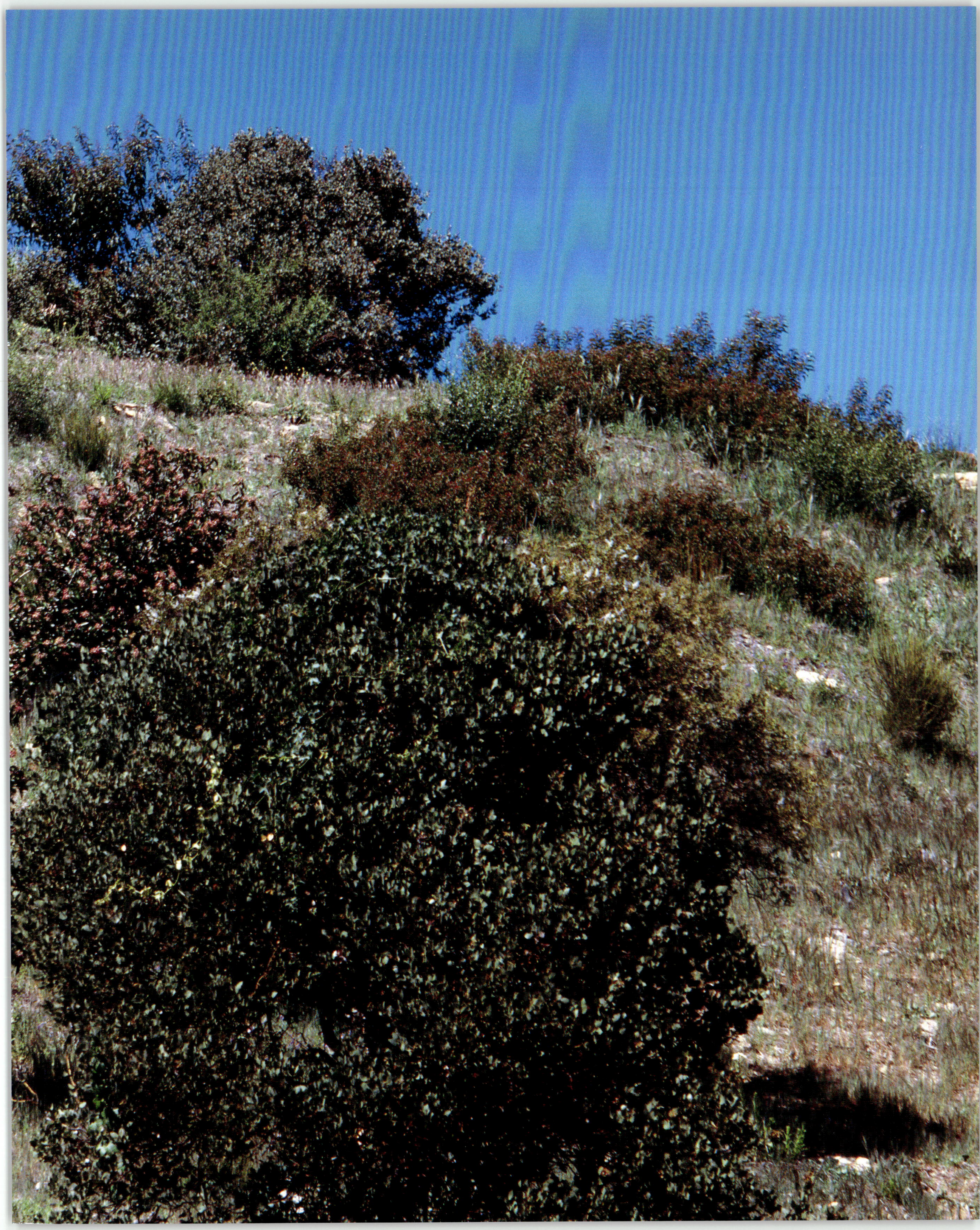

Work:

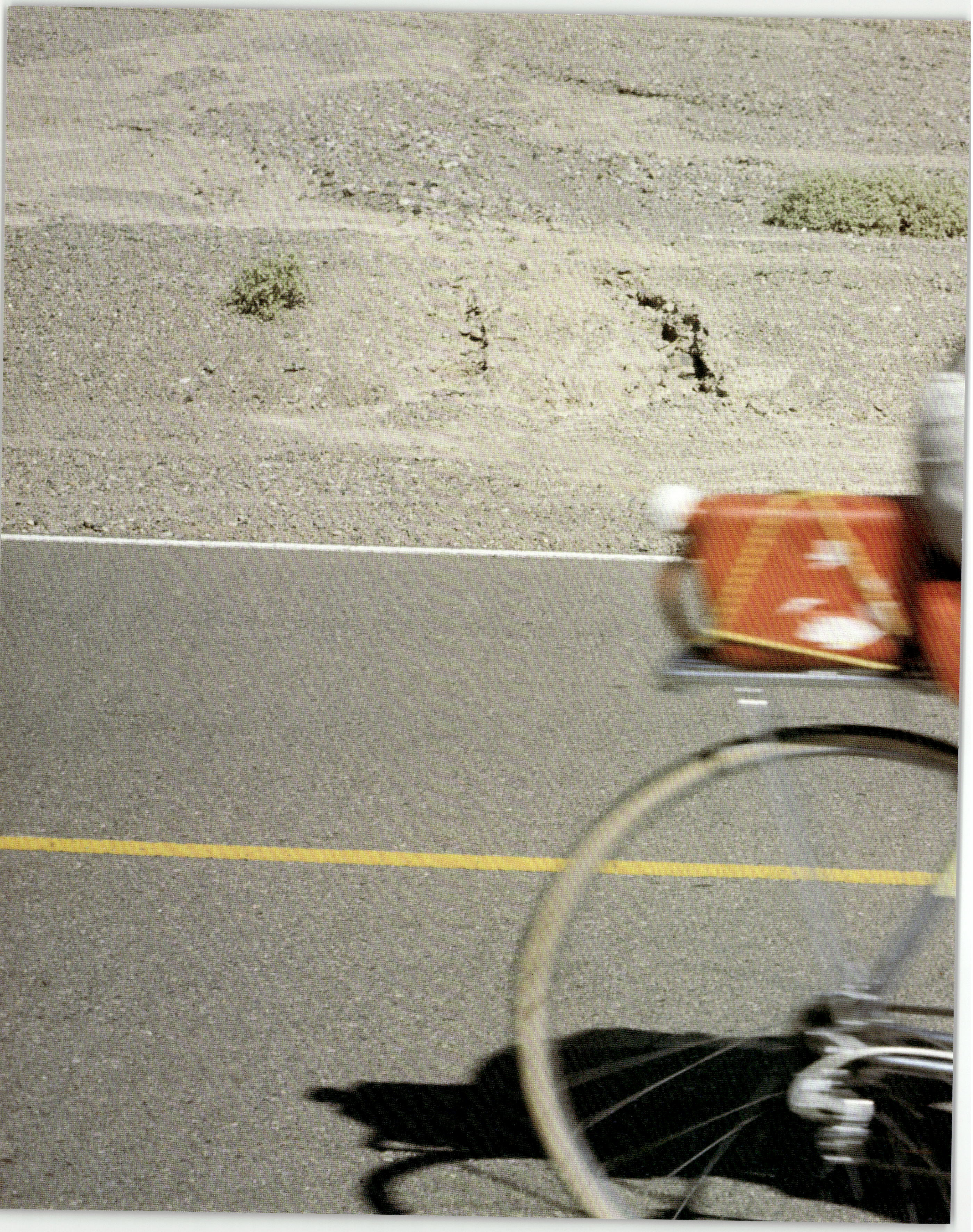

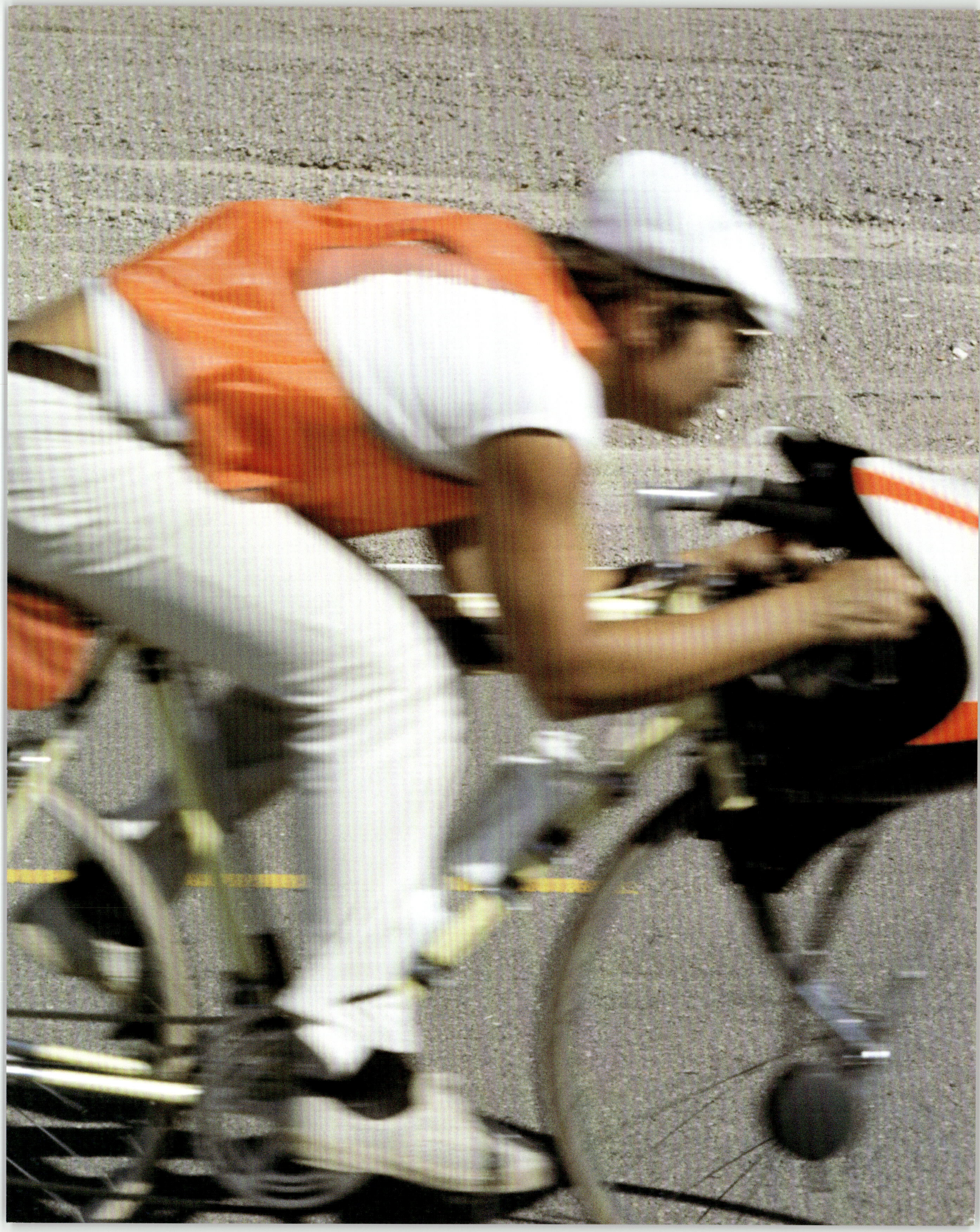

◁◁

Death Valley Run 1976

Death Valley, California, USA;
October 14, 1976

On October 14, 1976, I made the smallest motorized crossing of Death Valley on record. An ultra-light racing bicycle with fragile 'sew up' tires was equipped with a quality miniature bicycle motor. The 20cc. (approximately ½ cubic inch) Japanese TAS motor weighed 11 pounds, and was air cooled by a small fan. The engine and bicycle were streamlined with a special fairing. The whole motorized bike with extra tires, gasoline, water and tools weighed 40 pounds.

Because of the heat, the distance and the mirage effect, I wore white clothes and a luminescent orange vest for safety reasons. My speed along the 84-mile route from Scotty's Castle to Death Valley Junction ranged from a low of 16 mph to a high of 27 mph. The total trip including refueling stops took about seven hours.

RELIC: Customized bicycle

Medusa's Head 1990

Plywood, concrete, rocks, model railroad
trains and tracks
Five-ton sphere, 192 inches diameter

Medusa's Head *is a 16-foot, five-ton sphere which is encrusted with intertwining knots of different scale model railroad tracks and trains and buildings. In an obvious reference to the terrifying Greek goddess, Medusa, the sculpture is a metaphor for a world engulfed in its own technology.*

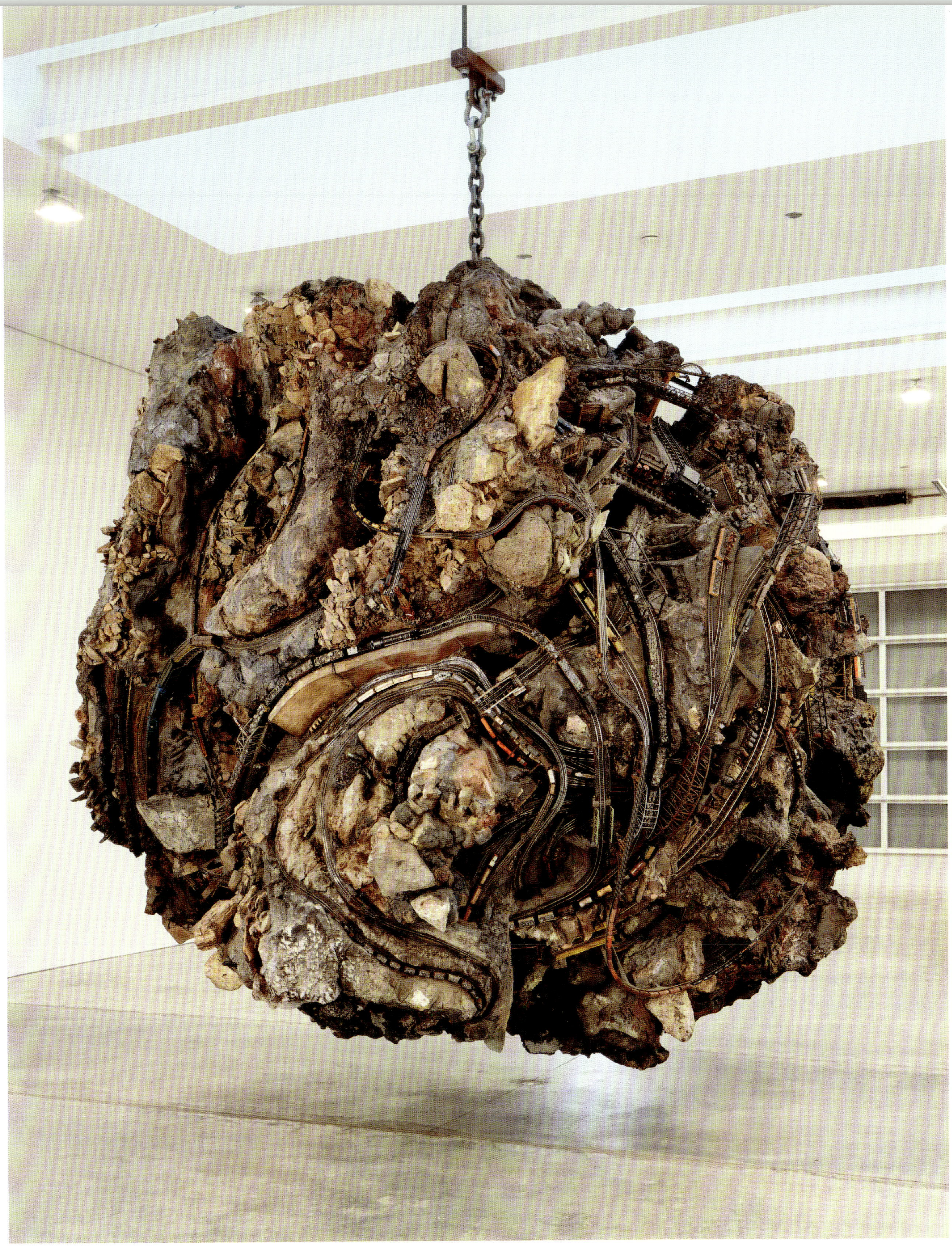

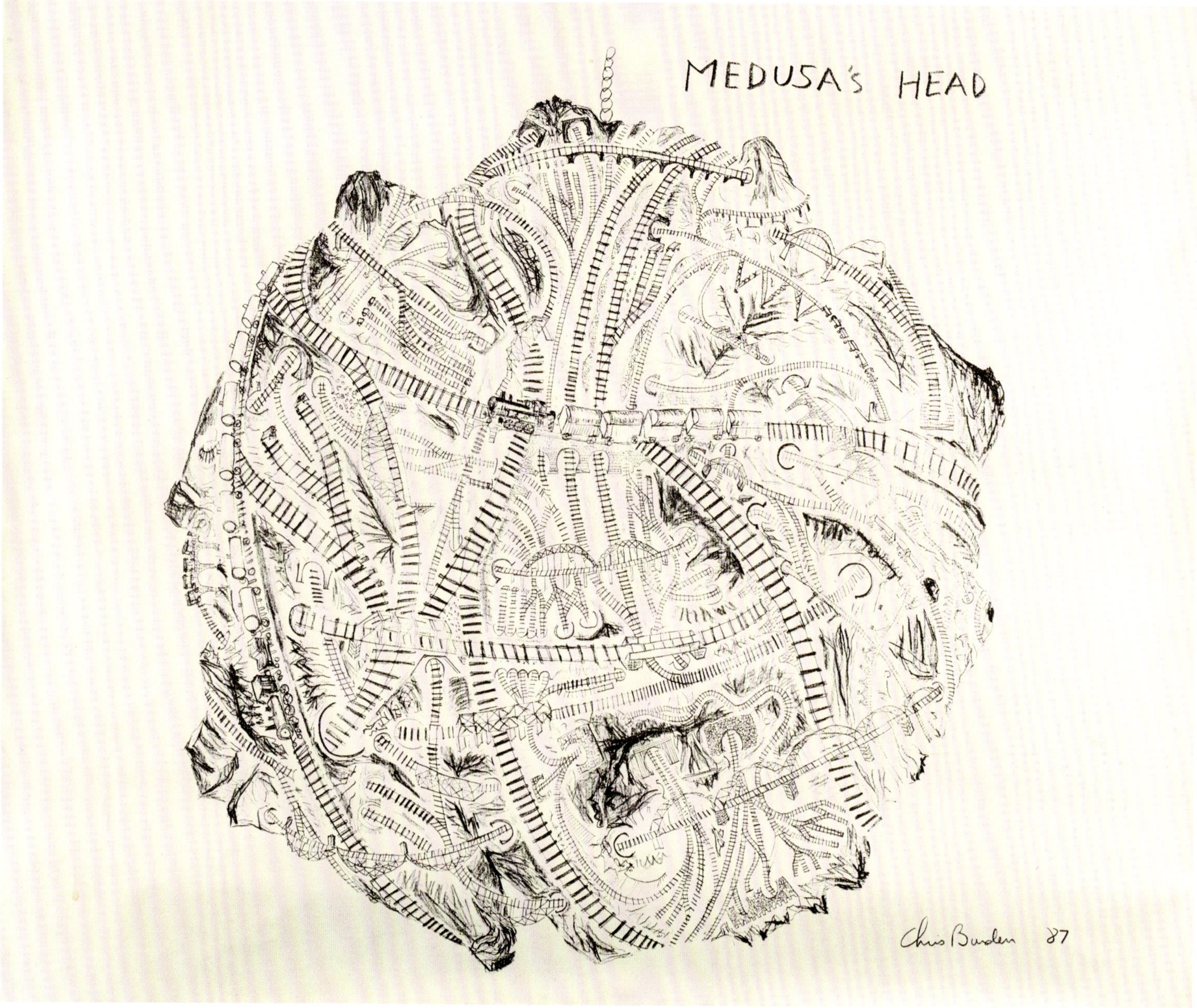

Medusa's Head 1987
Ink on paper, 20 × 23½ inches

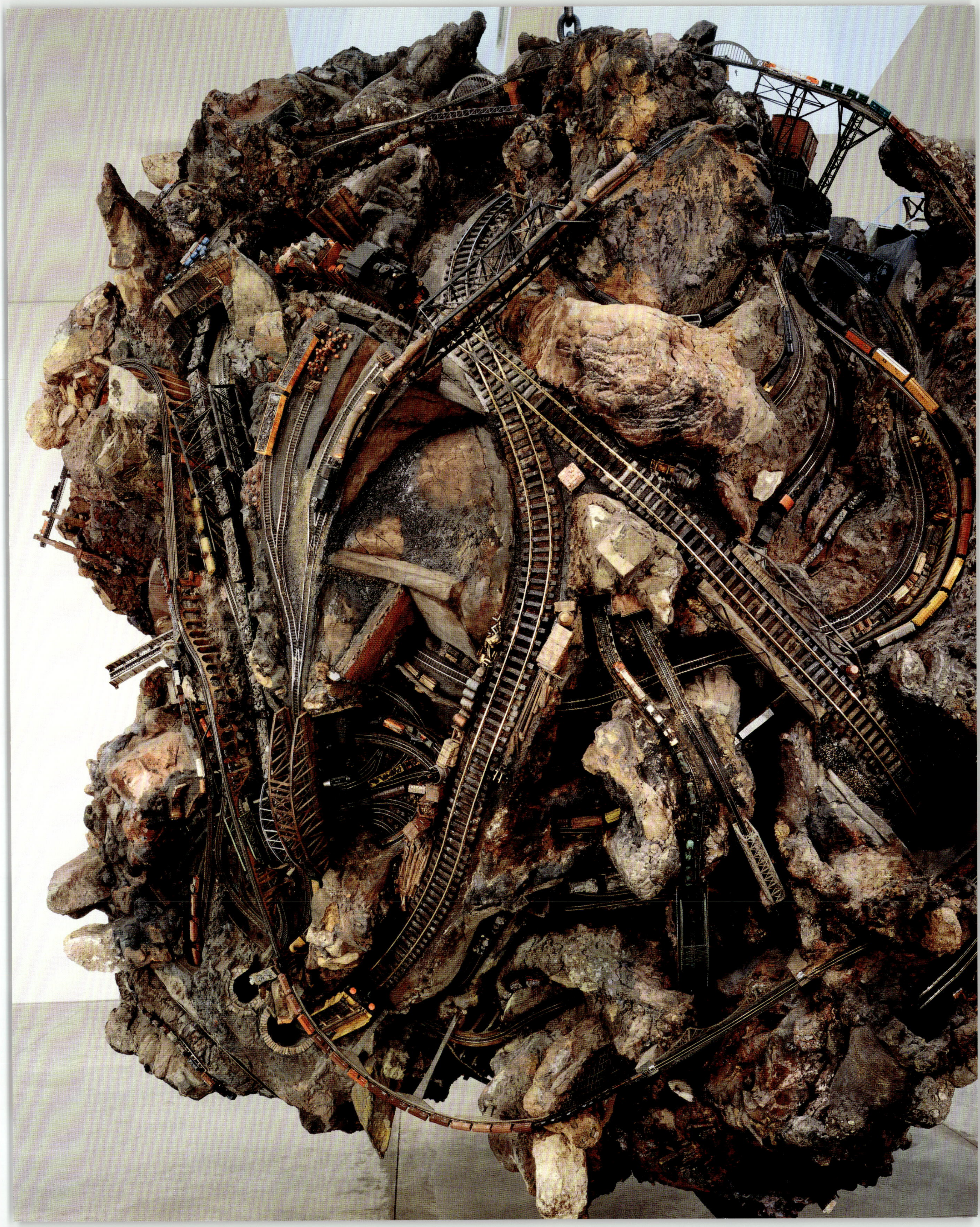

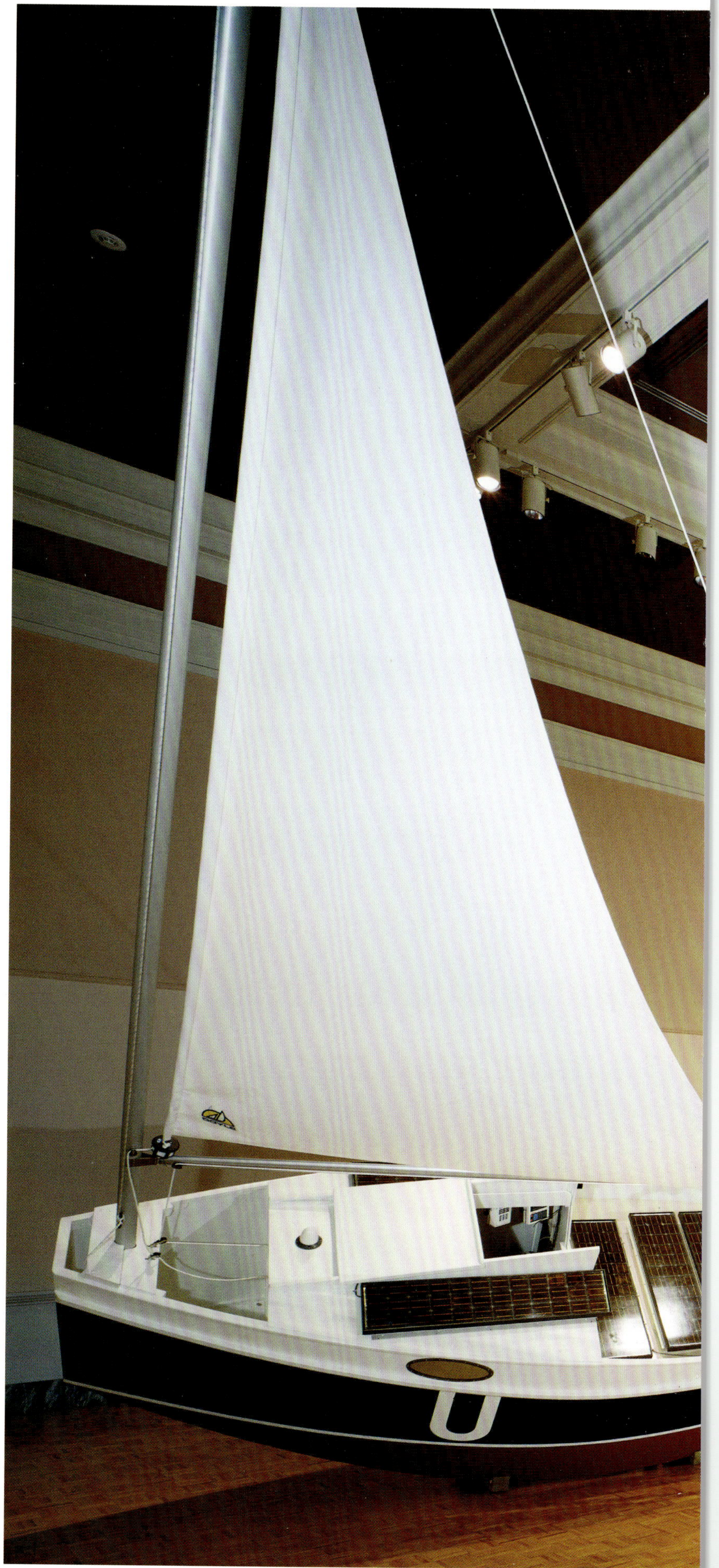

Three Ghost Ships 1991

Three micro 16 sailboats, one equipped with navigational satellite system, robotic sail and rudder controls, concept drawing
Each boat, 276 × 192 × 72 inches

Three Ghost Ships *was a project trying to combine American and British history, the romance of sailing and state of the art electronic gear. Three small, simple sailboats were to be equipped with automatic sail handling and a steering mechanism linked to a global positioning satellite system. They were to be launched from Charleston, South Carolina, carrying tea to Plymouth, England. The boats would sail with no human assistance and arrive, miraculously, in England.*

Three Ghost Ships I 1990
Ink on paper, 8½ × 13 inches

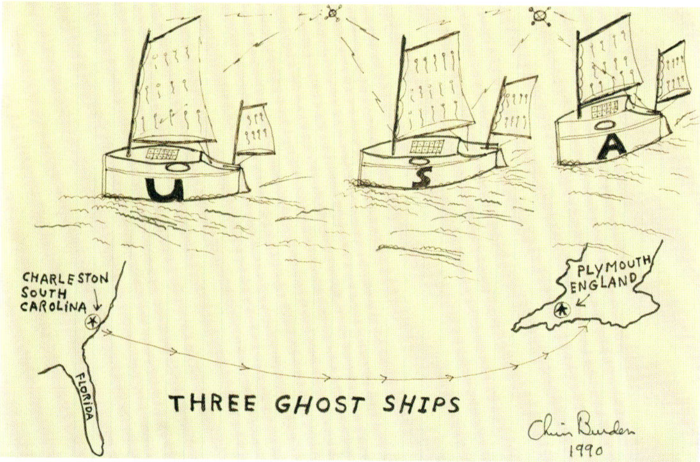

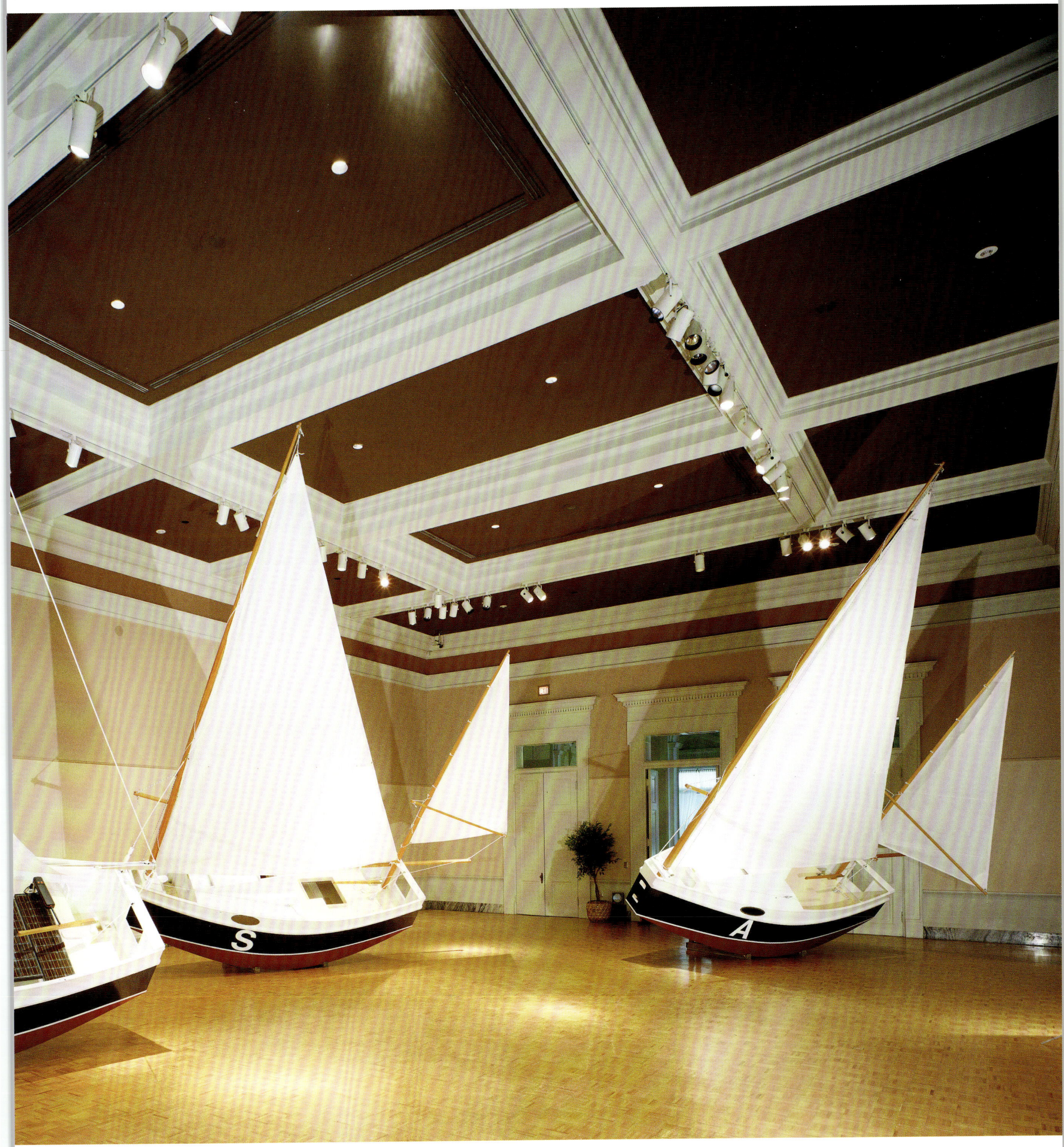
S
A

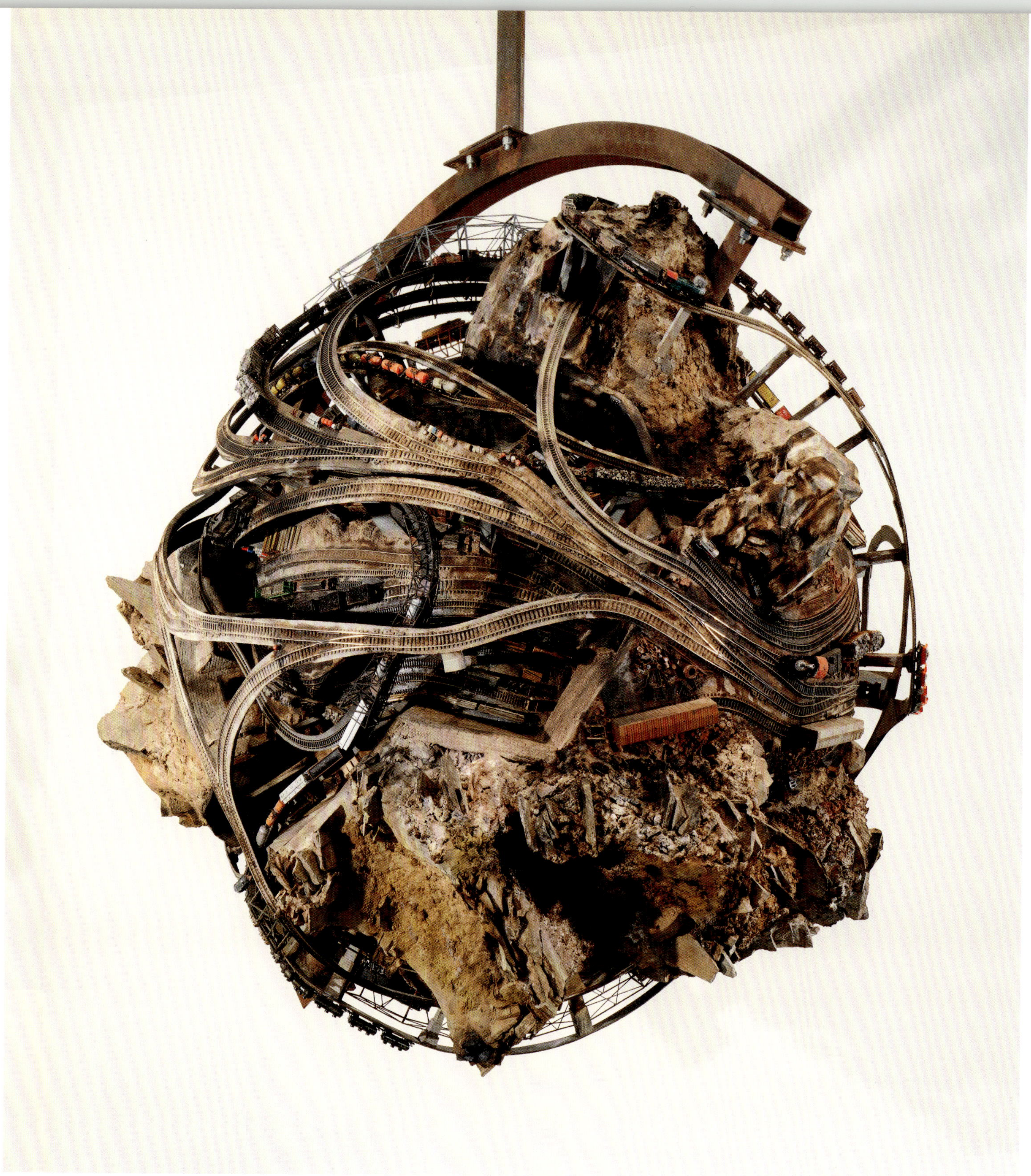

Medusa's Flying Moon 1992

Plywood, steel, tar, cement, rock,
plaster, plastic, wood, model railroad
trains and tracks, electric motor
72 inches diameter

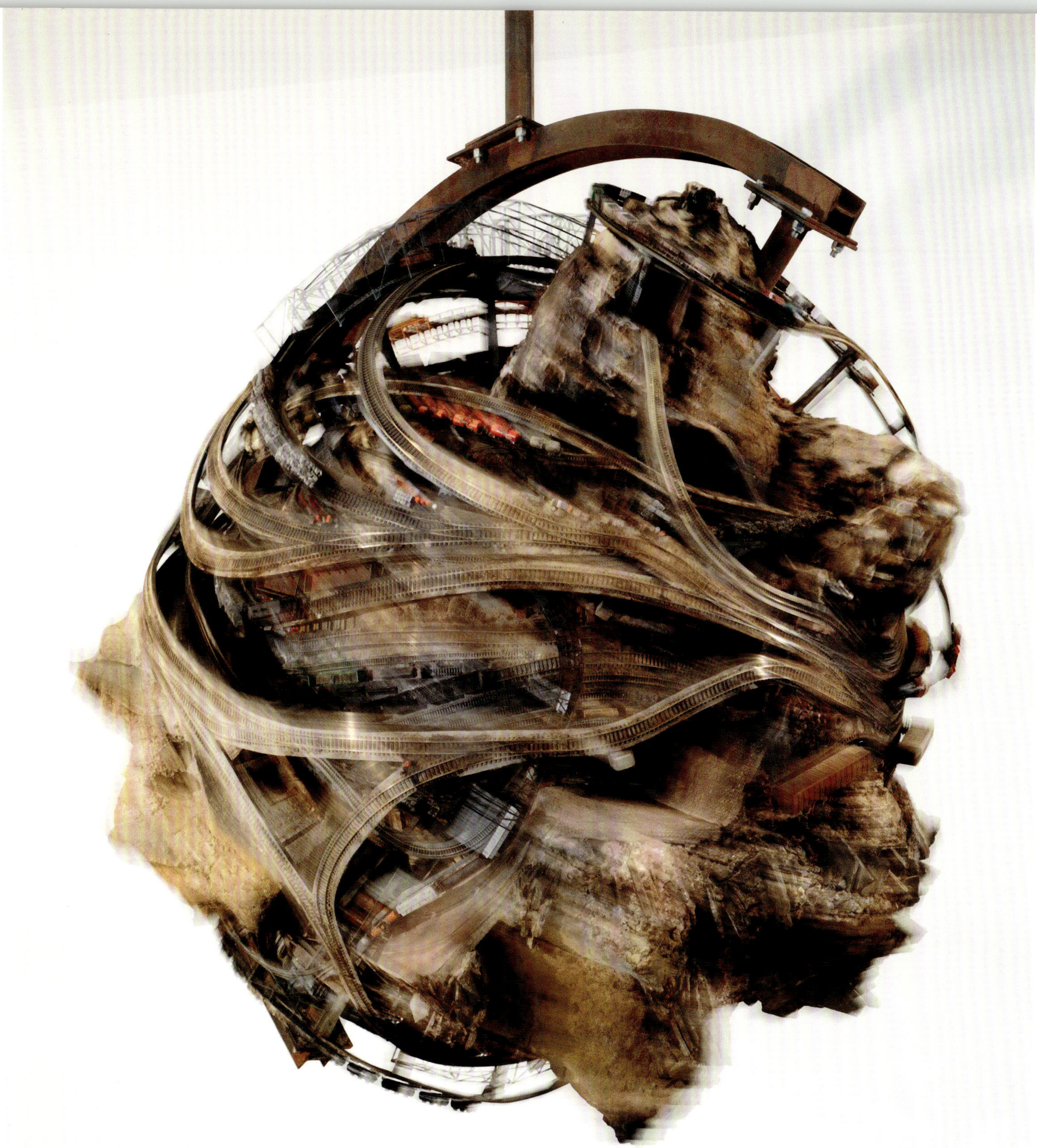

Medusa's Flying Moon *is a kinetic sculpture that is in the style of the huge sculpture,* Medusa's Head. Medusa's Flying Moon *is approximately six feet in diameter and contains an internal electric motor and drive mechanism that enables it to rotate, much in the manner of a traditional desk top globe. It is covered with varying scales of model railroad trains and tracks.*

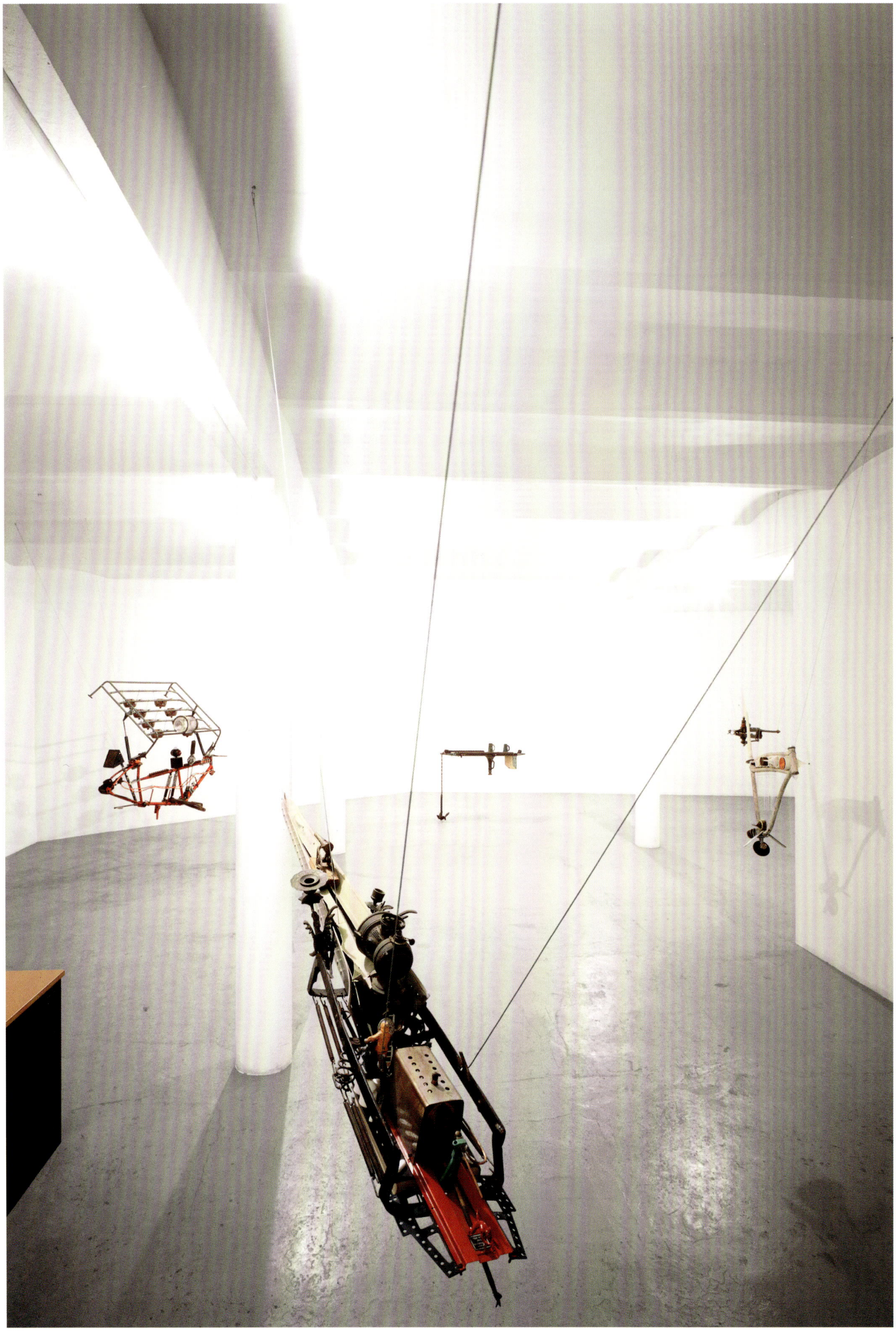

Five Ships 1992

◁ *(foreground)*

U2 Boat

Mixed media
12 × 30 × 10 inches

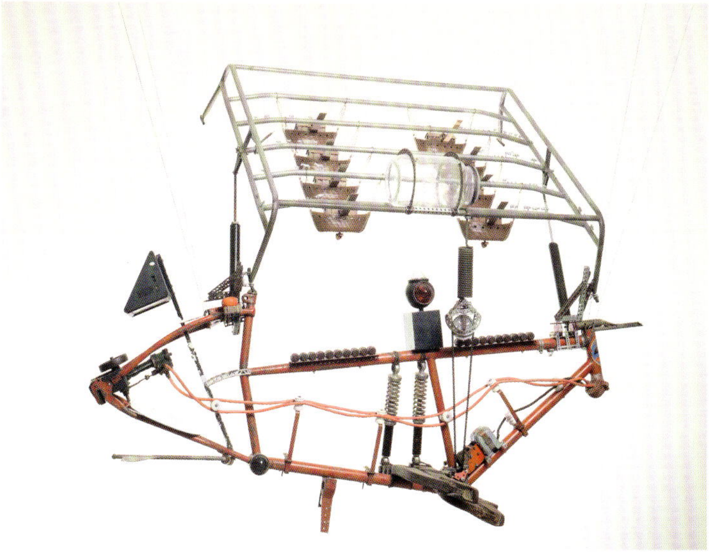

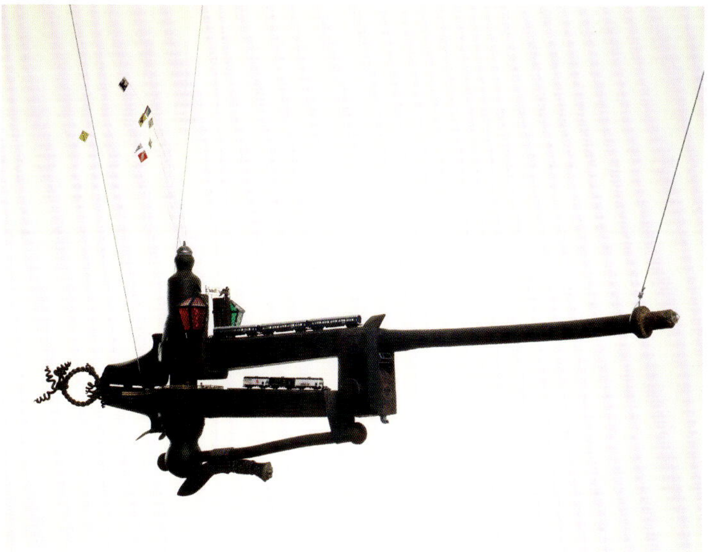

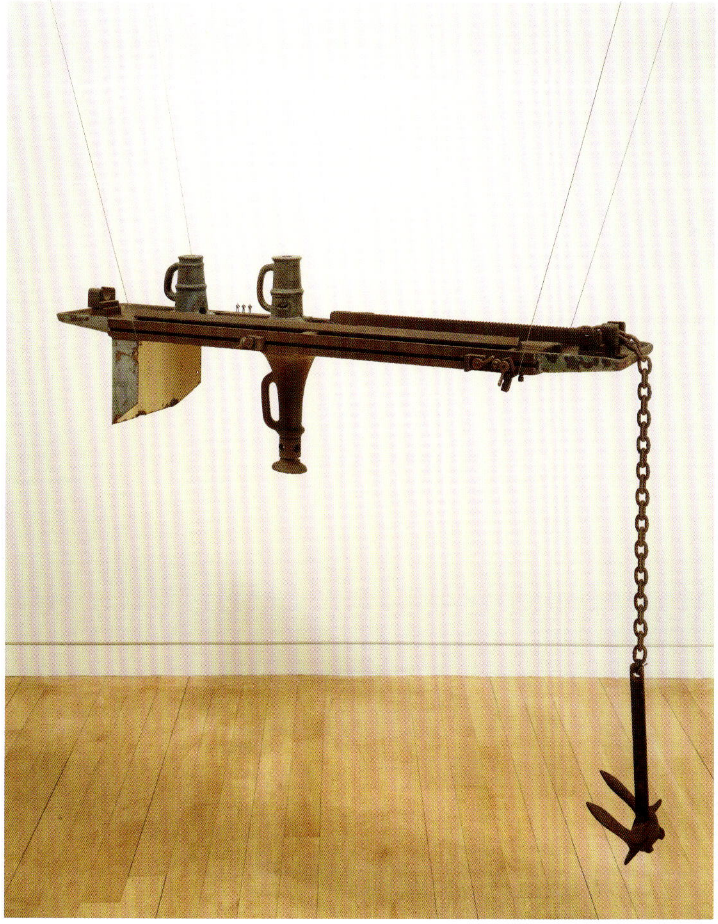

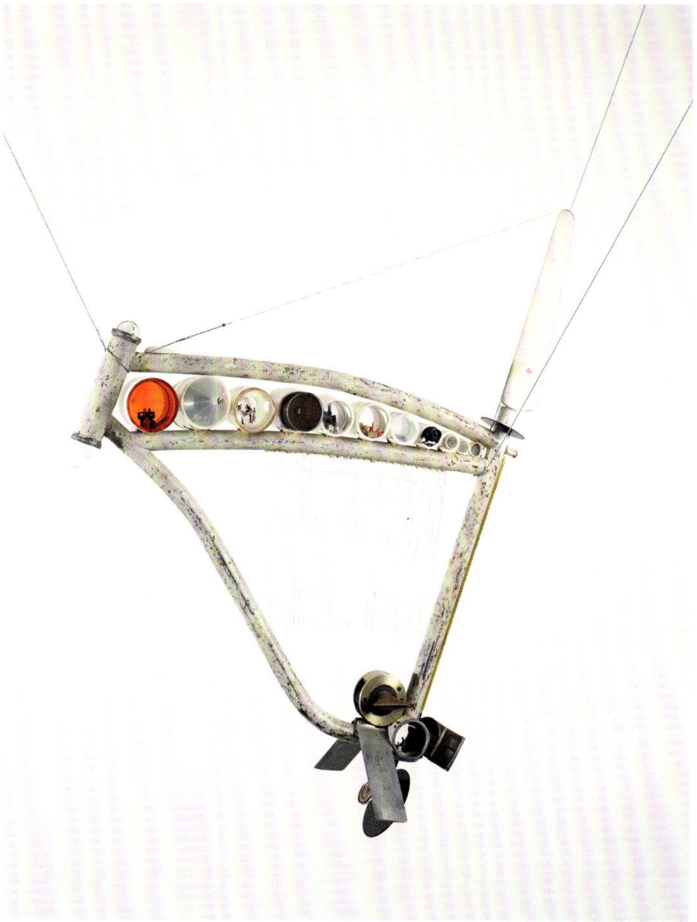

△△

Noah's Arks

Mixed media
58 × 63 × 42 inches

△

Two Cannon, Three Sailor Battleship

Mixed media
36 × 53 × 11 inches

△△

Grand Hotel

Mixed media
12 × 28 × 8½ inches

△

Hospital Ship

Mixed media
36 × 29 × 11 inches

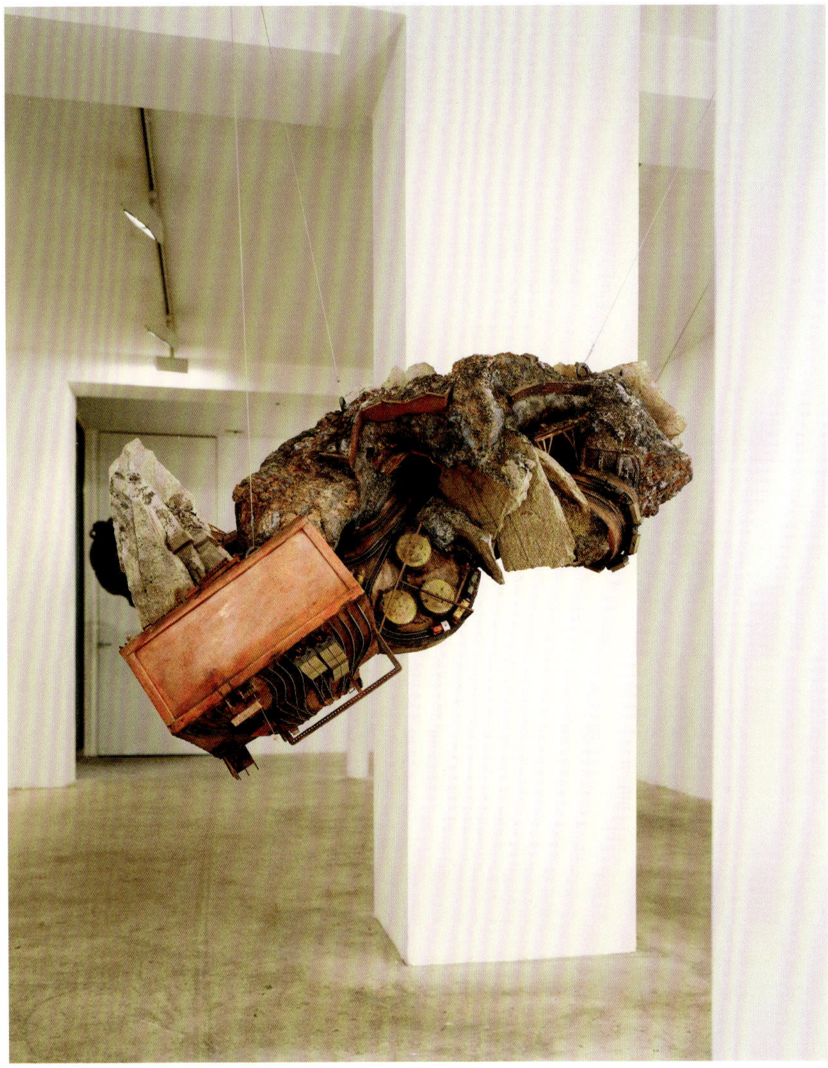 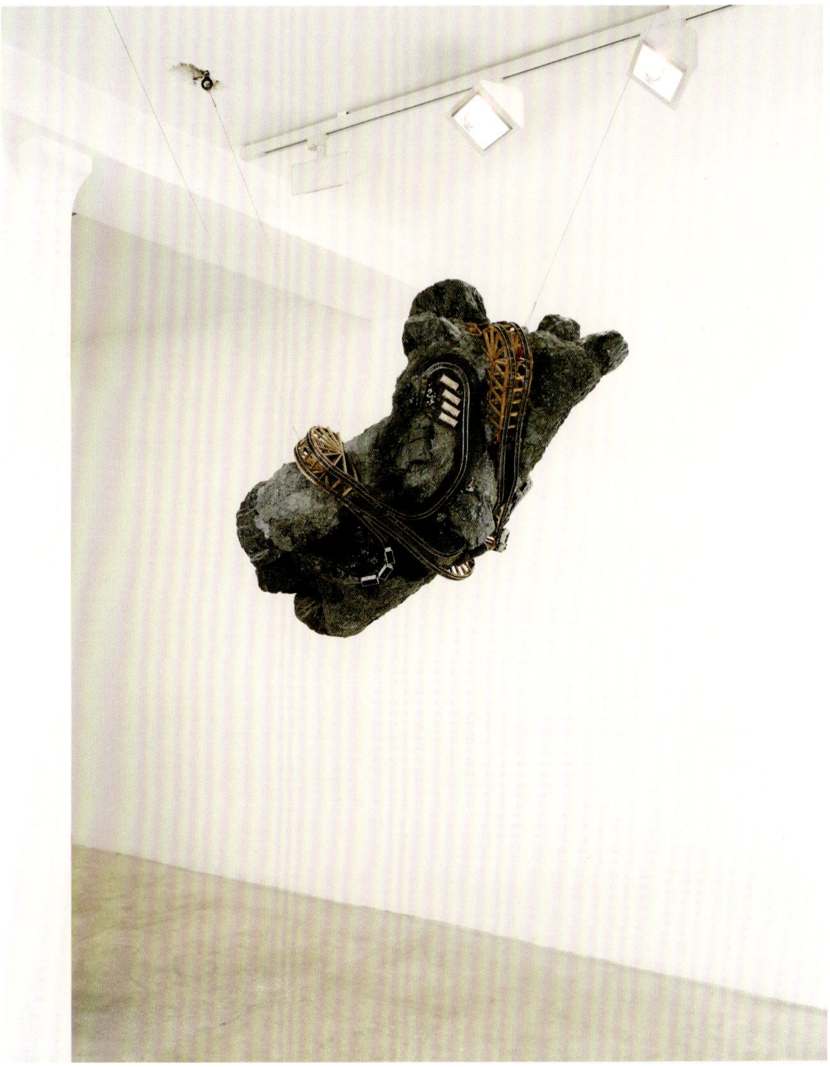

Five Moonettes 1994

The Five Moonettes *are irregularly shaped sculptures in the style of* Medusa's Head. *They vary in size from three to 12 feet and were first shown at the Galerie Anne de Villepoix in Paris, in September 1994.*

The Cubist

Cement, steel, model railroad trains and tracks
32 × 55 × 27 inches

The Coal Moon

Cement, steel, coal, model railroad trains and tracks
22 × 36 × 33 inches

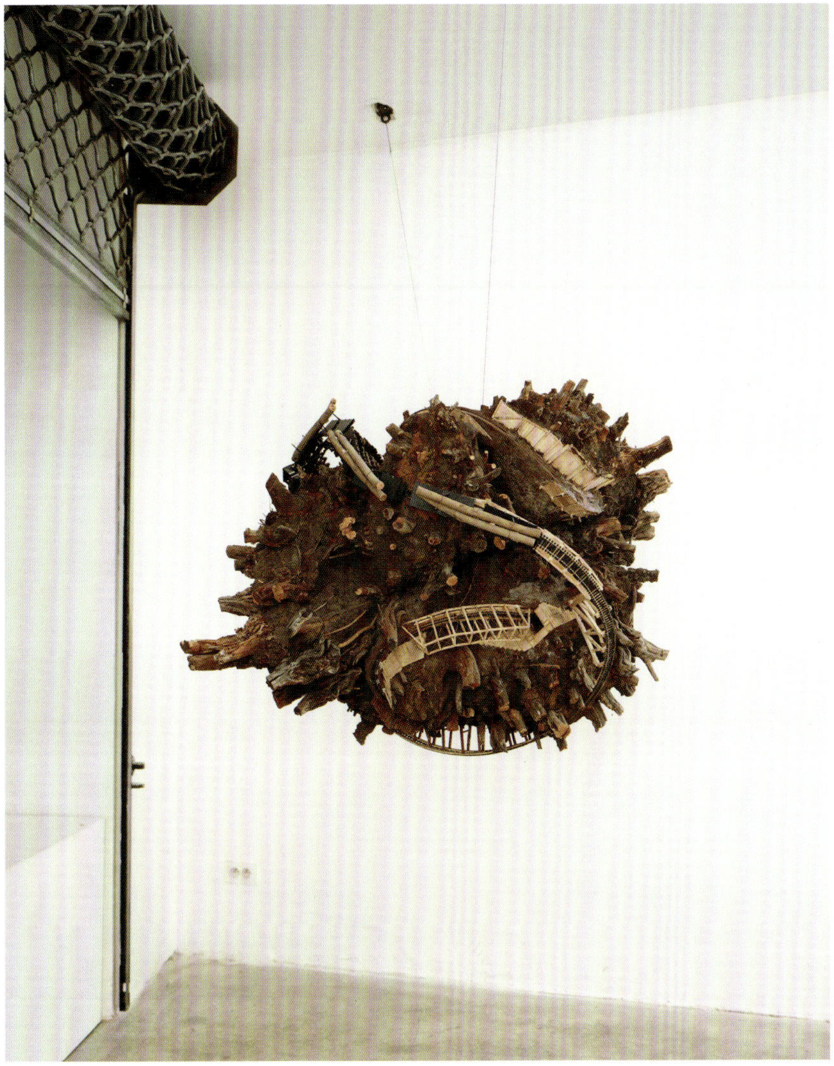

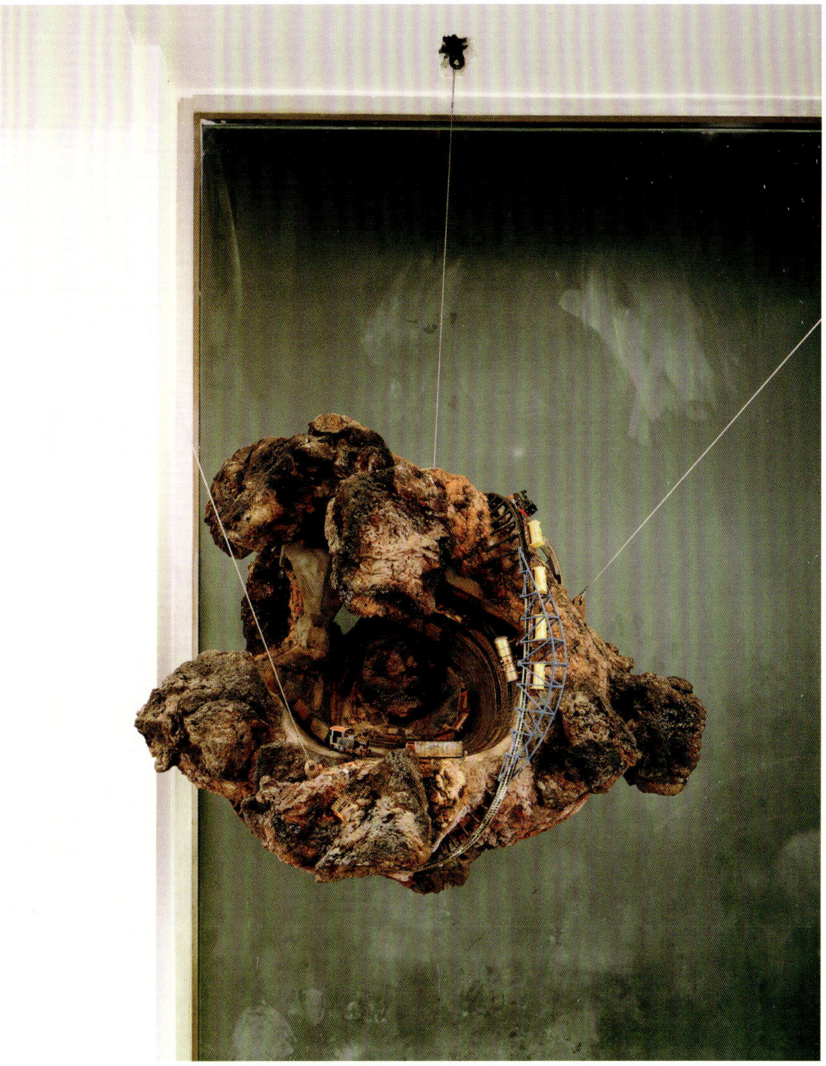

The Logged Moon

Cement, steel, model railroad trains
and tracks, wood
48 × 54 × 40 inches

The Deep Pit

Cement, steel, model railroad trains
and tracks
32 × 40 × 34 inches

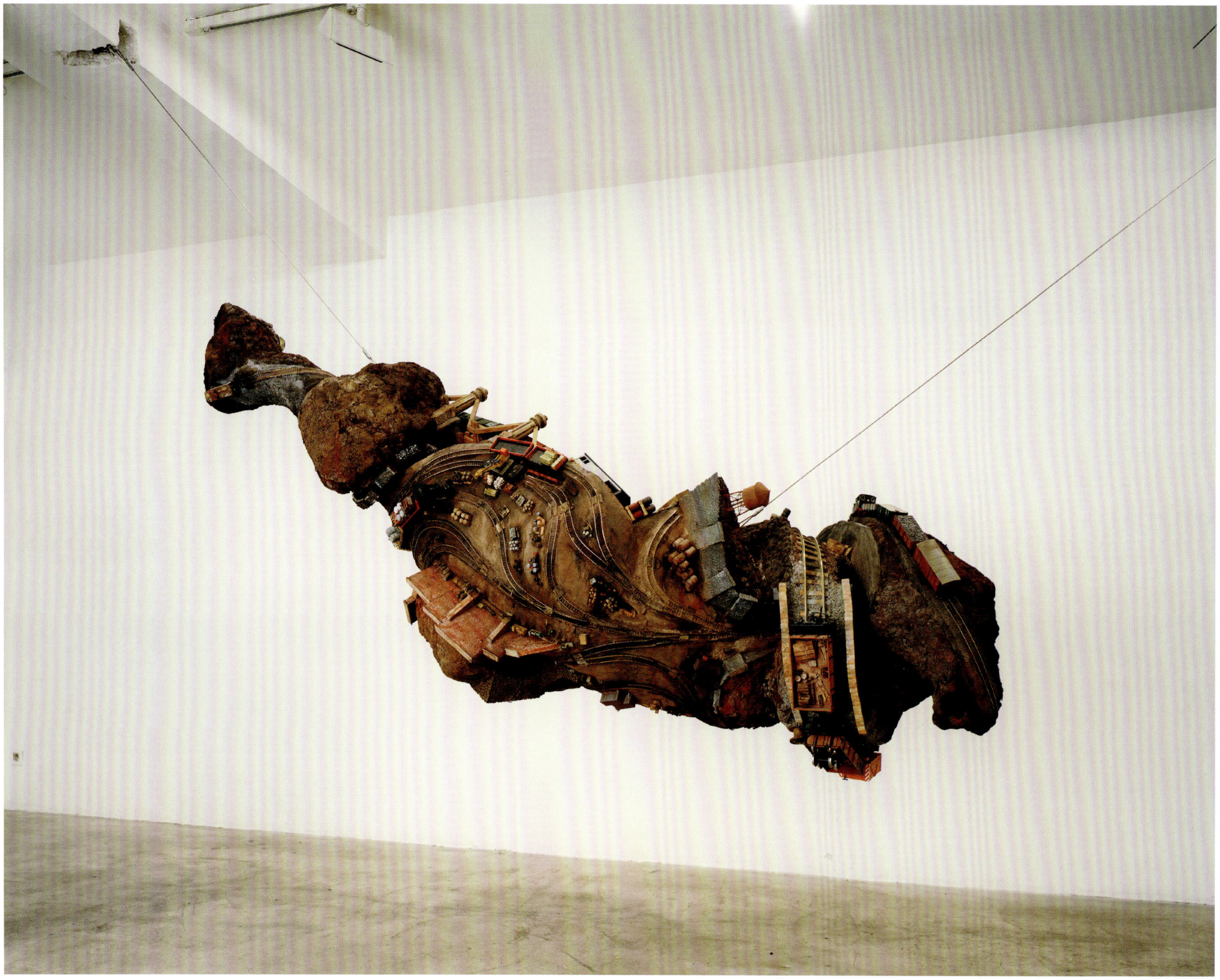

The Twist

Cement, steel, model railroad trains
and tracks
42 × 112 × 42 inches

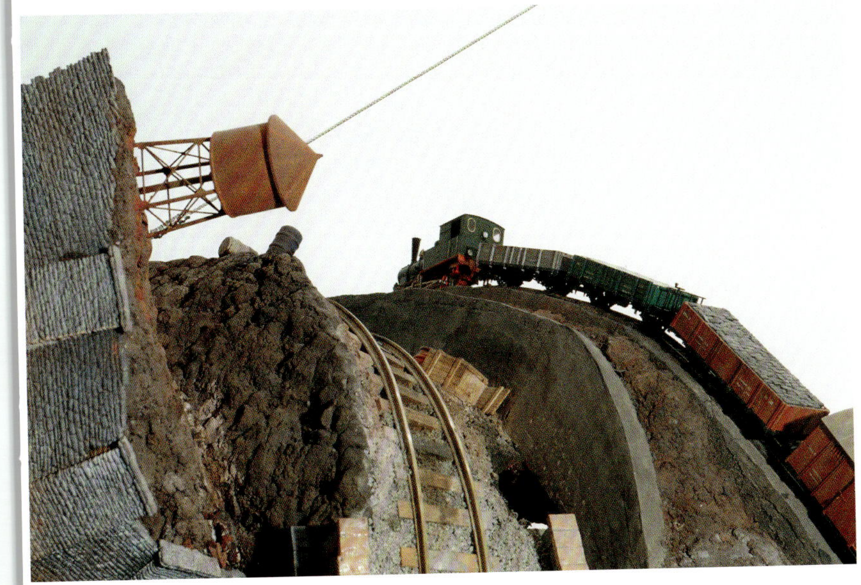
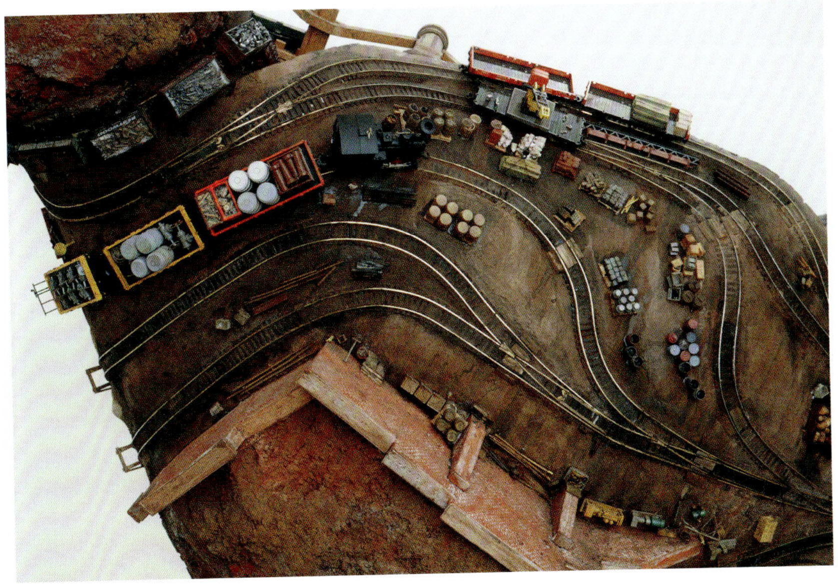
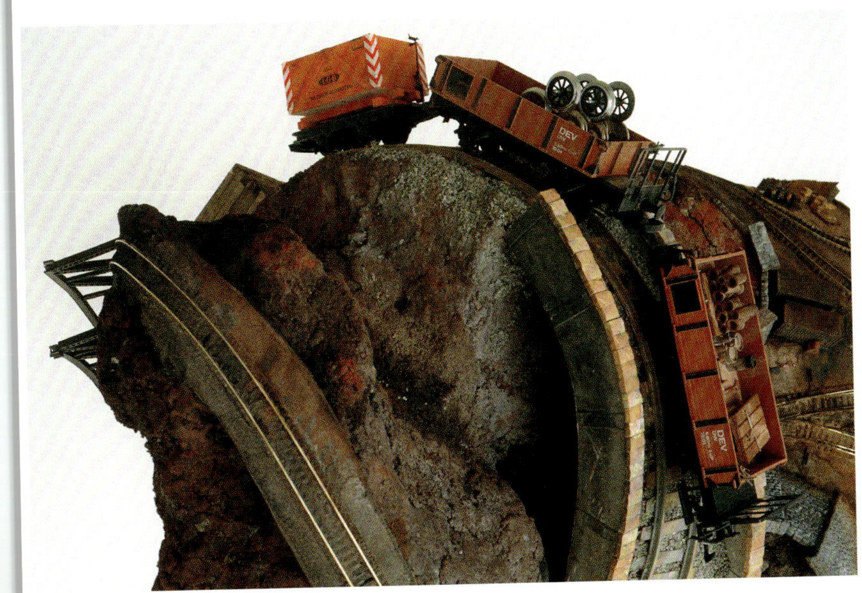
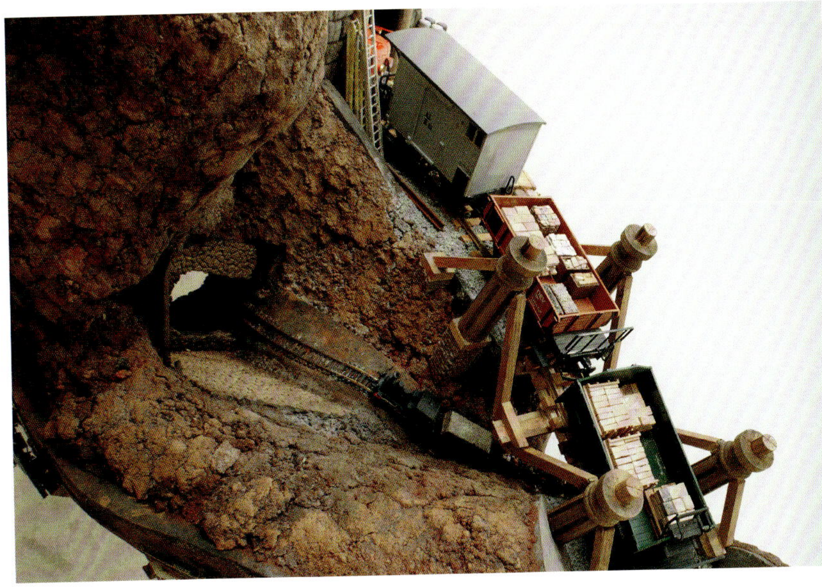

Five Day Locker Piece 1971

University of California, Irvine,
California, USA; April 26–30, 1971

I was locked in locker number 5 for five consecutive days and did not leave the locker during this time. The locker measured two feet high, two feet wide and three feet deep. I stopped eating several days prior to entry. The locker directly above me contained five gallons of bottled water; the locker below me contained an empty five gallon bottle.

RELIC: Padlock

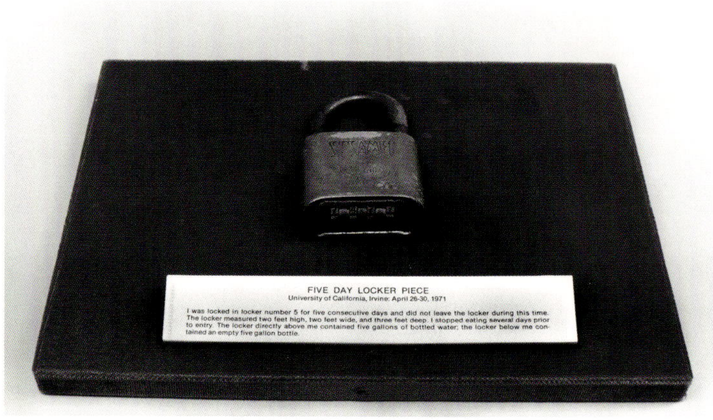

MFA Exhibition Announcement card, 1971

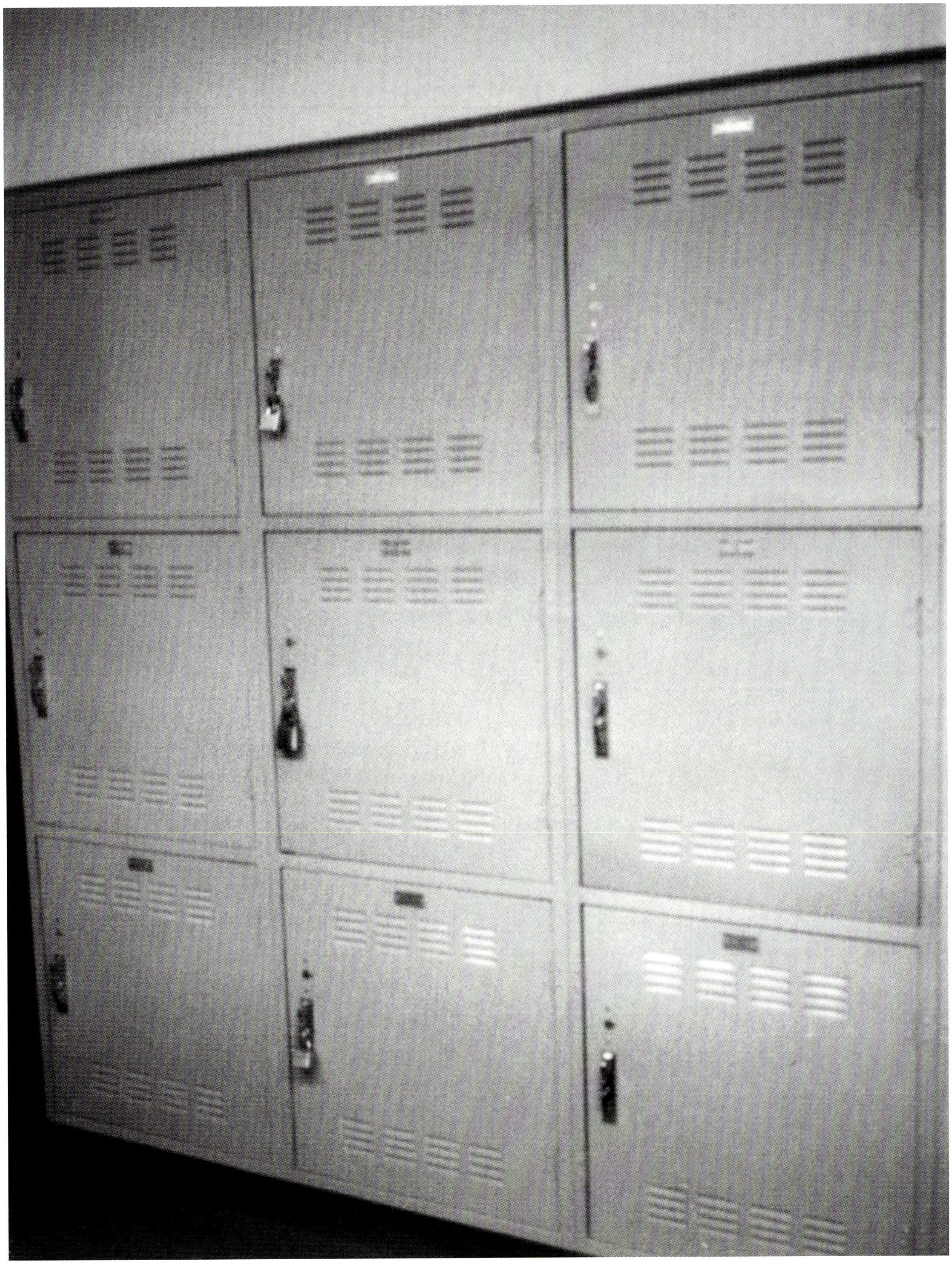

I Became a Secret Hippy 1971

Museum of Conceptual Art,
San Francisco, California, USA;
October 3, 1971

The piece began when I took off my clothes, jeans and a t-shirt, and lay on the floor on my back. A friend hammered a star-shaped stud into my sternum. I then sat in a chair and had all my hair cut off. Finally, I dressed in some FBI clothes I had bought for the piece.

RELIC: Tie, silver star

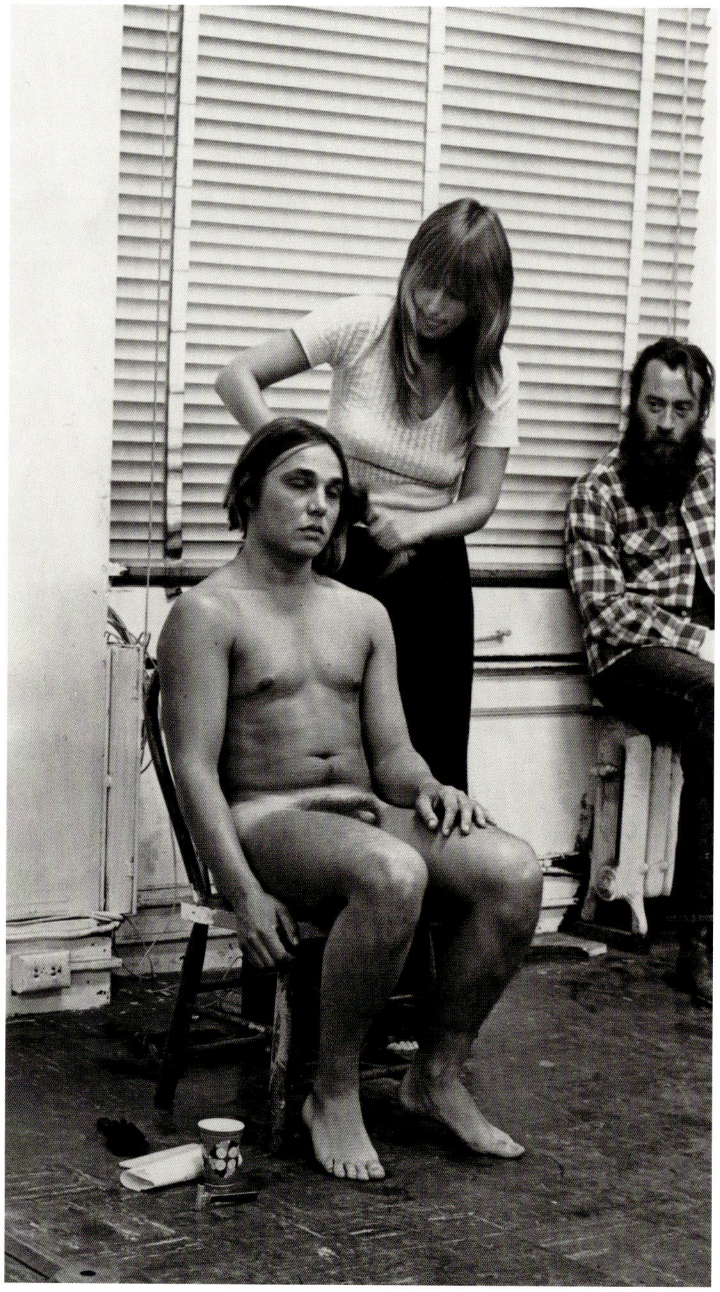

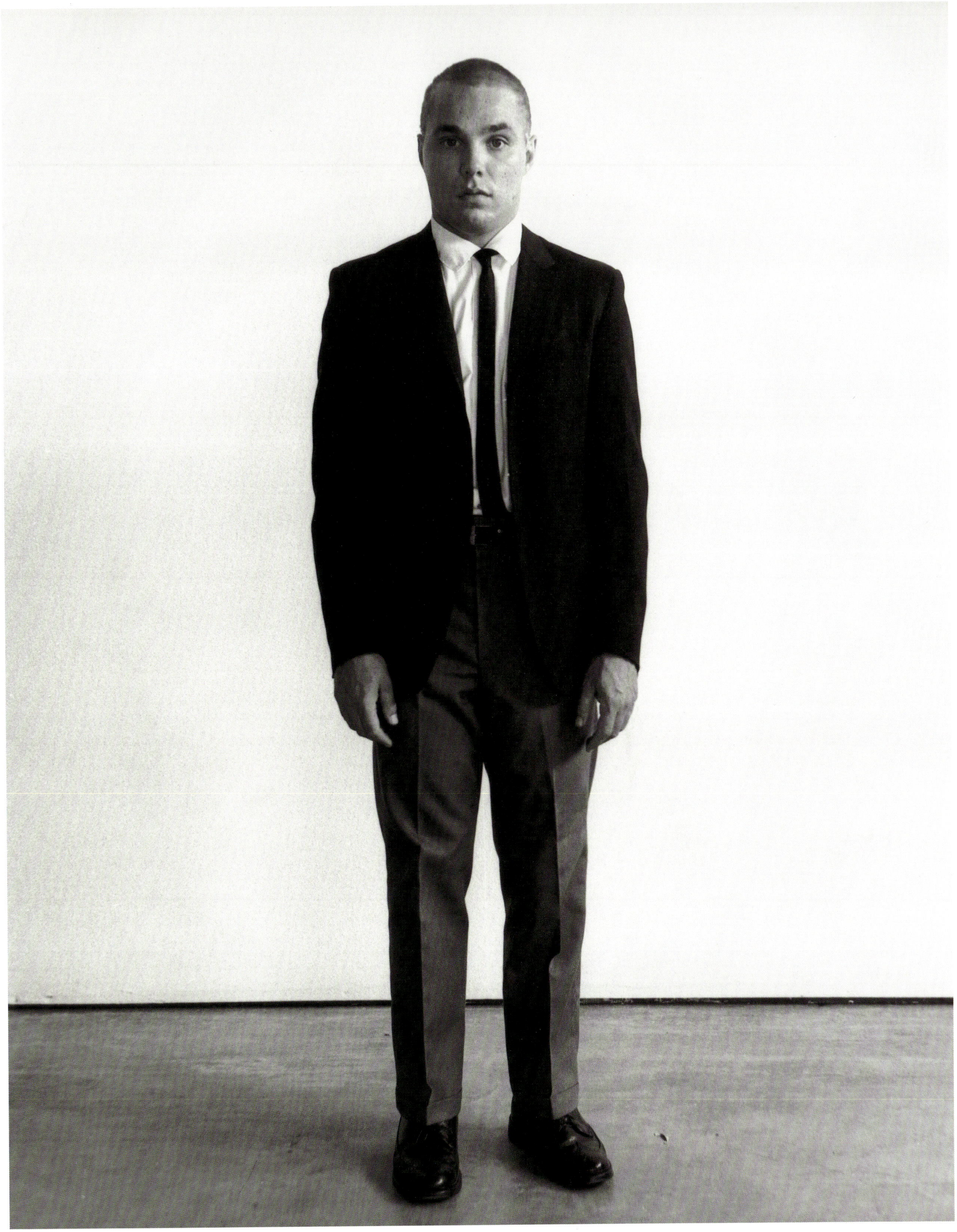

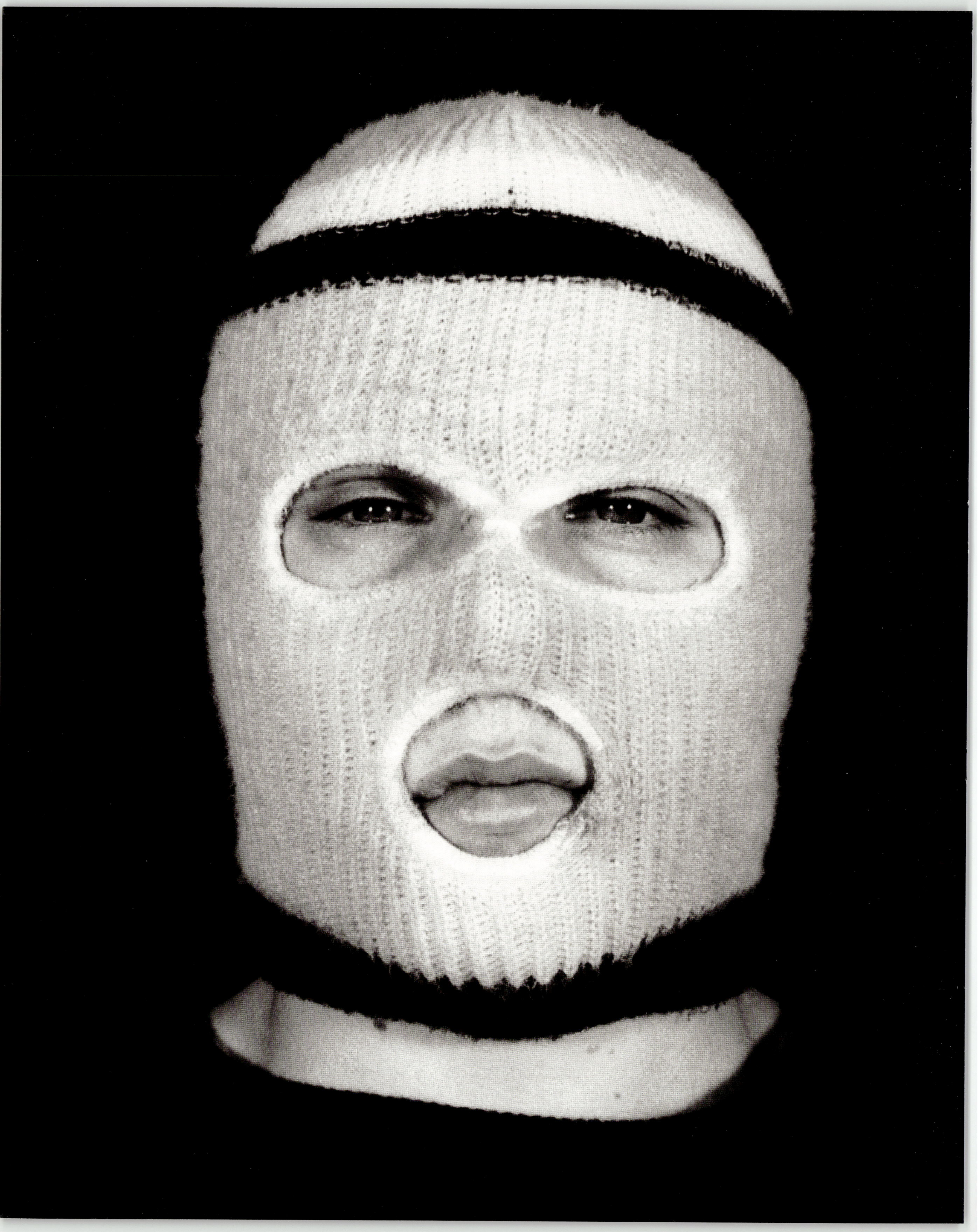

You'll Never See My Face in Kansas City 1971

Morgan Gallery, Kansas City, Missouri, USA; November 6, 1971

For three hours I sat without moving behind a panel which concealed my neck and head. No one could see behind the panel; a piece of board sealed the underside of the space. In conjunction with the performance, I wore a ski mask at all times during my stay in Kansas City from November 5–7, 1971.

RELIC: Ski mask

▷▷

Disappearing 1971

December 22–24, 1971

I disappeared for three days without prior notice to anyone. On these three days my whereabouts were unknown.

RELIC: Void (empty case)

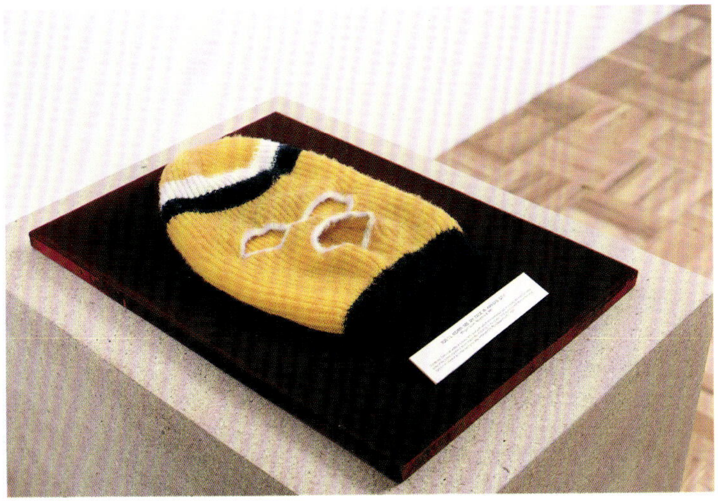

Dos Equis 1972

Laguna Canyon Road, Laguna Beach,
California, USA; October 16, 1972

On the evening of October 16, I placed two Xs constructed of 16-foot beams in an upright position blocking both lanes of the Laguna Canyon Road. The timbers had been soaked in gasoline for several days. I set the Xs on fire and left the area.

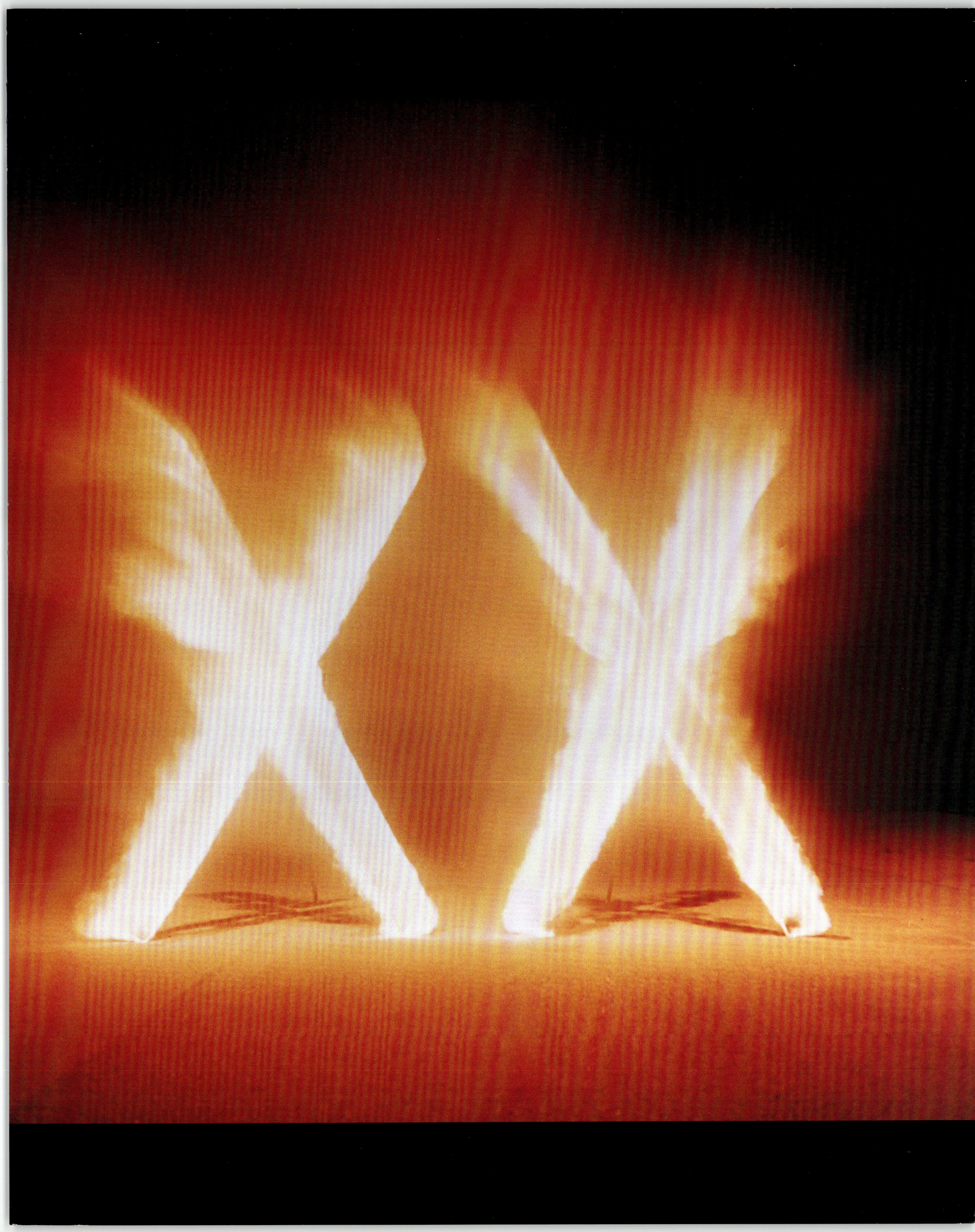

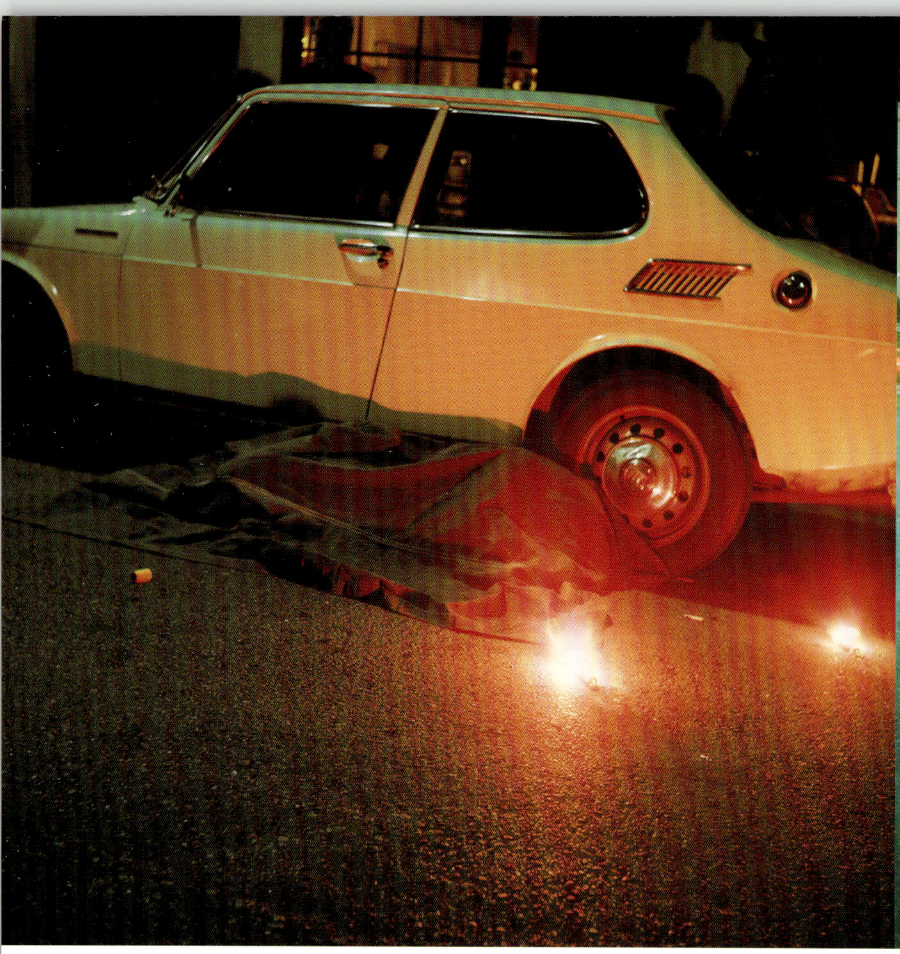

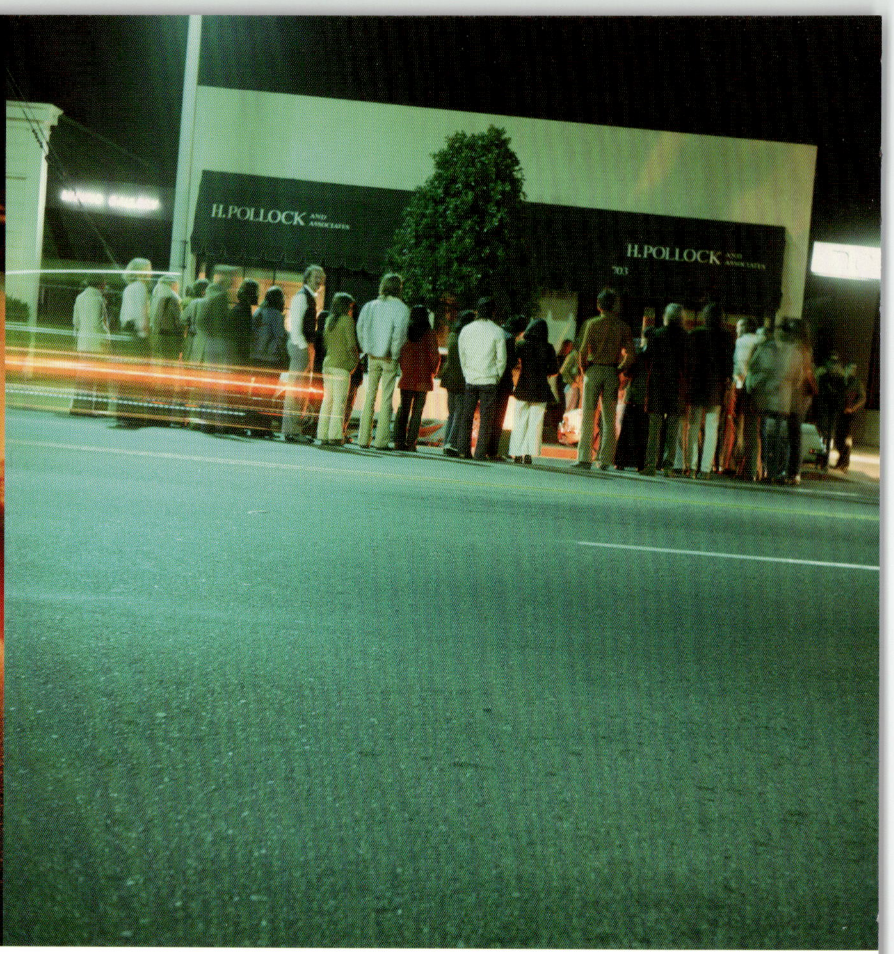

Deadman 1972

La Cienega Boulevard (Riko Mizuno Gallery), Los Angeles, California, USA; November 12, 1972

At 8 pm I lay down on La Cienega Boulevard and was covered completely with a canvas tarpaulin. Two 15-minute flares were placed near me to alert cars. Just before the flares extinguished, a police car arrived. I was arrested and booked for causing a false emergency to be reported. The trial took place in Beverly Hills. After three days of deliberation, the jury failed to reach a decision and the judge dismissed the case.

RELIC: Canvas tarpaulin

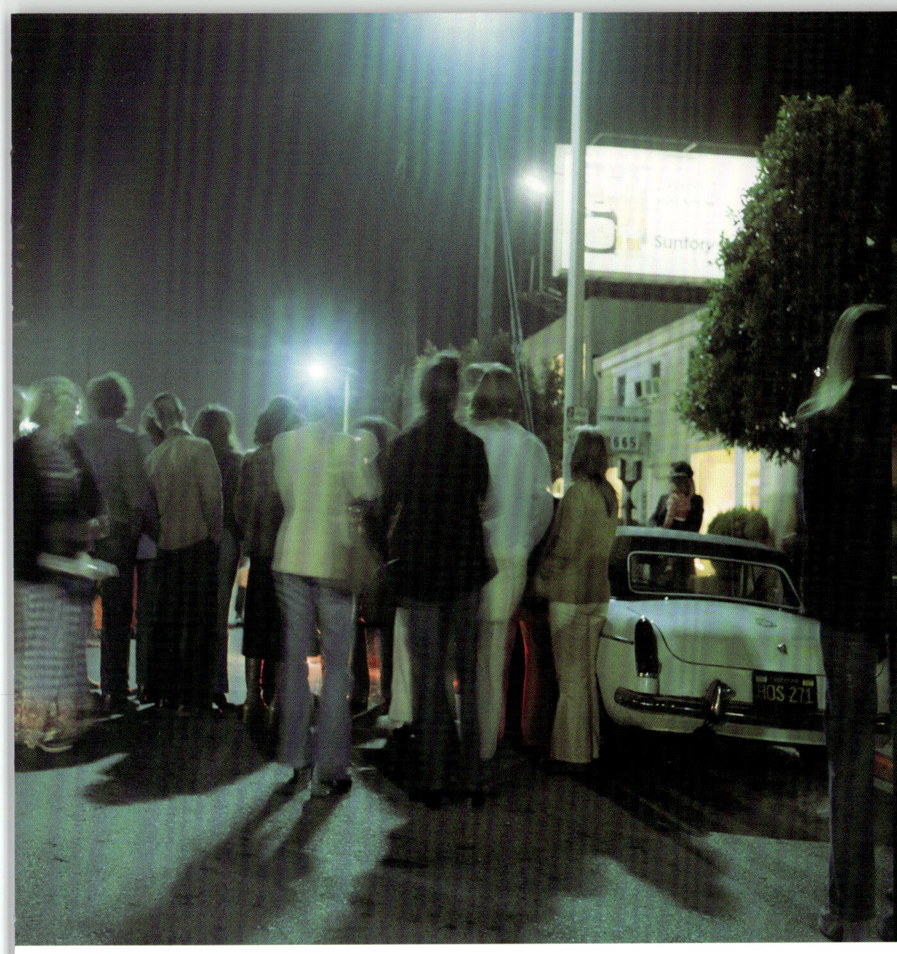
Suntory
665
HOS 271

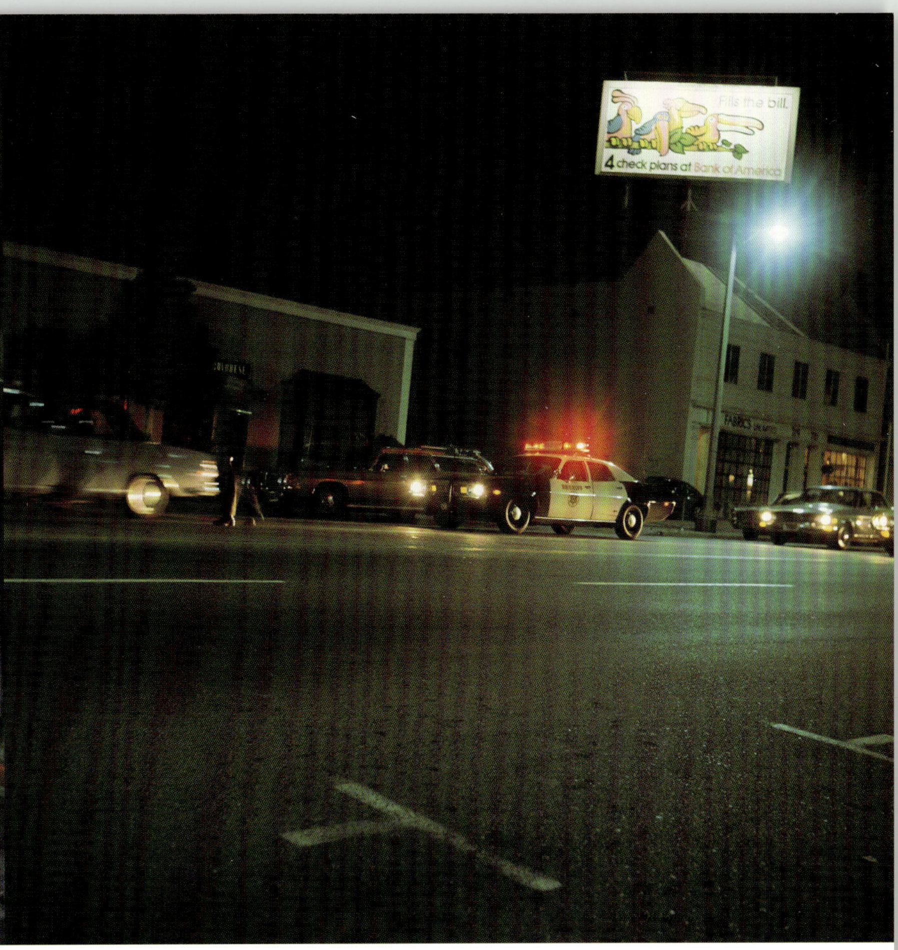
Fills the bill.
4 check plans at Bank of America

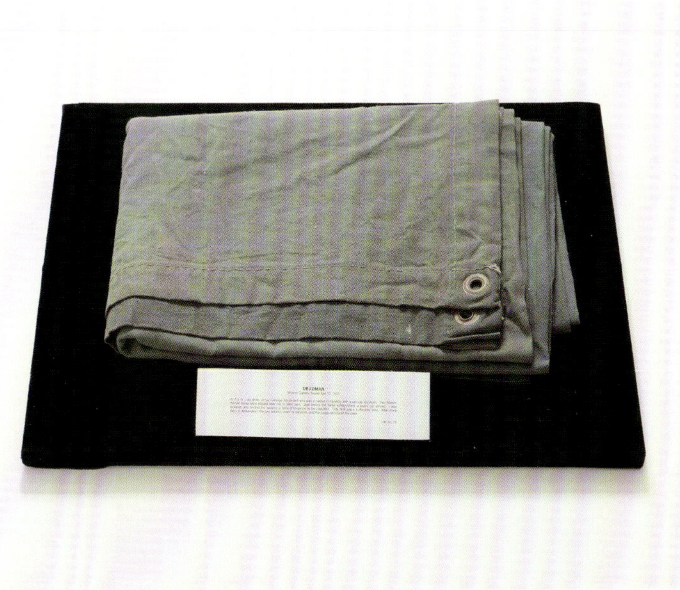

B.C. Mexico 1973

Newspace, Newport Beach, California, USA;
May 25–June 10, 1973

I was dropped off in San Felipe, Mexico on the Sea of Cortez. In a small canvas kayak I paddled southward to a remote beach, carrying some water with me. I survived there for 11 days; the average daily temperature was 120 degrees. On June 7, I paddled back to San Felipe and was driven to Los Angeles. The piece was announced as a show by Newspace and during my stay in Mexico a notice in the gallery informed visitors of my absence. On June 10 at Newspace, I showed a short movie of my departure and read a diary I had kept.

RELIC: Diary, seashell, stone

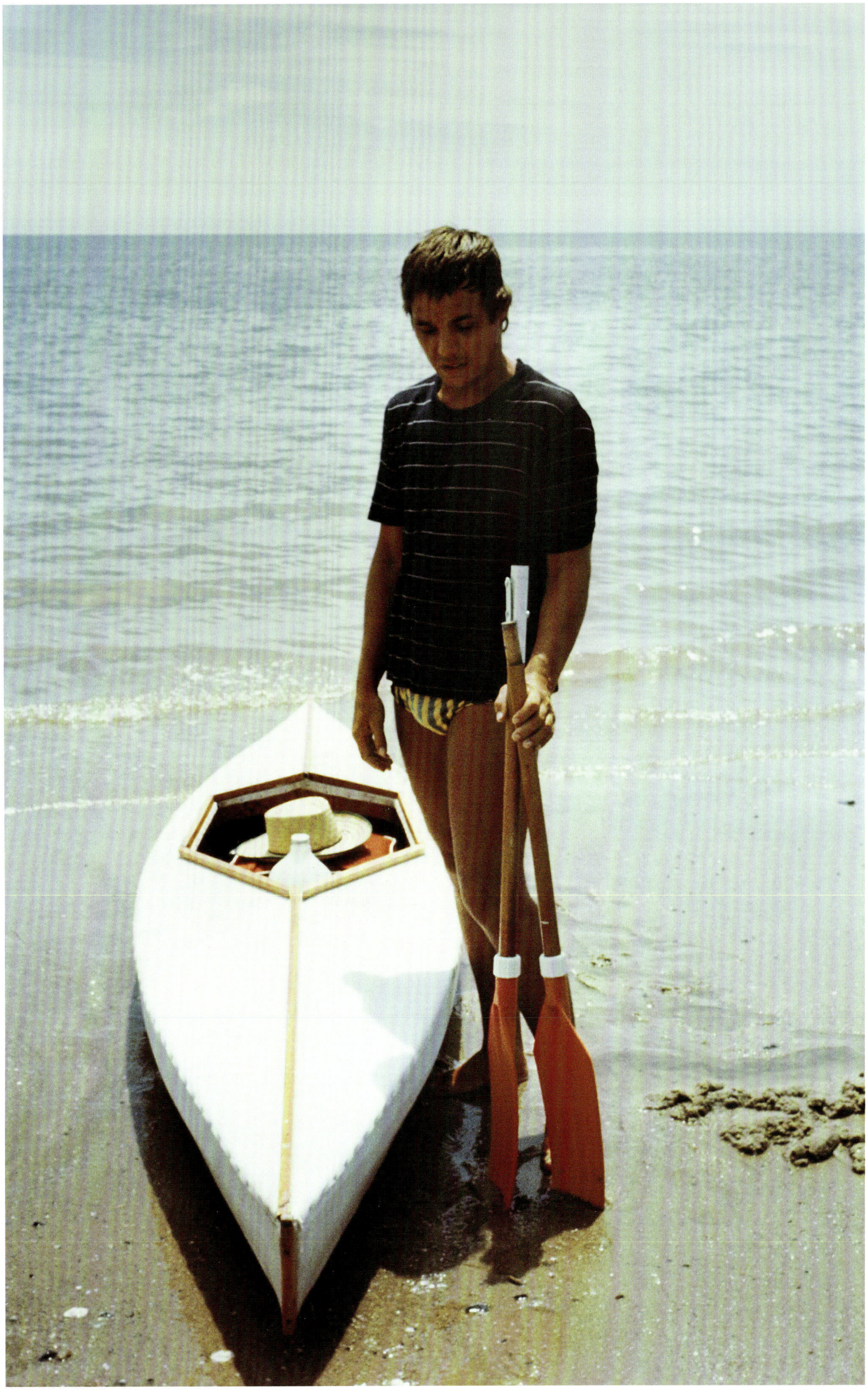

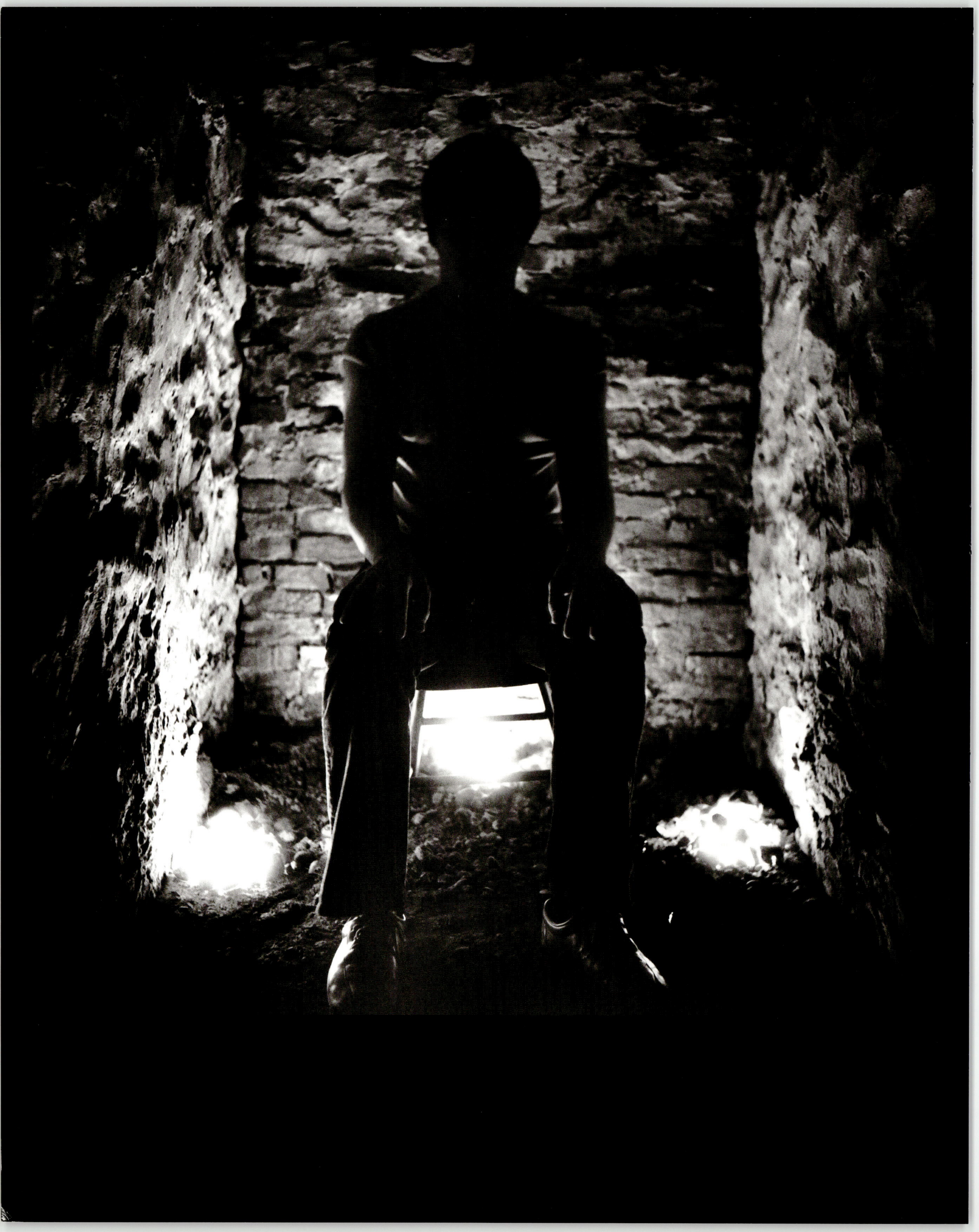

The Visitation 1974

Hamilton College, Hamilton,
New York, USA; November 9, 1974

The opening of 'California Climate', a show of painting and sculpture by young California artists, took place on Saturday evening. An unexpected crowd of 300 jammed the Art Center, an old house with many small rooms. I chose a very large room in the basement for my performance. The space had a low ceiling, a dirt floor and contained a massive stone fireplace support. One side of this huge block opened to form a niche. I was seated in the niche facing the opening with glowing coals around my chair. About a foot away an empty chair faced me. The room was black except for a small ray of light leading toward the niche from the next room in the basement. People who wanted to see the piece had to ask Michael Shapiro, the organizer of the show. He escorted each person, one at a time, to a locked door and through the lighted room of the basement, leaving them at the entrance to the large dark space and returning to the party upstairs. Each person was left to discover my presence and accept the invitation of the empty chair. Because each person spent about a half hour with me, only 15 people were able to participate in the piece. Although there was no indication by me that they should not discuss the piece, the participants refused to disclose their experiences to those waiting outside.

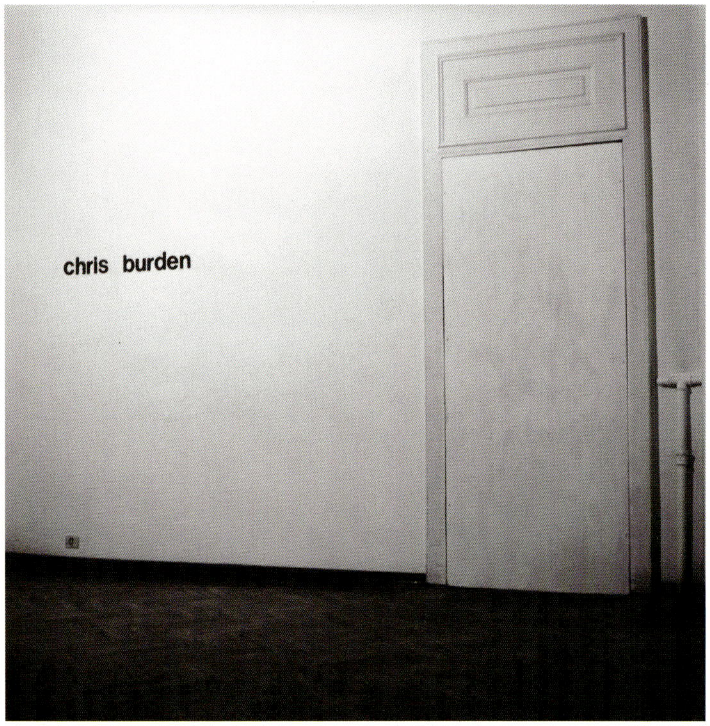

La Chiaraficazione 1975

Galleria Alessandra Castelli,
Milan, Italy; May 5, 1975

The Castelli Gallery consists of a series of rooms, all of different sizes and configurations. One room was unusual in that it had only one small entrance and no windows. In this room, I placed 25 chairs in four rows in the traditional manner of theater seating. I waited until 11 people had entered the room and then sealed off the entrance from the inside with particle board. An assistant placed a second panel on the other side which he painted white to match the gallery walls. The majority of the audience, about 150 people, was locked out of the room and could only imagine what was happening within. Inside the room, I spoke to the 11 people in Italian and convinced them to stay in the room until someone broke in from the outside. I told them that they were the sculpture and the responsibility for the success of the piece rested with them. I had provided 12 bottles of mineral water, candles and a makeshift toilet. After we had been in the room about an hour and half, the audience in the main gallery removed the outer panel and smashed the inner panel to gain access to the room. The room was left untouched for the remainder of the show.

RELIC: Hammer

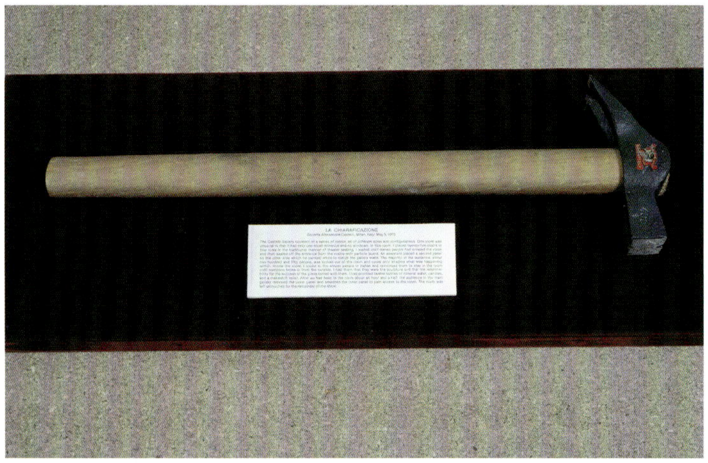

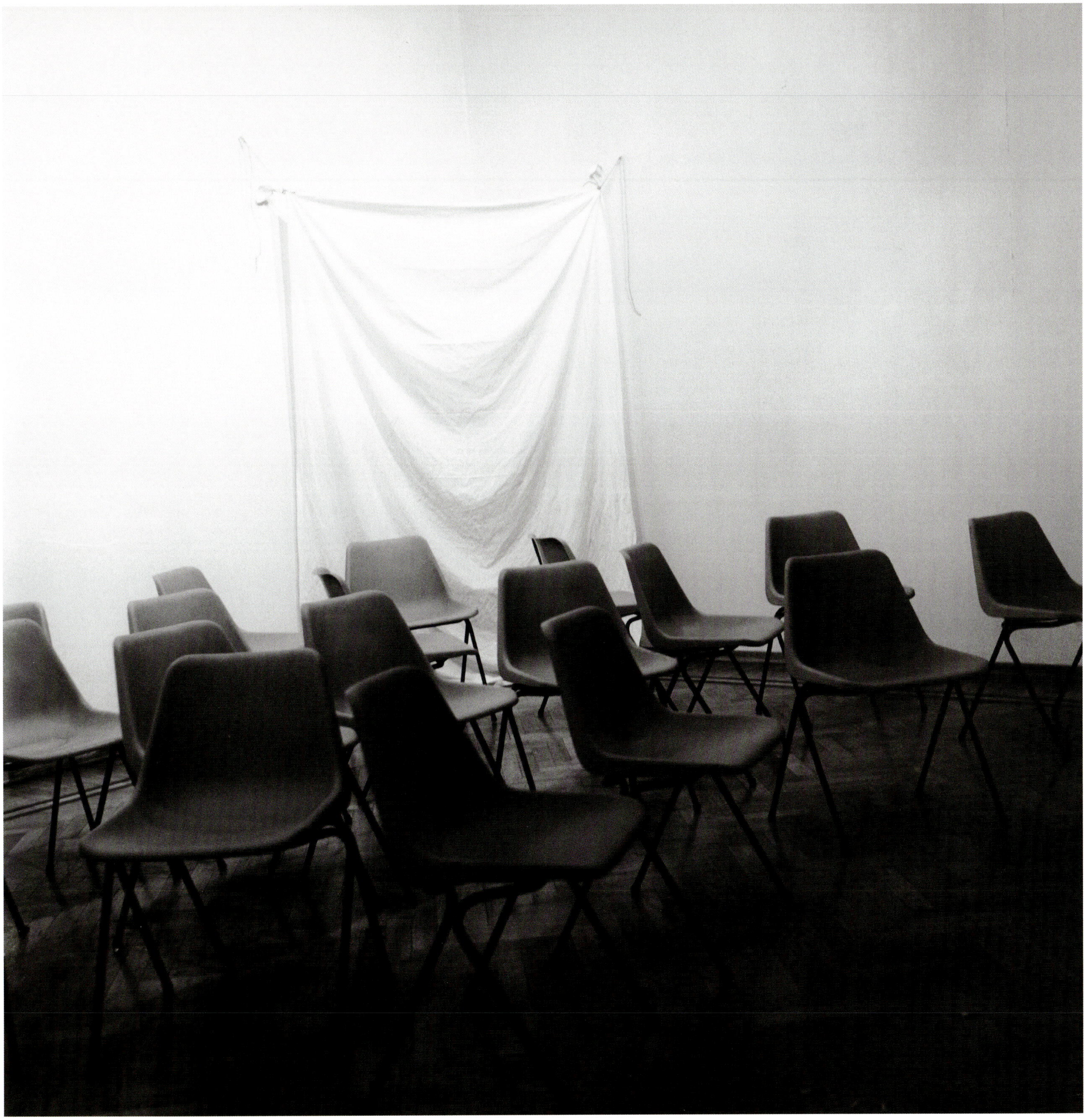

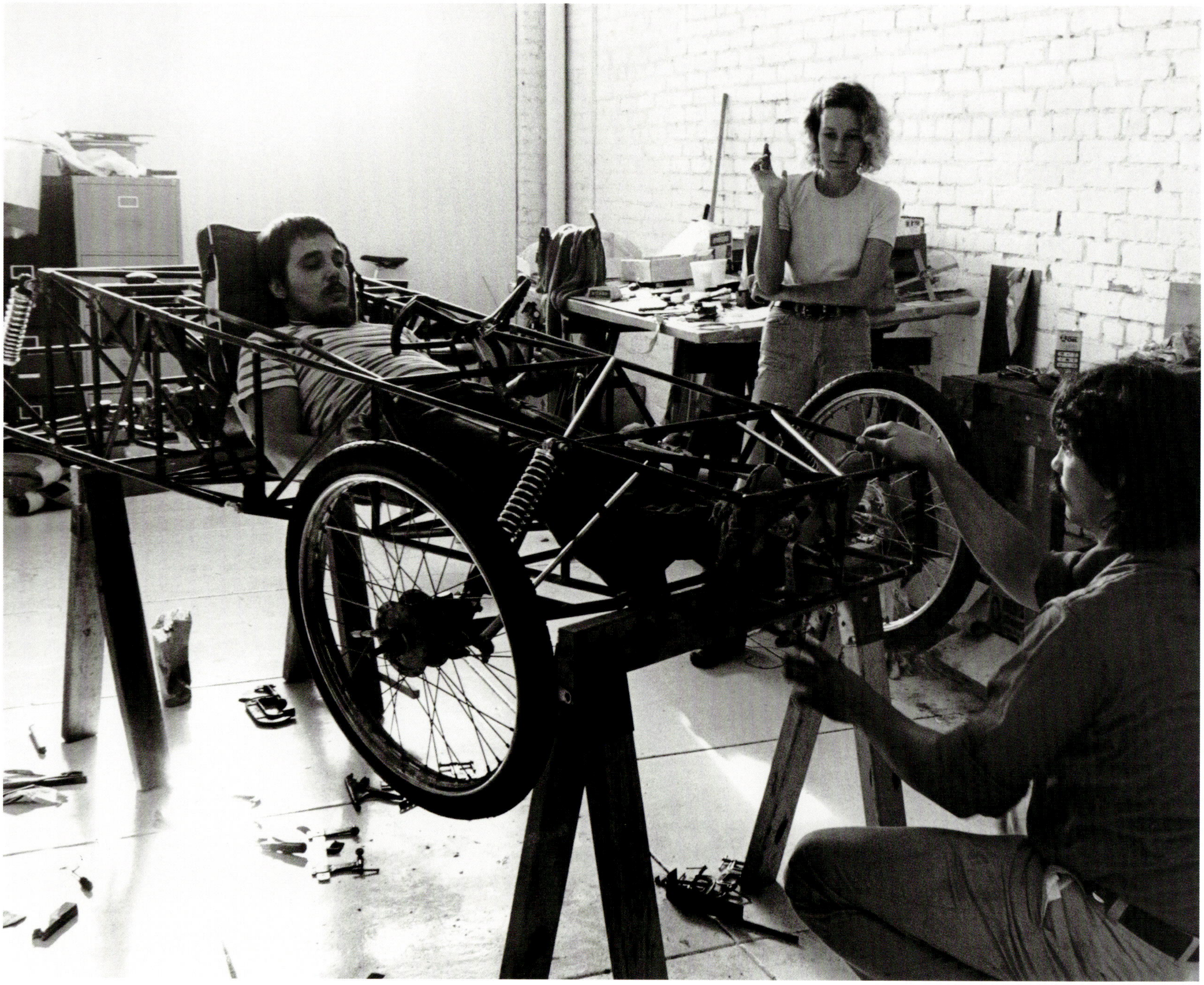

B-Car 1975

200-pound automobile
31 × 106 × 48 inches

During the two-month period between August 24 and October 16 1975, I conceived, designed and constructed a small one-passenger automobile. My goal was to design a fully operational four-wheeled vehicle, which would travel 100 miles per hour and achieve 100 miles per gallon. I conceived of this vehicle as extremely lightweight, streamlined and similar in structure to both a bicycle and an airplane.

▷
B-Car 1975
Ink on paper, 11½ × 8 inches
One of 121 drawings and related documents

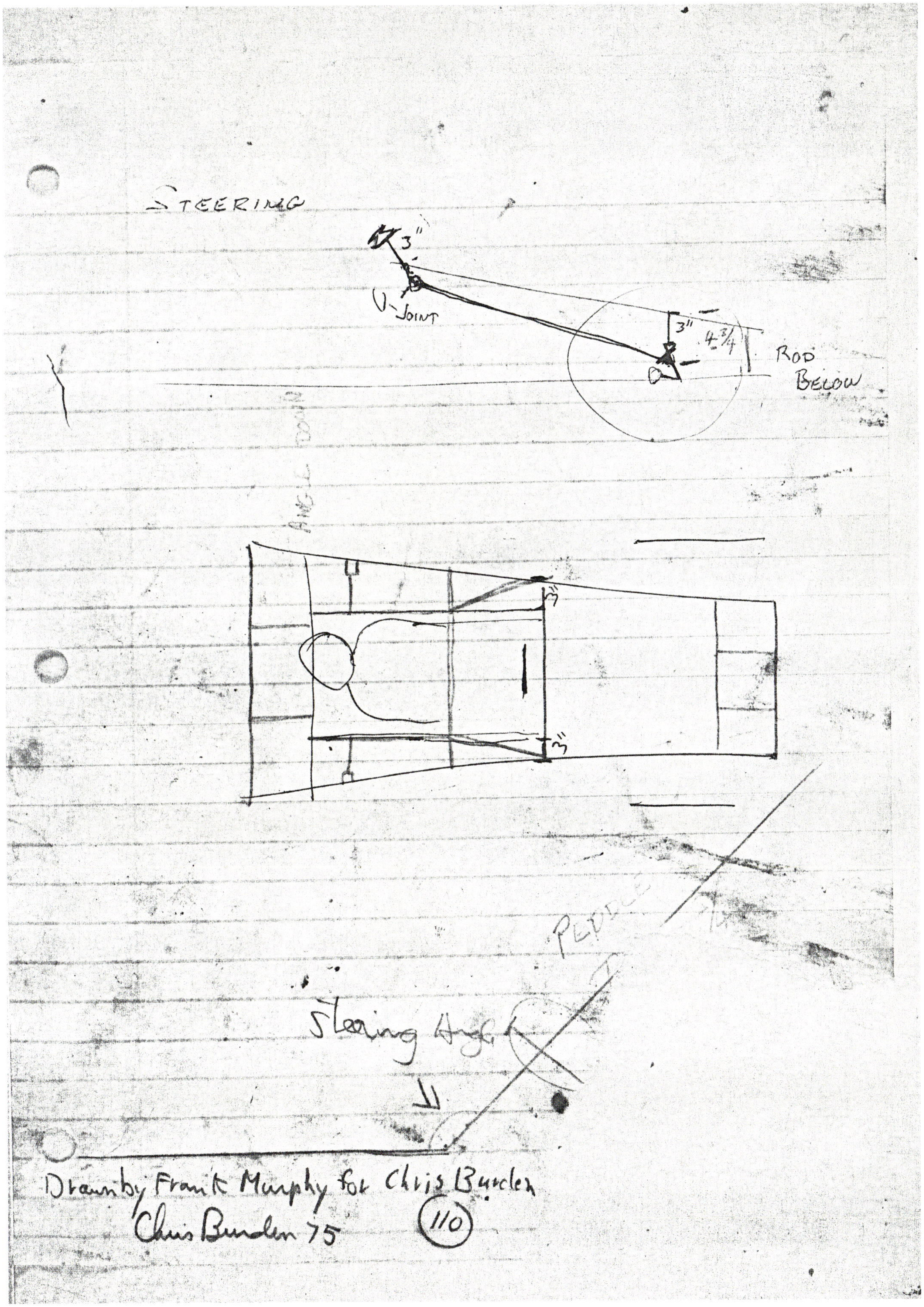
STEERING
3"
U-JOINT
3"
4 3/4
ROD BELOW
3"
3"
Steering Angle
Drawn by Frank Murphy for Chris Burden
Chris Burden 75
110

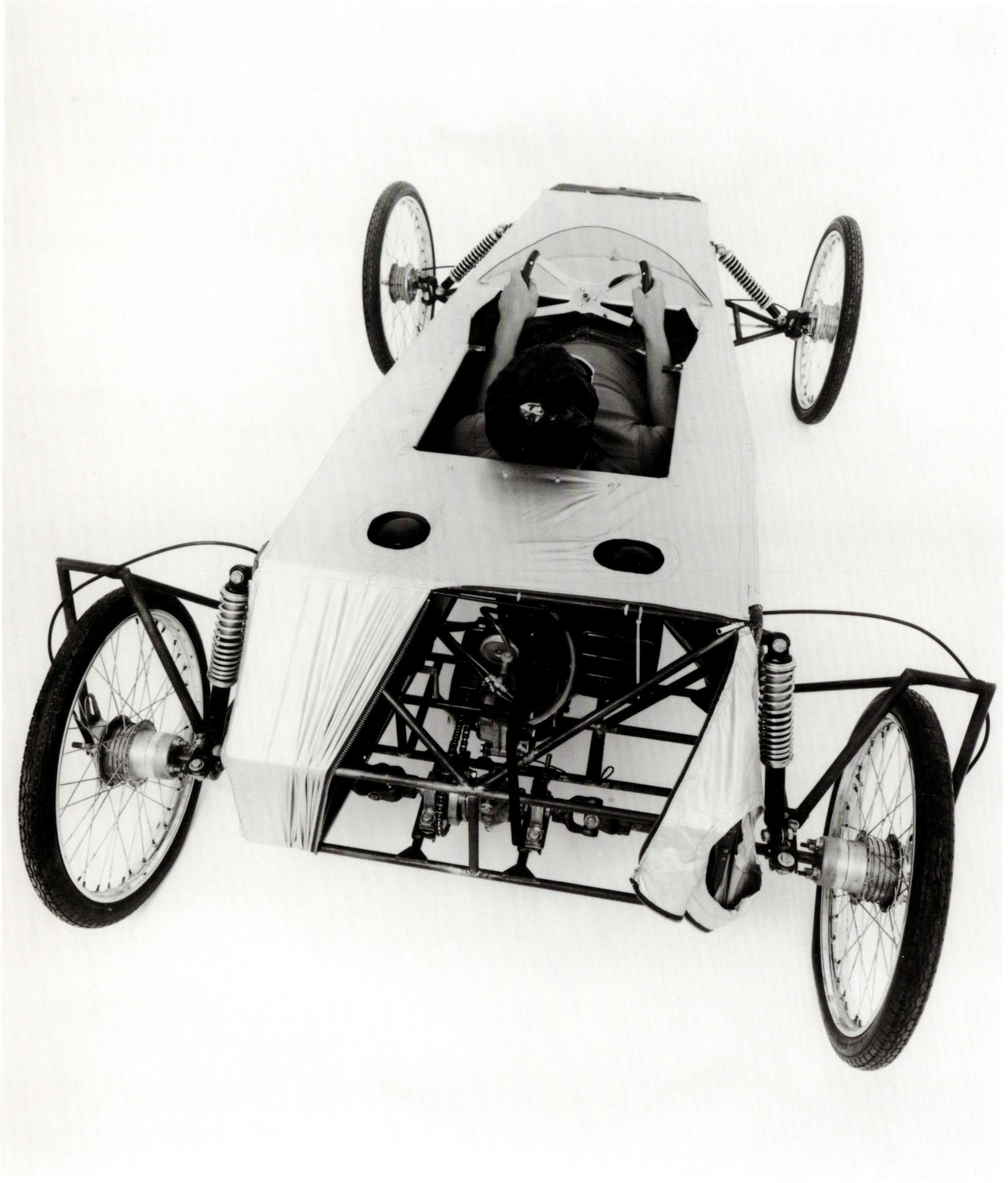

B-Car 1975

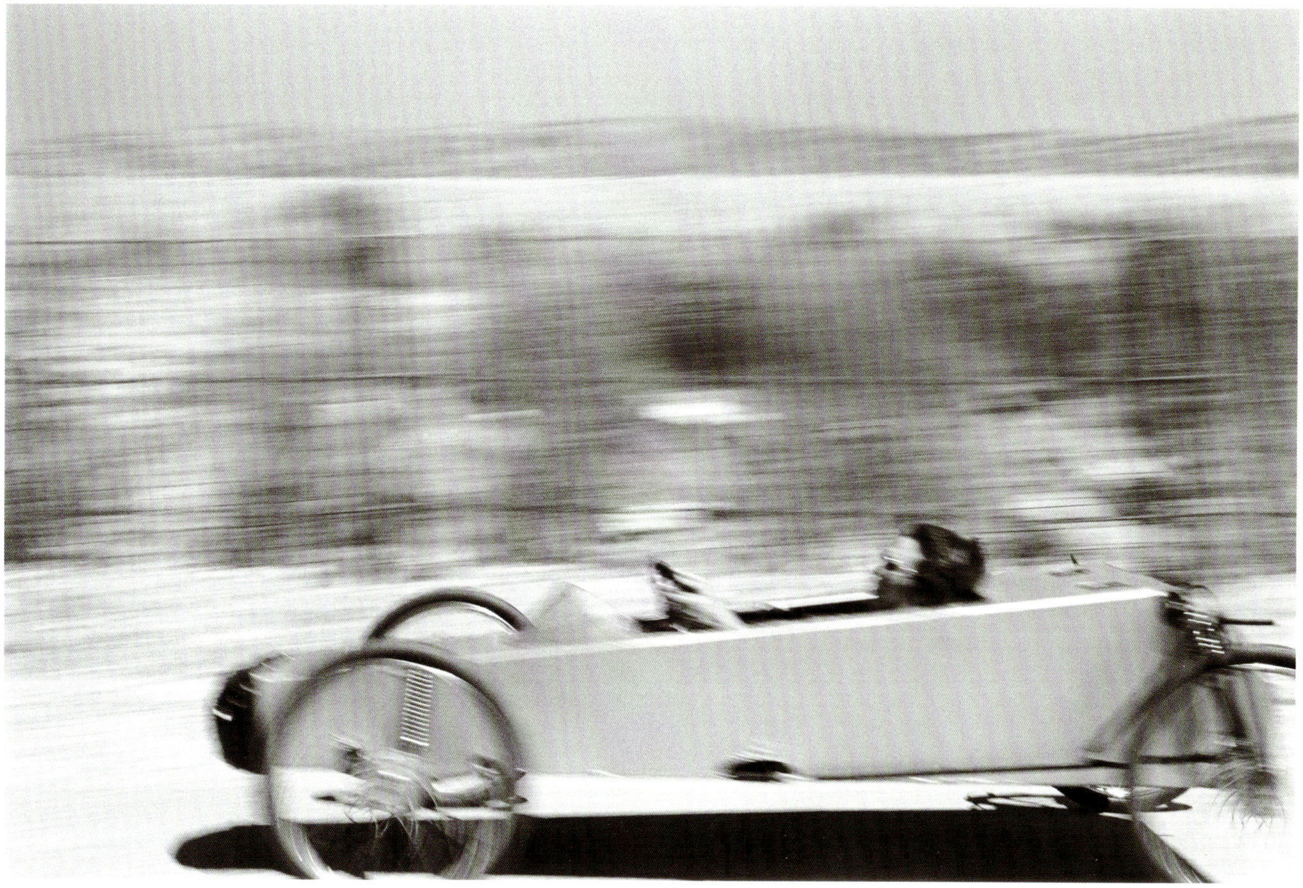

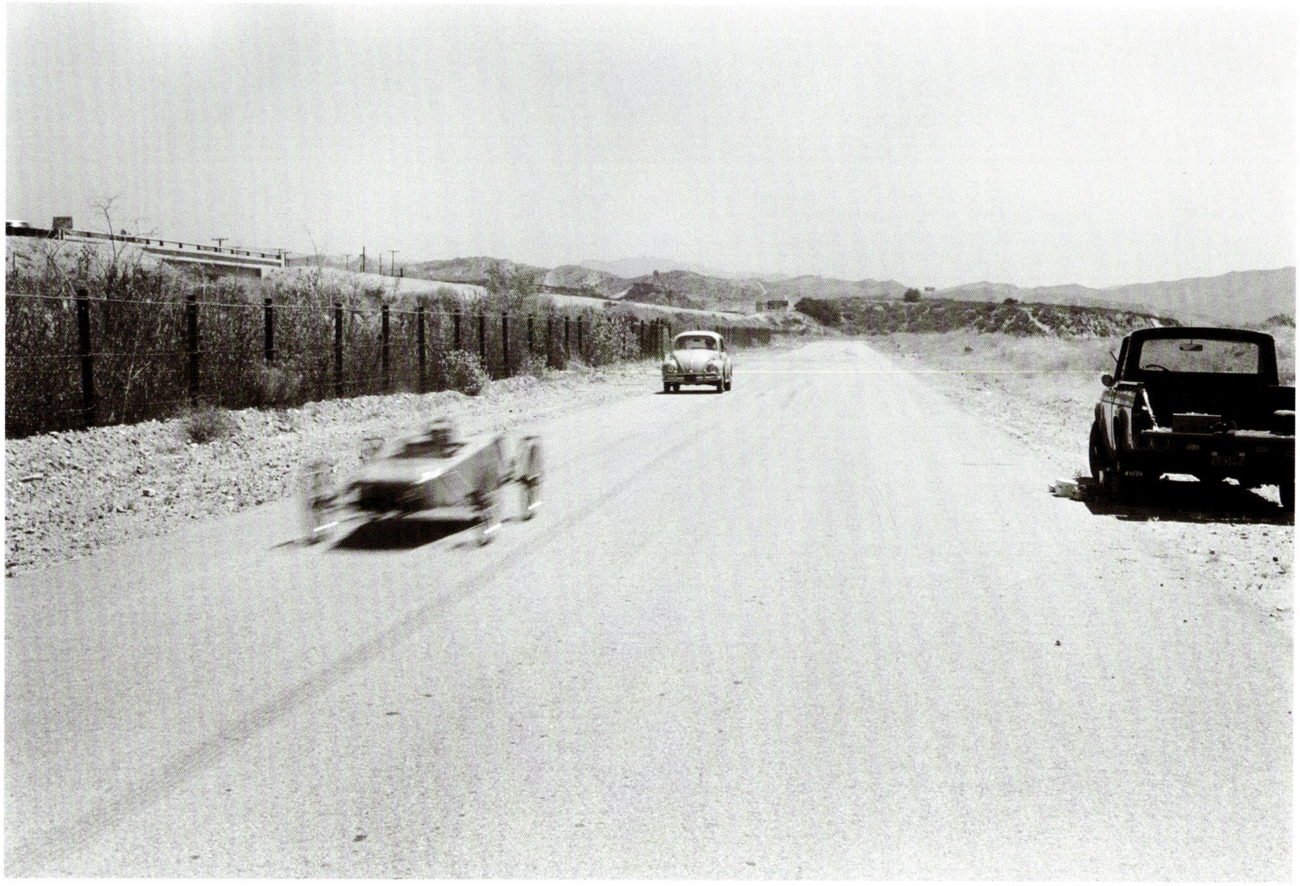

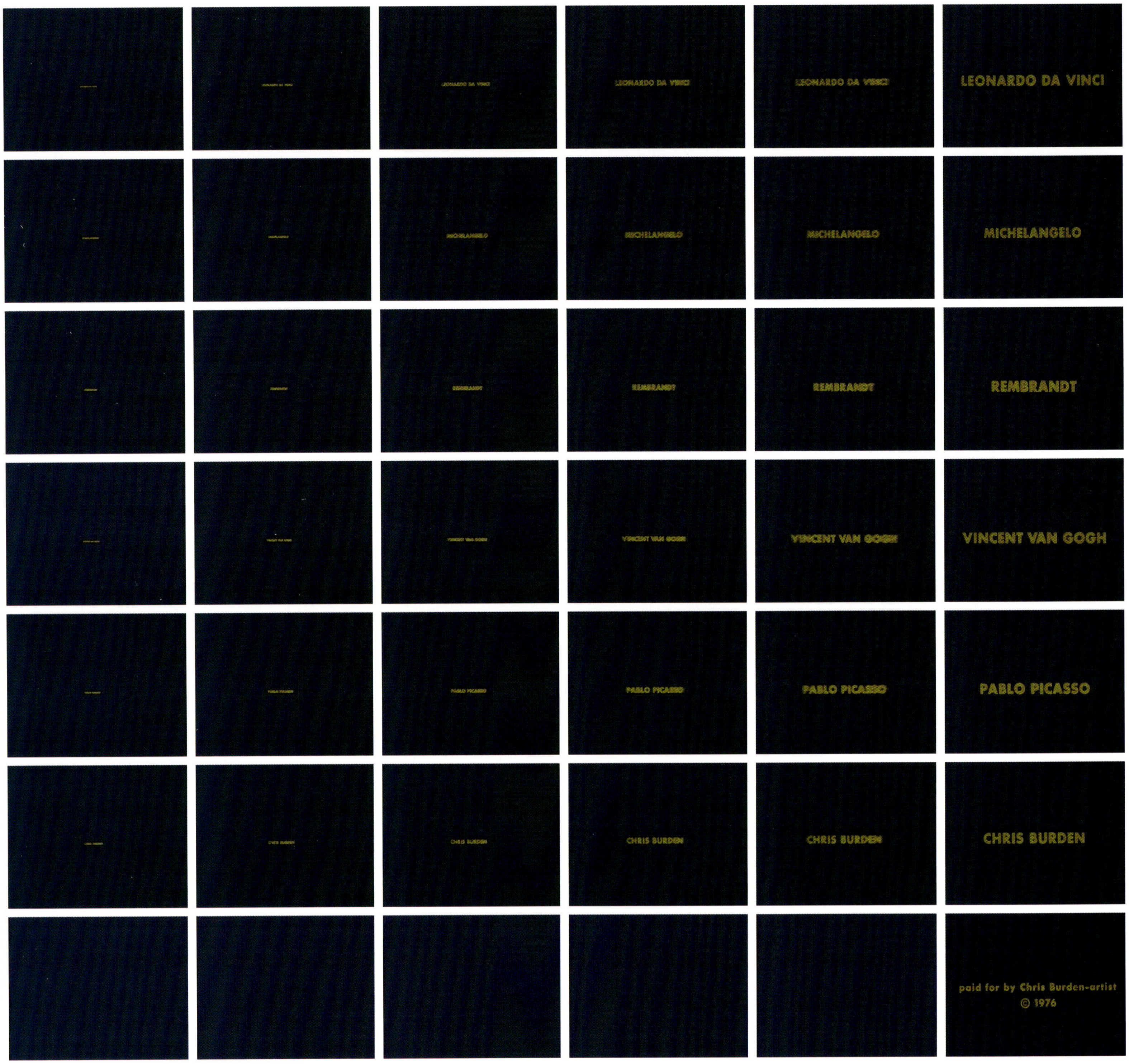
LEONARDO DA VINCI
MICHELANGELO
REMBRANDT
VINCENT VAN GOGH
PABLO PICASSO
CHRIS BURDEN
paid for by Chris Burden-artist
© 1976

Chris Burden Promo 1976

Channel 4 and Channel 9, New York,
USA; May 1–21, 1976
Channel 5, Channel 11 and Channel 13,
Los Angeles, California, USA;
September 17–24, 1976

I purchased twenty-four 30-second commercial spots on two New York television channels, Channel 4 and Channel 9, and 21 spots on three Los Angeles channels, Channel 5, Channel 11 and Channel 13. My 'ad' consisted of a series of names: Leonardo da Vinci, Michelangelo, Rembrandt, Vincent van Gogh, Pablo Picasso, Chris Burden. The series was repeated twice and followed by the disclaimer 'paid for by Chris Burden – artist'. The names were written in bold graphics – yellow letters on a blue ground. The individual names zoomed forward, starting very small and increasing in size until they filled the entire screen. As the names became readable, I spoke them aloud. The first five names were chosen from the results of a nationwide survey which showed them to be the most well known artists to the general public.

Studio Tour 1976

Venice, California, USA: October 24, 1976

My small studio was one of the many artists' studios in Venice, California, that an art tour group of 45 people planned to visit on Sunday, October 24. When the group leader and the first ten or 15 people knocked on my door, I met them wearing a gray orderly's jacket and holding a roll of tickets. I politely informed them that in order to gain access to my studio they would each have to buy a one-dollar ticket. The group leader grumbled that he had not been informed of this and that everyone had already paid the college that had organized the tour 13 dollars. Thus, he successfully discouraged some of the people who were already reaching for their wallets. However, word filtered back to the remaining 30 people about the studio with the extra one-dollar charge, and I was able to sell 12 tickets. Coming in small groups of two or three people, I gave them a thorough 20-minute tour of my studio – sleeping loft, moving mat couch, improvised shower, grocery list, file cabinet, desk, and an idea of how I spend my time in this small space.

RELIC: Roll of tickets

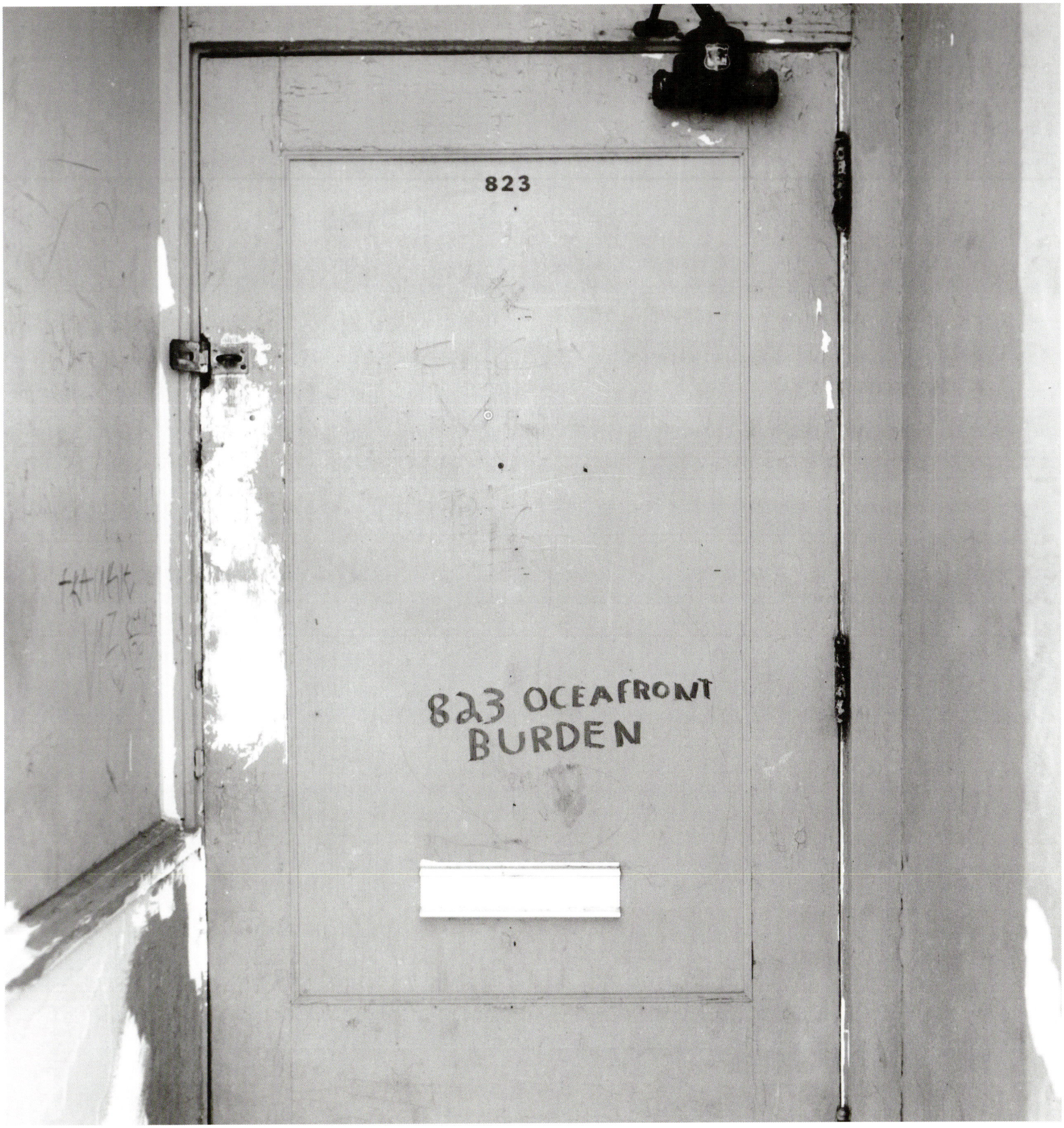
823
823 OCEAFRONT
BURDEN

C.B.T.V. (Chris Burden Television) 1977

Motor, lens, photoelectric cell,
two drums, two metal disks,
16 drawings in eight frames
Dimensions variable

The theory behind television, or the instantaneous transmission of a moving image from one place to another, was known for 60 years before it was physically possible to demonstrate it. Around 1915 John L. Baird, a Scottish inventor, succeeded in transmitting shadowy images from one room to another in his home.

Baird's primitive television was mechanical rather than electronic, and employed a rapidly revolving disk, perforated with a spiral of holes. Each tiny hole in the disk was able to scan a single line of the picture area. Behind the disk a condenser lens focused the light passing through the hole on to a single photoelectric cell. The photoelectric cell could turn on and off very rapidly corresponding to areas of light and dark. Thus, the image area was 'scanned', or broken down into a discrete number of on and off electronic impulses. The image could be reconstructed when the impulses were transmitted and decoded by a similar mechanism some distance away.

The system is extremely precise. The disk in the camera turns at 1,200 revolutions per minute or 20 times each second. There are 45 holes in the disk. Each hole passes the picture area in approximately one thousandth of a second. During this time (one thousandth of a second) the photo cell must turn on and off 50 times, in order that each scan line is broken down into a series of on-off signals. Thus, the photo cell turns on and off 50,000 times per second or 50kHz.

This on-off signal is sent down the wire or converted into a radio wave. The receiver is almost an exact copy of the camera. A very special light is turned on and off at 50kHz by the signal originating in the camera. If the disk in the receiver is turning at the exact same speed and the corresponding hole (i.e. hole #1 in the camera – hole #1 in the receiver) passes the screen area (the flashing neon plate in the receiver) at the exact same time as the camera, you are able to reconstruct the image originating in the camera.

I believe that as a technological invention this apparatus is of extreme significance, as it is a most successful solution to man's historic desire to 'see beyond' his immediate surroundings. As technology becomes more and more complex, fewer and fewer people have any understanding of how anything really works. By duplicating and demonstrating this complex piece of apparatus in its original 'simple' form, I hope to aid people to understand this complex instrument, which has made instant visual communication possible.

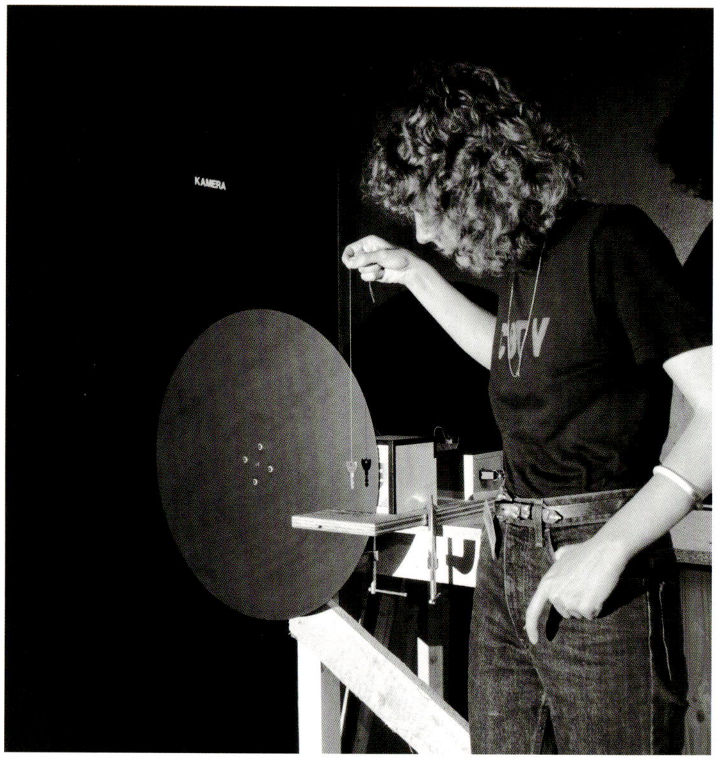

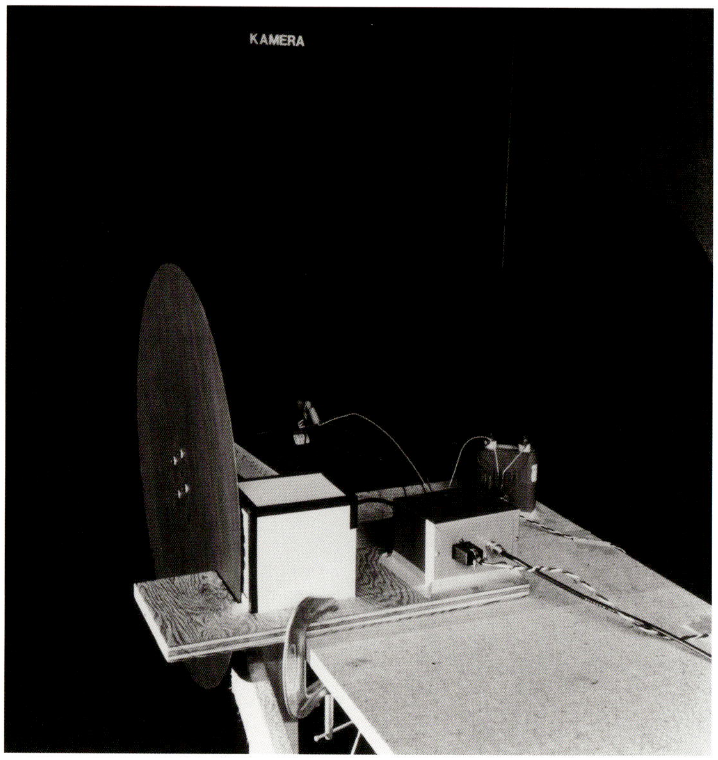

Camera

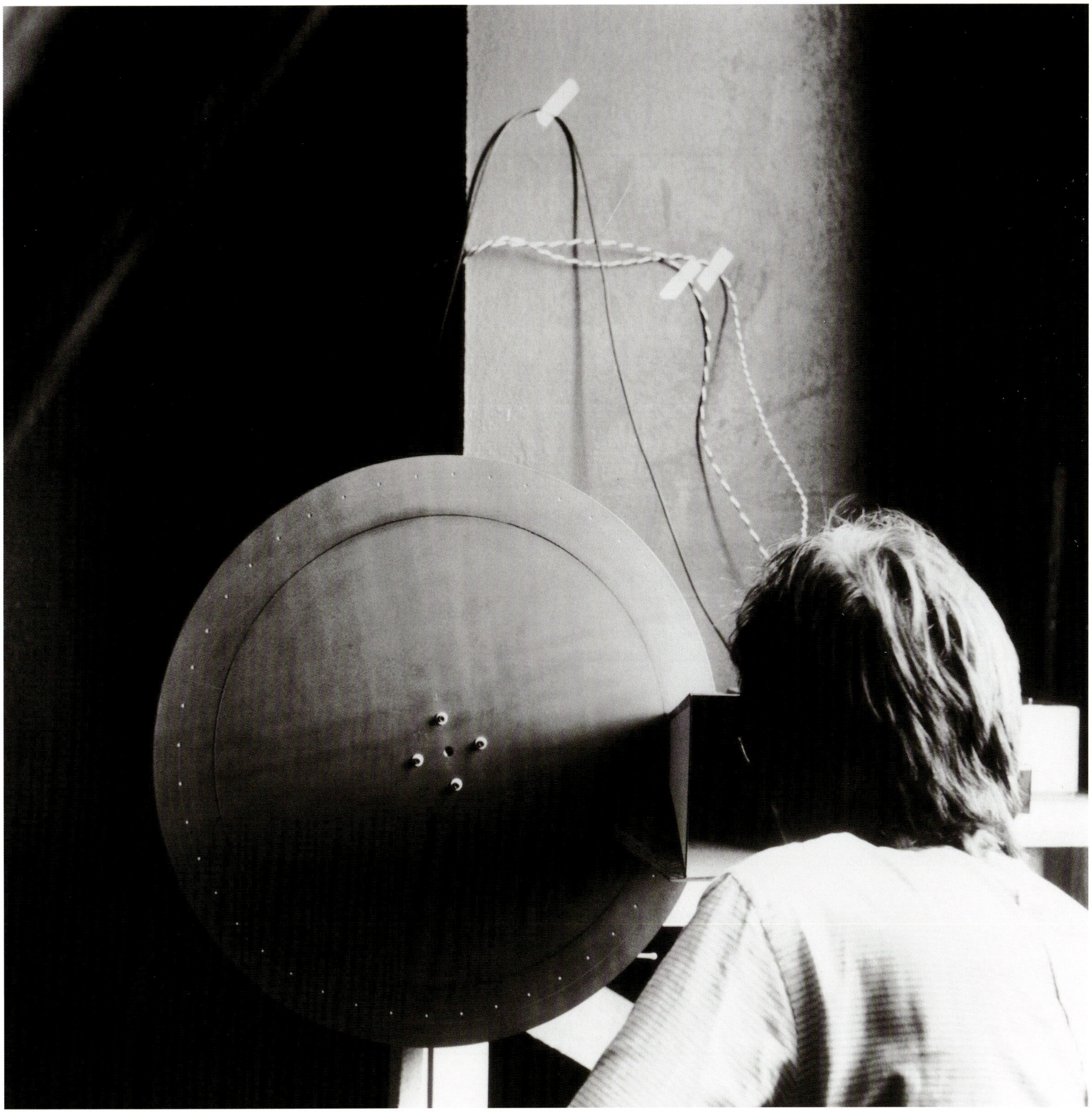

Receiver

The Curse of BIG JOB 1977

Venice, California, USA;
December 14, 1977–June 22, 1978

In an extreme state of anger and frustration at what I perceived to be the art world's inability to comprehend my two technological projects, B-Car *and* C.B.T.V.*, and having just suffered the loss of my girlfriend Alexis Smith, I purchased an antique 1952 Ford 'rig' (a tractor/trailer combination weighing 16,000 pounds empty). In large bold letters the words 'BIG JOB' were stamped on the chrome strips attached to either side of the truck's hood. The 35-foot black bat wing spray painted on either side of the trailer and the bent step bumper marking where a man had killed himself by ramming the back of the trailer in a small foreign car imbued BIG JOB with a sense of power and evil which I found irresistible. Using all the money I had, plus borrowing a thousand more, I paid the owner Jim Quaintance $3,000 in cash.*

With this huge truck I envisioned an almost endless series of projects that would free me from being an artist. My first plan was that I would drive to shopping centers with the B-Car *and the* C.B.T.V. *in the trailer and display them to members of the public for a nominal fee, much in the manner of an old fashioned road show. Another plan was that I would install a satellite receiving dish and transmitter, making the truck a rolling communication command post. I fantasized that BIG JOB would become the world's first mobile car factory: I would pull into a small Mexican village and produce the type of vehicle best suited for their specific local needs. I envisioned huge profits hauling antiques from New England, in a business partnership with my mother, and selling them to Hollywood decorators. Finally I planned I would take*

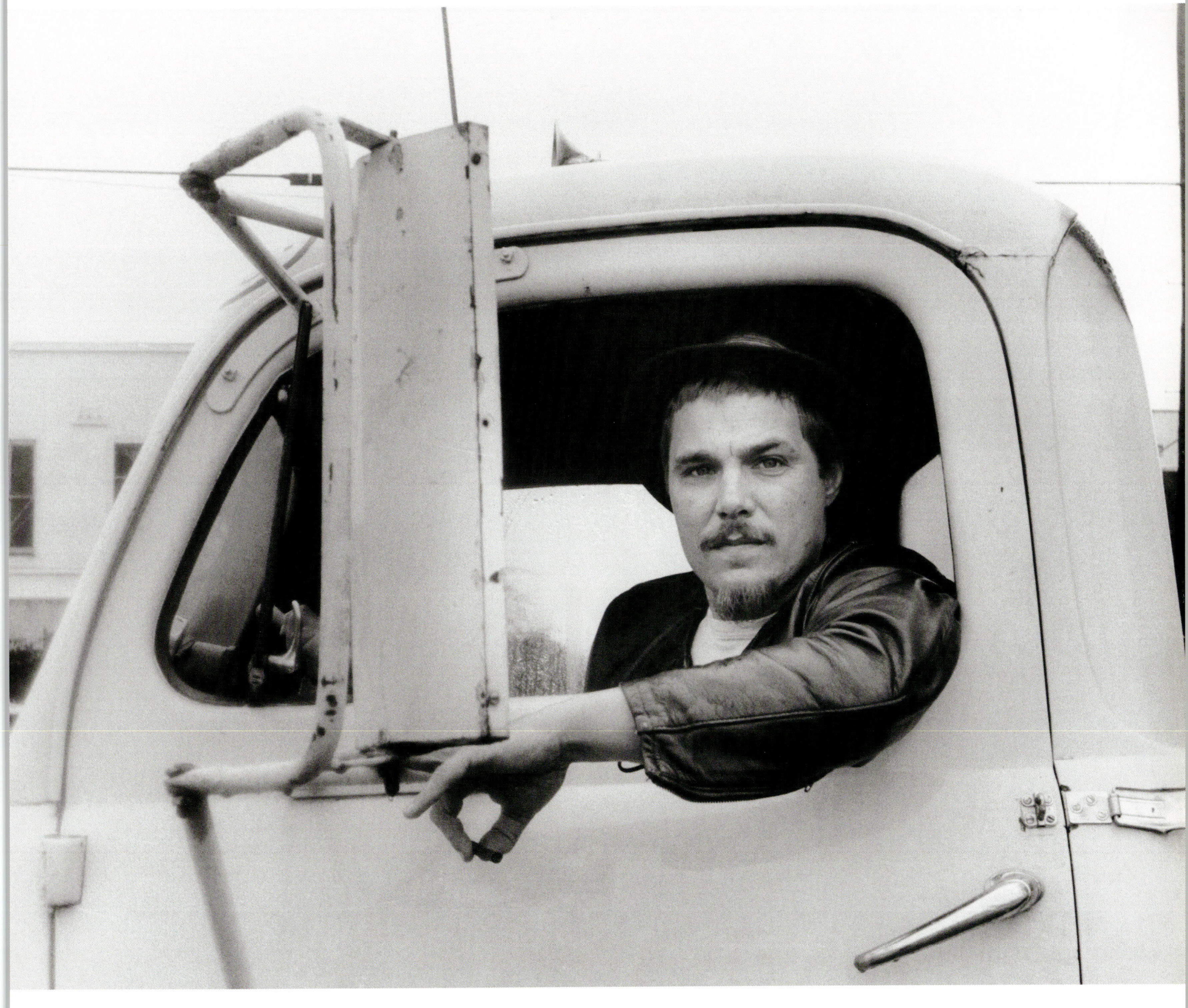

the truck to South America and that from inside the moving trailer using a catapult ramp I would launch a small airplane that would fly ahead and attack each new border station thereby expediting my exit or entry across each international border.

In fact, the truck was an obsolete wreck, barely able to drive around the block. The tires were bald, the brakes and connecting air hoses were in the last stages of disintegration. The electrical wiring hanging in a vast array of spaghetti-like confusion from under the dashboard would often start smoking whenever I turned it on. My energy for several months consisted of simply trying to keep the truck running and moving it from one side of the street to the other in order to keep it from getting parking tickets.

As I talked to more and more people familiar with the trucking business I realized that I did not possess, nor could I ever hope to obtain, the various state and federal permits necessary to operate the truck legally. In fact, merely driving the truck was an illegal act, since I did not possess a trucker's license.

At night I would have nightmares about driving the truck in small narrow Paris streets, wondering if the next old cobblestone bridge would collapse. I would dream that I had parked BIG JOB *on a steep hill and it would start to roll backwards. I would have to make an instantaneous choice between crashing into the parked cars behind me or rolling down the hill backwards and hoping that I could swivel the truck at the bottom into a side street.*

The truck had turned into a giant liability rather than the fantastic asset I first envisioned. I decided to sell BIG JOB*. This proved to be extremely difficult but after many weeks of advertising I was finally offered half the amount that I had paid just six months earlier. Realizing that the truck was truly worthless and that I might entirely lose all the money I had invested, I accepted this offer and sold the truck to Benny McBee. I rushed to the bank with the cash and to the Department of Motor Vehicles to notify them that the truck was no longer in my name.*

I thought that I had finally rid myself of BIG JOB*, but several weeks later I received a letter from the Los Angeles police notifying me that a warrant was about to be issued for me and that I was being sought for a hit and run accident. Apparently Benny McBee had been involved in an accident on the way home after purchasing the truck, had fled the scene, and had never transferred the truck's legal papers to his name. I appeared in person at the Los Angeles police station and talked to the detective in charge of the case. I explained to him that the truck no longer belonged to me and that I was not responsible for the accident. A few days later Benny McBee called to tell me that the serial numbers on the trailer did not match the numbers on the registration and that it appeared that the trailer might have been stolen. I assured him that I had not stolen* BIG JOB*, that I had simply purchased it from the former owner Jim Quaintance. I called Jim Quaintance and he assured me that it was simply a bureaucratic mistake, and that the numbers had been incorrectly transposed somewhere along the line.*

Several weeks later at 11:30 at night I received a phone call from an insurance investigator wanting to know the location of the truck so that they could assess an insurance claim that Jim Quaintance had lost $30,000 worth of trucking business because of the damage the truck had sustained when the small foreign car impaled itself on the rear step bumper. Benny McBee had still failed or been unable to register the truck in his name and the Department of Motor Vehicles still showed me as the legal owner. I explained to the insurance investigator that I sold the truck to Benny McBee several months earlier and that I had no idea of the whereabouts of the truck. The next morning the insurance investigator and an assistant came to investigate me. They asked me why I had bought the truck, was I in the trucking business, and how much I paid for it. Although I had done nothing wrong, I felt that I had become guilty by association and that BIG JOB *possessed a curse which I could not get rid of.*

About a month later Jim Hansen from the Highway Patrol Investigation Unit came to my studio. I was not in at the time, but he left me a card requesting that I contact him. With much apprehension I called him. To my surprise he seemed annoyed that he was ever assigned the case; the trailer as far as they could determine was not stolen. He asked me a few questions, seemed satisfied and told me that he considered the case closed.

RELIC: 24-inch pipe wrench

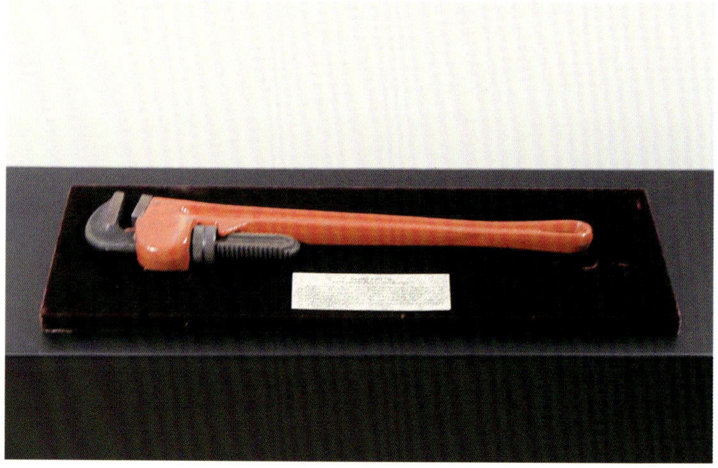

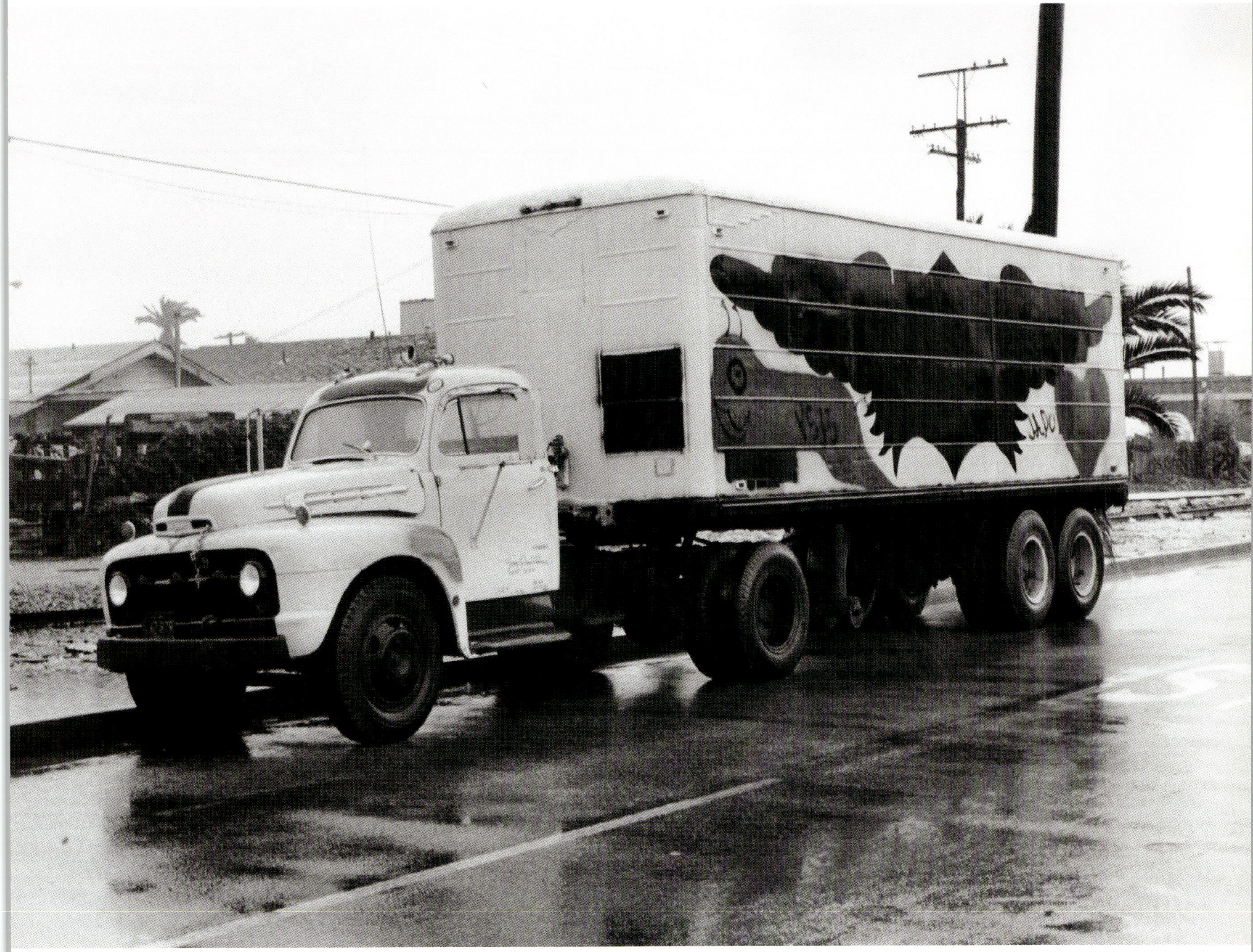

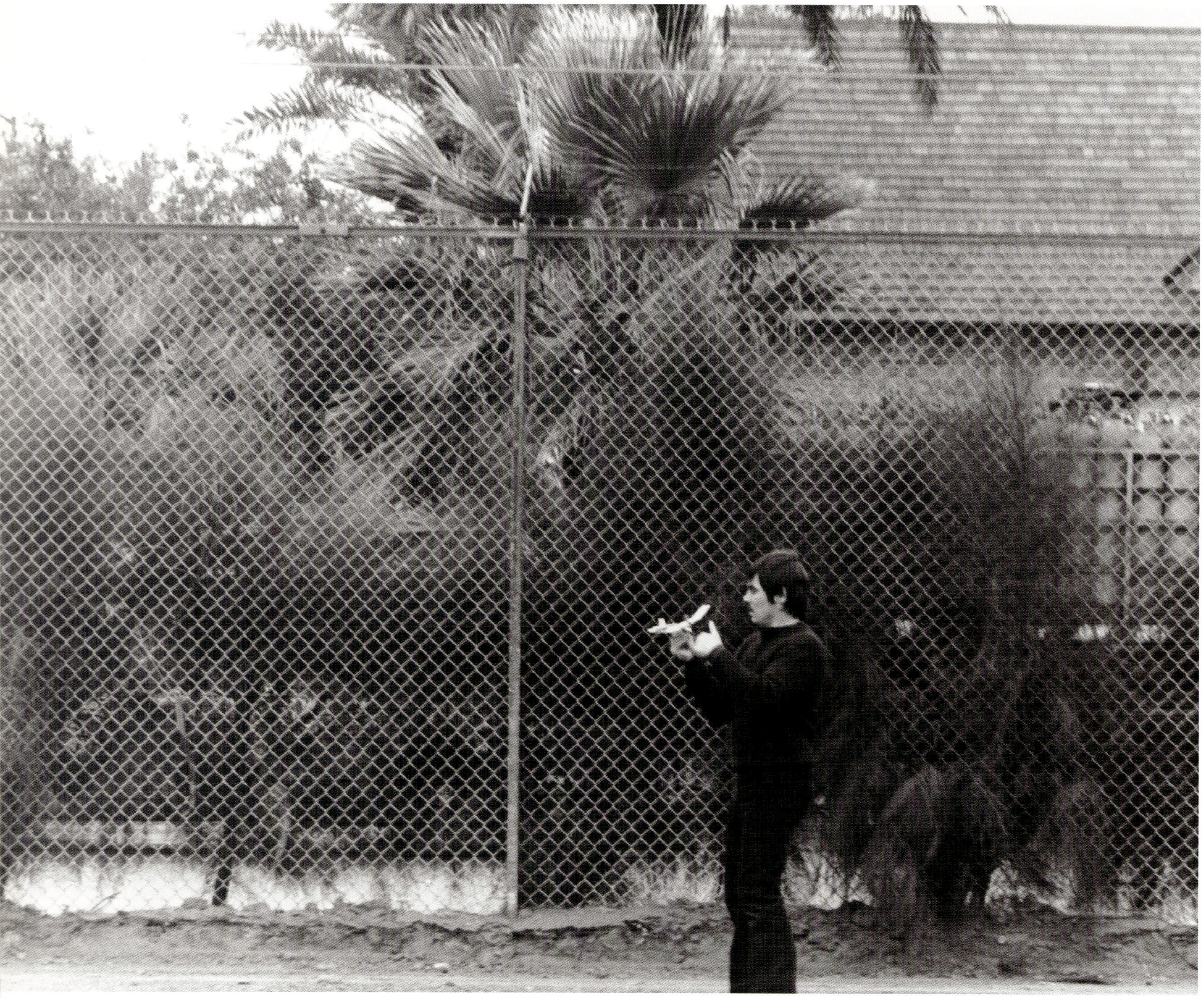

Coals to Newcastle 1978

Calexico, California, USA;
December 17, 1978

Calexico, California and Mexicali, Mexico are actually the same city separated by a tall steel and barbed wire fence demarcating the international border between the USA and Mexico. On the morning of December 17, standing on the American side of the border, I flew a small rubber band powered model airplane over the fence into Mexicali, Mexico. From each wing of the plane, like a miniature bomb, hung a cigarette of the finest seedless marijuana, 'sinsemilla', grown in California. The plane bore the following inscriptions: Hecho en USA (Made in USA), Fumenlos Muchachos (Smoke it Kids) and Topanga Typica (Typical Topanga).

RELIC: Two airplanes out of three

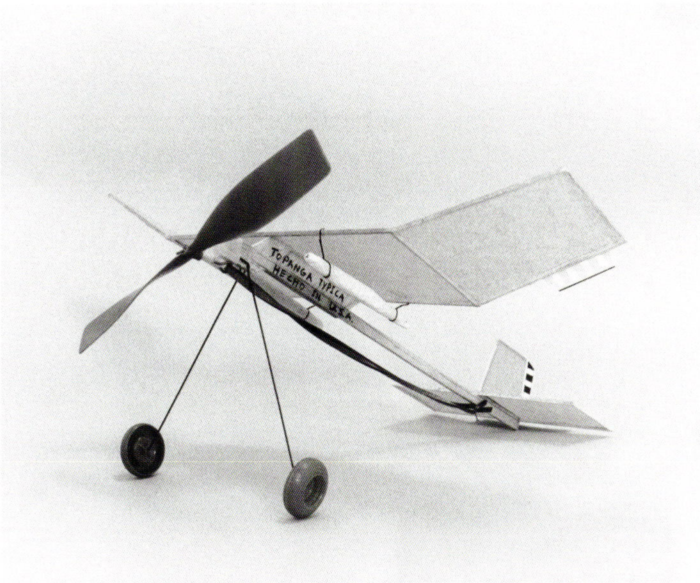

Honest Labor 1979

Vancouver, British Columbia, Canada;
March 26–March 30, 1979

I was invited to Vancouver for a week to be a visiting artist by the Emily Carr College of Art and Simon Fraser University. Rather than meet with students to present and discuss my past work in a teaching context, I requested that I be provided with a wheelbarrow, a shovel and pick axe. On the first day of my visit, I immediately began, in a vacant lot that had been provided for me, to dig a straight ditch about 2½ feet wide and 3 feet deep. Each following day students could find me digging from 9 am until 5 pm. I did not have a specific length or goal, except that I would be digging during the times of day that I had designated. Occasionally, someone would offer to dig for me, but after trying for a few minutes they would return the job to me.

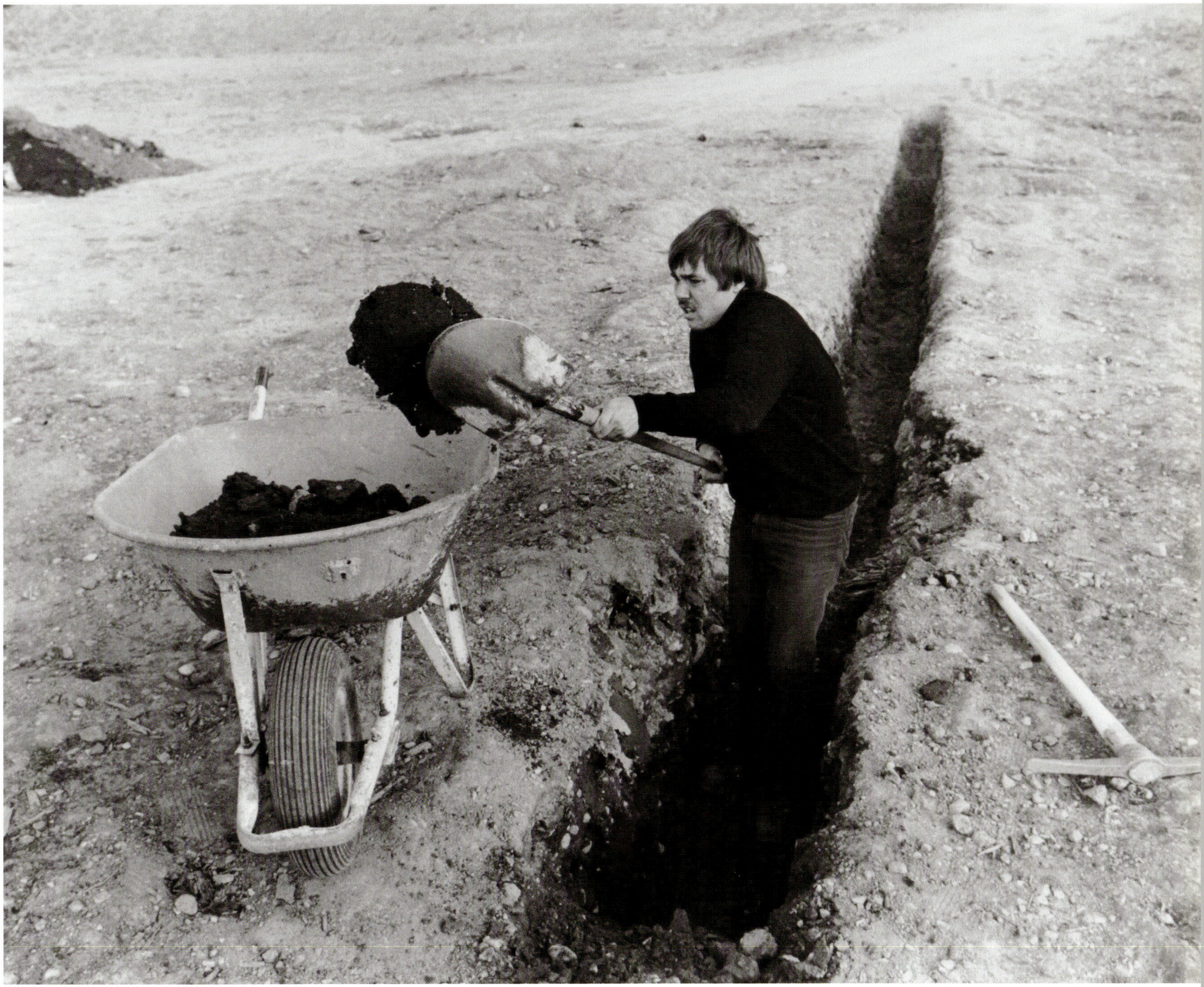

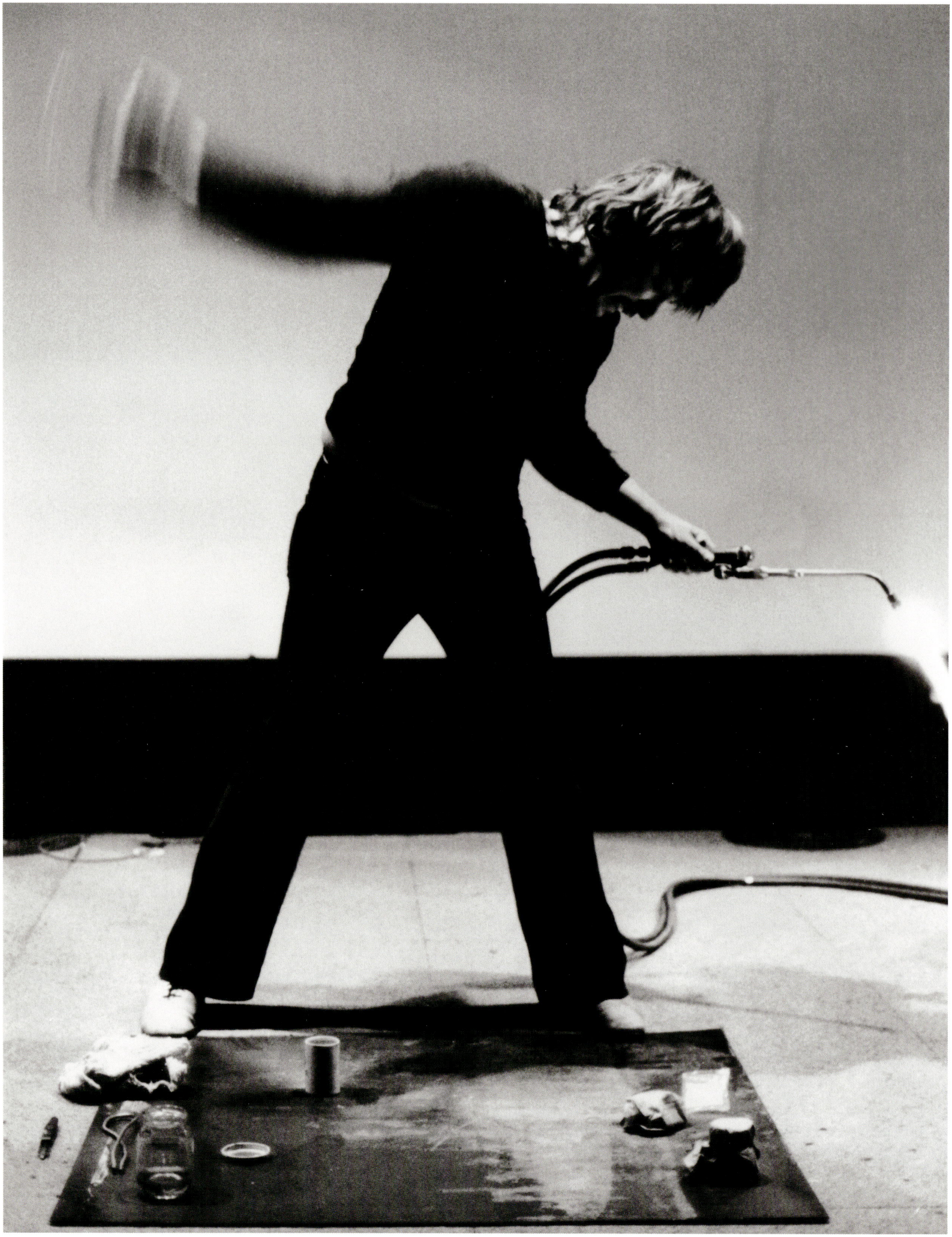

Napoleon d'Or 1981

Musée National d'Art Moderne,
Centre George Pompidou, Paris, France;
April 6, 1981

Napoleon d'Or *was a performance that I executed in Paris consisting of casting in gold a miniature Napoleon. The lost wax process used a plaster mold that I had prepared in England before my arrival in Paris. I chose the image of Napoleon because I feel that the French people regard the Napoleonic era as their most glorious hour. After the audience was assembled, the gold was placed on the top of the small plaster mold and heated to the melting point with a welder's torch. The mold was then swung vigorously in a circular pattern, forcing the molten gold into the mold. After several minutes the mold was broken open and the gold Napoleon was placed on a stand for viewing by the audience.*

RELIC: Gold figure on base

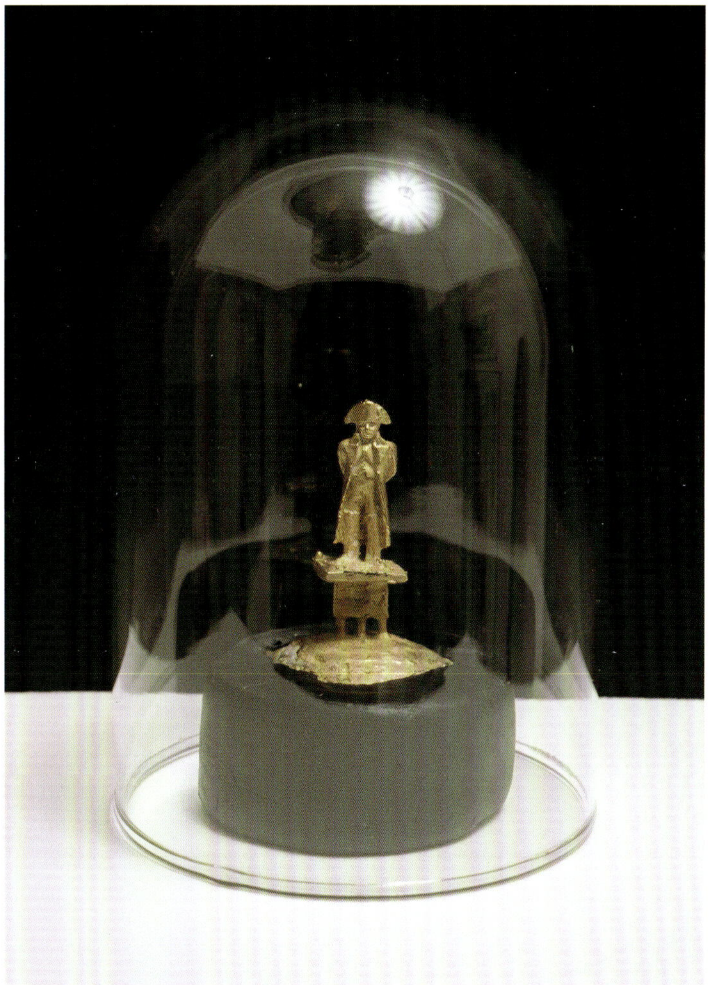

The Hard Push 1983

University of California, Los Angeles,
California, USA; May 25, 1983
114 × 48 inches

I constructed a large wooden wheel nine feet four inches in diameter out of plywood. At 12 noon I was tied into the center of the wheel at the bottom of Bruin Walk. Bruin Walk is the main pedestrian thoroughfare which goes up a steep hill for approximately 500 feet. I asked the gathered students to push me up the hill until I reached the top.

RELIC: Plywood wheel with attachment
points for hands and feet

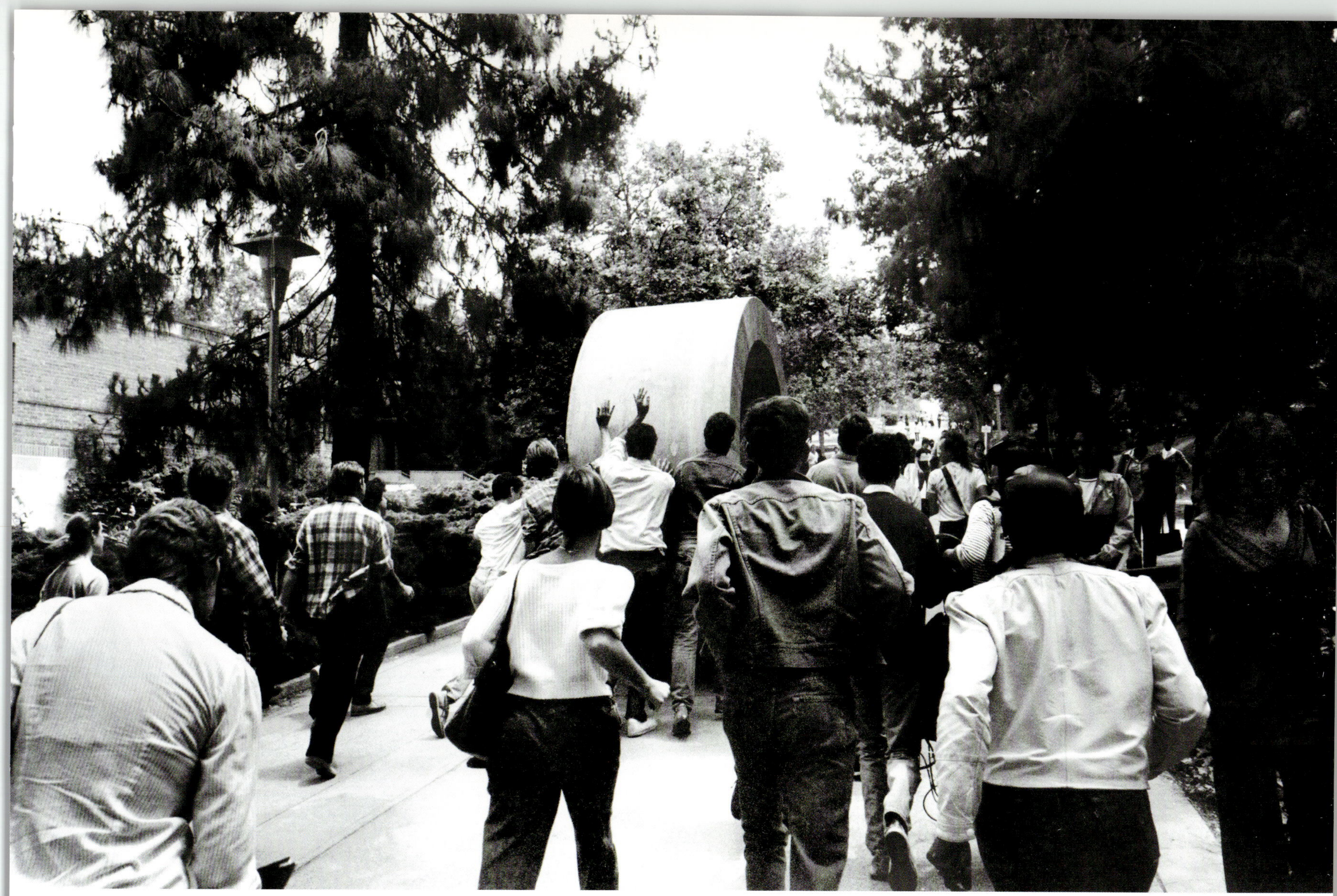

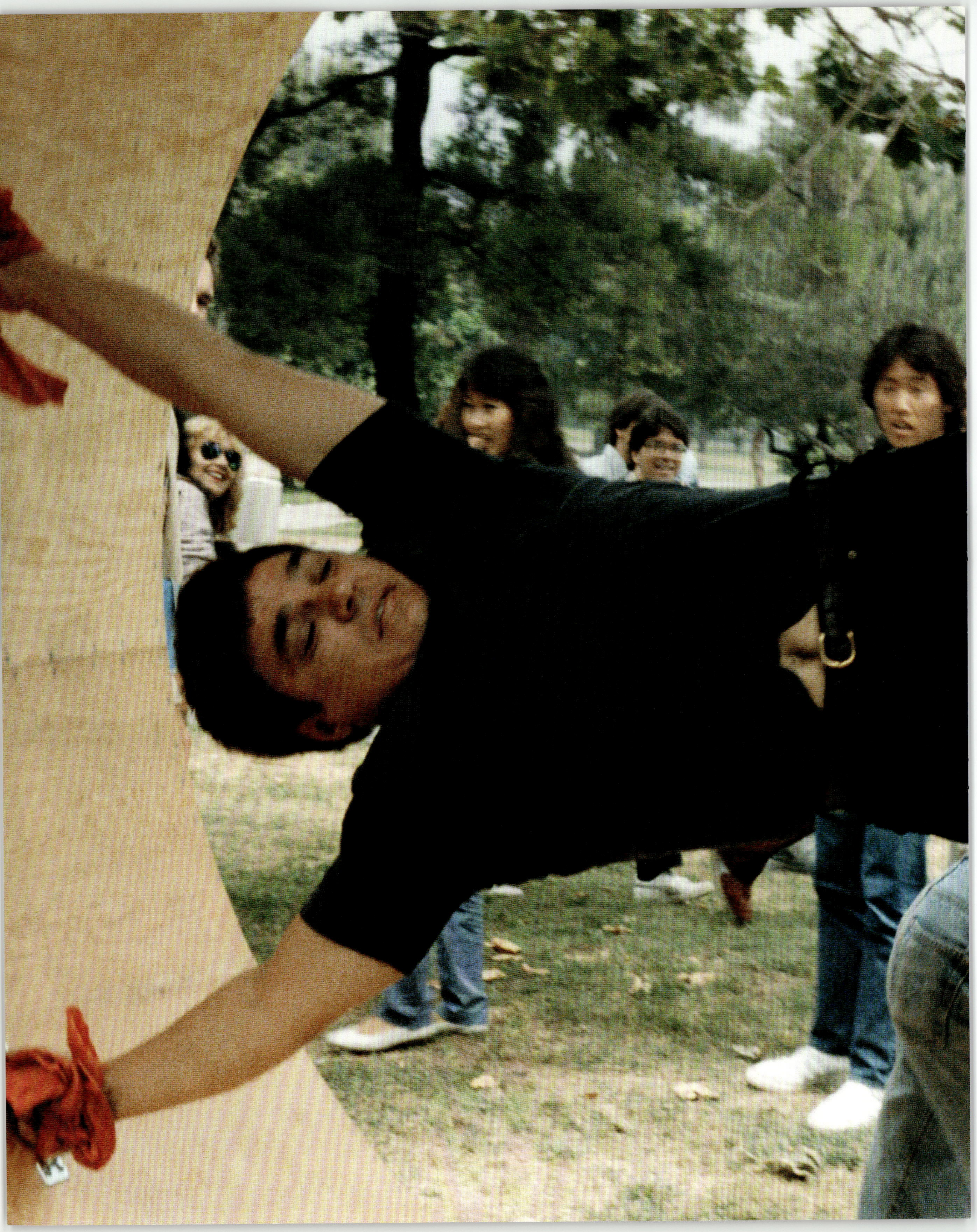

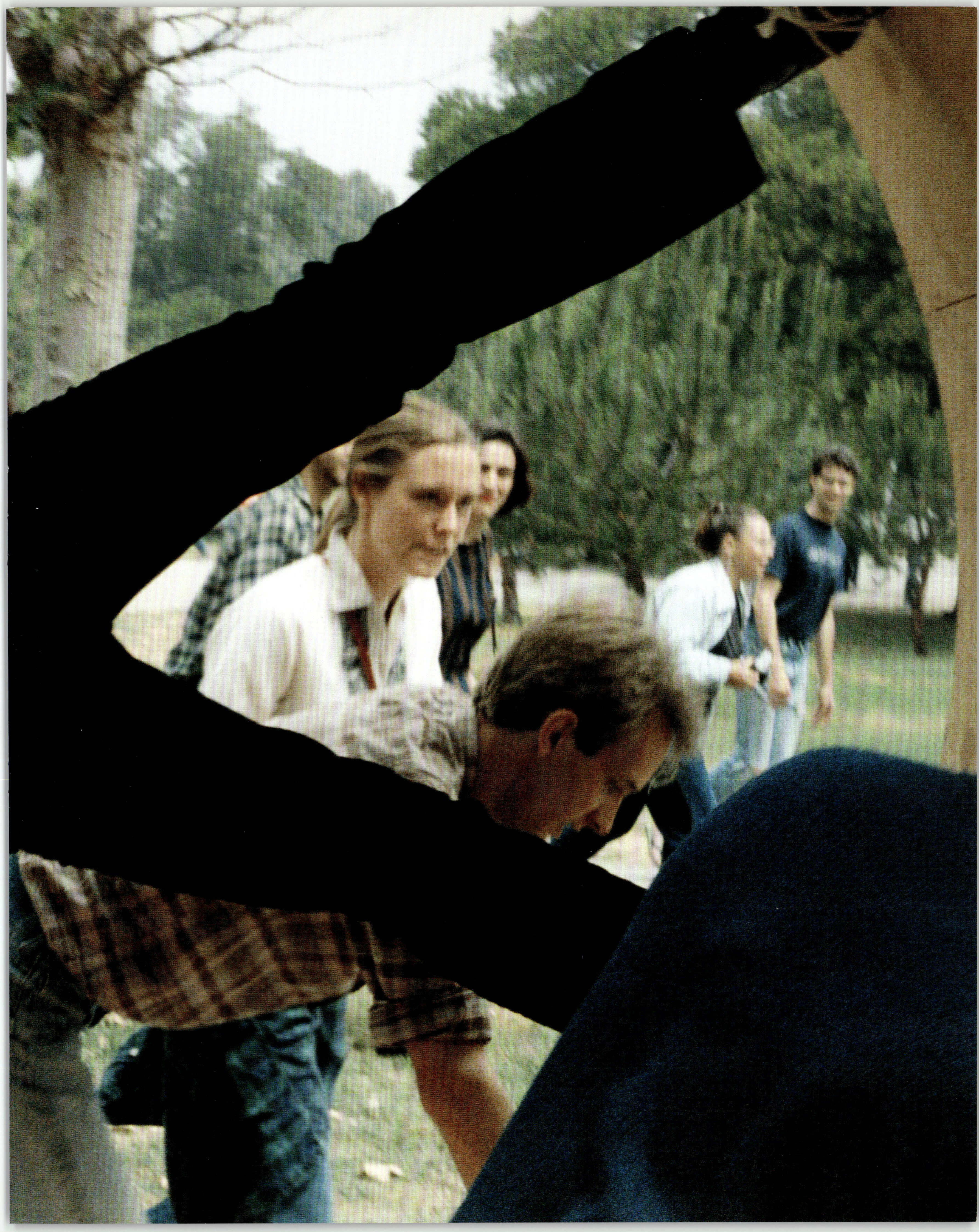

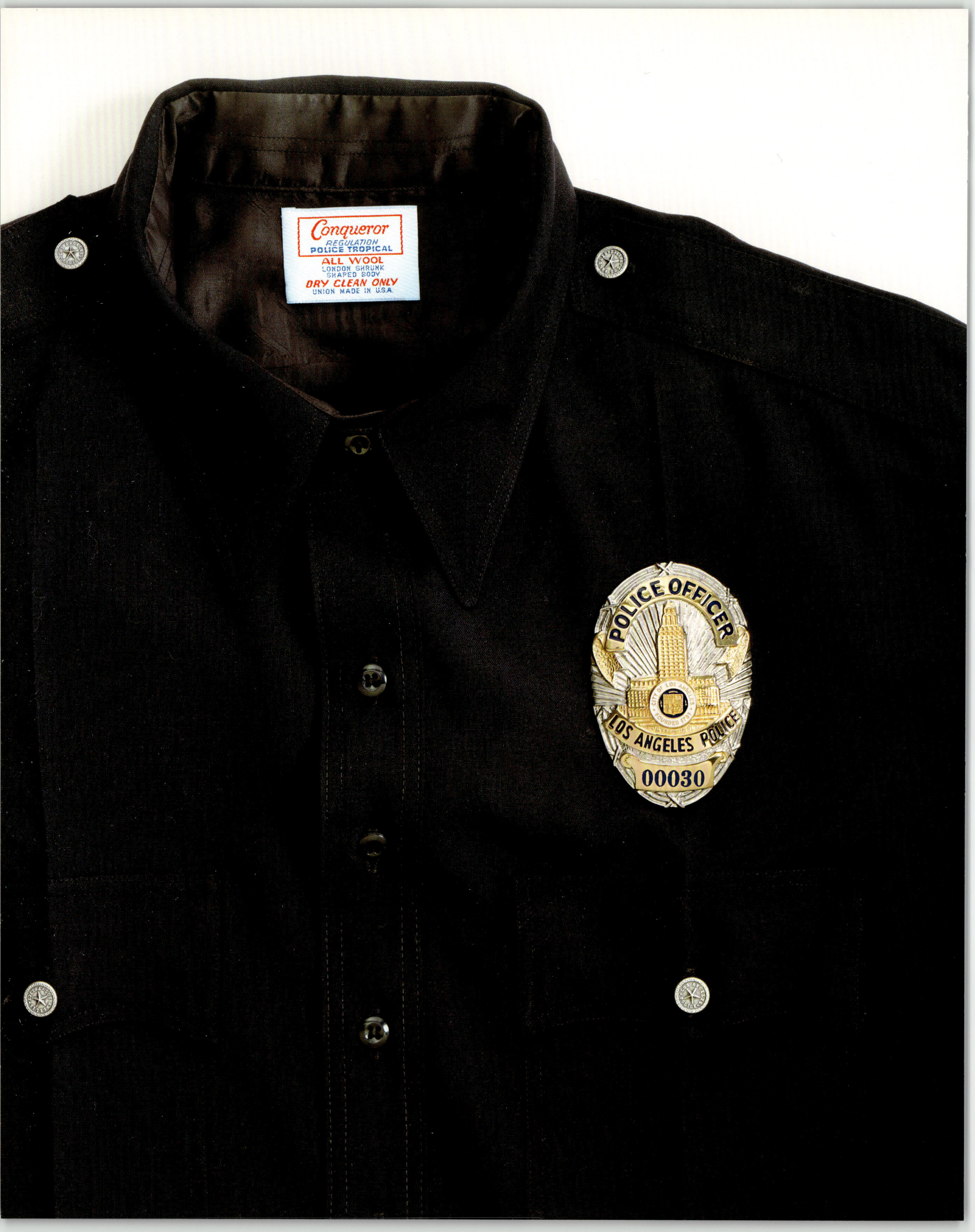
Conqueror
REGULATION
POLICE TROPICAL
ALL WOOL
LONDON SHRUNK
SHAPED BODY
DRY CLEAN ONLY
UNION MADE IN U.S.A.
POLICE OFFICER
LOS ANGELES POLICE
00030

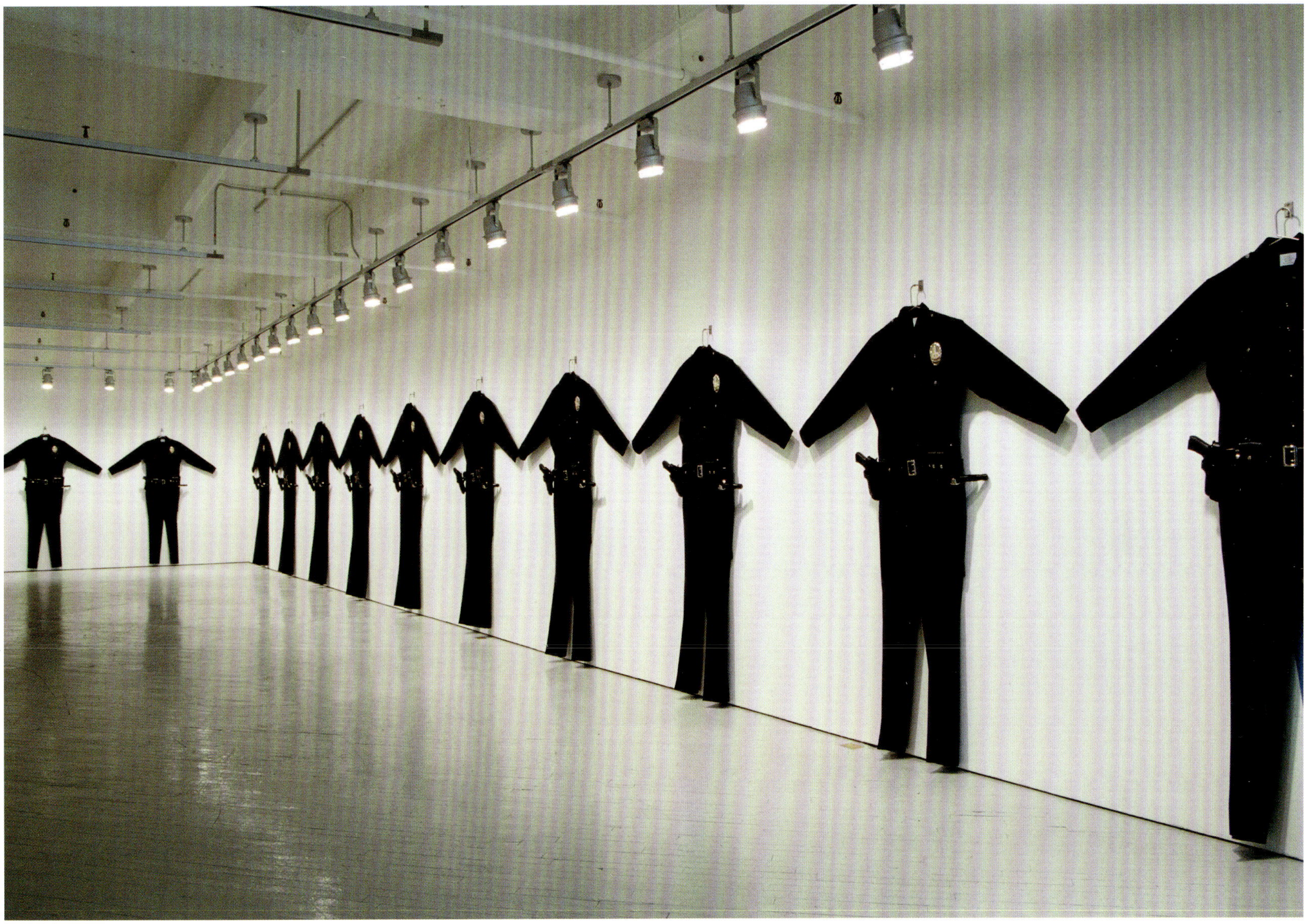

L.A.P.D. Uniforms 1993

(Edition of 30, with one artist's proof)
30 uniforms and 30 Beretta handguns
Wool serge, metal, leather, wood, plastic
Each uniform: 88 × 72 × 6 inches

L.A.P.D. Uniforms *is an edition of 30 oversized police uniforms, created in collaboration with the Fabric Workshop, in Philadelphia, during my 1992–3 residency. The seven-foot-tall uniforms are equipped with badges, belts, batons, handcuffs, bullets and 92F Beretta handguns. The uniforms replicate the official uniform of the Los Angeles Police Department. Viewed from a distance, the uniforms appear to be normal size; close up, they assume larger-than-life proportions.*

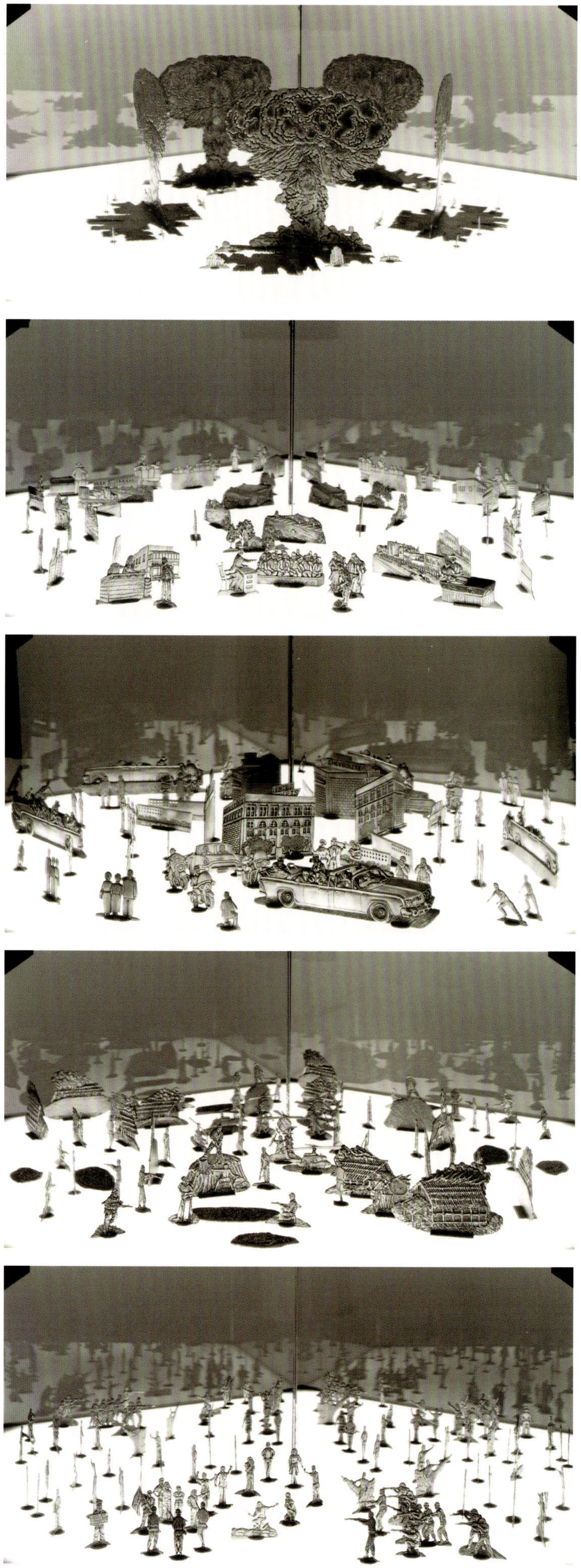

America's Darker Moments 1994

(Edition of three, with one artist's proof)
Painted cast tin figures, wood, glass and plexiglass vitrine
Each case: 56½ × 36½ × 36½ inches

America's Darker Moments *is a pentagon-shaped case, internally lit, depicting five notorious and shameful scenes from America's recent history: the bombing of Hiroshima, the murder of Emmett Till, the Kennedy assassination, the My Lai massacre and the shooting of protesting students at Kent State. Made out of miniature painted tin castings, in the style of antique German toy soldiers,* America's Darker Moments *was originally shown surrounded by 30* L.A.P.D. Uniforms.

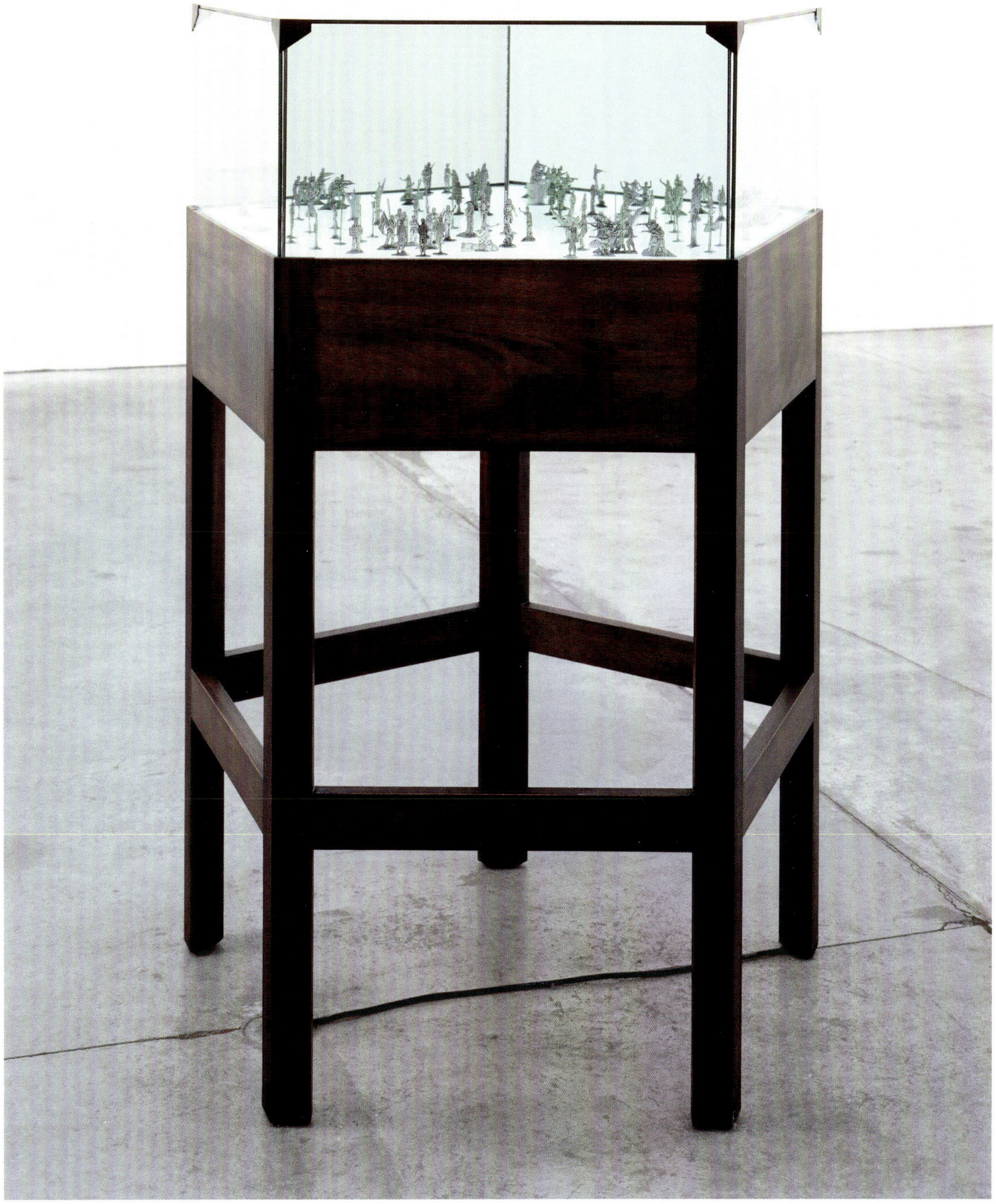

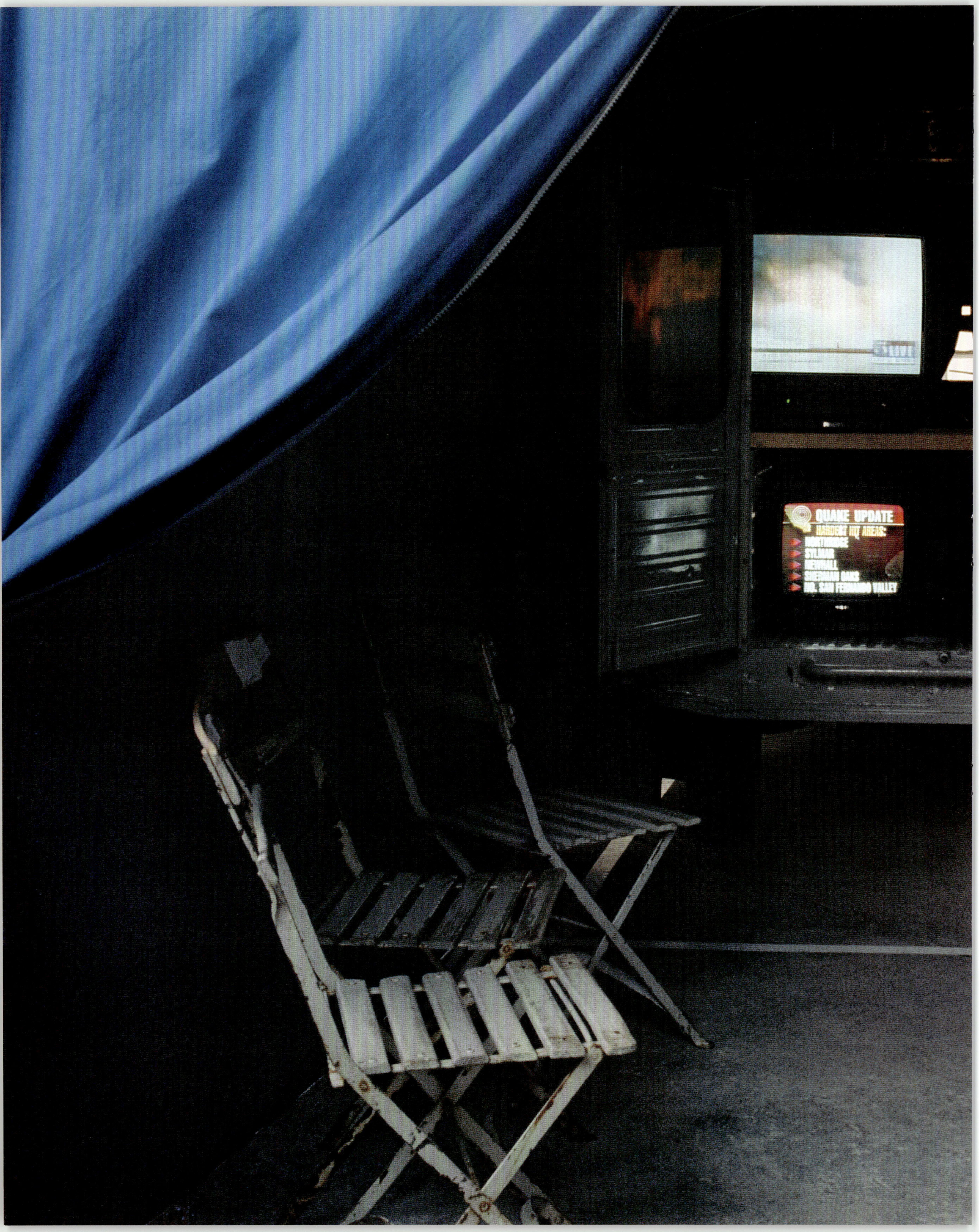
QUAKE UPDATE
HARDEST HIT AREAS:
NORTHRIDGE
SYLMAR
NEWHALL
SHERMAN OAKS
NO. SAN FERNANDO VALLEY

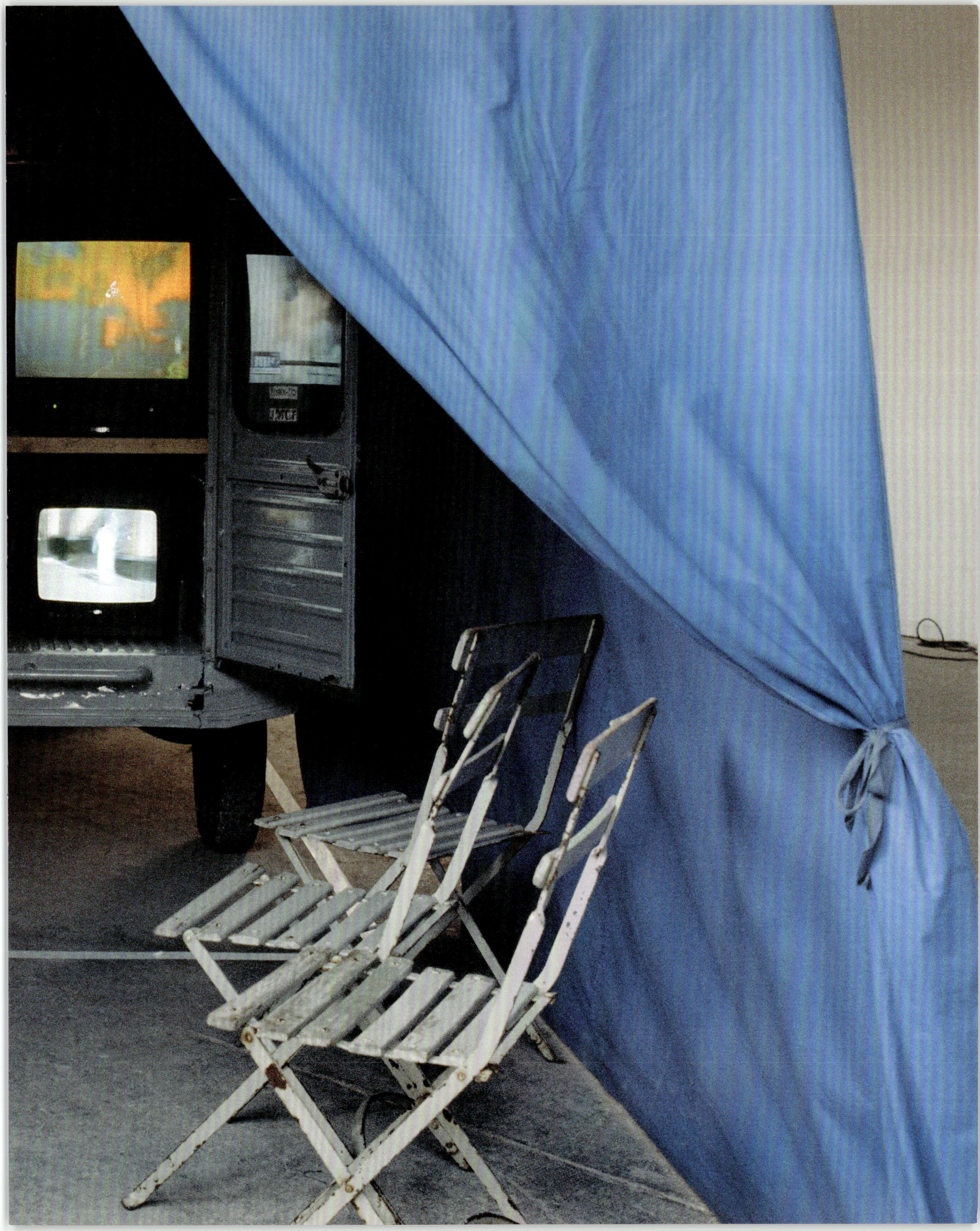

Mini Video Circus 1994

Three Citroën 2CV vans, each equipped with a canvas tent, six metal folding chairs, four video cassette decks, four TV monitors
Each van: 72 × 228 × 72 inches

The Mini Video Circus *installation/sculpture consists of three modified French Citroën 2CV vans. The back doors of each of the vans open to reveal four medium video screens. Each of the video screens is connected to a separate video deck. In addition, a tent structure pulls out of the back of each van and encloses the video screens. Six folding chairs are set up under each tent so that viewers can sit and watch the video. The chairs and the tent parts all fold up and are carried in the vans. On the sides of the vans are signs that read 'Les Actualités de la Californie et du Monde'. Each TV screen shows the most dramatic and visceral images of the recent disasters that have befallen California. The tapes show the Los Angeles riots, earthquakes, fires and the fourth tape is a mixture of the above three. The simultaneous tapes present rich, prolonged video visuals of these events that were likely shown only briefly in European news spots.*

My original plan was that the Mini Video Circus *would be a pilot program for unemployed French youths. Initially the youths would participate in restoring the derelict 2CV vans. The 2CV vans would be dismantled into separate components and used to build complete, running vans. These recycled 2CV vans would form a fleet of* Mini Video Circus *vehicles that would bring in-depth information about California to small French villages. The idea of circulating these* Mini Video Circuses *throughout the countryside, with youthful attendants charging a nominal entrance fee, is a symbolic gesture towards creative new enterprises providing innovative solutions for the unemployed and unskilled youth. The youths would learn video skills, car maintenance, salesmanship and basic small business skills. The video circus would also promote self initiative.*

Unlike Euro Disney, I believe these mini video circuses, with the never-ending California disaster footage, would be extremely popular and successful. Nothing makes people feel better and more content than seeing disaster fall upon a rich and excessive society in a distant place.

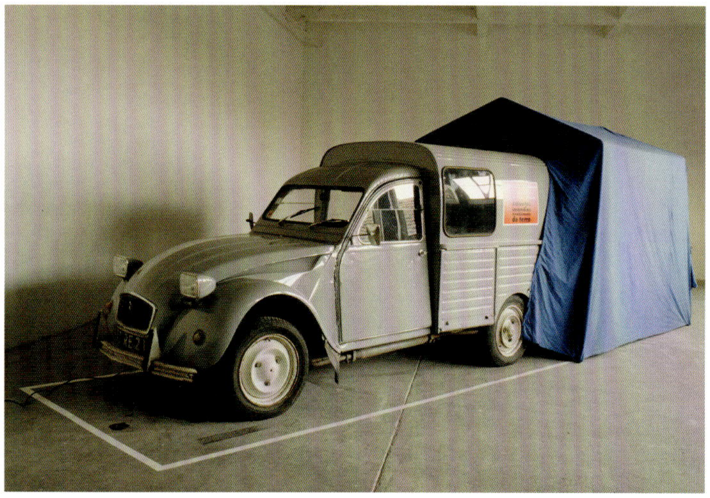

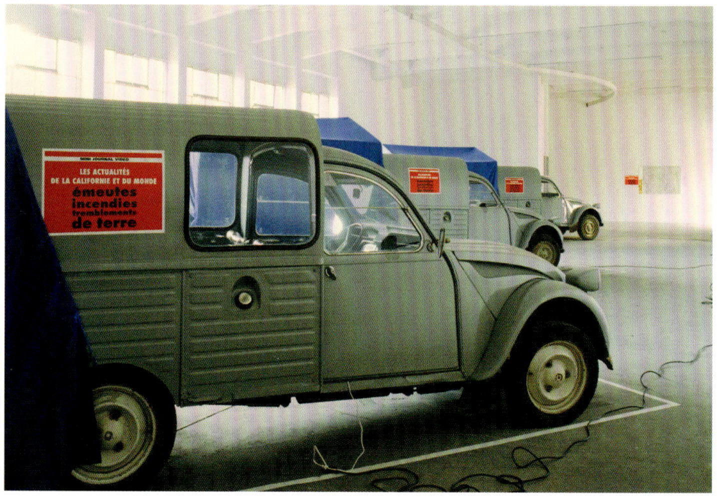

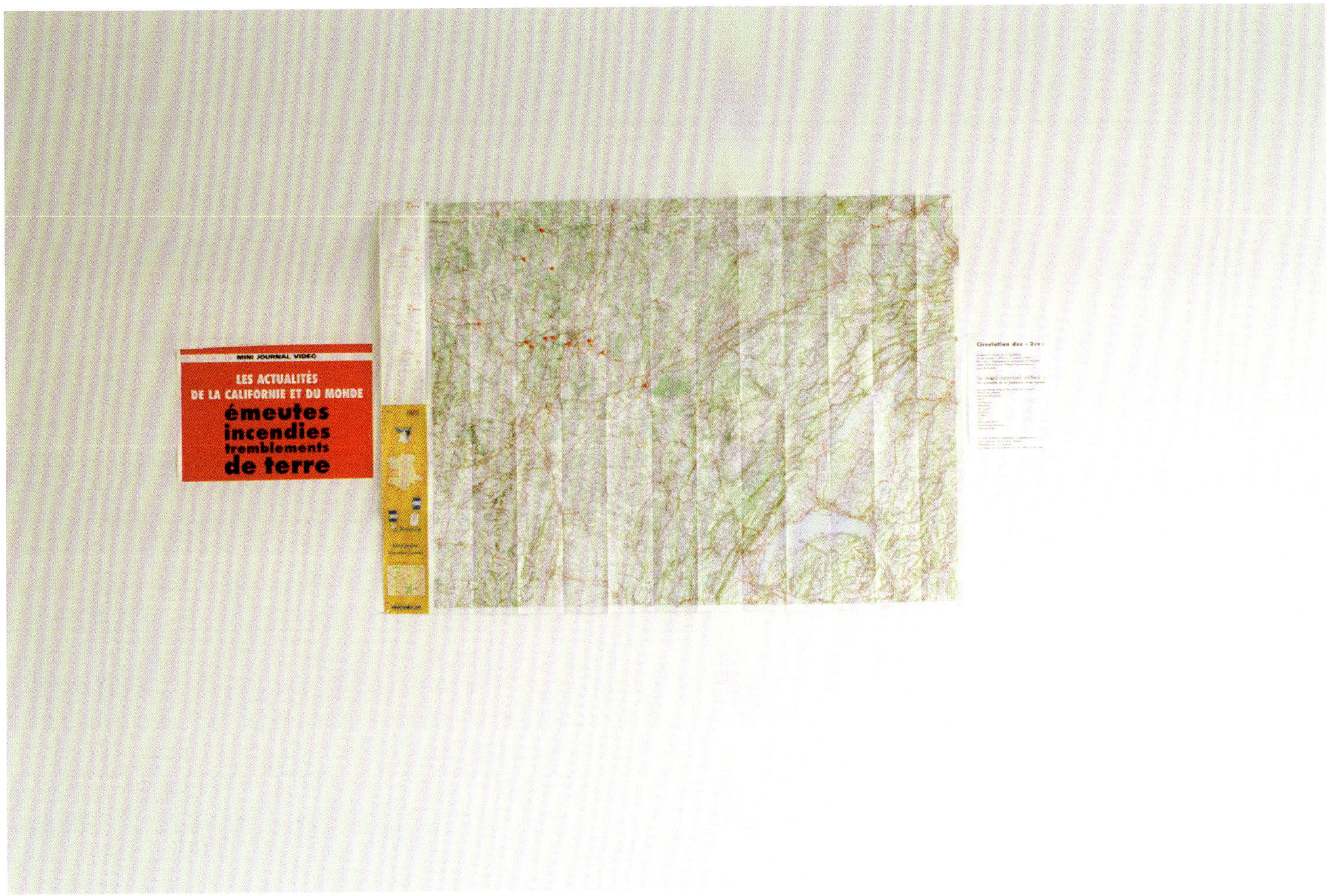
MINI JOURNAL VIDEO
LES ACTUALITÉS
DE LA CALIFORNIE ET DU MONDE
émeutes
incendies
tremblements
de terre
Circulation des « 2cv »

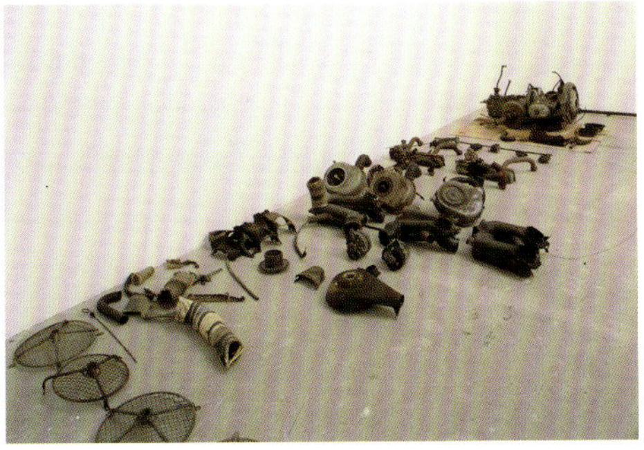

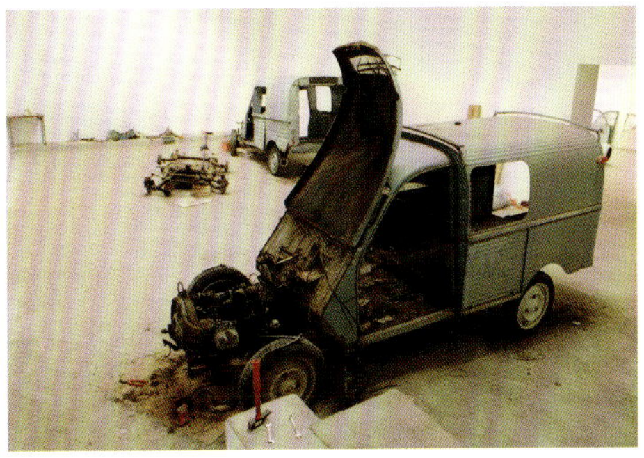

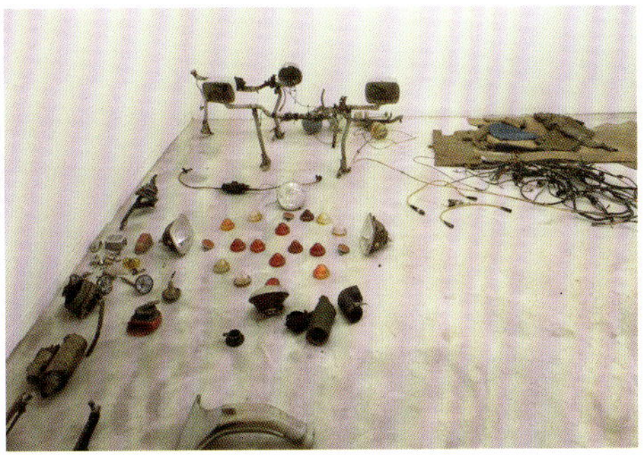

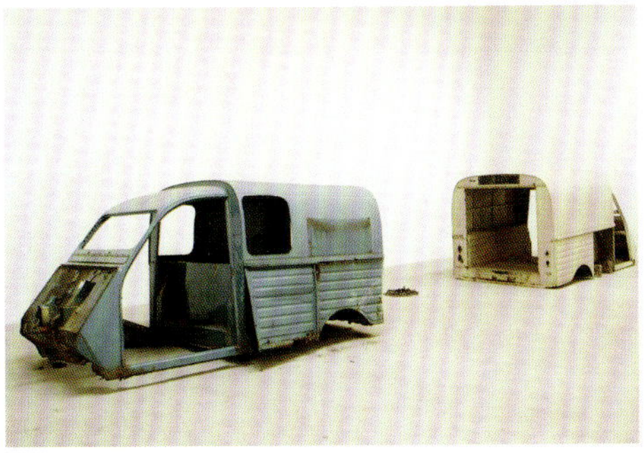

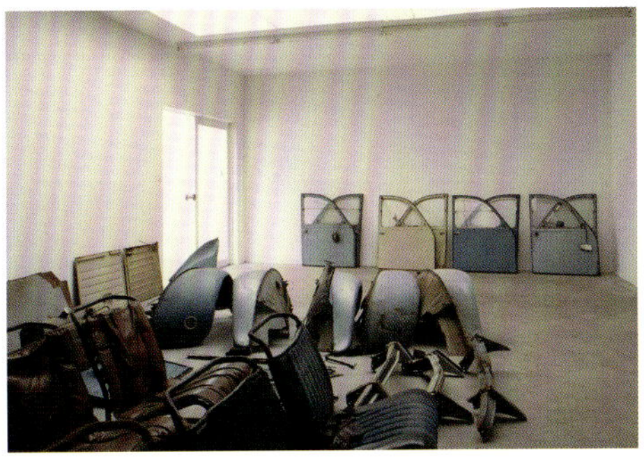

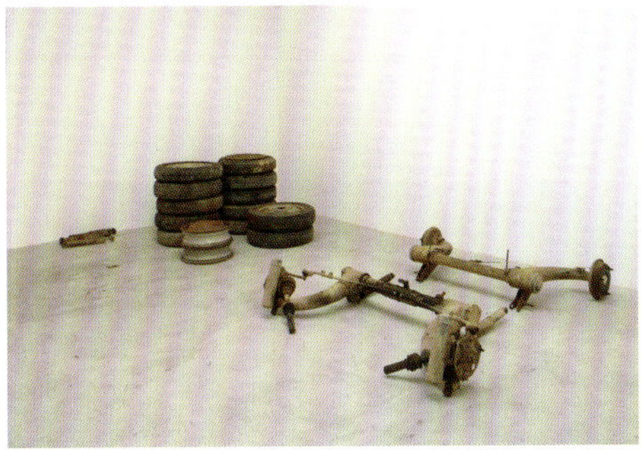

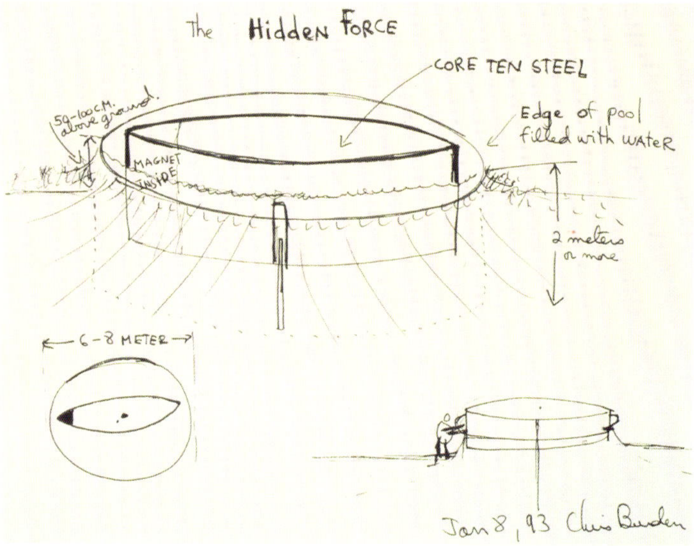

The Hidden Force II 1993
Ink on paper, 8½ × 11 inches
Initial proposal drawing

The Hidden Force 1995

Concrete, aluminum, water
Three pools with three floating
elliptical shapes
Each pool: 108 × 36 inches;
each elliptical shape: 18 × 84 inches

My artwork for the McNeil Island Correction Center consists of a sculpture made up of three identical elements. Each of the elements is placed on the grassy areas between the concrete walkways, one in front of each of the three new cellblocks. Each of these elements consists of a small, relatively shallow, circular concrete pool, approximately nine feet in diameter, with a depth of approximately three feet. Each of the pools is three-quarters submerged into the ground and the green grass rises up to the edge of each pool.

Floating in each pool is an elliptical shape, seven feet long and one-and-a-half feet high, made up of plate aluminum. This shape is roughly the size of a human body and can be seen as abstractly figurative. Concealed inside one end of each shape is a very large magnet. The floating elliptical shapes are held in place by a central pole on their undersides, which allows each shape to pivot within the pool and to rise and fall with the level of the water. This pole is not visible to the viewers. Each of the pools and the large elliptical shapes are essentially large compasses, with the magnetized end of the shapes pointing north. However, because of the large scale and the lack of directional markings, these sculptures' mechanisms, that of a large compass is not readily apparent to the viewers. Viewers can gently push or touch the aluminum floating shape and it moves easily to the left or to the right. Natural forces, such as the wind, also cause some slight movement. Invariably, the vast majority of the time, the magnetized ends of each of the three elliptical shapes are pointing north.

This sculpture is specifically conceived for the general prison population and the staff at McNeil Island Correction Center. Because the three elliptical shapes are always pointing in the direction of North, it will become apparent that they are guided by a strong hidden force. I think this unseen force, which is the magnetic field, is a metaphor for the 'right direction' or the 'right way'. The interaction between the three shapes becomes very important as a symbol for shared common values. For example, I would expect inmates to compare the position of one elliptical shape to the position of the other elliptical shapes as they pass by the sculptures on their way to the dining facilities three times a day and they would arrive at the conclusion that there is, in essence, one underlying, primary direction. My hope would be that the inmates might make the connection between this unseen but internalized force of nature and the unseen human values, i.e. the right way, that they must also internalize. The group of three compasses, all pointing in the same way, becomes a metaphor for the shared moral values of a group or a society. I think these three compasses have an added layering because of their location on an island. If the island were ever to break loose and float away, the three compasses would help the island find the right way.

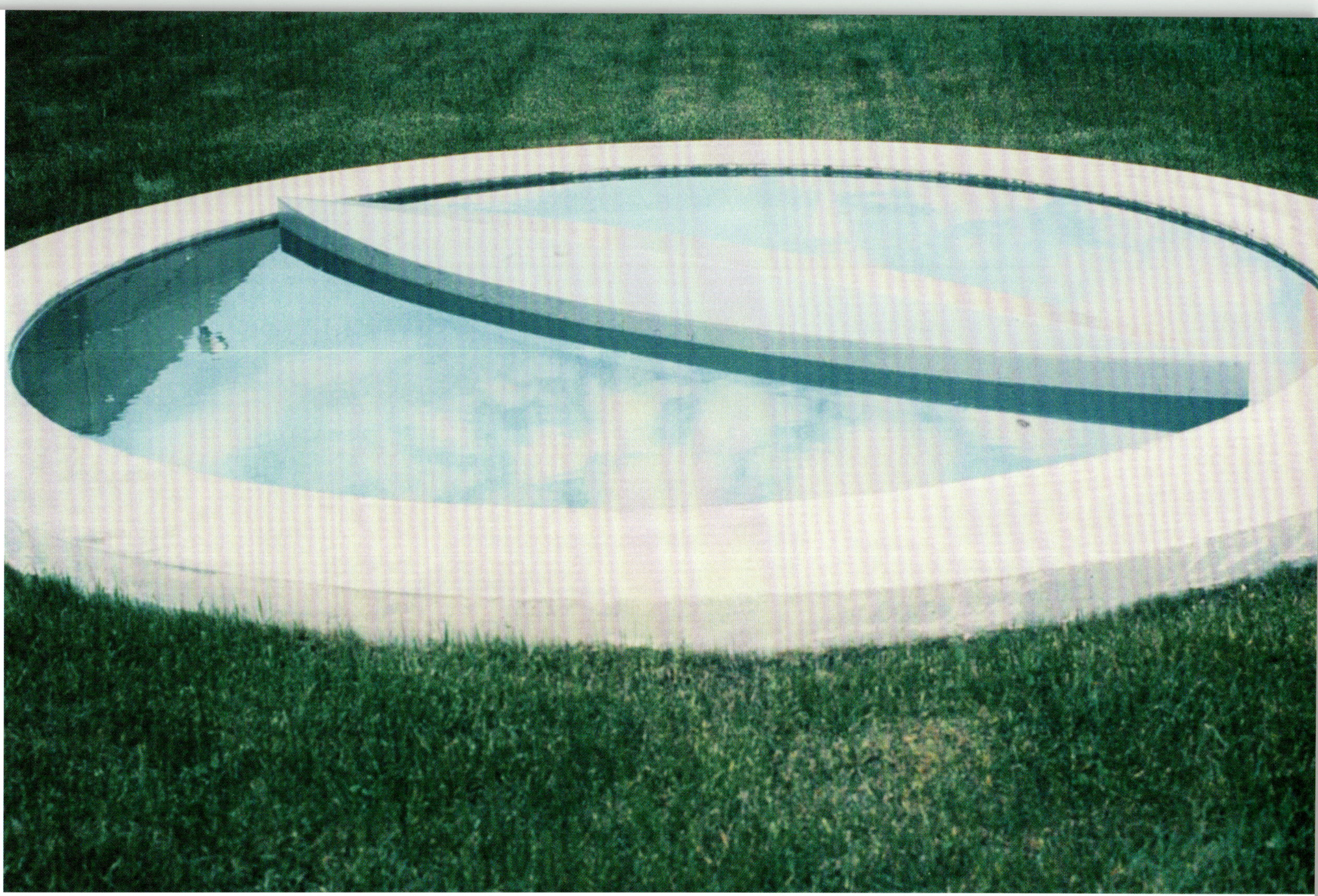

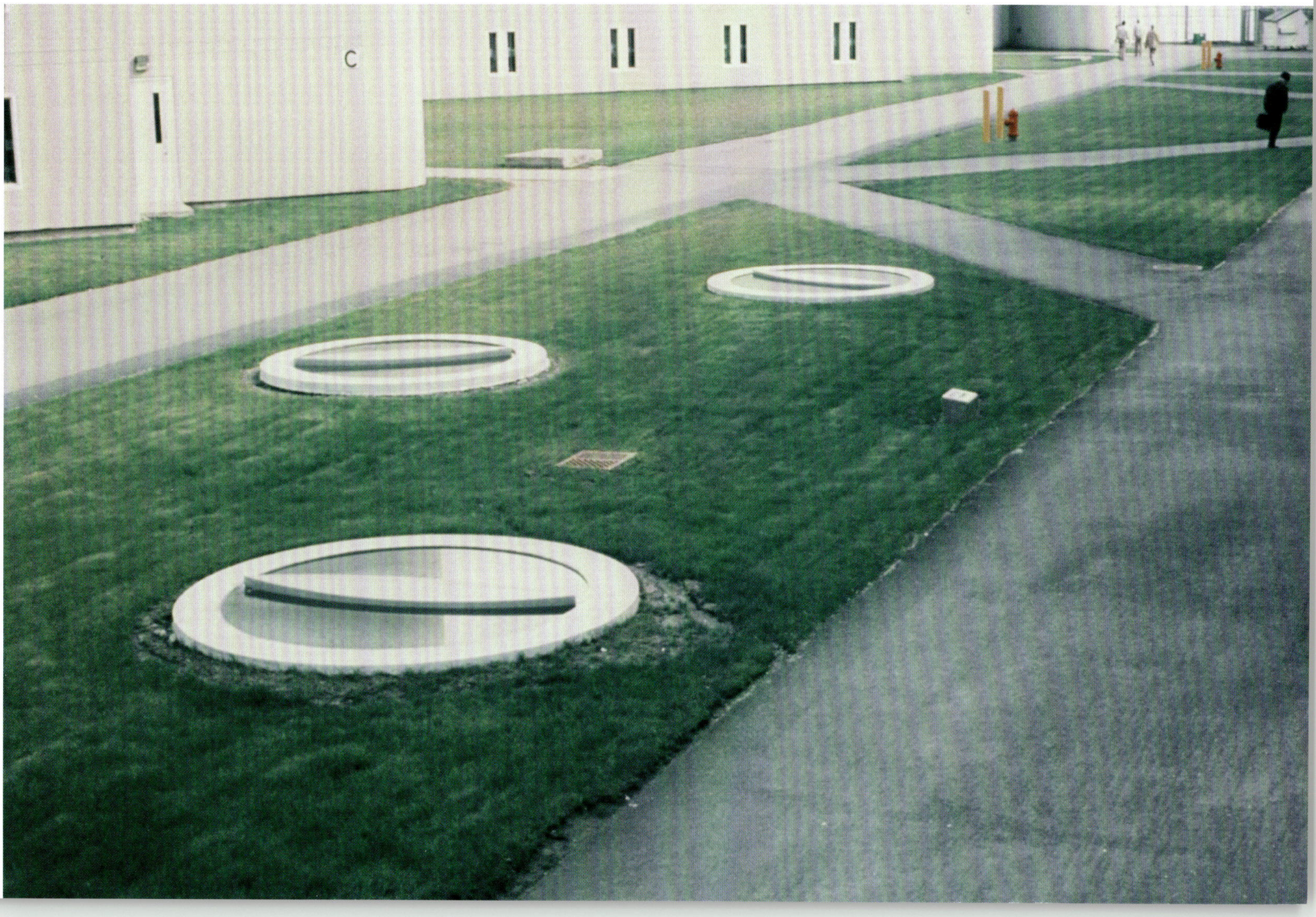
C

Work:

Bicycle Piece 1971

University of California, Irvine,
California, USA;
May 6–20, 1971

A black serpentine path one foot wide was placed on the gallery floor connecting the front and rear entrances of the gallery. During gallery hours, I continuously rode a ten-speed bicycle through the front entrance, along the path, out and around the building and back through the front door.

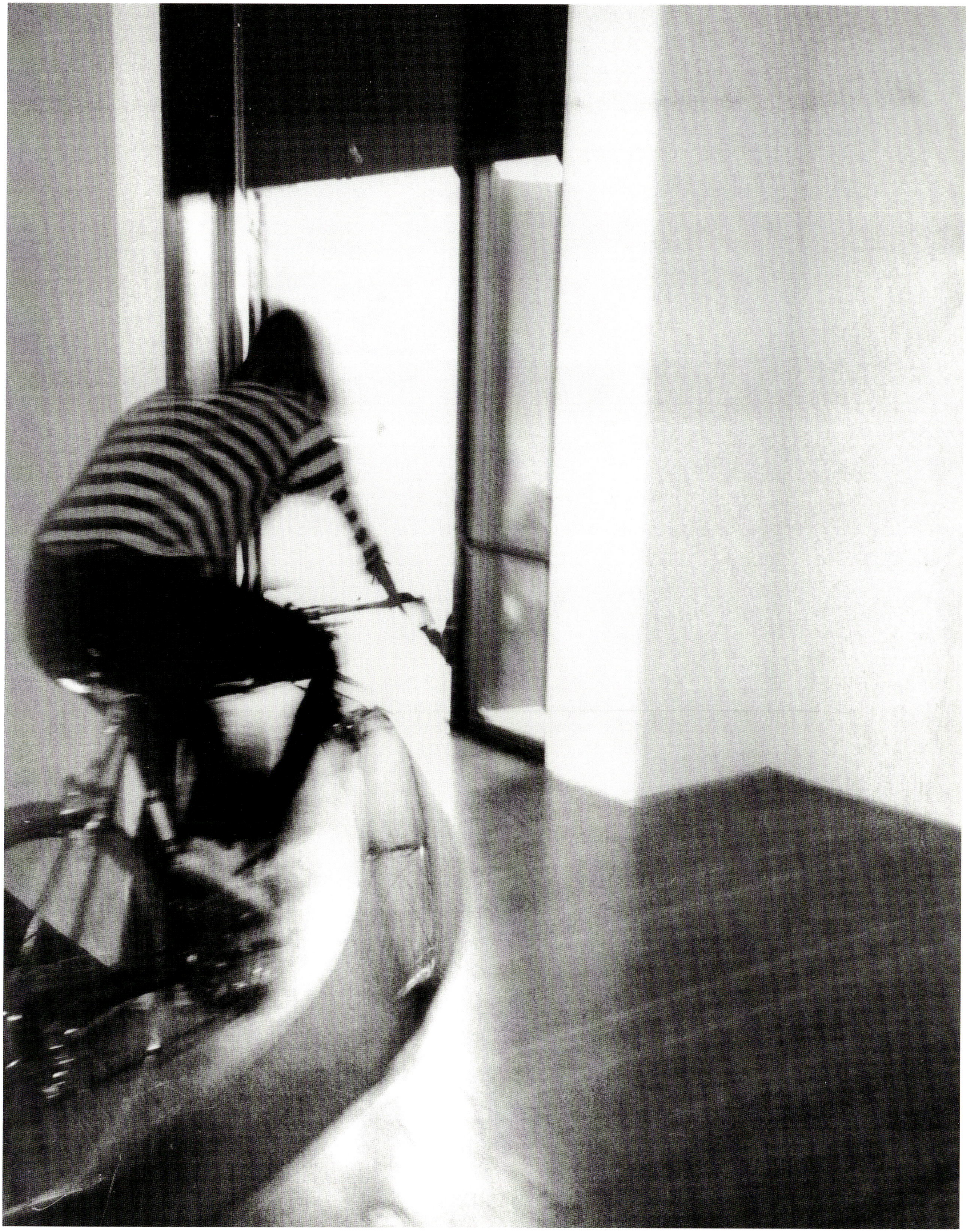

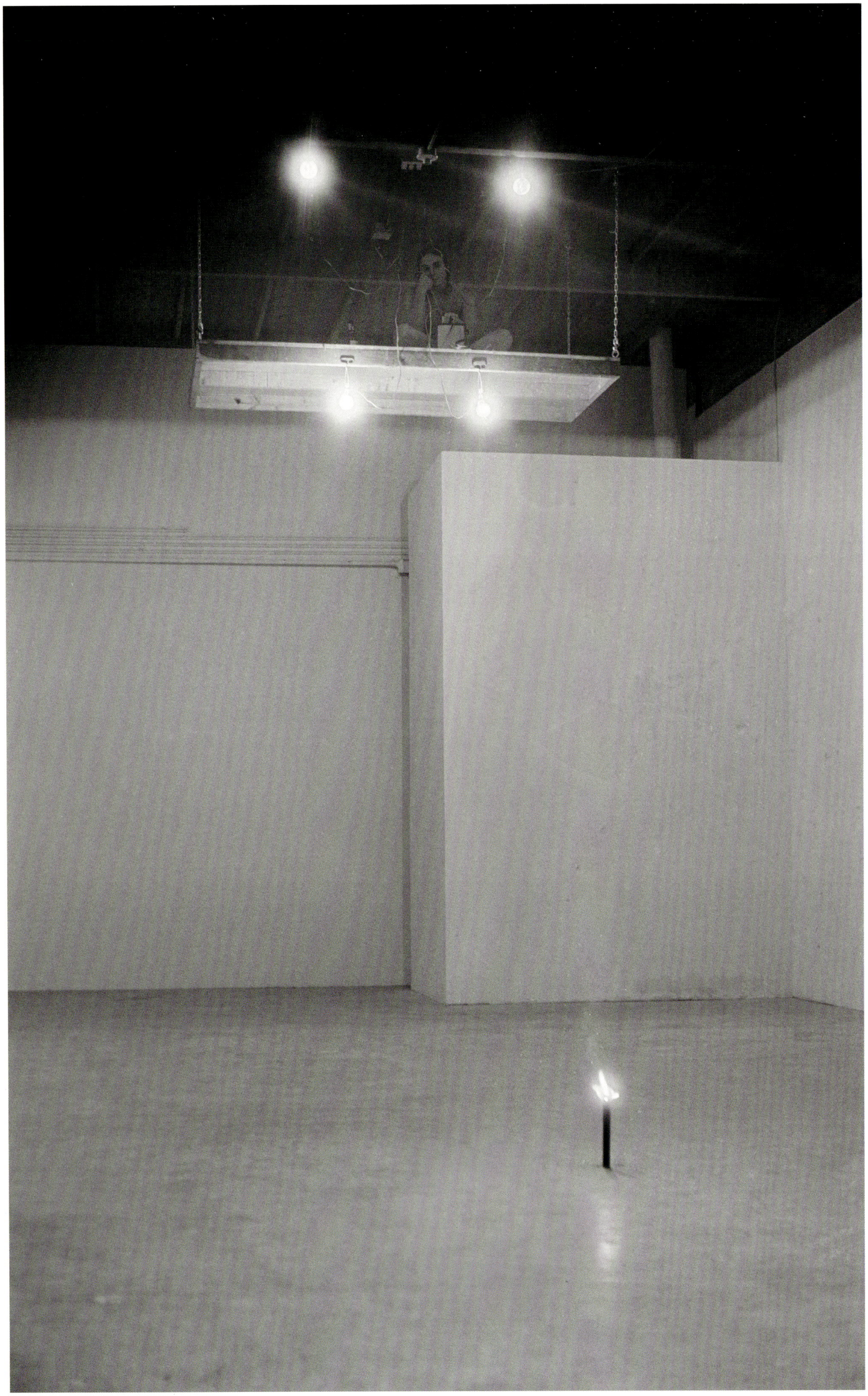

Shout Piece 1971

F Space, Santa Ana, California, USA;
August 21, 1971

I was seated on a platform suspended 14 feet above the floor. My hair was braided and my face was covered with red body paint. Four 500 watt movie lights were placed around me facing the front entrance of the space. My voice was amplified by three speakers. As people entered the gallery, I repeatedly yelled at them to 'get the fuck out, get out immediately.' Because the sound was very loud and contained high frequency feedback, most people left quickly.

Prelude to 220, or 110 1971

F Space, Santa Ana, California, USA;
September 10–12, 1971

I was strapped to the floor with copper bands bolted into the concrete. Two buckets of water with live 110 lines submerged in them were placed near me. The piece was performed from 8–10 pm for three nights.

RELIC: Copper band

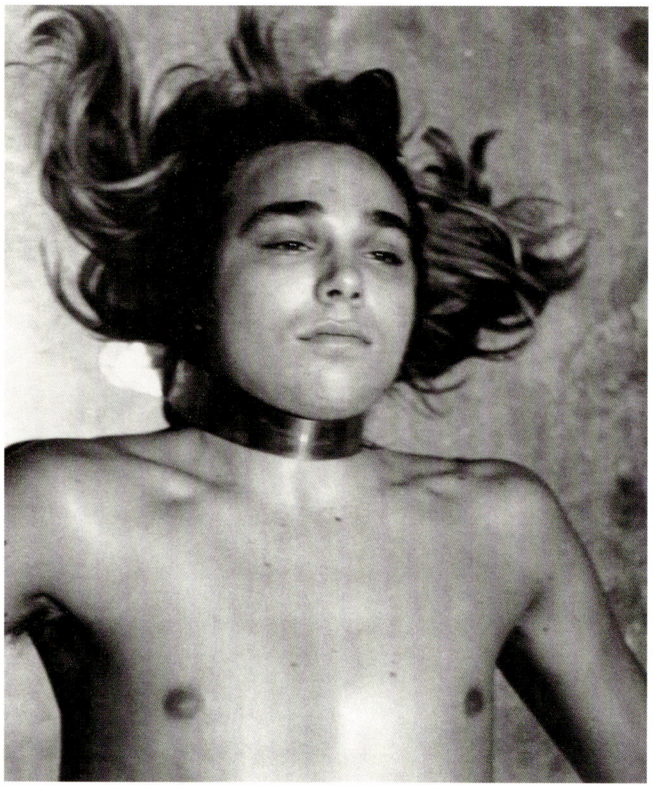

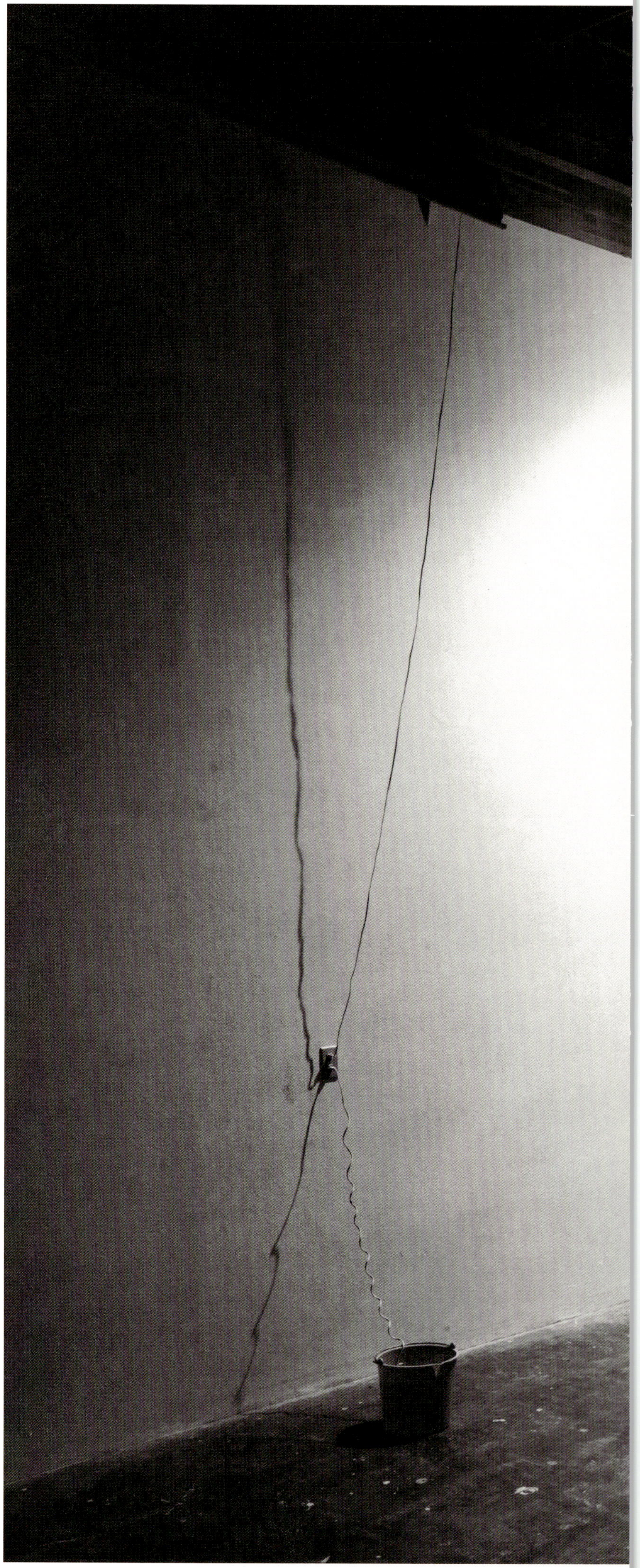

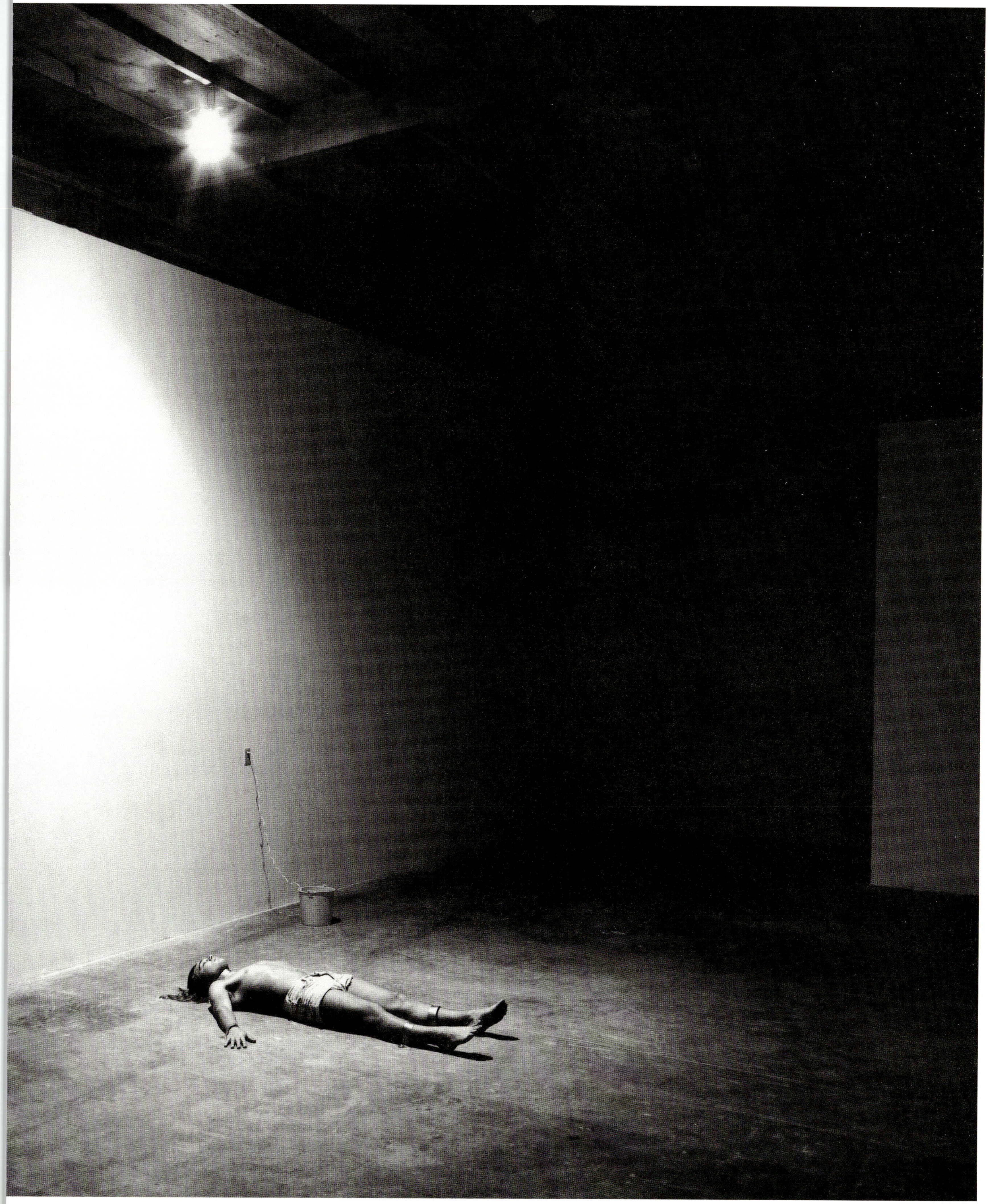

220 1971

F Space, Santa Ana, California, USA;
October 9, 1971

The gallery was flooded with 12 inches of water. Three other people and I waded through the water and climbed onto 14-foot ladders, one ladder per person. After everyone was positioned, I dropped a live 220 electric line into the water. The piece lasted from midnight until dawn, about six hours. There was no audience except for the participants.

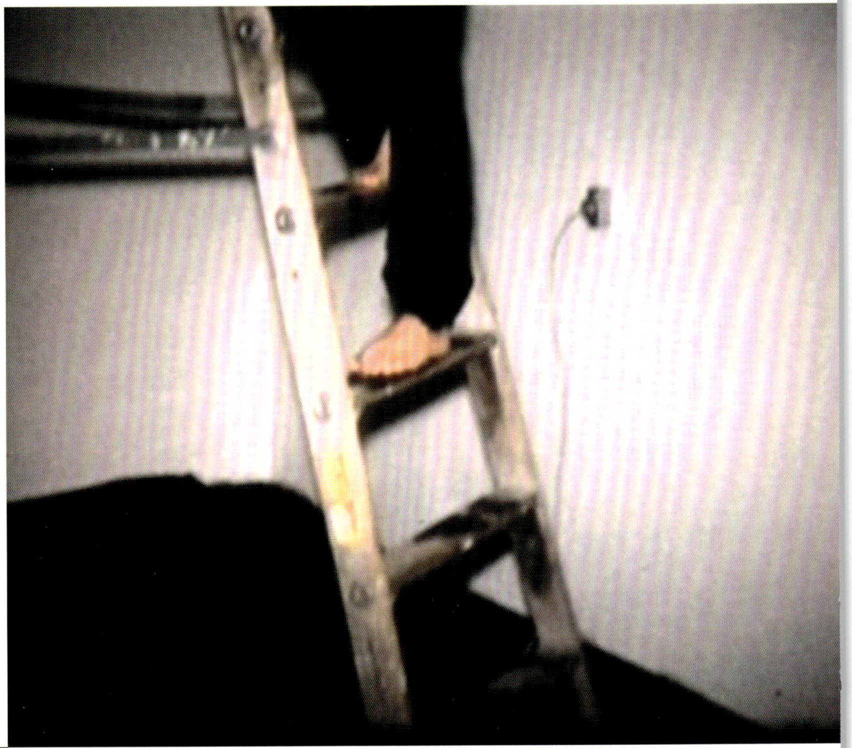

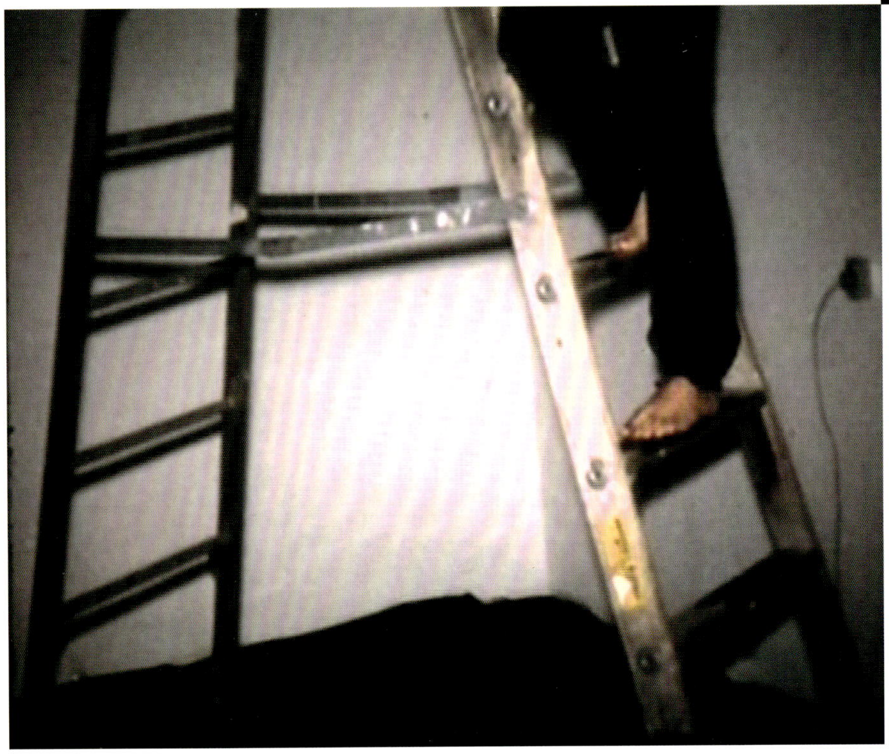

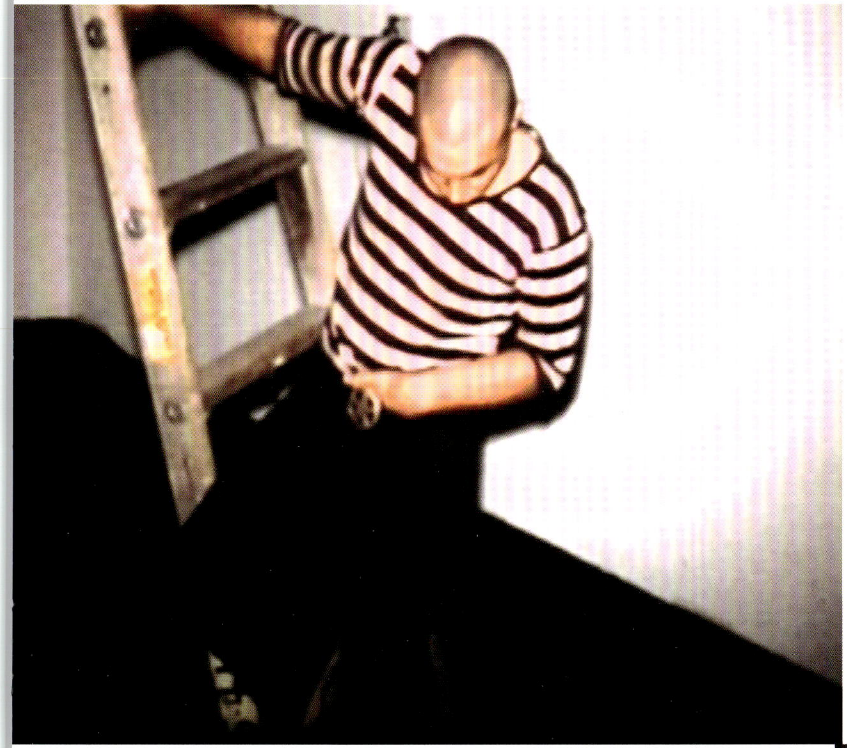

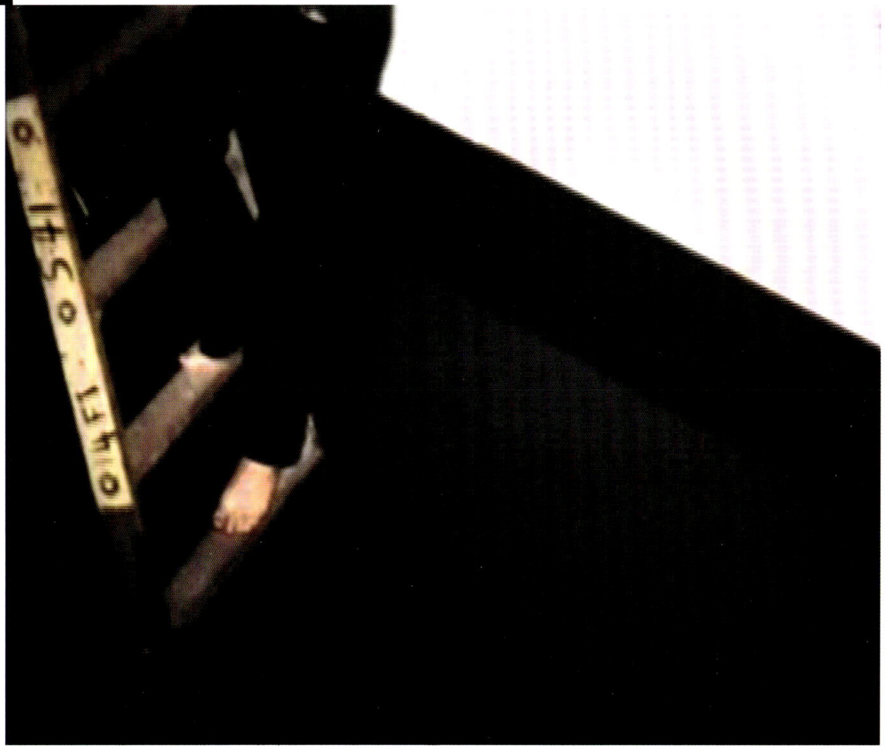

Shoot 1971

F Space, Santa Ana, California, USA;
November 19, 1971

At 7:45 pm I was shot in the left arm by a friend. The bullet was a copper jacket .22 long rifle. My friend was standing about 15 feet from me.

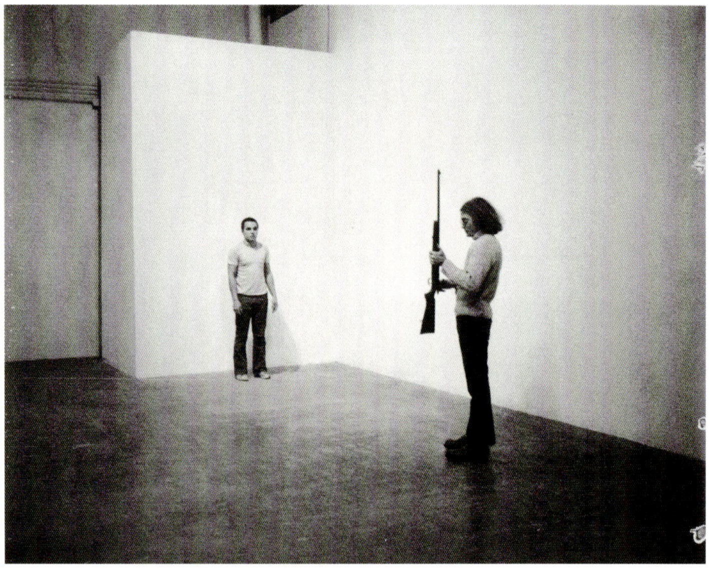

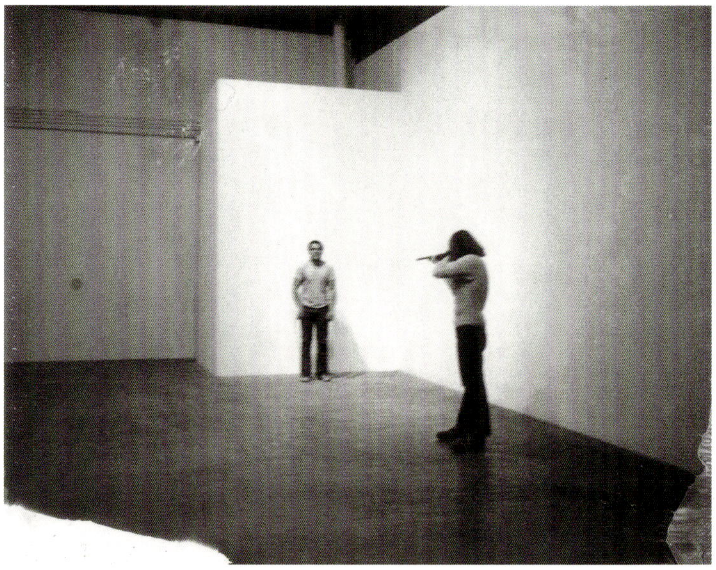

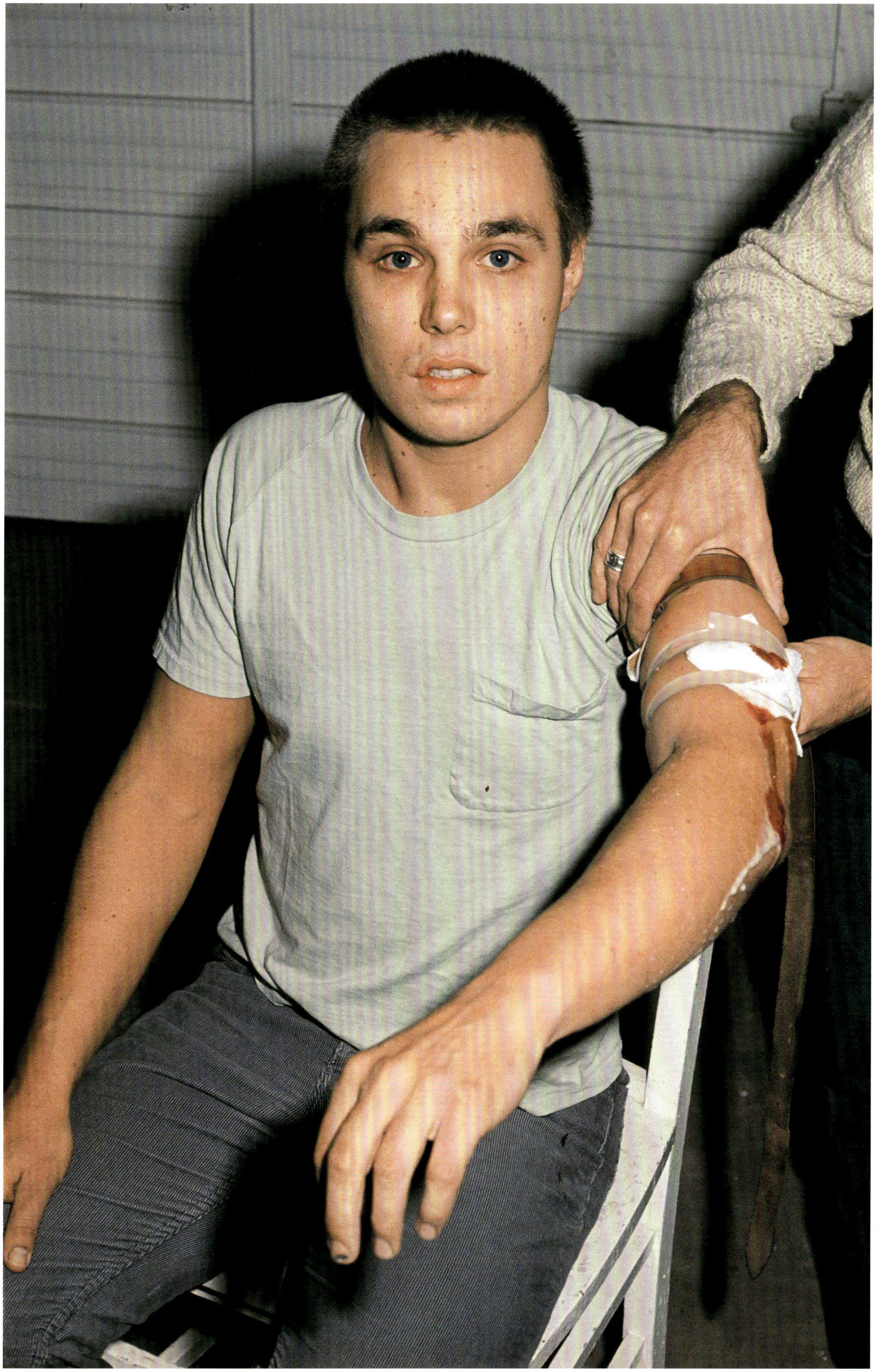

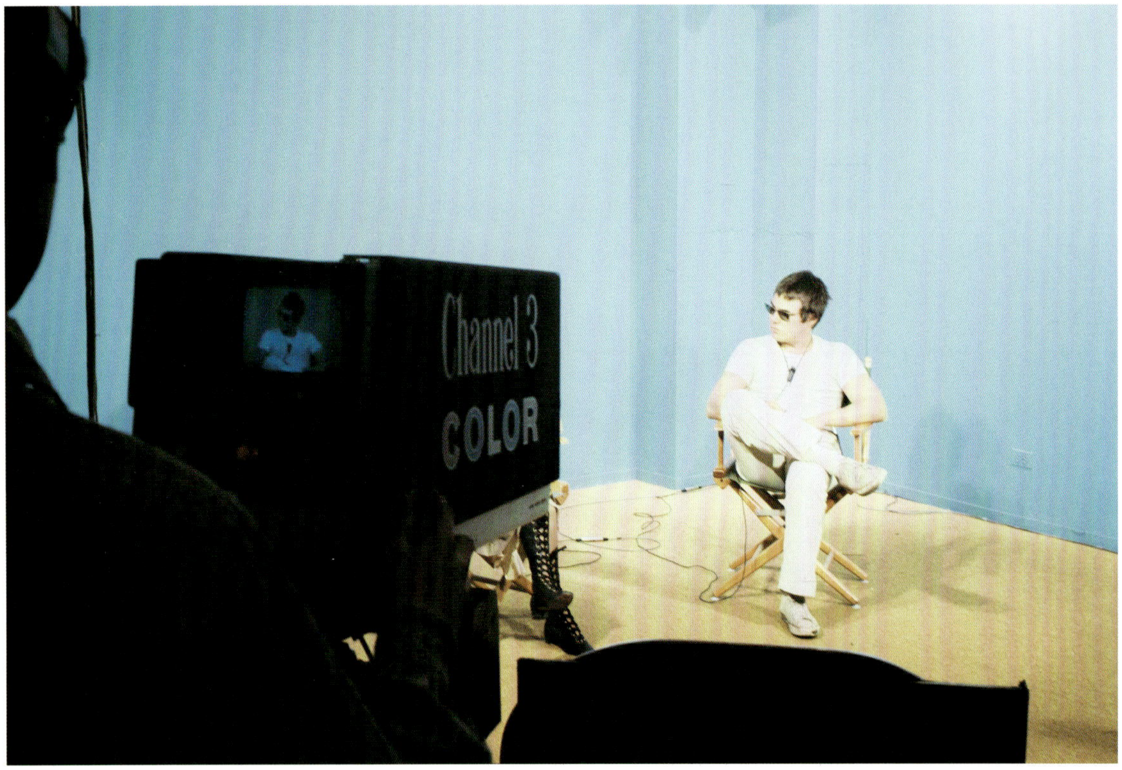

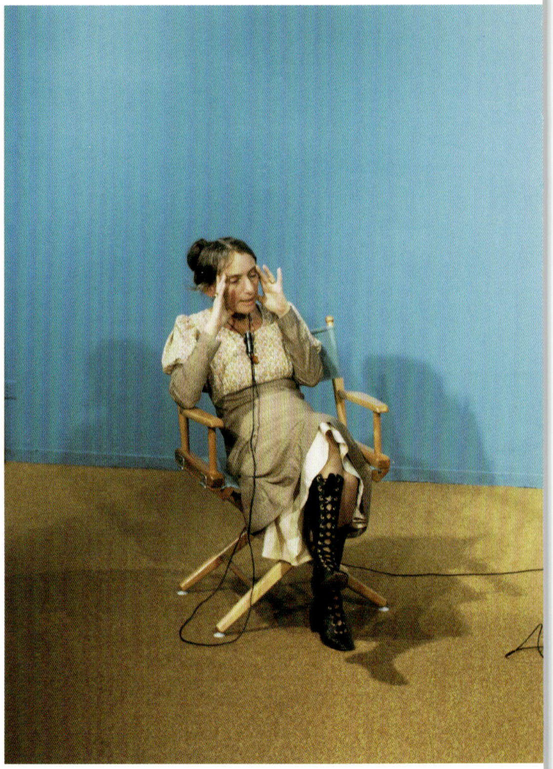

TV Hijack 1972

Channel 3 Cablevision, Irvine, California, USA; February 9, 1972

On January 14, I was asked to do a piece on a local television station by Phyllis Lutjeans. After several proposals were censored by the station or by Phyllis, I agreed to an interview situation. I arrived at the station with my own video crew so that I could have my own tape. While the taping was in progress I requested that the show be transmitted live. Since the station was not broadcasting at the time, they complied.
In the course of the interview, Phyllis asked me to talk about some of the pieces I had thought of doing. I demonstrated a TV hijack. Holding a knife at her throat, I threatened her life if the station stopped live transmission. I told her that I had planned to make her perform obscene acts. At the end of the recording, I asked for the tape of the show. I unwound the reel and destroyed the show by dousing the tape with acetone. The station manager was irate and I offered him my tape which included the show and its destruction, but he refused.

RELIC: Knife, scabbard

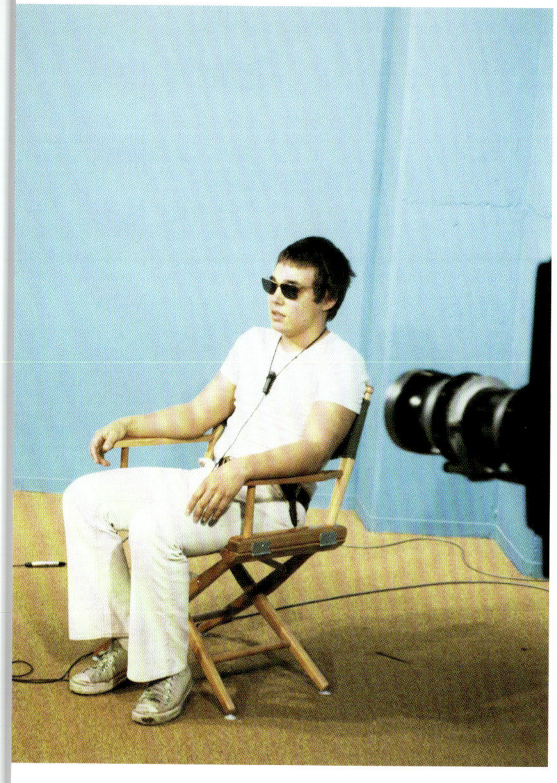

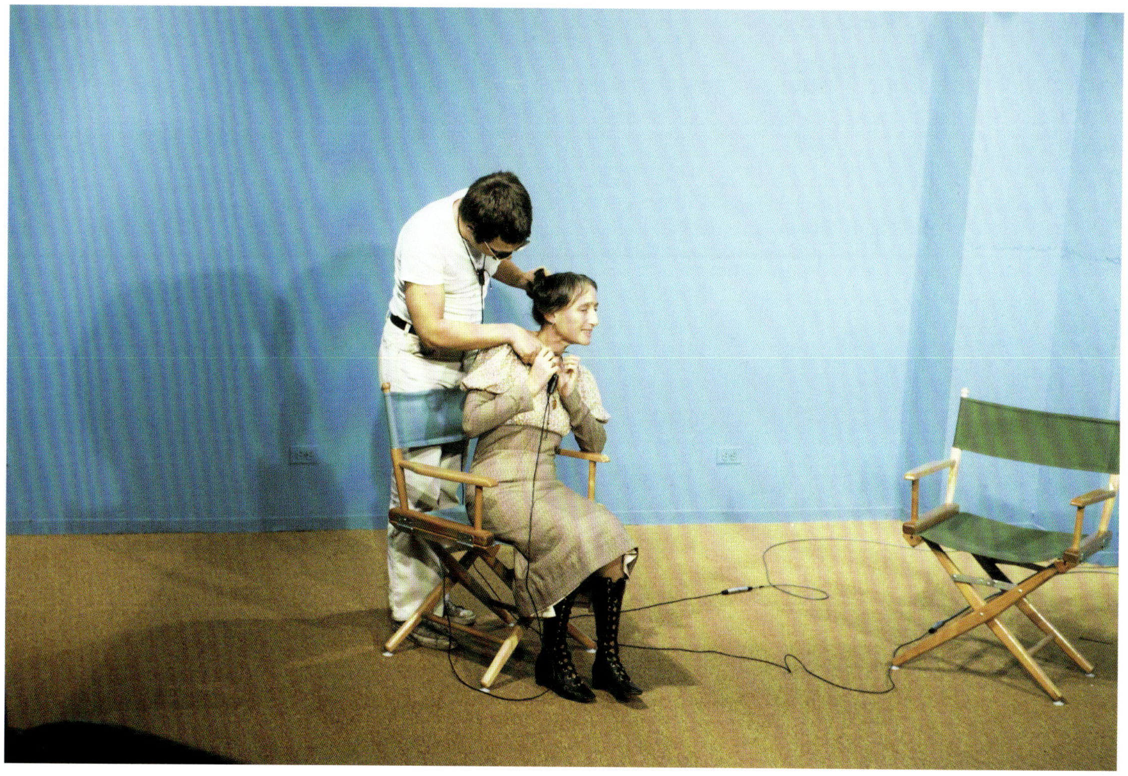

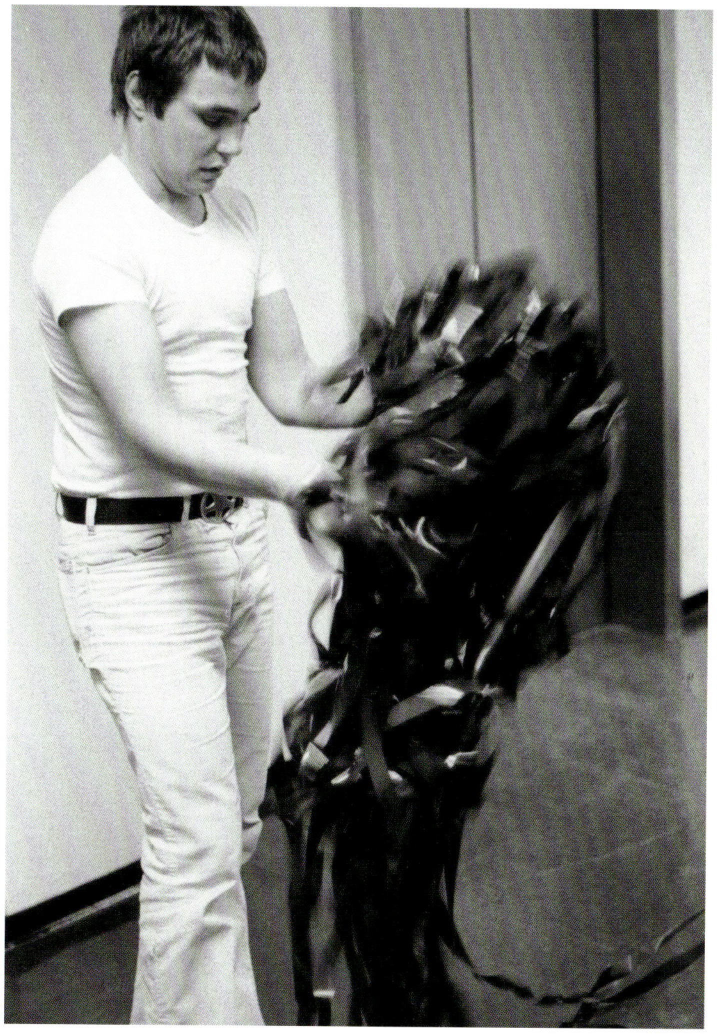

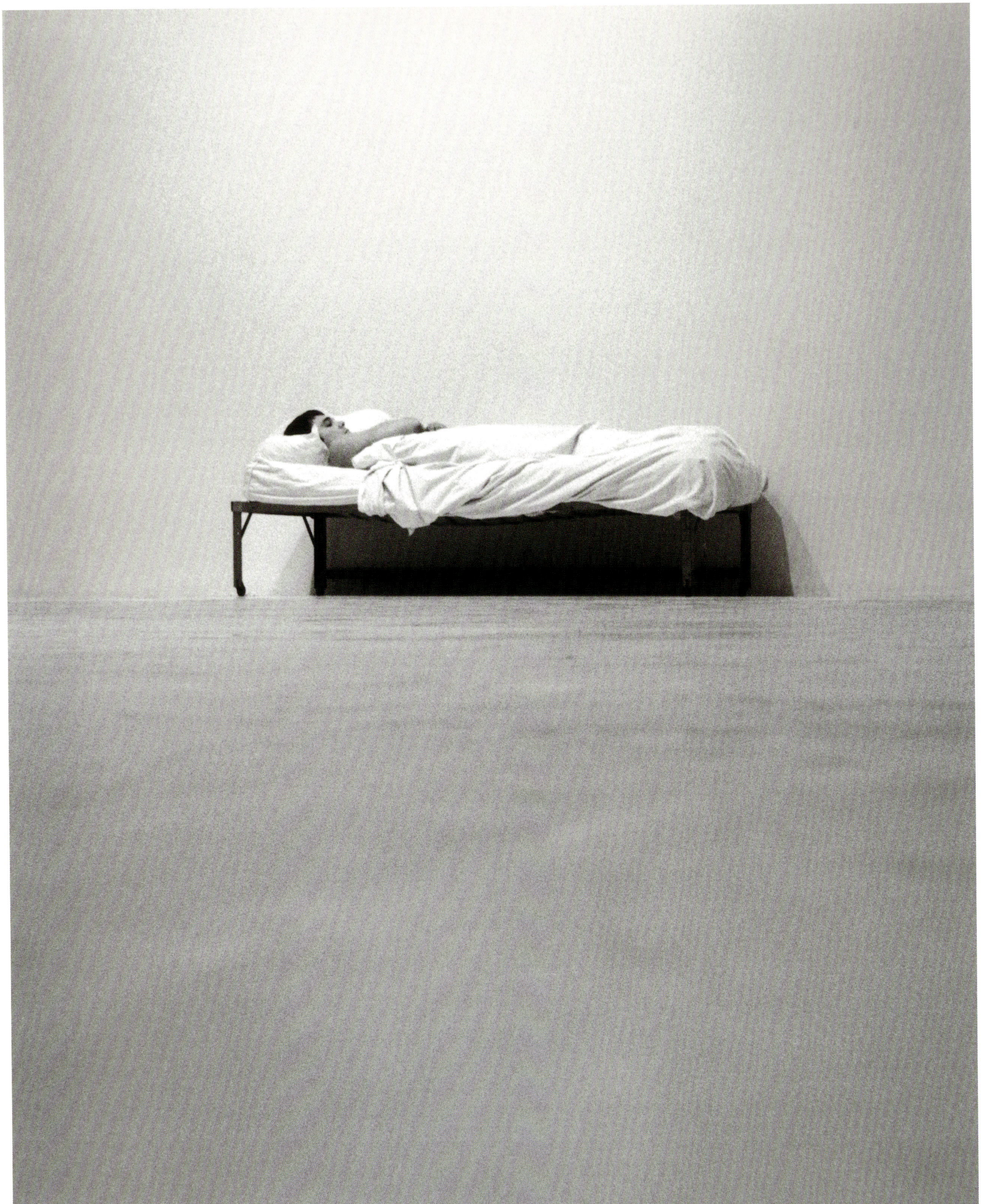

Bed Piece 1972

Market Street, Venice, California, USA;
February 18–March 10, 1972

Josh Young asked me to do a piece for the Market Street Program, from February 18 to March 10. I told him I would need a single bed in the gallery. At noon on February 18, I took off my clothes and got into bed. I had given no other instructions and did not speak to anyone during the piece. On his own initiative, Josh Young had to provide food, water and toilet facilities. I remained in bed for 22 days.

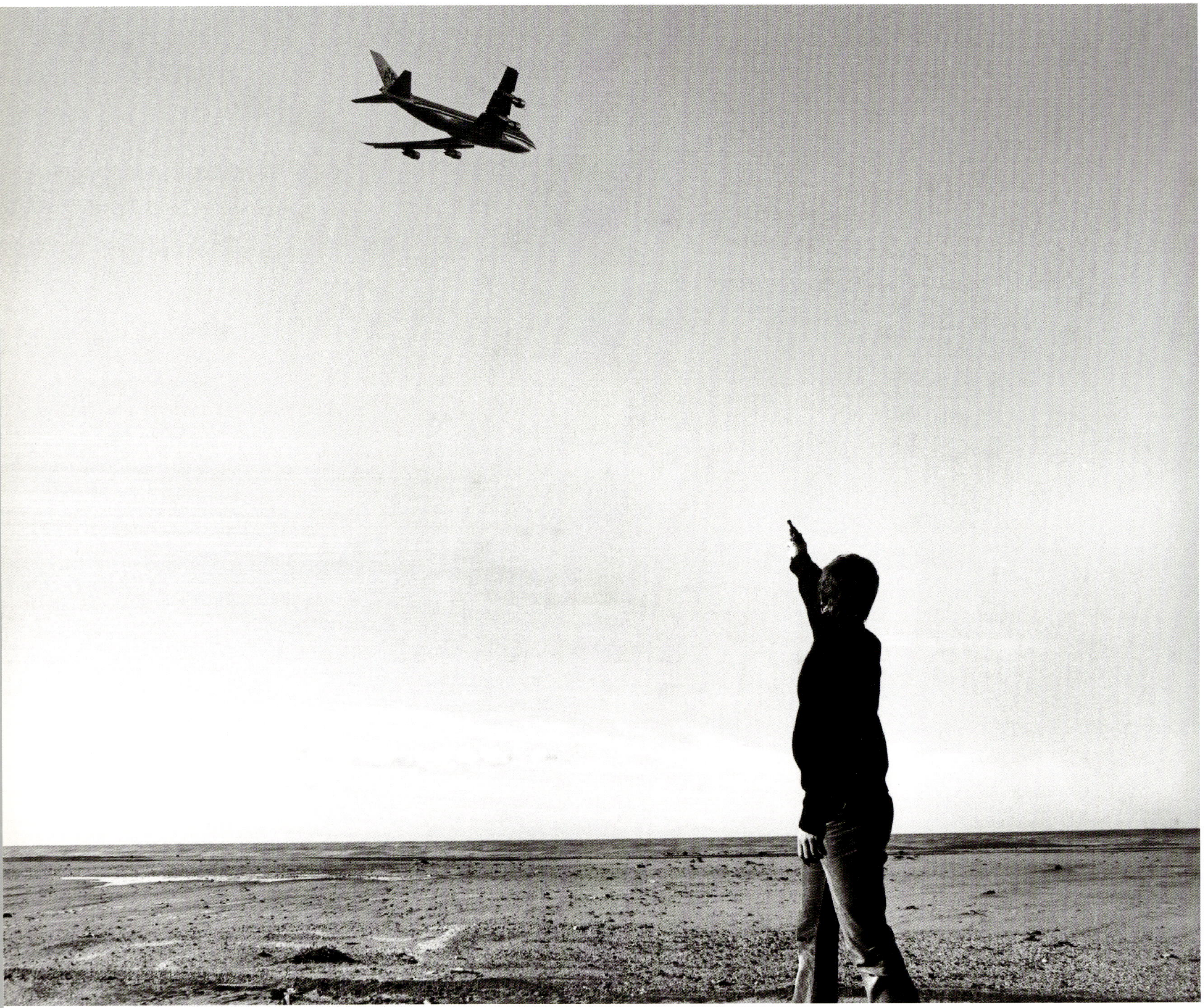

747 1973

Los Angeles, California, USA;
January 5, 1973

At about 8 am on a beach near the Los Angeles International Airport, I fired several shots with a pistol at a Boeing 747.

RELIC: Revolver

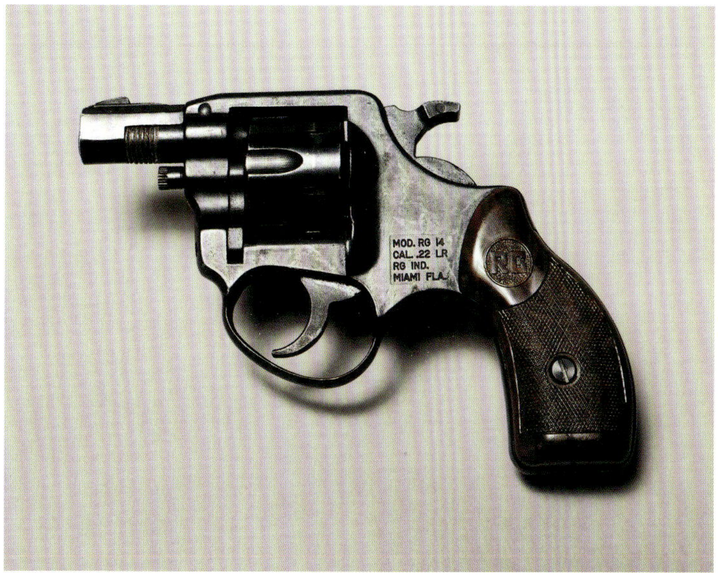

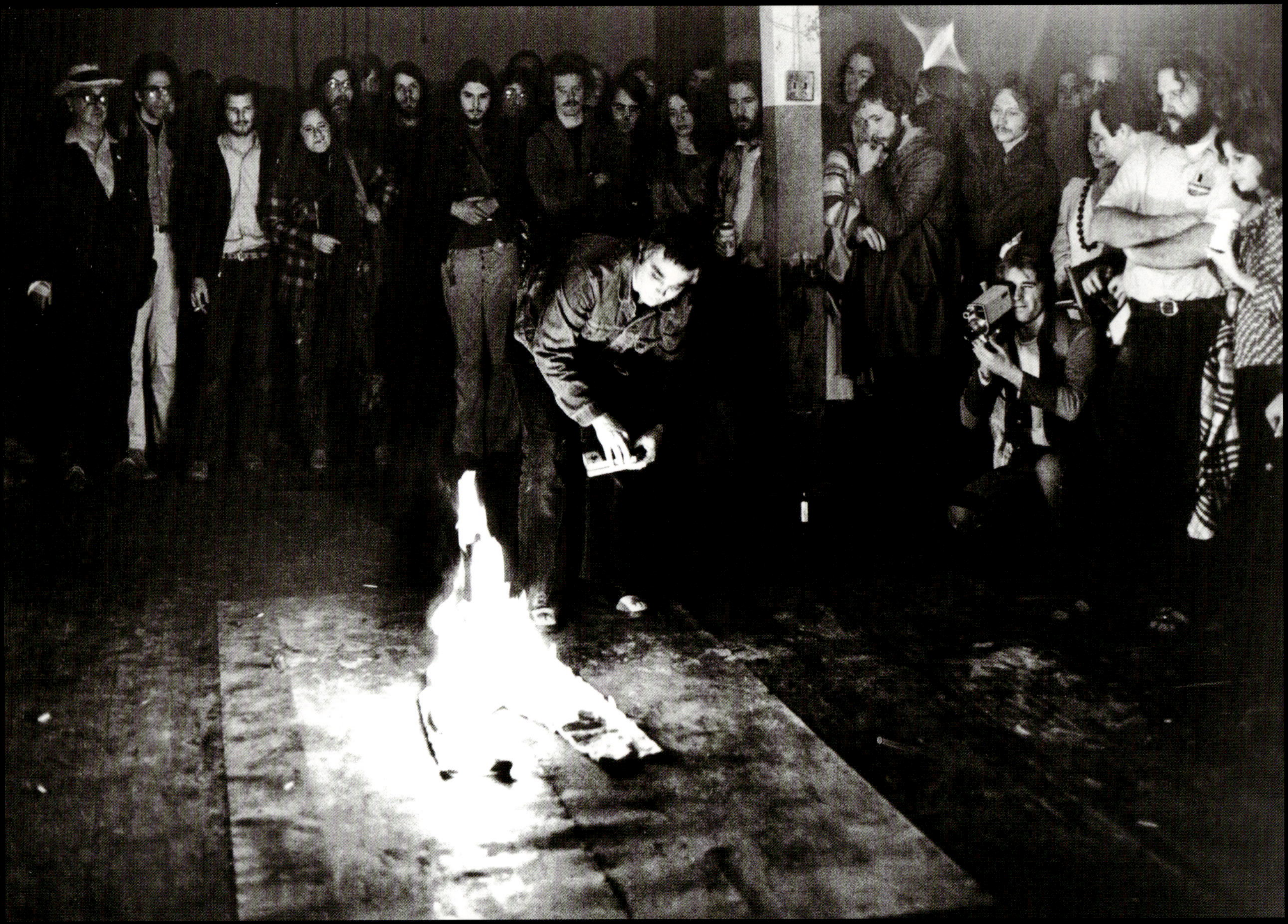

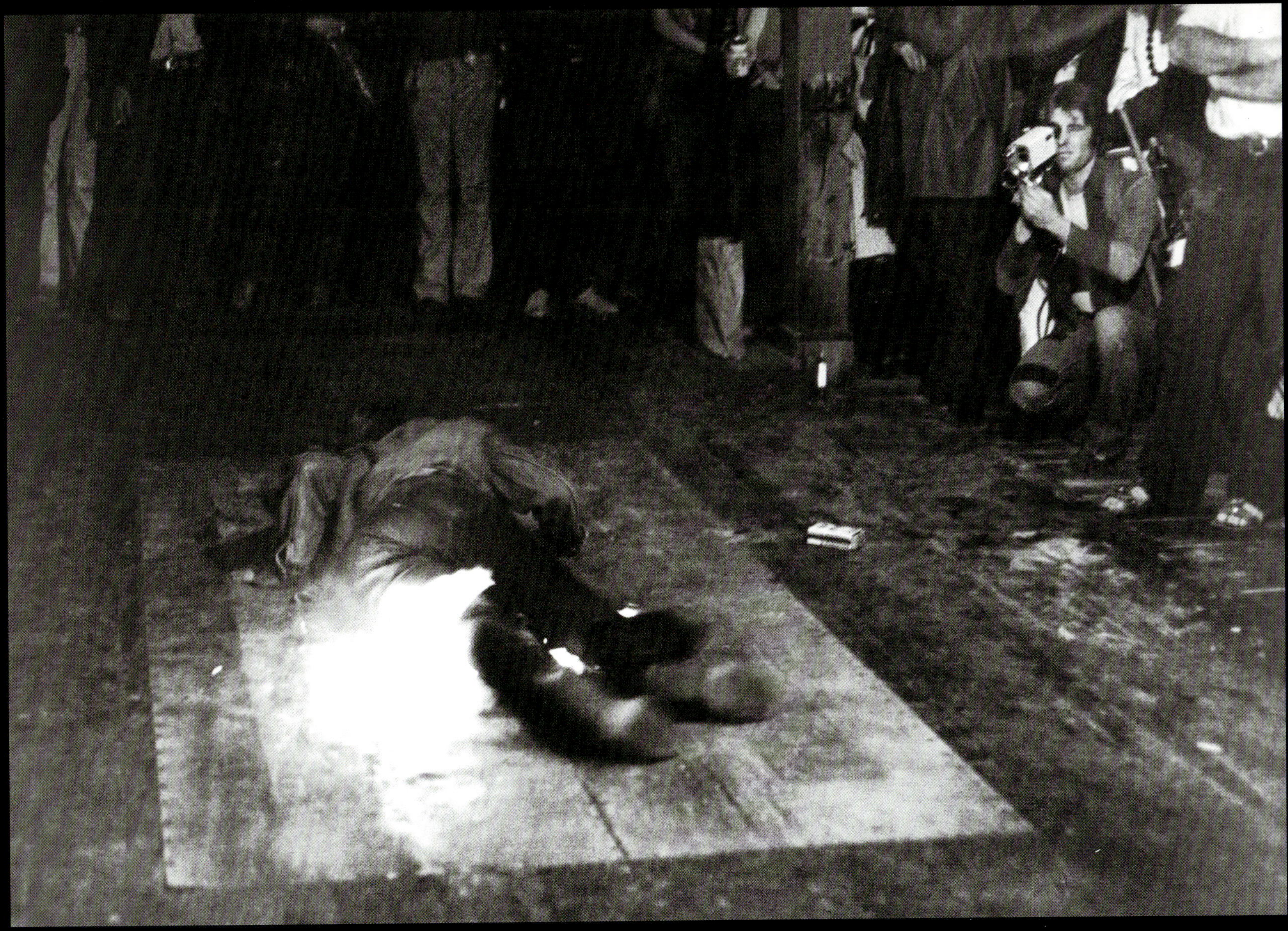

Fire Roll 1973

Museum of Conceptual Art,
San Francisco, California, USA;
February 28, 1973

I began the evening watching television, smoking and drinking beer. The other artists were preparing their pieces. People were filling the museum and my activity went almost unnoticed. After about an hour I got up and went around the room turning off all the lights. I had a pair of old pants which had been passed around by many of my friends. I placed the pants on the floor and saturated them with lighter fluid. I lit the pants on fire and extinguished the flames with my body. I turned the lights on and returned to watching television.

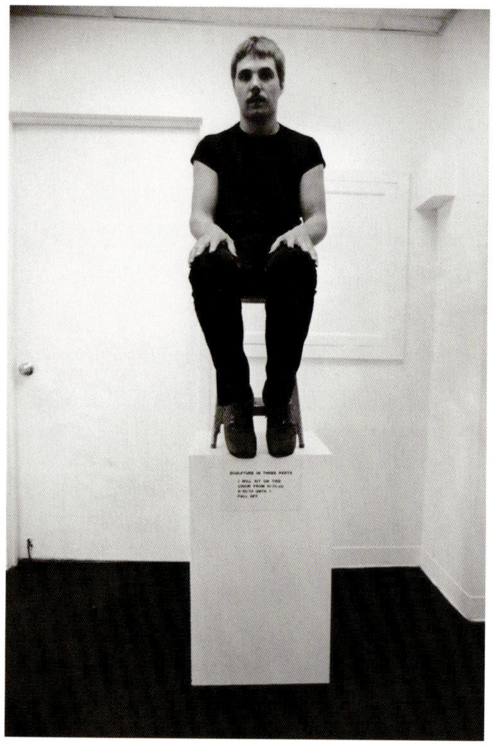

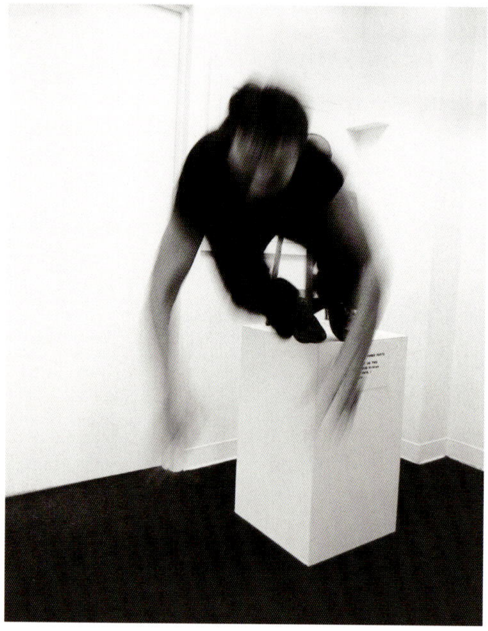

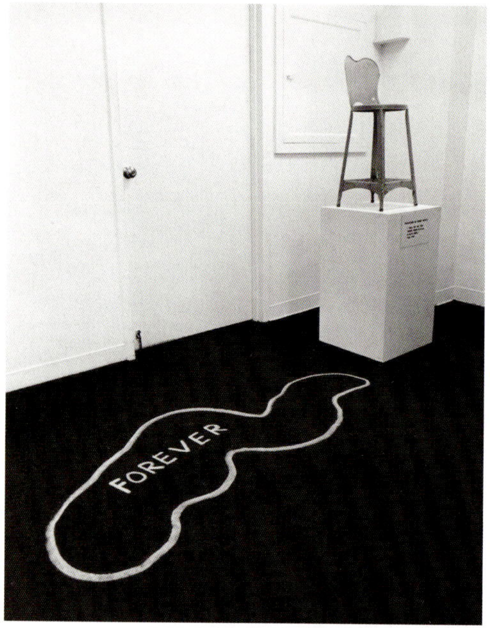

Sculpture in Three Parts 1974

Hansen Fuller Gallery, San Francisco,
California, USA; September 10–21, 1974

I sat on a small metal stool placed on a sculpture stand directly in front of the gallery entrance, an elevator door. A sign on the stand read 'Sculpture in Three Parts. I will sit on this chair from 10:30 am 9/10/74 until I fall off.' About ten feet away, a camera was constantly attended by changing photographers waiting to take a photograph as I fell. I sat on the chair for 43 hours. When I fell, a chalk outline was drawn on the floor around my body. I wrote 'Forever' inside the outline. I placed another sign on the stand which read 'I sat on this chair from 10:30 am 9/10/74 until I fell off at 5:25 am 9/12/74.' The chair, stand and outline remained on exhibit until September 21.

RELIC: Stool (destroyed)

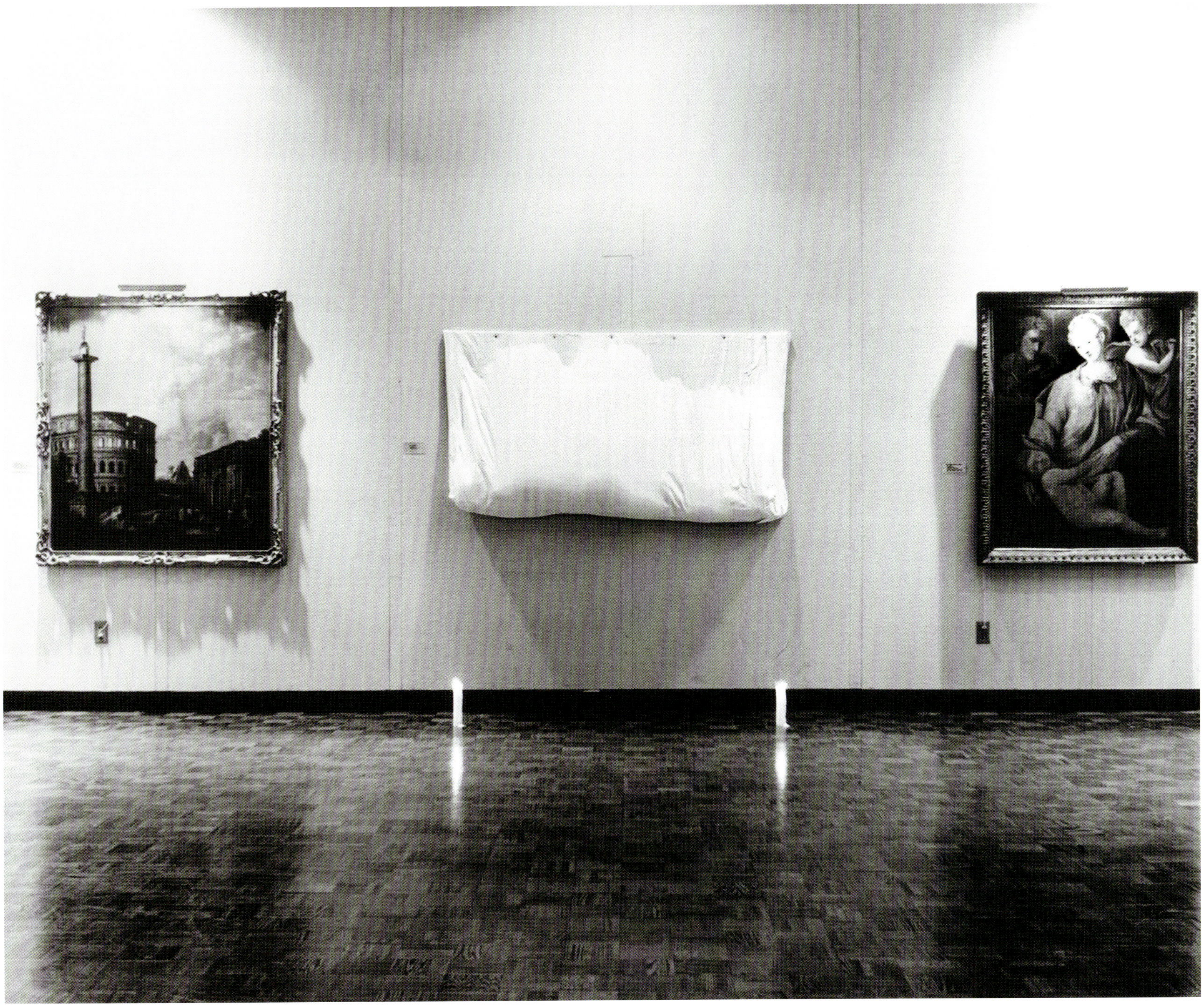

Oh, Dracula 1974

Utah Museum of Art, Salt Lake City,
Utah, USA; October 7, 1974

I was invited to do a piece in the foyer of the Utah Museum by the director E.F. Sanguinetti. The room was filled with Renaissance paintings of religious subjects. Using strips of adhesive tape, I made a large chrysalis for my body. I was mounted on the wall, replacing one of the paintings. A lighted candle was placed on the floor beneath my head and another at my feet. An engraved plaque, similar to those identifying the paintings, giving my name, title of the piece and the date was placed on the wall. I remained in the chrysalis during museum hours, 9 am to 5 pm.

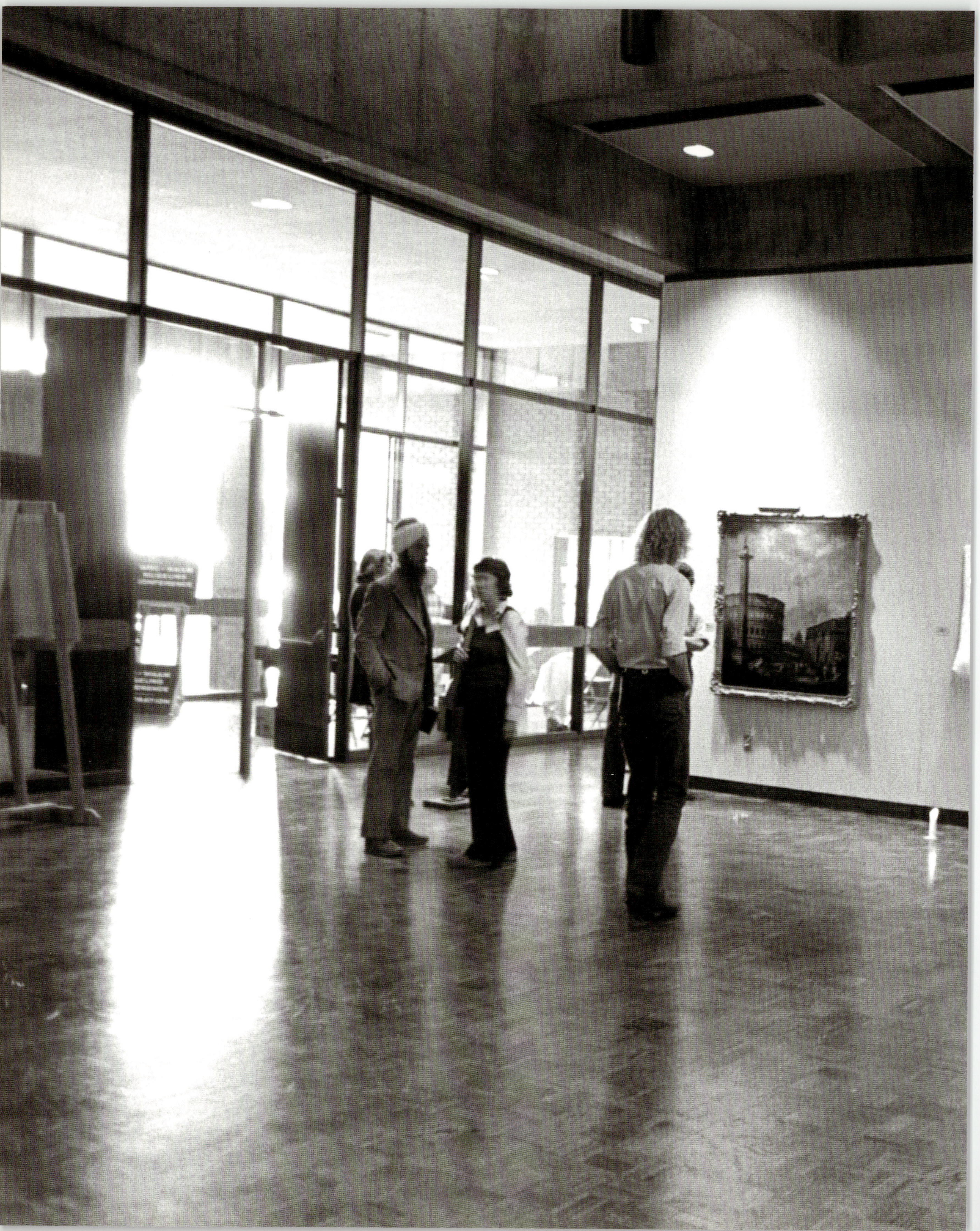

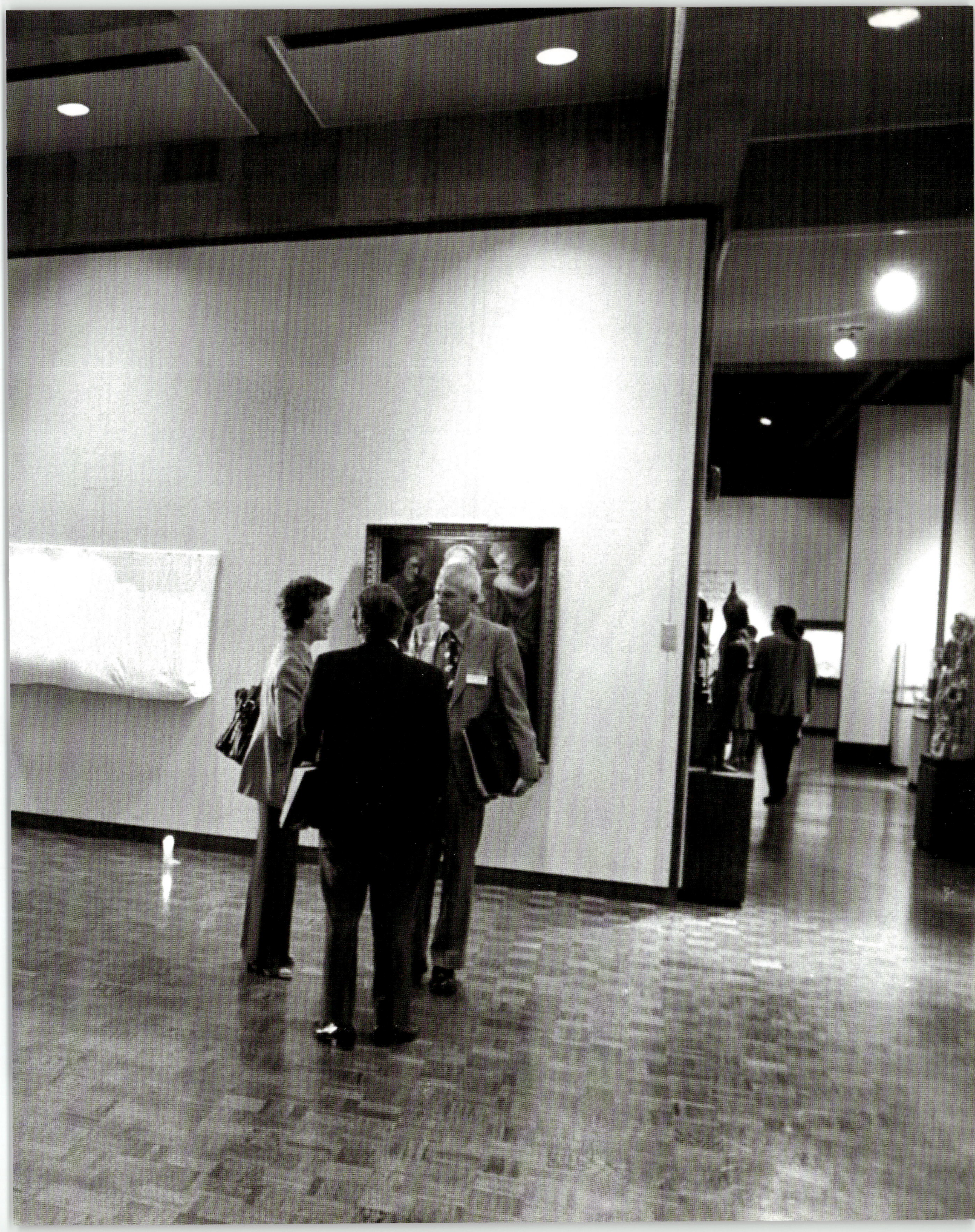

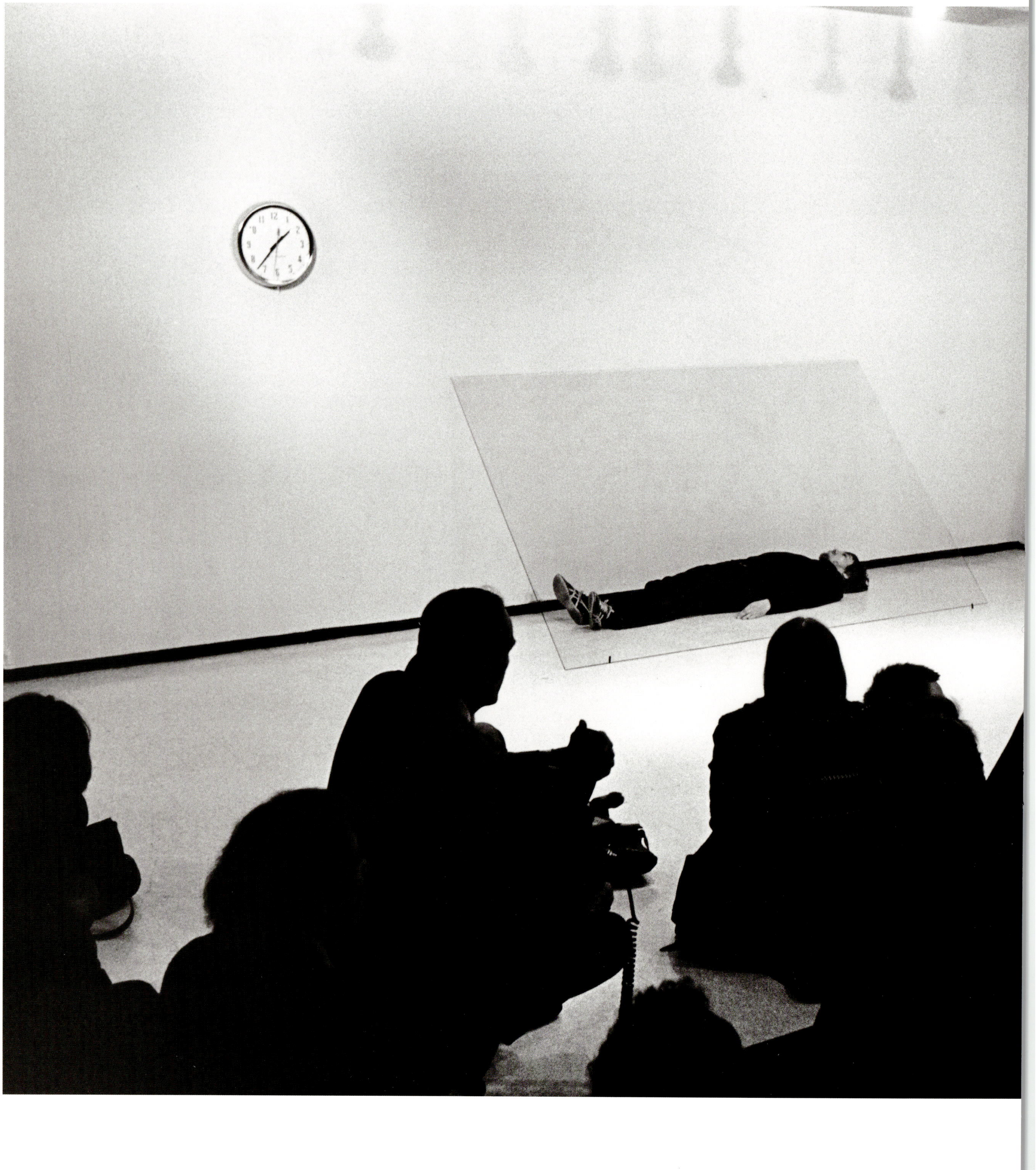

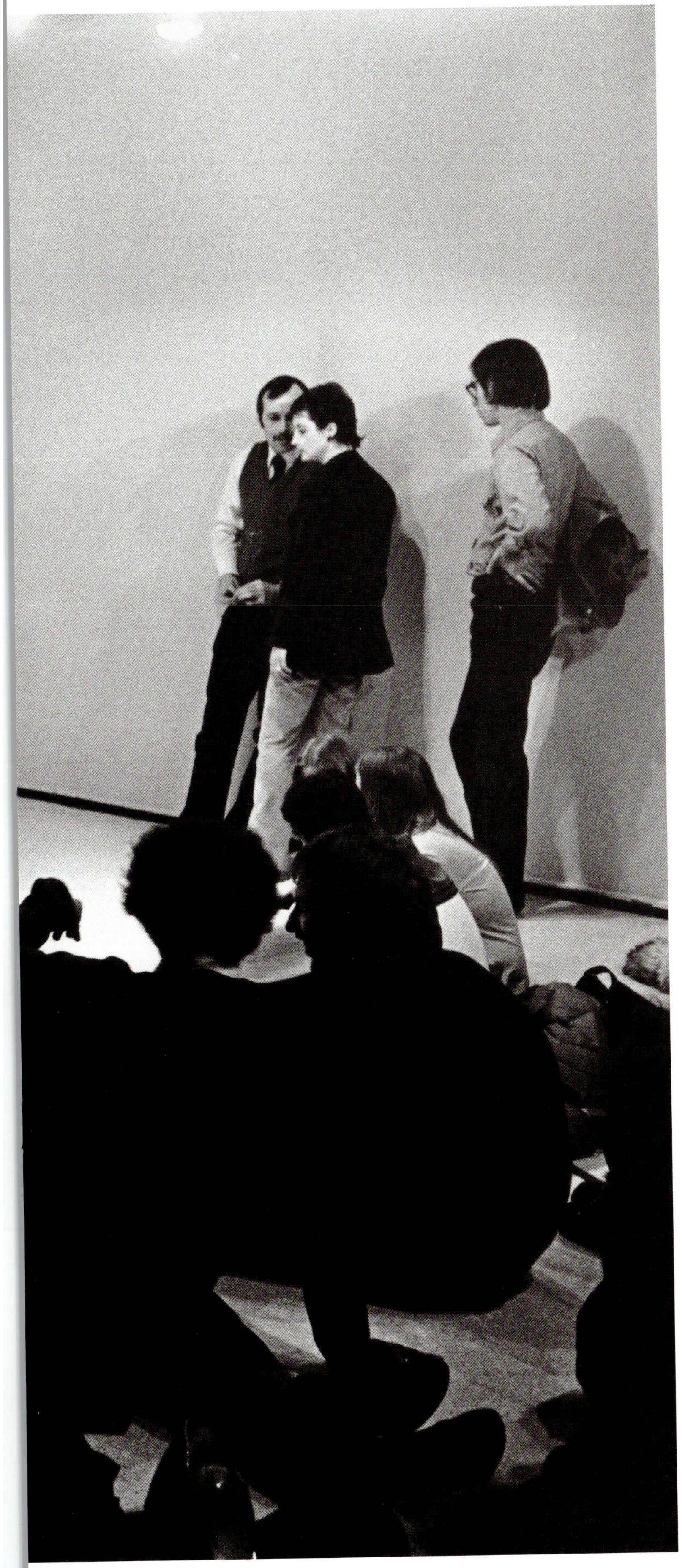

Doomed 1975

Museum of Contemporary Art,
Chicago, Illinois, USA; April 11, 1975

My performance consisted of three elements: myself, an institutional wall clock and a five by eight-foot sheet of plate glass. The sheet of glass was placed horizontally and leaned against the wall at a 45-degree angle; the clock was placed to the left of the glass at eye level. When the performance began, the clock was running at the correct time. I entered the room and reset the clock to 12 midnight. I crawled into the space between the glass and the wall and lay on my back. I was prepared to lie in this position indefinitely, until one of the three elements was disturbed or altered. The responsibility for ending the piece rested with the museum staff, but they were unaware of this crucial aspect. The piece ended when Dennis O'Shea placed a container of water inside the space between the wall and the glass, 45 hours and 10 minutes after the start of the piece. I immediately got up and smashed the face of the clock with a hammer, recording the exact amount of time which had elapsed from beginning to end.

Shadow 1976

Ohio State University, Columbus,
Ohio, USA; April 26, 1976

The piece began the moment I arrived at the airport and lasted the entire time I was in Columbus. I was dressed in clothes which I thought would fit people's preconceptions of an avant-garde artist, i.e. a fatigue jacket; pockets stuffed with notebooks, film and a tape recorder; opaque dark glasses with chrome rims; a black cap; Levis and a striped t-shirt. These clothes were in no way characteristic of my normal attire. During the course of the piece I acted distant and aloof, and had as little interaction with students and faculty as possible. The University had scheduled a particular time in the gallery for what they believed to be the performance. I had them erect a translucent screen to separate me from the audience. I sat on a chair behind the screen and a strong light illuminated my profile. I read the audience descriptions of the pieces I had done in the last six years. I allowed 30 seconds between each description for the audience to visualize the piece. The following day I was supposed to have a question-and-answer period with students. But I remained elusive, answering elaborate speculations with a simple 'yes' or 'no'. My intention throughout the piece was to make my personal presence almost superfluous by revealing little or no information about myself that was not already available publicly.

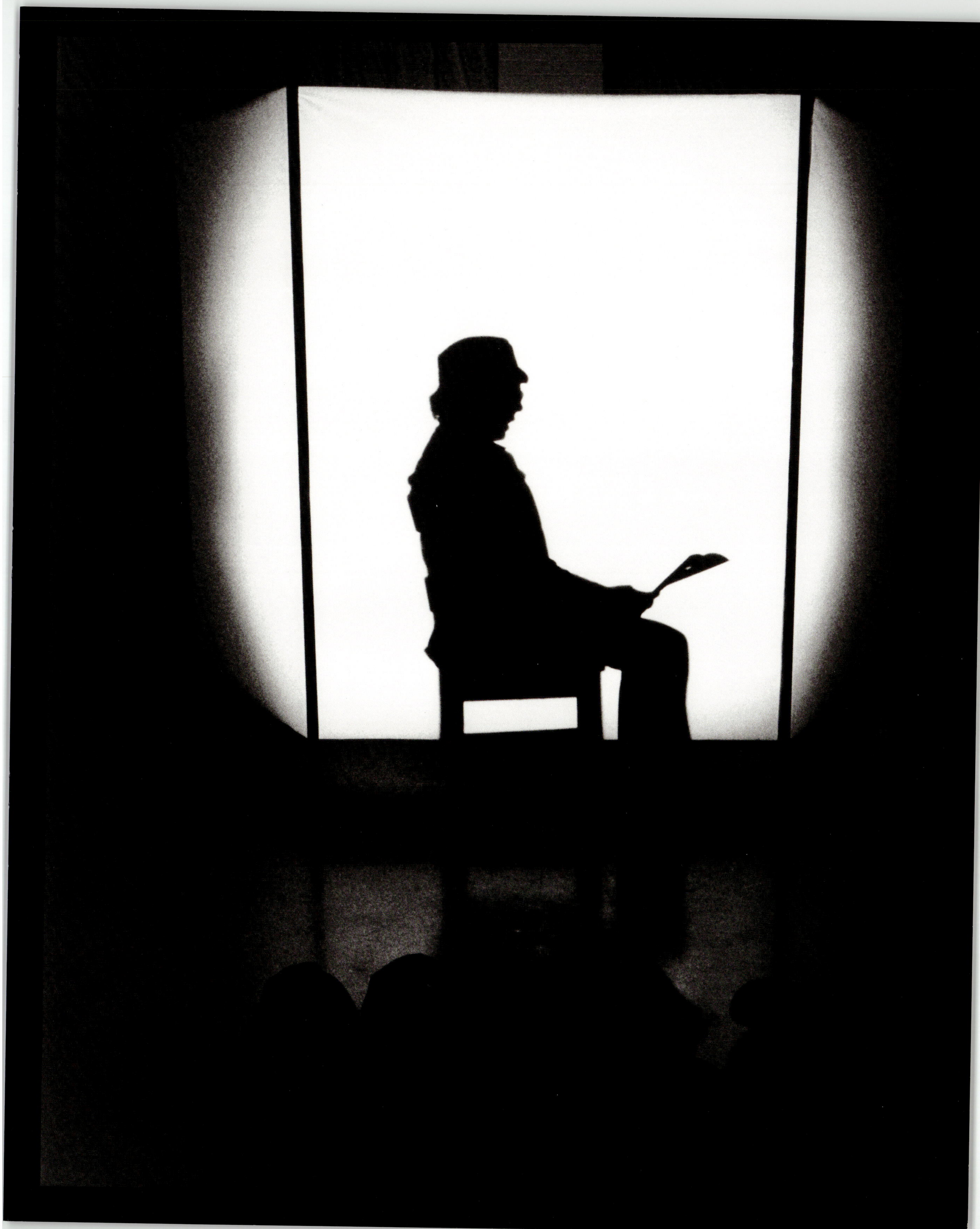

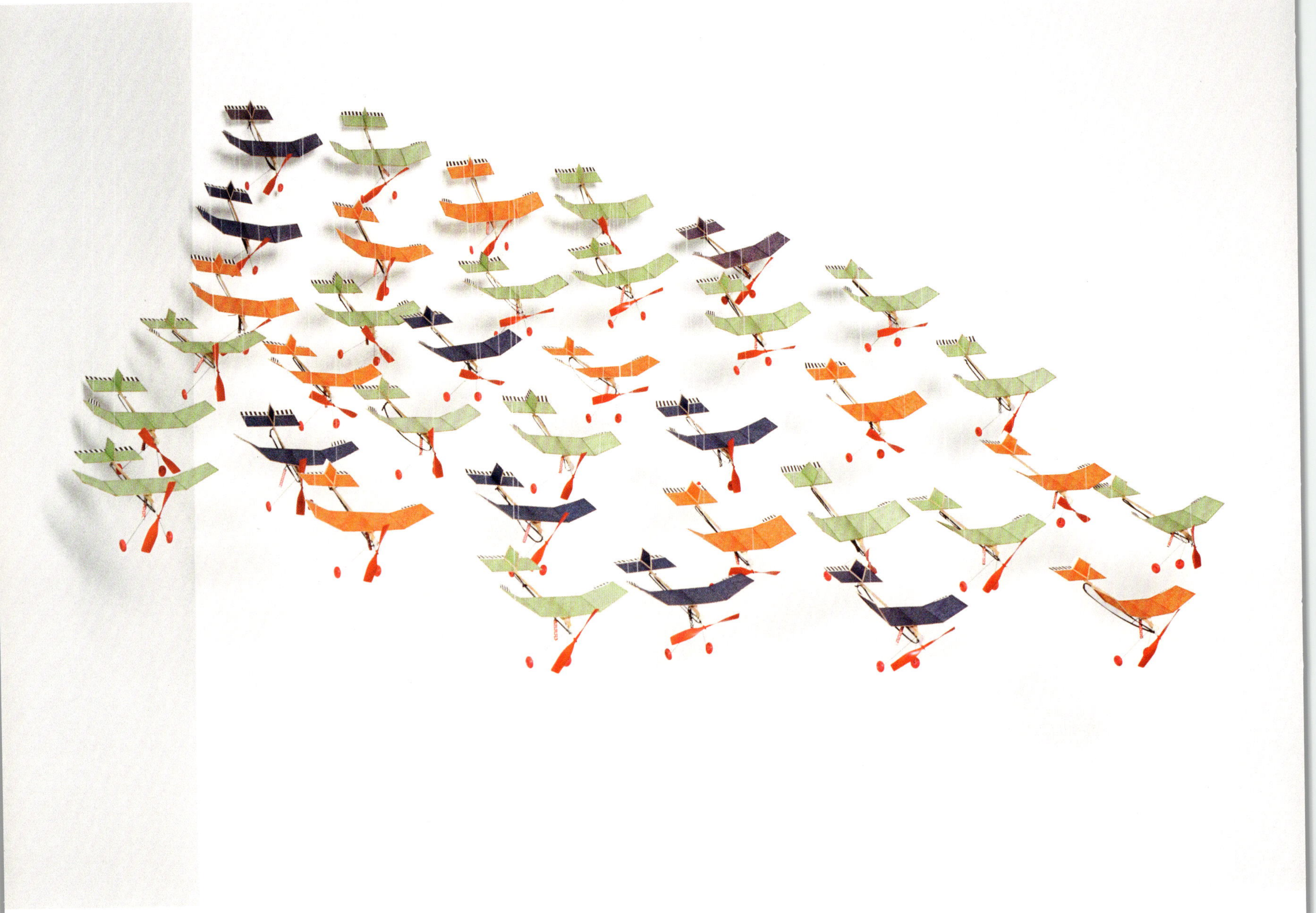

C.B. Air Force 1980

40 model airplanes of balsawood and paper, each equipped with a firecracker
Each plane: 10 inches long × 10 inch wingspan

The C.B. Air Force *(Chris Burden Air Force) consists of 40 Peck Polymer R.O.G. (Rise off the Ground) planes. These planes are of an extremely high performance, capable of flights lasting one-and-a-half minutes or more, and of obtaining altitudes of 60 to 80 feet. They are displayed in full-simulated flight. In 1979, the whole Air Force was displayed in Santa Barbara, California in the National Guard Armory during an action called* Pearl Harbor. *Over half the planes suffered some sort of damage. Four planes were totally lost in action. Plane #1 is permanently lodged in the apex of the 60-foot high ceiling. One plane was totally obliterated when four or five of the enemy (the audience) tried to simultaneously grab it out of the air. The other two planes were presumably captured intact and stolen by the enemy. The damaged planes have been rebuilt and the missing planes replaced and the* C.B. Air Force *has been restored to its full fighting strength, ready for more action.*

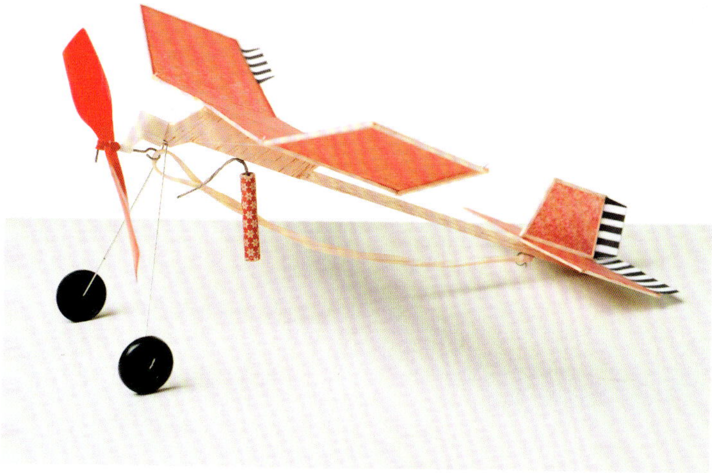

▷▷

A Tale of Two Cities 1981

Installation of two miniature cities with approximately 5,000 toys, sand, plants, boulders
Approximately 800 to 1,200 square feet

A miniature reconstruction of two city-states at war with each other using over 5,000 war toys from the United States, Japan and Europe. The whole tableau is set on a sand base which acts simultaneously as a metaphor for both the desert and the ocean. Each city is protected by the natural rock formations or 'city walls' formed by rows of actual bullets. Behind each city is a large collection of houseplants representing the jungle. The piece can be viewed in detail only through the use of a set of binoculars.

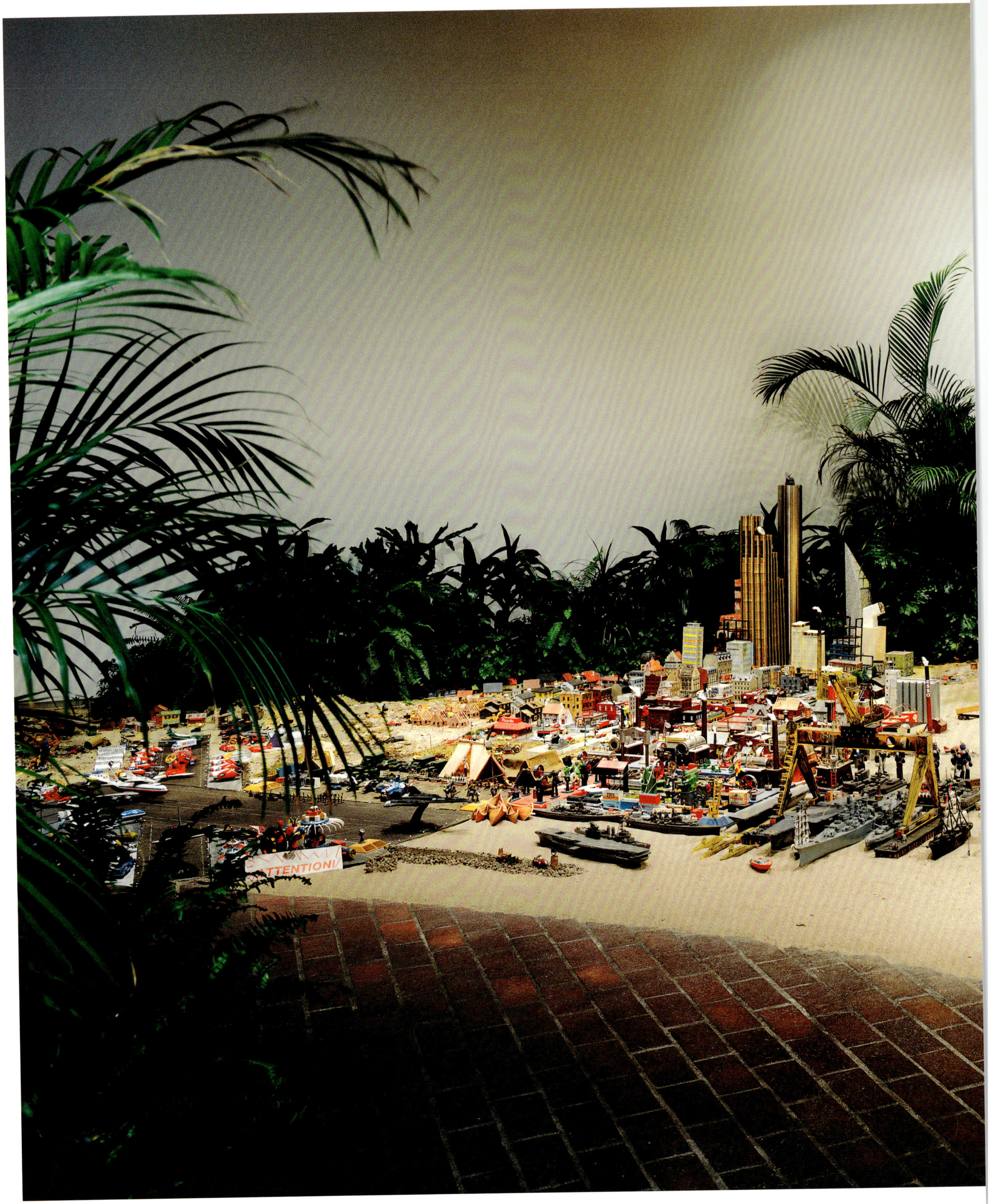
ATTENTION!

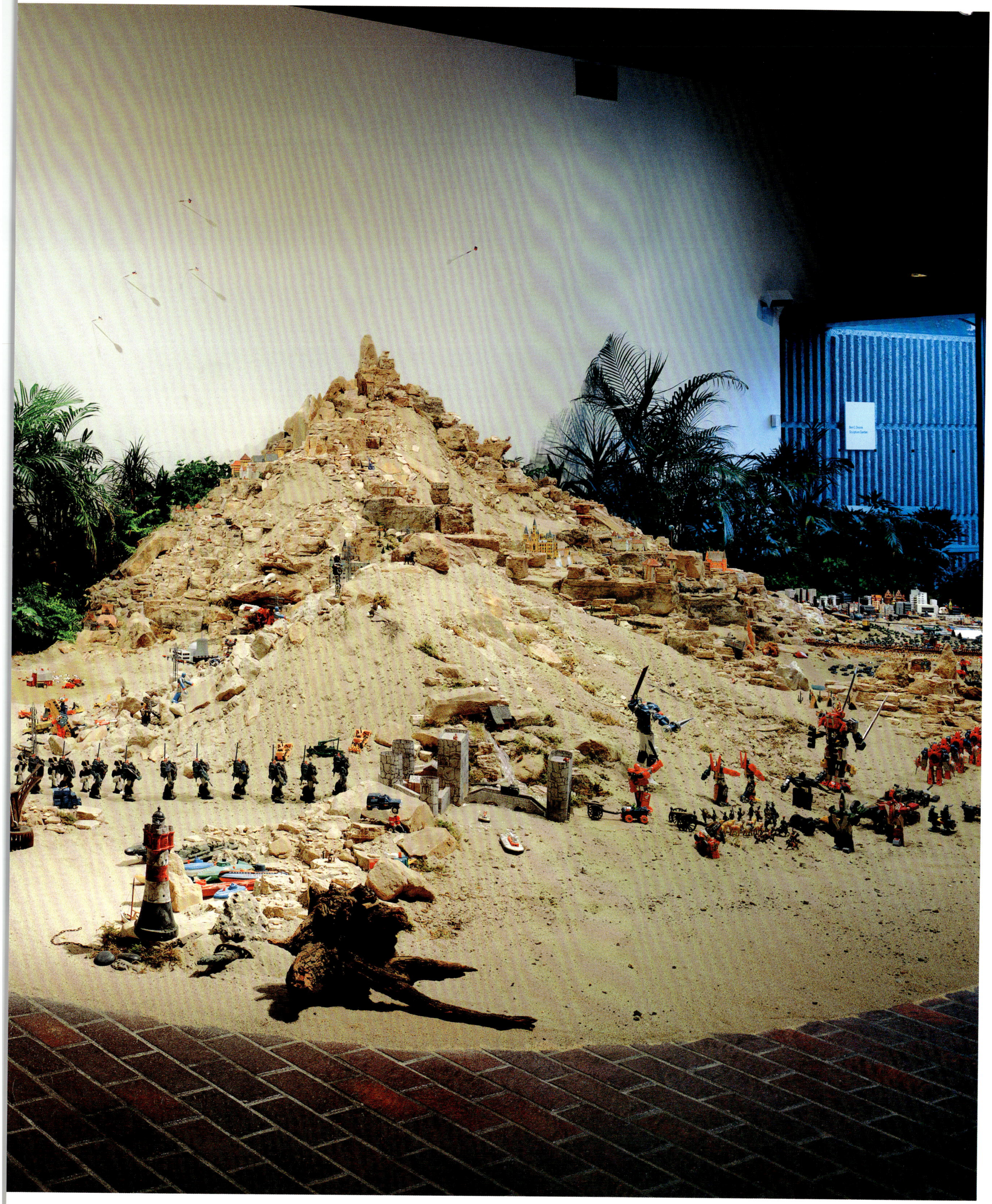

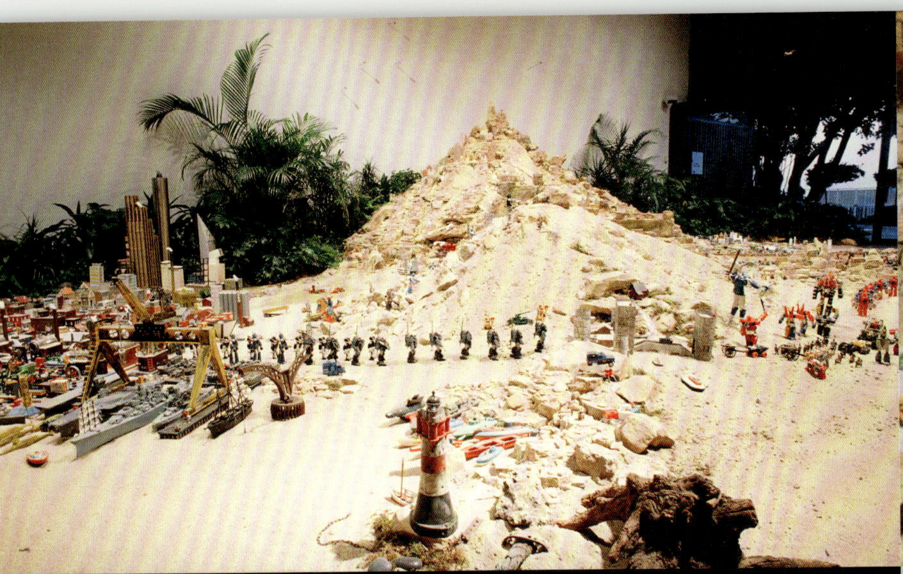
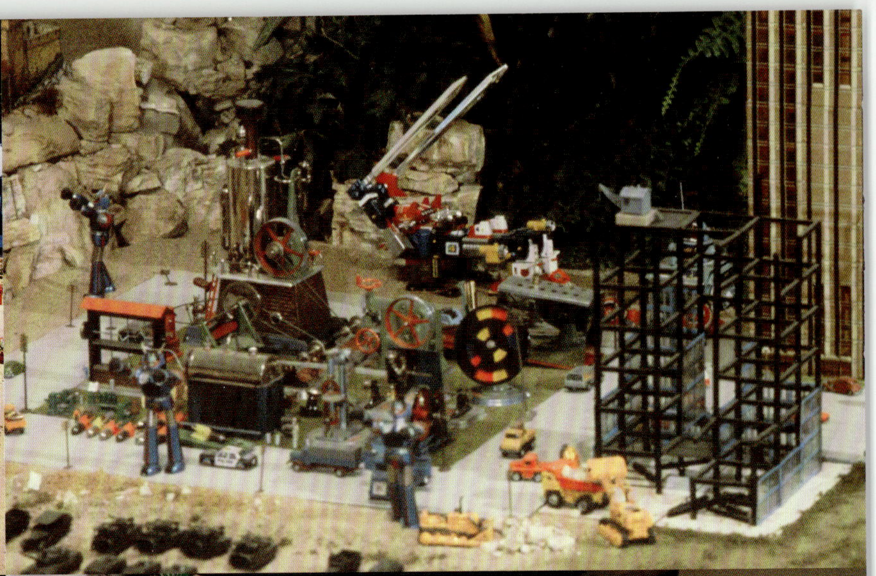
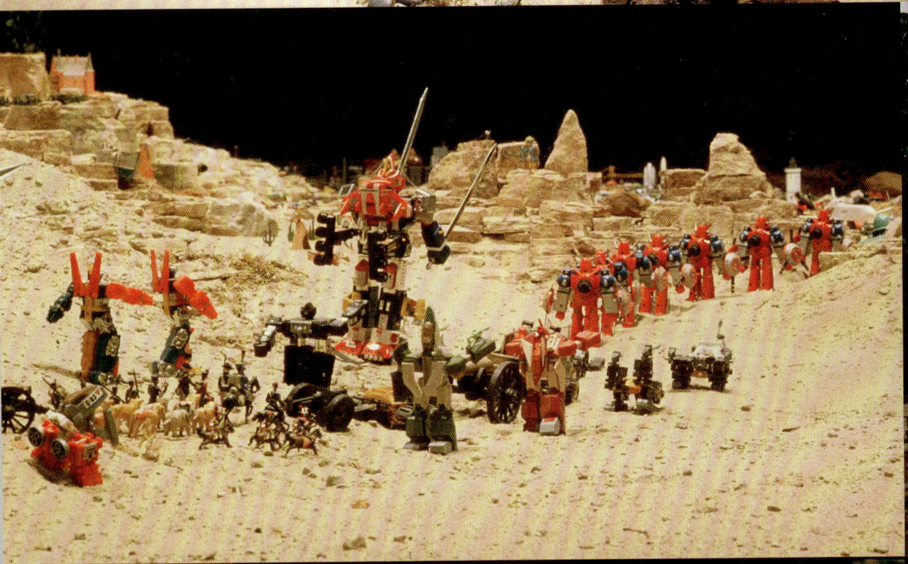
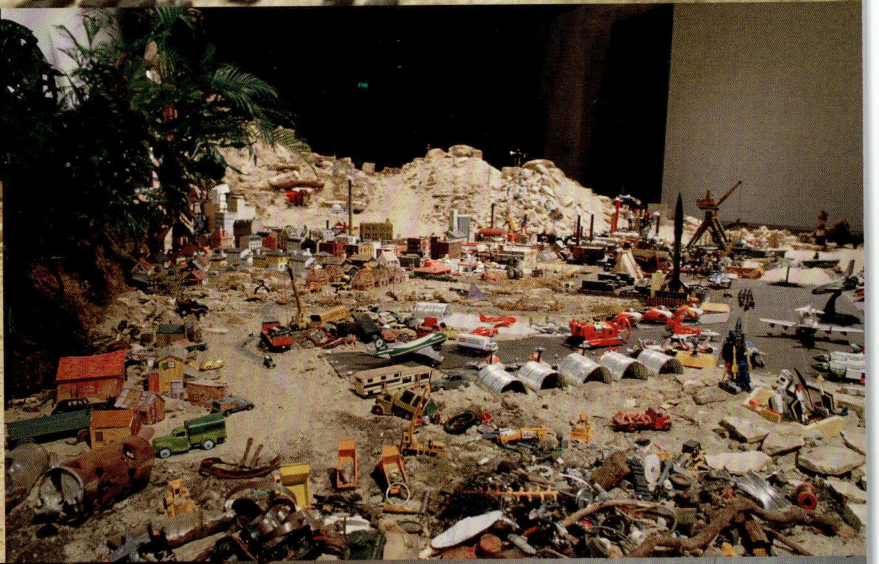
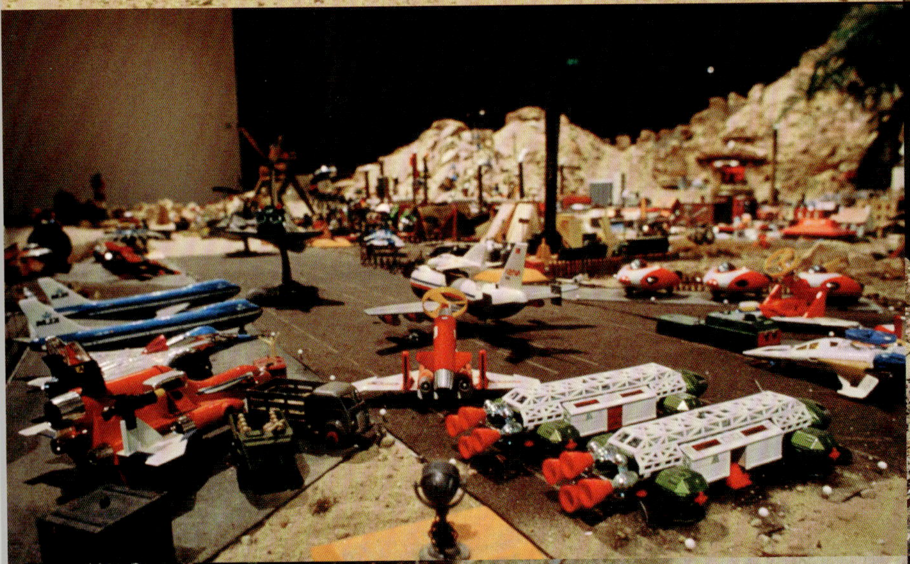
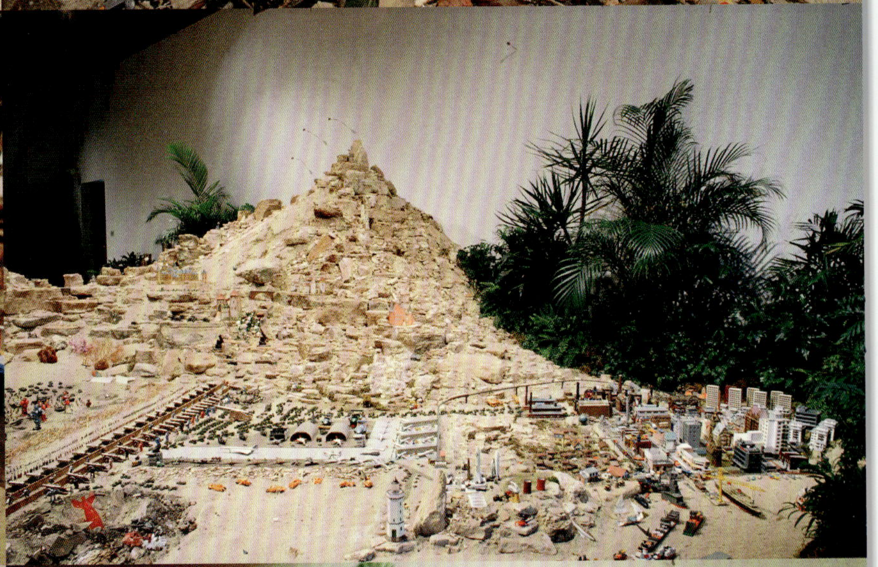
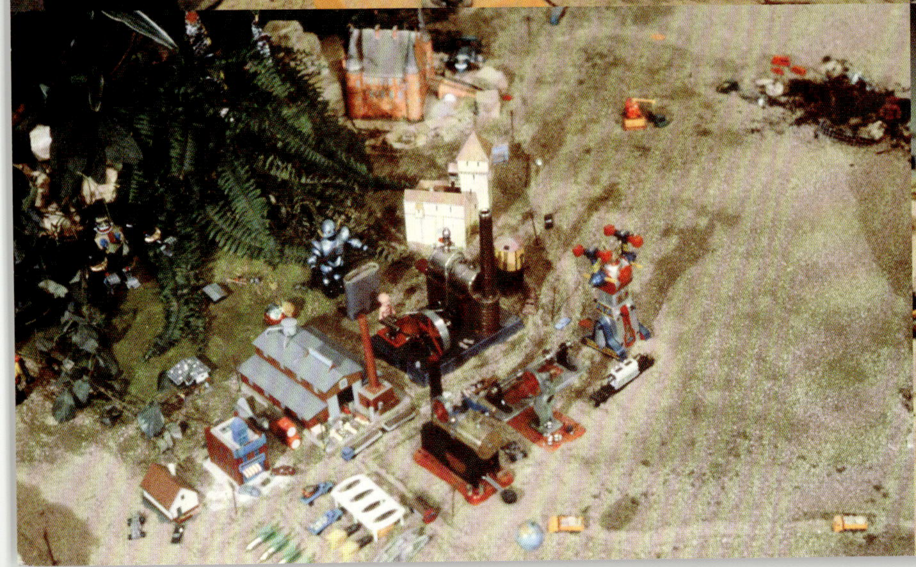
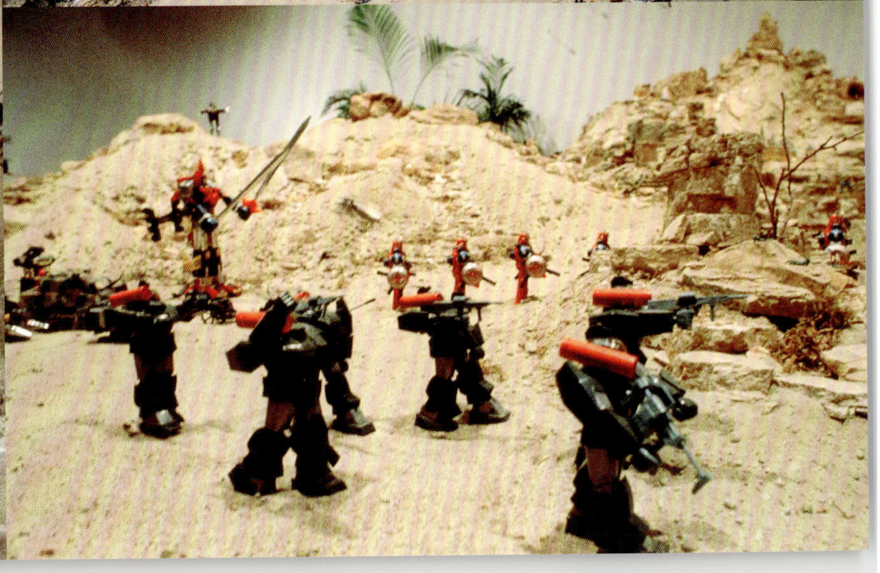

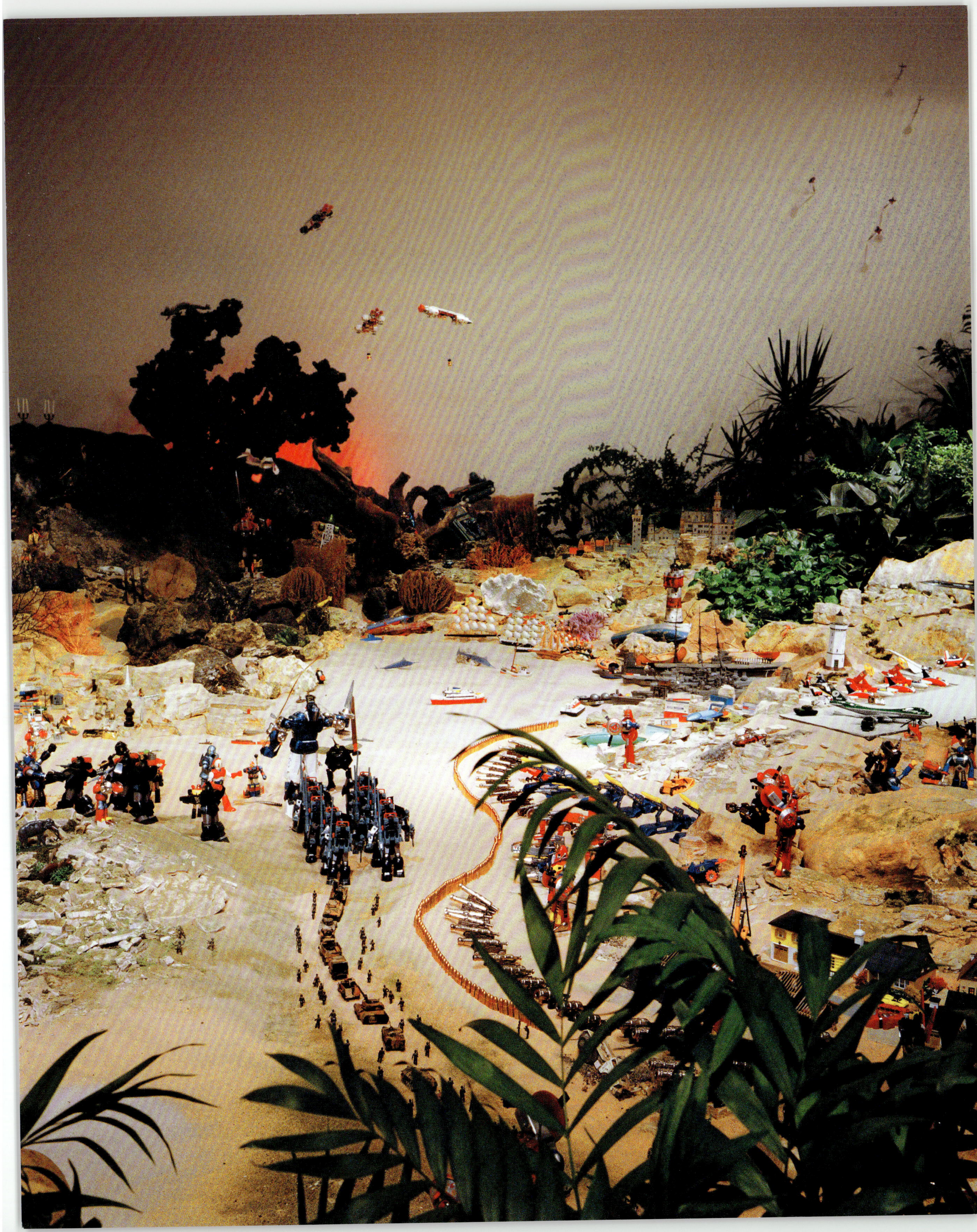

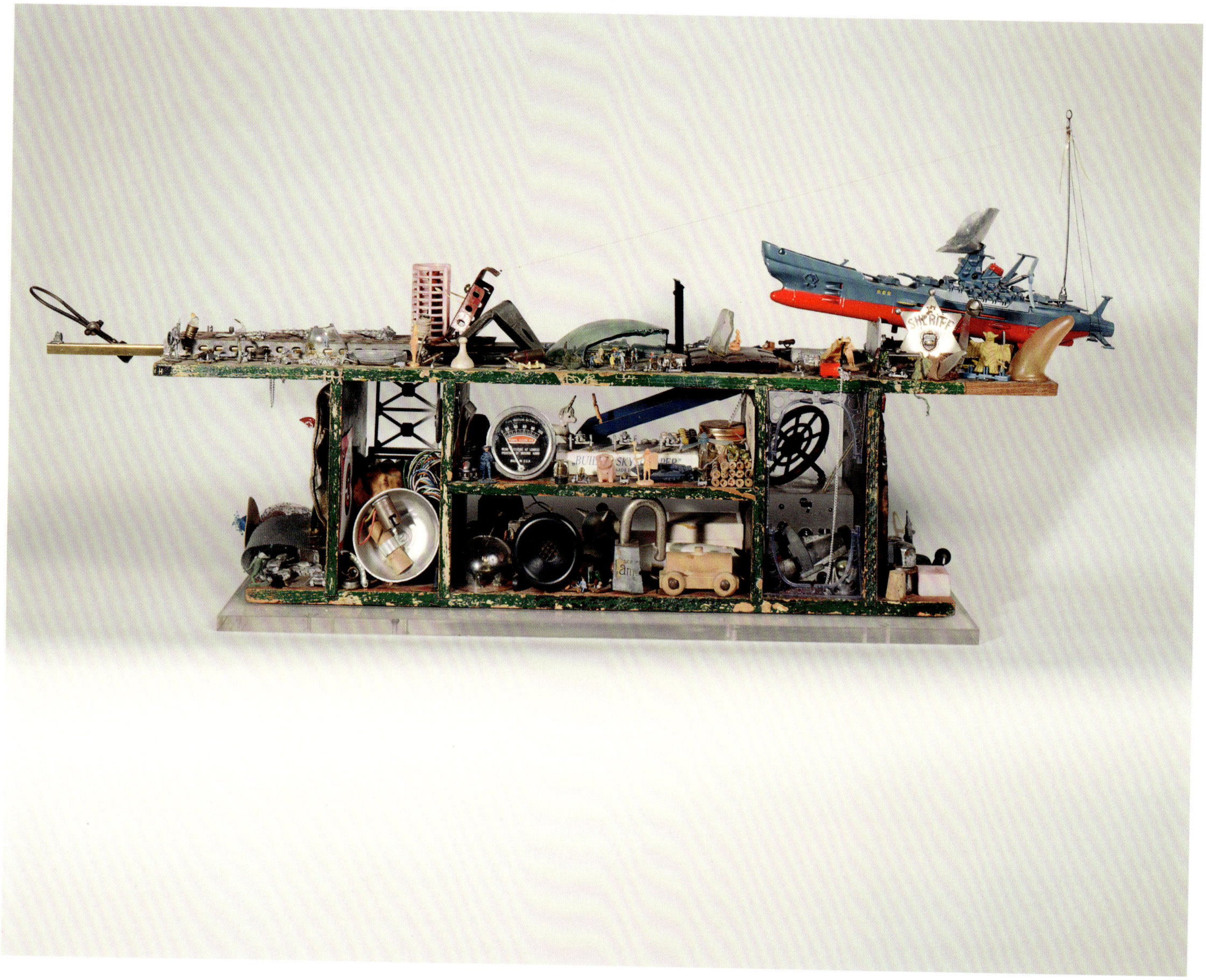

Warship 1981

Mixed media
10 × 33 × 6 inches

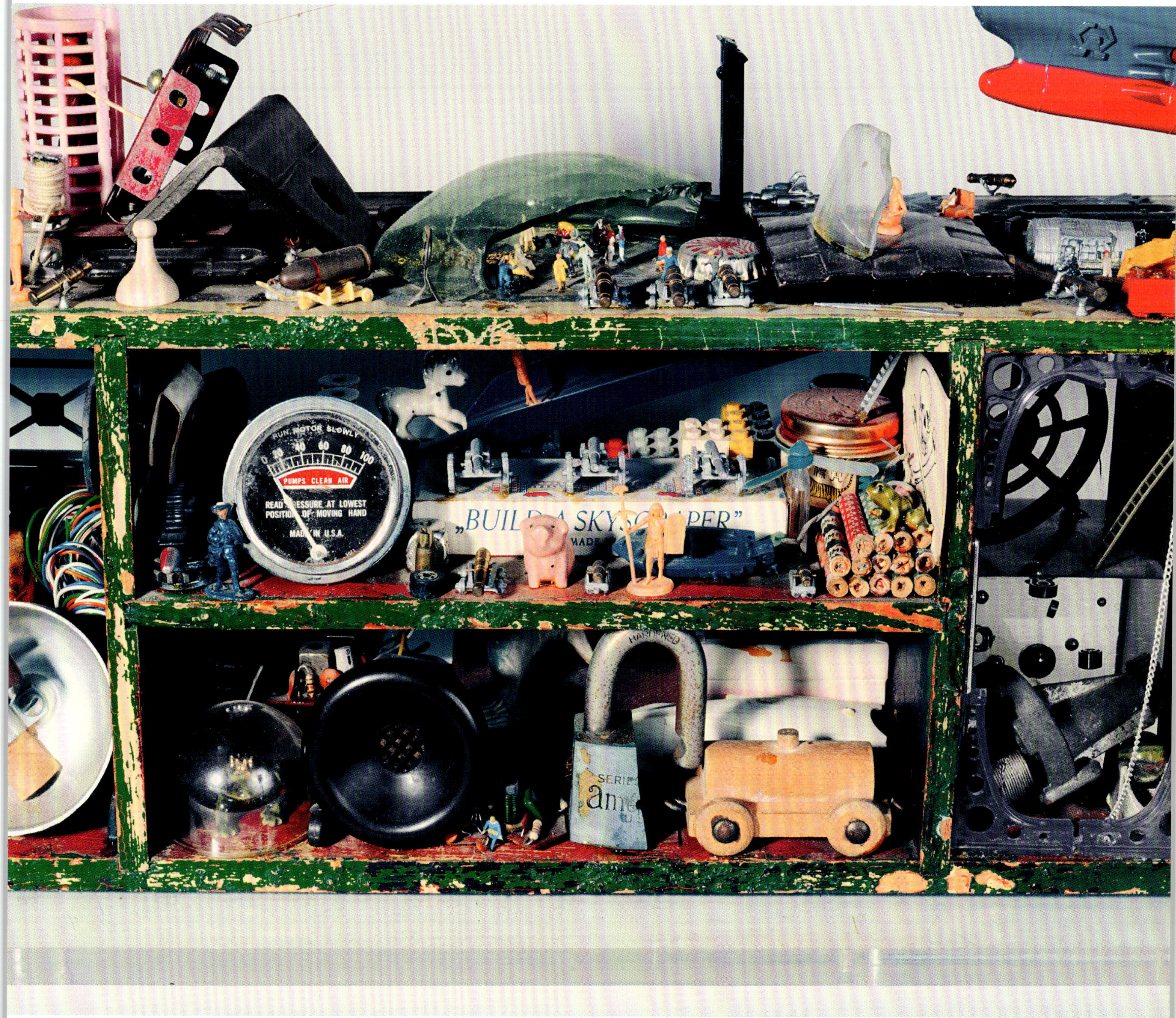
RUN MOTOR SLOWLY
PUMPS CLEAN AIR
MADE IN U.S.A.

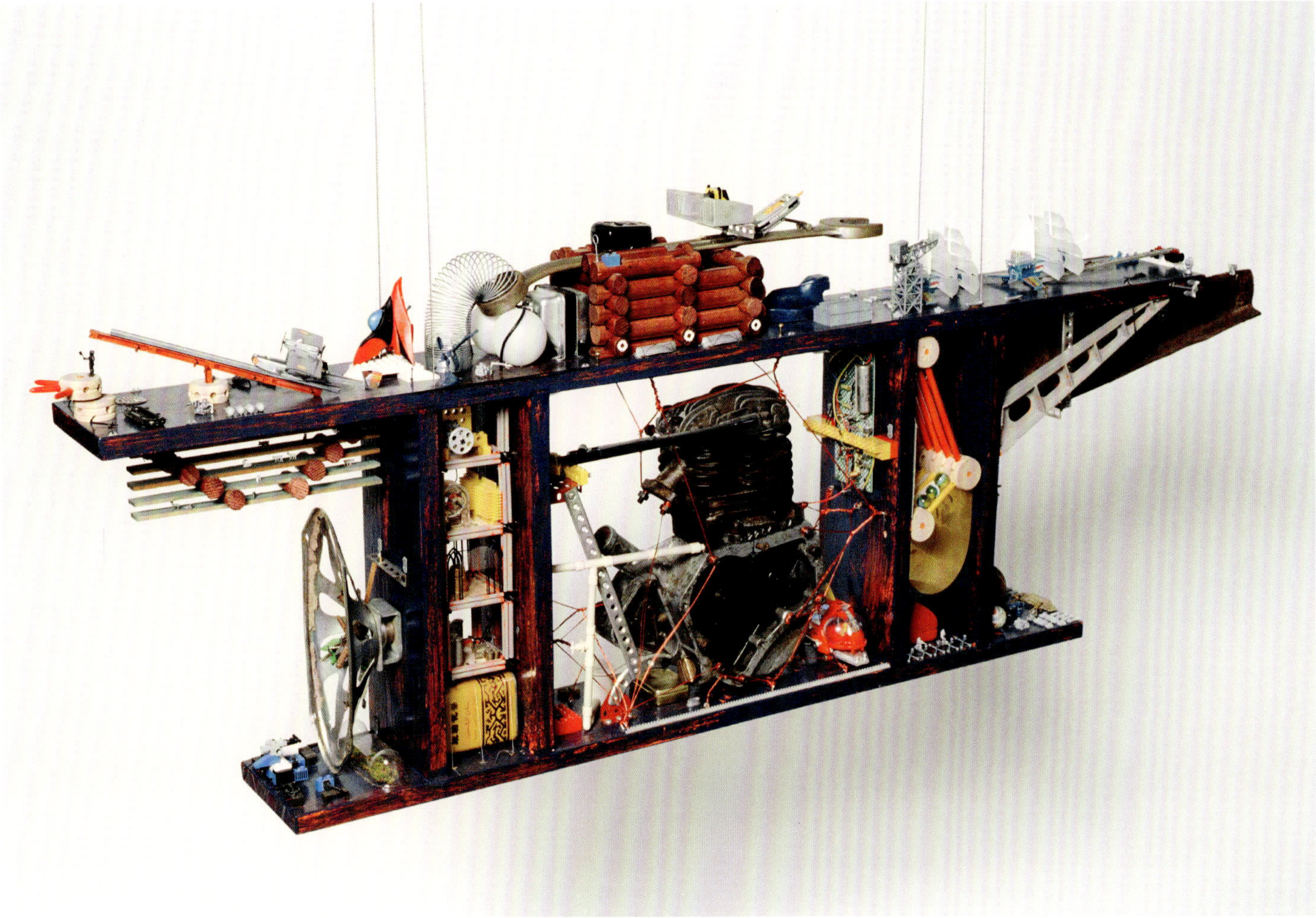

The Nina 1982

Painted wood, motorcycle engine, toys, glass, plastic, wood, metal, electronic circuitry
20½ × 55 × 7 inches

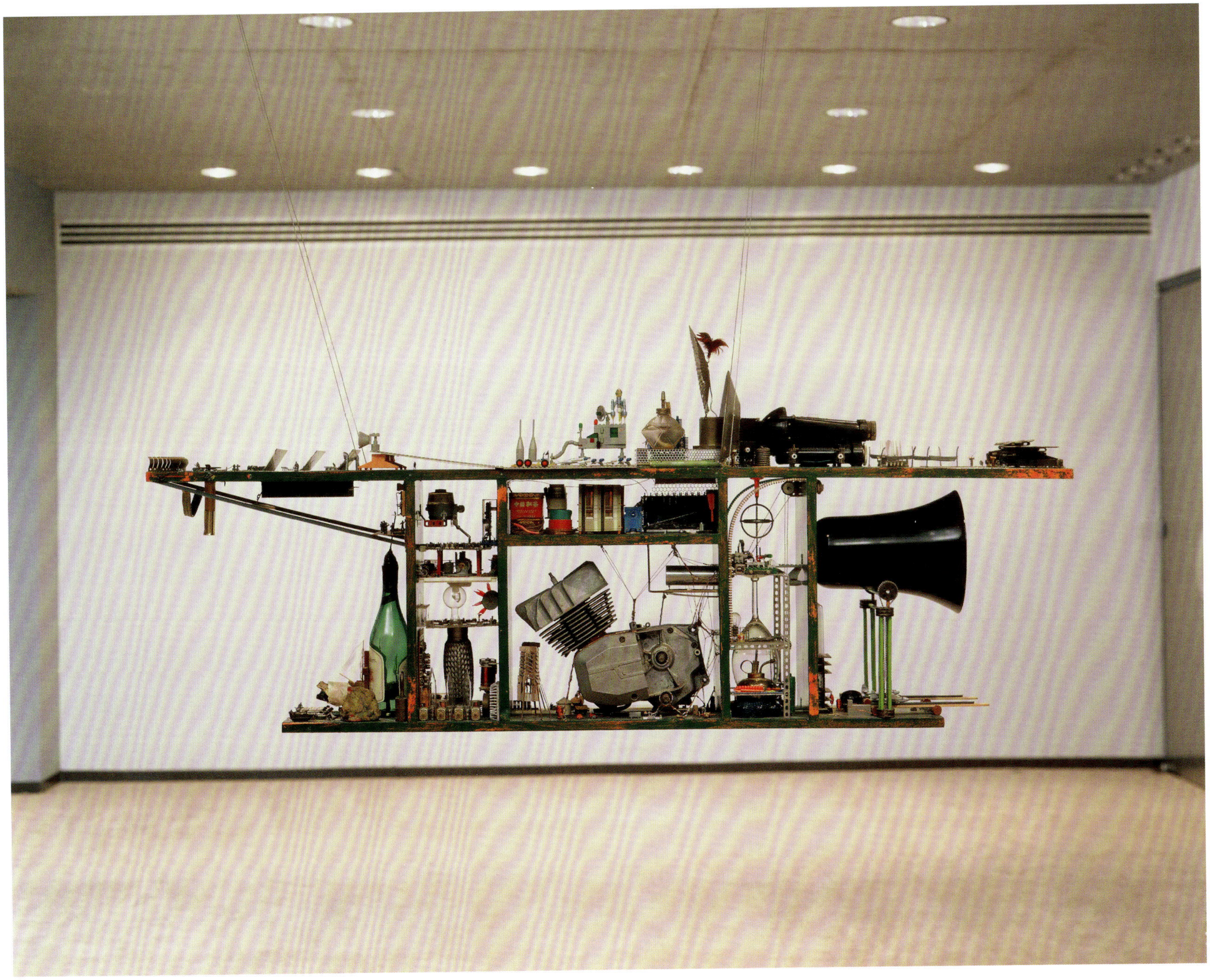

The Pinta 1982

Painted wood, motorcycle engine, toys, glass, plastic, wood, metal, electronic circuitry
29¾ × 70¼ × 11¾ inches

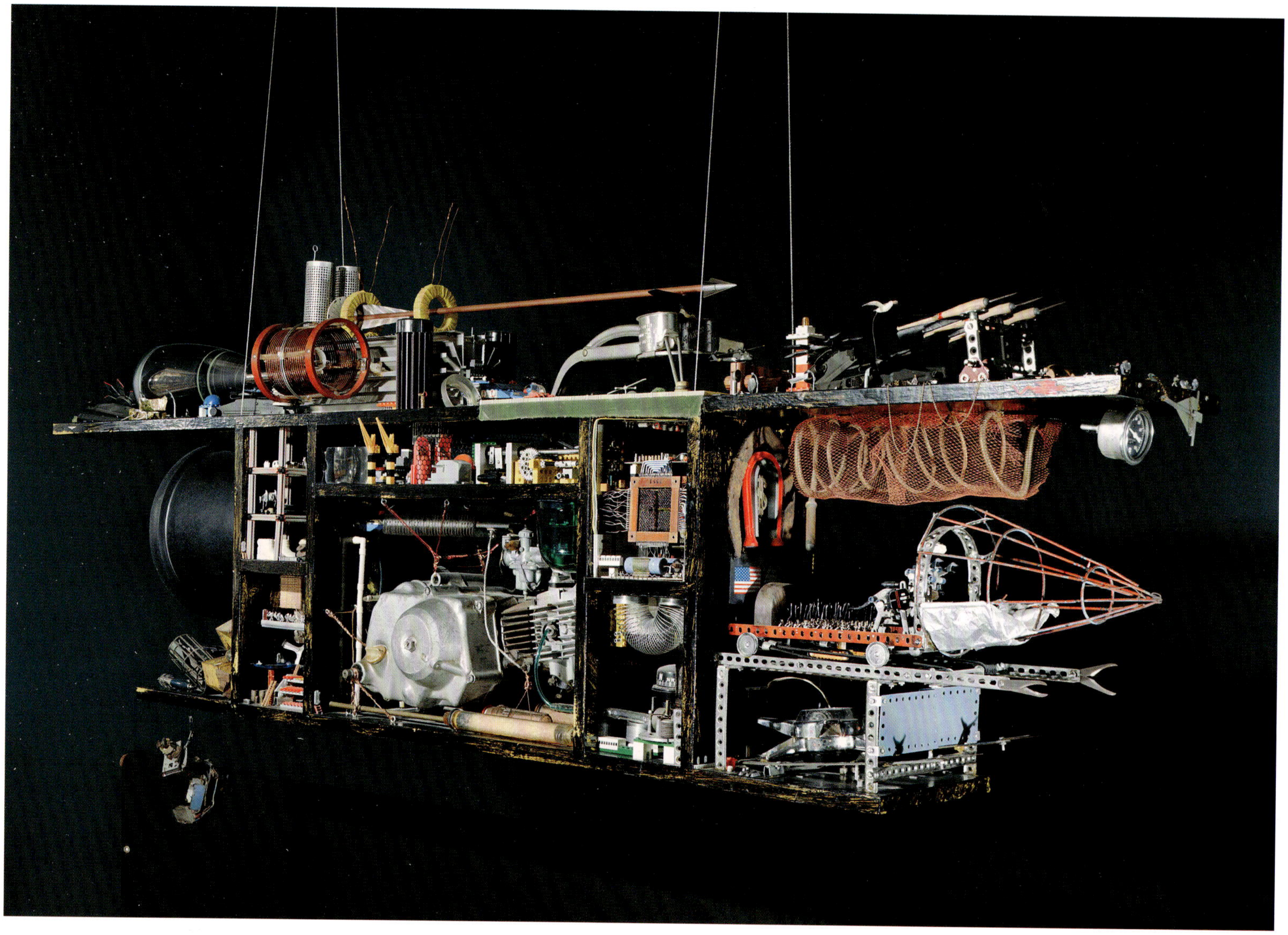

The Santa Maria 1982

Painted wood, motorcycle engine, toys, glass,
plastic, wood, metal, electronic circuitry
30 × 75½ × 15¼ inches

The Ship-O-Corks 1983

2,700 wine and champagne corks, copper wire, 12 dry cell batteries, wood, cardboard, child's nineteenth-century shotgun, eight paddle wheels, bamboo, nails, electric tape
12 × 54 × 12 inches

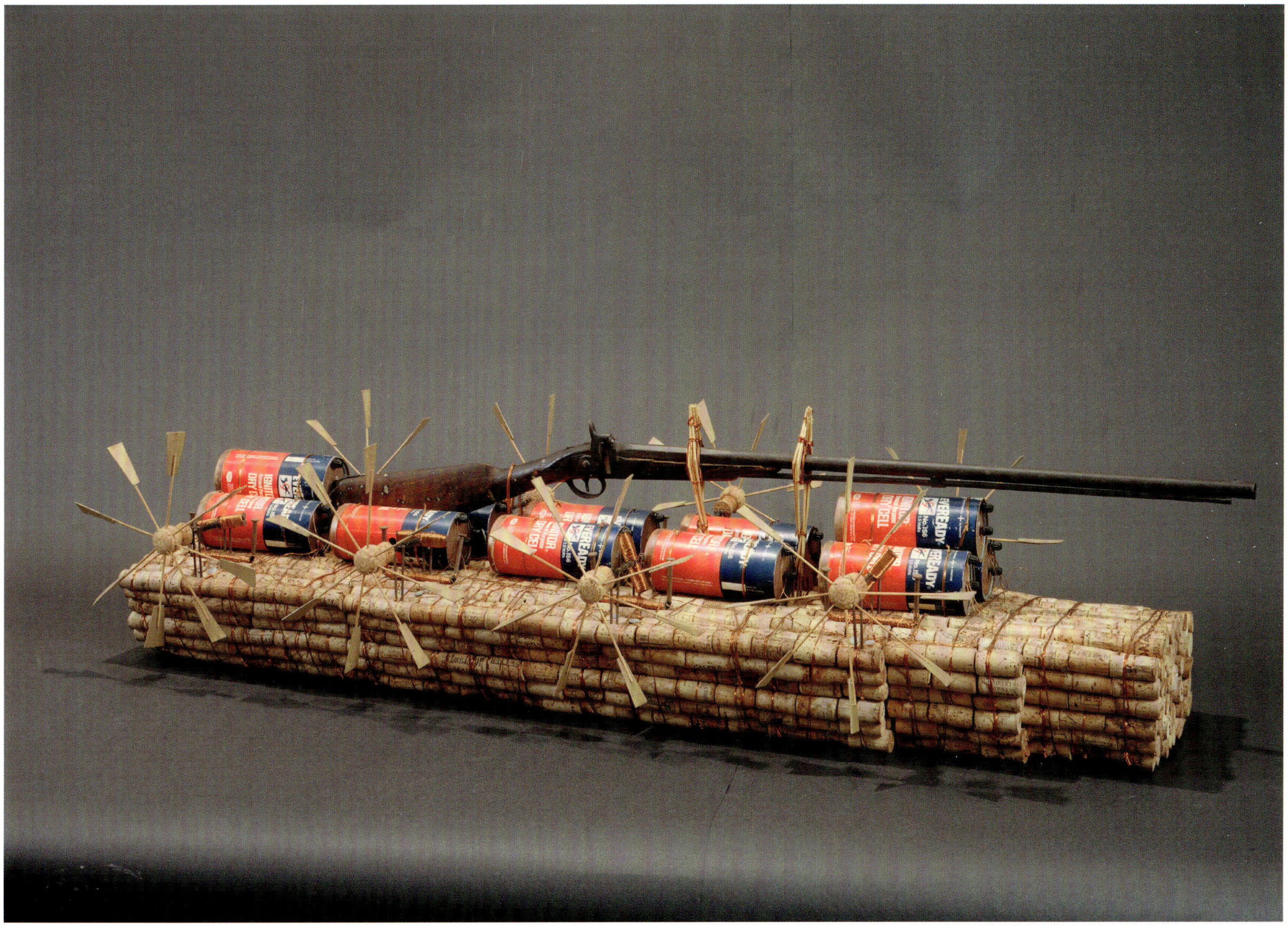

Exploding Subs 1983

Cardboard, metal, wood, batteries, three submarines
Each sub: 5 × 16 × 4 inches

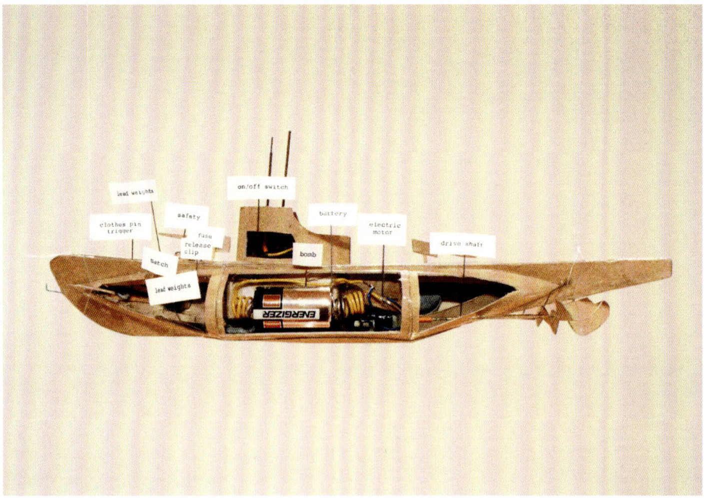

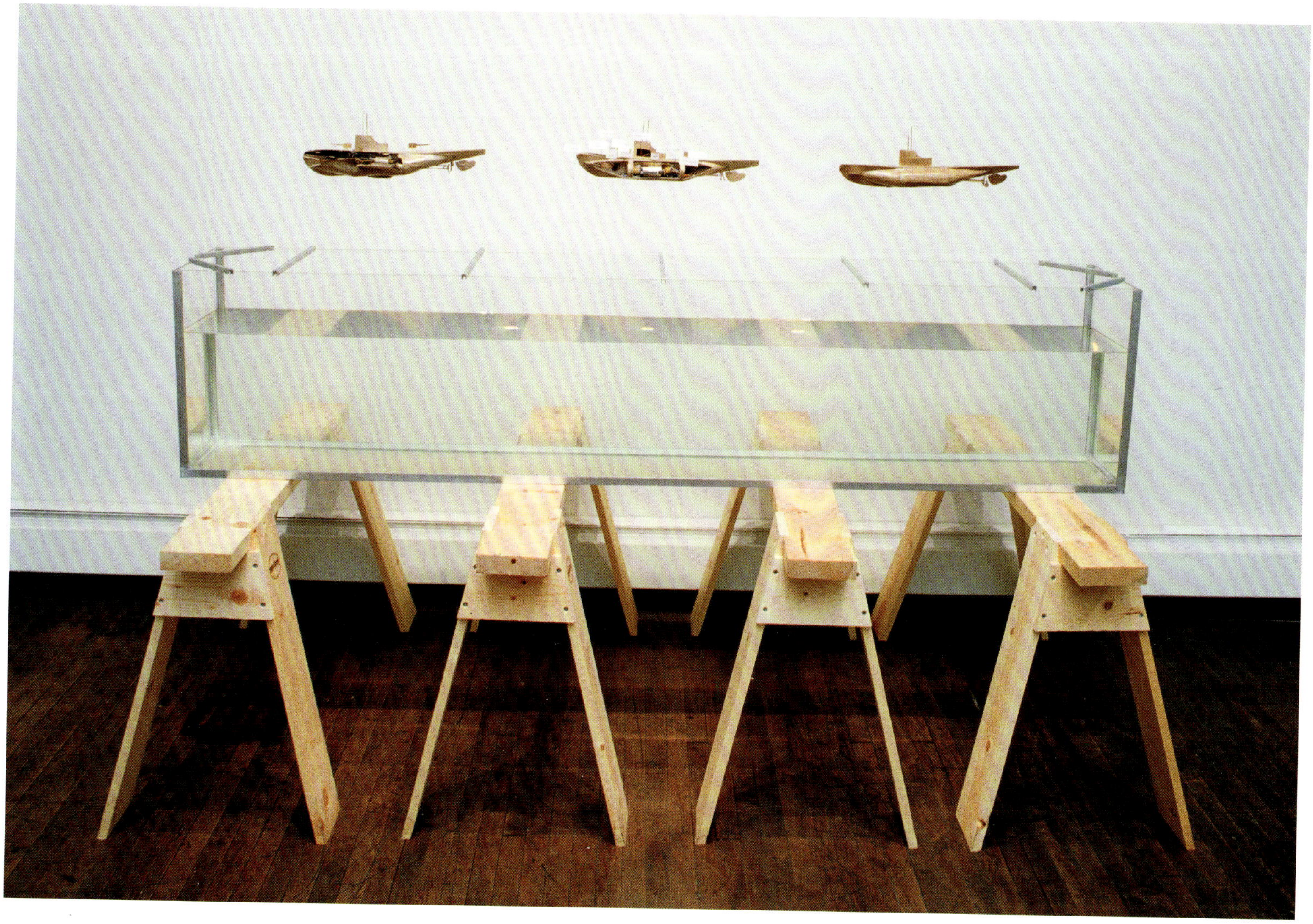

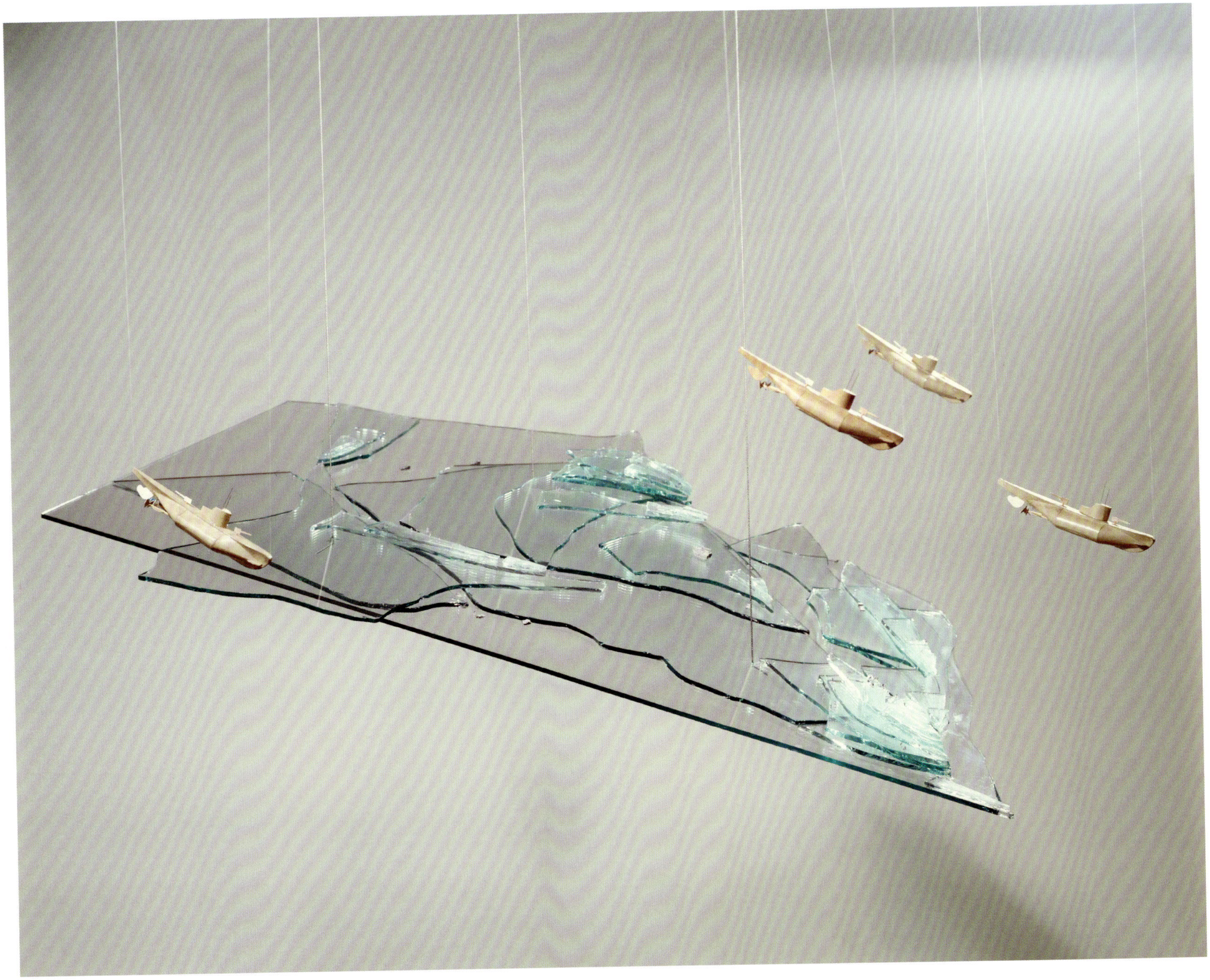

Large Glass Ship 1983

Glass, lead toy soldiers, four *Lucky subs*
2¾ × 51 × 39 inches

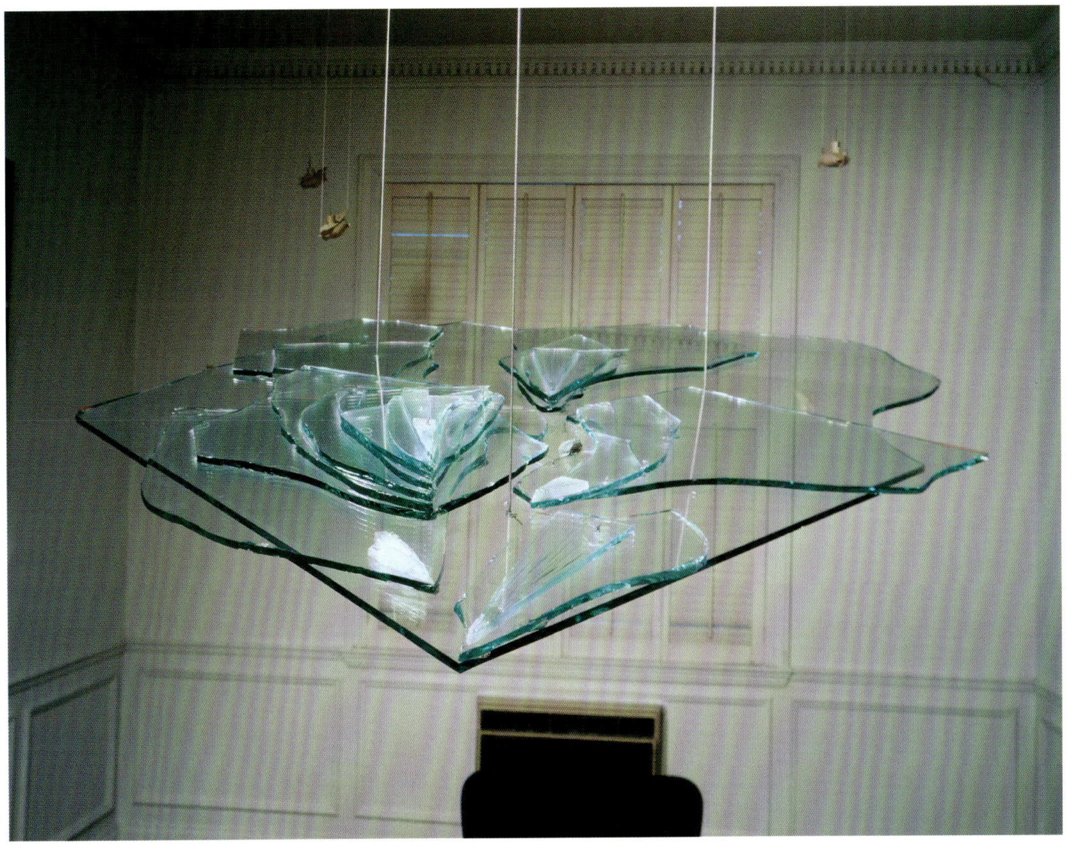

Small Glass Ship 1983

Glass, lead toy soldiers, five *Lucky subs*
2½ × 33 × 36½ inches

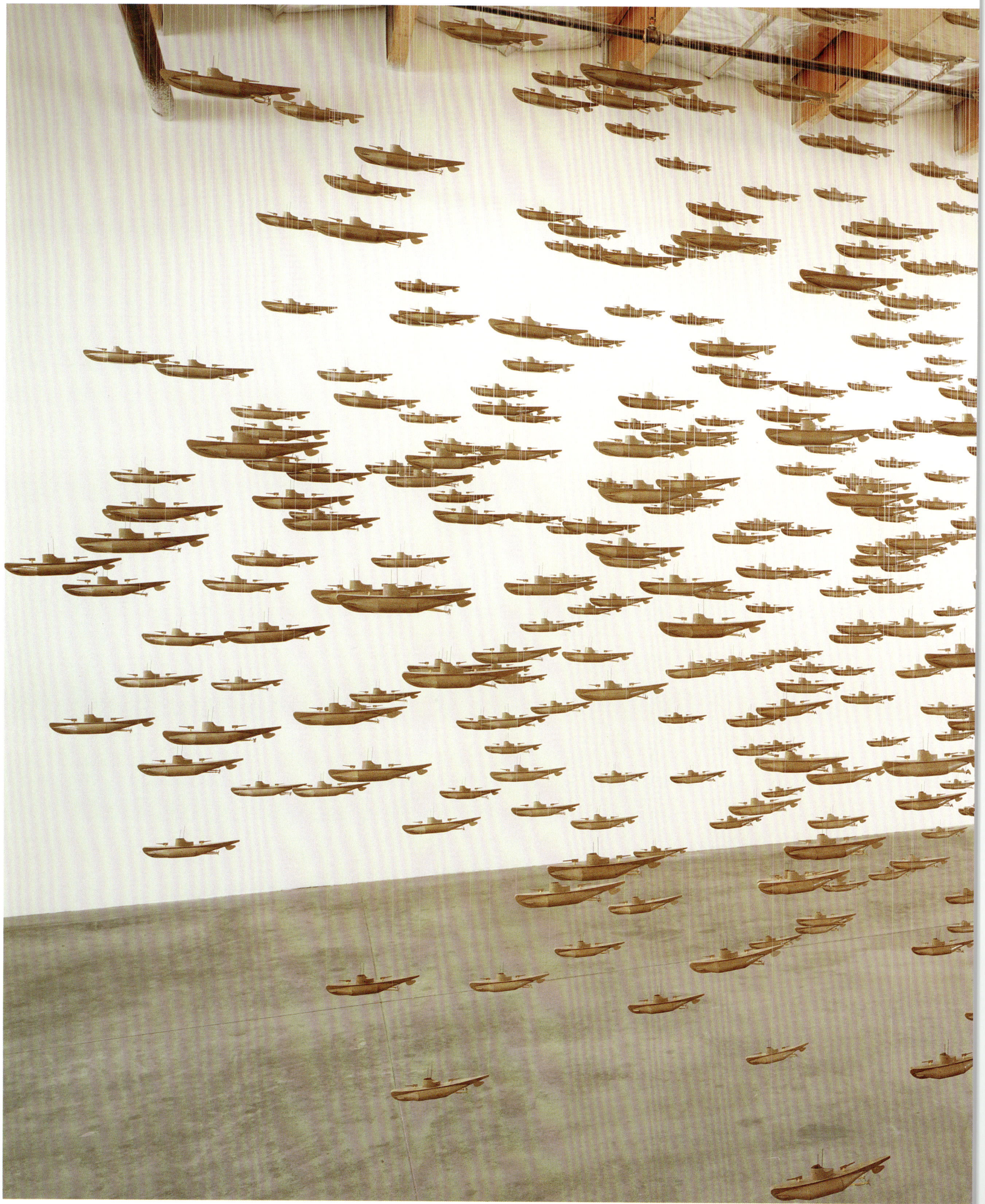

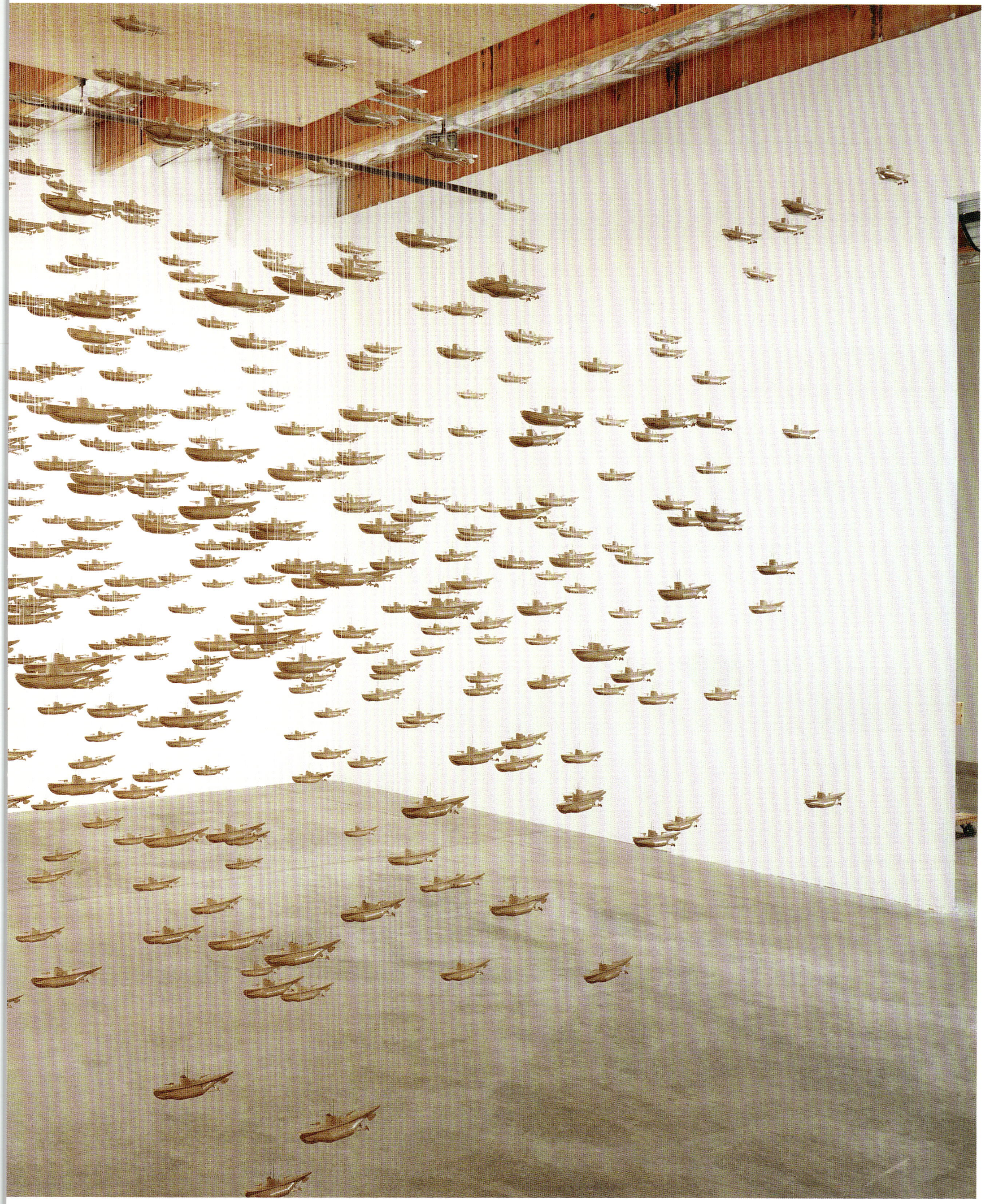

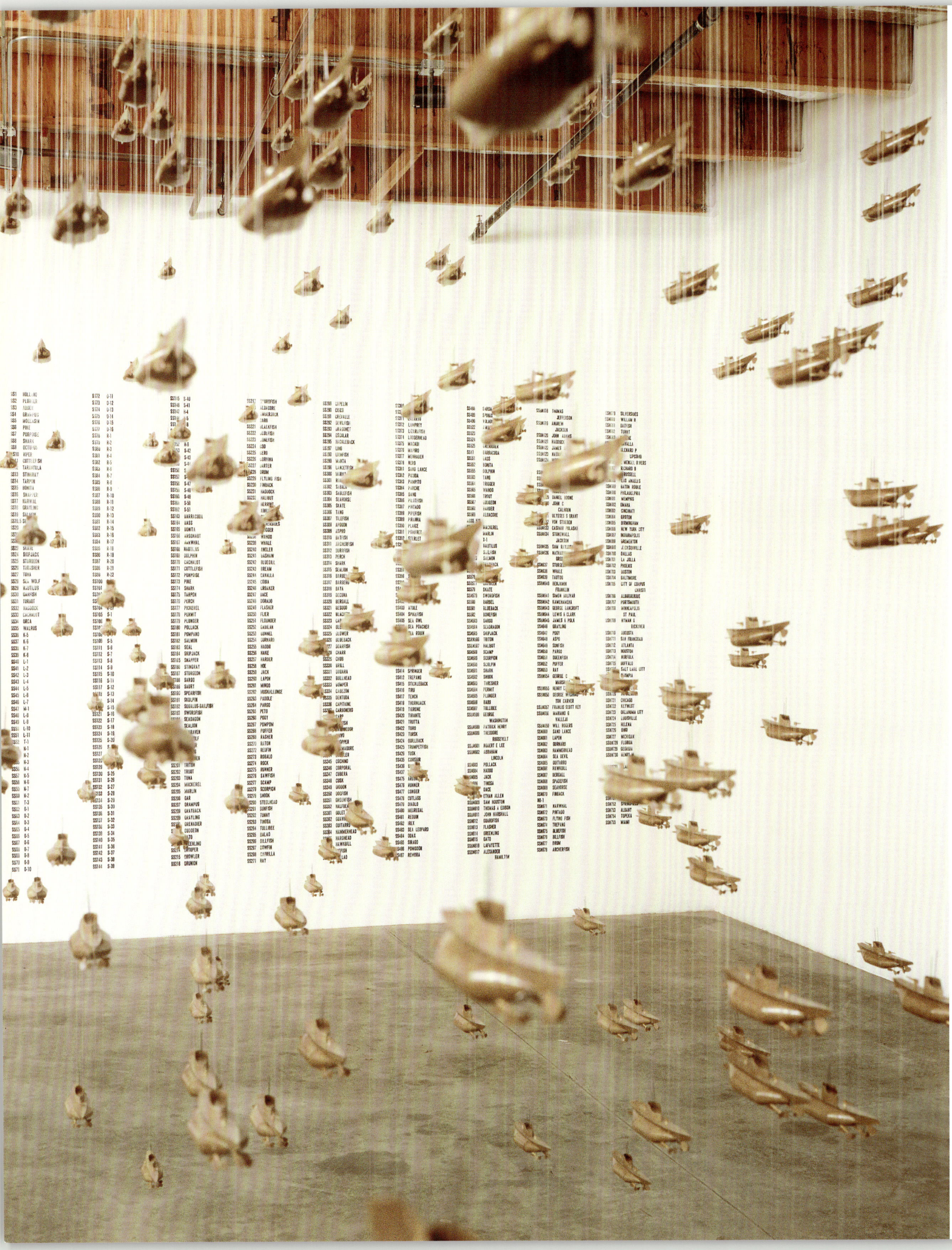

All the Submarines of the United States of America 1987

625 miniature cardboard submarines
96 × 240 × 144 inches installed;
each submarine 2¾ × 8¼ × 1½ inches

All the Submarines of the United States of America *is an installation I conceived and produced with New City Editions, Venice, California. It consists of 625 miniature cardboard submarines, each representing an actual submarine launched by the US Navy since the launching of the SS1 in 1897. It includes the US Polaris fleet of nuclear submarines which provided the US with nuclear superiority vis-à-vis the Soviet Union.*

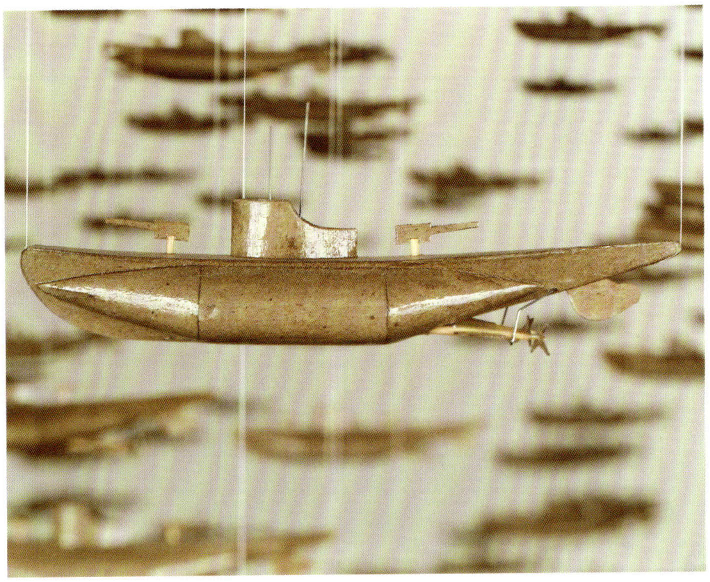

The Sailing Destroyer 1990

Model warship, metal table, framed drawings, blueprints, text
Model and table: 61 × 95 × 15 inches

The Sailing Destroyer *was an attempt to radically modify an existing, but obsolete warship into a sailing vessel. The intention was to actually sail the* HMS Cavalier *in the North Sea; however, due to financial constraints, only blueprints, calculations and a three-dimensional model were possible. Although, at first look, it appears to be the 'greening' of a warship, it could also be the prototype for a newer, more sinister stealth warship with no engine noise or heat.*

Working in conjunction with an American naval architect, Alan Andrews, we were able to devise a plan that would enable us to carry out these modifications on a shoestring budget. The sails would be borrowed from the jibs of MAXI *sailboats, large transatlantic racing boats. The mast would be simple steel tubing in an 'A' frame configuration, eliminating the need for side stays or existing structural bulkheads. The outriggers and leeboard are of a simple design and could be fabricated by relatively unskilled labor. All modifications could be accomplished without having to put the vessel in dry dock. The rough estimate for these modifications was $500,000. This figure contrasted sharply with the preliminary proposal by British naval architects to fit* HMS Cavalier *with a full keel at the cost of approximately $6 million. The modifications devised by Alan Andrews, while beyond the scope of the present project, are nevertheless simple, workable, cost-effective and within the realm of corporate sponsorship.*

Modifying HMS Cavalier *into a sailing vessel represents the 'greening' of a warship because it would no longer use fossil fuels as its power source. However, because its guns would still be functional, it is not a simple 'swords to plowshares' transformation. In fact, because the ship's engines would no longer be functional, the vessel would not produce the noise, vibration or the infrared heat signature commonly used by enemy ships and submarines to detect other vessels. Thus transforming an existing warship into a sailing vessel could actually be the forerunner of a new generation of 'stealth' warships.*

Sailing Destroyer 1988
Ink on paper, 8½ × 11 inches

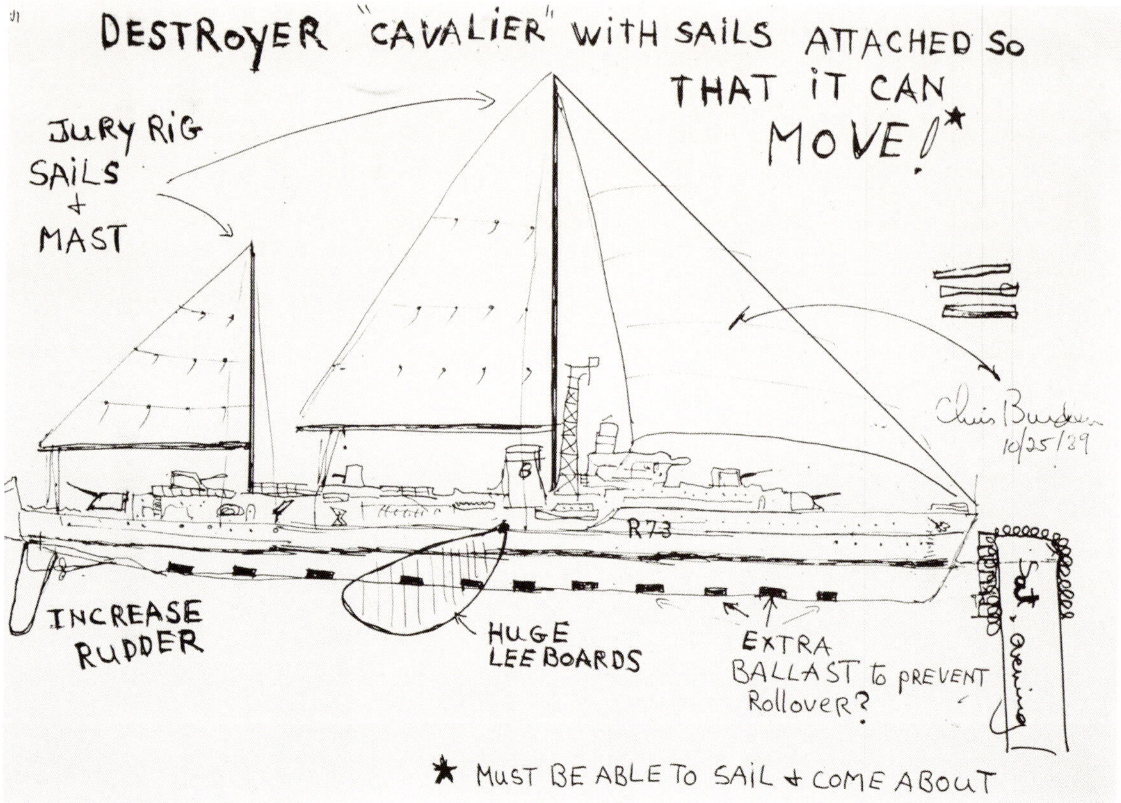

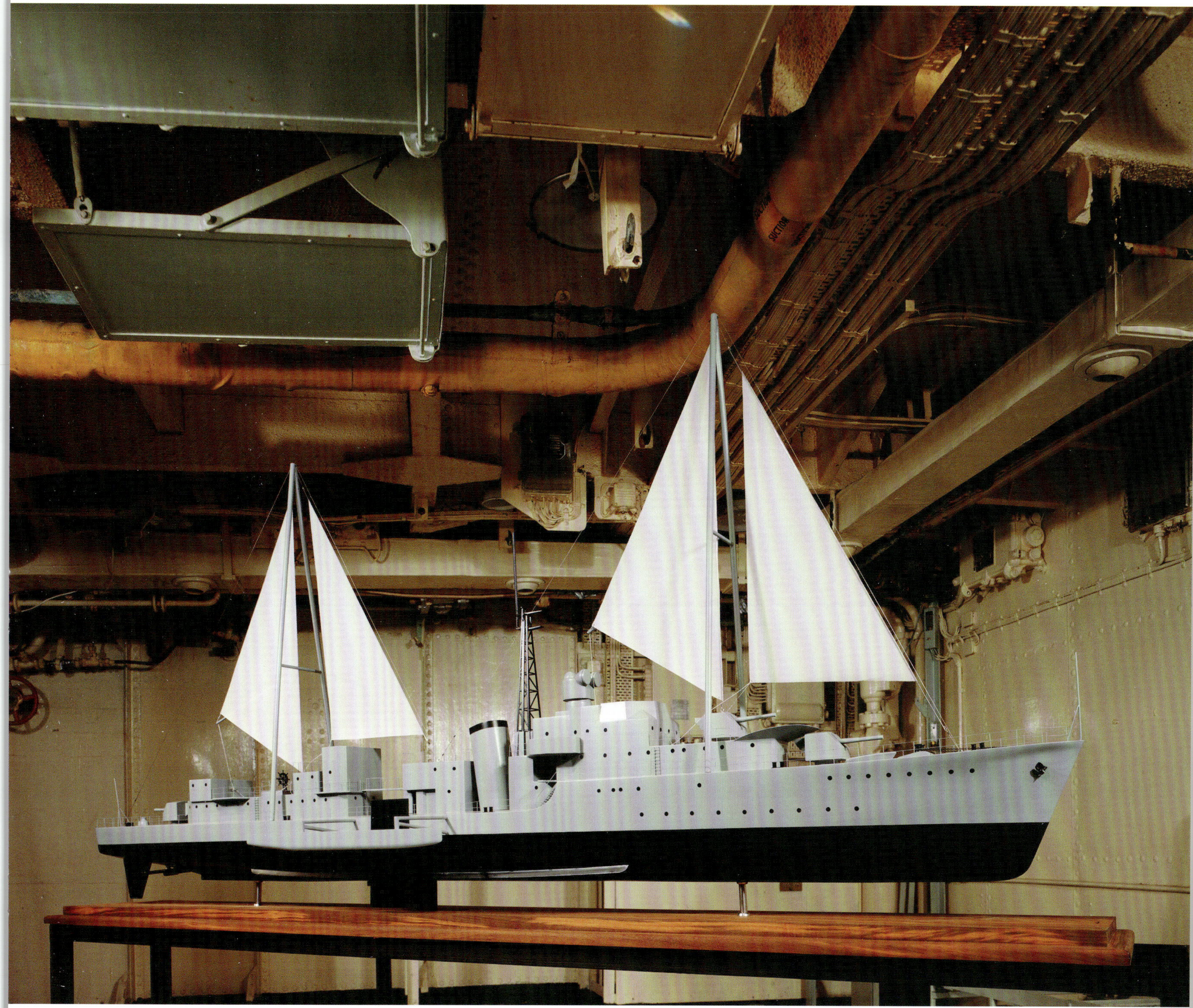

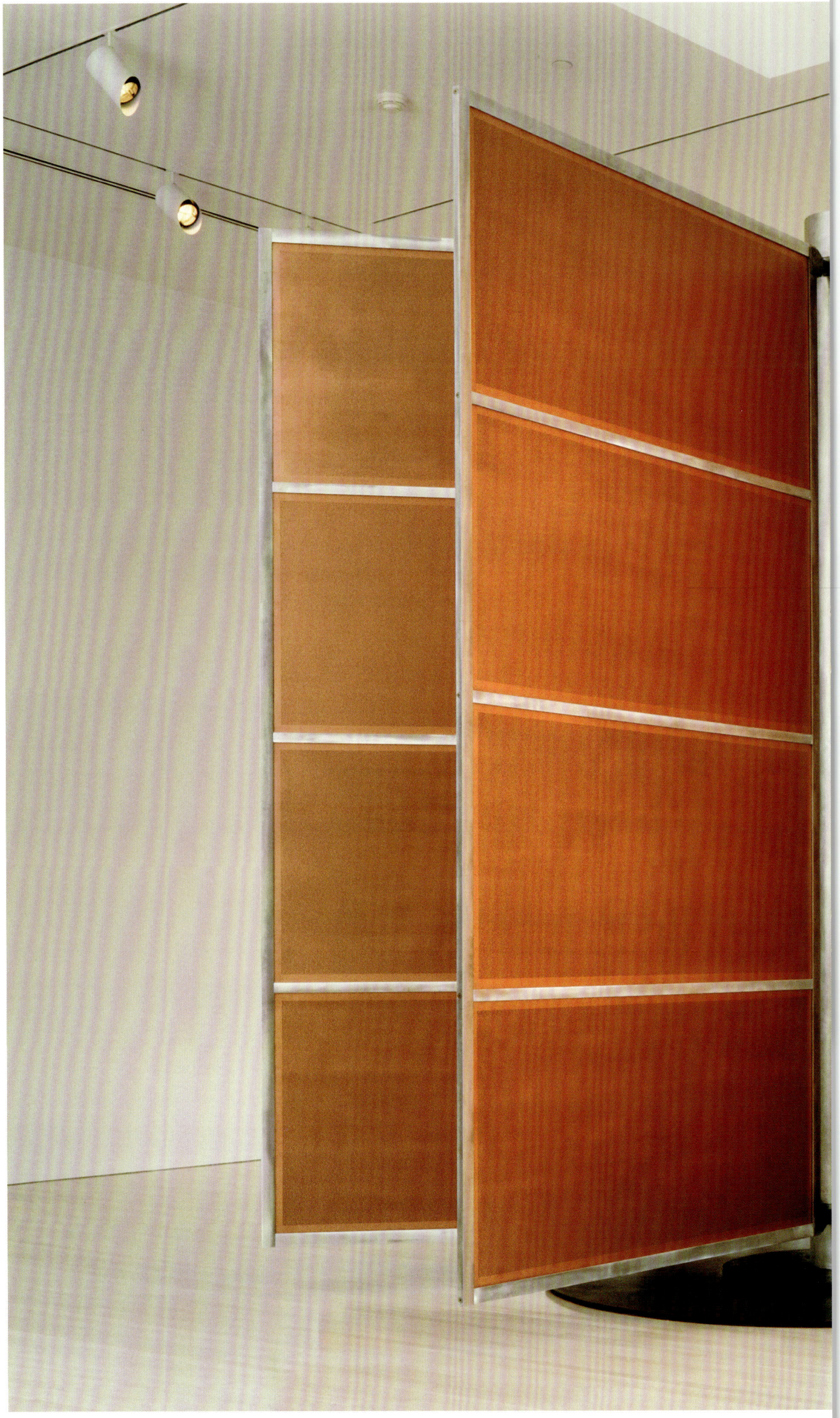

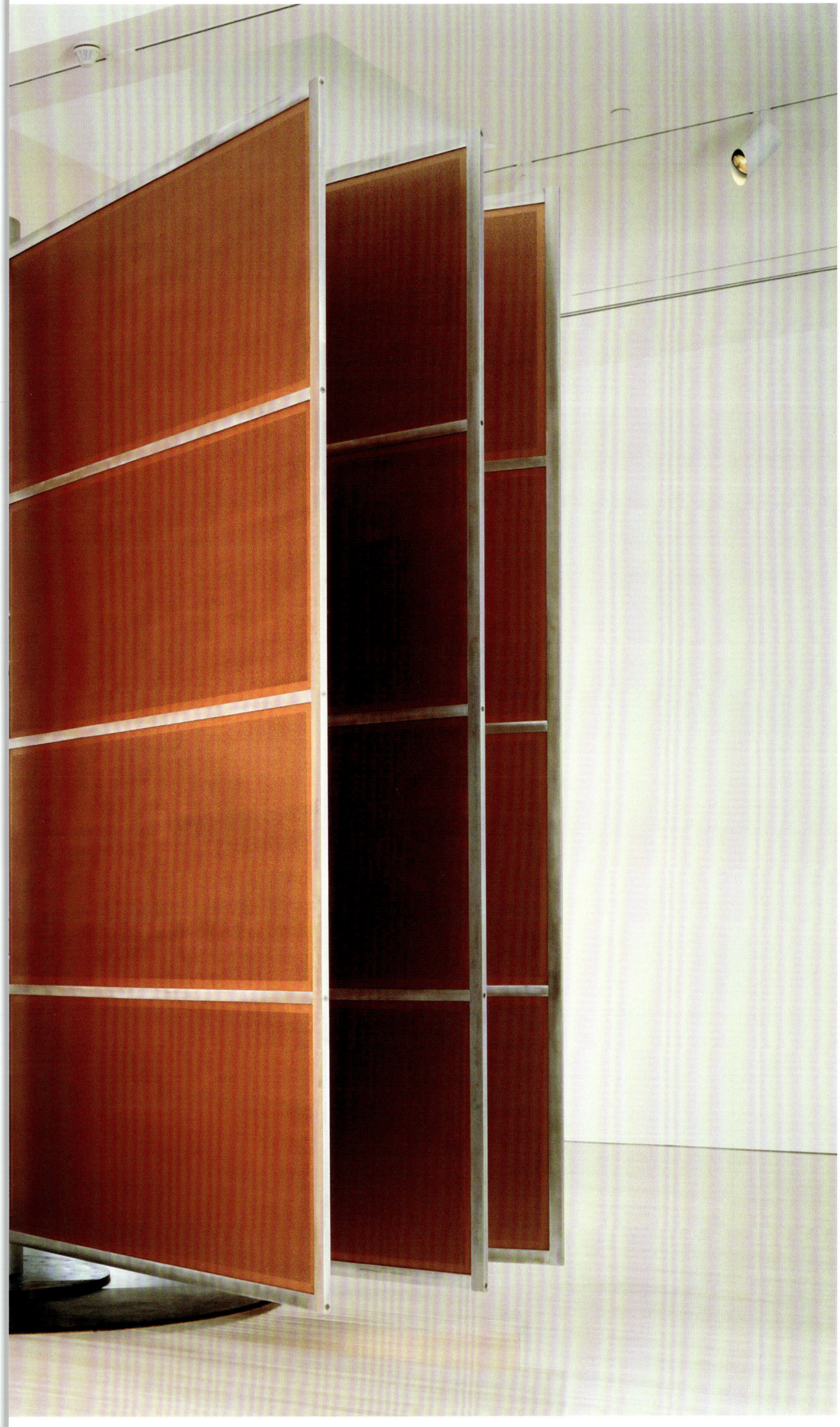

◁◁

The Other Vietnam Memorial 1991

Steel, aluminum, etched copper plates
164 × 119 inches

The Other Vietnam Memorial *consists of 12 huge copper panels, each seven by twelve feet, mounted on a central pole. The panels are hinged, like pages in a book, and can be turned. Etched into the copper panels, in a very small 6 point type, are three million Vietnamese names, symbolizing the North and the South Vietnamese killed during the US involvement from 1968 to 1973, in the Vietnamese Civil War. This memorial is obviously a counterpoint to Maya Lin's Washington, DC Memorial Wall.*

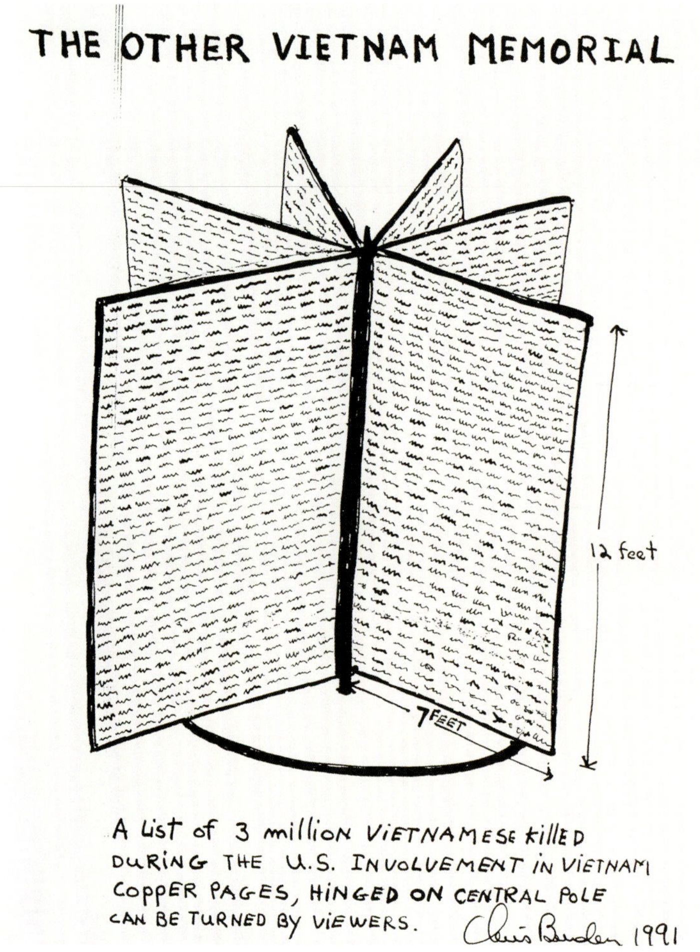

The Other Vietnam Memorial 1991
Ink on paper, 11 × 8½ inches

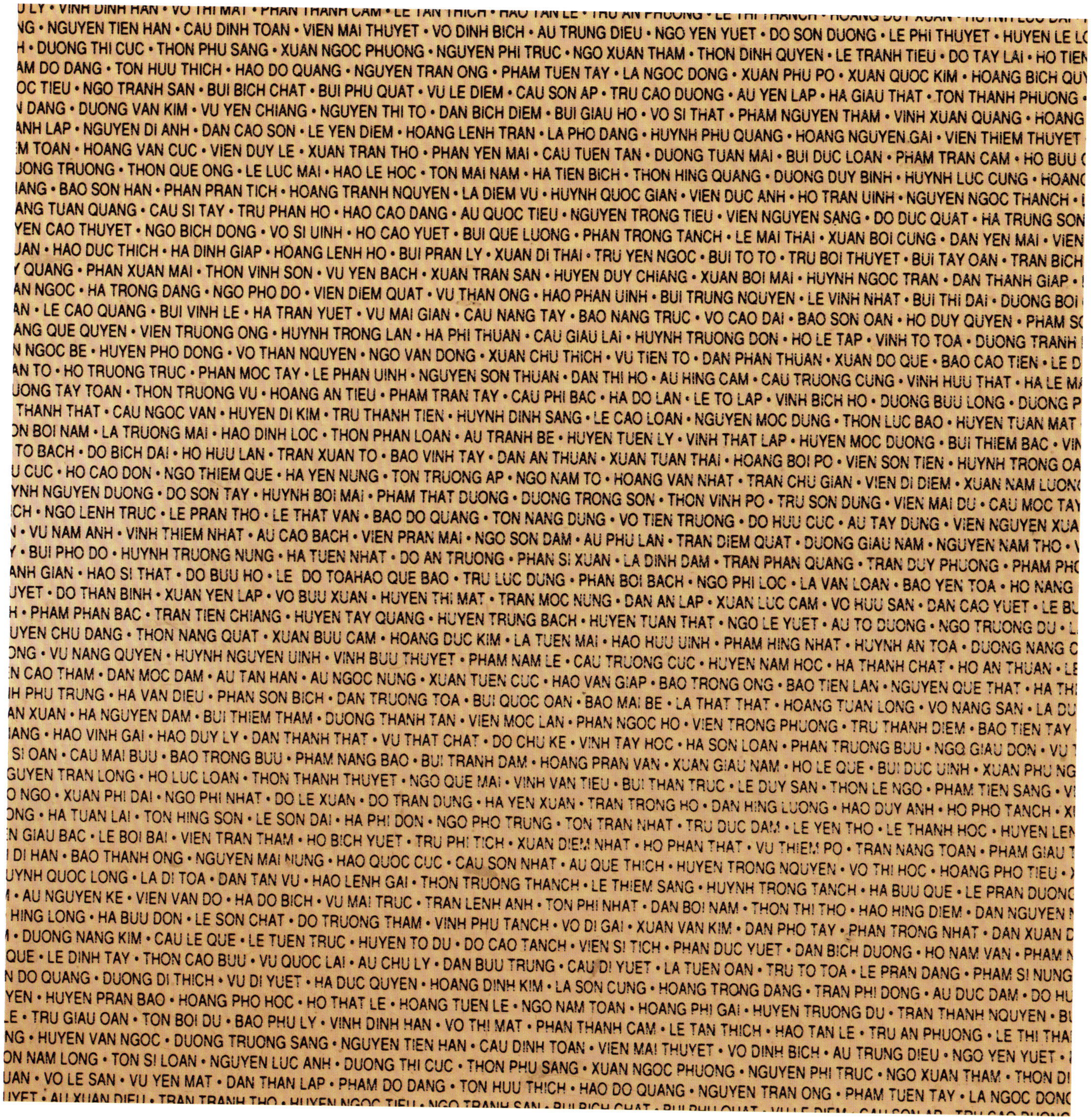

The Other Vietnam Memorial 1991 (detail, actual size)

Stealth Flying Wings 1994

Balsawood, tissue paper, CO_2 motor, pendulum balance system
Six airplanes, each with 30-inch wingspan
Two of six airplanes illustrated

The concept behind the sculpture, Stealth Flying Wings, *is that of a super-small, super-stealth model aircraft. The sculpture consists of six handmade stick and tissue flying airplanes, each with an approximate 30-inch wingspan, designed by Daniel Walton. They are equipped with a pendulum balance system which controls the outer elevons. They are also equipped with a CO motor, model number 120 TWI, built by Gasparin Co. They are to be displayed hanging, from two or three silk threads, in a flight-like formation.*

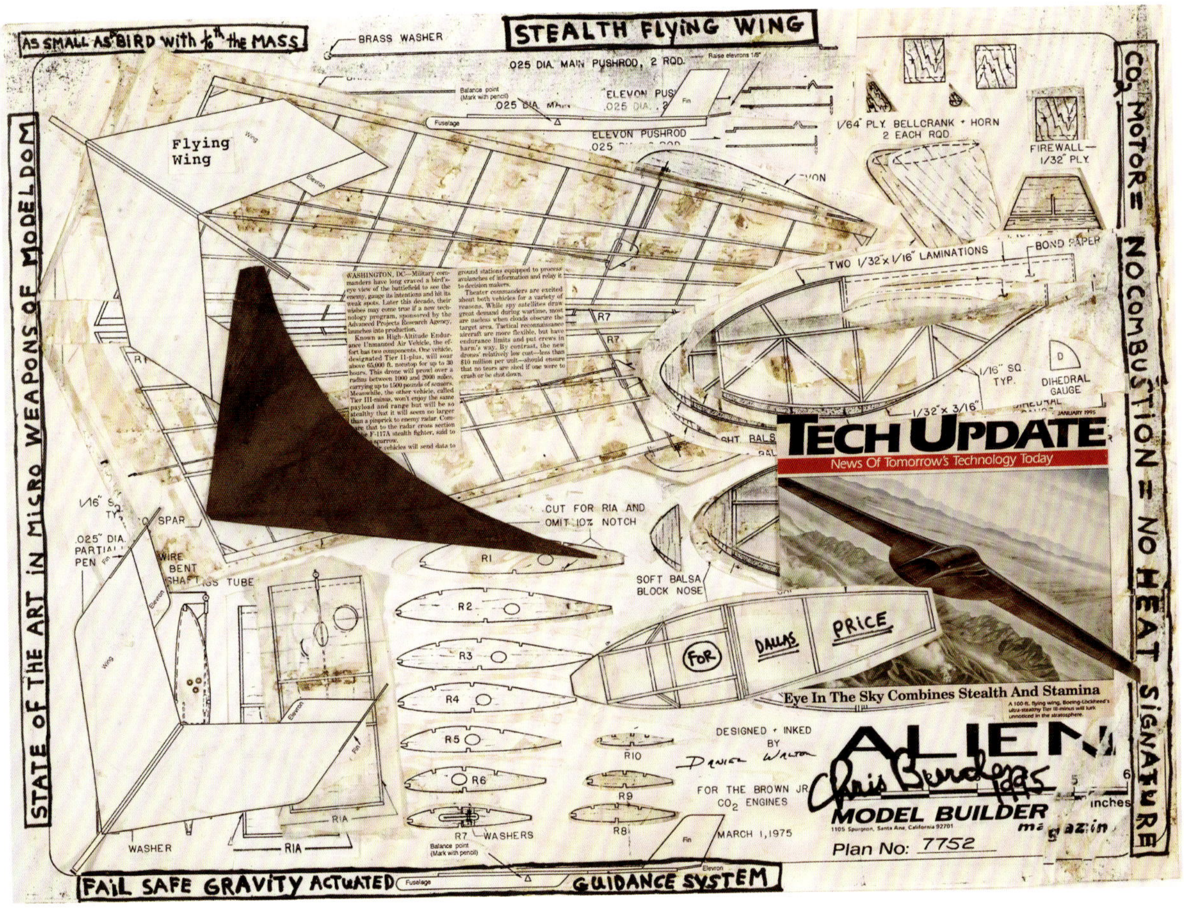

Stealth Flying Wing 1995
Ink and collage on paper, 24 × 30 inches

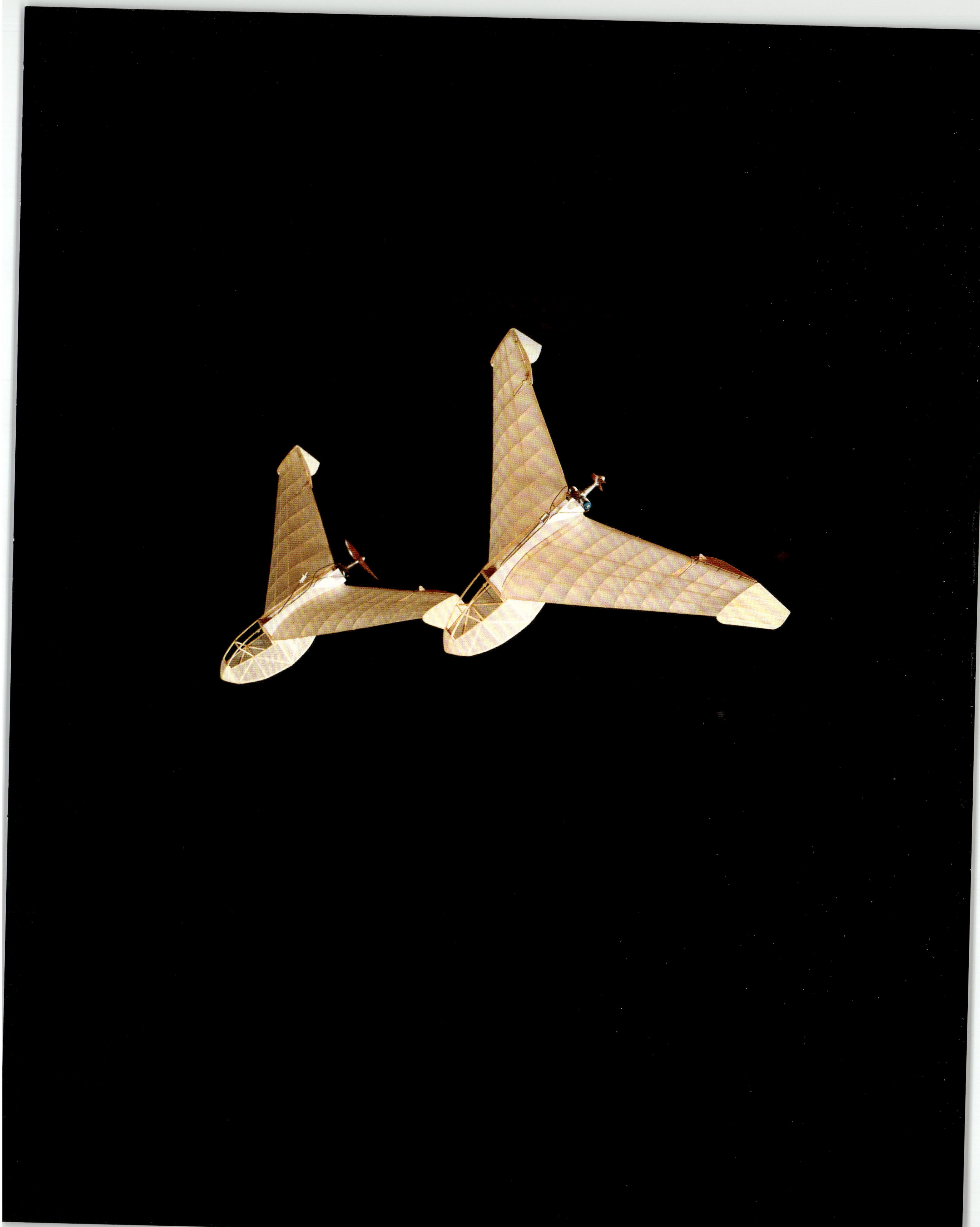

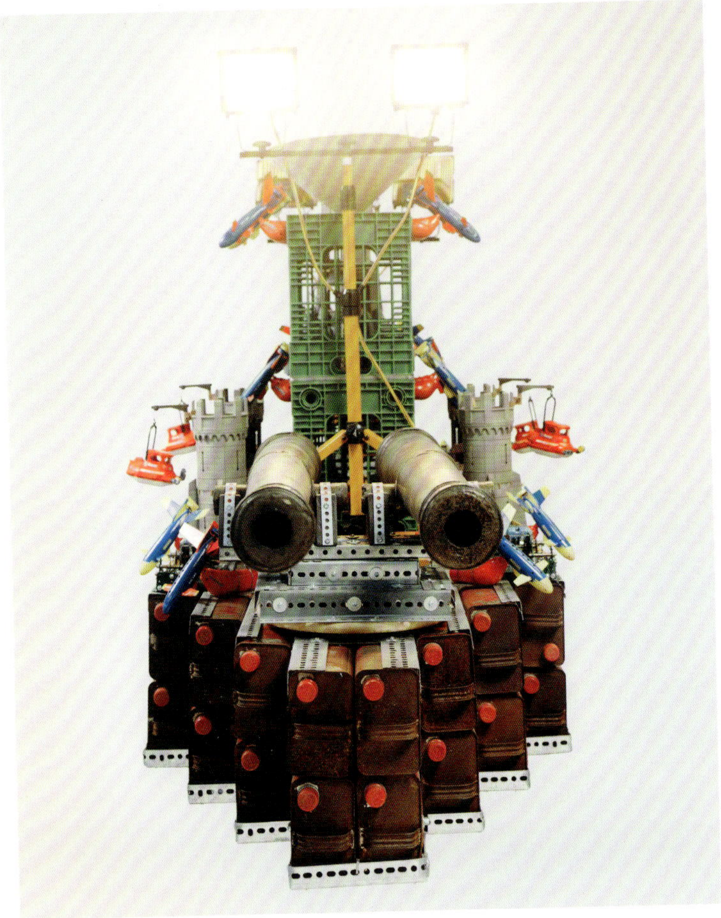

Bateau de Guerre 2001

172 metal Coleman gasoline cans, three cannons on wooden swivels, eight plastic torpedoes, 18 plastic submarine bombers, four plastic rescue submarines, two metal lamps, five plastic castle towers (two on each side, one on top) with attached weaponry, one straw Chinese radar hat, four plastic crates, metal framework
71 × 174 × 41 inches

I save, collect and store many items that are normally discarded, such as wine corks, coffee cans, glass bottles, plastic bottle caps, soap detergent boxes and metal Coleman gasoline cans. Bateau de Guerre *is constructed out of metal Coleman gasoline cans that I accumulated over a six-year period, from 1983 to 1989.*

The gas cans were used by my wife and I while we camped out on our property before our house was built. The cans were saved and stored for another 12 years. When I first started saving this particular group of cans, I did not know what I would ultimately use them for. Bateau de Guerre *was built in the spirit of another work, the* Ship-O-Corks, *1983, which was built from 3,000 wine corks.*

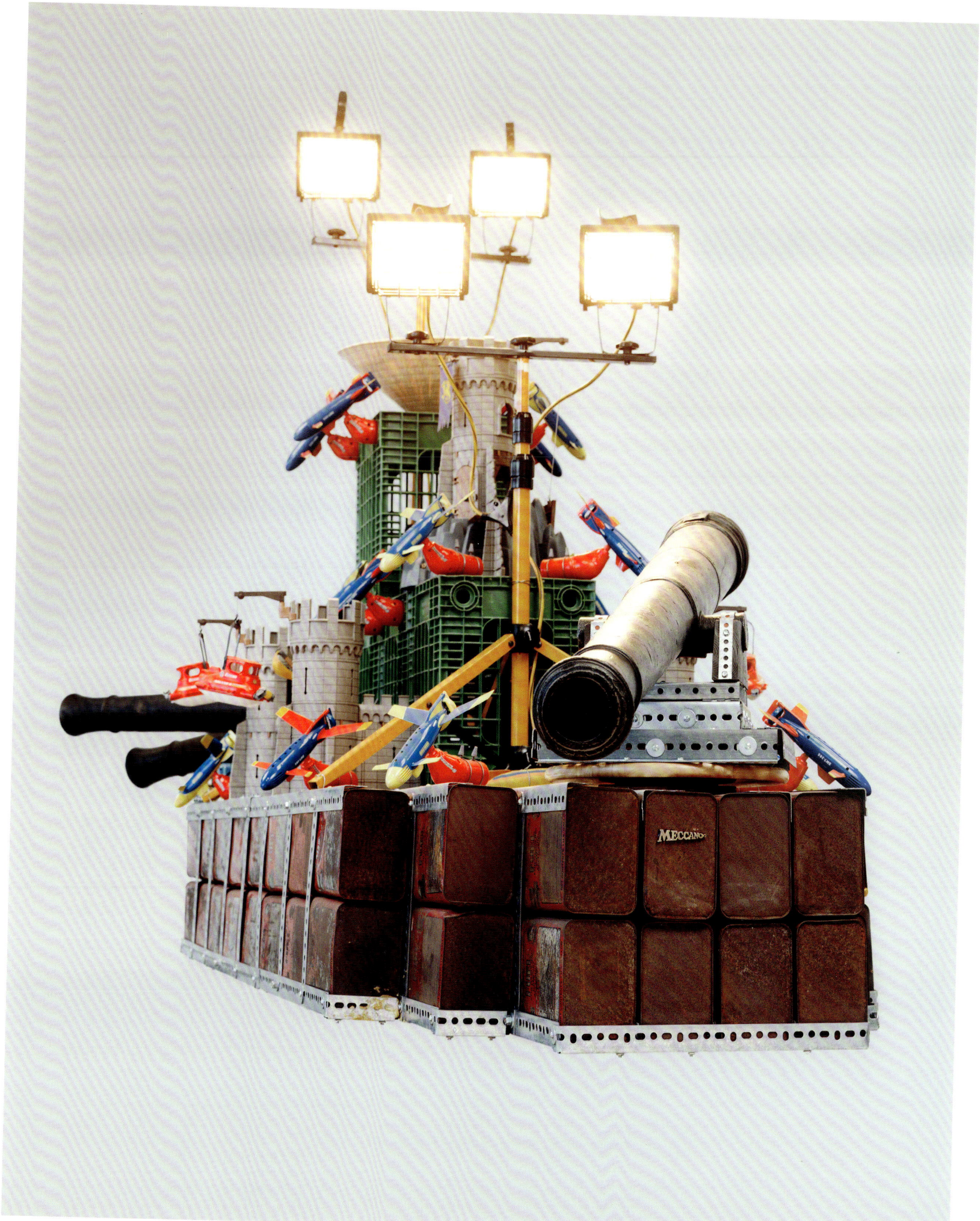
MECCANO

The Rant 2006

Edition of 10
DVD, color. Two minutes, ten seconds.
Monologue in French.

An extreme close-up of my face is projected onto a wall, several times larger than life size. Assuming the persona of a ranting xenophobic preacher, I deliver a short, intense monologue.

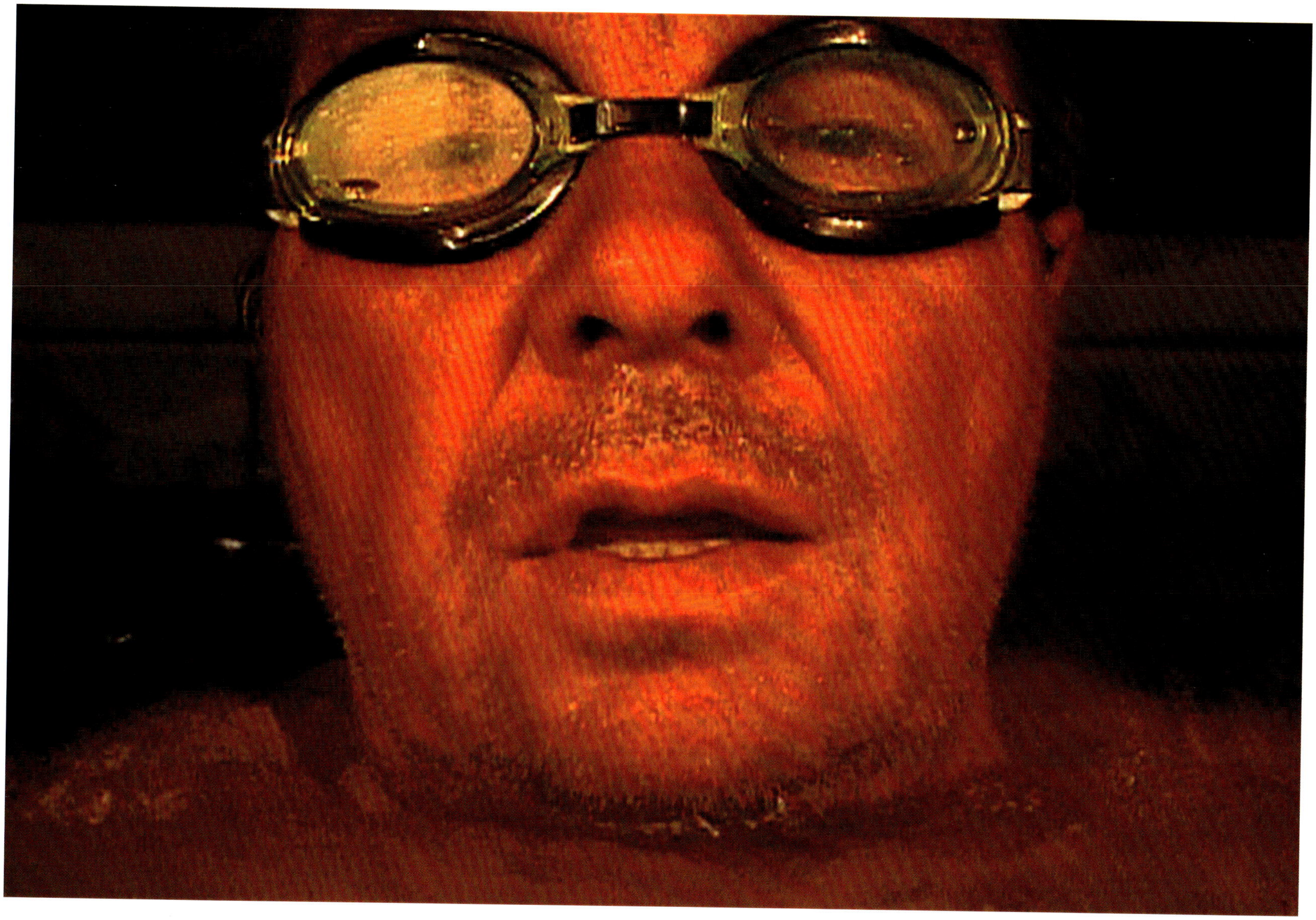

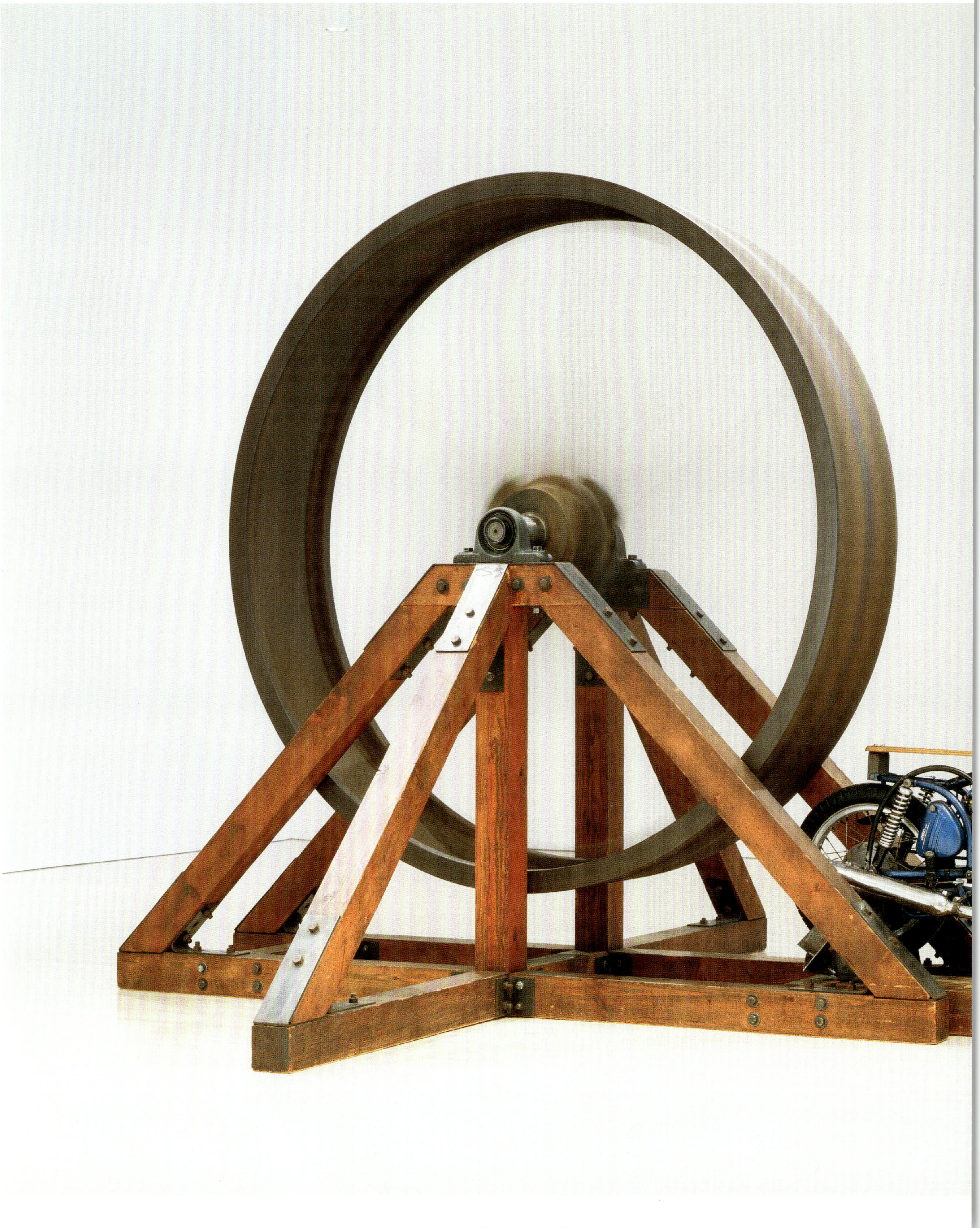

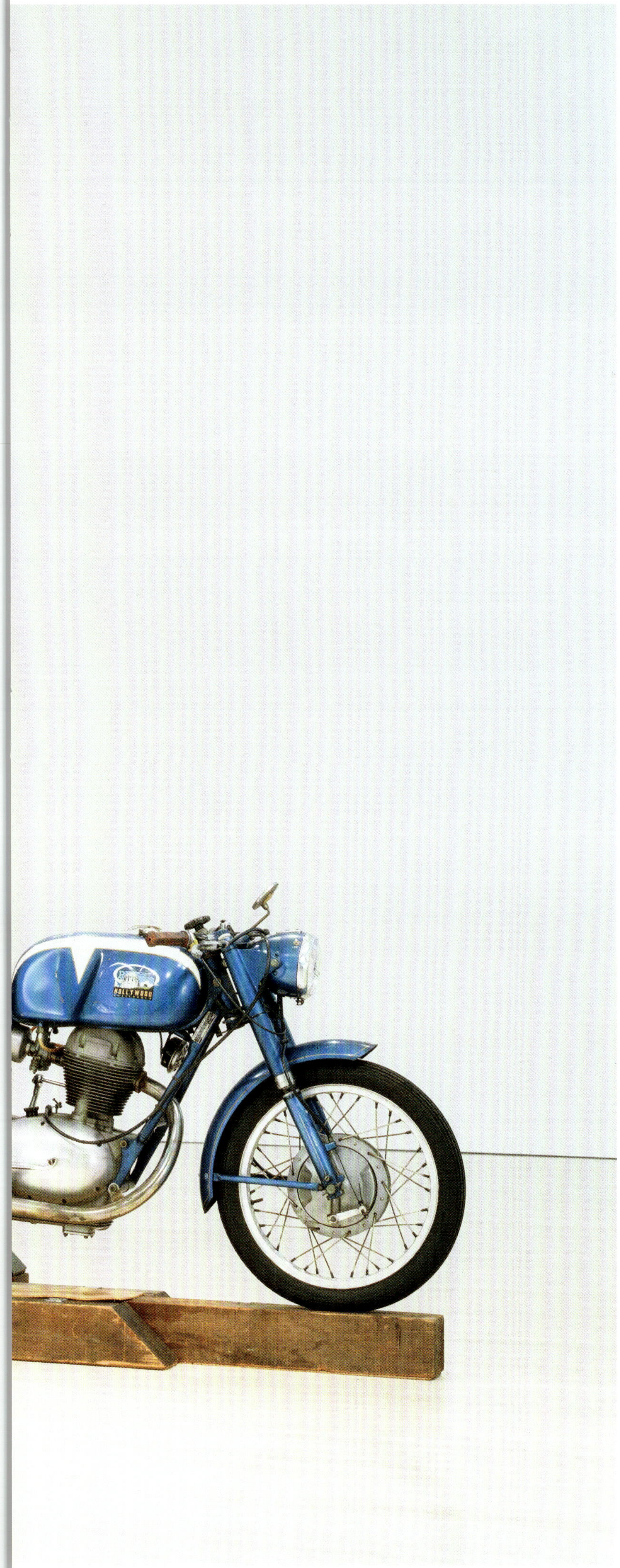

The Big Wheel 1979

Three-ton, eight-foot diameter, cast
iron flywheel powered by a motorcycle
112 × 175 × 143 inches

The Big Wheel *consisted of a three-ton cast-iron flywheel mounted in a vertical position and set in motion by the rear tire of a motorcycle. The iron wheel is accelerated to a speed of 200 revolutions per minute.* The Big Wheel *would then spin freely for two-and-a-half hours before it would need to be recharged.*

The Frictionless Sled 1983

Hollow aluminum bar, plastic, air compressor
37 × 256½ × 4½ inches

A physics experiment which demonstrates the dramatic effect of minimizing friction from an object in motion. The experiment consists of a 21-foot hollow aluminum rectangular tube in which minute holes have been drilled at regular intervals. Compressed air is pumped in the hollow tube, bleeding through all the tiny holes. A small three-sided plastic sled fits over the bar. When viewers to the gallery push the sled, it travels all the way down the length of the bar, bounces off one of the rubber bands at either end of the bar and continues to bounce back and forth numerous times. When the air compressor is turned off, the same push enables it to travel only a few inches, instead of several 21-foot trips.

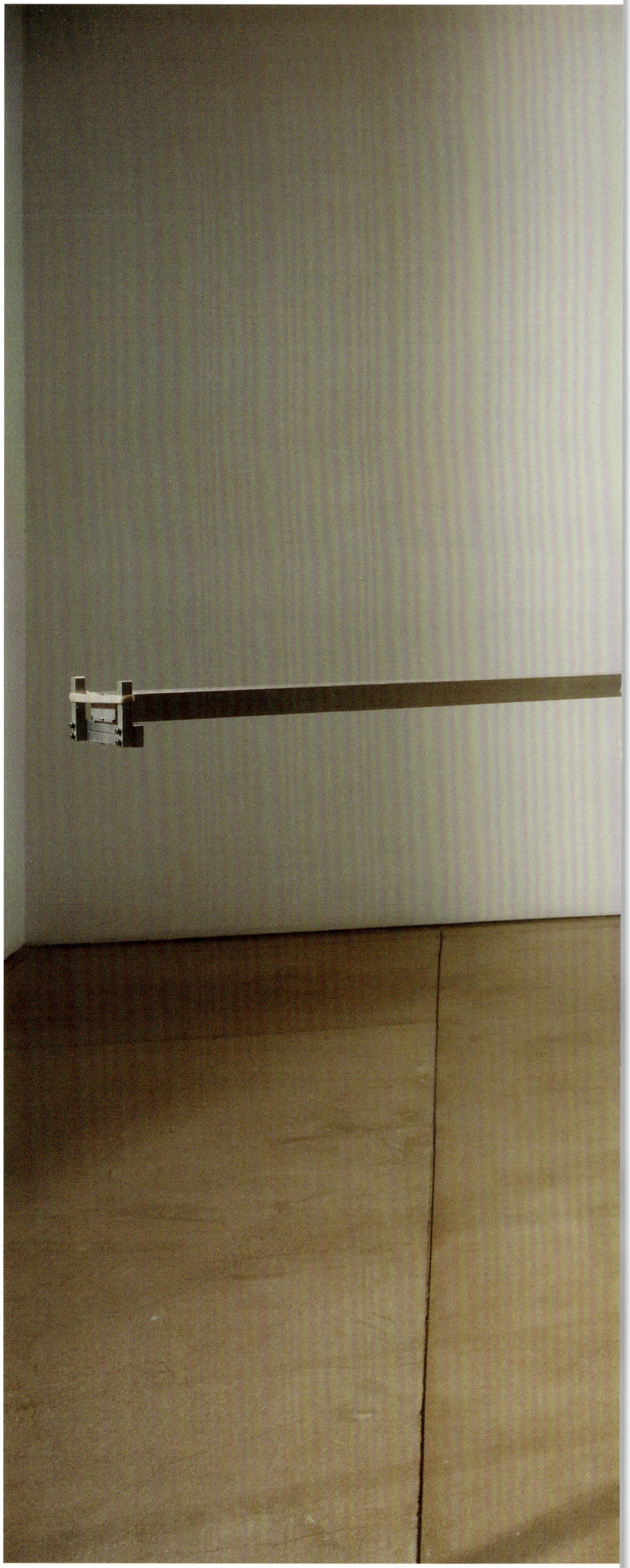

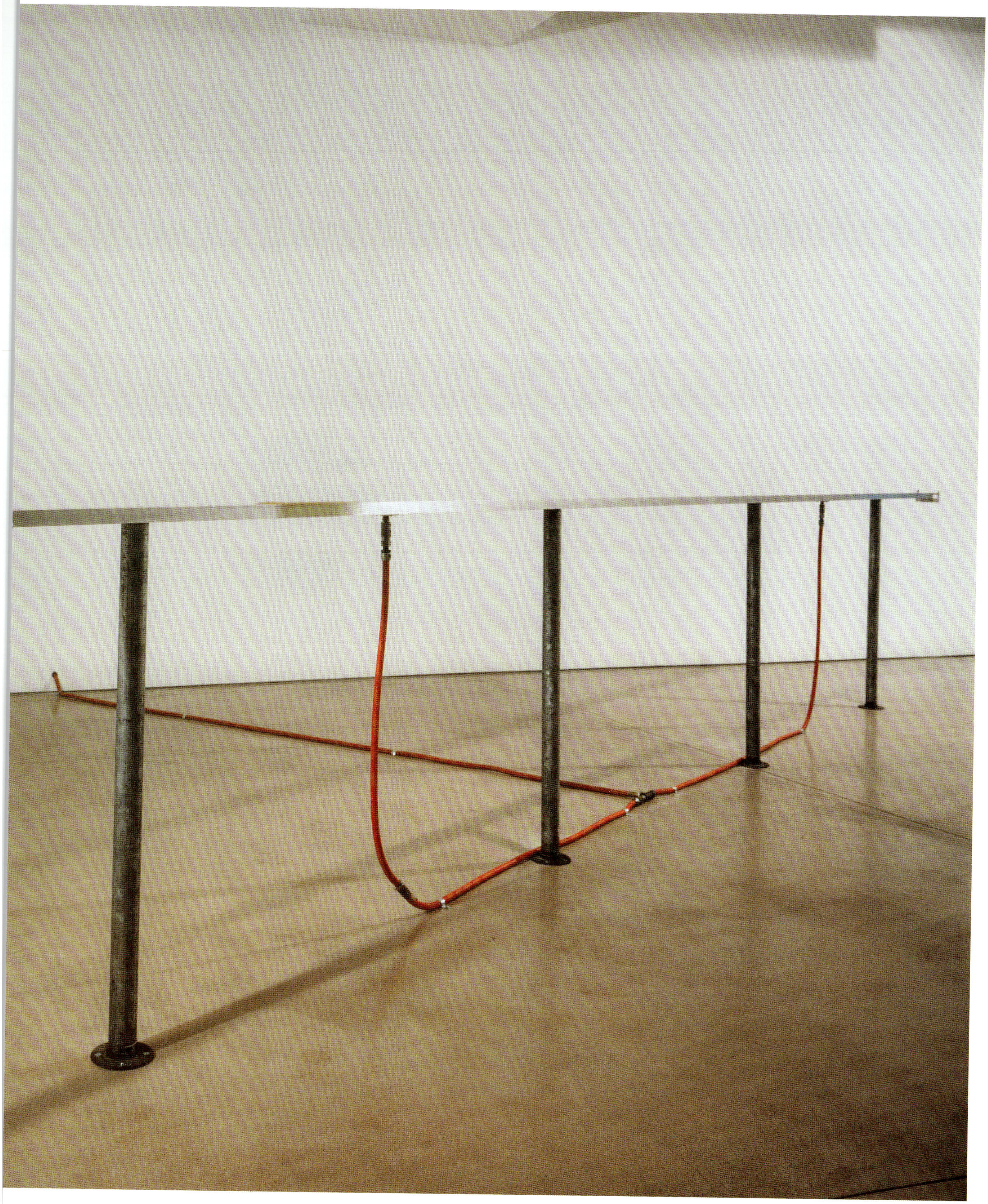

Beam Drop 1984

Approximately 60 steel I-beams, concrete
Approximately 35 square feet
Installation at Art Park, Lewiston,
New York, USA, August 2, 1984;
dismantled May 1987

Beam Drop *is a sculpture executed at Artpark in Lewiston, New York, on August 2, 1984. This sculpture was created by dropping approximately 60 large steel beams (some as large as 40 feet in length and weighing up to 2,000 pounds each) into a 35-foot square pit of wet cement. Each beam was lifted to a height of 100 to 120 feet by a large crane. With the aid of a specially designed trigger, each beam was released and allowed to free fall vertically into the wet cement below. Lodged into the concrete pit at different angles, all the beams formed a massive unpredictable abstract steel sculpture. The awesome force of gravity applied to these massive building materials (60,000 pounds of steel, 140 cubic yards of cement, 450 cubic yards of fill) is as self-evident to the viewers as the hand of the artist in a conventional abstract expressionist painting.*

Beam Drop 1983
Ink on paper, 11 × 8½ inches

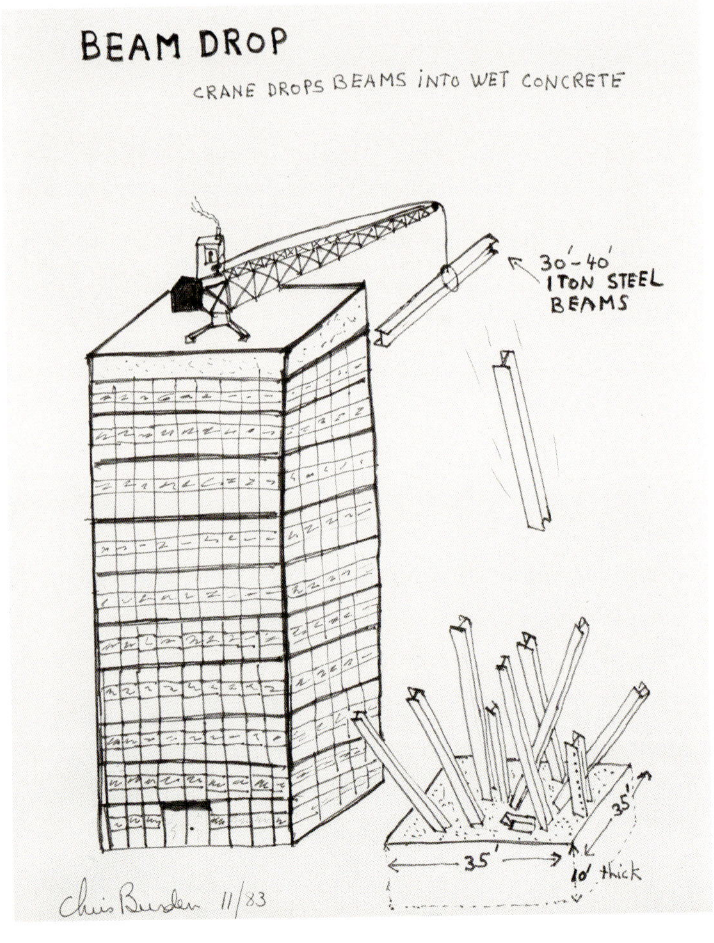

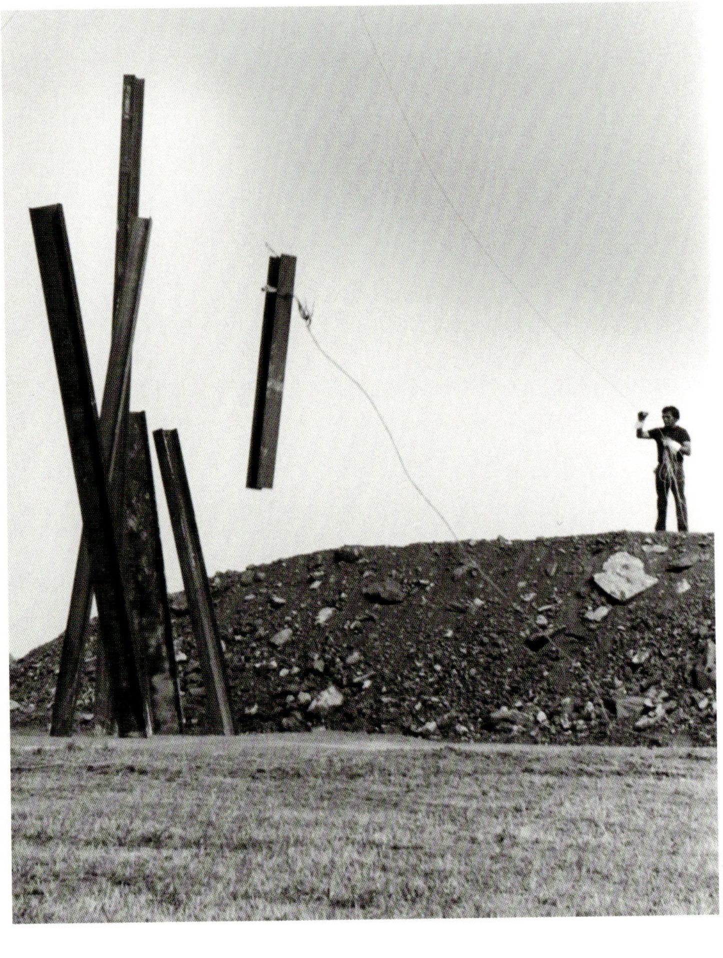

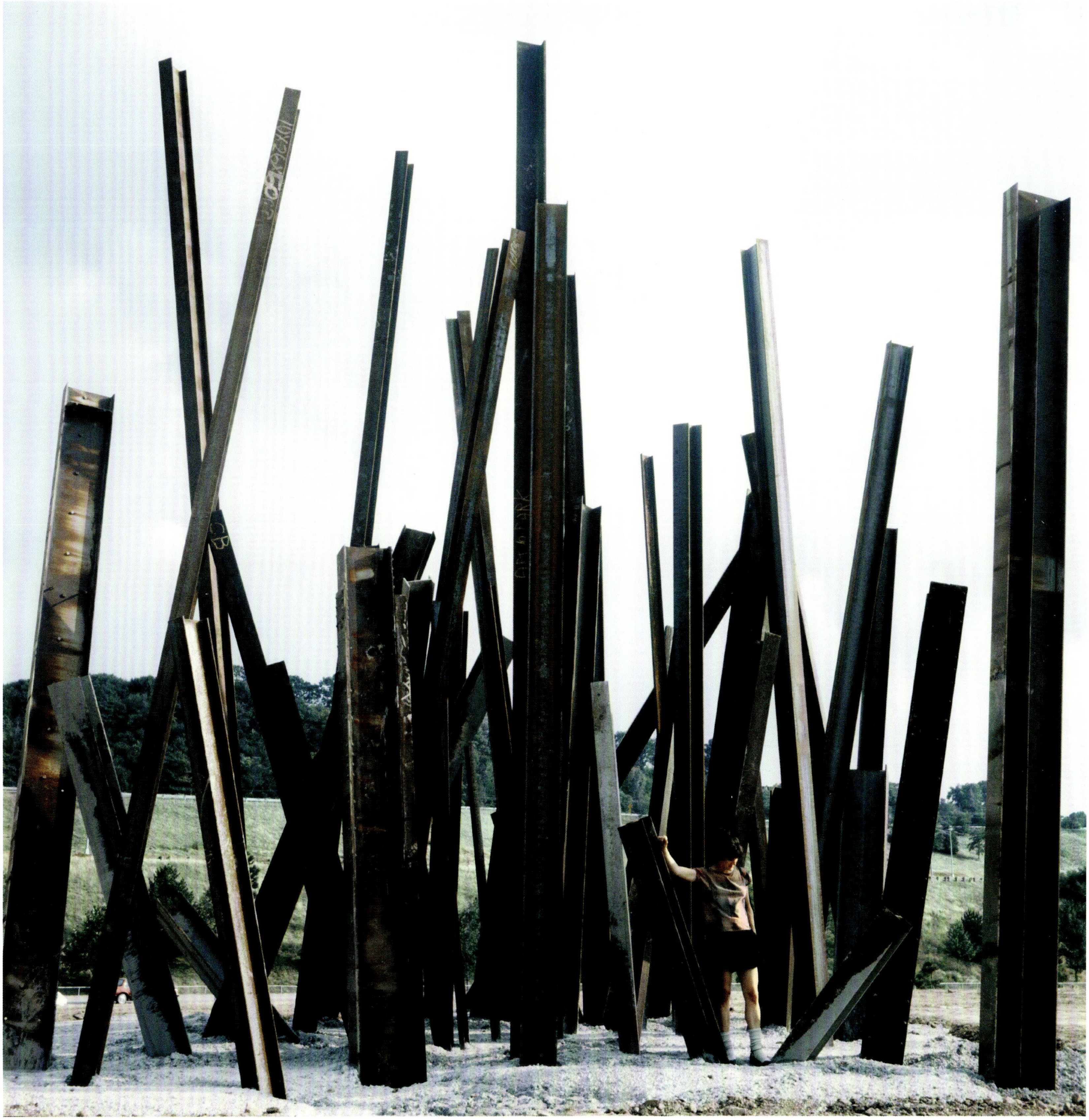

Another World I 1992

Wooden base, wooden block buildings,
glass river, two Titanic model boats,
metal Marklin model of Eiffel Tower, motor
96 × 60 × 60 inches
(tower: 72 inches high)

Another World I *is a kinetic sculpture based on the fantasy of using the Eiffel Tower as a vertical armature from which two Titanic ocean liners are suspended.* Another World I *consists of a wooden base, five feet square by two feet high. The base conceals an electric motor and controls and provides a support for an abstracted and compressed model of the city of Paris. The buildings in the city are suggested by simple blocks of wood. Using a piece of rippled glass and artistic license, the River Seine is depicted as meandering through the city of Paris and flowing under the Eiffel Tower. The Eiffel Tower itself is a six-foot-high Marklin metal Erector building set. The two 36-inch-long twin Titanics are highly detailed, modified plastic models.*

An electric motor, hidden in the base of the sculpture, spins the two Titanics around the Eiffel Tower at such high speeds that the ships are at right angles to the earth's gravitational field. Thus, 'passengers' aboard the ships, in 'another world', would observe the River Seine flowing at right angles to the wine in their glasses.

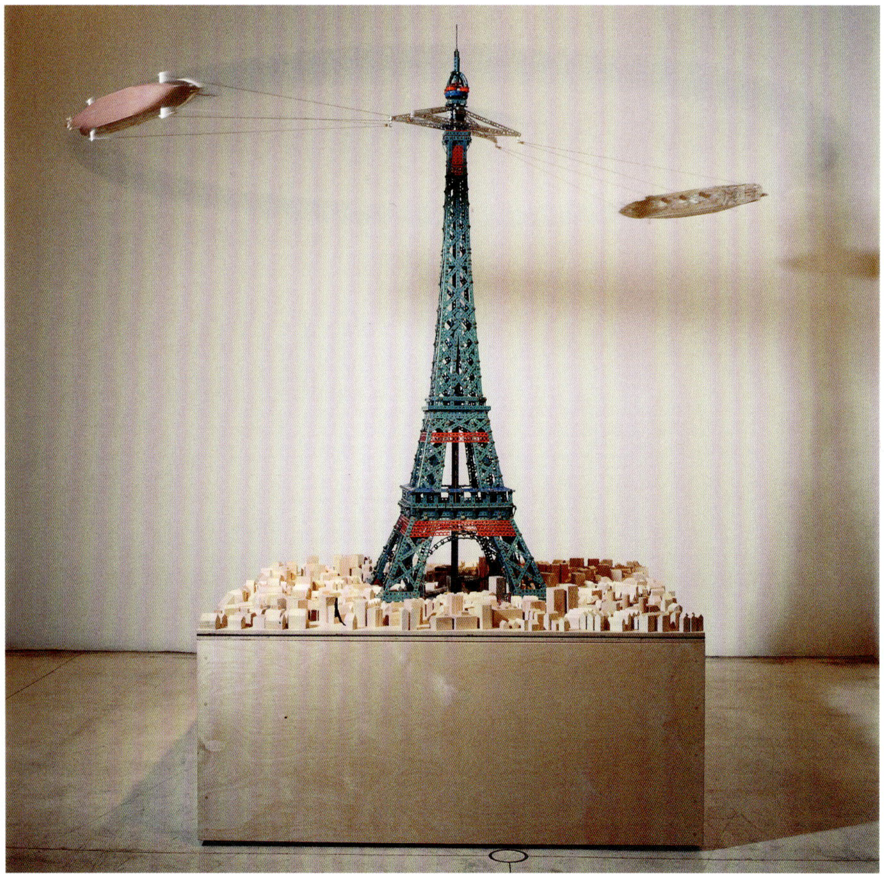

Another World II 1993

Wooden base, wooden block buildings,
glass river, two Titanic model boats,
metal Meccano building parts, motor
66 × 60 × 60 inches
(tower: 48 inches high)

Another World II *is the second version of a kinetic sculpture based on the fantasy of using the Eiffel Tower as a vertical armature from which two Titanic ocean liners are suspended.* Another World II *consists of a base that is five feet square by one-and-a-half feet tall. The four-foot-tall Eiffel Tower in* Another World II *is custom designed and constructed from Meccano parts. In* Another World II *the Eiffel Tower and the two Titanic models are two-thirds smaller than the tower and the ships in* Another World I. *The drive system and the attachment arms are strengthened and improved for greater durability in* Another World II.

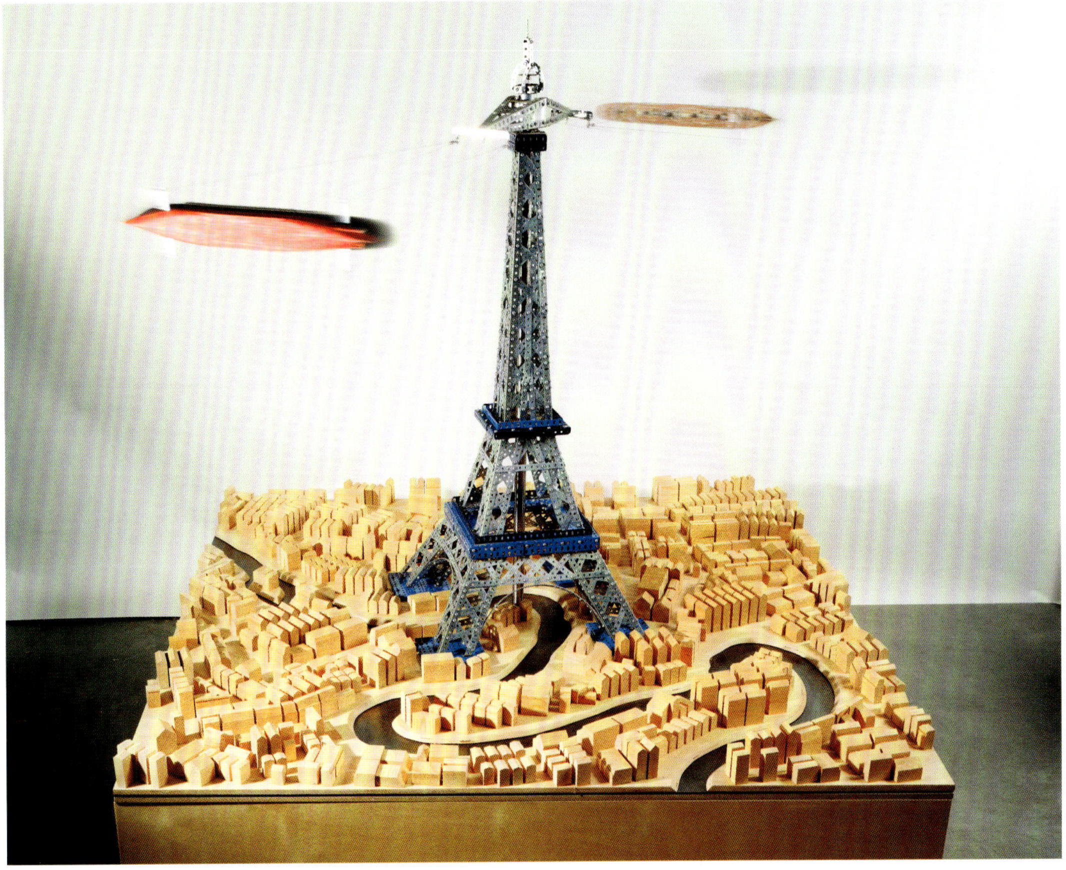

The Fist of Light 1993

Aluminum; heating, ventilating and air conditioning equipment; halide lights
129 × 153 × 130 inches

The Fist of Light *is a machine in the form of a chamber measuring eight by eight by ten feet on its inside dimensions. Placed on a two-foot grid pattern on the interior floor, walls and ceiling are 112 very high output metal halide lights. When all the lights are on the room is approximately three times brighter than the brightest, sunniest day at the beach. Because of the amount of heat generated by the lights inside the chamber, the exterior of the chamber is covered by cooling ducts and is connected to a high velocity five-ton air conditioning system. The public is not allowed to enter the actual chamber, because the intense light is a health hazard, both from the visible light and from the radiant output of energy. Thus, the elaborate machine exists in order to enable the public to conceive of the concept of there being so much light that black turns to white. This piece makes reference to some of the light and space artists, such as James Turrell and Robert Irwin. By pushing to an extreme what is conventionally viewed as a benign and positive material, I altered light into an unconventional, hazardous and powerful force.*

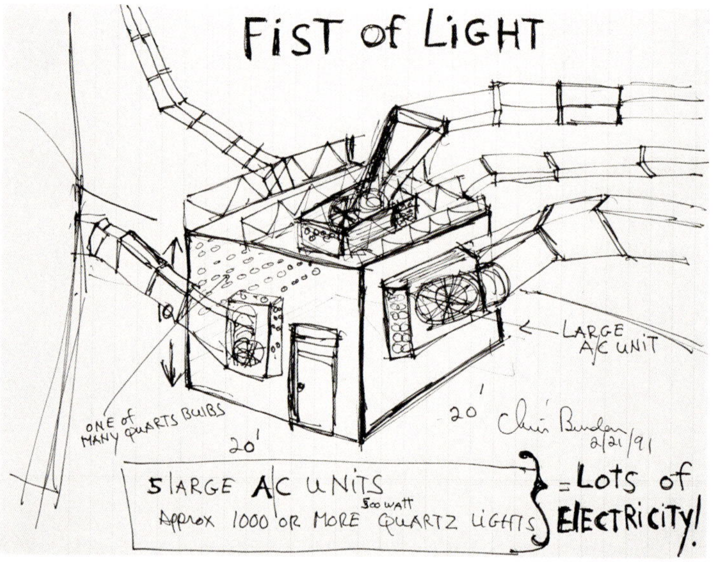

Fist of Light 1991
Ink on paper, 8½ × 11 inches

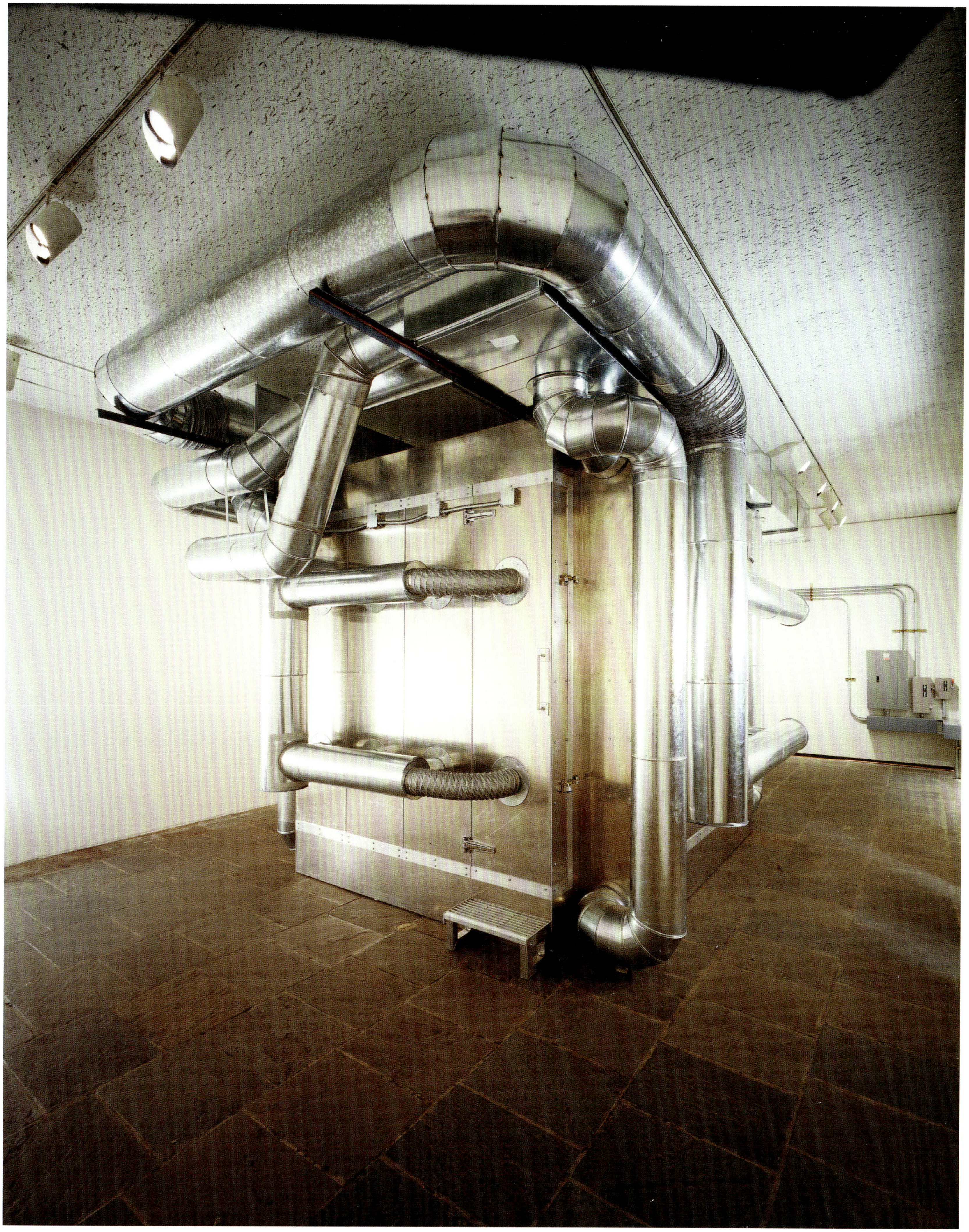

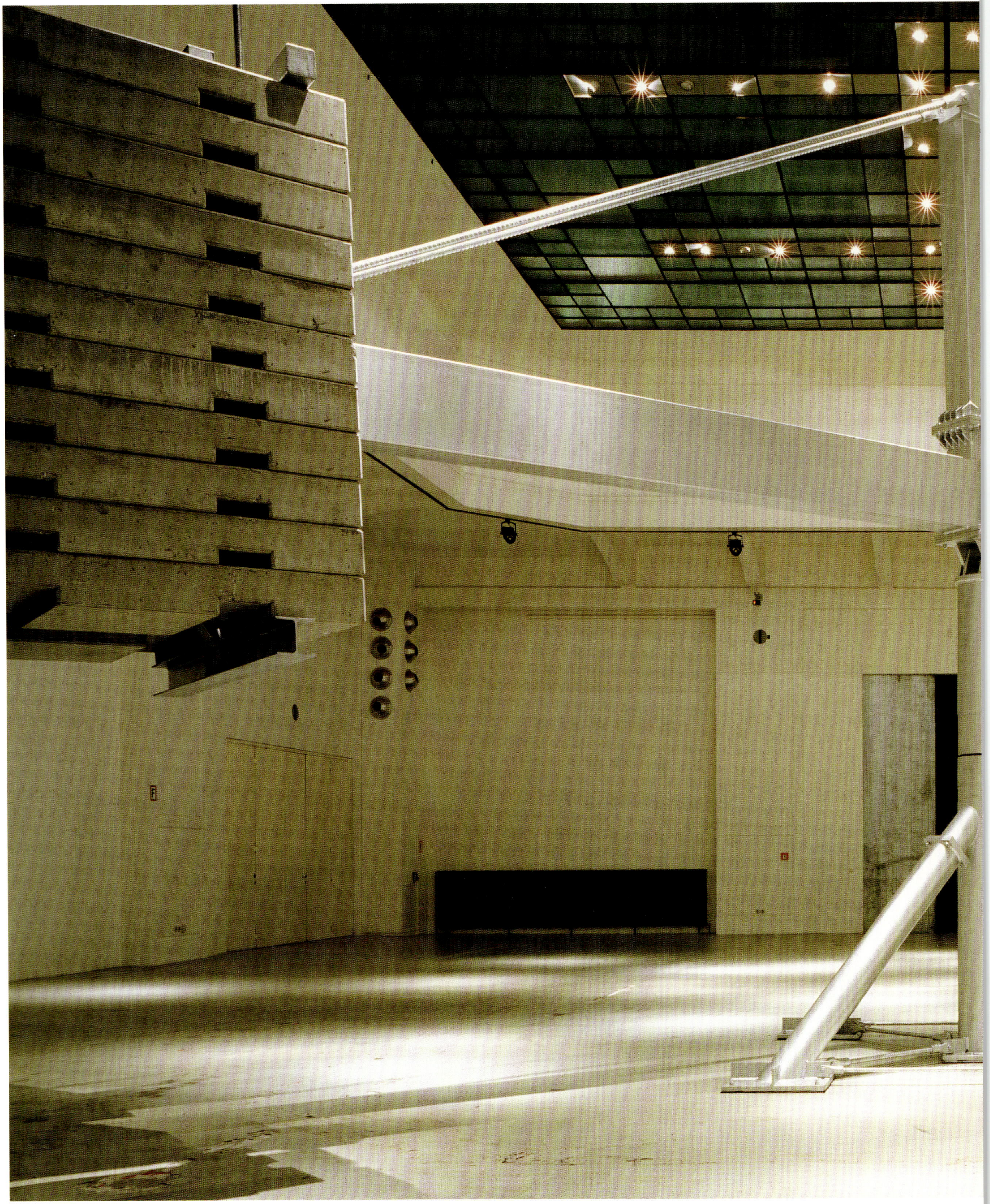

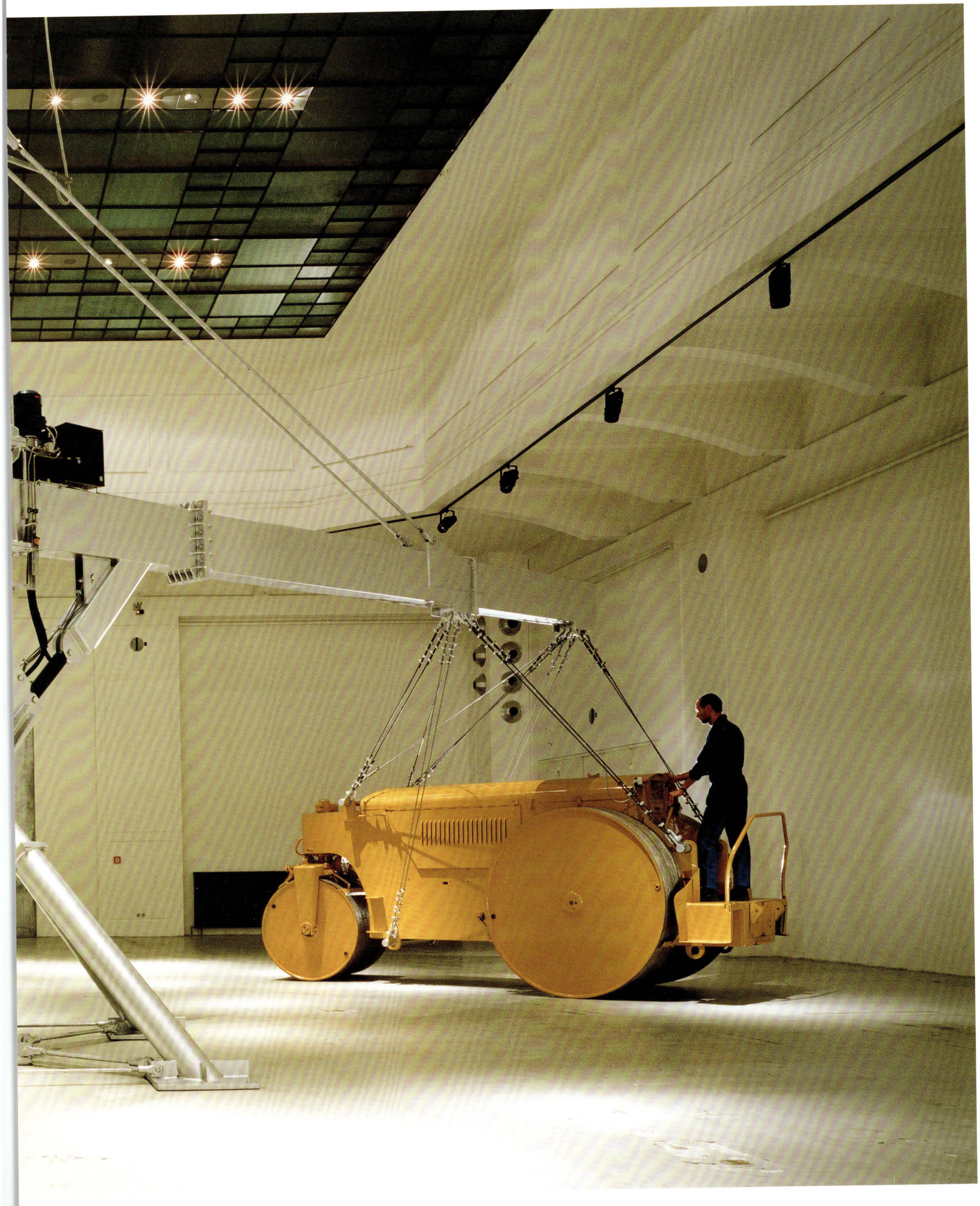

The Flying Steamroller 1996

Steel, concrete, 1968 Huber road grader
252 × 678 inches (diameter of circle)

The Flying Steamroller *is a huge sculpture which consists of a 12-ton steamroller that is attached to a pivoting arm with a counter balance weight. The steamroller is driven in a circle until its maximum speed is reached. At the same time, a hydraulic piston is activated and pushes up the beam from which the steamroller is suspended, causing the steamroller to lift off the ground. Because of the combined weight of the steamroller and the counter balance, which is approximately 48 tons, the steamroller, once lifted off the ground, continues to spin, i.e. 'fly', for several minutes. As the steamroller nears the end of its circular motion, or when the spinning momentum is exhausted, the hydraulic piston is slowly retracted and the steamroller slowly 'lands'.*

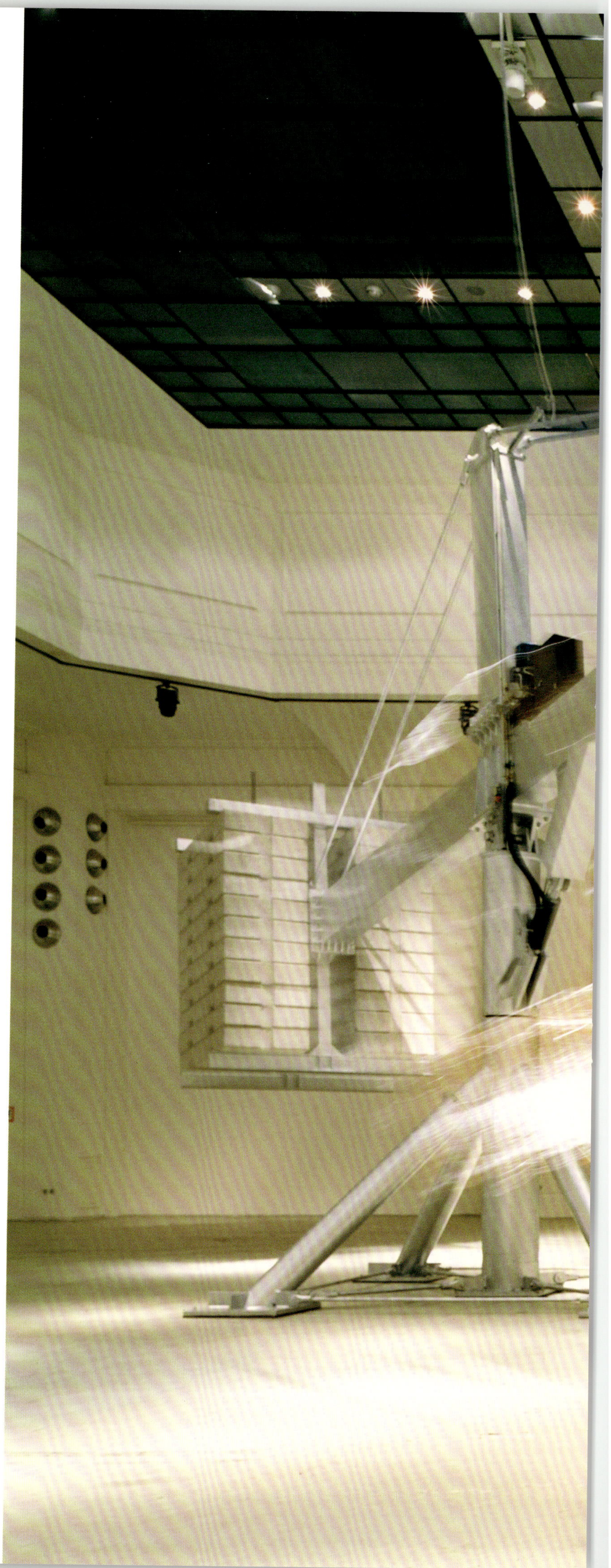

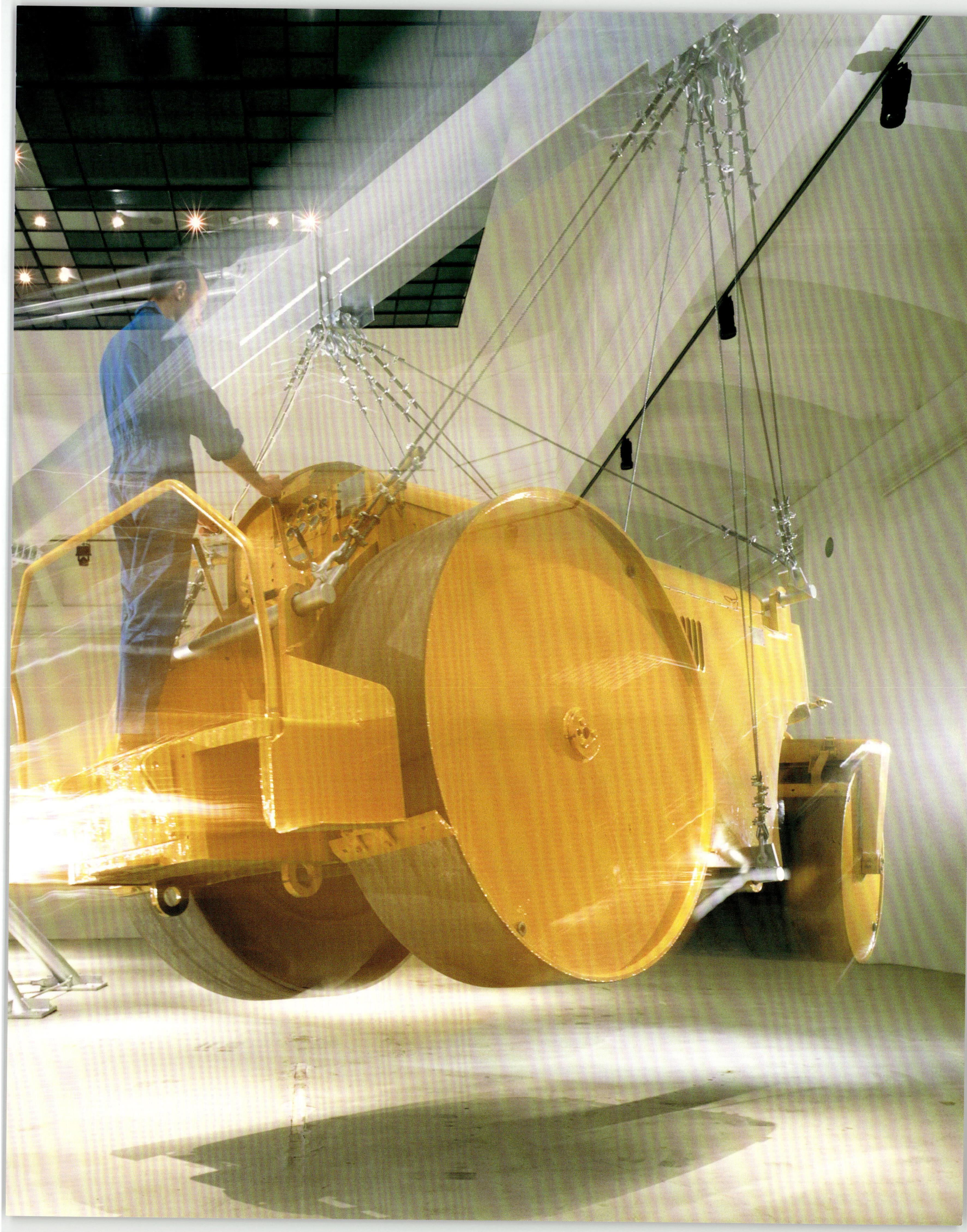

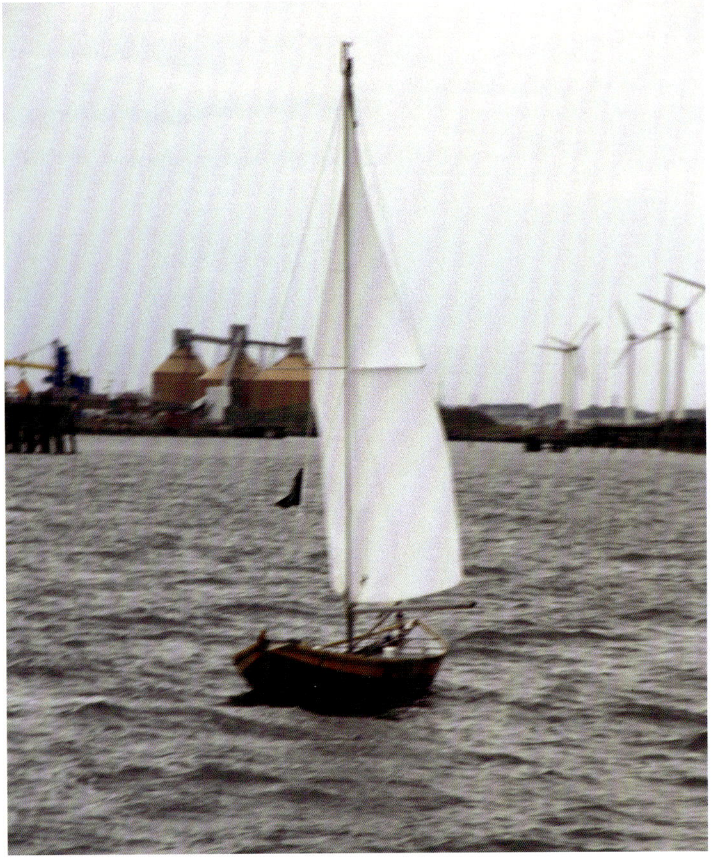

Ghost Ship 2005

30-foot, handmade sixareen, computers and software, hydraulics, Global Positioning System, auto-rudder, rigging
Dimensions infinite

In 2004 I was approached by Locus+, of Newcastle upon Tyne, England with the proposition of revisiting the original concept of Three Ghost Ships. *This sculpture consisted of three sailboats that could sail autonomously, without crew members, from Charleston, South Carolina to Plymouth, England. However, due to financial constraints, the sailboats were built and displayed as a static indoor sculpture, with simulated sail handling and navigational equipment. They were never were put to sea.*

Locus+ commissioned the building of Ghost Ship, *a traditional 30-foot, wooden, double-ended, clinker-built sailing craft called a sixareen, by a boat builder in Fair Isle, Scotland. Under the supervision of the University of Southampton, the boat was outfitted with a hydraulic system to control the sails and the rudder. A computer interfaced the various mechanical controls with a GPS navigation system. The boat sailed the approximately 400 miles from Fair Isle to the mouth of the River Tyne, arriving on the last day of the Tall Ships Festival. As the tall ships were sailing out of the harbor, the* Ghost Ship *sailed up the Tyne, under the Millennium Bridge and into Newcastle/Gateshead, to successfully complete its voyage on schedule.*

When I first discussed this project with Locus+, we all expected the Ghost Ship *could be a truly autonomous sailing craft. In other words, the boat could be programmed to sail between harbor 1 and harbor 2, without any input from the crew aboard the escorting mother ship, the* Bernicia. *However, the sails on the* Ghost Ship *had to be manually adjusted via remote control from the* Bernicia *and the entire system was not precise enough to literally sail from harbor 1 to harbor 2 without any human intervention. Although the* Ghost Ship *performed admirably in the rough North Sea, further development is needed in order to complete the absolutely autonomous sailboat as originally envisioned.*

The potential of a truly autonomous sailboat has tremendous implications for commercial cargo shipping. Huge crewless cargo sailboats could ply the trade routes delivering cargo without consuming any fuel. In addition to the financial savings from the reduction in manpower and fuel costs, a fleet of ghost ships ultimately portend a world where the existent forces of nature are harnessed in a benign and productive fashion.

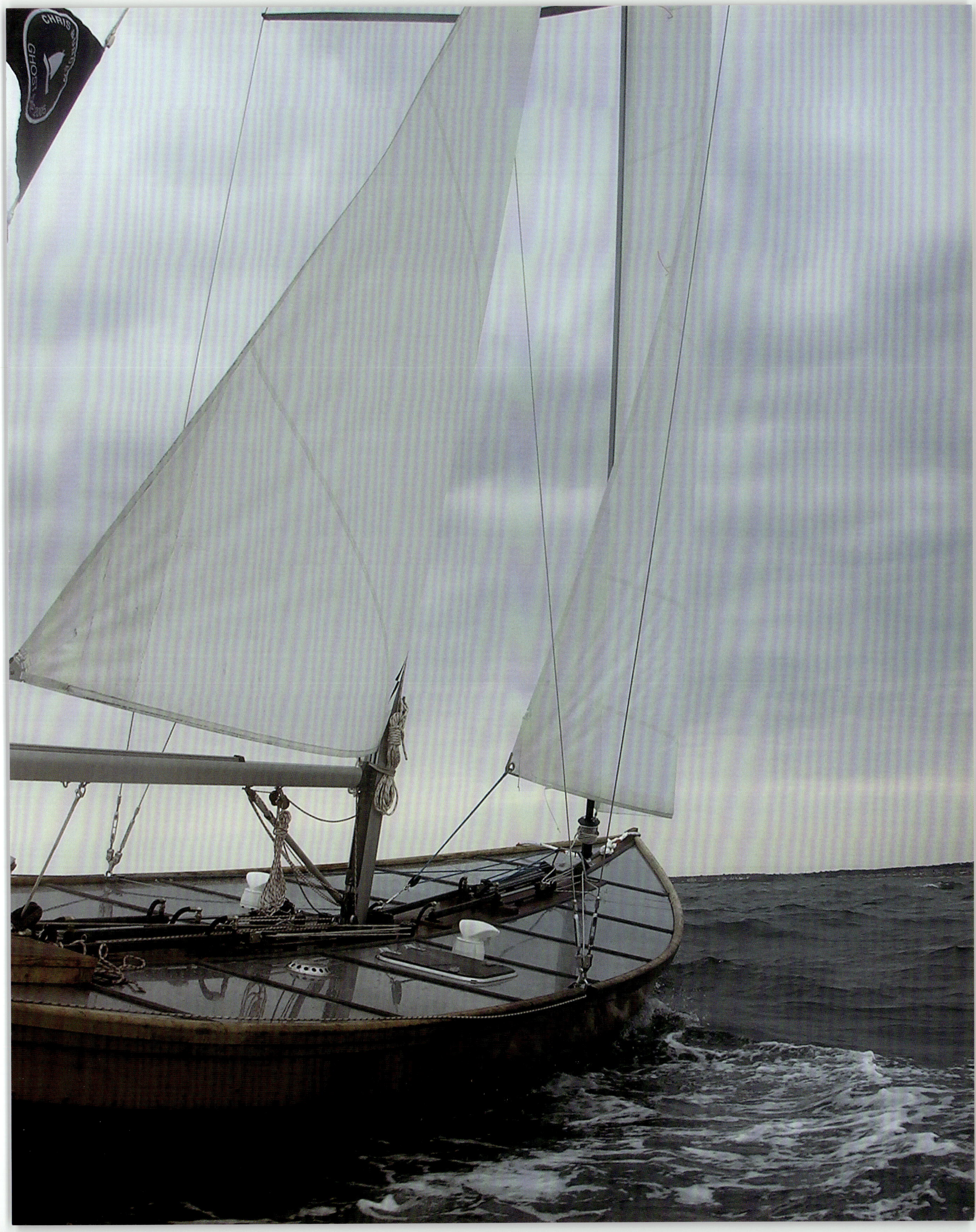

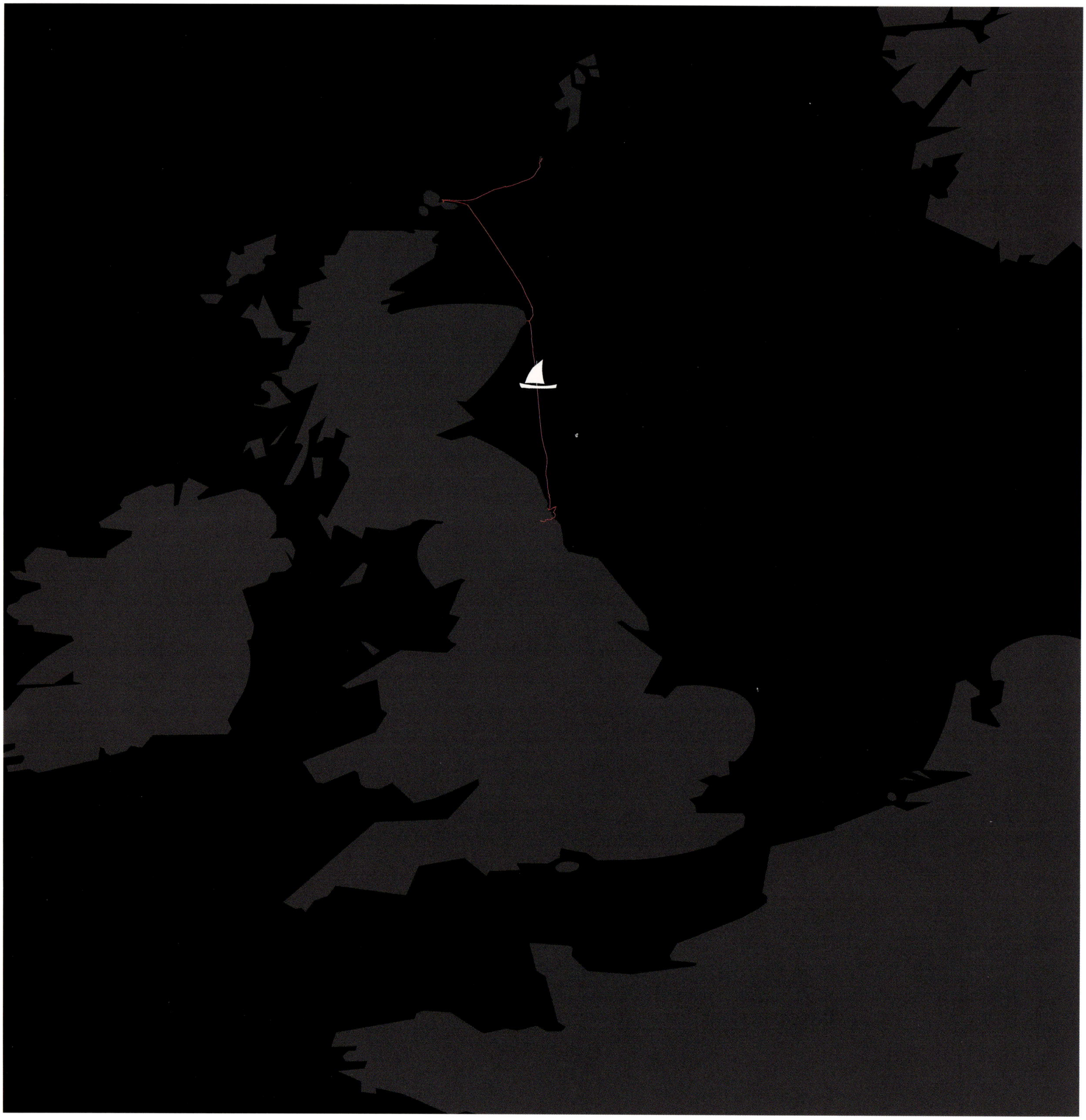

Ghost Ship's course as recorded on www.ghostship.org.uk

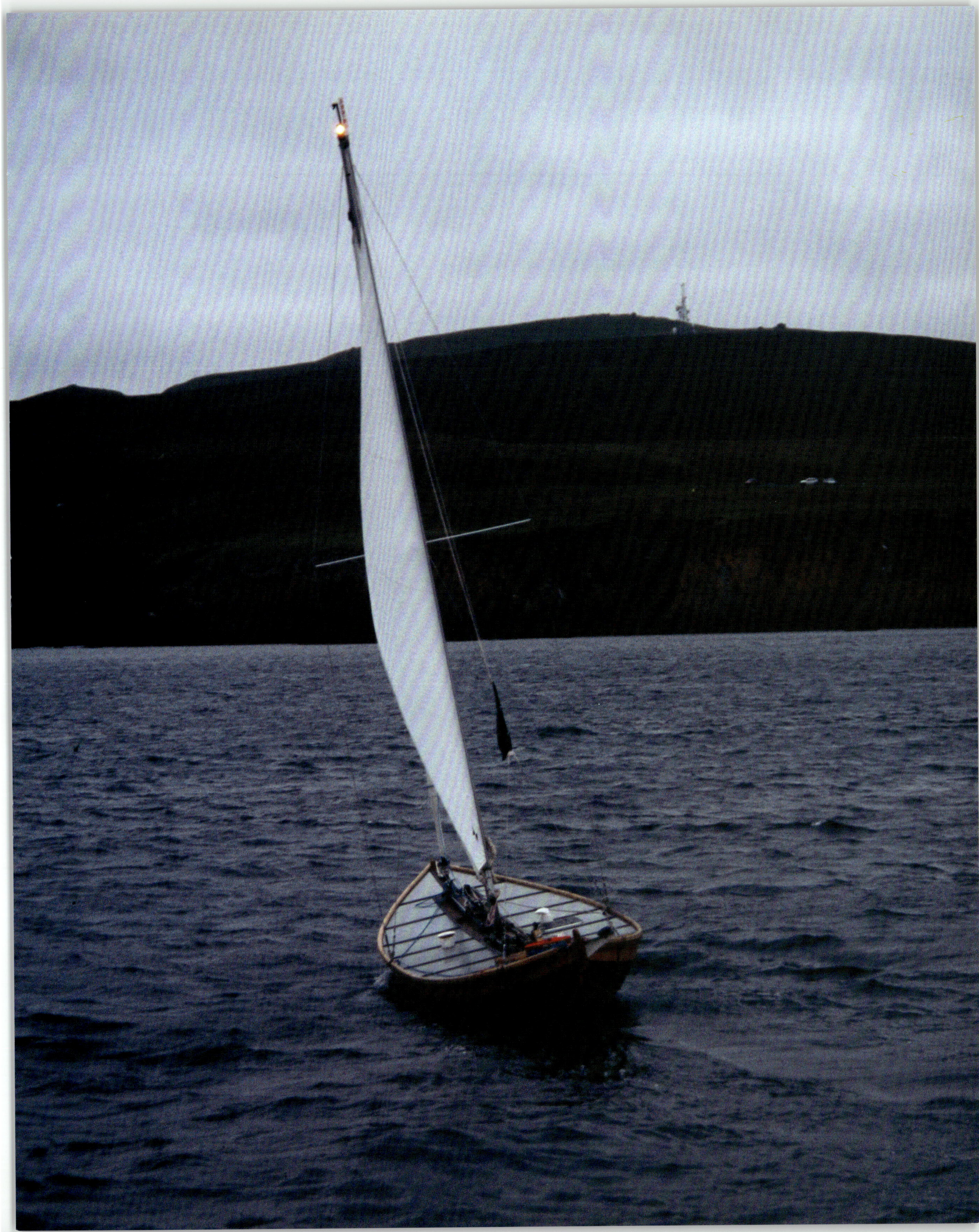

Match Piece 1972

Pomona College, Claremont,
California, USA; March 20, 1972

Two-thirds of the gallery floor was covered with white paper. A closed-circuit television system was installed in the room. The monitor was placed so that the audience could watch the piece or see it in the monitor, but could not do both at once. I sat on the floor at the opposite end of the room. Two miniature TVs were placed so that I could view them while I made match rockets and shot them at a nude woman lying on the floor about 15 feet from me. The rockets were made by wrapping the match head with foil and igniting it with another match. Range and accuracy were impossible to control. Some of the rockets landed on her body leaving small burns, others landed in the audience. The piece began before the audience arrived and ended when everyone had left, lasting about three hours.

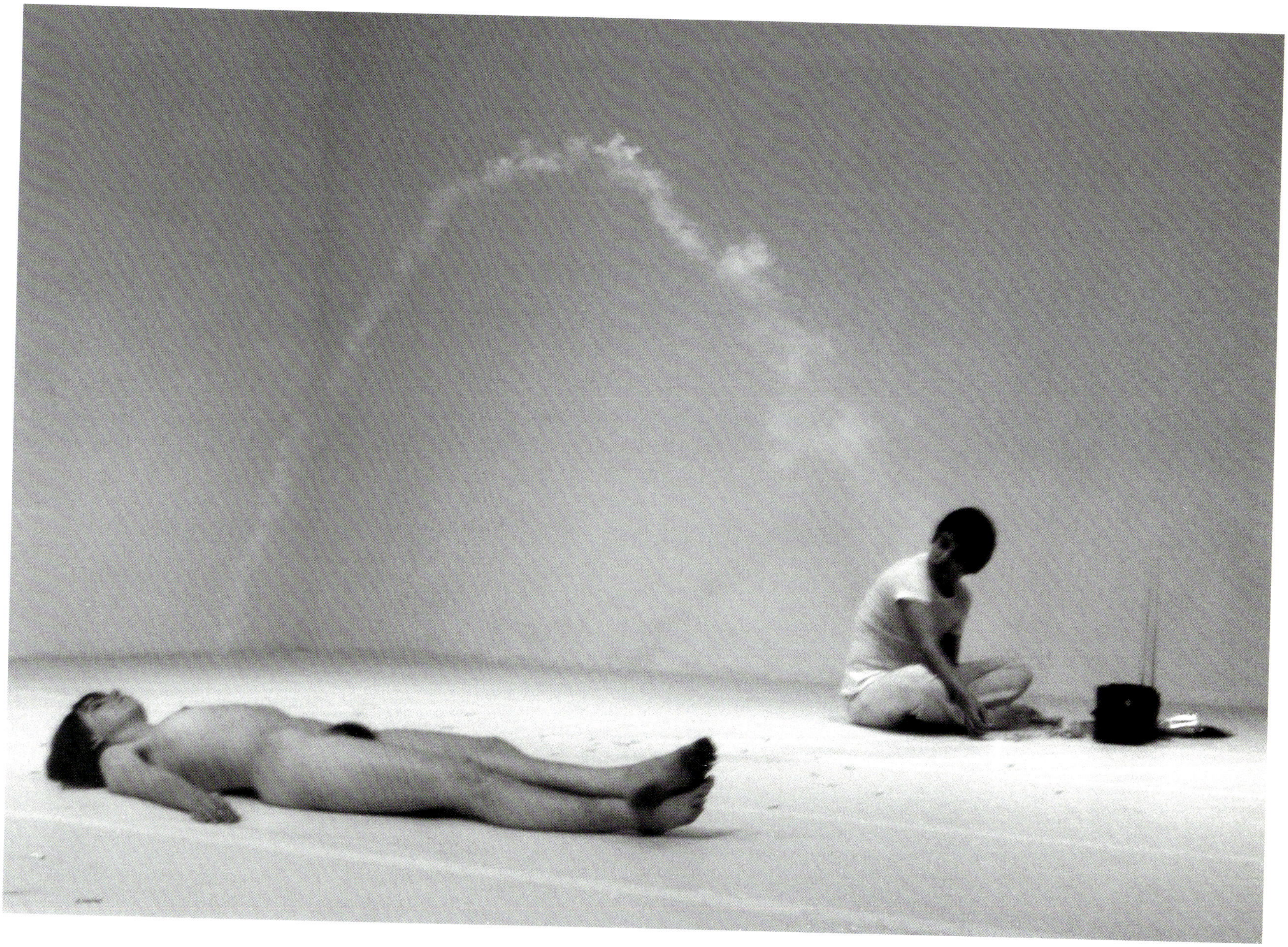

Icarus 1973

Venice, California, USA; April 13, 1973

At 6 pm three invited spectators came to my studio. The room was 15 feet by 25 feet and well lit by natural light. Wearing no clothes, I entered the space from a small room at the back. Two assistants lifted onto each shoulder one end of six-foot sheets of plate glass. The sheets sloped onto the floor at right angles from my body. The assistants poured gasoline down the sheets of glass. Stepping back, they threw matches to ignite the gasoline. After a few seconds I jumped up, sending the burning glass crashing to the floor. I walked into the back room.

RELIC: Glass wings

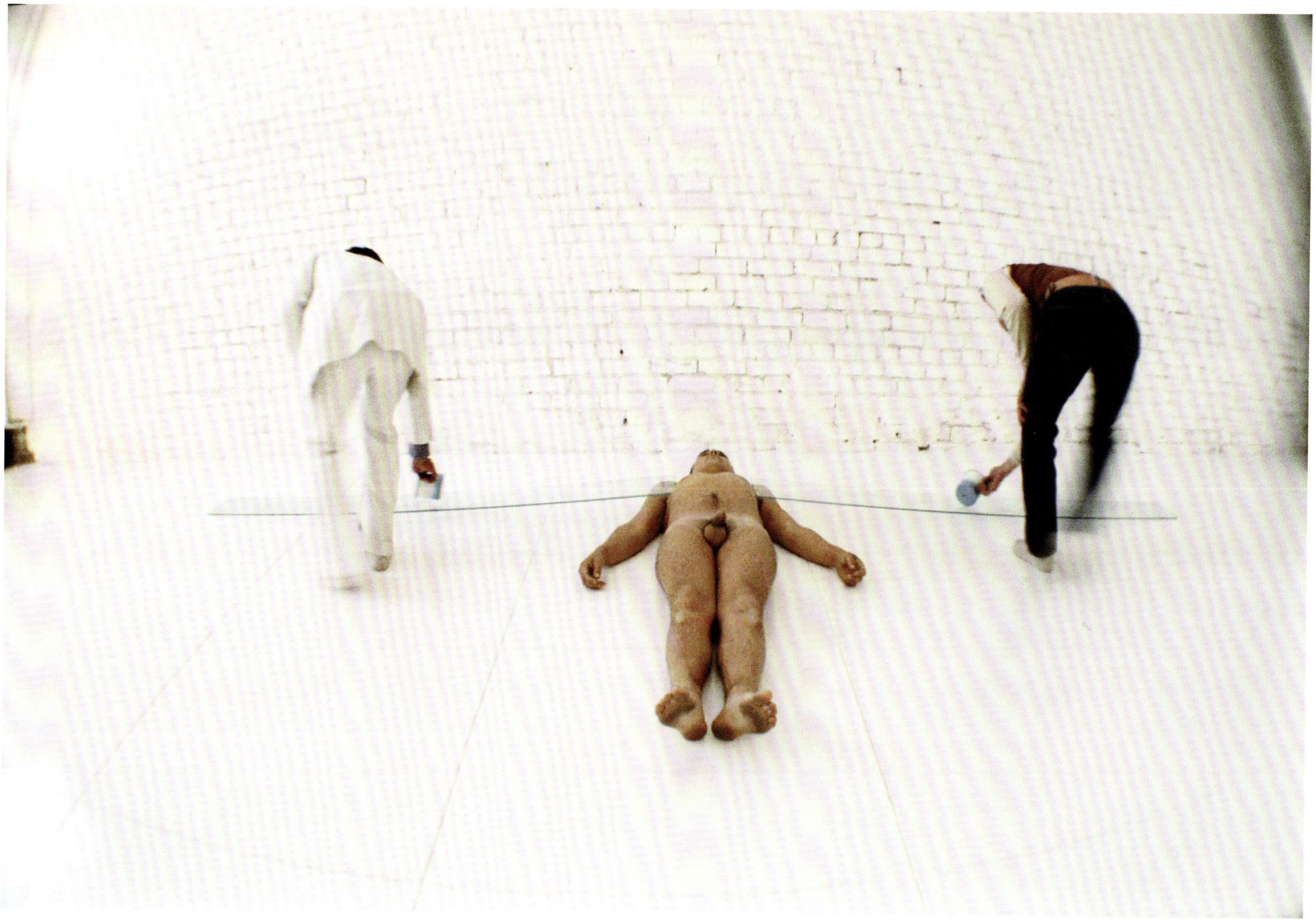

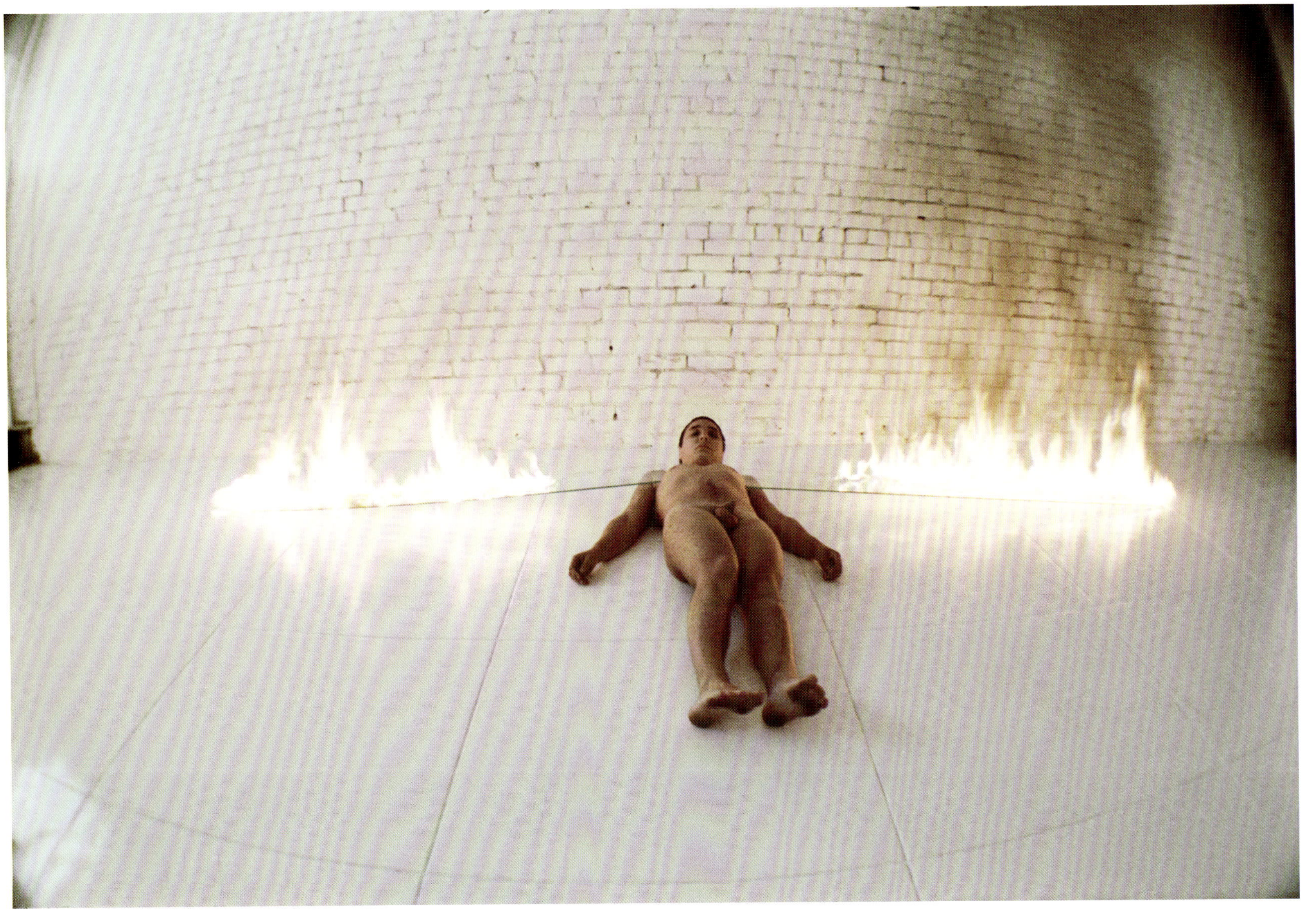

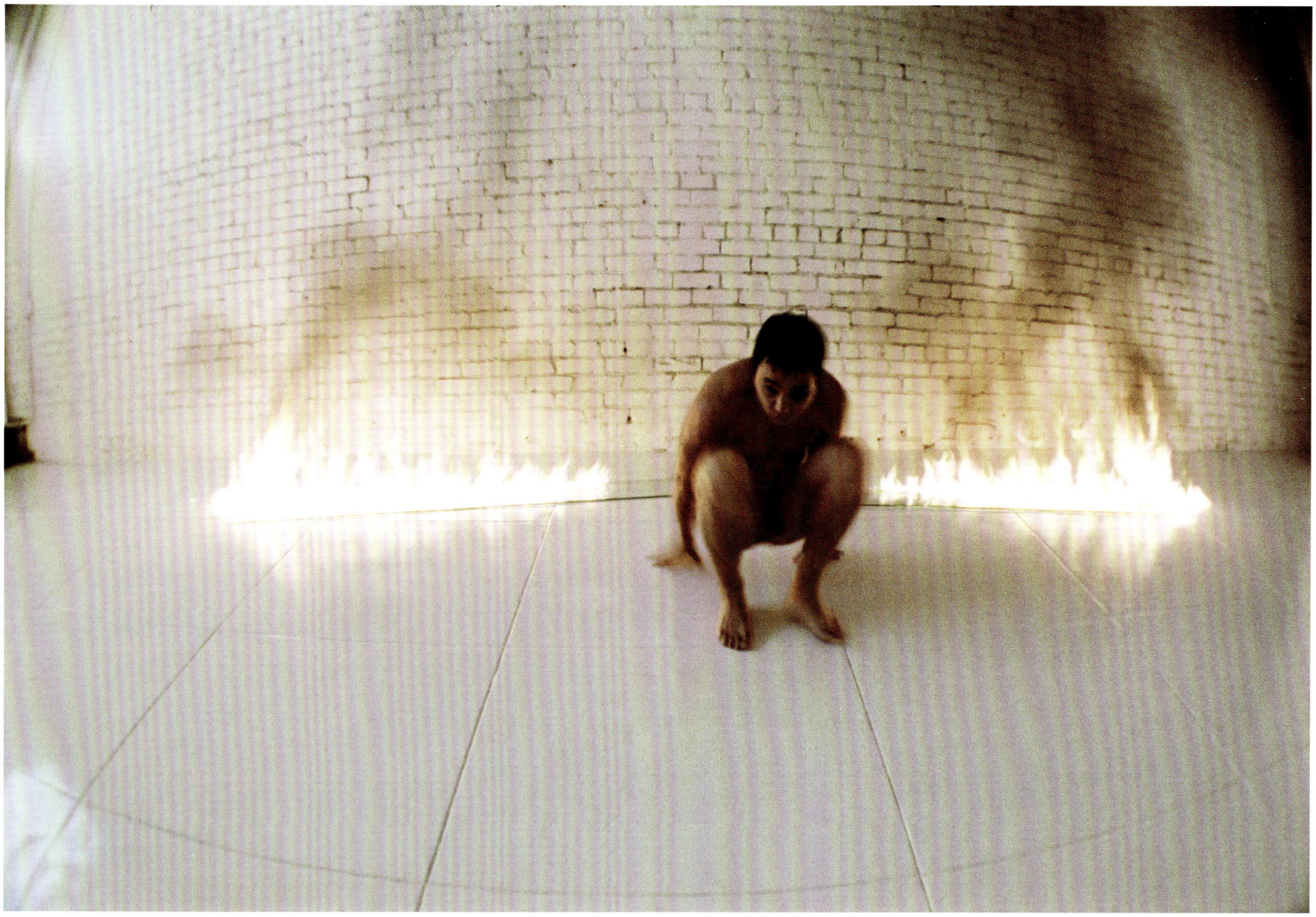

Movie on the Way Down 1973

Oberlin College, Oberlin, Ohio, USA;
May 1, 1973

Wearing no clothes, I was suspended by my feet with a rope tied to a ceiling crossbeam. I was hanging in the center of a gymnasium above basketball markings which suggested a target. I held a running movie camera pointed at the floor. In a far corner of the gym, a piano began a light melody and the audience was permitted to enter. The music lasted for a minute and a half. As soon as the music ended, an assistant in the rafters severed the rope with an axe blow. I crashed to the floor, got up, dressed and left.

RELIC: Kodak Super 8 movie camera

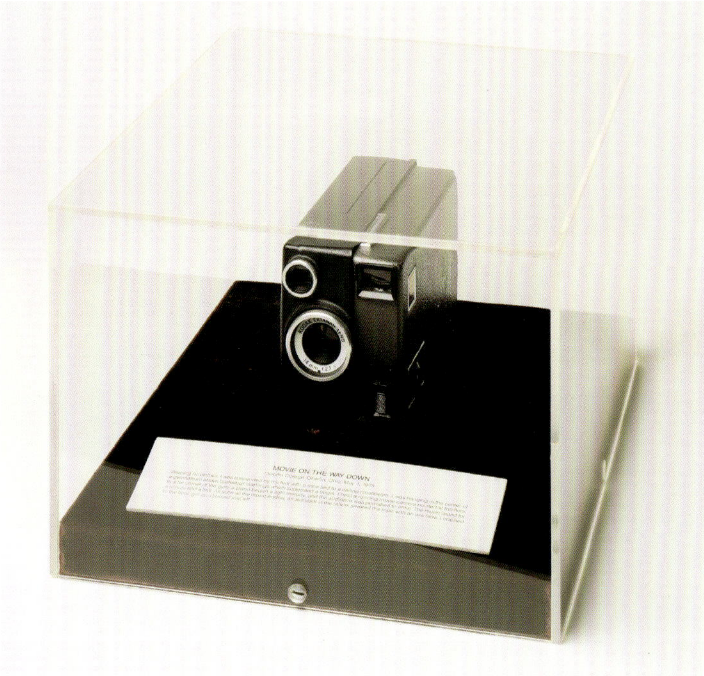

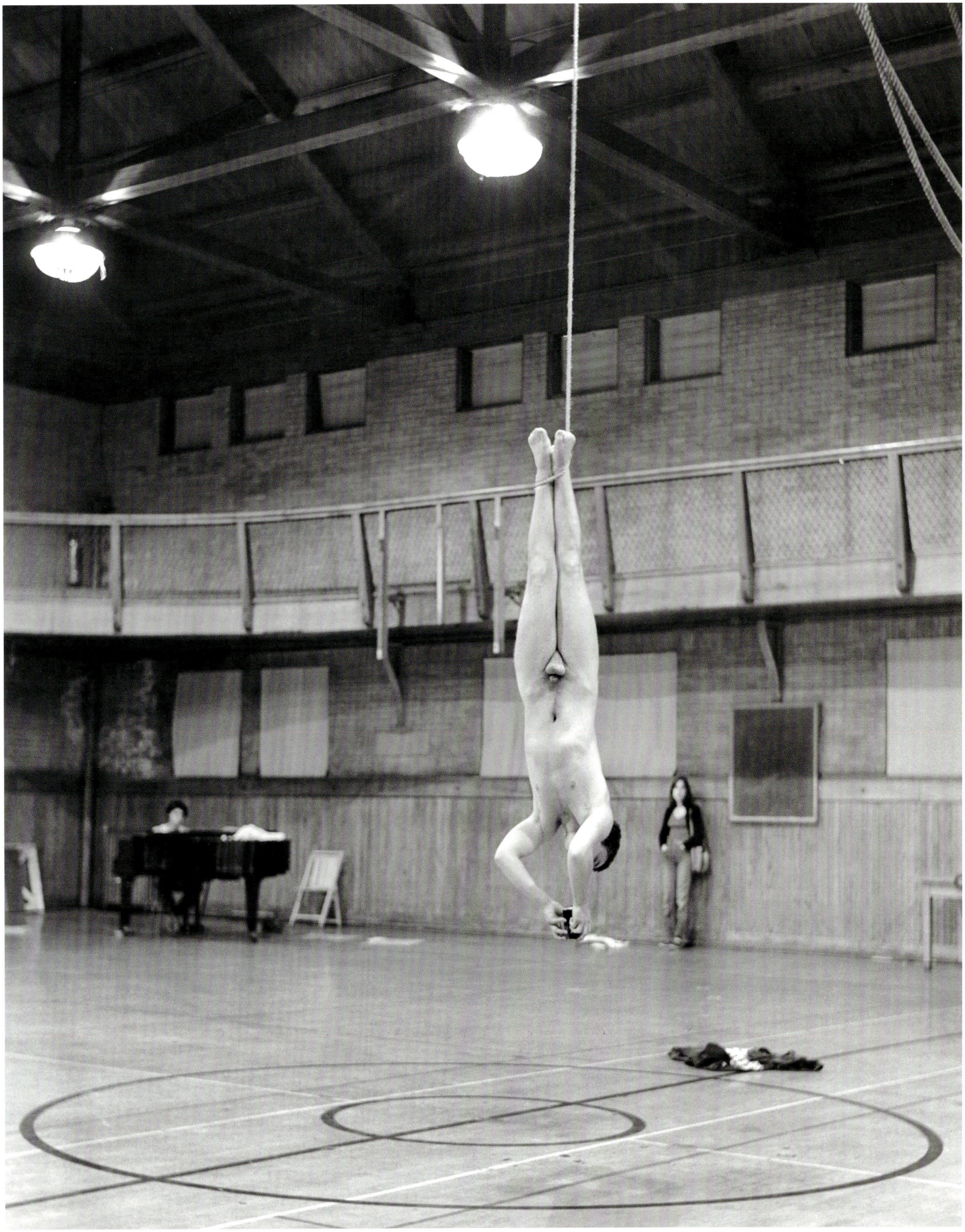

Through the Night Softly 1973

Main Street, Los Angeles,
California, USA; September 12, 1973

Holding my hands behind my back, I crawled through 50 feet of broken glass. There were very few spectators, most of them passersby. This piece was documented with a 16mm film.

RELIC: Broken glass

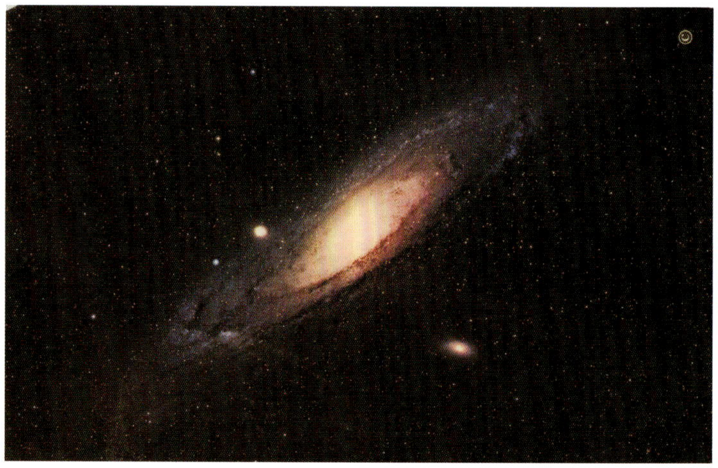

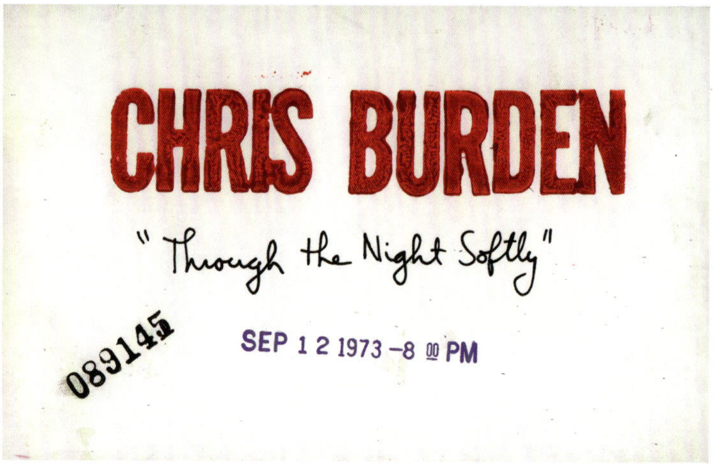

Announcement card
3½ × 5½ inches

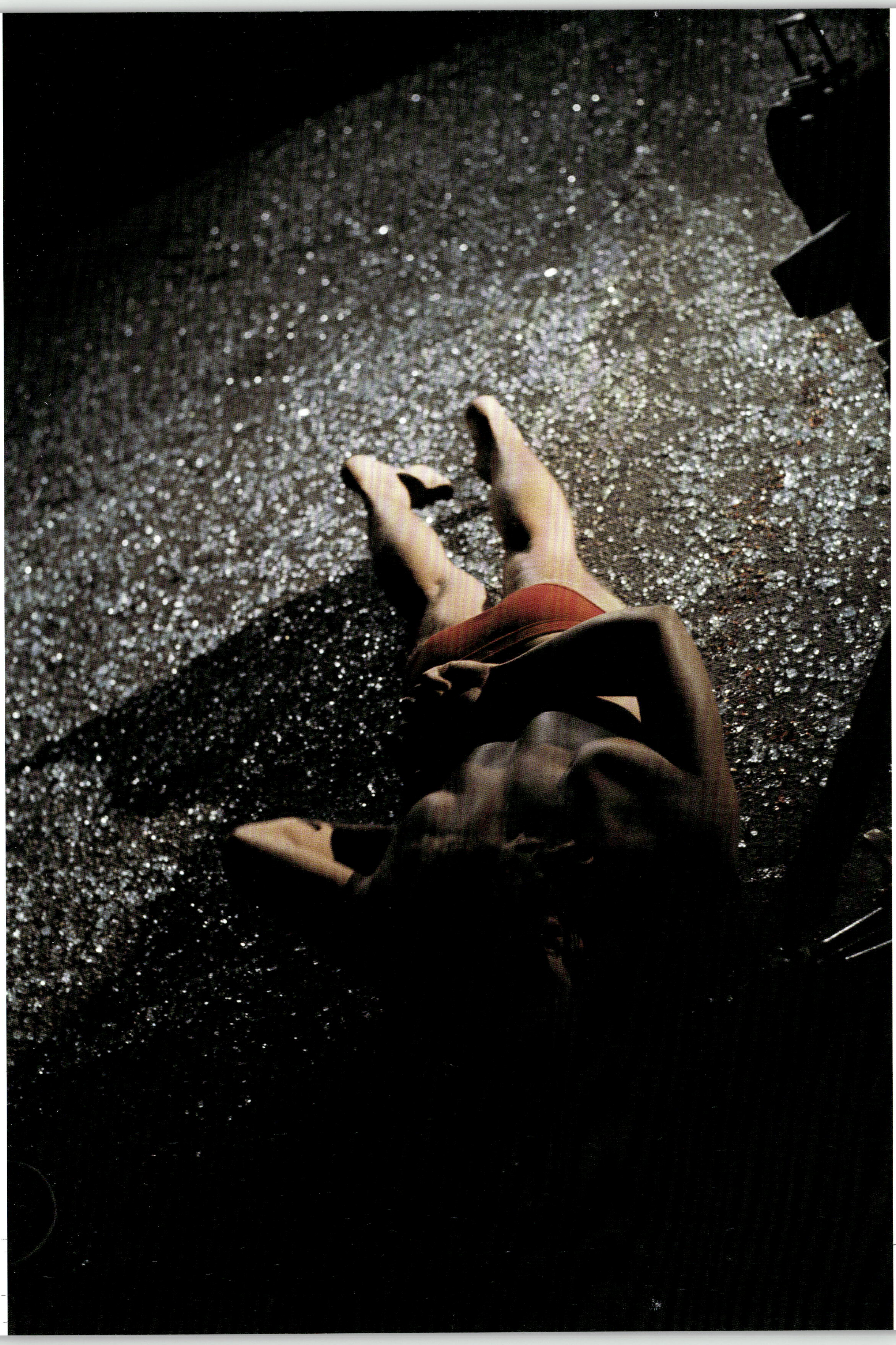

Doorway to Heaven 1973

Venice, California, USA;
November 15, 1973

At 6 pm I stood in the doorway of my studio facing the Venice Boardwalk. A few spectators watched as I pushed two live electric wires into my chest. The wires crossed and exploded, burning me but saving me from electrocution.

RELIC: Two wire coils

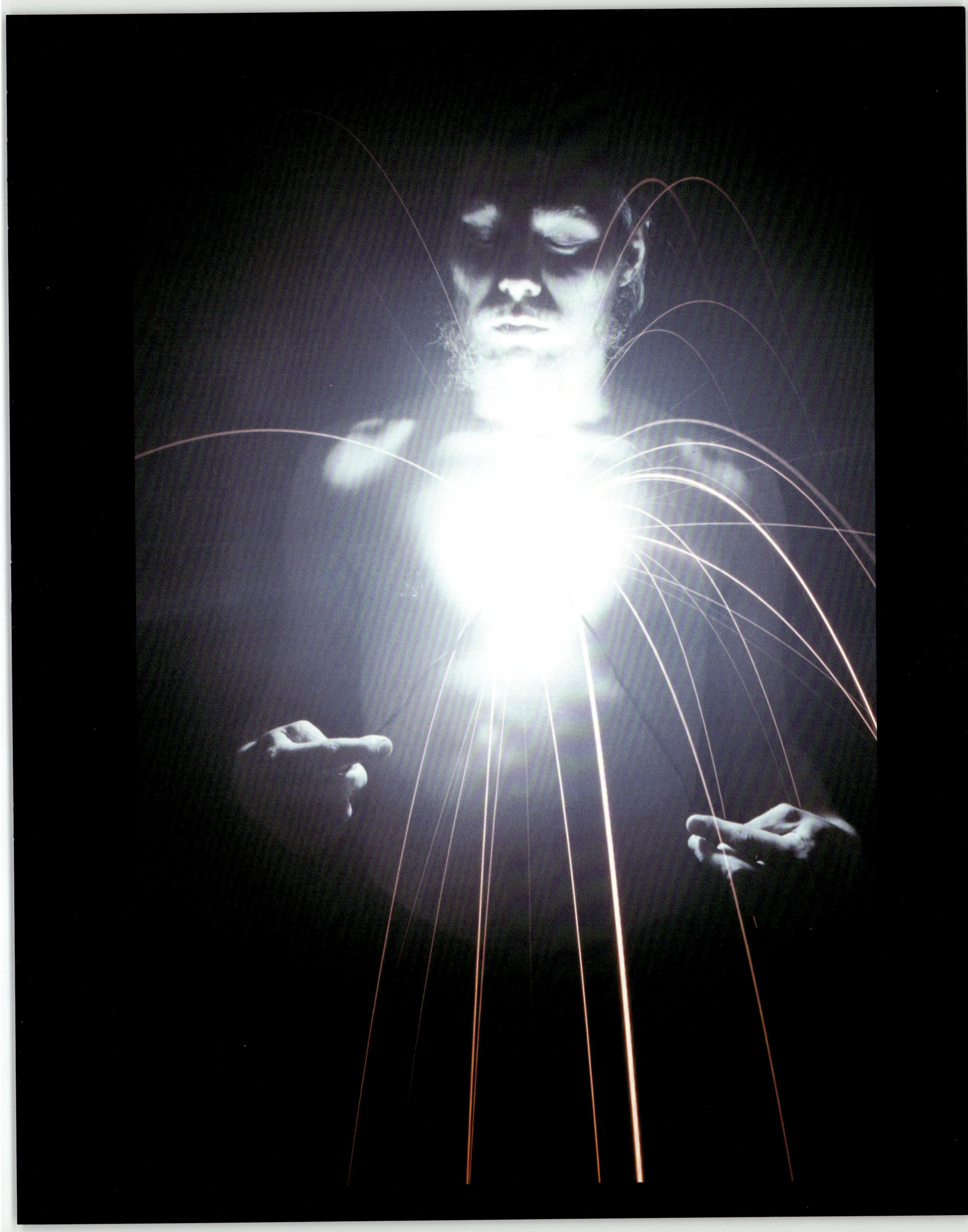

Trans-fixed 1974

Speedway Avenue, Venice, California, USA; April 23, 1974

Inside a small garage on Speedway Avenue, I stood on the rear bumper of a Volkswagen. I lay on my back over the rear section of the car, stretching my arms onto the roof. Nails were driven through my palms into the roof of the car. The garage door was opened and the car was pushed halfway out into Speedway. Screaming for me, the engine was run at full speed for two minutes. After two minutes, the engine was turned off and the car pushed back into the garage. The door was closed.

RELIC: Two nails

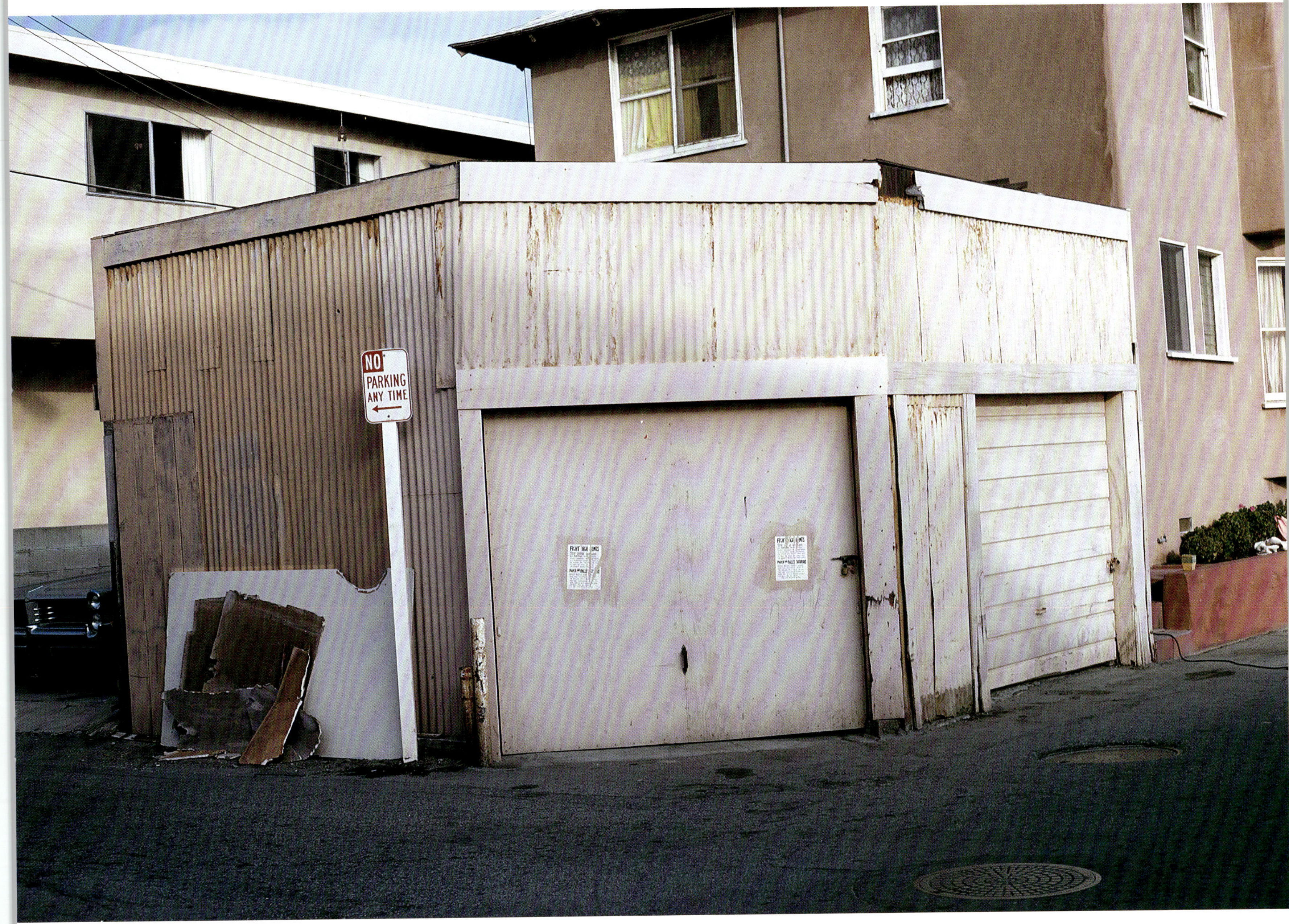
NO
PARKING
ANY TIME

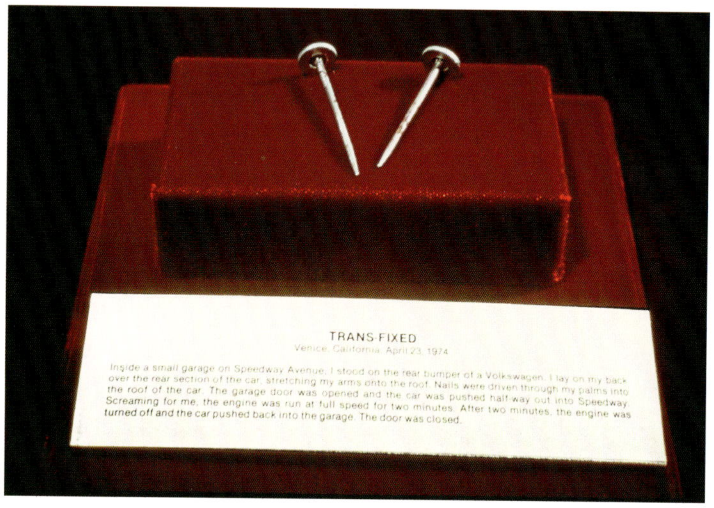
TRANS-FIXED
Venice, California, April 23, 1974
Inside a small garage on Speedway Avenue, I stood on the rear bumper of a Volkswagen. I lay on my back over the rear section of the car, stretching my arms onto the roof. Nails were driven through my palms into the roof of the car. The garage door was opened and the car was pushed half-way out into Speedway. Screaming for me, the engine was run at full speed for two minutes. After two minutes, the engine was turned off and the car pushed back into the garage. The door was closed.

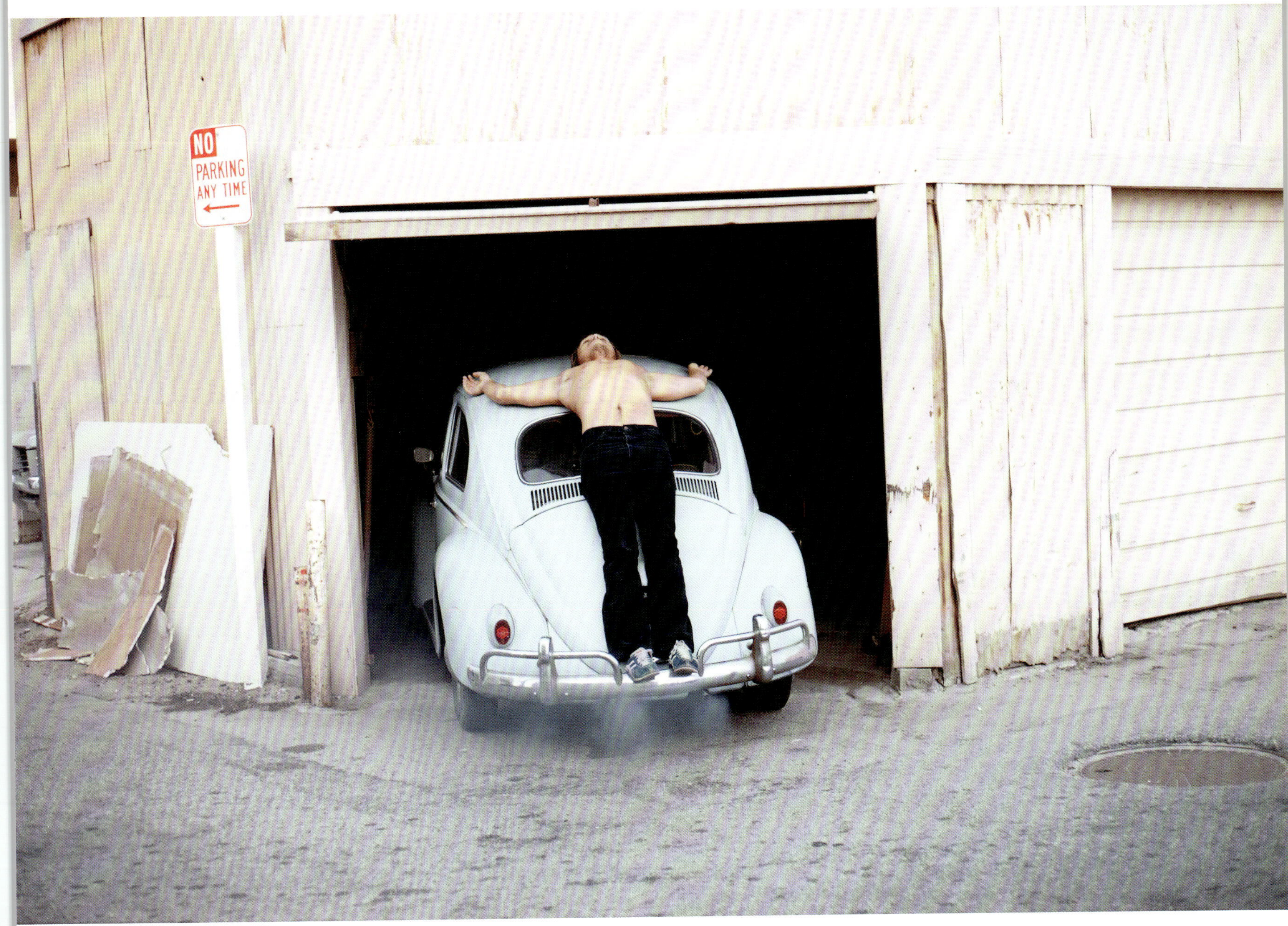
NO
PARKING
ANY TIME

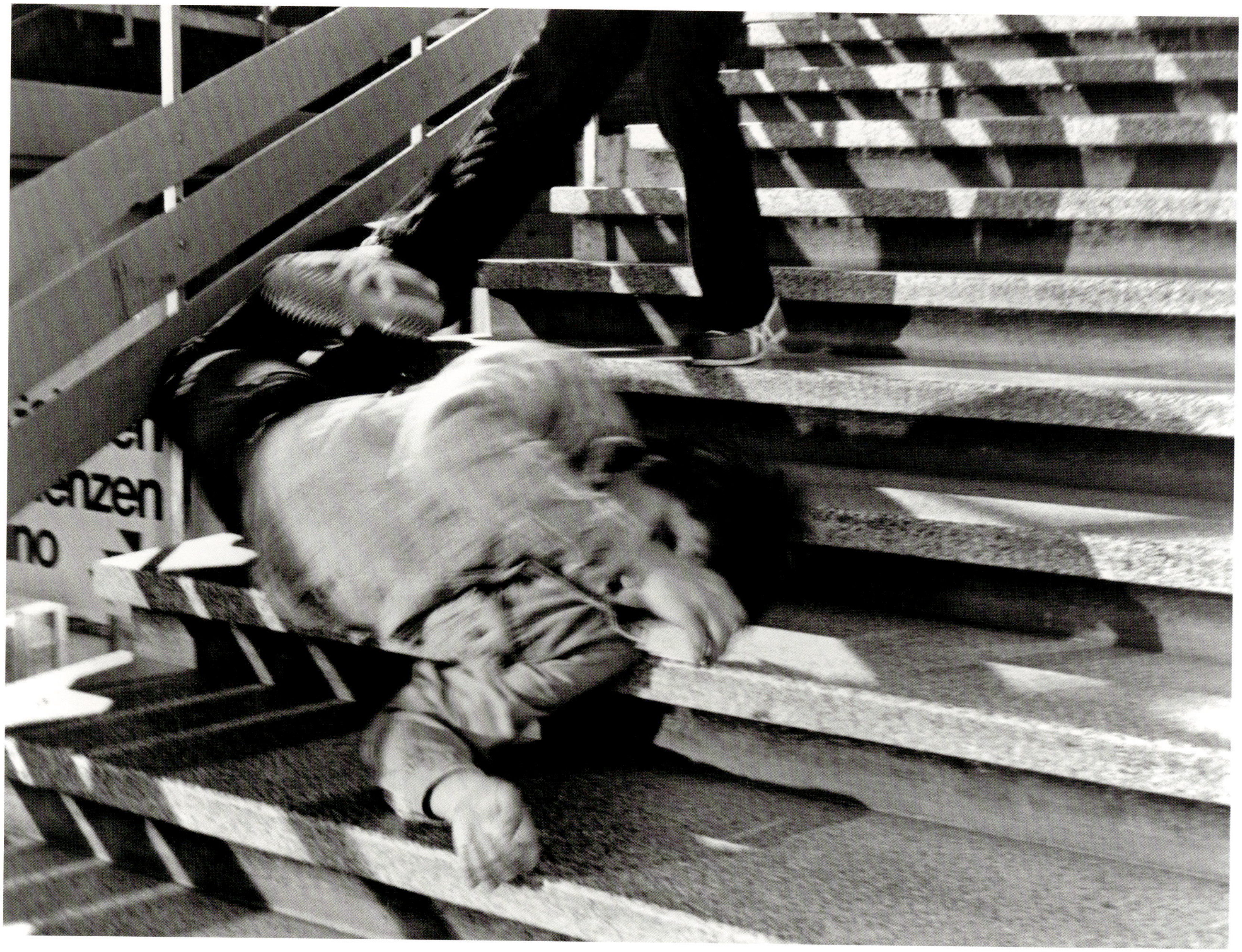

Kunst Kick 1974

Ronald Feldman Fine Arts, Basel Art Fair,
Basel, Switzerland; June 19, 1974

At 12 noon I was kicked down two flights of concrete stairs in the Mustermesse at the public opening of the Art Fair in Basel, Switzerland. I lay down at the top of the stairs and Charles Hill repeatedly kicked my body which fell two or three steps at a time.

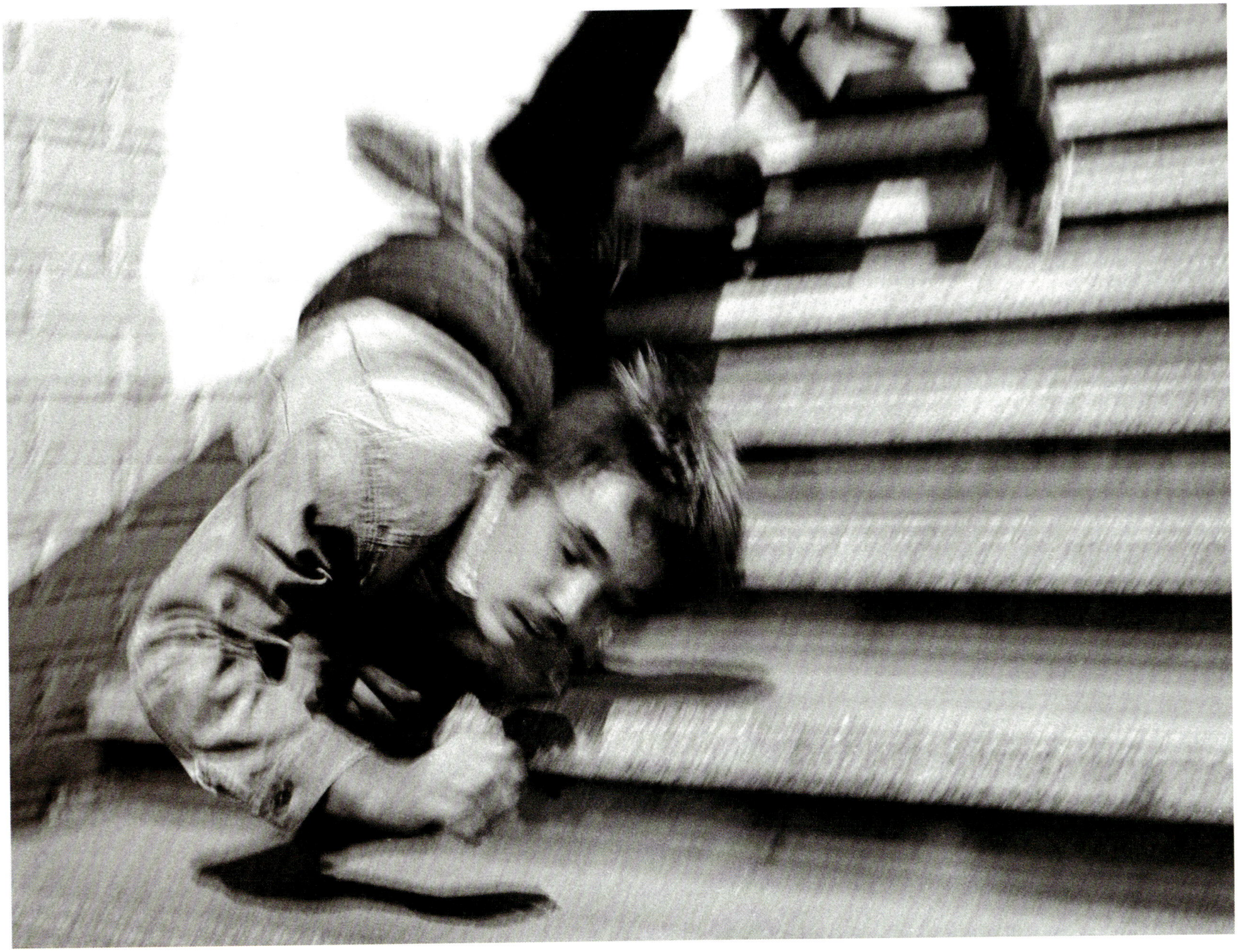

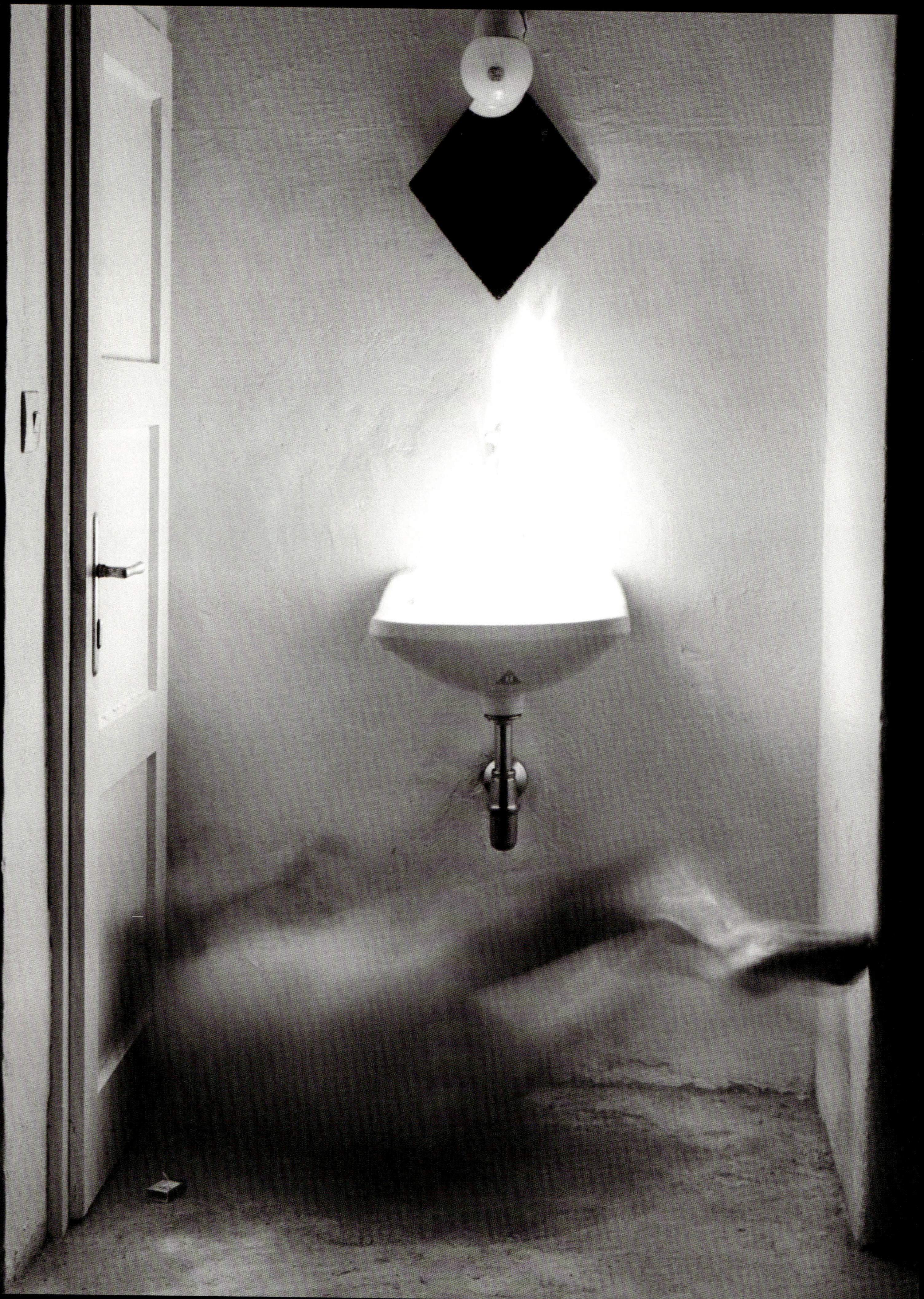

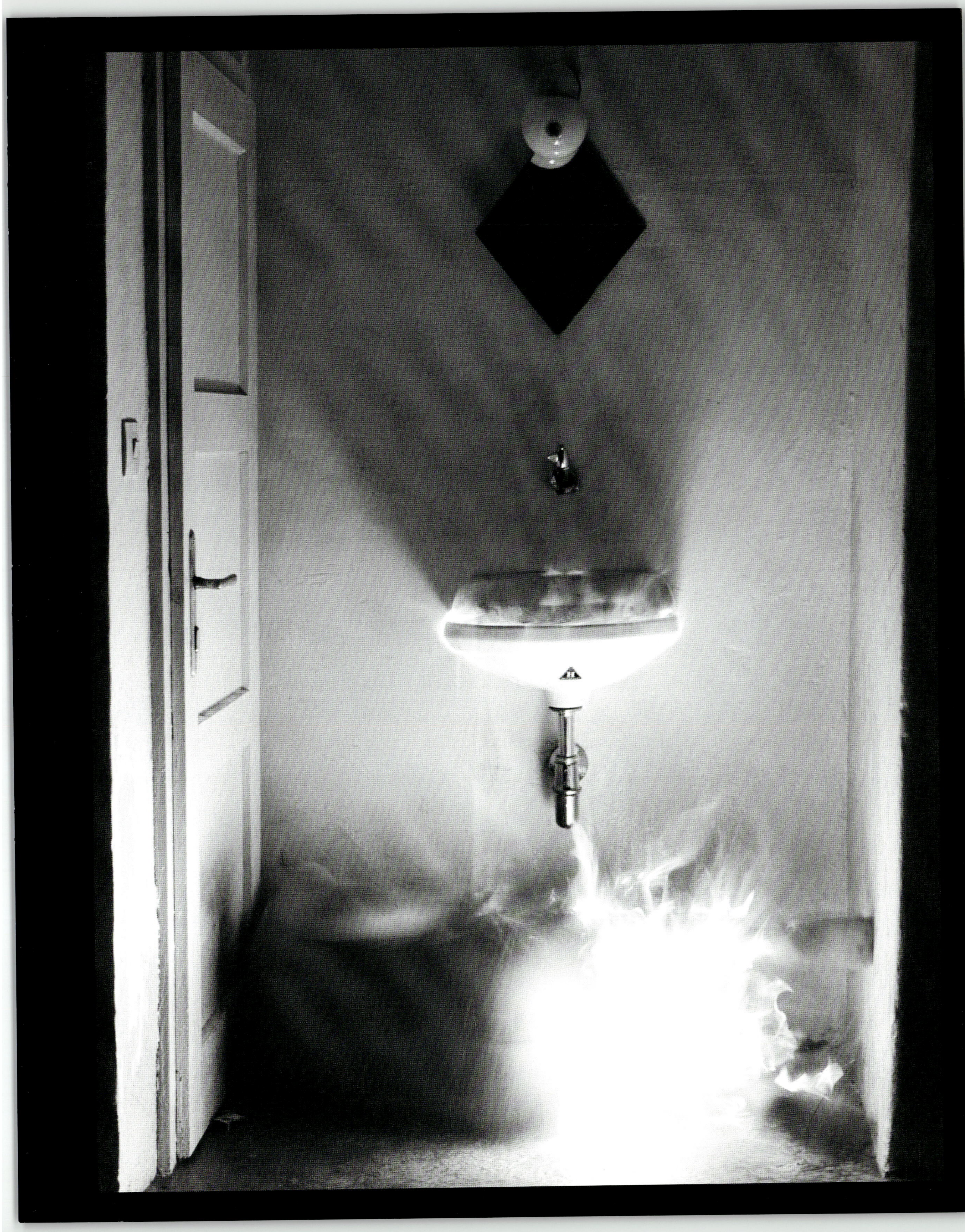

◁◁

Dreamy Nights 1974

Poolerie Gallery, Graz, Austria:
October 15, 1974

The gallery was dark. I covered my body with vaseline and walked into a small recess in the wall containing a sink filled with Spiritus (alcohol). I lit the Spiritus and lay underneath the sink with my back to the audience. I blew on a police whistle while writhing violently on the floor. After about a minute, an assistant threw water into the sink splashing the burning Spiritus onto my body. Water was thrown into the sink until the flames were extinguished.

RELIC: Corked bottle of Spiritus

Oracle 1975

Schema Gallery, Florence, Italy;
May 14, 1975

The performance was scheduled to begin at 9:30 in the evening. The first 35 people to arrive were let into the gallery and the door was locked. The gallery was dark except for one spotlight defining a circular area in front of one of three large windows. In front of each window hung a scrim that extended from ceiling to floor and obscured the window from view. The audience was asked to sit on the floor facing the windows and behind the spotlight area. After a few minutes, my shadow appeared on the scrim and said:

'In February I did a piece where I lay on a triangular platform for 22 days. The platform was built in a corner high above the gallery floor. During the piece I just lay on the platform. I didn't see anyone and no one could see me. I didn't eat, talk, or come down. After I had been there for three weeks, on the last night, I had a dream, a sort of a nightmare. In the dream, I was doing a piece on a large bunk bed. I was high on the top bunk, and nobody could see me. I was always worried that the sheets were coming untucked, hanging down, spoiling the piece by making it look messy. I couldn't look to see if the sheets were really hanging down, because then someone would see me. All I could do was lie there and worry. Then in the dream, the piece was over and I was down from the bed. I was sitting in a bar with two friends. It was the first time I had seen anyone. I couldn't talk and I didn't want anything. I could talk, really, but I didn't have anything to say. Nothing interested me. I knew that I was physically alright, but spiritually something had happened to me. It was as if I didn't need anything anymore; it wasn't just that I didn't want it. And it wasn't like I was crazy – it wasn't like that. It was like serenity. If there was ever a time when I should have been happy and relieved and wanted to talk, this should have been it. But it wasn't. It was like ennui or boredom, when nothing you think about is interesting or fun. I knew that people expected me to be happy, and they expected me to be glad to see them. I knew that it would be obvious that I was distant, and I couldn't hide the way I was feeling. It was like something had evaporated from me. I was sad and frightened. I realized what was wrong. I no longer had any desire to be part of the real world.'

After the dream was related, the shadow disappeared and the audience was asked to leave.

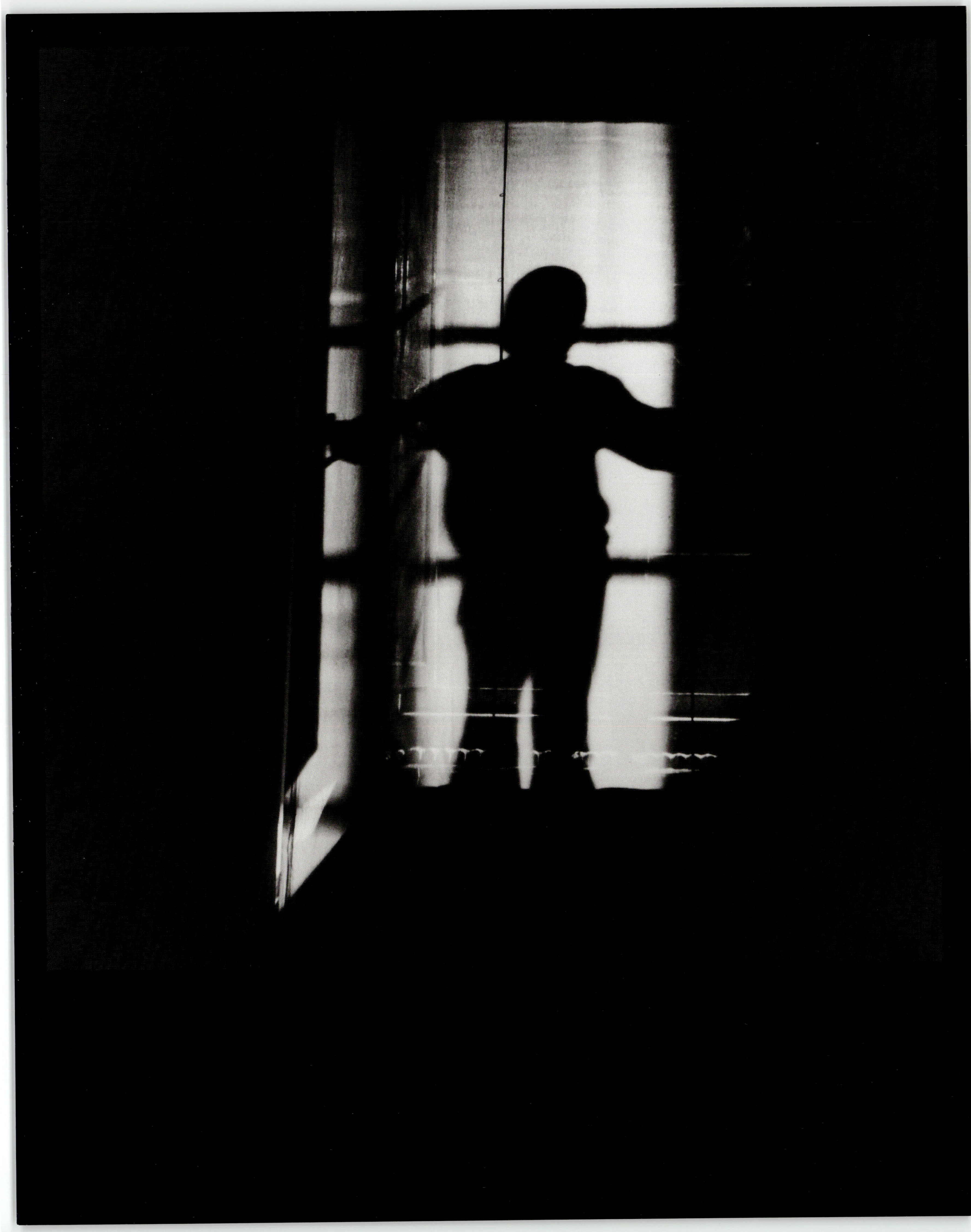

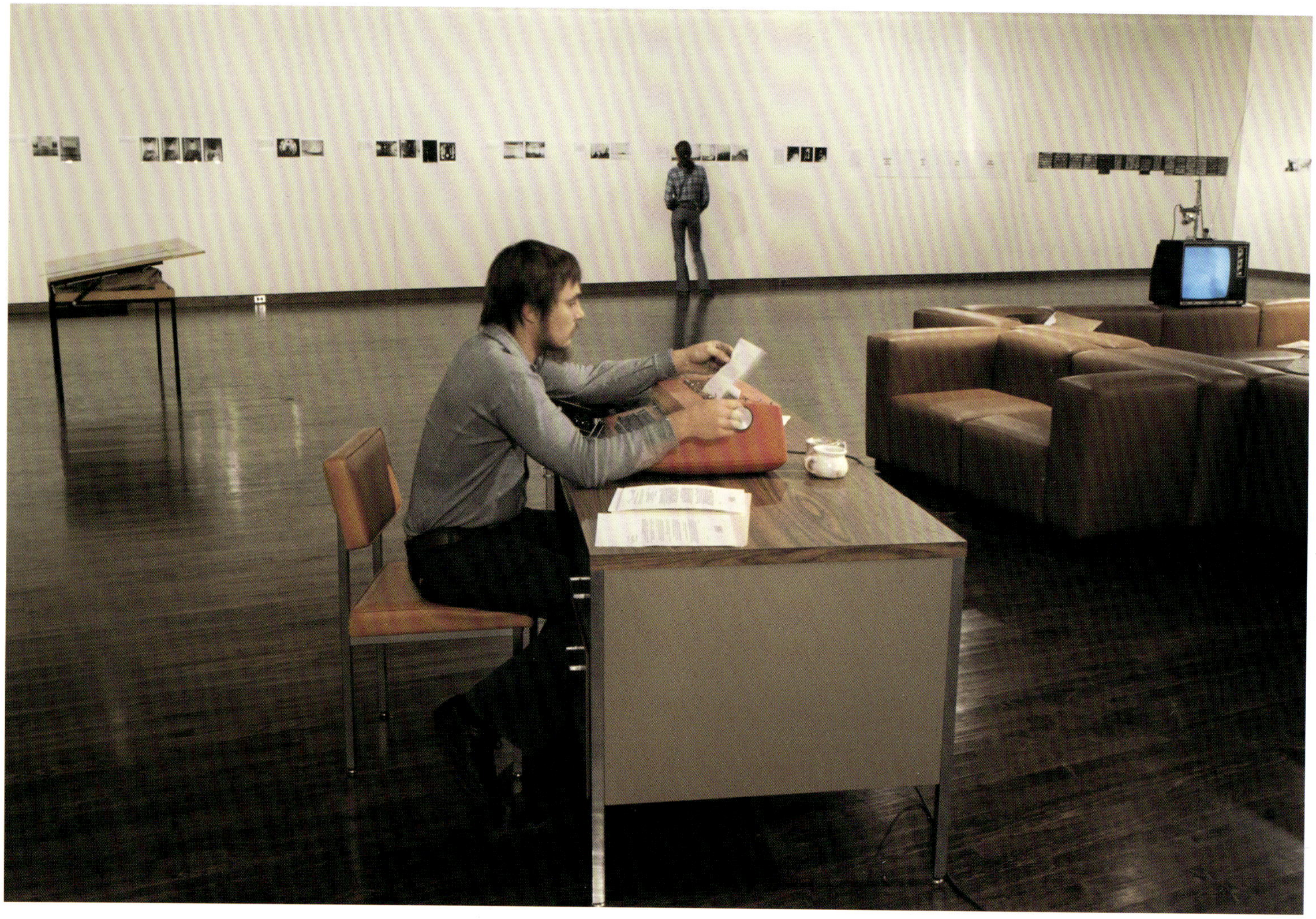

Working Artist 1975

University of Maryland, Baltimore,
Maryland, USA; November 22–24, 1975

Upon arrival at the University of Maryland, I had a poster printed which described Working Artist *as a three-day performance and exhibition of past works. In the University Gallery, which was quite large (measuring 64 feet square), I hung photographs and written explanations of all my past performances in a continuous chronological line around the gallery walls. In the center of the room was an island of expensive modular leather furniture. In addition to this existing furniture, I requested that a desk, a telephone, an electric typewriter, a television set, a photo copystand and a drafting table be installed in the space. During the three-day period from November 22 to 24, I lived in the gallery, sleeping on the leather couches, and attempted to conduct my affairs as if I were in my own studio. Visitors to the gallery were treated as my guests, and I talked freely with them and answered their questions. My accessibility and the routines of my daily existence contrasted sharply with the extraordinary activities depicted on the walls.*

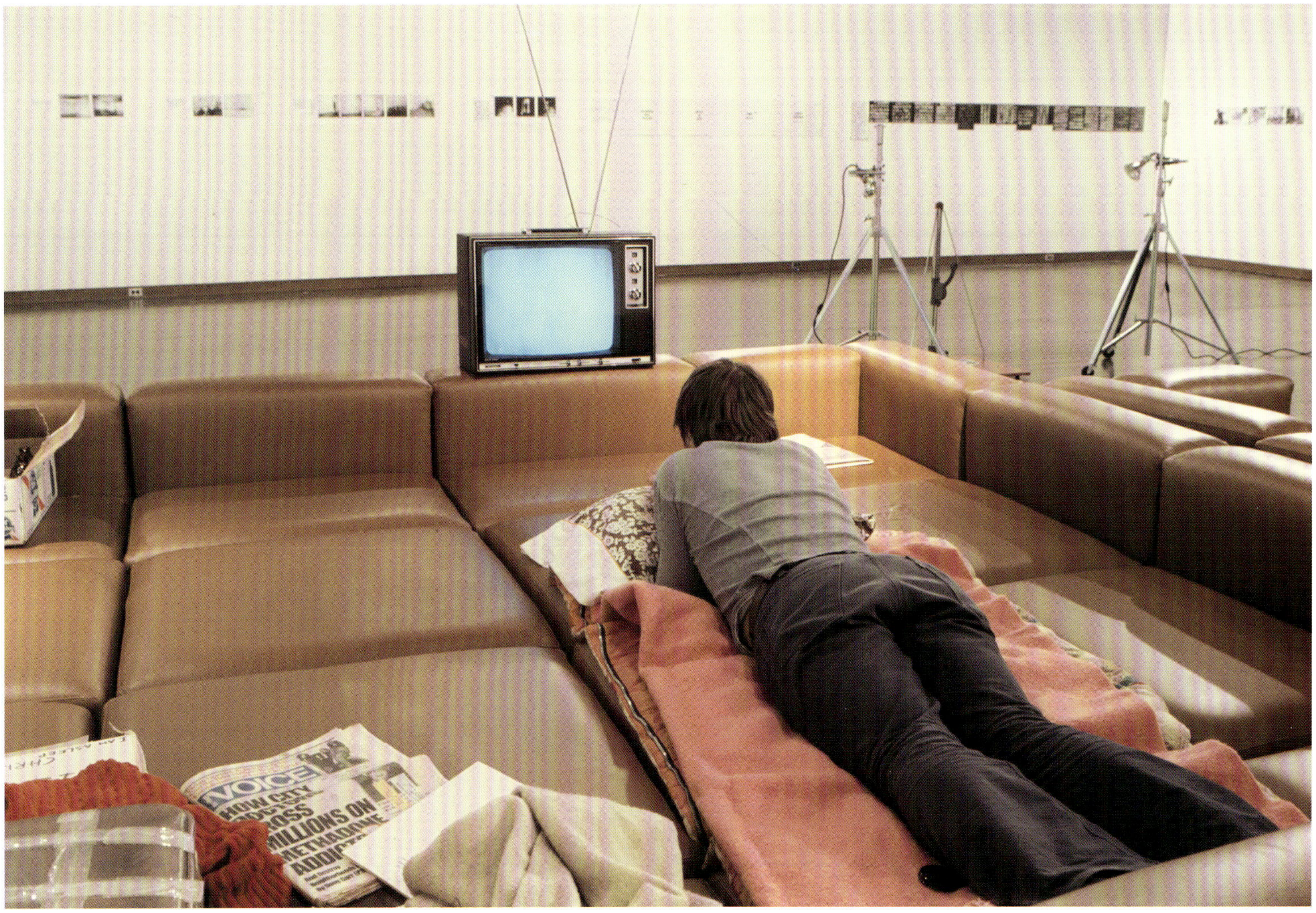
VOICE
MILLIONS ON

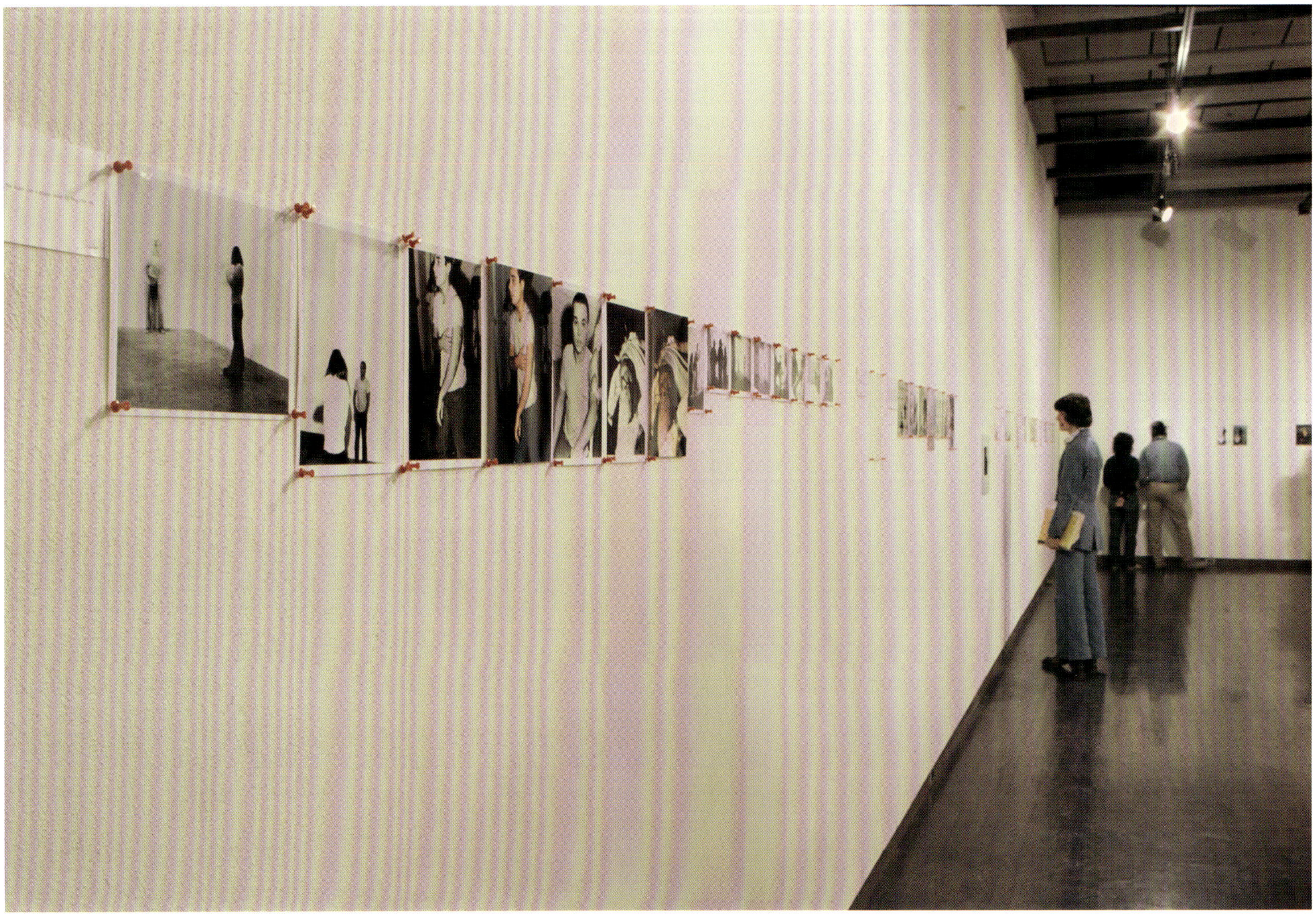

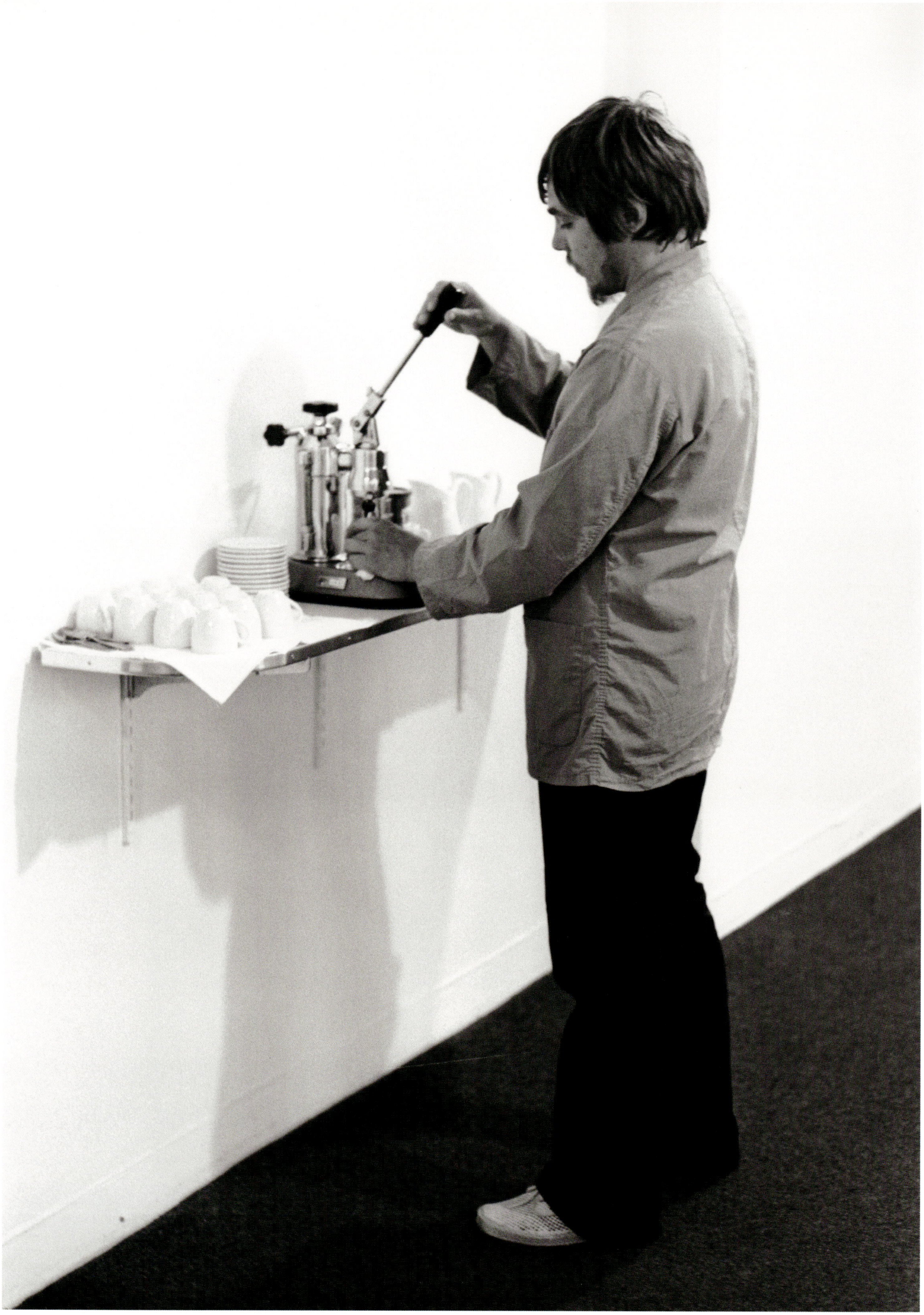

Garcon! 1976

Hansen Fuller Gallery, San Francisco,
California, USA; August 3–7, 1976

The week of August 3–7, I served cappuccino and espresso to visitors of the Hansen Fuller Gallery. I did this during gallery hours, 10:30 am to 5:30 pm, for an entire week, serving more than 300 cups of coffee. The gallery made no announcement of the performance, and a group painting show opened concurrently with my piece.

I installed a white mini-bar, complete with cappuccino machine, demi-tasse cups, espresso spoons, etc. on a wall near the entrance to the gallery. Attired in a gray cotton orderly's jacket and carrying a silver tray, I approached entering visitors and politely asked them if they would care for either a cappuccino or an espresso, which I would serve to them while they looked at the paintings. My attire and demeanor were such that only a handful of people out of the hundreds who attended the show recognized me as 'Chris Burden'.

RELICS: Pitcher, shirt

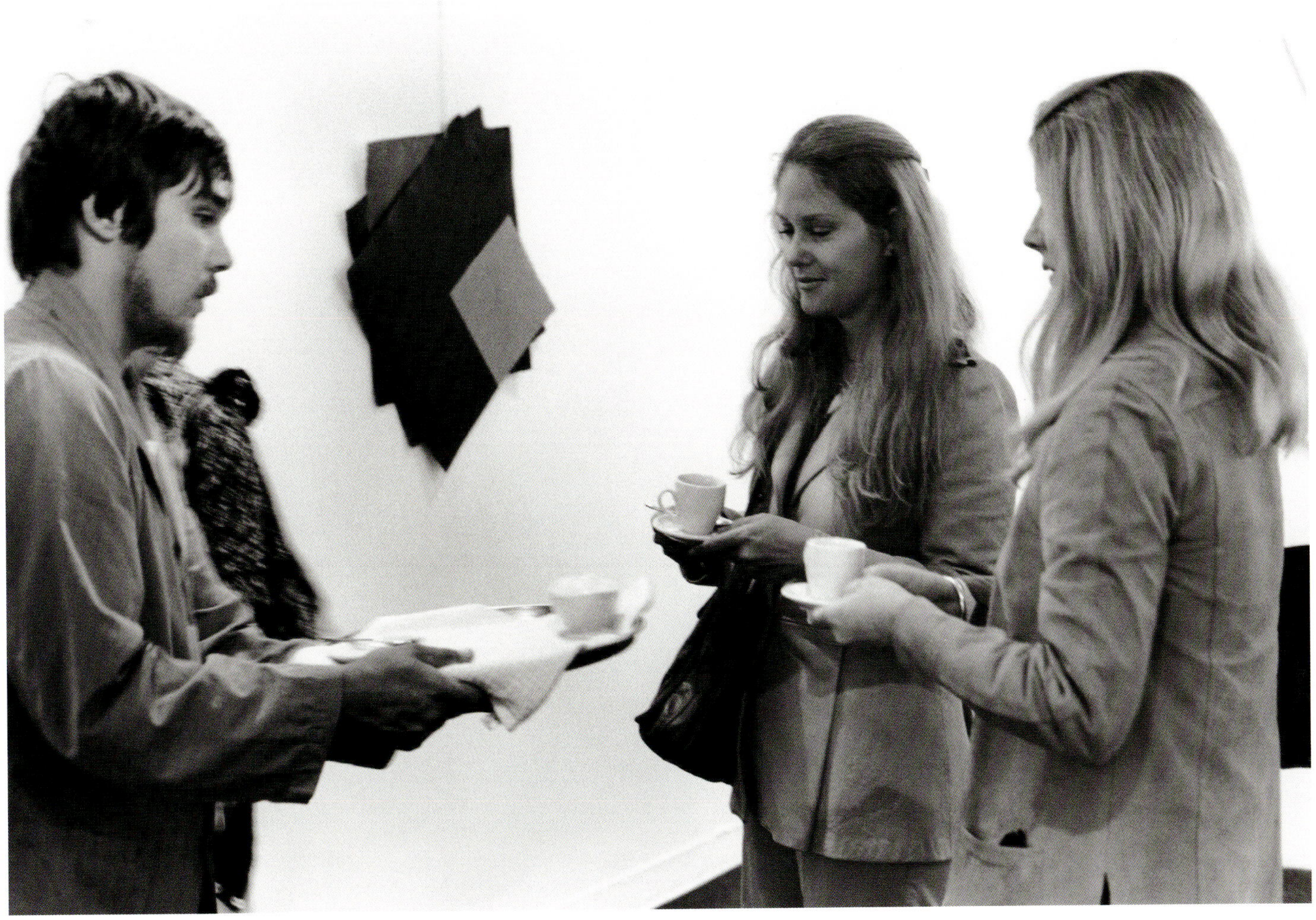

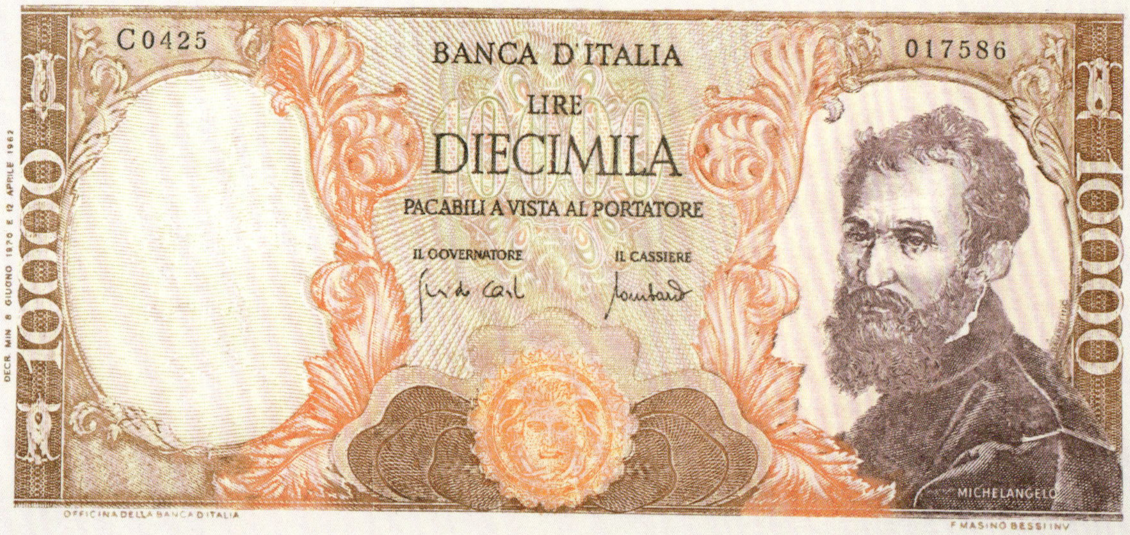
C0425
BANCA D'ITALIA
017586
LIRE
DIECIMILA
PAGABILI A VISTA AL PORTATORE
IL GOVERNATORE
IL CASSIERE
10000
10000
MICHELANGELO

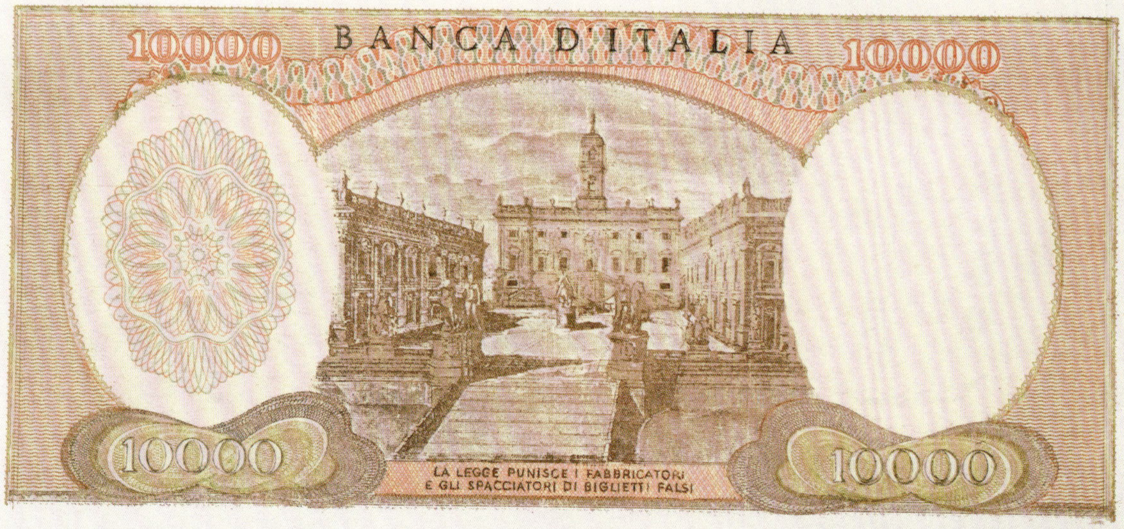
10000
BANCA D'ITALIA
10000
10000
LA LEGGE PUNISCE I FABBRICATORI
E GLI SPACCIATORI DI BIGLIETTI FALSI
10000

Diecimila 1977

(Edition of 35 with ten artist's proofs)
Crown Point Press, Oakland,
California, USA; May, 1977
Photo etchings of 10,000 lire note on
handmade paper.
Front and back: image 2⅝ × 5⅞ inches;
paper 10 × 14 inches

I was invited by Kathan Brown of Crown Point Press to produce a print. I chose to reproduce as carefully as possible an Italian 10,000 lire note (worth approximately 12 US dollars). Crown Point Press worked several months on this extremely difficult project. The finished print required handmade paper with appropriate watermark and 14 separate colors. Although the bill is reproduced to actual size, it is printed on a larger sheet of paper, leaving a large white border around the facsimile bill. In the photograph on the right three rejected prints have been 'cut out' and are being held with two real 10,000 lire notes.

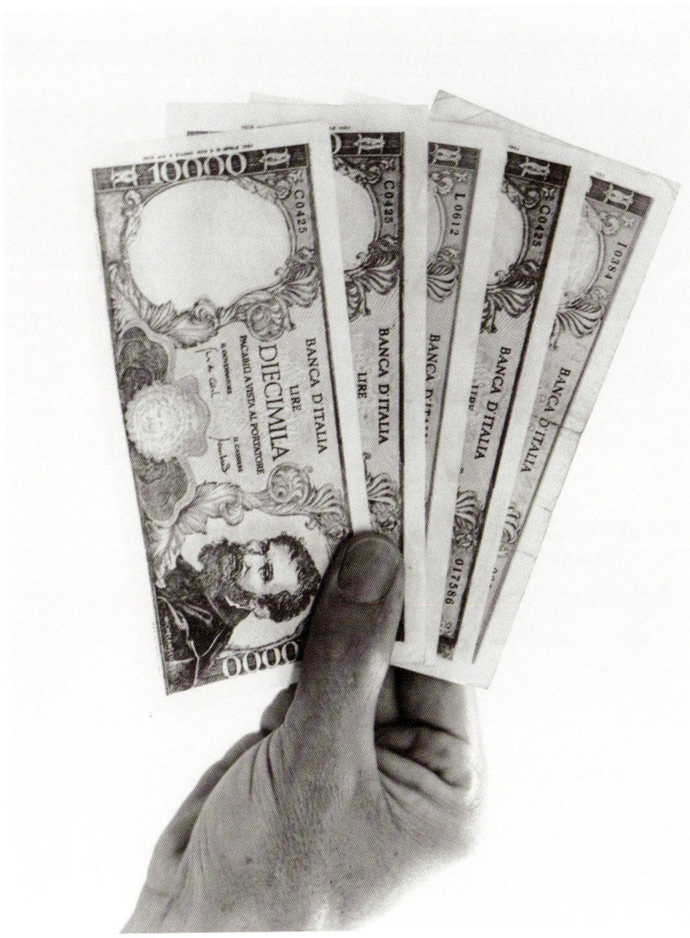

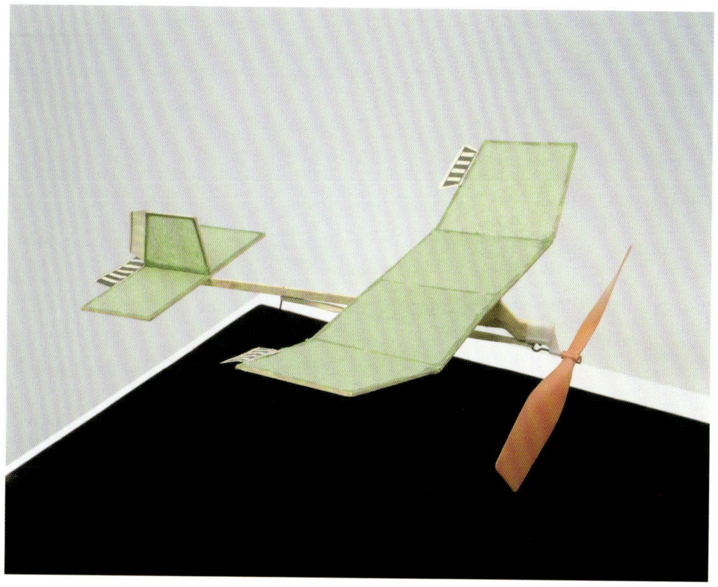

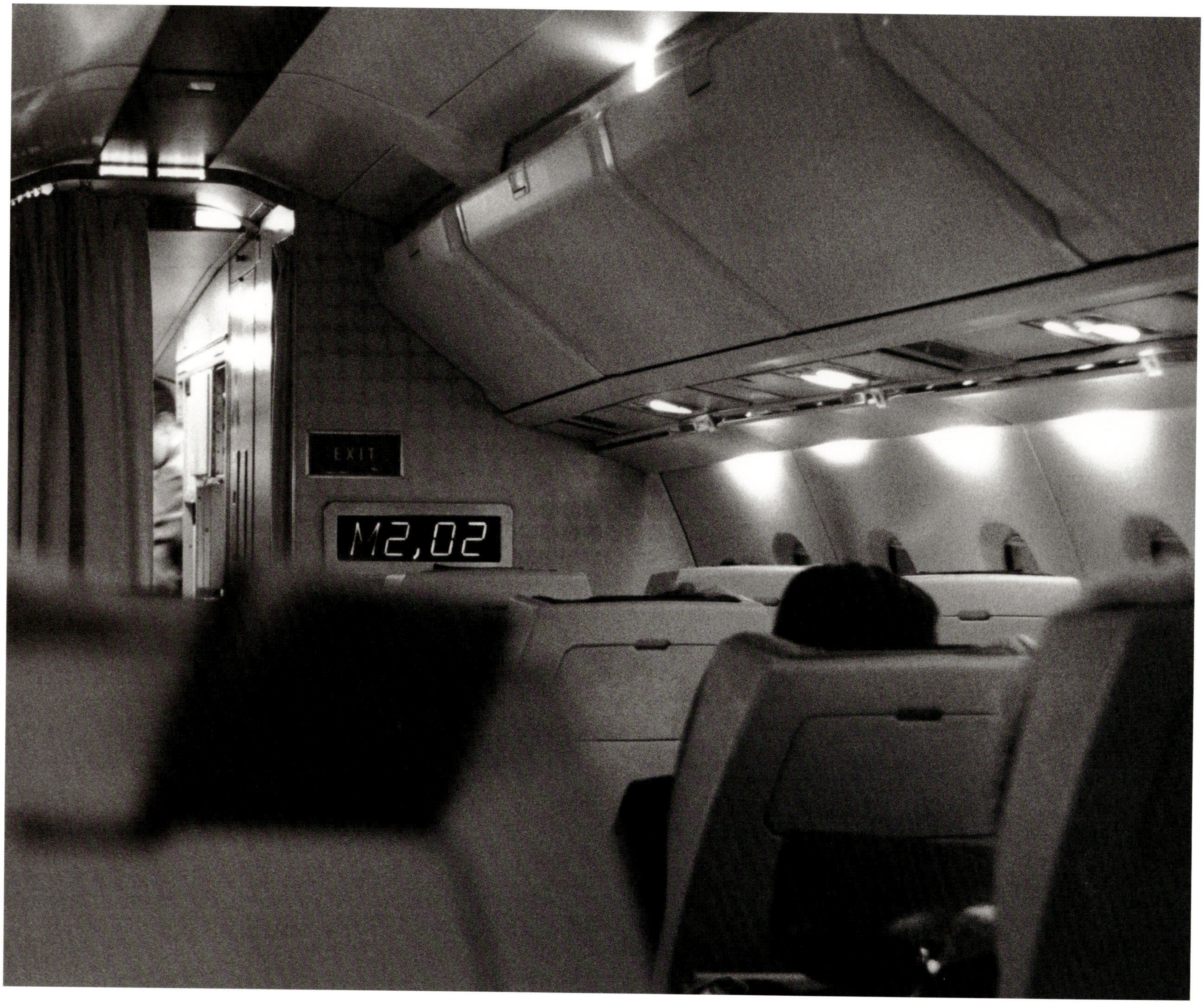
EXIT
M2,02

C.B.T.V. to Einstein 1977

Air France Concorde flight between Paris, France and Washington, DC, USA; December 28, 1977

While seated aboard the Concorde at Mach 2.05 and 60,000 feet, I flew a small stick and tissue rubber band powered model airplane from the rear of the Concorde towards the front. In accordance with Einstein's theories, the velocity of my model airplane, as seen from Earth, is the sum of the velocity of the Concorde (approx. 1,400 miles per hour) plus the velocity of my model airplane (approx. 10 miles per hour). My model airplane thus traveled faster than the supersonic Concorde.

RELIC: Model airplane flown on Concorde

▷▷

The Citadel 1978

Private studio, Los Angeles, California, USA; August 8–12, 1978

The Citadel *was a combination installation and performance dealing with outer space. A small, oddly-shaped room with a rear brick wall was made completely light-tight and painted black. Over 500 extremely detailed miniature metal spaceships ranging in size from one quarter of an inch to four inches were hung from the ceiling using black thread. Four folding chairs were provided for the audience.*

Each group of four was let into the pitch black room and was seated by an assistant. Because they had been waiting outside in the bright sunlight they could not see anything. I turned on two tape recorders. One tape was a recording of a steam jet on a cappuccino machine, repeated over and over. This noise simulated rocket noise. The other tape began with the message that 'these starships have assembled here from all corners of the universe to investigate the infinite, inexplicable Citadel Wall, the end of the universe.' At the same moment, I lit a candle which illuminated a small portion of the spaceships. While the rocket noise continued and the audio tape related a series of excerpts from outer space war games, such as: travel in suspended animation, the use of the Jump Drive for interstellar travel, atmospheric conditions, names and uses of the different types of ships, the vast array of different types of weaponry, etc, I moved slowly back and forth through the suspended ships. Slowly, as the audience's eyes adjusted to the candlelight they could see more and more of the small ships, which were hovering in front of them, above them, and on either side of them. Towards the end of each performance I moved to the rear of the room revealing the brick wall (the Citadel Wall). The candle was extinguished. The two tapes came to an end and the audience was ushered out. Each session lasted ten minutes and was repeated continuously from 11 am to 1 pm during the days August 8–12, 1978.

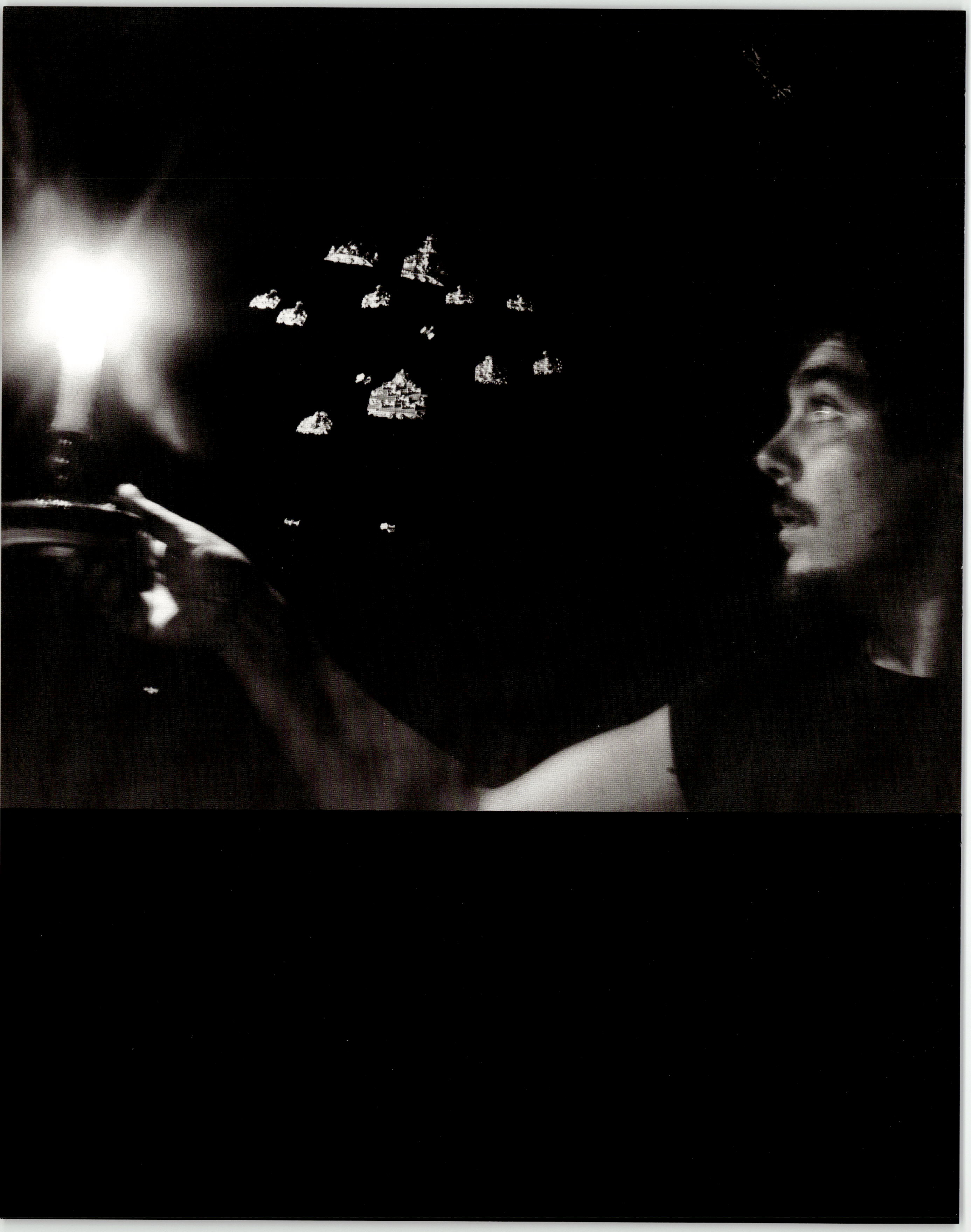

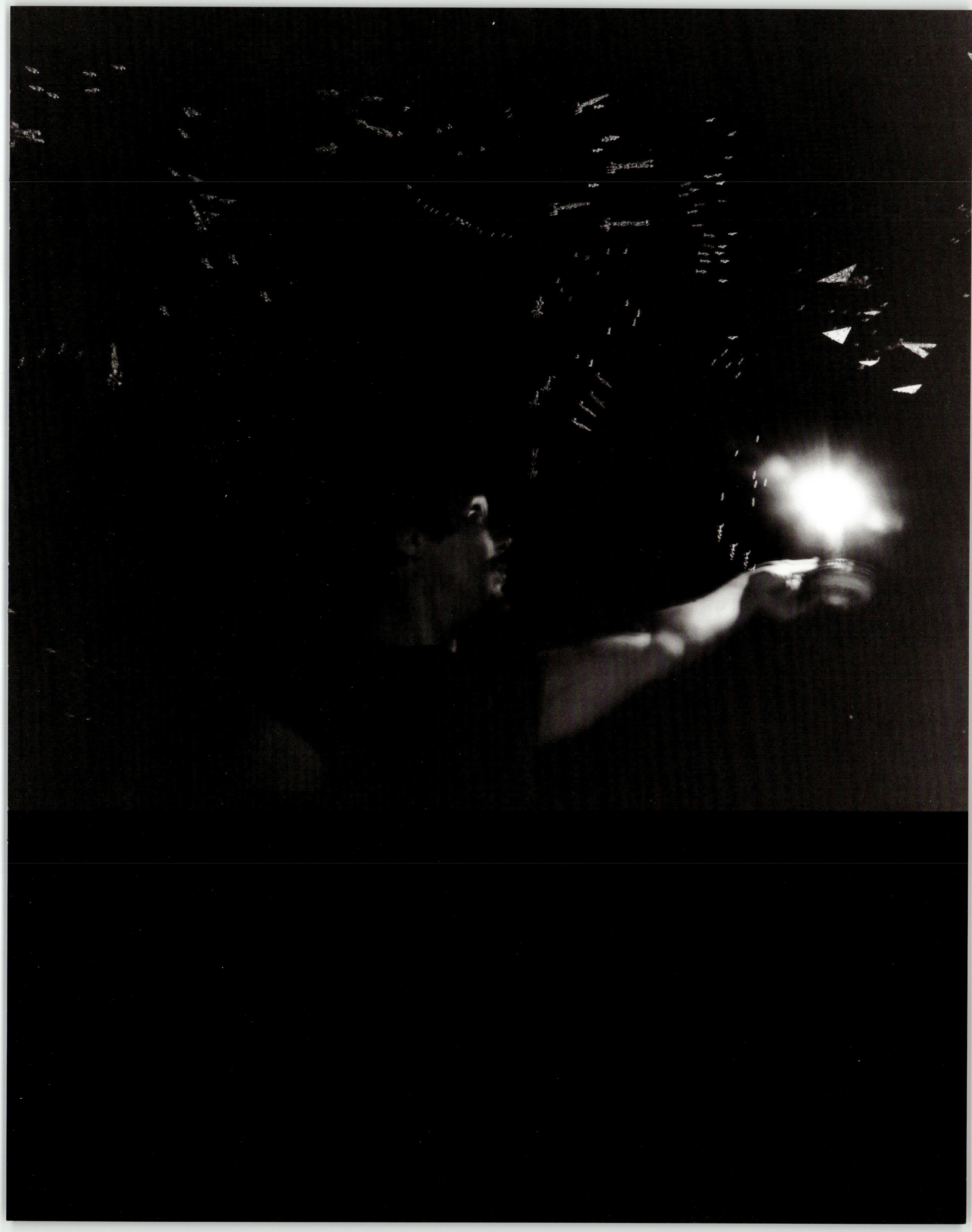

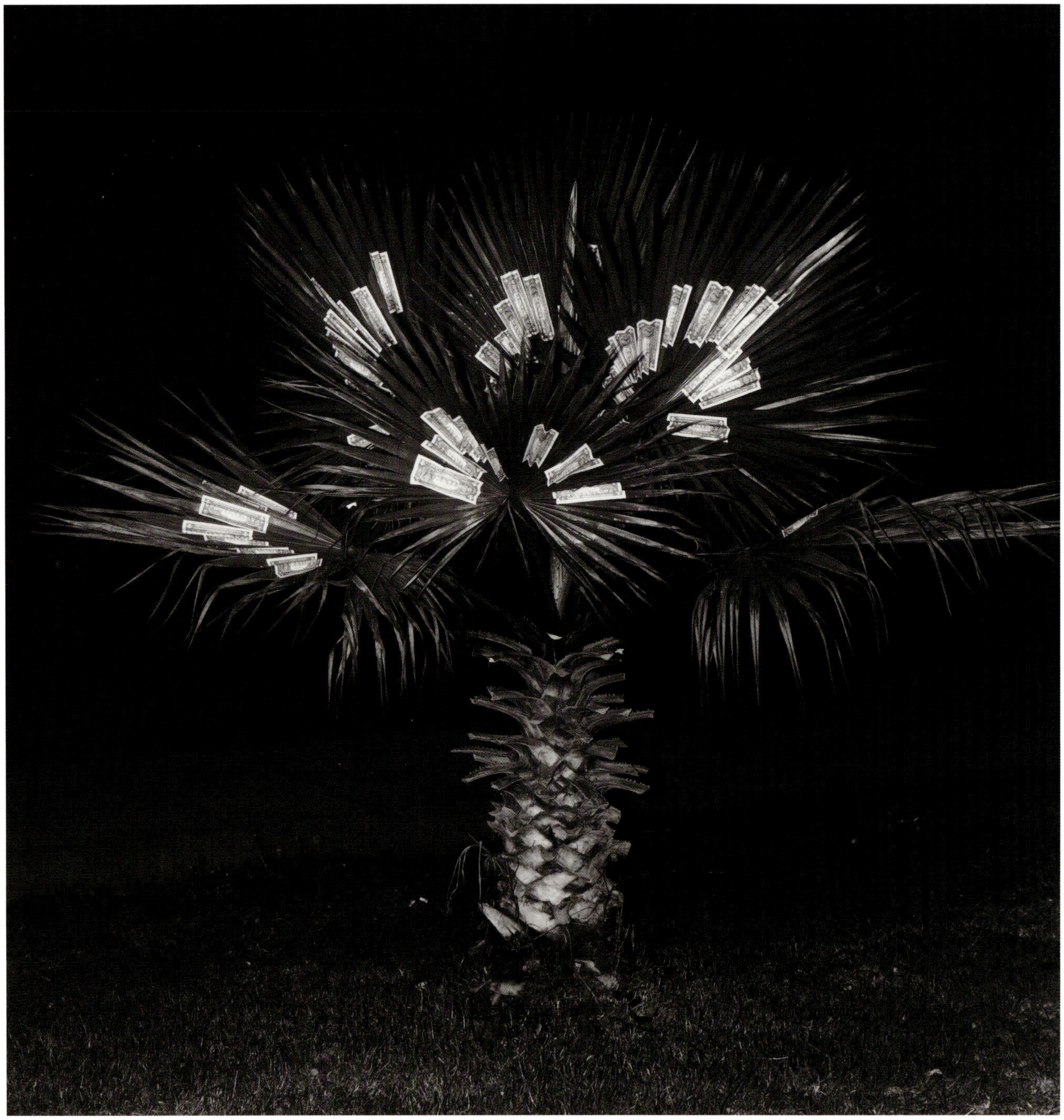

In Venice Money Grows on Trees 1978

Venice, California, USA; October 6, 1978

Just before sunrise two friends and myself glued 100 brand new one-dollar bills to the leaves of two very low palm trees on the Venice boardwalk. The bills were folded lengthwise several times so that they fit into the creases on each palm leaf. Although in plain sight and within arm's reach some of the money remained untouched for two days.

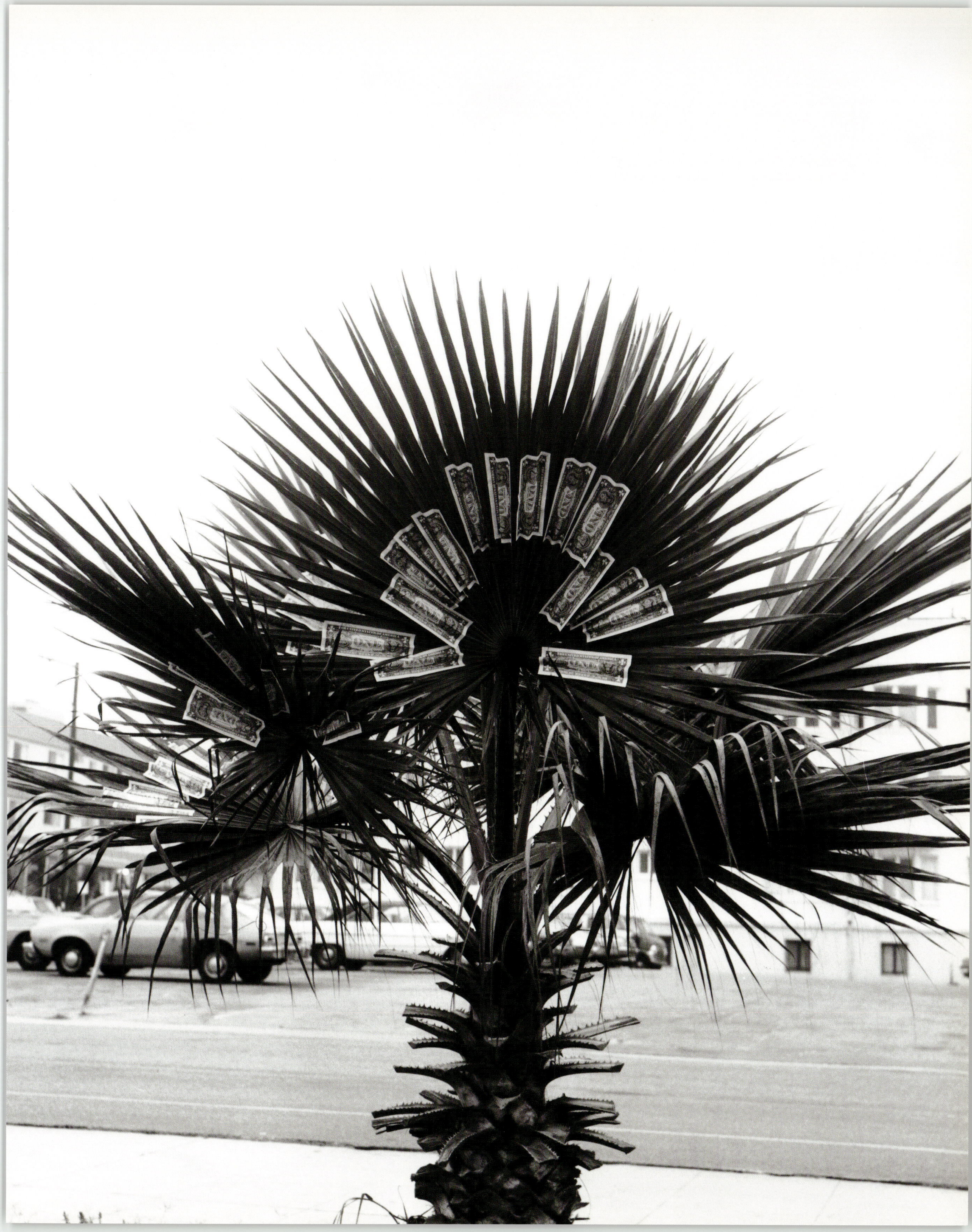

The Reason for the Neutron Bomb 1979

50,000 nickels, 50,000 matchsticks
368 × 210 inches

The Reason for the Neutron Bomb *was an installation that attempted to physically represent 50,000 Russian tanks. Each tank was symbolized by a nickel across which was placed a shortened wooden safety match. 50,000 of these 'tanks' were placed in parallel lines like toy soldiers. Altogether they occupied a space that measured approximately 20 × 30 feet. Across the back wall in six-inch-high letters was the statement '*THE REASON FOR THE NEUTRON BOMB*'. On either side of the piece, glued on the wall, was the following statement:*

'Behind the Iron Curtain, along the border between Eastern and Western Europe, the Russians maintain an army of 50,000 highly sophisticated tanks. The United States possesses only 10,000 tanks and the combined strength of all the Western European nations, including the NATO forces, is estimated to be no more than 20,000 tanks. The Western European forces are outnumbered by more than two to one. This numerical imbalance is the reason given by our military for the existence of the neutron bomb.'

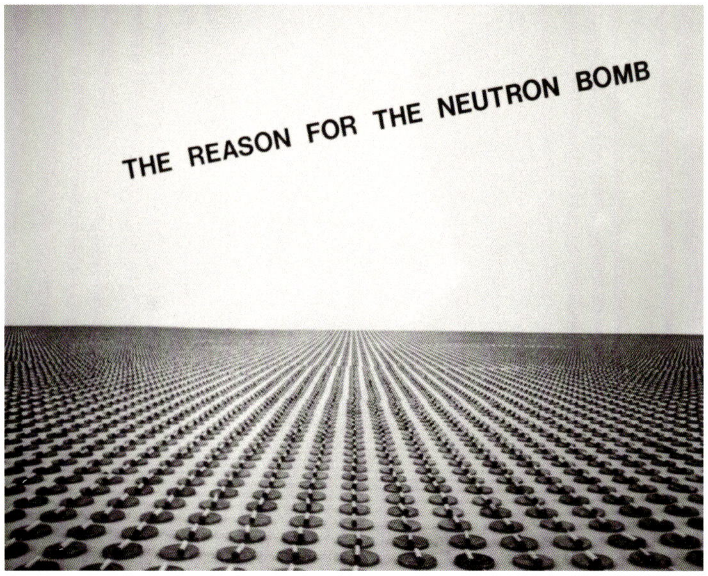

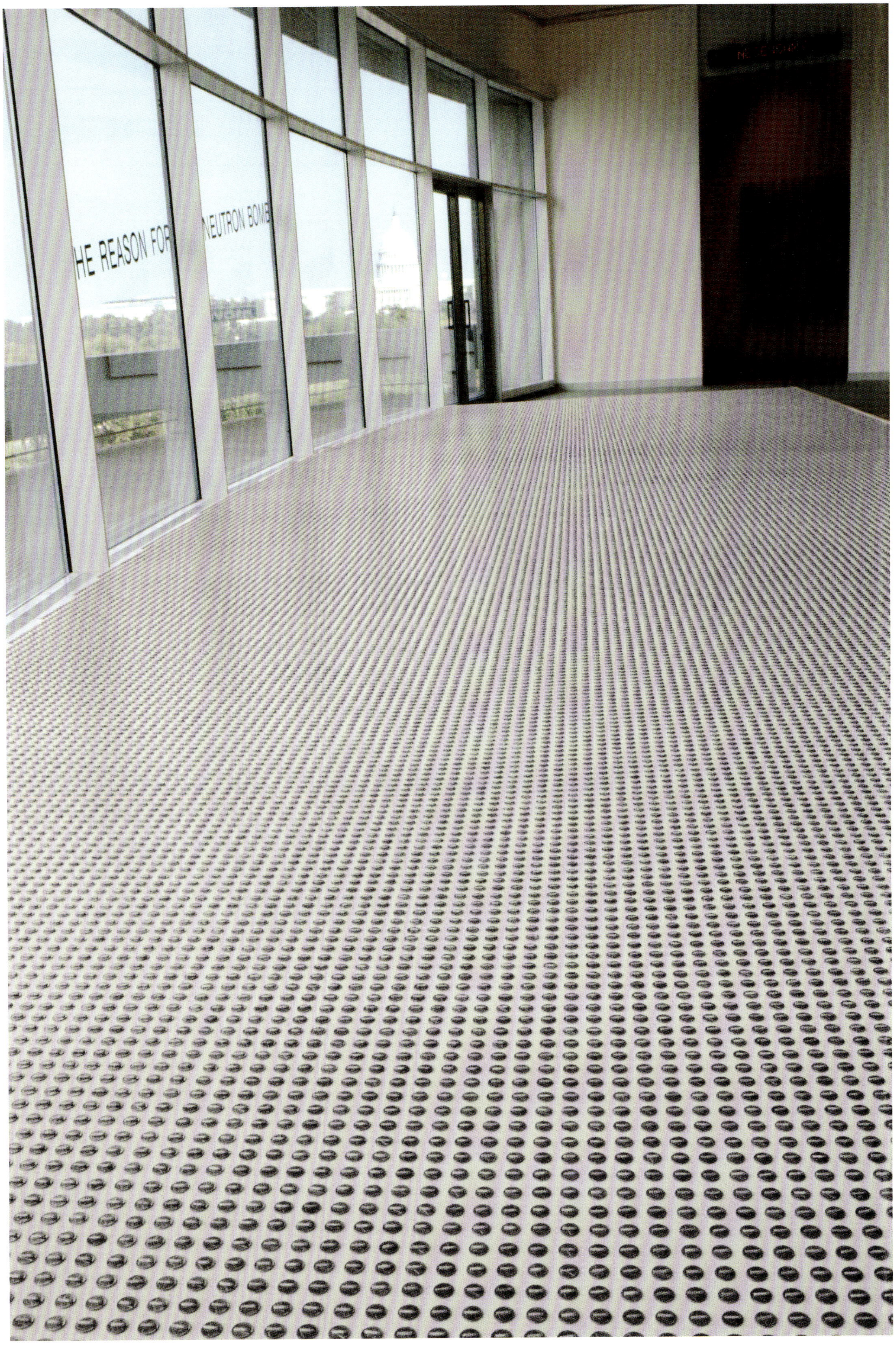
HE REASON FOR
NEUTRON BOMB

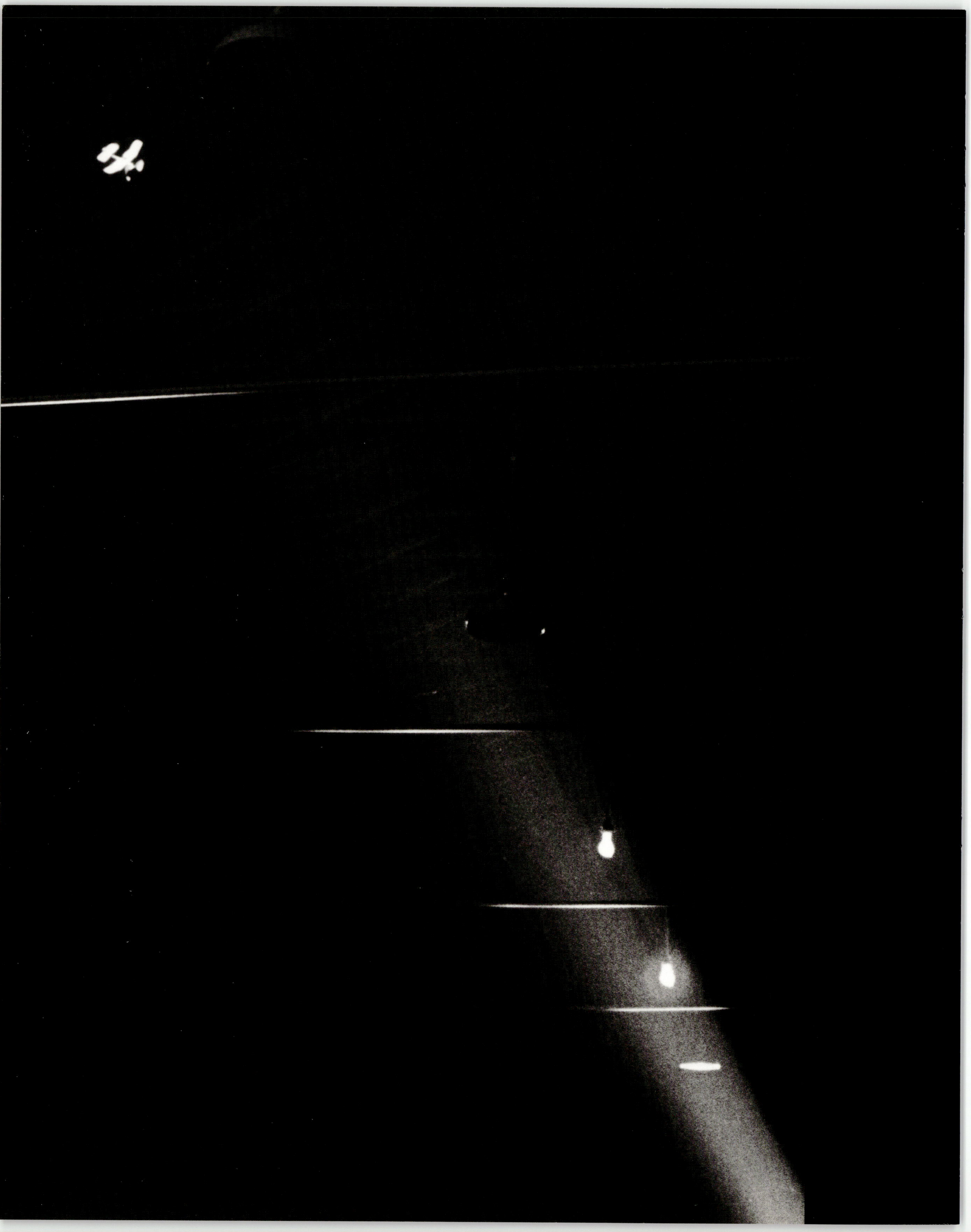

Pearl Harbor 1979

National Guard Armory, Santa Barbara,
California, USA; December 8, 1979

For this performance a fleet of 40 stick and tissue rubber band powered flying model airplanes was constructed (later to become C.B. Air Force*) At one end of this large vaulted space (which contained three basketball courts) eight assistants and I tried to keep the fleet of miniature planes airborne and circling through the beam of a large searchlight. The searchlight, parked outside, was aimed through open doors so that the strong beam of light traveled through the space toward the ceiling. Attempts to keep the fleet of planes constantly airborne and circling were only partially successful and many planes behaved erratically, kamikazeing into the audience seated in the bleachers at the far end of the armory space. After an hour the fleet of planes was depleted and damaged, and the performance came to an end.*

Cinque Cinque Cento (Five Five Hundreds) 1980

Italian Per/form/ance Festival, Rome,
Italy; March 9, 1980

Five Fiat 500s, the smallest, cheapest and most popular Italian car, were attached to the plow of a bulldozer using long nylon cords. The cars were all driven by their owners who had volunteered to participate. After the spectators arrived, at a given signal, the cars all started their motors, were put in gear and driven forwards. At the same time the bulldozer proceeded to drive backwards. The motors and small wheels of the Fiats spun furiously, but to no avail as the bulldozer slowly dragged the running cars backwards about 500 feet. The piece took place inside the large courtyard of an abandoned slaughter house, the long rows of arches, the evening darkness, and the smoke from the burning tires, clutches and motors combined to give the atmosphere of an ancient spectacle at the Coliseum.

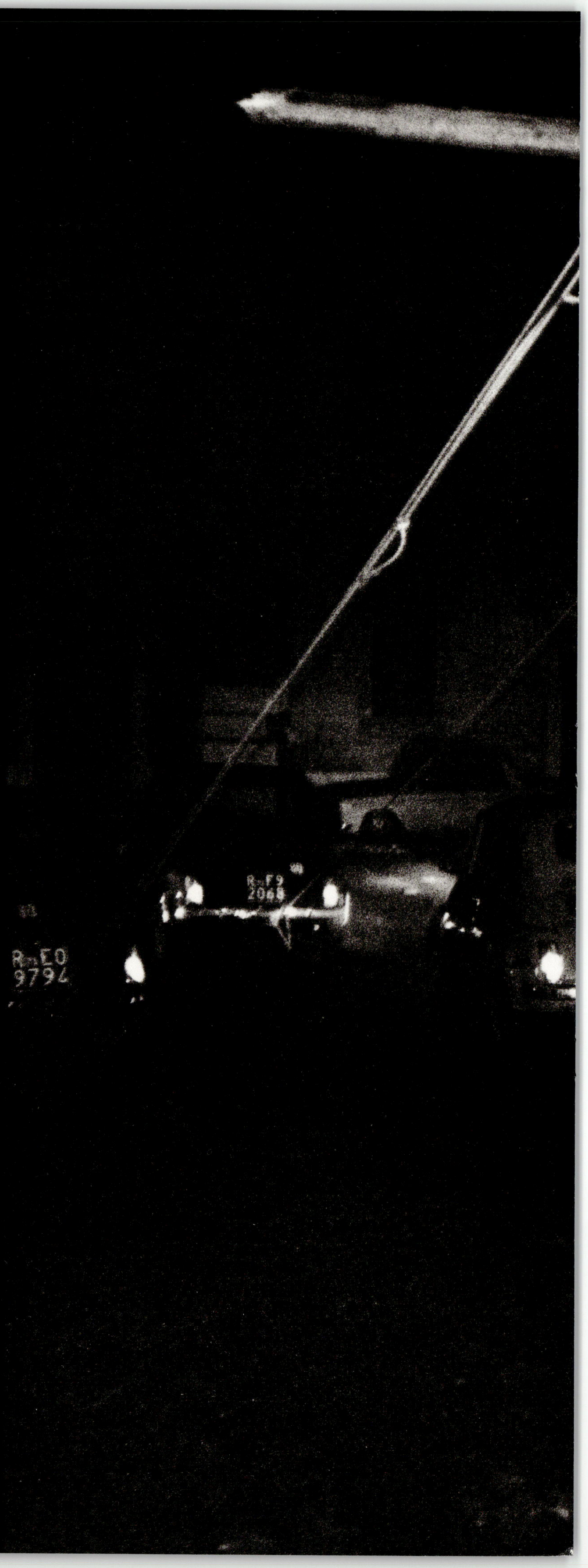

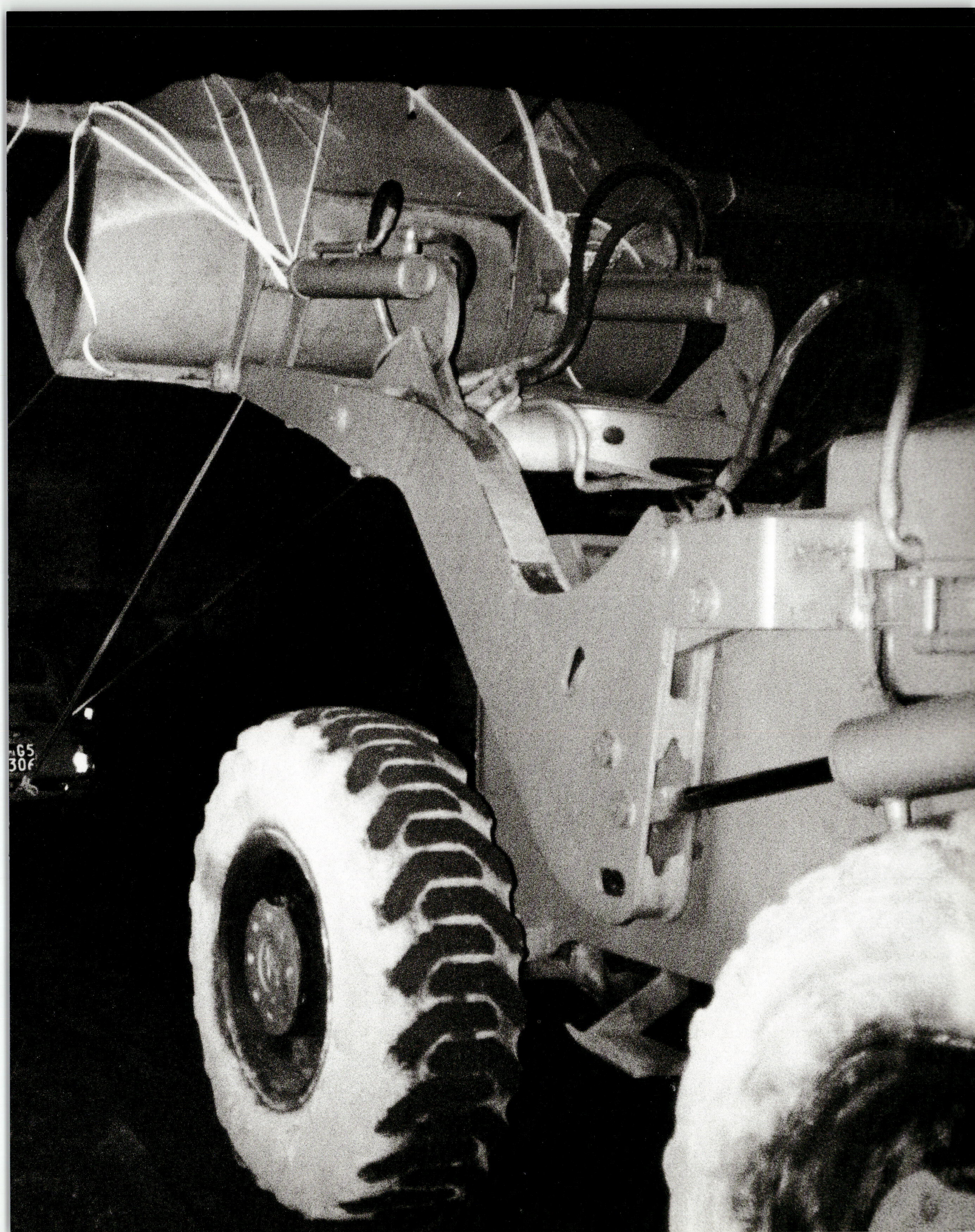

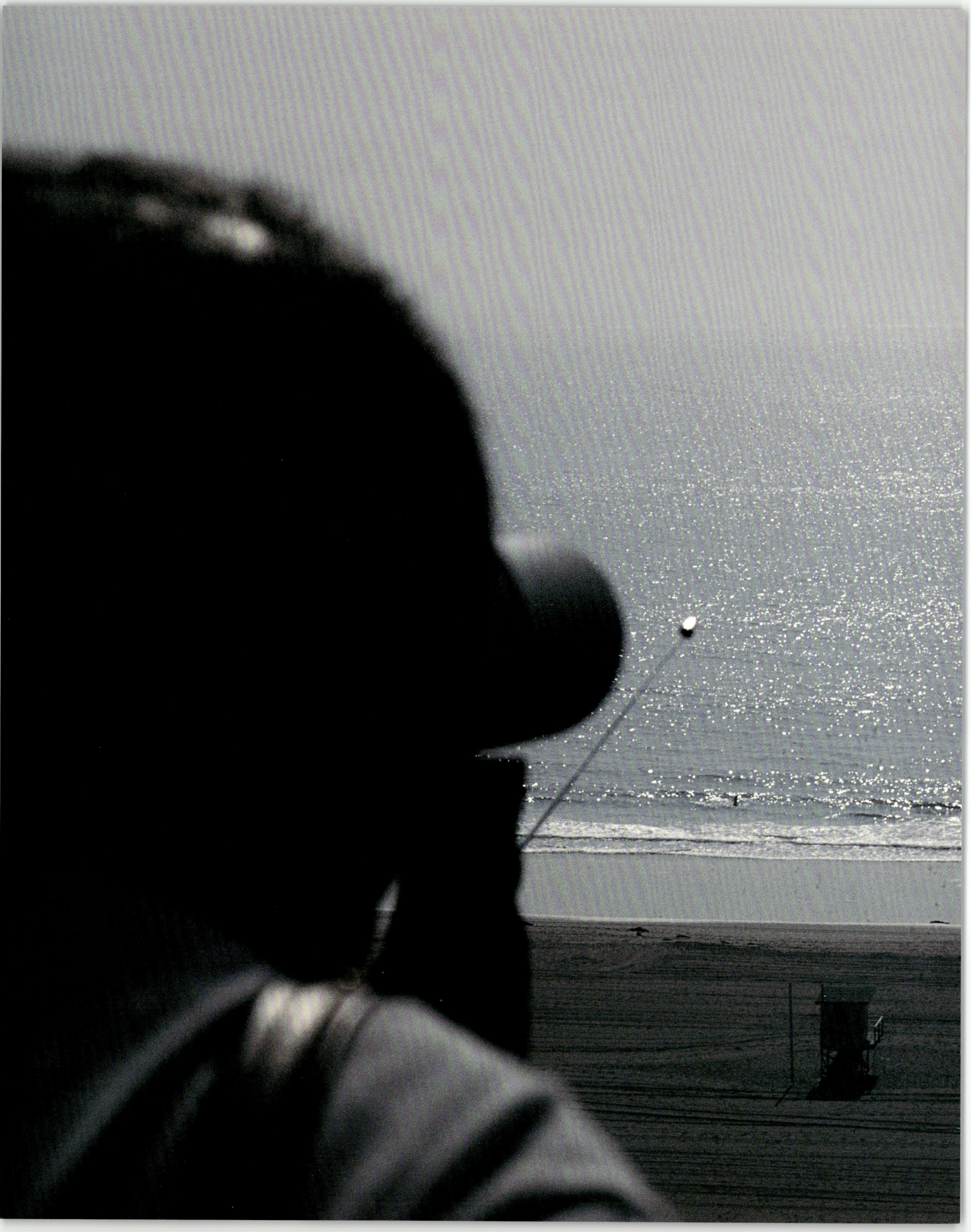

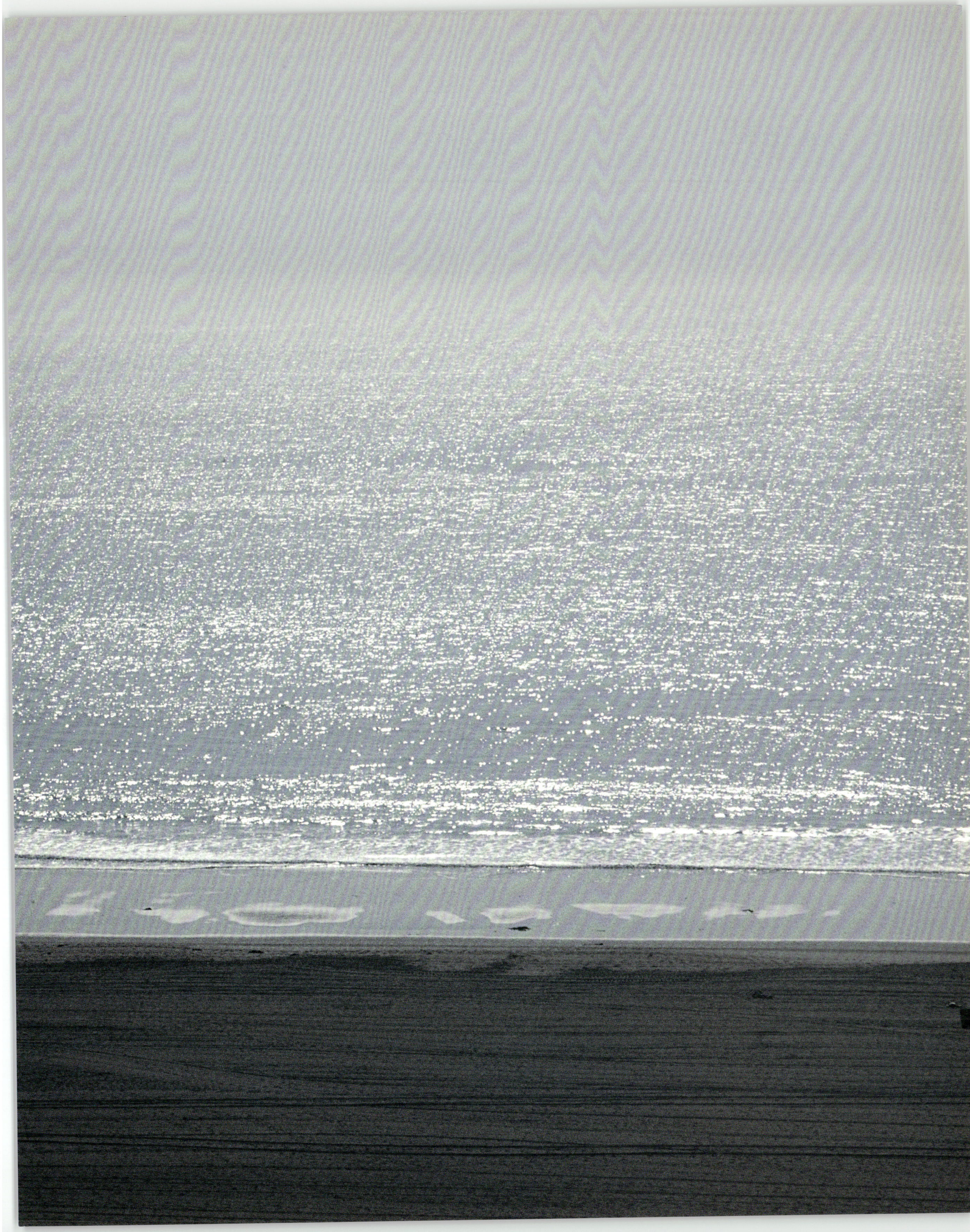

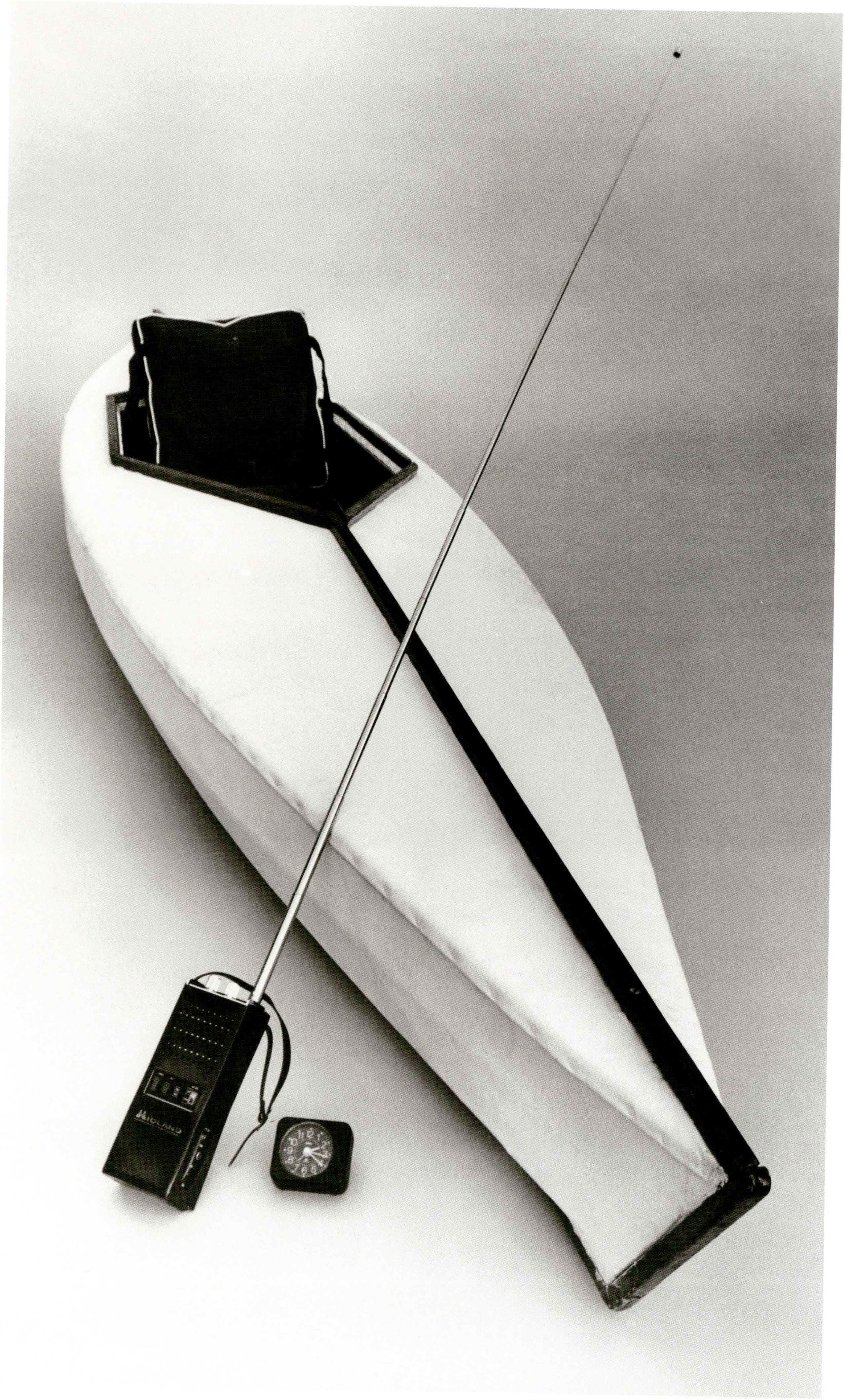
MIDLAND

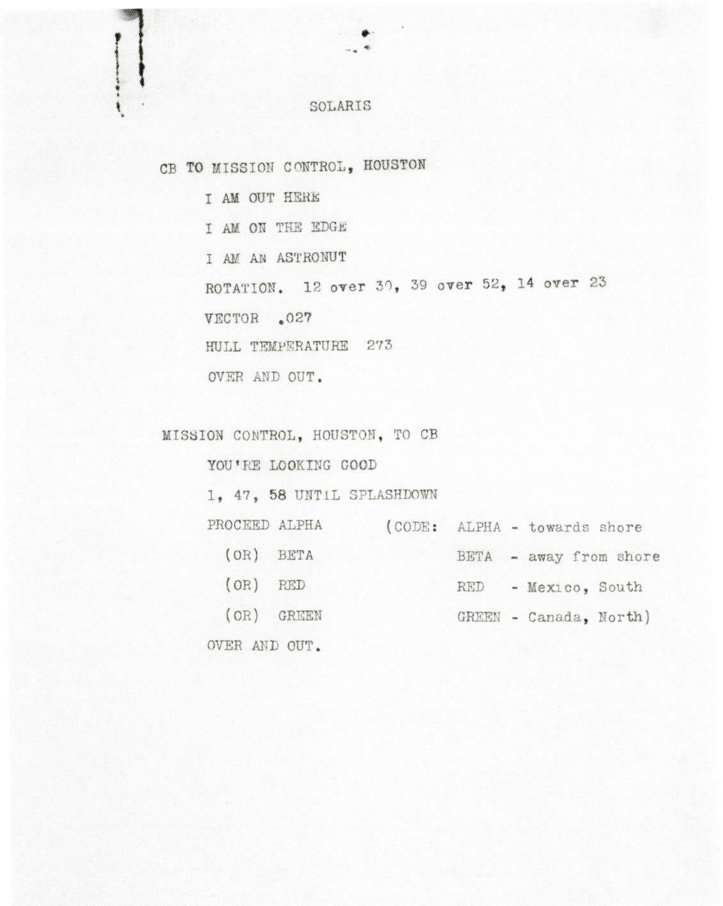

SOLARIS

CB TO MISSION CONTROL, HOUSTON

I AM OUT HERE

I AM ON THE EDGE

I AM AN ASTRONUT

ROTATION. 12 over 30, 39 over 52, 14 over 23

VECTOR .027

HULL TEMPERATURE 273

OVER AND OUT.

MISSION CONTROL, HOUSTON, TO CB

YOU'RE LOOKING GOOD

1, 47, 58 UNTIL SPLASHDOWN

PROCEED ALPHA	(CODE: ALPHA - towards shore
(OR) BETA	BETA - away from shore
(OR) RED	RED - Mexico, South
(OR) GREEN	GREEN - Canada, North)

OVER AND OUT.

Performance script
Typed script on paper, 11 × 8½ inches

◁◁

Solaris 1980

Pacific Ocean, Santa Monica,
California, USA; October 23, 1980

Visitors were requested to come to a specific location on the Santa Monica bluffs overlooking the Pacific Ocean between the hours of 2 pm and 4 pm. Equipped with a walkie-talkie, I was floating in a small canvas kayak two to three miles out in the ocean, directly in the glare of the setting sun. I was invisible to the naked eye and visitors could only view me by looking through a powerful telescope. The foreshortening and glare provided the illusion that I was floating through some highly volatile gaseous substance. On shore near the telescope, a small metal table equipped with a black clock, a walkie-talkie and a small tape recorder provided the symbolic materials for Houston 'Mission Control'. Using the walkie-talkies I could communicate with Mission Control. A typical transmission would consist of:

C.B. to Mission Control, Houston.
I am out here.
I am on the edge.
I am an Astronut.
Rotation 12 over 30, 39 over 52,
14 over 23.
Vector .027.
Hull temperature 273
Over and out.

At four o'clock, splashdown was announced and the telescope was removed.

RELIC: Card table, walkie-talkie

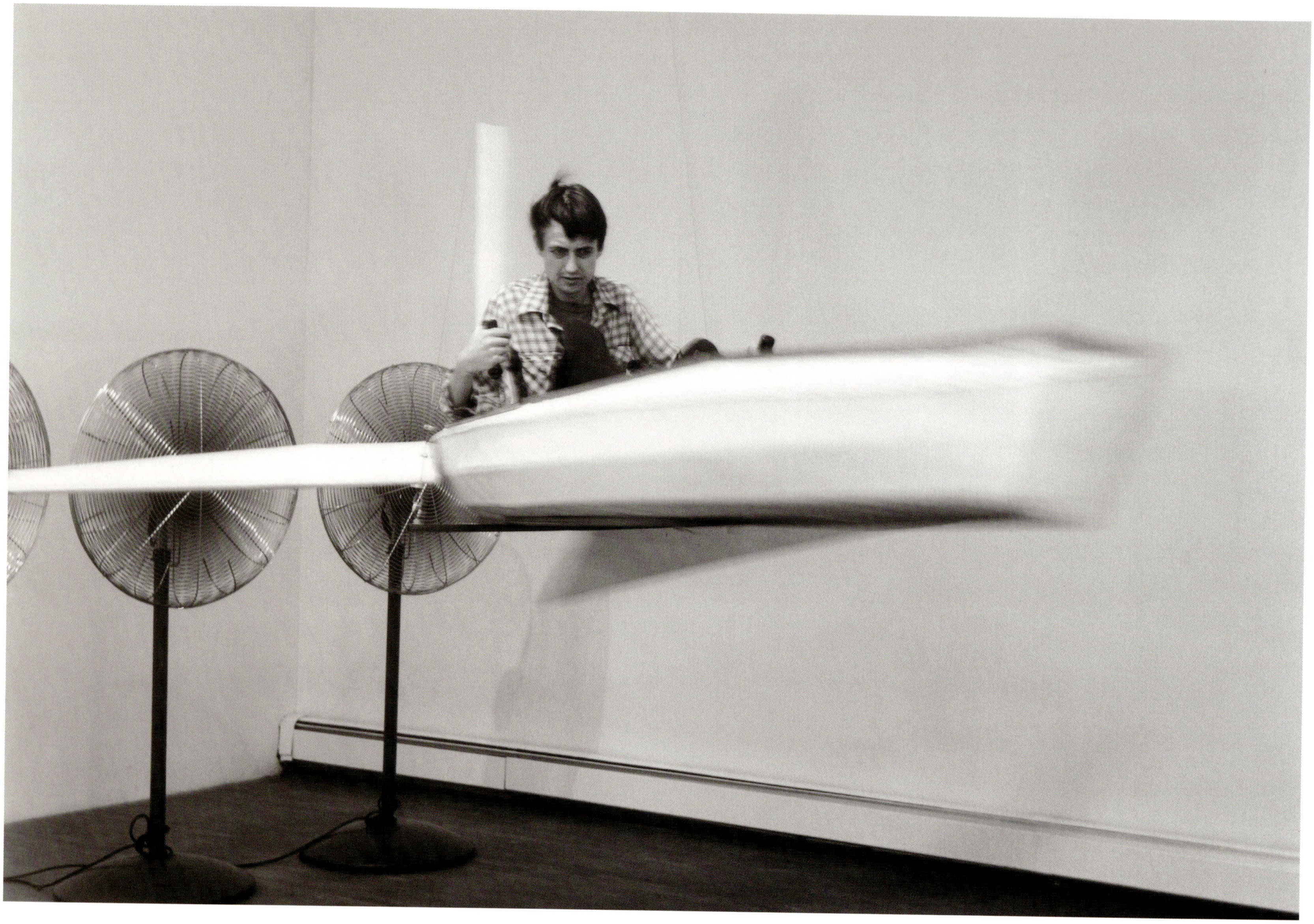

The Flying Kayak 1982

Canvas, wood, wooden set of stairs,
fans, film, wire
46 × 156 × 120 inch wingspan

A small canvas kayak equipped with a set of wings and a rudder was suspended on steel cables about six feet above the gallery floor. Placed directly behind the kayak were four industrial pedestal fans. Visitors to the gallery could enter the kayak with the aid of a strong wooden set of stairs which would then be removed by the gallery attendants. The wings and rudder were movable through a set of controls inside the kayak and when the fans were turned on the kayak would be 'flown' (i.e. moved around the gallery space). In addition, while the kayak was being 'flown', a film loop of a hovering helicopter was projected on the wall facing the 'pilot', heightening the illusion of flight.

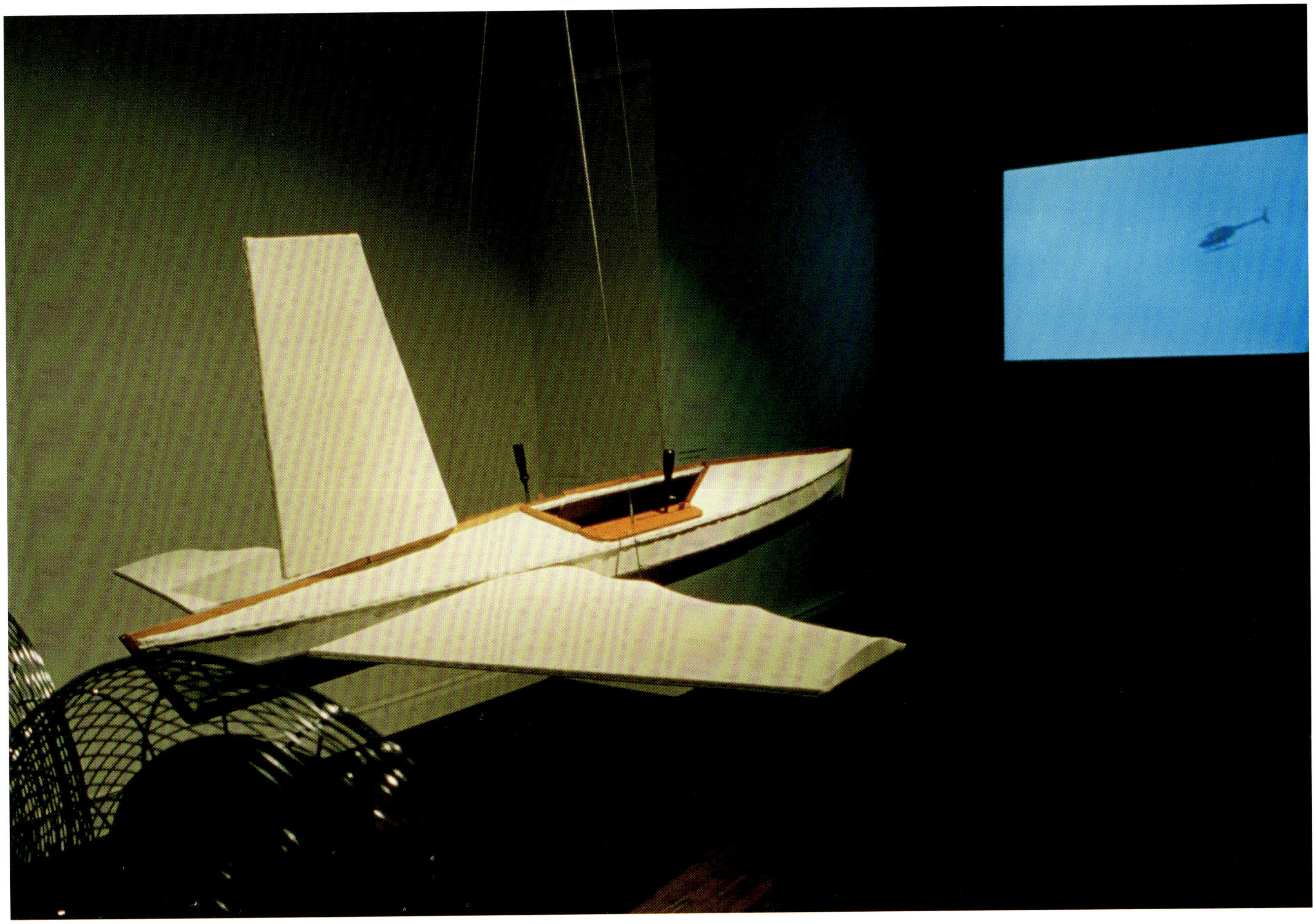

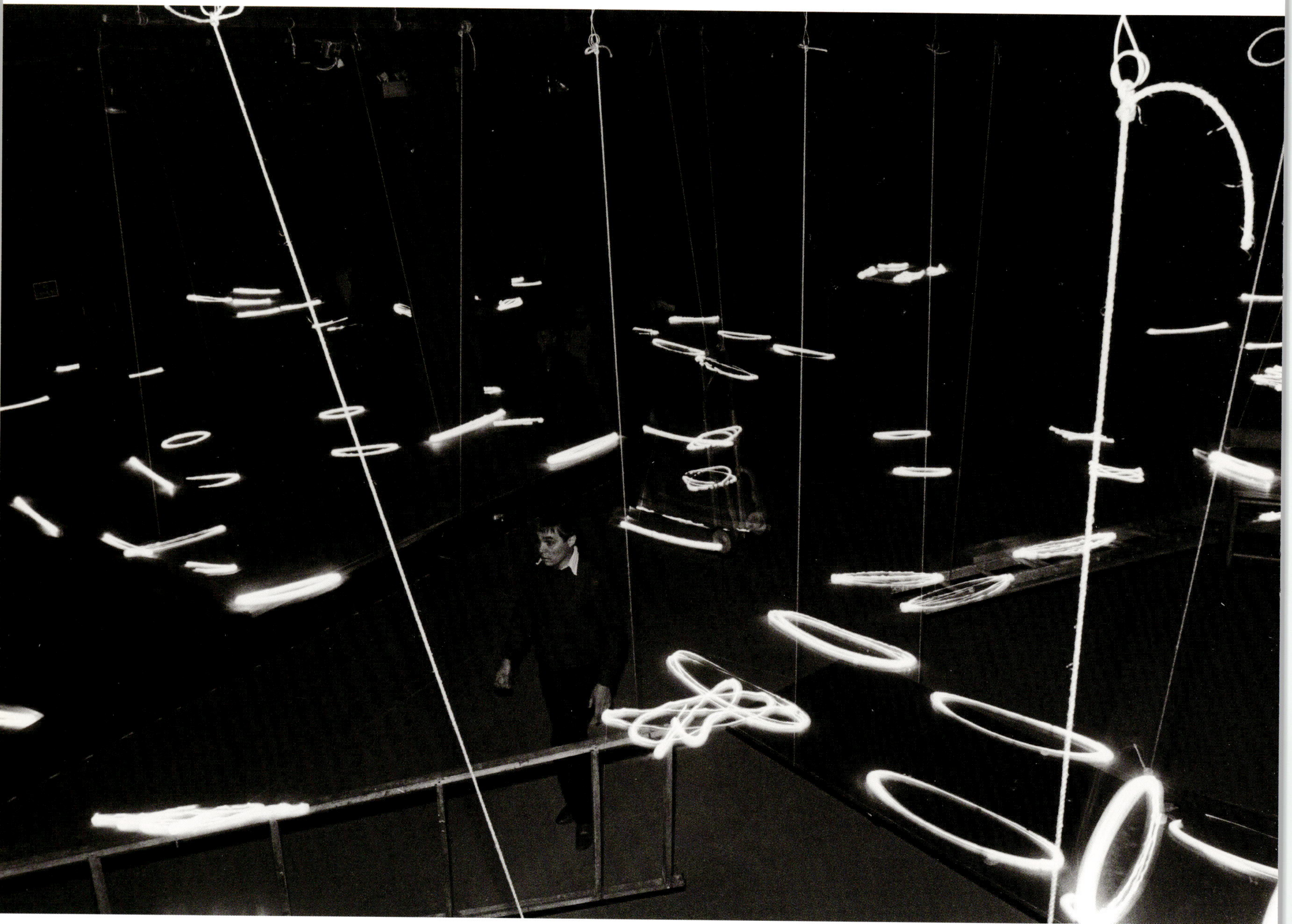

Hercules 1982

Washington Project for the Arts,
Washington, DC, USA; March 27, 1982

Over 30 large objects: doors, window panes, tables, chairs, metal ladders and a hand truck, were suspended parallel to the floor in a large theater space which had been painted black. Several small votive candles were placed along the perimeter of each object and lit. During the two hours of the performance/installation I would continuously circulate throughout the room pushing the platforms so that they all continued to move and swing in erratic patterns. Visitors to the gallery were initially disoriented by the moving spots of light and felt as though they were on a rocking ship. Movement through the space had to be done very carefully in order not to be hit by one of the swinging objects. The effect was that all of these doors, window panes, tables, chairs and ladders, which had been stored in space for a long time, had been suddenly and magically levitated by an unseen 'Herculean' force.

▷▷

From Neanderthal to the 20th Century 1983

International Performance Festival,
Rotterdam, Holland; April 6, 1983

A ten-foot steel I-beam was suspended horizontally from the ceiling approximately six feet off the floor using eight pieces of heavy twine. From the I-beam the lengths of twine passed through eyelets screwed into the ceiling and then returned to a central fastening point on the floor. Underneath the focal point of all the strings was a pile of dry straw. For approximately 40 minutes I repeatedly attempted to make fire using a small bow and shaft. When I was finally able to create fire, I lit the straw, which burned through the cords, and the steel I-beam crashed to the floor.

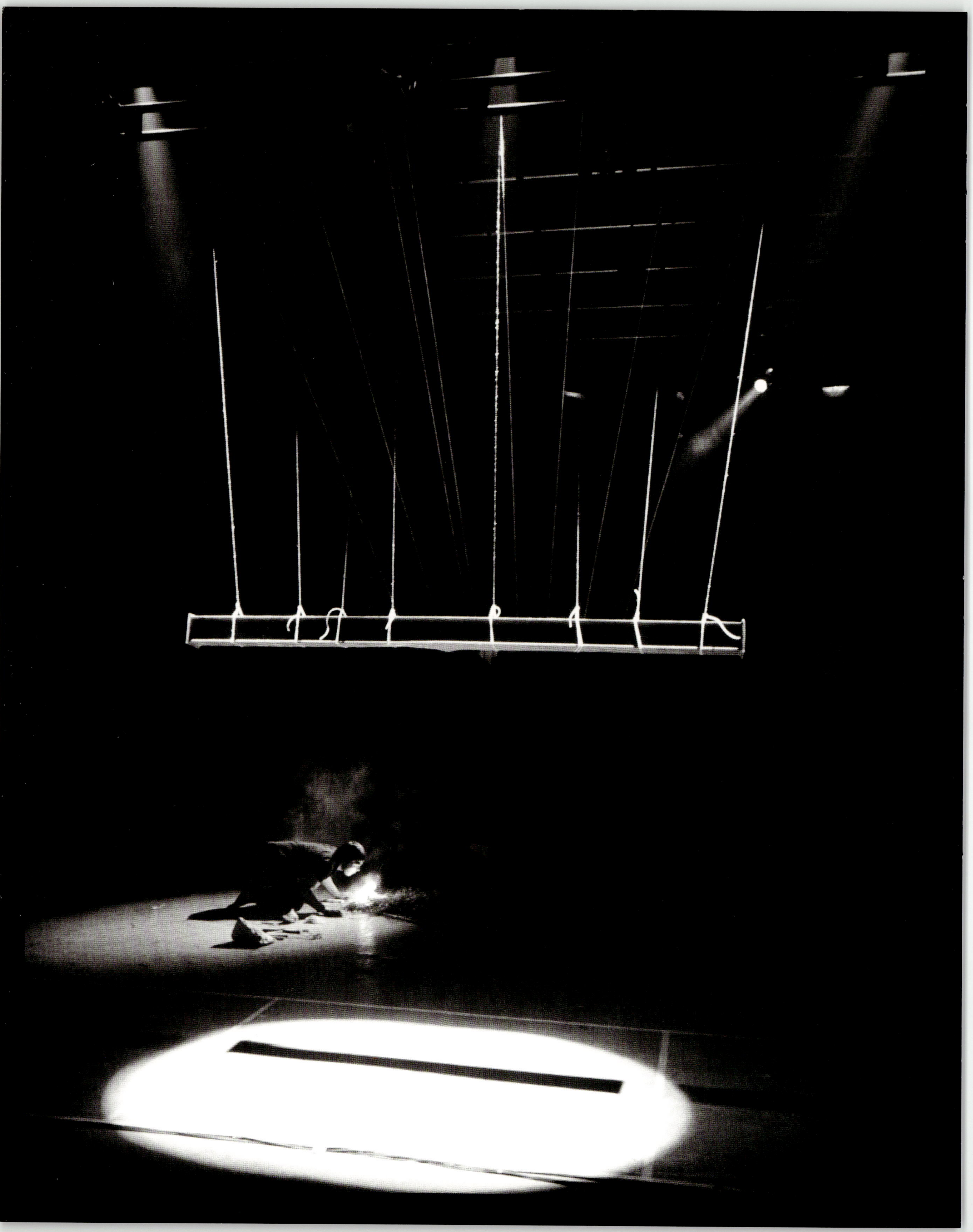

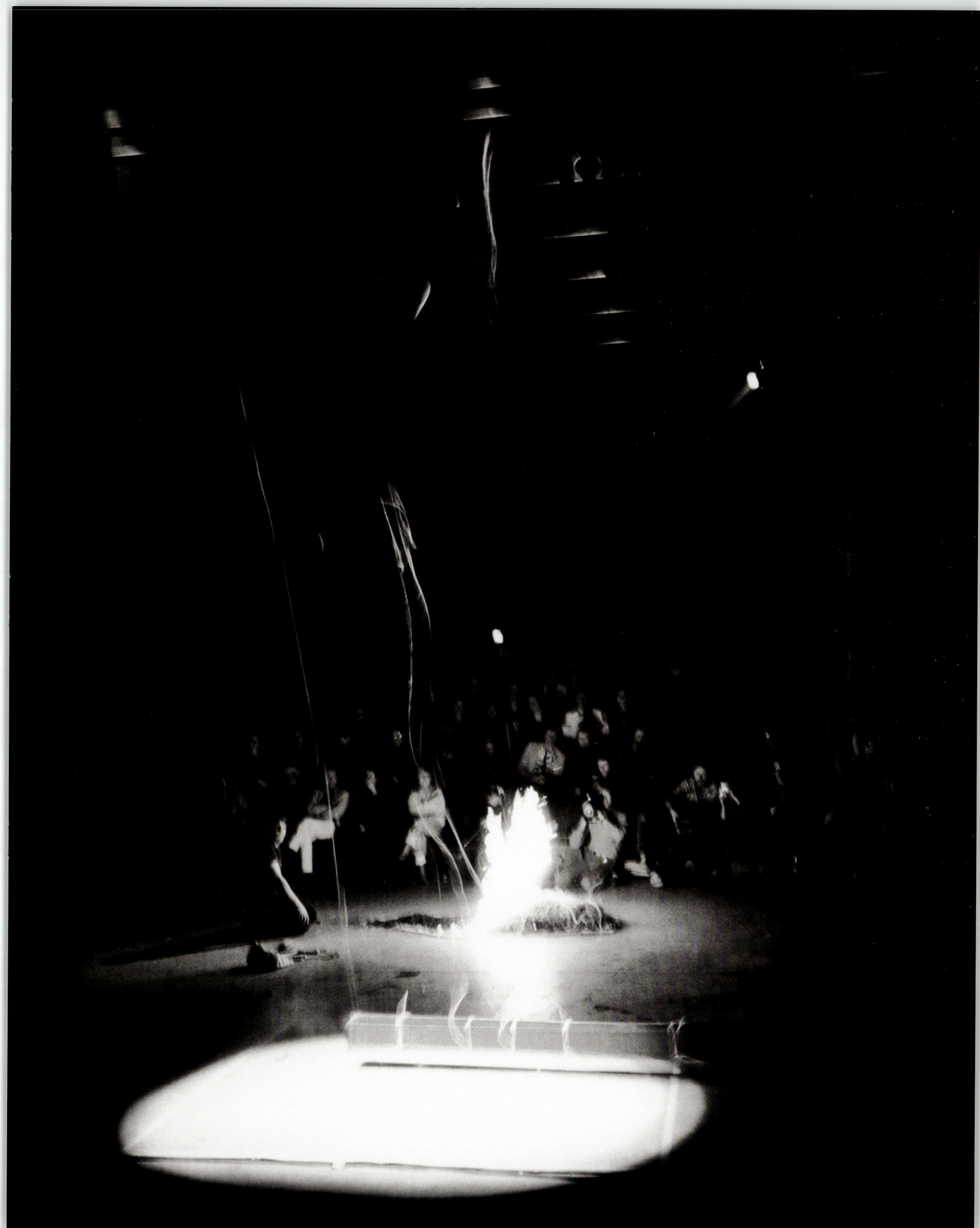

CHRIS BURDEN

Scale Model of the Solar System, 1983

A scale model, both in size and distance, of the Solar system. The Sun (865,000 miles in diameter) is represented by a sphere 13 inches in diameter and 40 inches in circumference. The planets of the Solar System, constructed to the correct scale, are placed at the correct scale distance across the city. The distance from the sun varies from 36 feet for Mercury, the closest planet, to almost a mile away for Pluto, the farthest planet.

— Chris Burden

CHRIS BURDEN was born in 1946. He obtained a B.F.A. at Pamona College, Claremont and a M.F.A. at the University of California, Irvine in 1971. Since 1978 he has been the Head of New Genre at the University of California, Los Angeles. In the early seventies, Burden became widely known for sensational performances involving his body. Since then, he has produced a multitude of assemblages, installations, kinetic and static sculptures and scientific models. He has had major retrospectives at the Newport Harbor Art Museum, Newport Beach, CA (1988) and MAK-Austrian Museum of Applied Arts, Vienna (1996). In 1999, Burden exhibited at the 48th Venice Biennale and the Tate Gallery in London.

PLANET LOCATOR

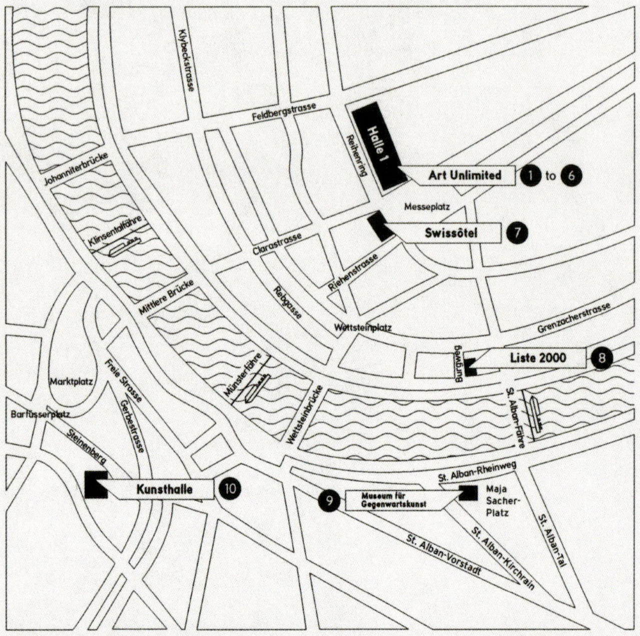

GAGOSIAN GALLERY Hall/Stand **2.0/G2**
Stand Phone +41/61-699 50 57 | Fax +41/61-699 50 58

USA-New York, NY 10021 | 980 Madison Avenue
Phone +1/212-744 23 13 | Fax +1/212-772 79 62

USA-Los Angeles, CA 90210 | 456 North Camden Drive
Phone +1/310-271 94 00 | Fax +1/310-271 94 20

USA-New York, NY 10011 | 555 West 24th Street
Phone +1/212-741 11 11 | Fax +1/212-741 96 11

GB-London W1R 7LH | 8 Heddon Street
Phone +44/20-72 92 82 22 | Fax +44/20-72 92 82 20

info@gagosian.com | www.gagosian.com

1 THE SUN [865,000 miles (1,392,000 km)] in diameter) is represented by a sphere 13 inches (33 cm) in diameter and 40 inches (101.6 cm) in circumference. The planets of the Solar System, constructed to the correct scale, are placed at the correct scale distance across the city of Basel. The distance from the Sun varies from 36 feet (10.9 m) for Mercury, the closest planet, to almost a mile for Pluto, the farthest planet. The location of each planet, installed at its correct scale distance, is indicated on the map.

2 MERCURY [3,100 miles (4,880 km) in diameter] would be the size of a sphere 0.05 inches (.127 cm) in diameter. In this installation Mercury is located in **Art Unlimited, Halle 1**, since its distance from the Sun would vary, due to its elliptical orbit, between a minimum of 36 feet (10.9 m) [28.6 million miles (45.9 million km)] and a maximum of 55 feet (16.75 m) [43.5 million miles (69.7 million km)].

3 VENUS [7,700 miles (12,104 km) in diameter] would be the size of a sphere 0.12 inches (.305 cm) in diameter. Venus is located in **Art Unlimited, Halle 1**, since its distance from the Sun would vary between a minimum of 83.6 feet (25.5 m) [66.8 million miles (107.4 million km)] and a maximum of 84.8 feet (25.8 m) [67.7 million miles (109 million km)].

4 EARTH [7,900 miles (12,756 km) in diameter] would be the size of a sphere 0.12 inches (.305cm) in diameter. Earth is located in **Art Unlimited, Halle 1**, since its distance from the Sun would vary between a minimum of 114 feet (34.7 m) [91.3 million miles (147.1 million km)] and a maximum of 118 feet (35.9 m) [94.4 million miles (152.1 million km)].

5 MARS [4,200 miles (6,787 km) in diameter] would be the size of a sphere 0.063 inches (.16 cm) in diameter. Mars is located in **Art Unlimited, Halle 1**, since its distance from the Sun would vary between a minimum of 160 feet (48.7m) [128.2 million miles (207 million km)] and a maximum of 193 feet (58.8 m) [154.6 million miles (249 million km)].

6 JUPITER [88,770 miles (142,800 km) in diameter] would be the size of a sphere 1.33 inches (3.38 cm) in diameter. Jupiter is located in **Art Unlimited, Halle 1**, since its distance from the Sun would vary between a minimum of 576 feet (175.5 m) [460.2 million miles (740 million km)] and a maximum of 634 feet (193.2 m) [506.4 million miles (816 million km)].

7 SATURN [75,100 miles (120,000 km) in diameter] would be the size of a sphere 1.13 inches (2.87 cm) in diameter. Saturn is located in the **Swissôtel,** since its distance from the Sun would vary between a minimum of 1,047 feet (319 m) [836.5 million miles (1,346.4 million km)] and a maximum of 1,172 feet (357 m) [935.8 million miles (1,511 million km)].

8 URANUS [11,470 miles (51,800 km) in diameter] would be the size of a sphere 0.17 inches (.43 cm) in diameter. Uranus is located at **Liste 2000**, since its distance from the Sun would vary between a minimum of 2,126 feet (647.7 m) [1,698 million miles (2,742 million km)] and a maximum of 2,336 feet (711.7 m) [1,866 million miles (3,800 million km)].

9 NEPTUNE [10,540 miles (49,500 km) in diameter] would be the size of a sphere 0.16 inches (.41 cm) in diameter. Neptune is located in **Museum für Gegenwartskunst**, since its distance from the Sun would vary between a minimum of 3,465 feet (1,055.7 m) [2,767 million miles (4,460 million km)] and a maximum of 3,528 feet (1074.9 m) [2,817 million miles (4,540 million km)].

10 PLUTO [3,370 miles (6,000 km) in diameter] would be the size of a sphere 0.05 inches (.13 cm) in diameter. Pluto is located in the **Kunsthalle** since its distance from the Sun would vary between a minimum of 3,440 feet (1,048 m) [2,748 million miles (4,425 million km)] and a maximum of 5,720 feet (1,742.7 m) [4,569 million miles (7,400 million km)].

Information sheet from installation at Basel Art Fair, 2000

Scale Model of the Solar System 1983

Plastic, steel ball bearings, plexiglass
Dimensions variable

The Sun (865,000 miles in diameter) is represented by a sphere 13 inches in diameter and 40 inches in circumference. The planets of the Solar System, constructed to the correct scale, are placed at the correct scale distance across the city. The distance from the Sun varies from 36 feet for Mercury, the closest planet, to almost a mile for Pluto, the farthest planet. The location of each planet, installed at its correct scale distance, is indicated on the map.

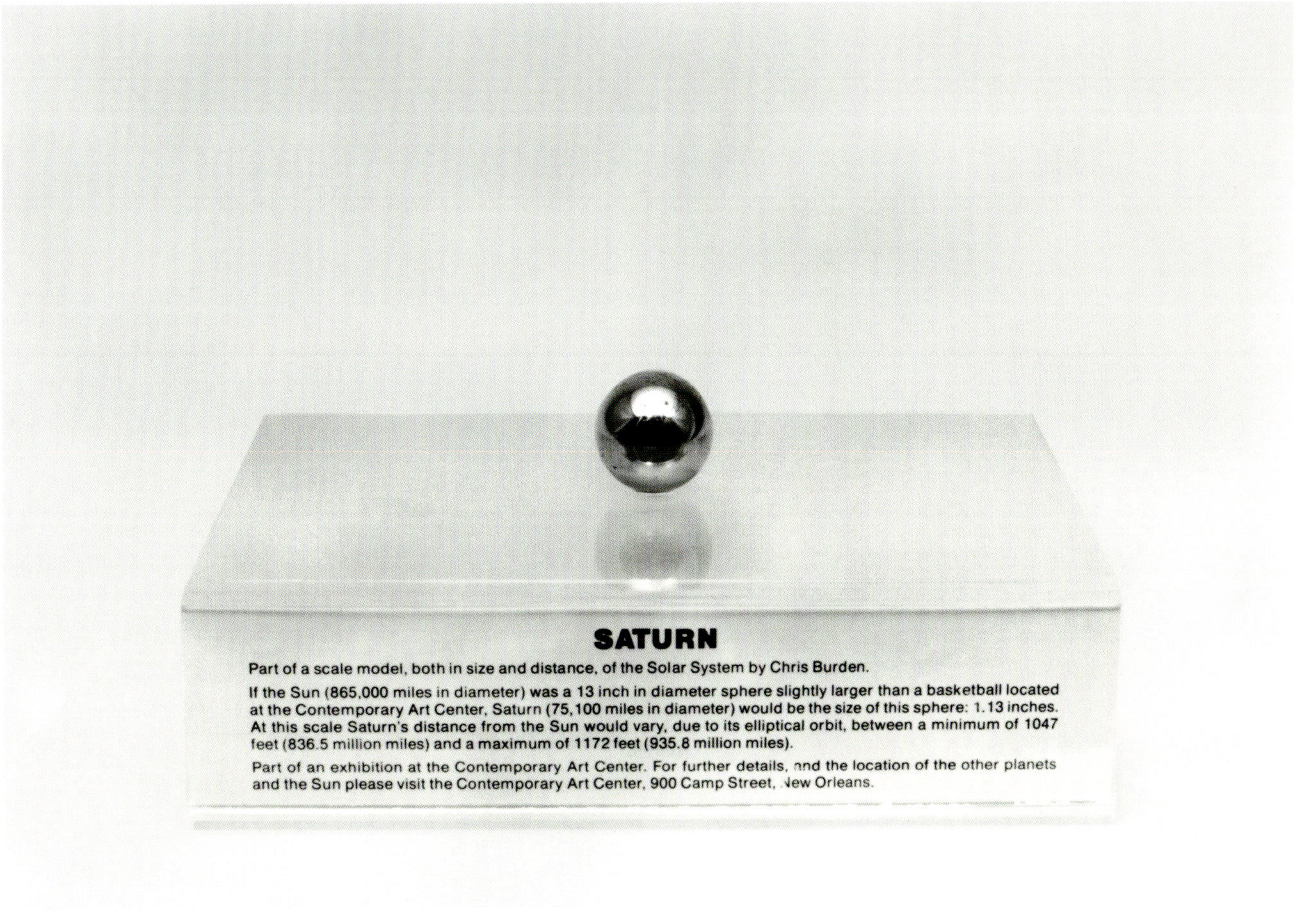

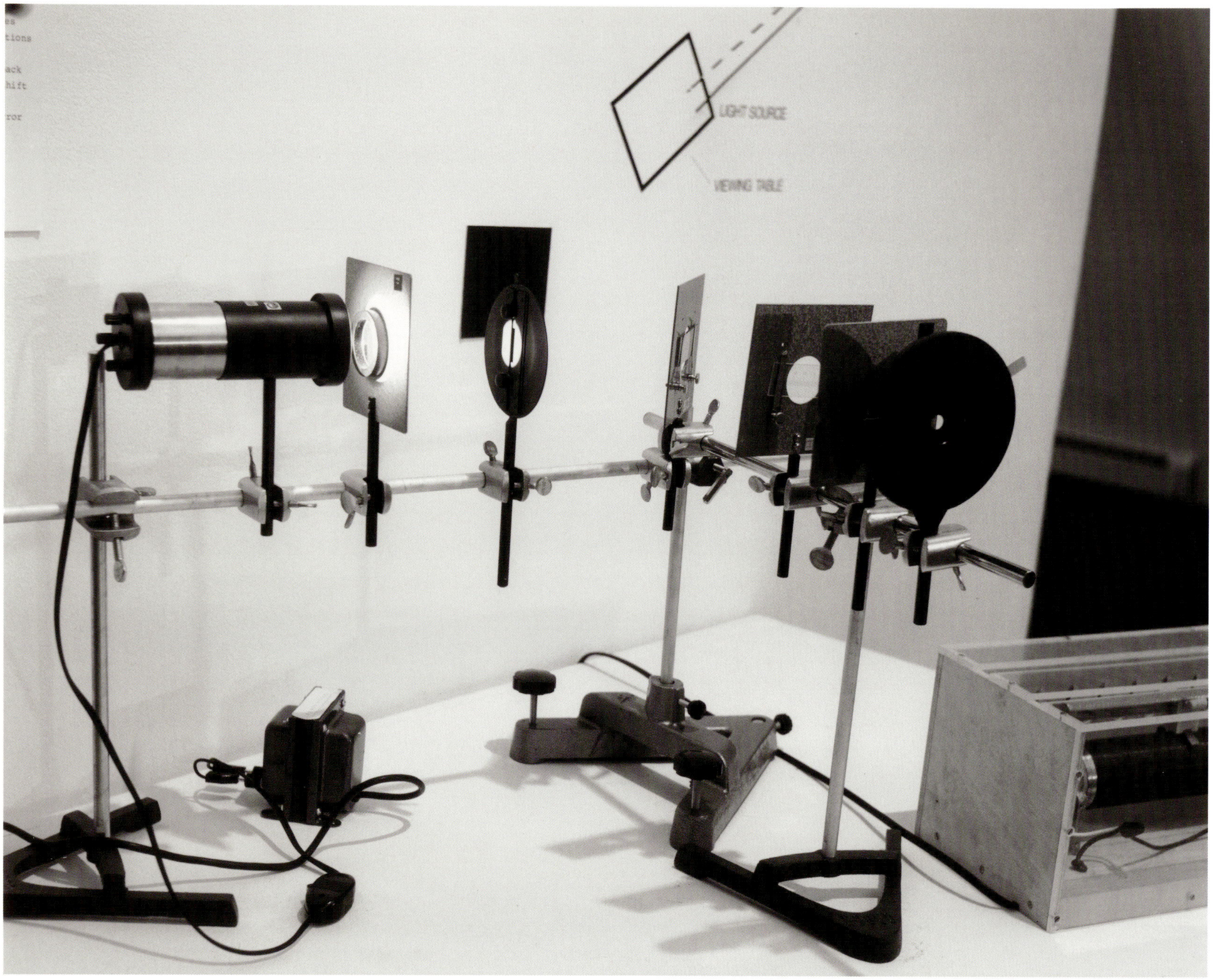

The Speed of Light Machine 1983

Optical apparatus, lenses, mirrors
180 × 540 inches

The Speed of Light Machine *is a re-creation of the original nineteenth-century apparatus used to accurately measure the speed of light in the small confines of a laboratory. A beam of light is bounced through a series of lenses and mirrors, and the viewer, by looking through an eyepiece at the control table, can see finite proof that light travels at the extreme speed of 186,000 miles per second, or 669 million miles per hour. If man is ever to travel to the distant stars, he will have to travel at speeds approaching the speed of light.*

The speed that light travels is approximately 186,000 miles per second or 770 million miles per hour. According to Einstein's theories of relativity, the speed of light is one of the fundamental absolutes of the universe, nothing can travel any faster. If mankind is ever to travel the vast distances between the stars, spaceships that travel close to the speed of light will have to be developed.

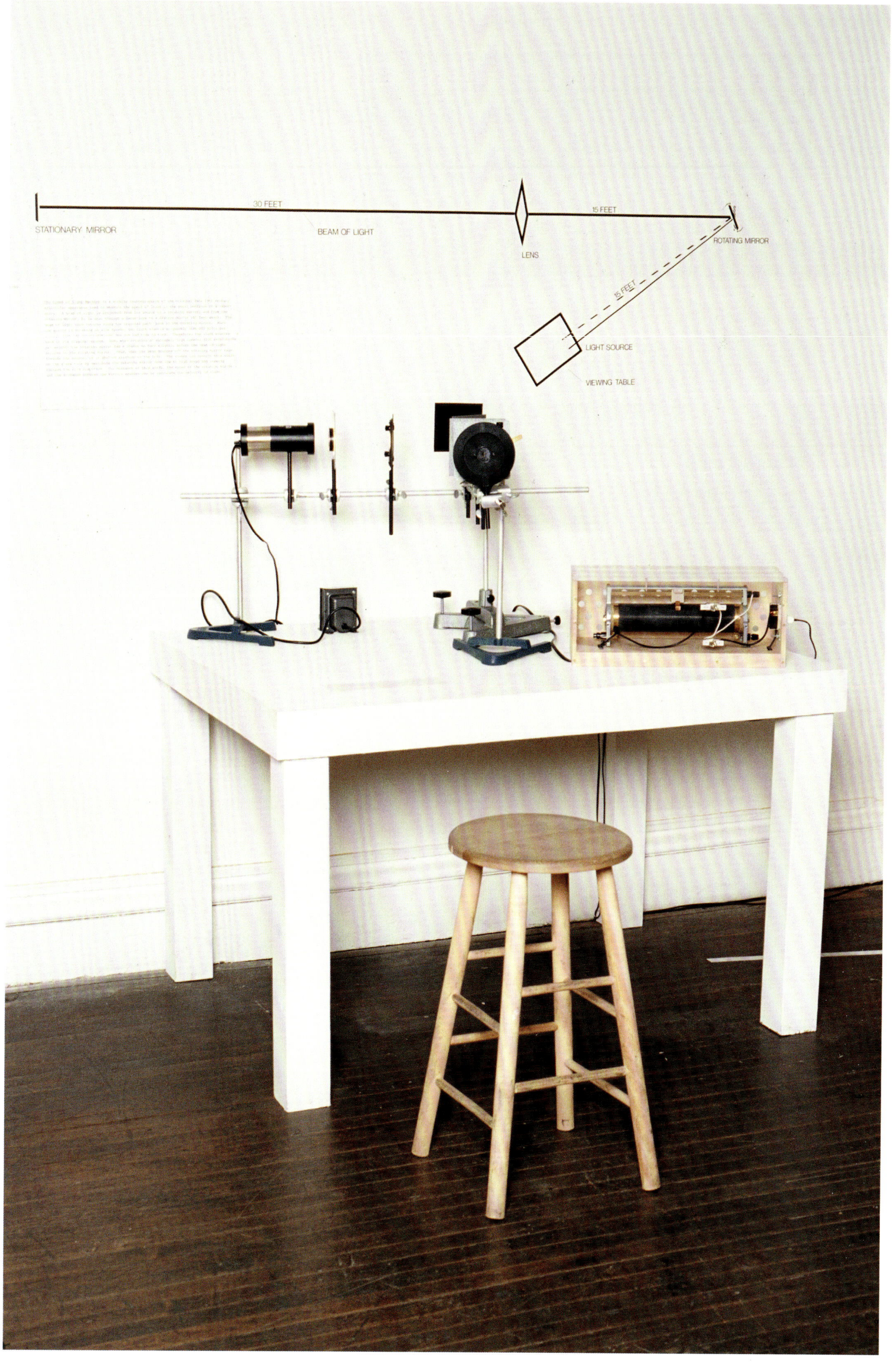
30 FEET
STATIONARY MIRROR
BEAM OF LIGHT
LENS
15 FEET
ROTATING MIRROR
15 FEET
LIGHT SOURCE
VIEWING TABLE

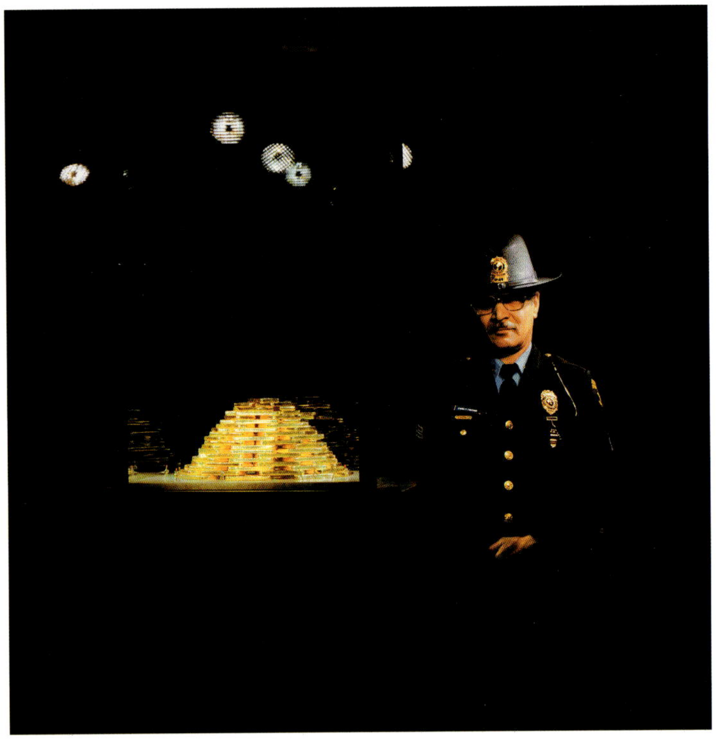

Tower of Power 1985

100 one kilo (32 oz.) pure gold bricks, matchsticks
Dimensions variable

The Tower of Power *is a sculpture built out of 100 one kilo (32 oz.) bars of pure gold. On the marble surrounding the tower are several paper matchstick men in various forms of tribute. At the present rate of exchange, this tower is equivalent to a million US dollars. Like the matchstick men, our lives are relatively transient and consumable in relationship to the ascribed and lasting power of gold.*

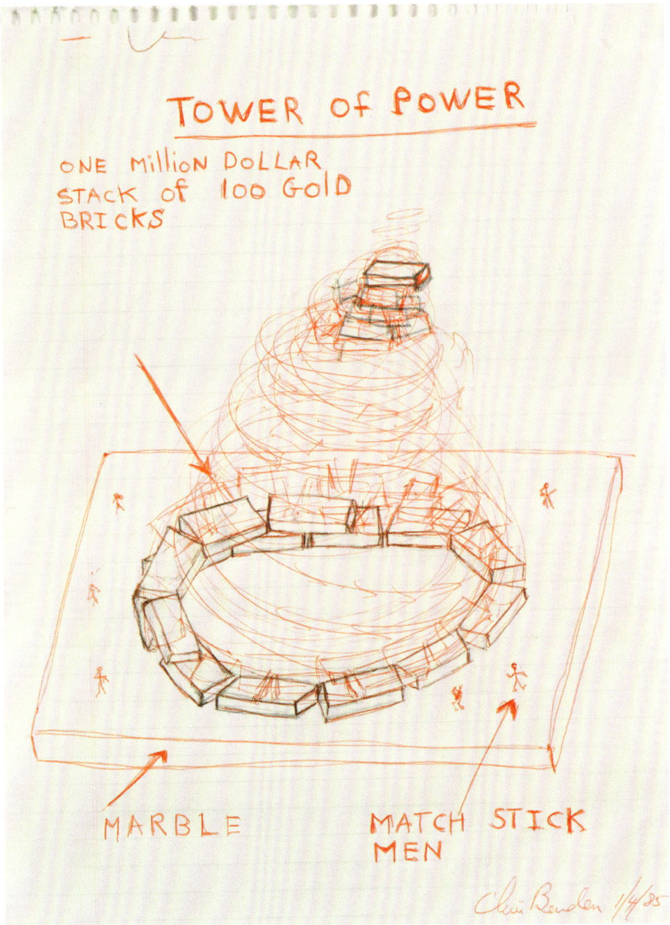

Tower of Power II 1985
Ink on paper, 11 × 8½ inches

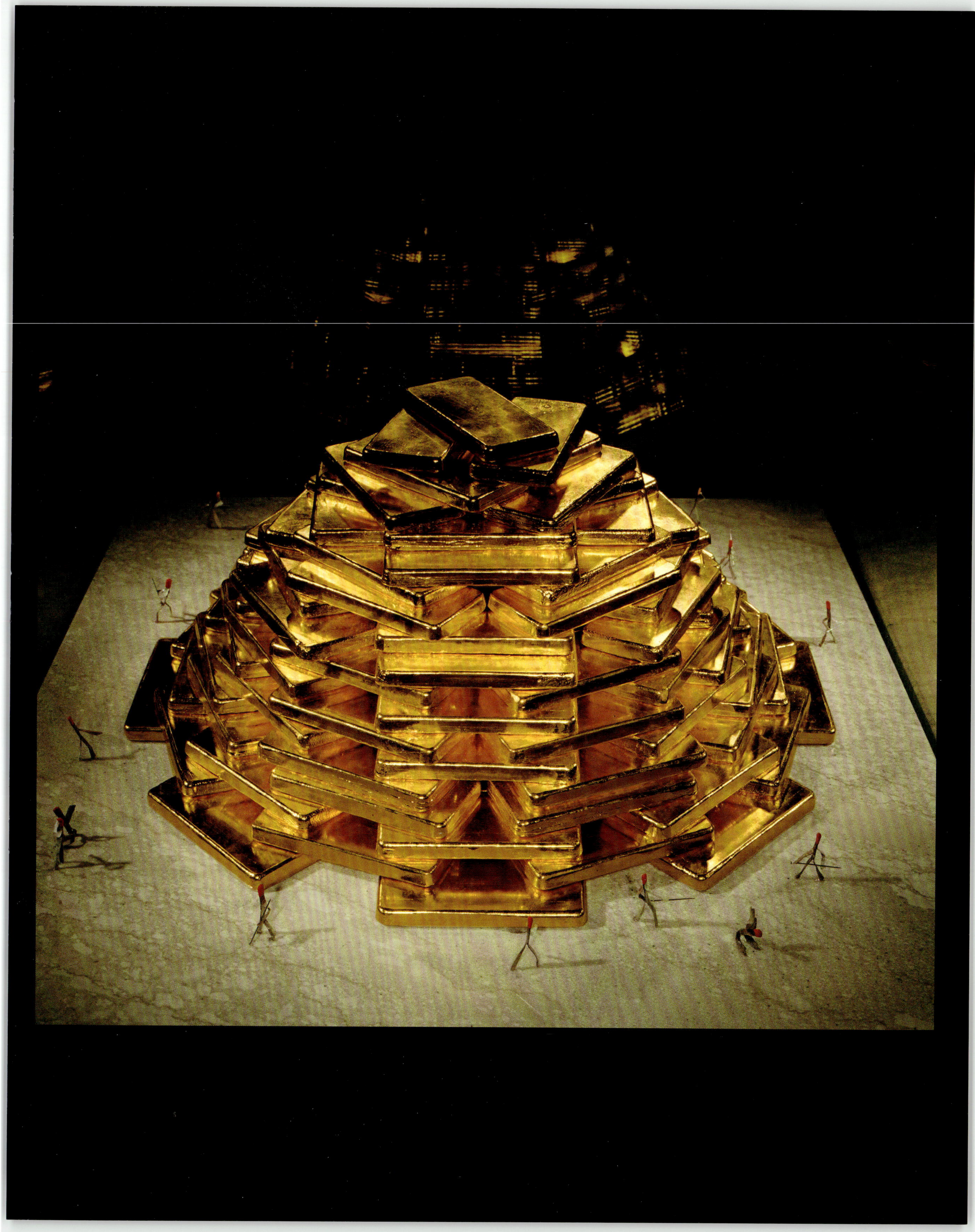

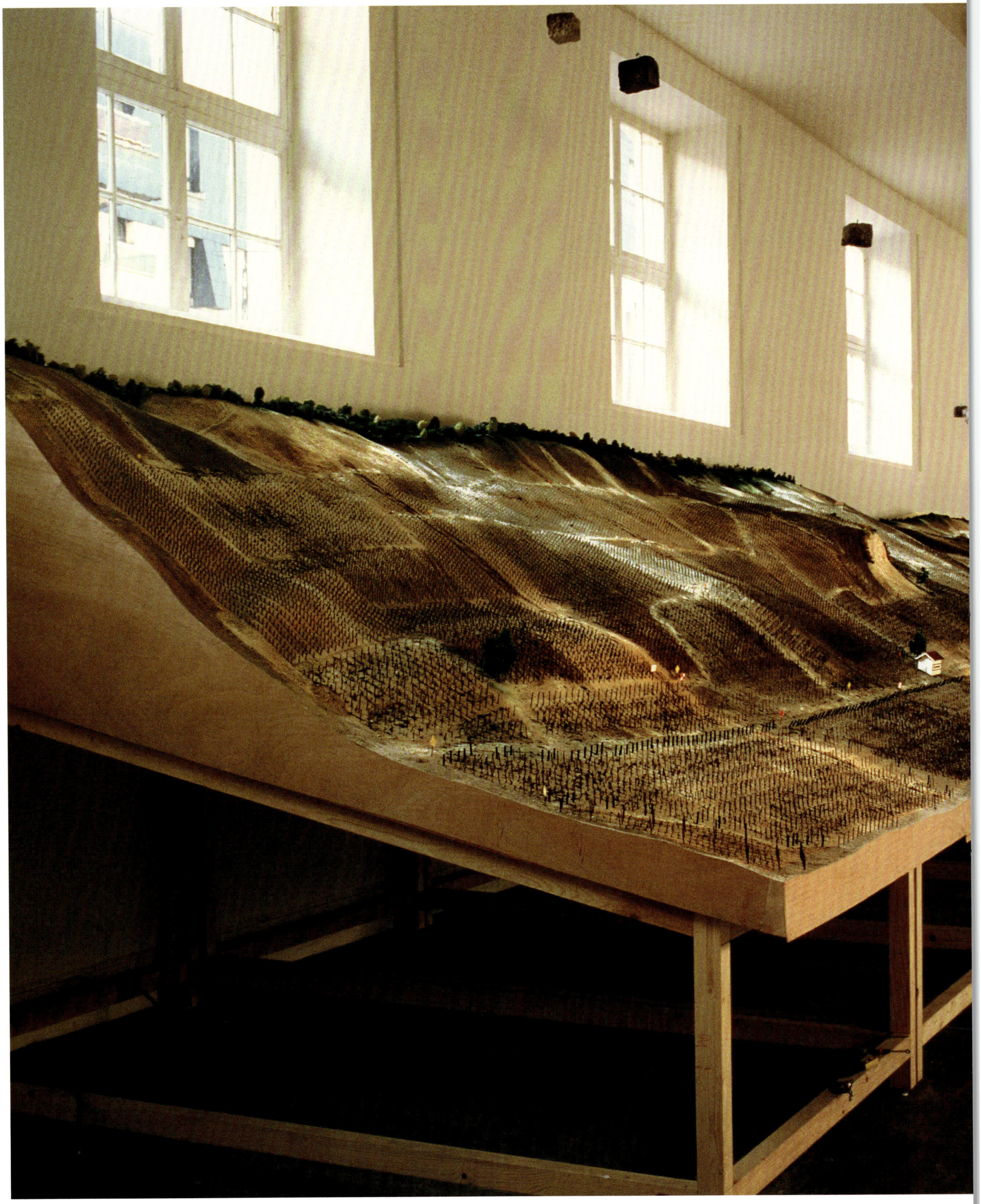

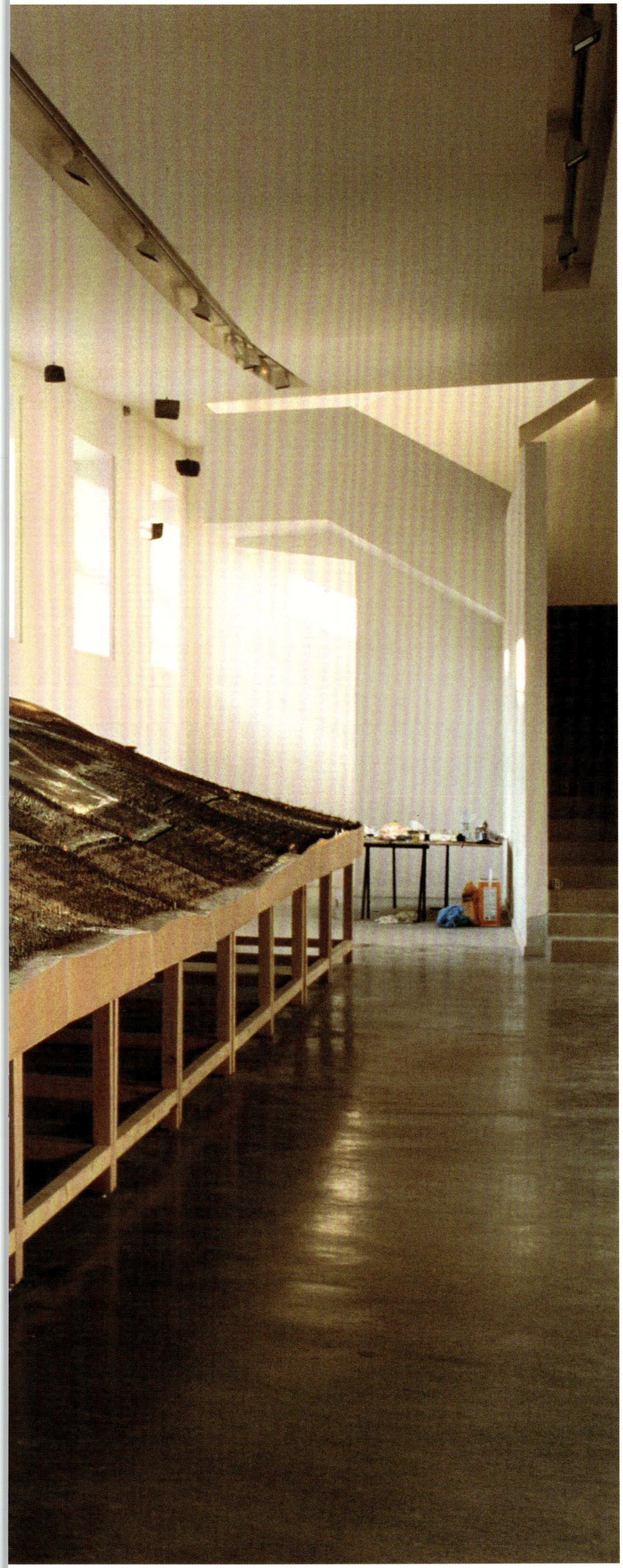

The Spirit of the Grape (L'esprit du vin) 1994

Wood, foam, paint, toothpicks, thyme
86 × 531 × 120 inches

Whilst traveling through the Champagne-Ardenne region of France, I was struck by the beauty of the bare vineyards and the light through the rolling valleys. In trying to recreate a sense of that beauty, I made a diorama of the rolling hills and the bare grapevines on their stakes. The undulating landscape is constructed from modeled foam and rests on a wooden frame. The vineyards are replicated, in a very small scale, using toothpicks and thin twisted pieces of wire. Suspended from the ceiling and floating over the rolling landscape at regular intervals, are four or five cobblestone-like pieces of real rock. These stones represent the gray skies of the Champagne-Ardenne region. The stones also represent the heavy weight of history and tradition that hangs in the air, throughout all of Europe, that is reassuringly comforting, while at the same time, oppressively inhibiting.

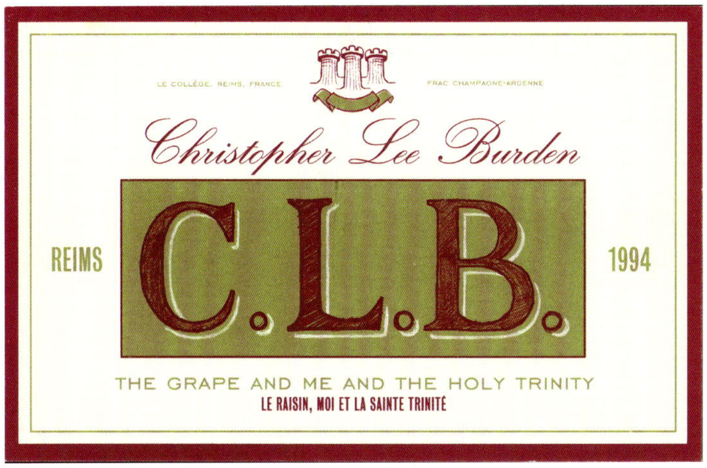

Label from C.L.B. champagne, 1994
3⅝ × 5¾ inches

Pizza City 1996

Toys, buildings (plastic, wood, metal, paper), foam, paint, mounted on 25 wooden and metal tables
Each table 36 × 84 × 48 inches

Under construction for nearly seven years, Pizza City *is a 70-foot-long by 30-foot-wide model of a miniature city and its surrounding landscape.* Pizza City *contains the permanent accumulation of thousands of tiny European, Oriental, North African, American and futuristic sci-fi styles of buildings and other elements of an archetypal city.* Pizza City *is an imaginative fantasy, a spiritual model of Los Angeles. Like Los Angeles, its urban sprawl knows no bounds. City centers, complete with skyscrapers, suddenly appear at the very edges of the suburbs. Oversize office buildings are adjacent to small single family homes. Elevated expressways bisect through neighborhoods. Throughout* Pizza City, *as in Los Angeles, one finds enclaves of thematic architecture, i.e. adobe villages, Swiss villages, faux chateaux, which provide psychological comfort and respite from the omnipresent megalopolis.*

Pizza City *is composed of approximately 25 table-high modules that are joined together in groups of threes and fours. These groupings enable the viewer to actually enter the city from a variety of places and view the city and its minute detail from many different vantage points. The scale of the buildings is very small. The scale of* Pizza City *is 1 to 220. A scale mile is 24 feet. The thousands of model buildings and objects that have been collected and modified by the artist were produced and originally sold as Christmas ornaments, paper models of historical buildings, collectibles, model train components, toys and fantasy war game accessories. The buildings and objects were produced by manufacturers to serve a need in society, to serve as touchstones to an idealized world. By accumulating and organizing the mass quantities of these pre-existing architectural models and objects, the rich and textured quality of Los Angeles is captured.*

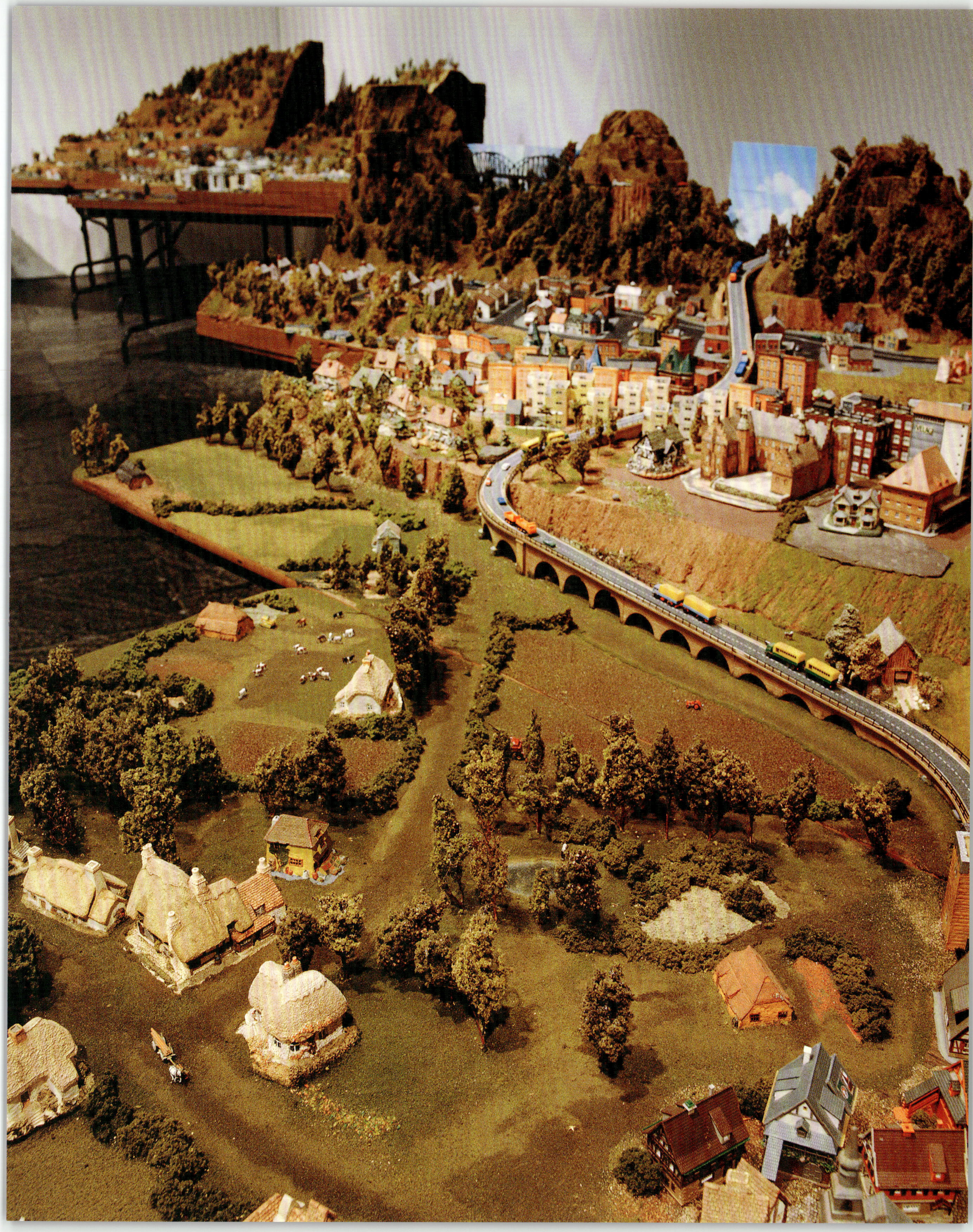

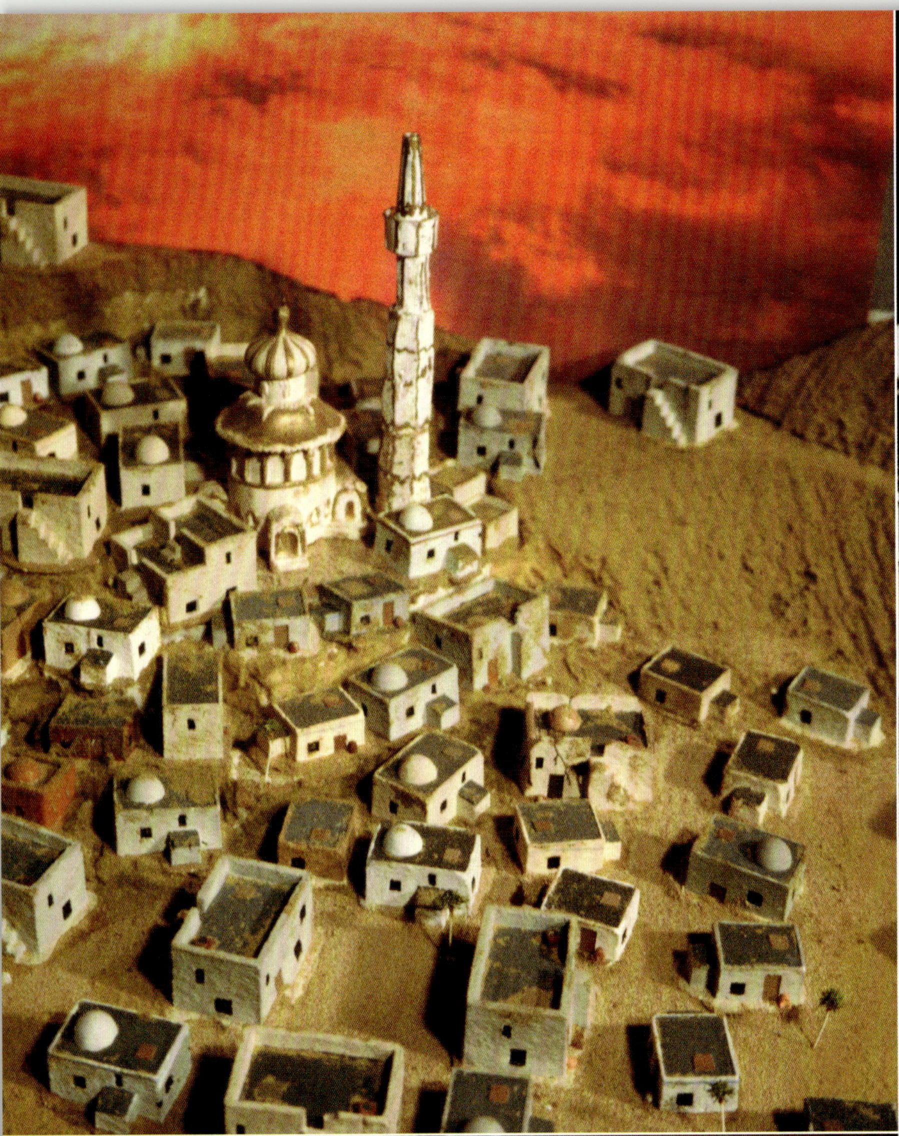

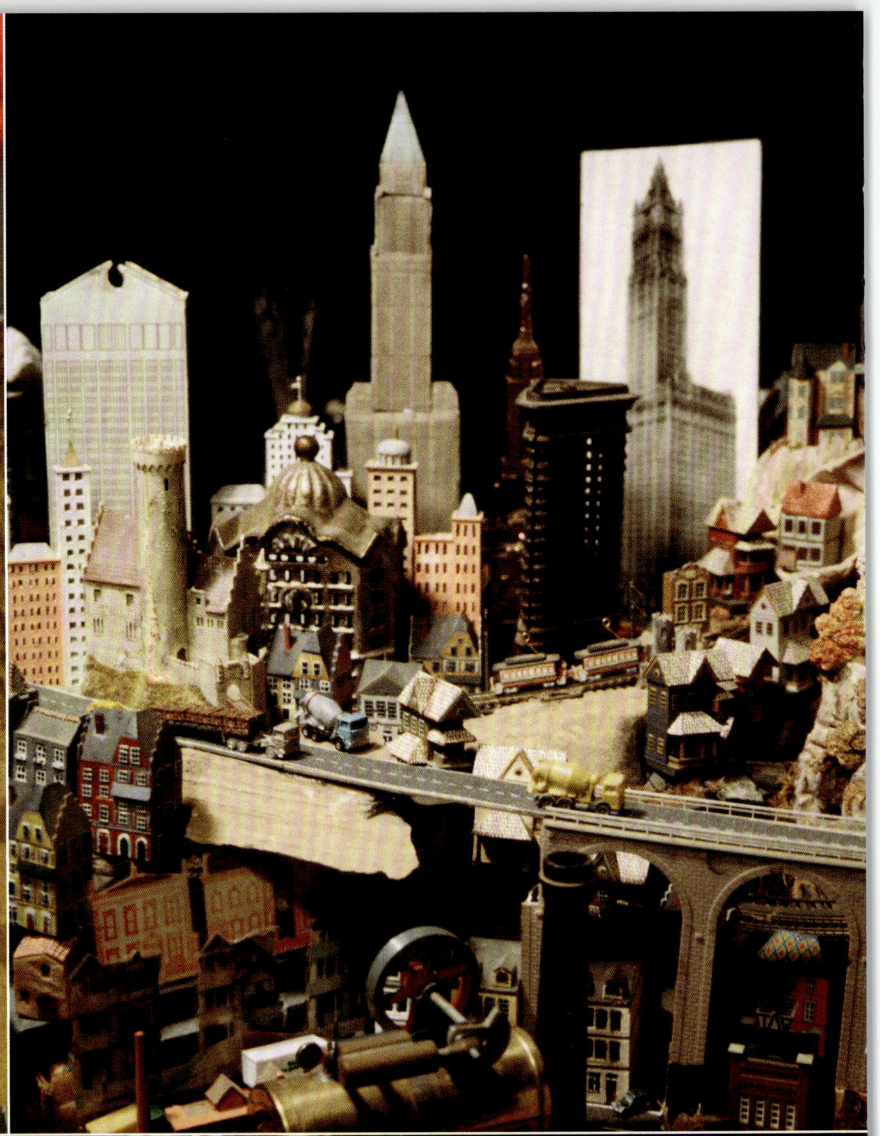

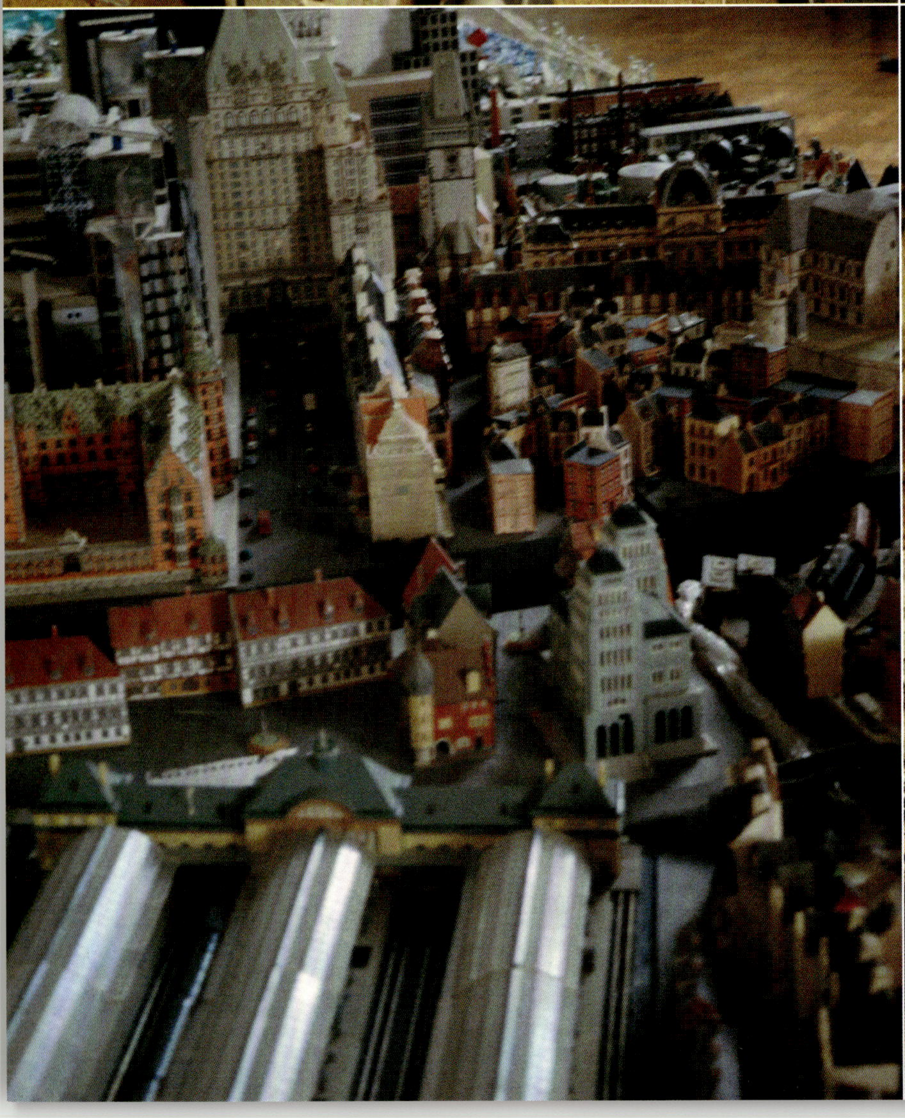

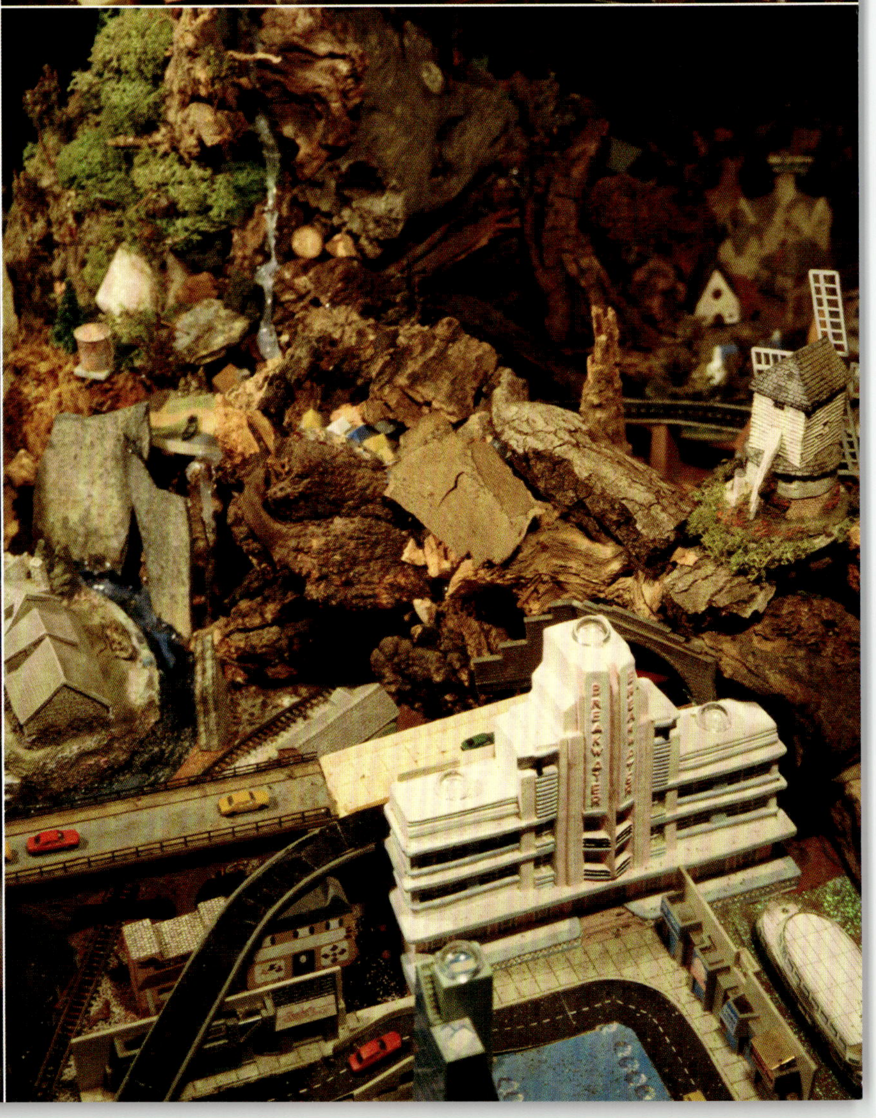

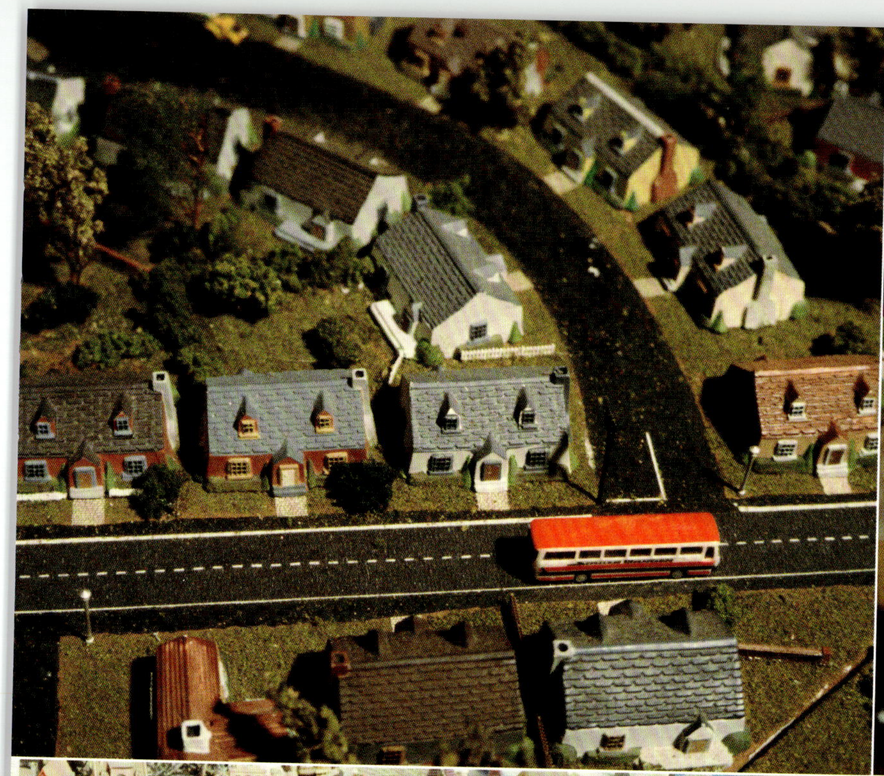

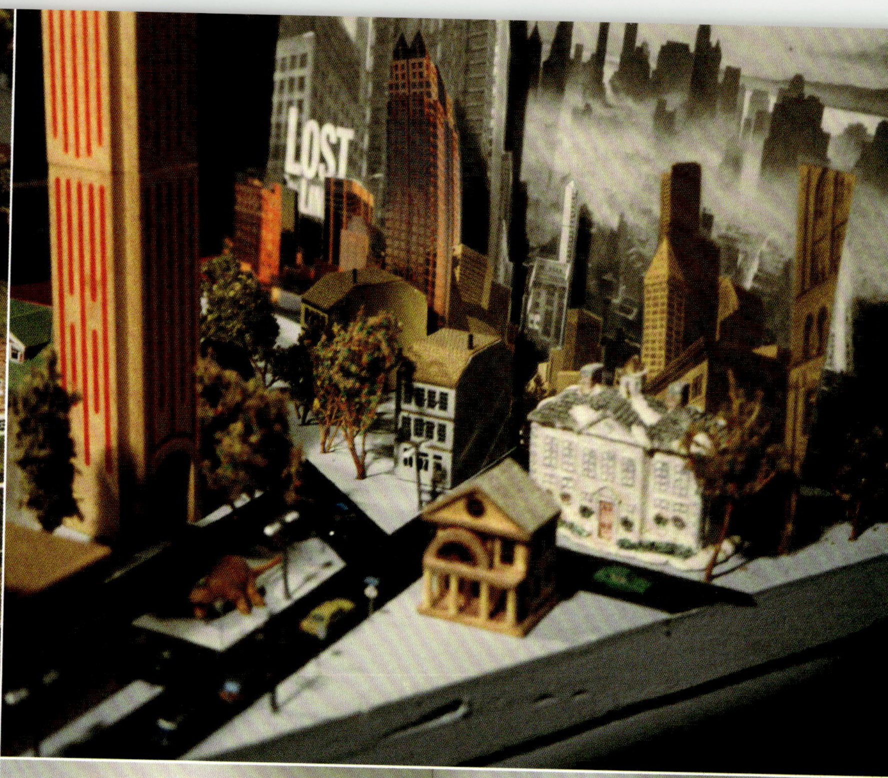
LOST

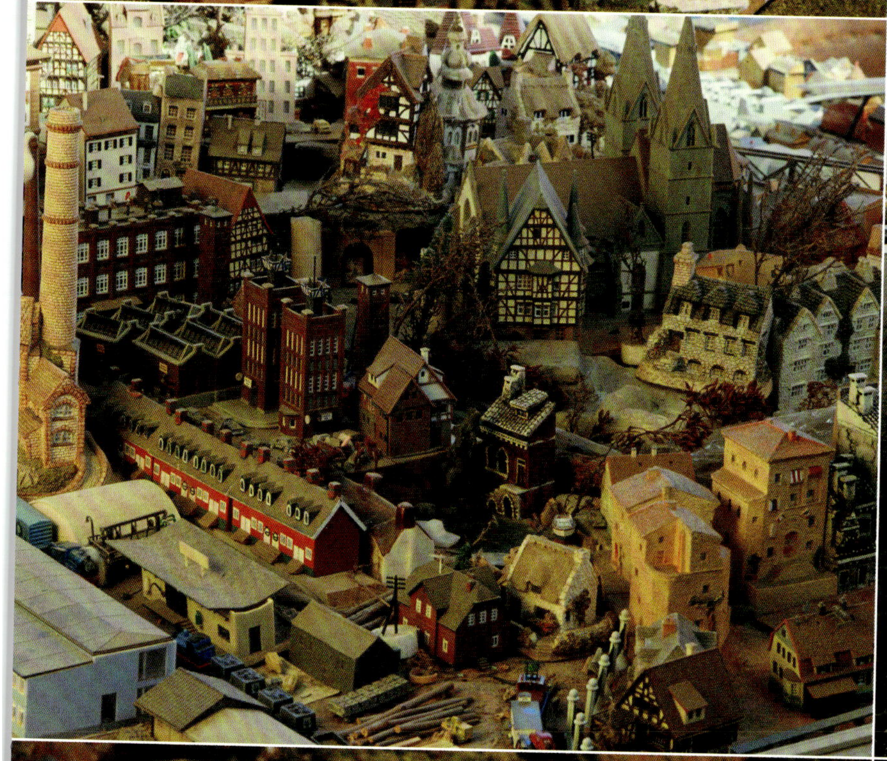

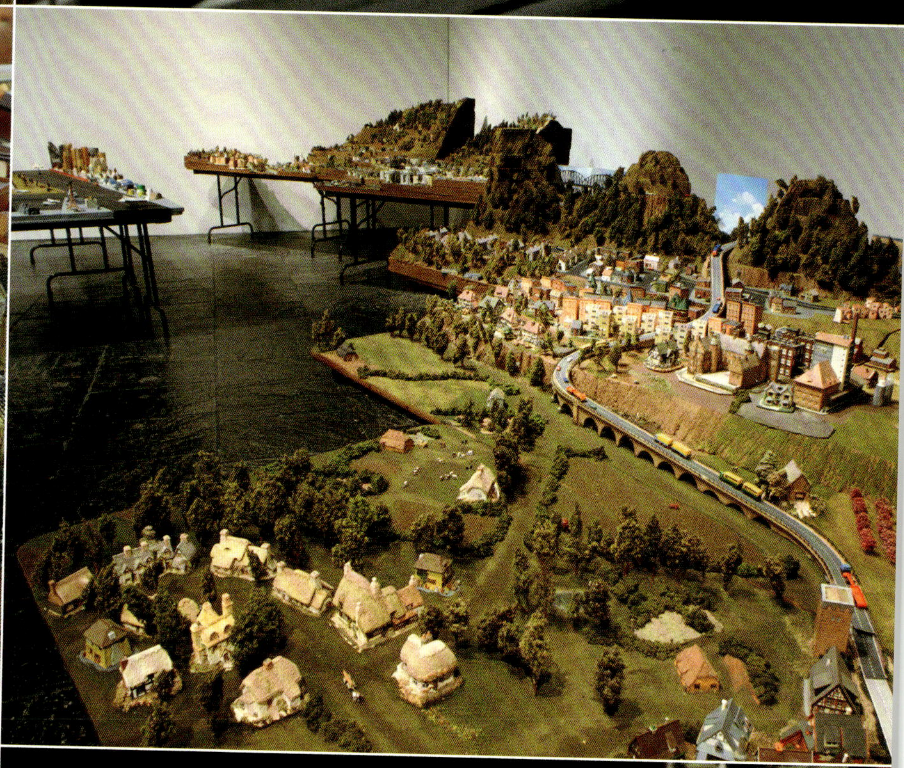

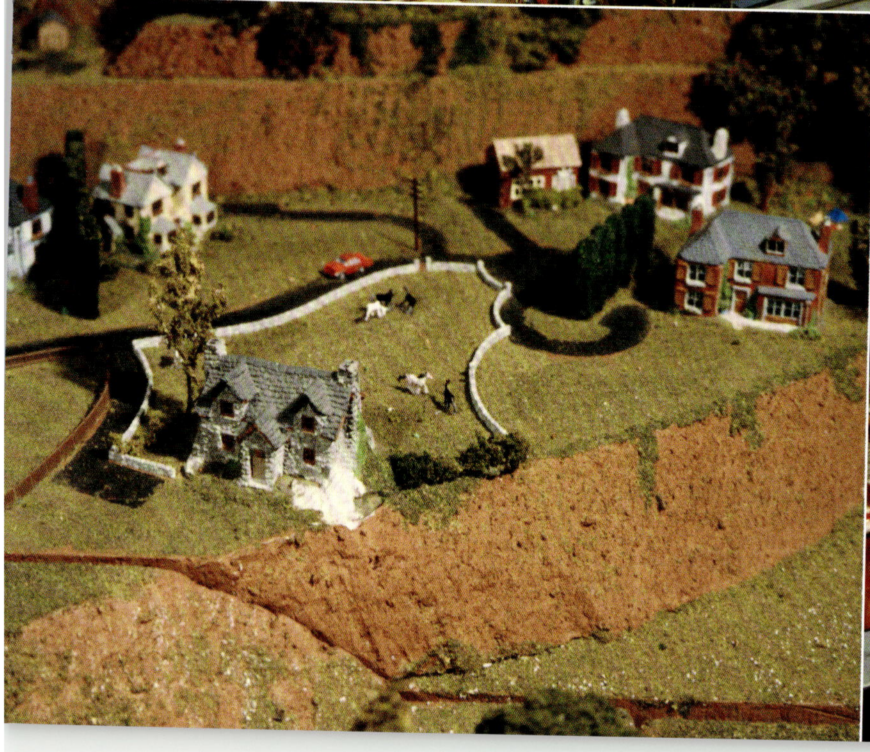

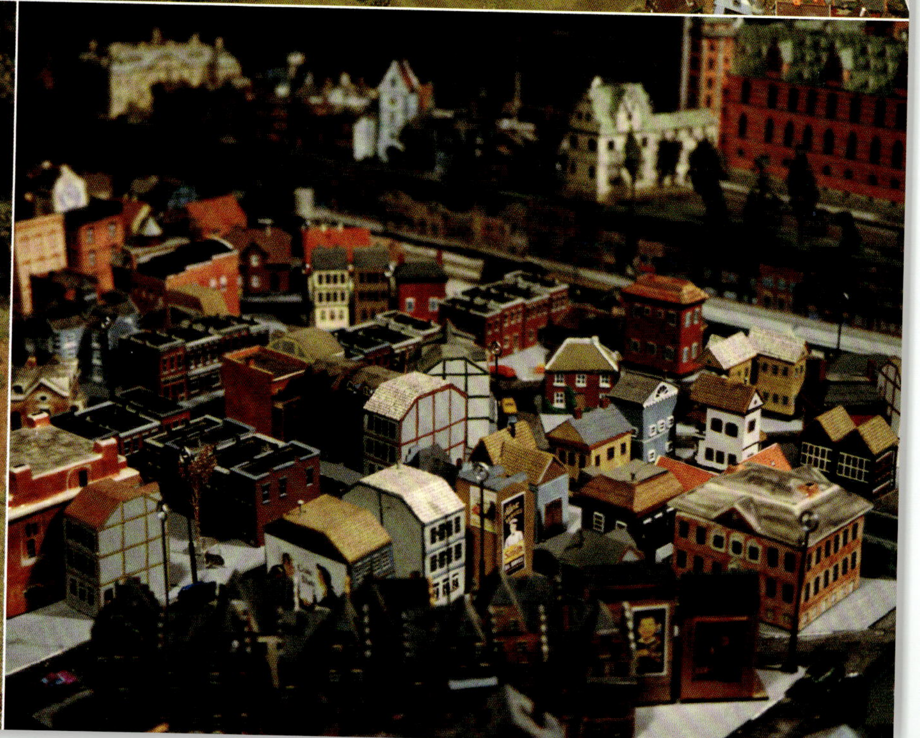

When Robots Rule: The Two-Minute Airplane Factory 1999

Dimensions variable (requires minimum exhibition space of 60 × 25 feet)

When Robots Rule: The Two-Minute Airplane Factory *is an assembly line factory that manufactures a small stick and tissue rubber band powered airplane. After being assembled and built, the model airplanes, with their rubber bands pre-wound, are launched off the production line every two minutes.*

The airplane that is produced by the factory is based on the design of a model airplane called the 'Rise Off the Ground', or 'R.O.G.' The R.O.G. is able to rise to heights of 60 to 70 feet and flies so well it is wondrous to behold. In addition to building and flying the R.O.G. recreationally, I have incorporated this plane into five of my earlier artworks. These artworks are: C.B.T.V. to Einstein *(1977);* Coals to Newcastle *(1978);* Pearl Harbor *(1979);* Airplane and Barbed Wire *(1979); and* C.B. Air Force *(1980).*

When I conceived the idea for the airplane factory, I fantasized how miraculous it would be to build a machine that would transform the tedious manual eye-hand dexterity necessary to hand-build an airplane into a fluid and precise mechanical process. The airplane factory was initially exhibited at the Tate Gallery in London in 1999. It was designed to be as automated as possible. Humans needed only to load the raw materials into the totally computer-controlled factory. The factory would take the materials, build and ultimately launch a finished airplane. Each plane was to spiral upward until its power was dissipated and then glide back to the floor. Immediately the planes would be retrieved by a gallery attendant and offered for sale to the public at a nominal price. With an airplane being produced and launched every two minutes, the total production over the 110-day span of the exhibition at the Tate Gallery would be approximately 22,000 planes. The labor required to build one airplane at a time by an individual is four hours. Thus, building 22,000 airplanes would consume 88,000 man hours. The miracle of the airplane factory is that in building 22,000 airplanes, it would liberate 88,000 man hours of tedious hand labor. In a microcosm, this is the dream and the promise of the Industrial Age; much, much more for much, much less.

In the construction of the airplane factory there are parallels between my toy airplane factory and the world of finance, production and marketing with all the promises of success and the attendant problems. What at first appears to be a playful, albeit expensive, machine which produces a wonderful, delicate, inexpensive toy is, in fact, a real model of capitalism. Could the machine, When Robots Rule: The Two-Minute Airplane Factory, *from the sales of the airplanes, pay for itself and ultimately start making a profit?*

The factory was worked on continuously during the four month exhibition at the Tate Gallery. However due to a computer program that proved to be far too complex, slight variations in the balsawood, and the fact that the machine had no feedback system to monitor each step of the construction process, the sculpture, When Robots Rule: The Two-Minute Airplane Factory *proved to be a heroic, but unsuccessful attempt at building a factory that could continuously build and launch airplanes.*

Airplane Factory 1998
Pencil on paper
19 × 24 inches

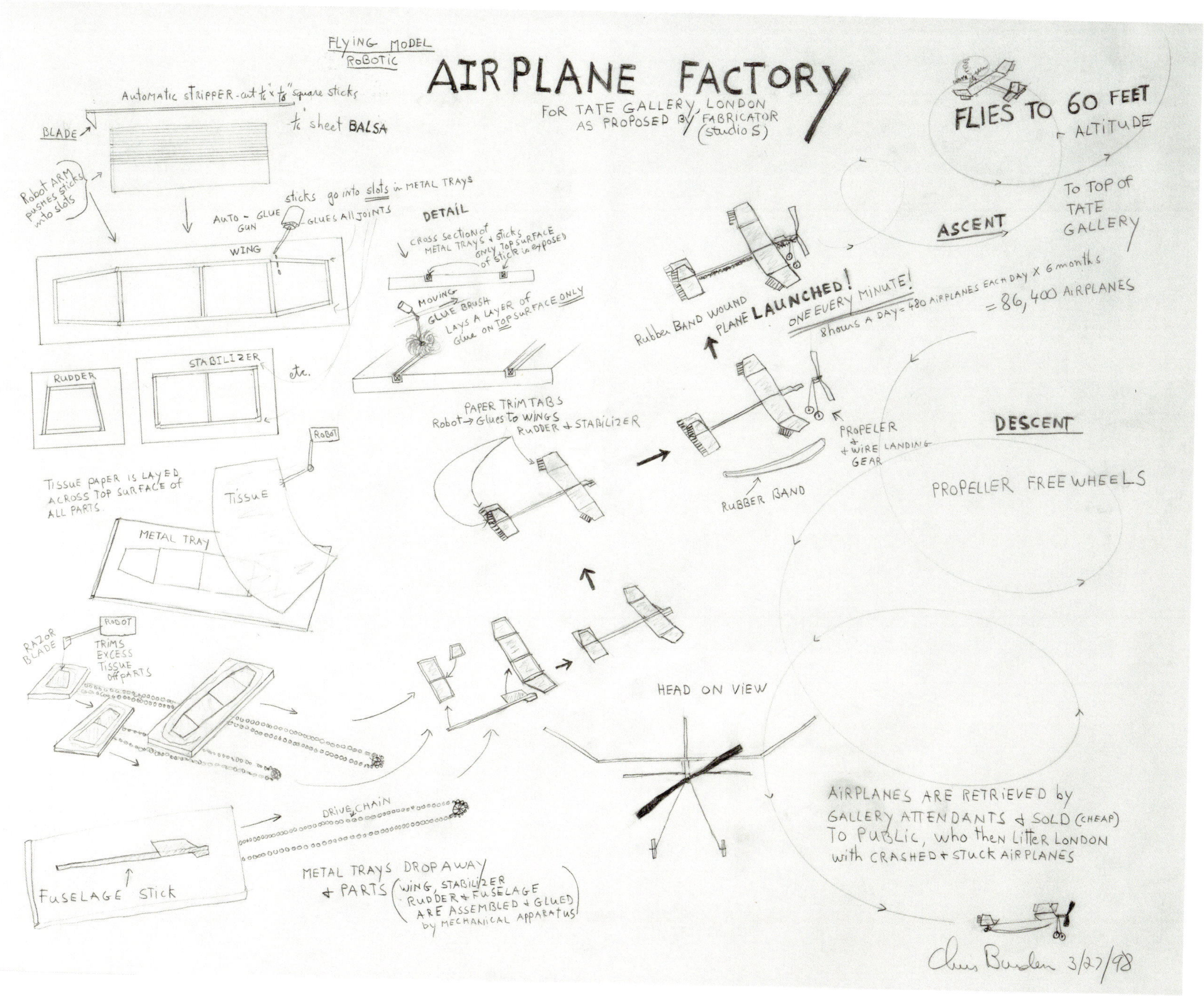

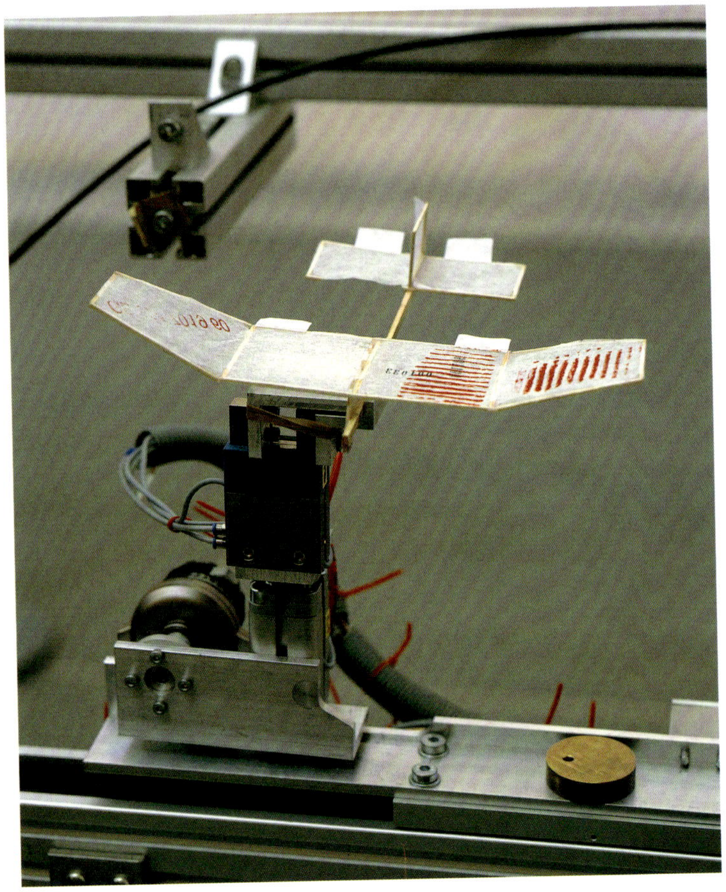

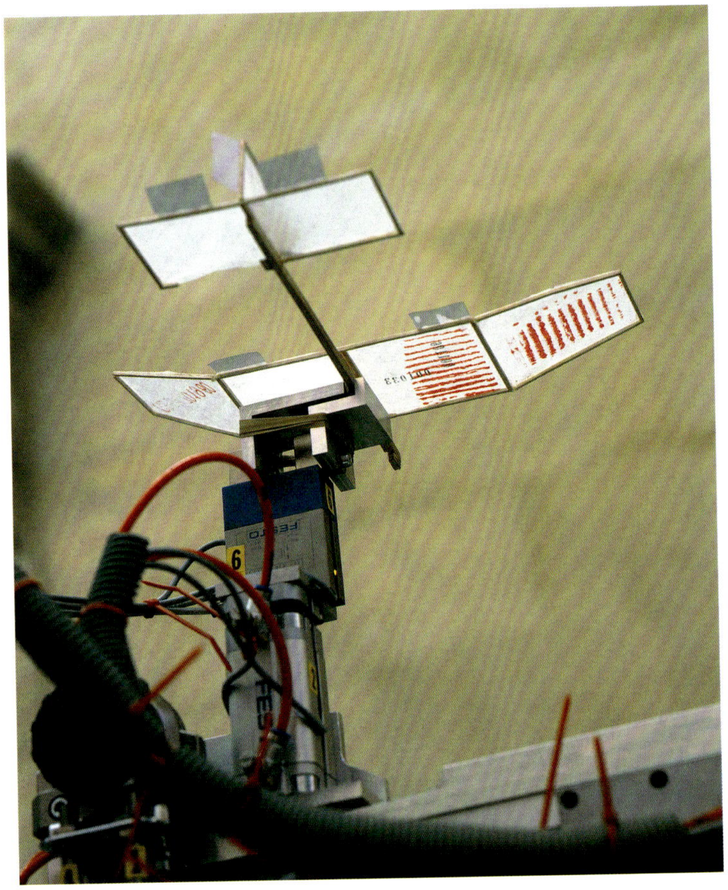

Production

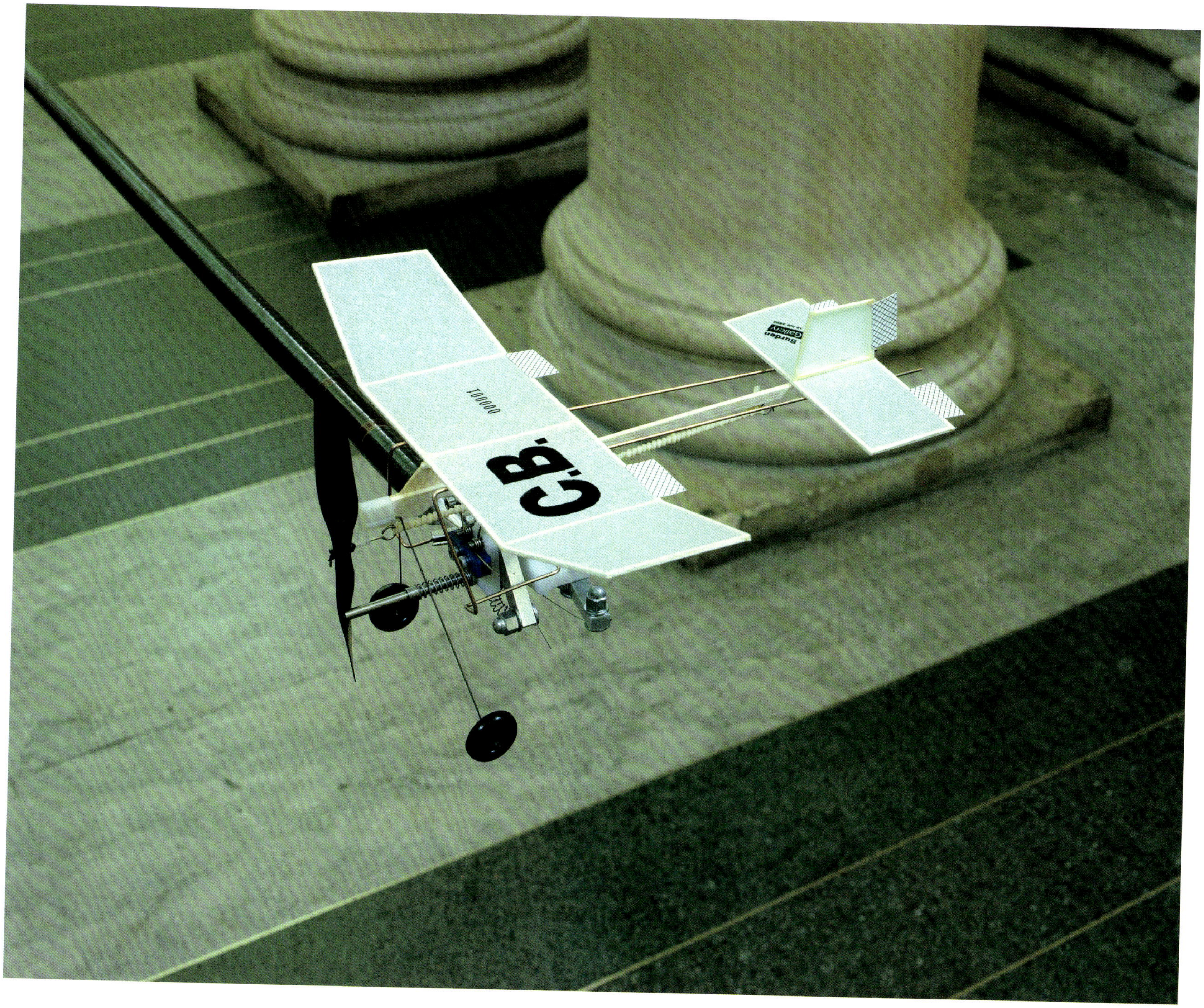
C.B.

Gold Bullets 2003

(Edition of ten, with two artist's proofs)
Ten 22-karat gold bullets in two wood and plexiglass display cases
Bullets: dimensions variable
Each case: 6¼ × 10¼ × 5¾ inches

Each set of Gold Bullets *consists of ten different 22-karat gold bullets, displayed in two wood and plexiglass display cases. The bullets are separated into five 'Roundies' and five 'Pointies', referring to their predominant physical characteristic. Each bullet is stamped with a 22K stamp and a Chris Burden stamp.*

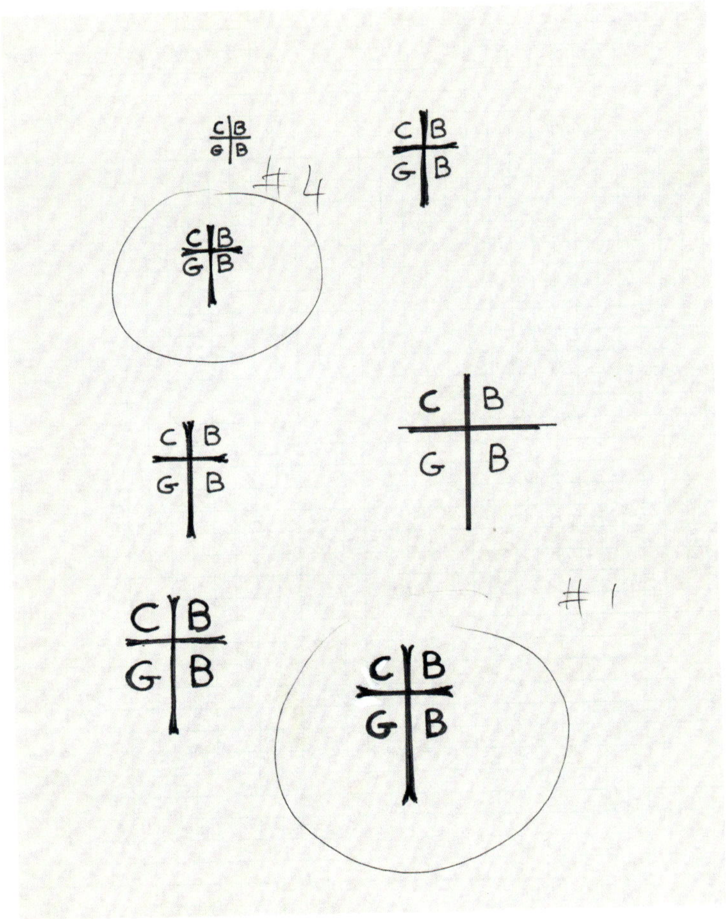

Designs for CBGB stamp 2003
Pencil and ink on paper, 11½ × 8 inches

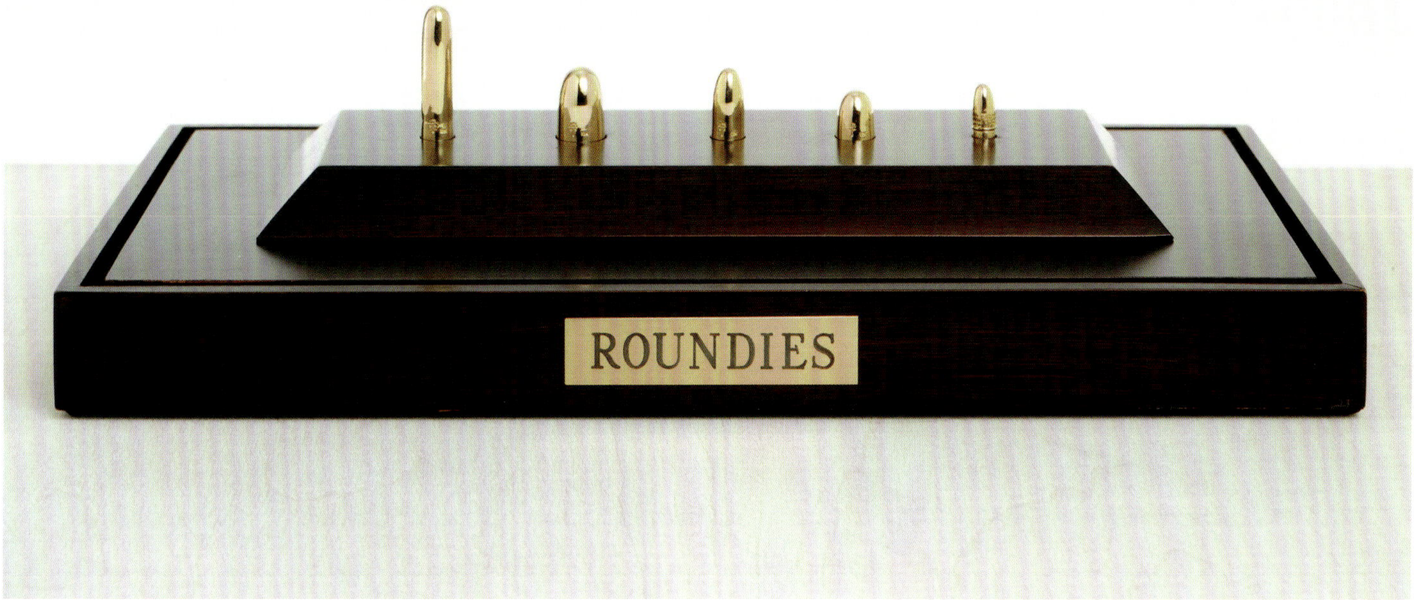
ROUNDIES

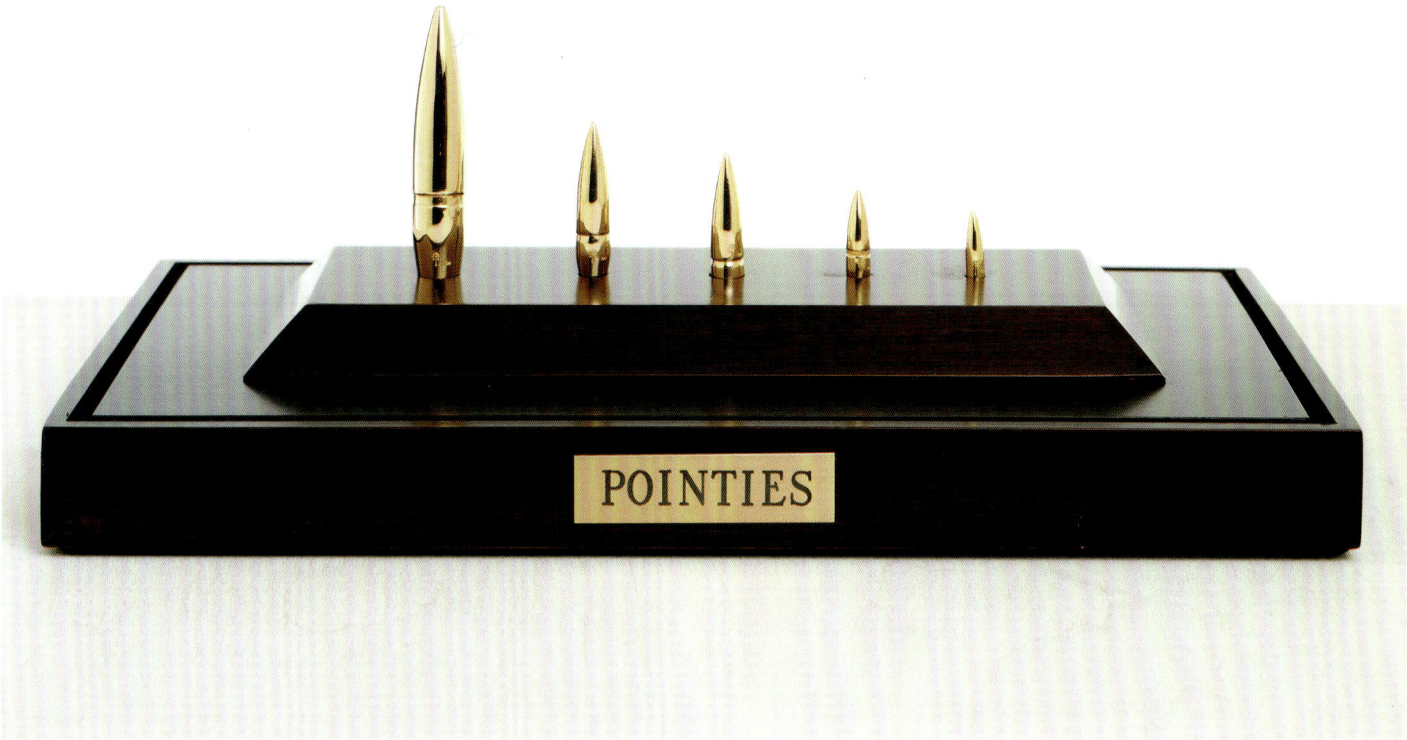
POINTIES

Metropolis 2004

Two one-twelfth-horsepower DC motors with motor controllers, four electric transformers, wood, plastic, steel, aluminum, magnets, cement, glue, Lego, Lincoln Logs, fired clay bricks, Hot Wheel cars and tracks, Monorail trains and track
87 × 194 × 130 inches

Metropolis *is an intense and complex kinetic sculpture. It measures approximately 7 × 16 × 10 feet and is modeled after a fast-paced, frenetic modern city. The armature is constructed of steel beams that form an eclectic grid. The grid is interwoven with an elaborate system of Hot Wheel roadways and Monorail train tracks. Hot Wheels are inexpensive small toy cars that are available in many different styles. They are designed to speed downhill on specially designed plastic roadways. Also attached to the grid are various structures built from Lego, Lincoln Logs, Playmobile, Mini Bricks, wood blocks, metal building kits and Meccano and Erector components. Situated at opposite ends of* Metropolis *are two electrically-powered conveyor belts, each studded with magnets at regular intervals.*

The 80 Hot Wheel cars are modified with rubber bumpers and with magnets glued to their undersides. The magnets on the conveyor belt and the magnets on the cars lock together and enable the cars to be brought to the top of the sculpture. At the top of the sculpture, the Hot Wheel cars are released one at a time and race down the roadways, weaving in and out of the structure, simulating rapid traffic and congestion. Occasionally a disastrous multi-car crash forces an immediate emergency shutdown of one of the conveyor belts in order to stop the pileup and to retrieve the crashed cars from the floor. The noise, the continuous flow of the Monorail trains, the speeding Hot Wheel cars and the random car crash, produces in the viewer the stress of living in a dynamic, active and bustling twenty-first century city.

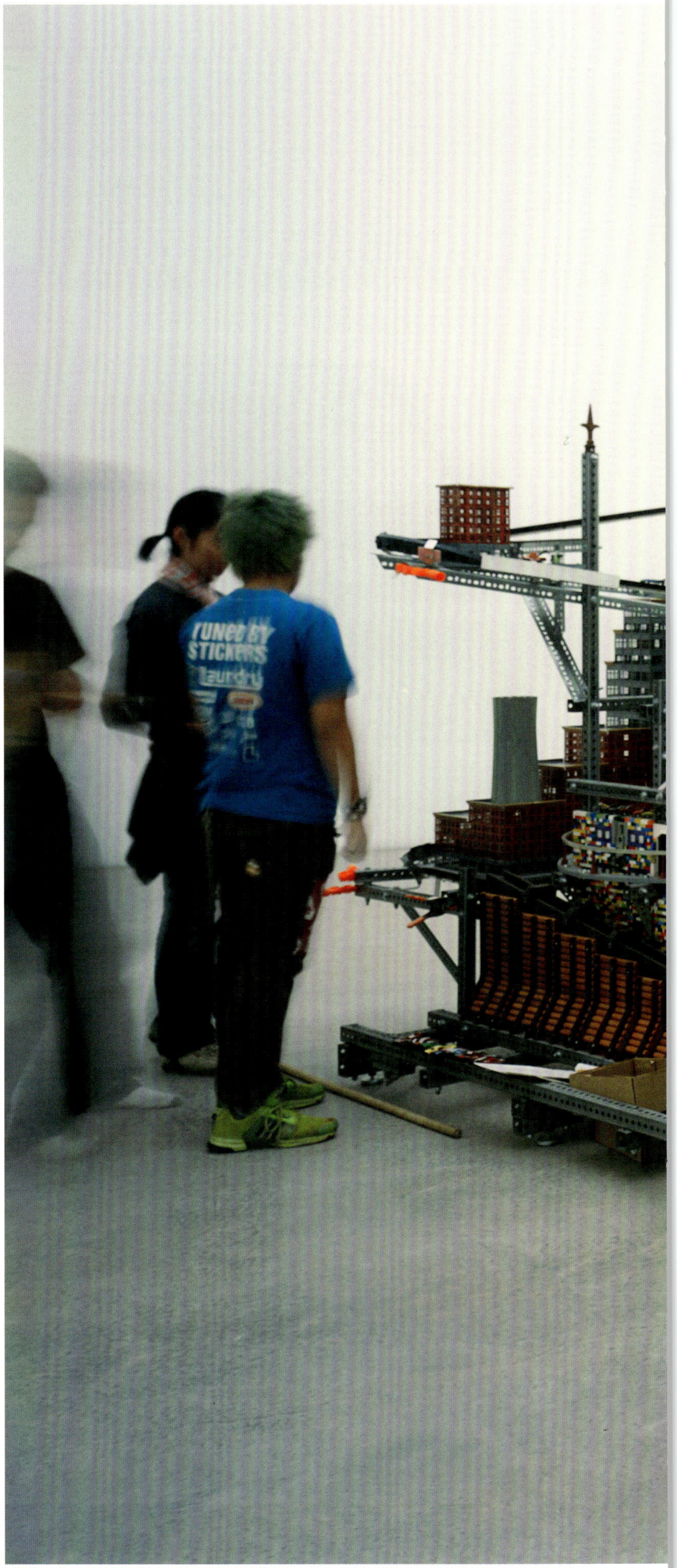

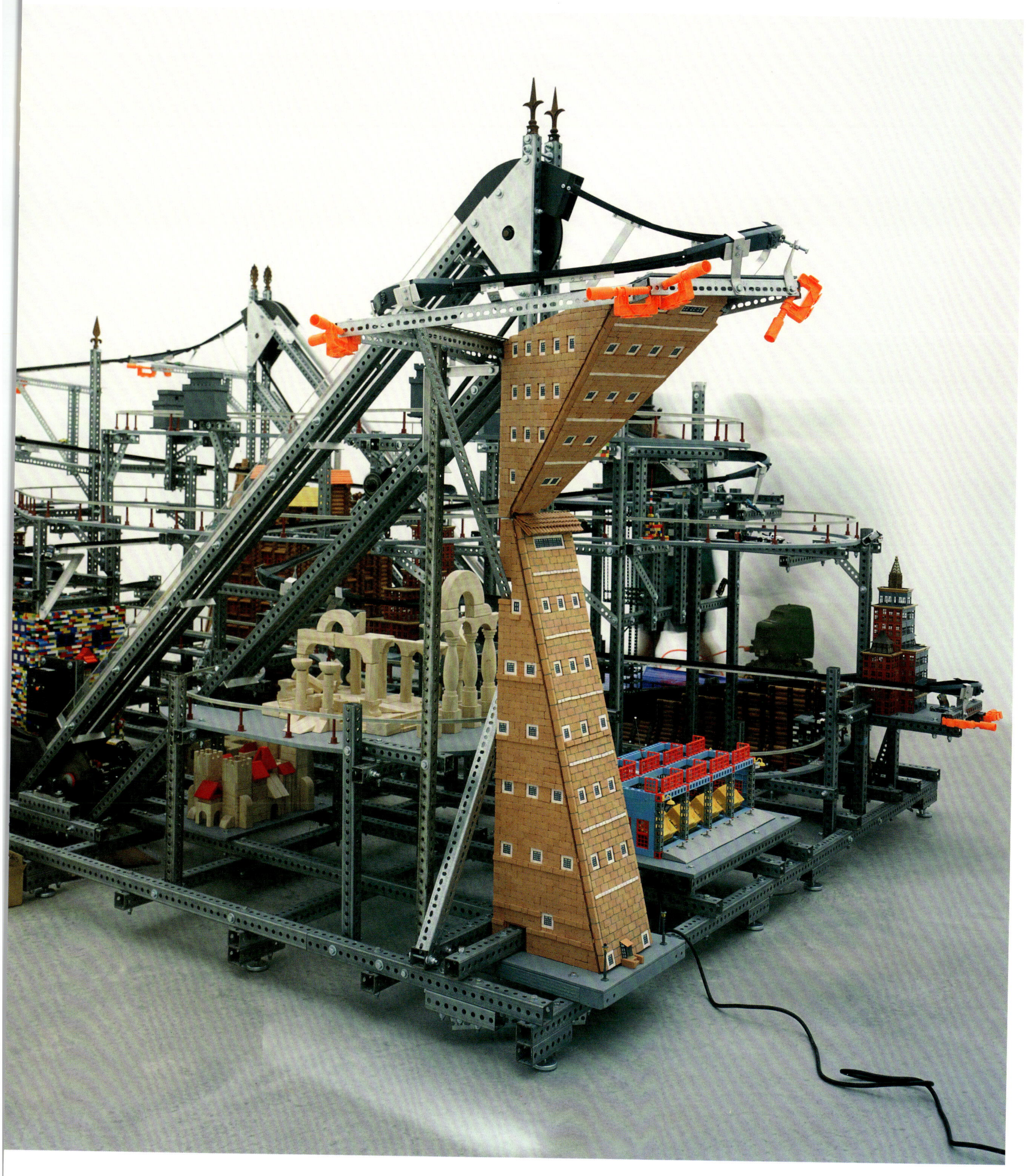

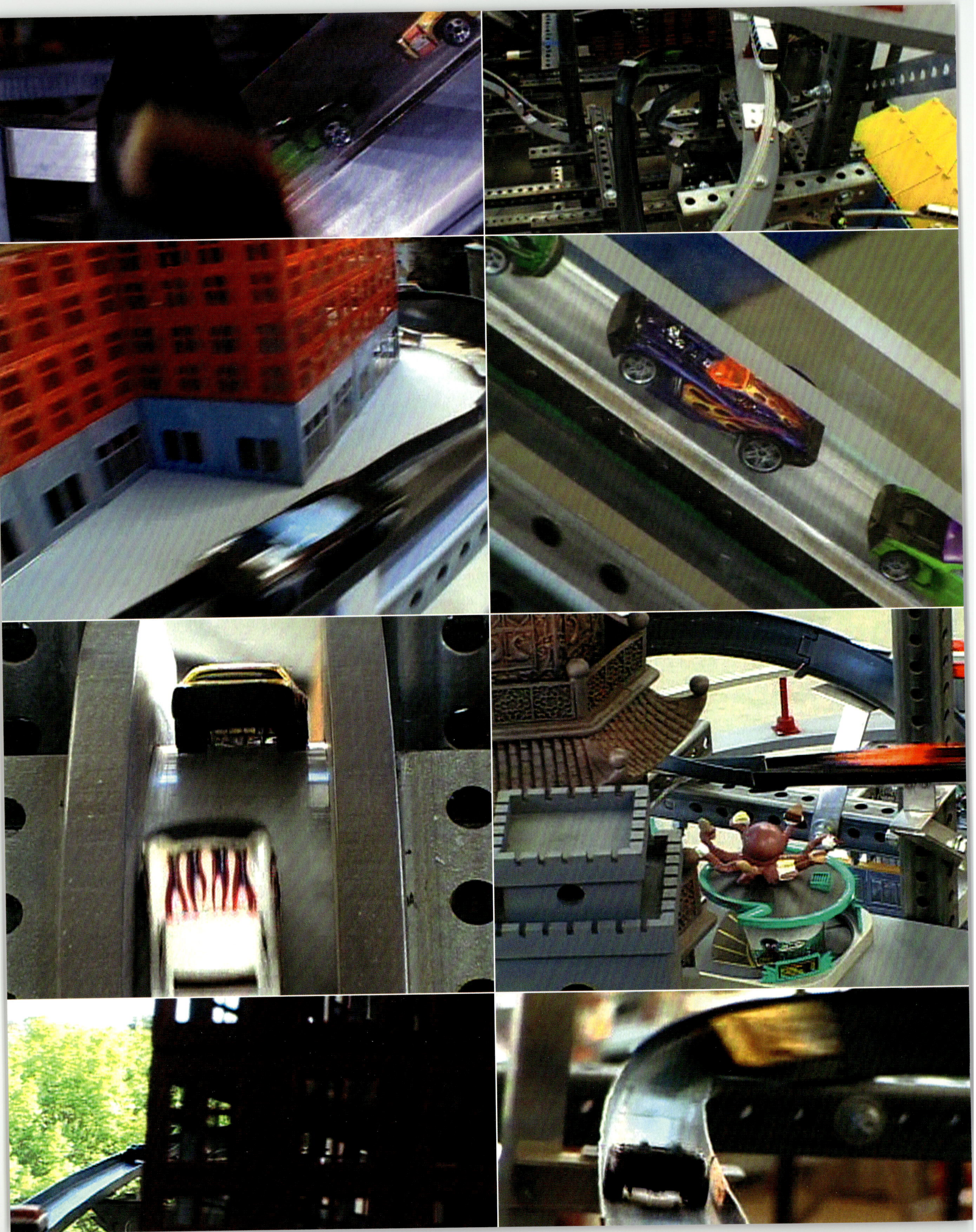

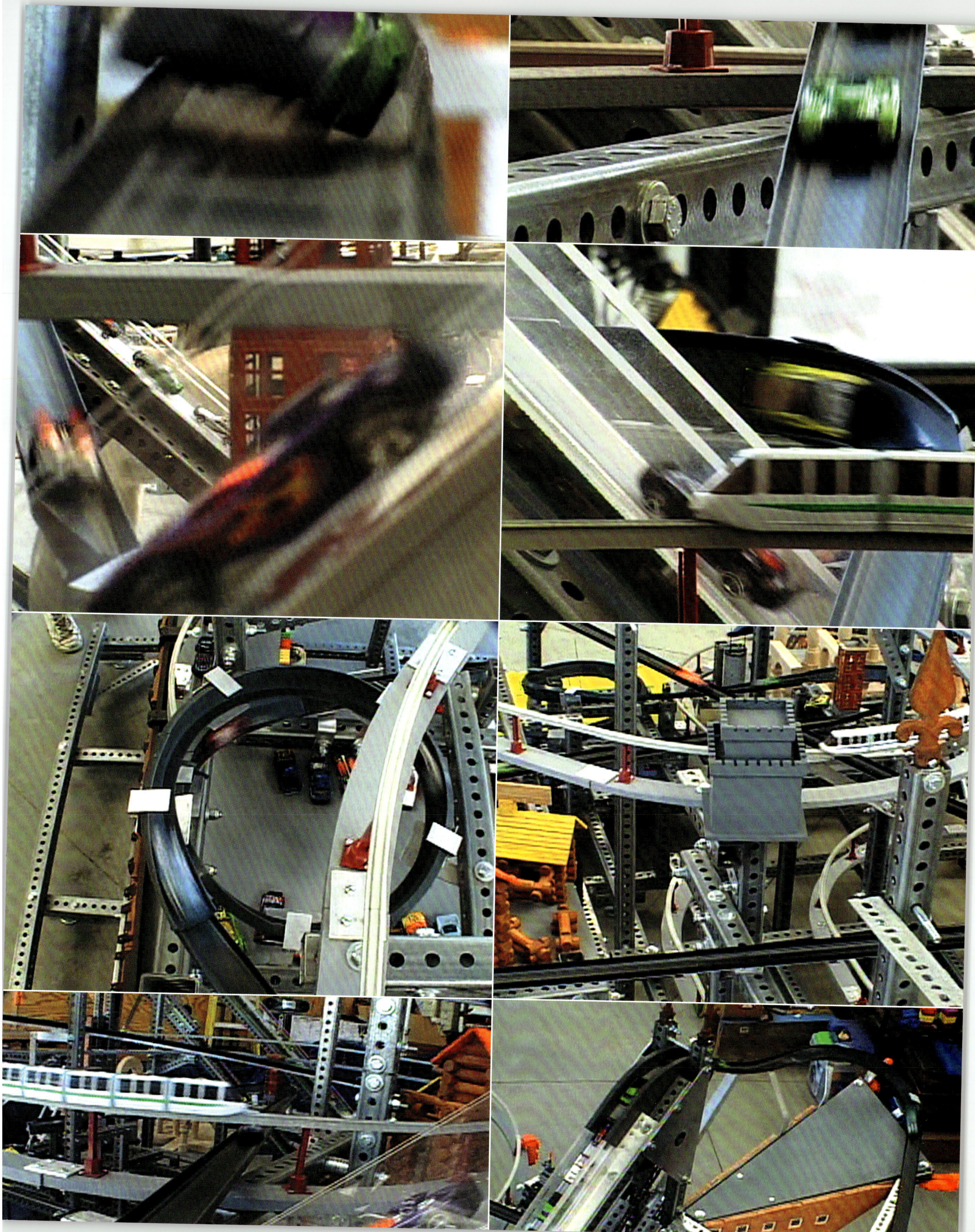

Fred Hoffman

'My art is an examination of reality …
I think my art is an inquiry, which is what all art is about.'
Chris Burden, 1974

Chris Burden: Some Reflections

The first time I met Chris Burden he was lost in the process of setting up a new artwork. While he was friendly, it was difficult for him to verbally communicate much of anything about what was going on. Here was a man of action rather than words, about to unveil the first major sculpture to link up with his now historic performances of the early 1970s. This was over 25 years ago, in 1979, when as an art critic for *Artforum* I went to the Rosamund Felsen Gallery in West Hollywood to review the first exhibition of *The Big Wheel*. I met Chris while he was adjusting something on his motorcycle for its eventual engagement with his giant flywheel construction. From that day on, every time I have been around Chris as he worked on his art I have witnessed a man who is completely and totally absorbed in his work.

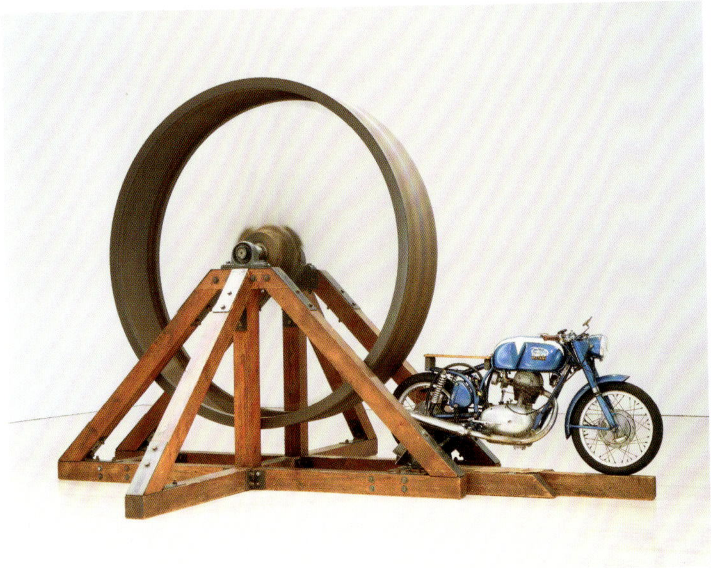

The Big Wheel 1979

Unbeknownst to me at the time of my initial encounter with the artist, I was about to begin an active dialogue with Chris concerning his art production. In 1981 I included *Warship*, the first of his ship assemblages, in a group exhibition titled 'California: A Sense of Individualism', which I curated at L.A. Louver Gallery in Venice, California. After starting my first print and multiples company, New City Editions, Chris and I began considering a possible production project to undertake together. Between 1984 and 1987 we collaborated on the construction of a group of small cardboard submarines we envisioned as a series. After completing this group of works, we realized that they would make an important statement as one overall installation. These works subsequently became *All the Submarines of the United States of America*, the subject of my first gallery exhibition with Chris. Approximately three years ago, I again undertook a project with the artist for the production of a series of bridges conceived as multiples. Based on the original Erector set elements, we recreated the parts in stainless steel and used these for the creation of seven bridges, ranging in size from 12 × 18 inches to 9 × 34 feet. While my background as an academic makes me fully equipped to think critically about Chris's work, I feel that my unique position as a collaborator with the artist has given me insights into his creative process as an innovator in sculpture, conceptual and installation art.

I

The common perception of Chris Burden is tied to his work as a performance artist who has undertaken a diverse array of actions, all placing his own body at risk to harm, injury and possibly even death. In fact, over the last 30 years this artist's output has taken many forms, ranging from very large room-sized installations to more collectable sculptural objects, from works based on conceptual documentation to the creation of visionary drawings. All of these diverse modes of practice address a number of important art historical, social, political and cultural concerns. No one work or period of his career captures the totality of Burden's oeuvre. It has been interesting to watch the art world's response to Chris Burden's heterogeneity of production. At times, even respected cognoscenti have expressed dismay at the disparity between practices and periods. On more than one occasion I have been asked by fans and supporters to reconcile 'unrelated' objects or actions. Coupled with whatever response I may have provided is a chuckle, my means of expressing the challenge of negotiating the complex relations of form and content that characterize Burden's work. It is instructive to identify some of the general operating principles that inform and drive the artist's formal and conceptual choices.

Chris Burden's creative motivation can best be described as the pursuit of knowledge. Whether he is planning the assembly of a group of urban street lamps, engineering an almost life-size bridge construction, or designing a one-person automobile, Chris Burden approaches each project with intense observation, reflection and scrutiny. With full acknowledgement and respect for the mystery of the unknown, he initiates each work with a need for inquiry and invention reminiscent of an Enlightenment thinker.

With complete confidence and conviction in the possibility of discovering something new and/or unexpected, the artist then proceeds by what may be characterized as an intuitive investigation. Combining the planning of an inventor with the inspiration of dreams, Burden seeks to realize in constructed form the intangibles of imagination and empathy, the fantastical and the socially engaged.

II

As noted above, I first came to know Chris Burden personally in 1979 when he exhibited *The Big Wheel,* a 6,000-pound cast iron flywheel mounted in a vertical position on a wooden support structure of 6 × 6-inch timbers. Accompanying this unexpected and mesmerizing object was an Italian Benelli 250cc motorcycle, positioned in front of the flywheel. The back wheel of the bike had been raised off the floor and suspended by a small wooden device. Upon closer inspection one realized that this device's function was to enable the bike's back wheel to become engaged with the larger flywheel construction. The first exhibition of this key work was at the Rosamund Felsen Gallery on La Cienega Boulevard in Los Angeles. At that time this street was still the main place to see contemporary art in that city. It was more or less the town's 'gallery row.' The Felsen Gallery was located at the end of a long driveway, set back from the heavily trafficked street. Off to the side of the main viewing room the artist had installed the *Big Wheel* in a fairly tight space, approximately 25 × 15 feet, with reasonably high ceilings. Walking down the driveway and entering this space, my initial impression of this massive object was somewhere between shock and wonder. I recall that when I first encountered the piece, it was at rest. Burden and one assistant were huddled over the motorcycle, making some adjustments to its motor. Soon thereafter Burden had mounted the bike and the engine was fired up. The sound was overwhelming, significantly enhanced by reverberation pounding against the confines of the room and heightened by the sheer improbability of having to deal with a roaring motorcycle in an art gallery. Burden slowly and methodically revved the engine, seeming to take the bike to its maximum capacity in first, then second, then third gears and finally opening the throttle full blast. As the speed of the engine increased, the artist maintained his total and undivided focus on achieving the maximum amount of horsepower from each gear. The sound was almost deafening. It was both fascinating and forbidding. While you were physically drawn to the power that this vehicle was creating, your ears rebelled against your eyes' desire to witness the absorbing spectacle. As the bike's back wheel generated torque, it was transferred to the flywheel, both increasing speed in unison. Burden maintained the bike's maximum speed in its highest gear for a couple of minutes, after which time he decelerated and turned off the bike, rocking it forward to disengage from the wheel. By this time the flywheel had taken on an overwhelming presence of its own. Here again it became a matter of attraction and repulsion. Watching a 6,000-pound flywheel spinning at about 30 miles per hour is hardly something that you are prepared to experience so close at hand,

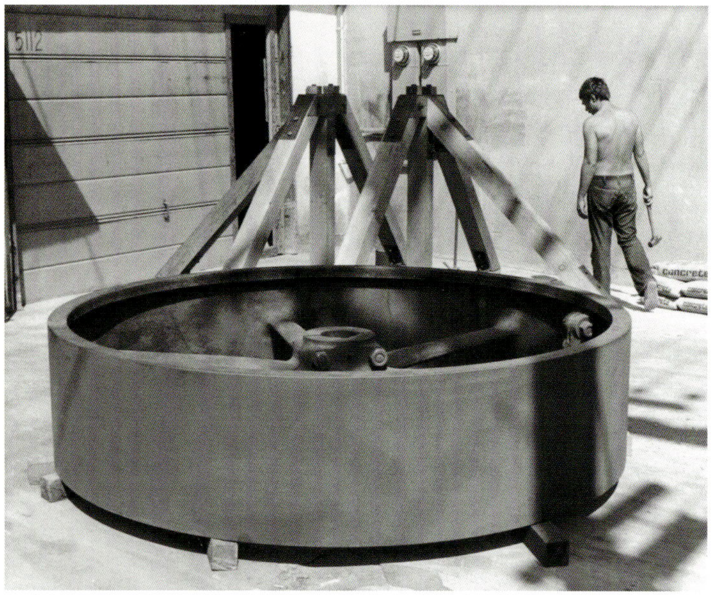

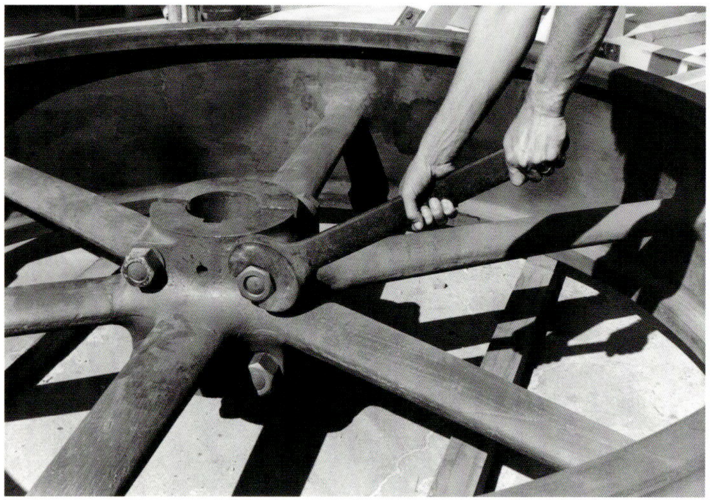

The Big Wheel under construction 1979

let alone in an interior space. Not only was the size of the object formidable, but now all kinds of thoughts raced through my mind, especially what might happen if the object's force caused it to become separated from its supporting base. Visions of the wheel busting out of the gallery and racing down the street were just one of my fantasies. What was particularly disconcerting was how quiet this massive object was even at its peak power and speed. The sound coming off of the wheel was like a light, whispering wind. It was a sound that was not only seductive, but also virtually hypnotic. You just stood there as if in a trance, consumed, neither moving nor talking. All of the fantasies of danger and destruction were nullified by the actual peacefulness of one's sensory experience, which was heightened to an intense degree through contrast with the previous roar of the engine as Burden ground through the gears. The conflict between the thoughts of the mind and the feelings of the body and senses seemed to be resolved, ultimately, in favor of visceral response.

I have seen five or six subsequent installations of this work, both in museums and in my own art gallery in 1989. While every installation of this work has been exciting, none has been more memorable than the initial experience. Obviously the first time you encounter something as unusual and unexpected as *The Big Wheel*, the reaction will be deeply impressed into sensory memory. In the setting of Rosamund Felsen's gallery, the scale of the space and proximity of city traffic conjured up visions of the artwork's crashing escape into the world outside. In this particular setting you never forgot that 'the real world' was just behind the white walls. The potential for destruction seemed much more than an aesthetic sensation and it is this feeling of sublime danger that Burden uses to disrupt any passive consumption of his art.

III

When I saw this work at its initial showing, I did not recognize how much this single exhibition marked a decisive turning point in the artist's career.[1] Up to that moment Chris Burden's work had been focused primarily on performance. While *The Big Wheel* (along with the *B-Car* created four years earlier) clearly acknowledged the artist's earlier concerns, it also marked the arrival of the artist's engagement with dynamic objects. While *Five Day Locker Piece* (1971), *Shoot* (1971), *Doorway to Heaven* (1973), and *Trans-fixed* (1974) each helped usher in and define the dematerialization of art in the 1970s, *The Big Wheel* announced the artist's pursuit of the materialization of ideas. Now, some 25 years later, it becomes clear that Burden's entire career has addressed the nature of force, both bodily and mechanical. Culminating, then, with *The Big Wheel*, conceptual motivation is resolved

1 Almost concurrently with this exhibition, the artist presented *The Reason for the Neutron Bomb* in New York (1979). While not as object-oriented as *The Big Wheel*, this installation also had strong sculptural properties.

through the more traditional manipulation of object and form.

From the moment of my initial encounter with *The Big Wheel* two themes quickly emerged. First, Chris Burden's approach to object making/object presentation was consistent with many of the fundamental attitudes of the Minimalists of the late 1960s. Especially notable was Burden's purist sensibility, driving him to seek out and subsequently present only basic and essential forms. For example, an underlying economy of means is evident in the artist's use of his own motorcycle as the source of power for his massive flywheel. This is equally apparent in *The Reason for the Neutron Bomb* (1979) where 50,000 nickels embossed with the portrait of President Lincoln are arranged in a highly ordered configuration, with a single matchstick placed on top of each coin. Taken together, this vast plane of tiny identical components creates a unified, holistic field. This project demonstrates his astute understanding of the aesthetic possibilities offered by the Minimalist object-makers.

It is informative to compare Burden's piece with Walter De Maria's *Broken Kilometer* (1979). Both works share a formal concern with part to whole relations that ultimately resolve into an overall, field-like composition. Both works also recognize the non-hierarchical relationship between part to whole in Pollock's dripped maze, where no individual stroke or gesture distinguishes itself (as being more or less important) from any other stroke. In the case of Burden and in contrast to De Maria, however, the creation of a 'holistic field' as the organizing principle for the presentation of a room-sized sculptural installation serves his goal of metaphorically commenting upon a particular political reality. That is, Burden's work addresses the power and might of the Russian nuclear arsenal at the height of the Cold War. In his use of such rudimentary forms as the Indian Head nickel and simple wooden matchsticks, now presented with such insightful formal clarity, Burden is able to shed the weight of the tired and used-up illustrative symbolism from which modernism sought so desperately to escape. In his simplicity, the artist has been able to re-inject social and political content back into the art-making dialogue.

Chris Burden's concern for formal clarity also directed the evolution of *All the Submarines of the United States of America*. Continuing his interest in the theme of warfare, which he initiated with *The Reason for the Neutron Bomb* in 1979, he began producing assemblage sculptures of warships in 1981 (as will become clear from both this text and this publication, the warfare theme is of continuing interest to the artist). As part of the installation of *Large Glass Ship* of 1983, which for the most part consisted of large shards of broken sheets of glass, Burden included four small model cardboard submarines painstakingly crafted by hand. Not only had the artist chosen the most generic of materials – cardboard – as the skin of his submarines, but with only a few small pieces of wire and parts of toothpicks he captured enough essential details of form to make them feel credible and believable as surrogates. A year later two more of these subs made an appearance in the second and smaller of the glass ship installations. Fascinated by these small paper forms, Burden envisioned a much larger grouping of these objects. While it was surely possible for the artist to continue his painstaking creation of these miniature models, the production of numerous examples became much more viable when the artist approached New City Editions to consider a large-scale project. Agreeing that the cardboard submarines would be distributed in different-sized groupings placed in vitrines, the artist and his collaborators produced around 625 of the objects in two years. While in retrospect this production seemed rather straightforward, it was, in fact, laborious, tedious and a test of commitment. Realizing the output from 'the sub factory' was like running a marathon: lots of preparation, pacing and resolve. In the end it became apparent that there was a much bigger idea contained in this group of objects that went beyond the distribution of a set of beautiful, intriguing multiples. What the collaborators recognized was that a display of all the submarines produced would not only create a truly captivating installation, but would drive home the intended meaning of the project. While each submarine model existed as a simple, almost generic surrogate, the experience of all 625 submarines installed in a unified field could create a sense of the anonymous, inexorable power inspired by real weaponry and warfare.

Even in some of Chris Burden's most 'obsessive' installations – such as *A Tale of Two Cities* (1981) and *Pizza City* (1996) – in which additive and accumulative processes dictate decisions as to overall form, one always senses that a rigorous minimalist-deductive process underlies his aesthetic decisions. When a work contains tens of thousands of minute pieces, each is approached with the same concern for its essential nature and how it might best support or enhance the overall effect that the artist hopes to convey. Burden's resolution in defining detail and organizing minutiae became evident to this writer when he accompanied the artist to Miami for a later installation of *A Tale of Two Cities* in 1984 at the Lowe Museum of Art. After a couple of days of preparation by the artist and a small team of assistants in which a general configuring of the larger landmasses was established, the artist spent 72 continuous hours first mapping and then methodically placing one tiny object after the next into the installation, systematically building up groupings of toy figures, buildings and landscape elements into panoramas. In retrospect, the density and complexity Burden was able to achieve feels like the same aesthetic that contemporary animators have been able to capture through digital technology. Here in the 'pre-digital age' Burden literally lost himself in his work. In fact, his resolve was so complete that over the time that I observed him at work, he barely recognized my presence. Only by having maintained such a high degree of focus, which in turn sustained his commitment to each object and act of placement, was the artist able to achieve the resulting look and feel he desired.

As a somewhat different example of Chris Burden's aesthetic rigor, we can turn to his interest over the last several years in the toy Meccano-Erector set building system and, specifically, its applications for creating both small and large-scale bridge constructions. With the standardized Meccano-Erector set parts, Burden saw the possibility of using a pre-existing system. Created almost 100 years ago for the purpose of enabling children to become acquainted first-hand with the technologies then driving Western industrialization, Meccano-Erector provided Burden the means of generating a series of new, highly refined and totally unexpected sculptural forms. Simply, Burden saw the potential for combining architectonic and cultural references, technology and geography, through a medium that had previously signified 'toy' and 'play'. The objects Burden has created out of this 'toy technology' have enabled the artist to link his creative pursuits to both the historical past and to the uninhibited, highly intuitive life of the child. Take just one of several examples, possibly the most radical of all of the artist's bridge constructions – the large *Curved Bridge* (2003). Although the production of a group of bridges using newly created stainless steel reproductions of the original Erector parts was conceived for the purpose of creating modest-sized works of art to be distributed in editions, the artist's initial use of the material necessarily led him to consider other, even more ambitious projects. Thus, when the Beverly Hills branch of the Gagosian Gallery proposed an exhibition of the stainless steel bridges, Burden immediately seized the opportunity to push the Erector set technology to its limits. Inspired by a small photographic reproduction in an historical study of Western bridge design, the *Curved Bridge* uses these simple parts in such an ambitious fashion that the resulting bridge defies logic and rational expectations. The artist's creative process became a study in how far he could stretch the structural and aesthetic capacities of the material. Equipped with the confidence that the act of construction itself would lead to a set of as yet unrecognized formal solutions, the artist committed himself to seeing how far he could extend the physical and compositional potentialities of the work. Not resting content until his investigation had been fully 'played out', the resulting object manifests a purity and simplicity that could never have been envisioned at the outset of the process. While it reads as a 'bridge', it exists equally as a pure abstract form. In going further than any of his previous bridge designs in liberating form from historical-narrative content, it spans a similar gap between art and life as that achieved in the early performative works.[2] Without the artist's trust in the process – that his combined technical/formal investigation would lead him into new, unexpected terrain – the resulting radicalism of *Curved Bridge* would never have been achieved.

IV

Chris Burden approaches a subject in much the same way as a scientist. This implies that while Burden never abandons his identity as an artist, he applies an objective method of ordering knowledge as it pertains to his aesthetic aims and he is committed to the 'rational and logical investigation of the concepts in which a particular phenomena (whether it be a form, a system, an idea) is expressed'. Burden goes where the data from the examination of a problem leads him. His aesthetic decisions are often reached by means of deductive reasoning. For example, if the artist's concern is the creation of a multi-layered track and self-retrieval system for Hot Wheels cars (*Metropolis*, 2004), his design solution (the shape, height, angles and curves of the track) will be based on countless hours of testing the capacities of Hot Wheels cars. The form of the resulting construction represents the labor of his investigation. Take Burden's new installation of early twentieth-century urban street lamps. Their current installation surrounding Burden's studio is the result of the artist's astute recognition of the innate power of these forms. This recognition resulted from the artist's slow and tireless process of accumulating over 150 of these objects – both entire lamps and their disparate parts – over a period of several years. Because this process was so slow, it enabled the artist to recognize aesthetic properties in the lamps that might otherwise have been overlooked. While the artist obviously recognized the historical significance of these urban, public objects, his method of inquiry also enabled him to discover new aesthetic, formal and even psychic possibilities in their individual structure and their mass arrangement. What I find particularly intriguing and relevant is that throughout the process of accumulation, the artist provided little if any explanation of his vision for these objects' eventual display. He simply moved forward, more or less systematically, with his goal of acquiring the maximum number of objects possible. Being around Burden throughout this period, one never questioned his intent. His irrefutable conviction seemed to negate any doubts. From the outset I do not think that even Burden knew what he would do with these objects. It was not even clear how many he

2 Paul Schimmel offered this comment during the opening for the first exhibition of *Curved Bridge* at Gagosian Gallery, Beverly Hills, July 10–August 29, 2003.

3 Sir William Cecil Dampier, *A History of Science* (Cambridge: Cambridge University Press, 1952): xiii.

could potentially acquire. Nonetheless, with an instinctive leap of faith, he made a significant commitment (time, energy, money) to the multi-year project of their acquisition, restoration, reassembly, and re-installation. From the outset Chris Burden clearly appreciated the beauty of these individual forms. While fascinated by their formal qualities, he never could have imagined their potential to become such an expressive and monumental gesture until he had assembled a corpus of individual specimens into a dense unified field. Without the mindset of the scientist, it is hard to imagine the artist trusting that his initial instincts would result in something new and unexpected. What Burden has therefore achieved is an installation that pays tribute to these objects' historical function while at the same time becoming an expression of his own individual identity. That is, in the way that Chris Burden has closely clustered these now almost 100-year-old urban street lamps around his studio, they function as a beacon directed at both the surrounding mountains and the heavens above. They become the artist's declaration of his own presence and vitality. Their illumination and radiance become Chris Burden's means of declaring that he is alive and well, charged with energy and fully engaged with the surrounding world.

Considering those factors which separate Burden's working process from that of the scientist, foremost among them is the playful way in which he approaches a new work or idea. Toward this end it is not uncharacteristic to find Burden seemingly absorbed in an imaginary game, gathering and manipulating objects for an unspecified and open-ended period of time. Such a process can go on for weeks, months, and in some cases years. Often, the objects Burden uses have been collected for years prior to being considered by the artist as part of a designated sculpture or installation. At what point Burden's playfulness shifts to 'art production' is hard to assess. There is no predetermined program that guides him towards completion of a work. Burden's process is slow and intensely considered and the development of a project is not determined by external factors such as exhibition commitments or the pressure to produce for the market.

Again, let me recount another experience with the artist. When visiting Burden and his wife, the sculptor Nancy Rubins, in their newly-completed home in the late 1980s, one noticed that the living room was beginning to fill up with thousands of collected objects such as toys, scale model buildings and figures, and accompanying landscape elements. The initial groupings were set up on a number of tables placed in their living room. Burden was creating a slice of the ideal small city, rendered more or less like an architectural model in Z scale, or 24 feet to one mile. As surfaces became filled with objects, additional areas were installed, allowing the city to grow. Soon, the tops of the filing cabinets

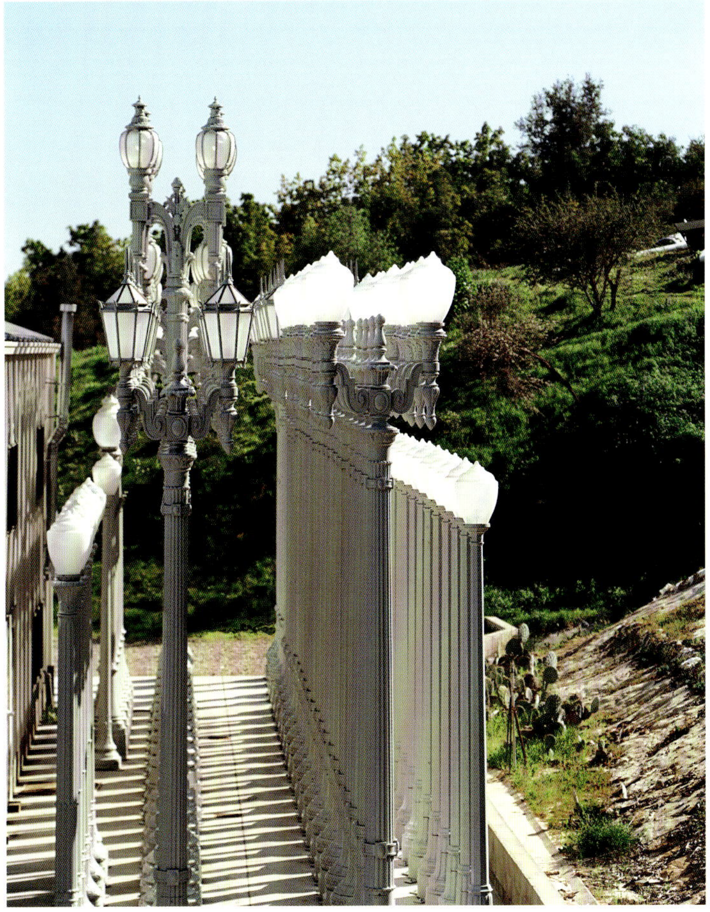

Urban Light 2005 (detail)

lining portions of the living room became extensions of the artist's playful accumulation and arrangement of objects. While this project started with the objective of rendering something fairly specific, the actual process of collecting and placing inevitably led the artist to create vignettes and accumulations of form that he had not initially envisioned or expected to include. The process of building up this extended tableau occupied Burden over the following four to five years. When you visited his home, he would rarely call attention to anything he had done in the living room. You pretty much had to explore on your own and attempt to get him to comment on what he was doing. While this amazing accumulation was there to explore, Burden never referred to it as an 'artwork'. Then one day, really without much explanation, he realized that his ideal architectural model had become transformed into 'Los Angeles' – a densely-packed section of an urban setting sprawling out into suburbs and then rural environs. For the outsider, the objects arranged on these surfaces seemed to refer to differing, at times competing, cultural or social geographies. For example, one group of objects might form a complex and dense section of urban landscape; another might refer to an army garrison; another to a housing complex; and yet another to a more rural environment. What had been confined for a great period of time to private play had now taken on a specific conceptual focus and become an object/installation for eventual public display. It still remains unclear what triggered this change of focus. With this shift, all kinds of issues had to be dealt with, including how to transform tens of thousands of playful, fanciful objects into a manageable (secure, permanent, transportable) assemblage. These practical issues were only considered once Burden switched mindsets from 'play pen' to art. I would venture to note that had he started with the idea of an artwork, the resulting accumulation could never have contained the feeling of playfulness and immediacy that the final work conveys. This work, an accumulation of 25 tables, is known as *Pizza City*. It is the artist's representation of the concept of a 'slice of life', transposed from the 'oven' of his private domain to a space of aesthetic consumption, the art museum.

V

Chris Burden has from the outset attempted to close the distance between art and life by challenging the viewer to confront his discomfort with things either unknown or considered taboo to our daily lived experience. Pollock's paintings expanded modernist pictorial aesthetics by making the emotive content of a painting more credible. Chris Burden went further by introducing the experience of his own mortal flesh into the creative arena. He did this through the number of challenges he presented to his own body. In so doing, the element of risk became a central concern in the judgment and recognition of the creative act.

When Burden shifts away from performance beginning in the late 1970s and throughout his subsequent art production, this same element of risk plays a key role in both what he produces and how we have come to evaluate it. Foremost, Burden rarely if ever takes on a project that from the outset has any guarantee of successfully being realized. Because so many of his projects are conceived as a challenge to what is commonly considered possible, the element of chance and the effects of duration on the structuring of the work link Chris Burden's objects and installations to his historic performances. What both share is the commitment to search for a deeper, contextual meaning that develops as new issues present themselves in the course of both the creative process and the activity of viewer reception. Along with Burden, the audience is prompted to re-evaluate its aesthetic objectives and goals. This way of working comes out of a world-view of 'non-attachment' and is accompanied by the constantly gnawing risk of failure. While the artist may start down one path, his careful scrutiny and evaluation of newfound realities as they present themselves reduces any guarantee of where his analysis will eventually lead him. Just as there are no guarantees when you place yourself in a locker for five days, or drop a live 220-volt wire into a pool of water beneath a ladder upon which you are standing, there are equally no guarantees when you rather innocently, almost half-consciously, start placing objects one after another on tables day and night after day and night. Driving all these activities and any resulting objects is an underlying commitment to present something (an action, a form) that is credible in terms of daily, lived experience. In performing these acts of incremental negotiation, Burden invests his objects and installations with what I like to call 'an aesthetic of plausibility'. While we surely have neither the background nor experience of the artist with his diverse array of interests and subjects, we feel comfortable around his work, sensing that we could have encountered these objects and installations numerous times throughout our lives. They perform in ways which we expect objects to perform. They seem rational, mostly logical. While they may depart from common expectation in terms of scale, complexity and choice of materials, objects such as *The Big Wheel*, *Metropolis*, *The Flying Steamroller* (1996), *Samson* (1985) and even *Medusa's Head* (1991) share enough features with the objects we use and confront on a daily basis to cause us neither fear nor alarm. While Chris Burden's artworks may not be part of our quotidian experience in the way that simple readymades – or even 'Koonsian' objects – might claim to be, they nonetheless feel basic and real. What ensures the plausibility of his projects is the artist's highly deductive working procedures. By applying critical-analytic methods in his decision making processes, Chris Burden guarantees that his production is not speculative fantasy. Rather, because the artist's forms share enough features with objects and experiences we encounter on a daily basis, we trust that his work will lead us to a deeper understanding of ourselves and our world.

Let me introduce one final example from Chris Burden's recent production in order to convey how an 'aesthetic of plausibility' underlies both his artistic intent and the art world's reception of his efforts. Recently Burden was approached by the Museum Boijmans Van Beuningen in Rotterdam to propose a new work. In keeping with his customary practice, Burden began by visiting both the city and the museum. The notion of 'visiting' already has some interesting connotations for this artist's way of realizing a new work. While you think you are focused on the realities of the place you are visiting (observing/assessing), the reality is that you encounter that place carrying the baggage of all your thoughts, impressions and feelings of the places from which you've come. Chris Burden has always recognized this truth. His response to the environment of Rotterdam was in part a reflection on some specific concerns of his daily life in the remote environs of the Santa Monica coastal mountain range. Maybe it was the reality of Rotterdam's own connection to the sea that caused Chris Burden to conjure up thoughts of his own 'backyard', for the artist seemed to immediately respond to his hosts by proposing an outdoor sculptural installation which commented on both an important aspect of the local environment as well as on the artist's own residence some 6000 miles away. Chris Burden's own words best convey his perspective:

I live in a rural section of Los Angeles and several times a week, for the last 15 years, I hike with my dogs into the hills and along a dirt road that follows a ridgeline. There are no houses and – usually – no people on this one-hour walk. The road dead-ends at the top of a small mountain that has a 360-degree view stretching from the Los Angeles basin to the Pacific Ocean and the San Fernando Valley. At the end of the road there are approximately 11 derelict and abandoned cars and trucks. These automobiles date from the 1960s and represent the golden era of

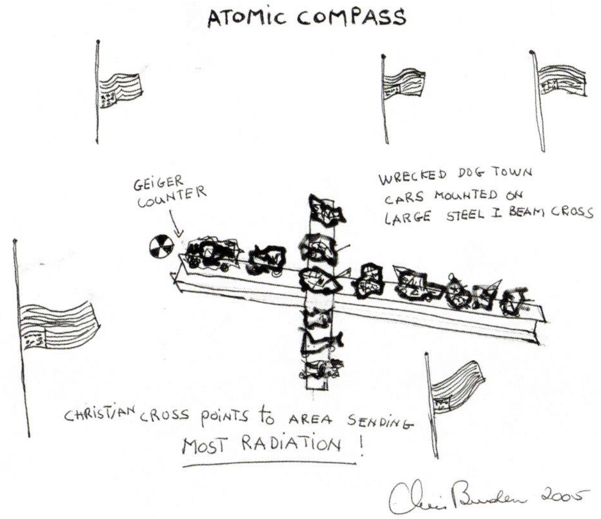

Atomic Compass I(a) 2005
Ink on paper, 8½ × 11 inches

American automobile manufacturing. They are heavy and overbuilt. One is a Lincoln continental, like the car J.F. Kennedy was assassinated in. The chrome plating is so thick on many of the parts, it has not yet started to rust. The cars have become filled with sticks and debris from animal nests and the cars are covered with graffiti, such as DOGTOWN and VALS SUCK, referring to local gang and surfer lingo. These decomposing carcasses are of a great curiosity to me and lend a somewhat ominous and spooky feeling to the area. People go to this area to be alone, take drugs, or to work out their hostilities on the derelict cars.

The *Atomic Compass* would consist of a large I-beam structure in the shape of a cross. The 11 or so DOGTOWN automobiles would be mounted onto the large I-beam cross, like precious gemstones on a royal scepter. At the center of the cross, a pivot would be installed and the whole swinging cross would be laid flat, a few feet off the apex of the cross and connected to an electric motor so that the cross would swing towards any detected radiation. ... In addition, numerous large flagpoles would be placed around the park, flying the US flag, the Stars and Stripes. The flags would not only be mounted upside down, an international sign of distress, they would also be flown half-mast, a sign of mourning.[4]

According to this proposal, Chris Burden would create a giant compass responding to the movement of radioactive material through the port and connecting waterways of Rotterdam. In large part this work is a strong commentary on the fragility of the world's political and social order and the increasing risk of mass, worldwide destruction. Secondarily the piece functions as a critique of the ever-present power and reach of the United States. My immediate concern, however, is the artist's choice of objects and the materials used to convey his intended meaning. Through the utilization of a group of objects with which the artist has had such long term personal interaction, Burden demonstrates the real-world plausibility of nuclear environmental threat. The concept of an *Atomic Compass*, which in itself might be viewed as an elaborate folly, is brought back into the realm of credibility. The artist is completely confident that this totally unexpected construction, with no precedent, will be able to convey his intended metaphors and associations. While old Lincoln Continentals might not be part of the daily Dutch experience, Burden rightfully understands the symbolic potential of these burnt out wrecks shipped from the Santa Monica mountains. Not only does their current state conjure up associations of both economic and psychological decay, but in the process of slowly rusting away, they make subtle reference to the long half-life of nuclear material.

None of the elements that would make up this work are really unexpected or extra-ordinary. Because each component comes from our daily lived experience, we accept their presence even when the combination of elements and their shift in scale invite a reassessment of our simple acceptance. We are curious and intuitively motivated to explore further and at the same time our 'better' sense reminds us to be cautious. Having achieved this tension between 'do' and 'don't', Burden's object comes alive, challenging us psychically, even spiritually. In so doing we cannot help but investigate the social and even political content of what we have confronted. Because Burden's projects are so convincingly able to stimulate our curiosity and passion, we are led away from the doubts and fears that are the residue of our attachment to the conclusions of our rational mind.

4 Chris Burden, *Atomic Compass*, 2005. Unpublished text by the artist presented as part of his proposal to the Museum Boijmans Van Beuningen, Rotterdam.

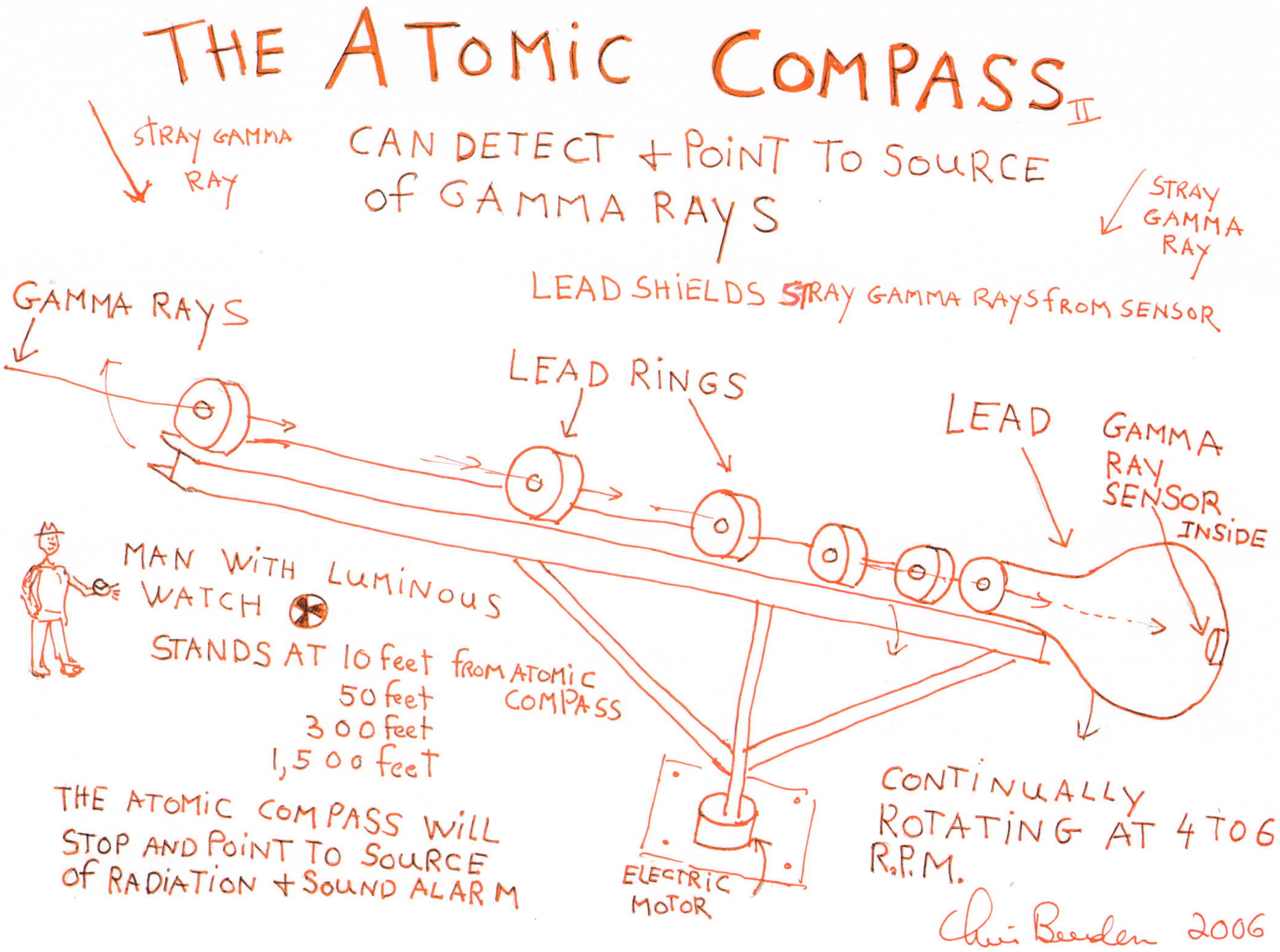

The Atomic Compass II 2006
Ink on paper, 8¼ × 11⅝ inches

Chris Burden's Ghost Ship

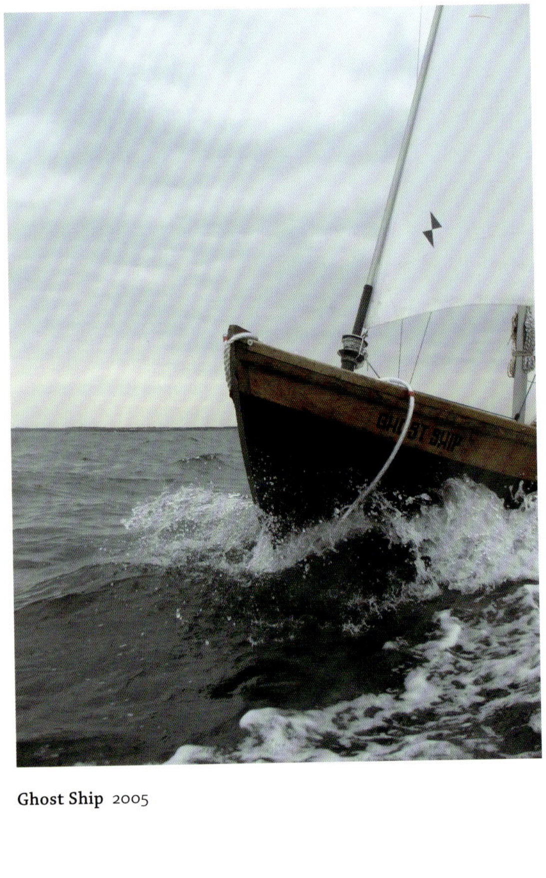

Ghost Ship 2005

In the last week of July 2005 the Newcastle upon Tyne and Gateshead quayside hosted the Tall Ships Race, an annual event celebrating nineteenth-century maritime technology with all the associated scale, power and bravado. Thousands of visitors lined the River Tyne to admire the, well, very tall ships amid a carnival atmosphere. The flotilla of over 100 ships, their decks filled with activity, left Newcastle to a backdrop of waving flags, music and more onlookers than the city ever expected. As the ships disappeared from view and the crowds departed, a small boat sailed past the Baltic Centre for Contemporary Art and through the specially raised Millennium Bridge. At odds with the fuss and hub of activity on the sailing vessels, this simple boat, its deck empty, quietly made its way up the river. Those watching made a double-take as the crewless craft slipped through the waters.

The poetic quietude of this moment took those who witnessed it by surprise, not simply because of the seeming impossibility for a boat to operate with no one on board. Self-sustainable yet vulnerable, it evoked some kind of unexpected emotion – a sort of mix of the romantic myths of loss associated with the sea intermingled with the possibilities of the power of modesty over spectacle.

This was the arrival of Chris Burden's *Ghost Ship*, a reworking of a piece entitled *Three Ghost Ships* made for the 1991 Spoleto Festival, in which three sailboats were built to the specifications of marine architect Phillip Bolger. Often referred to as 'instant boats', the designs were cut out of plywood parts following pre-drawn patterns, each numbered for easy assembly. These simple seaworthy boats are built to be reconstructed as soon as the plywood rots away. Burden designed these vessels to transport a small amount of tea from Charleston (home to US air, naval, and submarine bases) to Plymouth, England (from where the

Mayflower left to take a group of Puritans to what was referred to as the New World), unmanned. The boats had never actually encountered the sea until Locus+ invited Burden to explore the project further, this time using one boat in the context of the Tall Ships Race.

Powered by the wind in two sails (main and jib) *Ghost Ship* left from Fair Isle on its maiden voyage, traveling over 400 miles south to reach Newcastle upon Tyne eight days later. A small island in the Shetlands bordered by cliffs rising to almost 200 meters, Fair Isle has been a shipping landmark for thousands of years. The coastline and surrounding rough sea conditions have made it the location of many shipwrecks. *Ghost Ship* was hand-built following a traditional Shetland design, known as a sixareen, developed for fishing in the local, difficult waters that the skipper would navigate using the sun, stars, sea swell and wind direction. The ship measures just over 29 feet in length, with the inner skeleton made from oak and the fluid lines of the hull crafted from Scottish larch. Tradition deems the sixareen to be built by eye, working from the notion that 'if it looks right, it is right'.

In *Ghost Ship* this long history of boat-building is brought into conversation with new technology. Beneath deck-level transparent sheeting, the hull holds a laptop and a GPS system. Way-points were designated and located digitally, mapping out the journey through the ports of Peterhead, Stonehaven, Anstruther, Eyemouth and the Farne Islands, docking each night. Keeping a distance of one kilometer, a support vessel trailed behind, ready to take radio control if needed.

All of these technical details are important, yet they reveal very little of the actual artwork itself. As an engineering experiment, the research will head off in other directions, but in terms of the work these are *effects* rather than *affects*. *Ghost Ship* engages with and exists within the question 'Where is the work?' Is it in the trip, or the boat itself, or in the factual details of the moment of arrival at 15.15 on 07/28/05? Or is it in the anecdotes that surround the journey, in the rumor of the project created through its documentation, or in the website (www.ghostship.org.uk) tracking its daily progress along the coast? Or is it in the surprise and disbelief of the individuals who caught a glimpse of the crewless boat riding the waves? Maybe it is in the act of asking if it would be possible to create a ghost ship? Individually, these elements provide only a partial sense of the project. *Ghost Ship*, importantly, is a proposition, evoking speculation and the imagination.

It brings to mind the myths of haunted wrecks that fuel fables and movies, as well as the 'ghost fleets' that sail from port to port transporting hazardous waste. In locations like Fair Isle, the ghost ship is not a fantasy, as empty fishing vessels returning to shore are a historical fact of the local economy – the treacherous local seas have resulted in the loss of many crews at sea.

As with much of Burden's practice, *Ghost Ship* pushes at the limits of perceived possibilities. Early works such as *Shoot* (1971) or *Five Day Locker Piece* (1971) took Burden to the boundaries of his own physicality, while *Samson* (1985) tested the stability of architecture and *Small Skyscraper* (2003) strained the limits of Los Angeles County building regulations. *B-Car* (1975) was an important departure from his early body-works, initiating an exploration of the boundaries of technology within the realm of the social. The goal was to make a one-passenger, four-wheel vehicle, similar in structure to a bicycle or airplane, capable of travelling 100 miles per hour at 100 miles per gallon. Using the potential of engineering and technology, *B-Car* proposed to realize the potential of existing technical achievements and, like *Ghost Ship*, the work was built through intuition. The act of creation, rather than the actual driving of the car or the sailing of the boat, is where the definition of the works lies. Proposal and process are paramount, as Burden noted in 1973: 'In some of my pieces I am setting up situations to test my own illusions or fantasies about what happens.'[1] Burden considers the success of *Ghost Ship* to be the invitation from Locus+ to return to the project and attempt to make it happen – in other words, where the edges of the known are extended.

Burden's work offers a series of proposals to be realized – some remain at that stage while others become possible as technology catches up with his ideas. In an earlier Newcastle-based project, *The Sailing Destroyer* (1990), Burden proposed to radically modify the obsolete 1943 warship HMS *Cavalier* into a sailing vessel, effectively making it invisible to enemy vessels and submarines through the elimination of the rumbles usually made by the engine. References to the sea weave through Burden's practice; examples include *The Nina, The Pinta and The Santa Maria* (1992), *All the Submarines of the United States of America* (1987), *B.C. Mexico* (1973), *Solaris* (1980) and *The Blacklisted Ten* (1991). In *Another World I* (1992) a metal Marklin model of the Eiffel Tower is turned into a fairground attraction as two 30-inch models of the famously 'unsinkable' *Titanic* are thrown into orbit around this nineteenth-century symbol of progress. Ships are markers of exchange, trade, communication, adventure, technological advancement and power. They are entirely vulnerable to the surrounding unpredictability of the sea while operating as micro-societies where particular rules and social conventions are adopted, be it the glamor of the cruise-liner or the discipline of the military. Michel Foucault described the ship as a perfect example of the heterotopia: 'a place without a place, that exists by itself, that is closed in on itself and at the same time is given over to the infinity

1 See 'The Church of Human Energy: Chris Burden', an interview with Willoughby Sharp and Liza Béar, in *Avalanche* 8 (Summer/Fall 1973): 54

of the sea.'[2] As a site both radically contingent and autonomous, the ship, like Burden's proposals, represents both possibilities and limits.

Burden's practice acts out the simple question 'What happens if you...?', making the risk of failure an active space of opportunity. This perhaps can be seen most explicitly in *When Robots Rule: The Two-Minute Airplane Factory* that took the form of an assembly line manufacturing model airplanes to be launched into the cavernous space of Tate Britain's Duveen Galleries in 1999. Although, like *Three Ghost Ships*, on paper the machine was capable of the task, in practise only a single plane made the flight, with visitors confronted with technicians carrying out tests and adjustments. Technology is dumb: it has no intuition or reflexivity, yet the purpose of machines is to increase efficiency beyond the ability of the human hand. Unlike *Ghost Ship*'s builder, a machine cannot intuitively know if something 'looks right'.

At Tate the apparent 'failure' made the work all the more poignant. Of course the artist and museum were disappointed that planes in flight did not fill the gallery, but the inability of the machine to replicate human endeavor became a poetic philosophy of failure. *Ghost Ship* can be seen to have succeeded – it made its trip to the delight of all involved, despite severe weather conditions – but the work itself lies in endeavor.

Burden's critically engaged practice proposes questions that are manifested through actions and events interrogating structures of power and assumptions. As with George Brecht's event-scores or Andreas Slominski's elaborate action sequences, Burden introduces doubt and never fully eliminates the unknown. The potential of each event, from its announcement to its documentation, is a space where objective and supposedly incontrovertible facts collide with the subjectivities of individuals and wider political and sociological contingencies. Much art reaches us through the mediation of magazines, books, lectures, documentation and anecdote. Fully aware that the recording cannot stand in for the event of the work, Burden maintains a tight control, generally picking a single image and a short, to-the-point text to represent his works. Bring to mind a Chris Burden work. That memory has probably been constructed from a single black-and-white photograph, backed up by a succinct textual description. If the 'memory' of a Burden work becomes mediated by the texts and images that recount it, then this very text has a responsibility. I am aware that my own inevitably inadequate description will form an impression of this work, as will making a choice of images for these pages. With *Ghost Ship*, the collaborative and long-distance process has made Burden less concerned with fixing a single image of the work. However, in spite of this, a 'trademark' image will emerge nonetheless as editors and writers settle on a recognizable, iconic means to communicate the nature of the work visually.

In a 1973 interview Burden discussed his interest in engaging with the preconceptions created by the announcement of a work or exhibition. Talking of a planned work (in which 'My wife will drive me to Baja, drop me off and do a U-turn back to California') he explains that the piece will be activated through its enunciation, describing how a flyer will suggest that 'some sort of recording' will take place.[3] This initiates a potential work that will 'exist as a fantasy', as individuals imagine it for themselves. Once the event of the work has taken place and been documented, each exhibition visitor or reader 'will be able to test the two, then go away and mesh the two. They will think that they have got it, but of course they won't: they are both illusions.'[4] In this space of speculation lies the potency of the work.

The absence at the core of *Ghost Ship* is filled with the same immediacy as Burden's earlier works and the event of each piece poses an open question: Can it happen again? So, if one unmanned boat can follow a coastline, can another? If one person can occupy a locker measuring 2 × 2 × 3 feet for five days, could another? With an adjustment, could countless model airplanes be manufactured in a day? (In fact, Burden is currently returning to the *Airplane Factory* to see if changes in engineering over the past seven years now make it realizable.) The answer is not the point, nor is the importance of first-hand witnessing. Burden's is a practice suffused with possibilities where questions are posed as a consideration of how structures and limits shape the world.

2 Michel Foucault, 'Of Other Spaces', *Diacritics* vol. 16 No.1 (Spring 1986): 23
3 'Willoughby Sharp Videoviews Chris Burden', *Avalanche* Video (1973) 27.45 minutes.
4 *Ibid.*

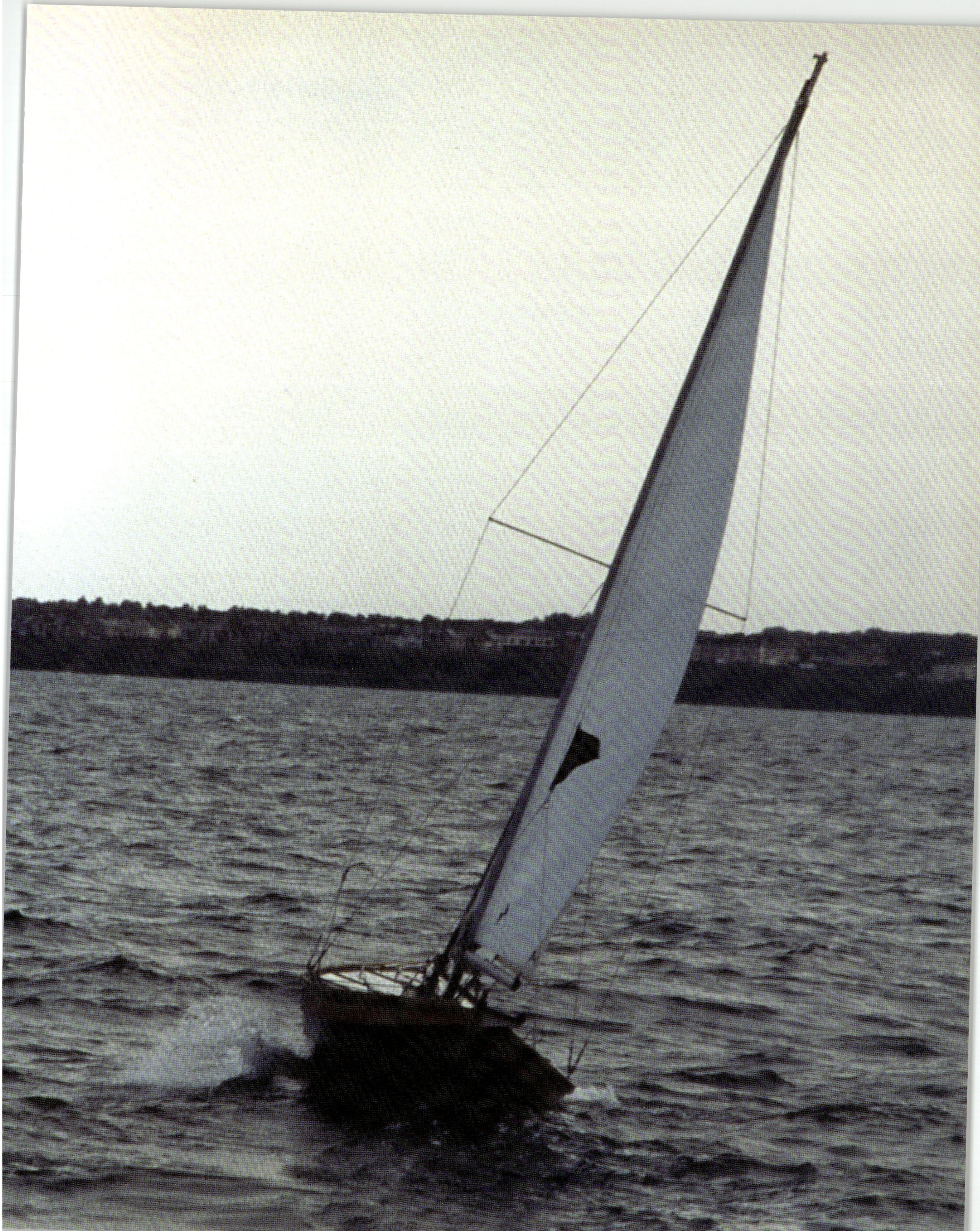

Paul Schimmel

Working Drawings: Chris Burden on Paper

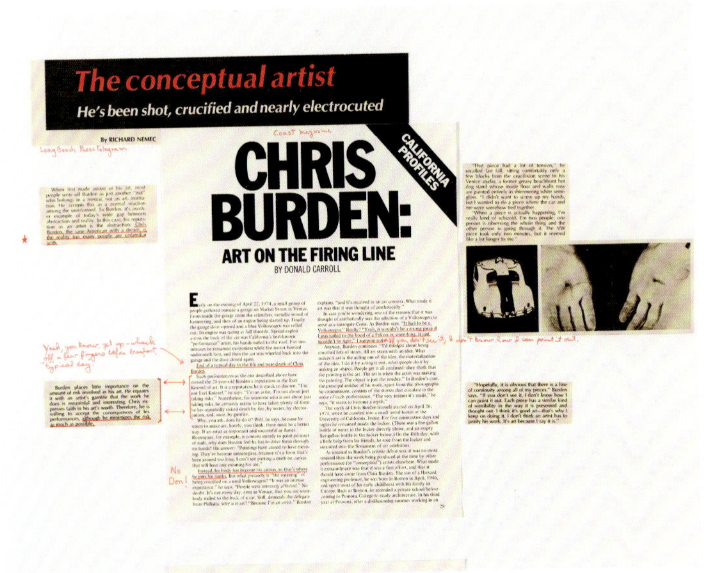

Sane American with a Dream 1975 (detail)
Collage, 30 × 40 inches

Over the past 20 years, a reputation first built on profound and often shocking performances has evolved into an understanding of Chris Burden as one of the leading sculptors and installation artists of the late twentieth century. This evolution comes with the development of Burden's increasingly complex oeuvre of handcrafted, labor-intensive studio sculptures, as well as another significant body of work that is industrially fabricated, often using off-the-shelf parts and involving a direct collaboration with both art and commercial fabricators. Each of these bodies of work alone would define a significant, at times breathtaking, accomplishment. Yet to truly understand the breadth of these investigations – the parallel, dual-track nature of Burden's practice over the last two decades and its origins in the performative actions of the 1970s – one must appreciate the works' foundation. This might be described as a quasi-scientific examination of psychology, social behavior, science, engineering, business, finance and architecture, among other fields. As viewers of Burden's brave and varied yet coherent oeuvre, we are always presented with the relics of performances or the finished sculptures and installations, but it is in the processes of conceptualization and development that we see the true origins of these works and the real underpinnings of his art.

Burden's works on paper – preparatory drawings, sketches, engineering plans and photographs with text – form a quite significant (though less known and appreciated) body of work in their own right. Neither as complete nor perhaps as complex as the performances, sculptures and installations, these vital works nonetheless reveal conceptual thought processes and provide the basis for much of Burden's art from the mid-1970s to the present. Drawings serve an important role in many artists' practices. For Burden, they provide the underpinnings of his

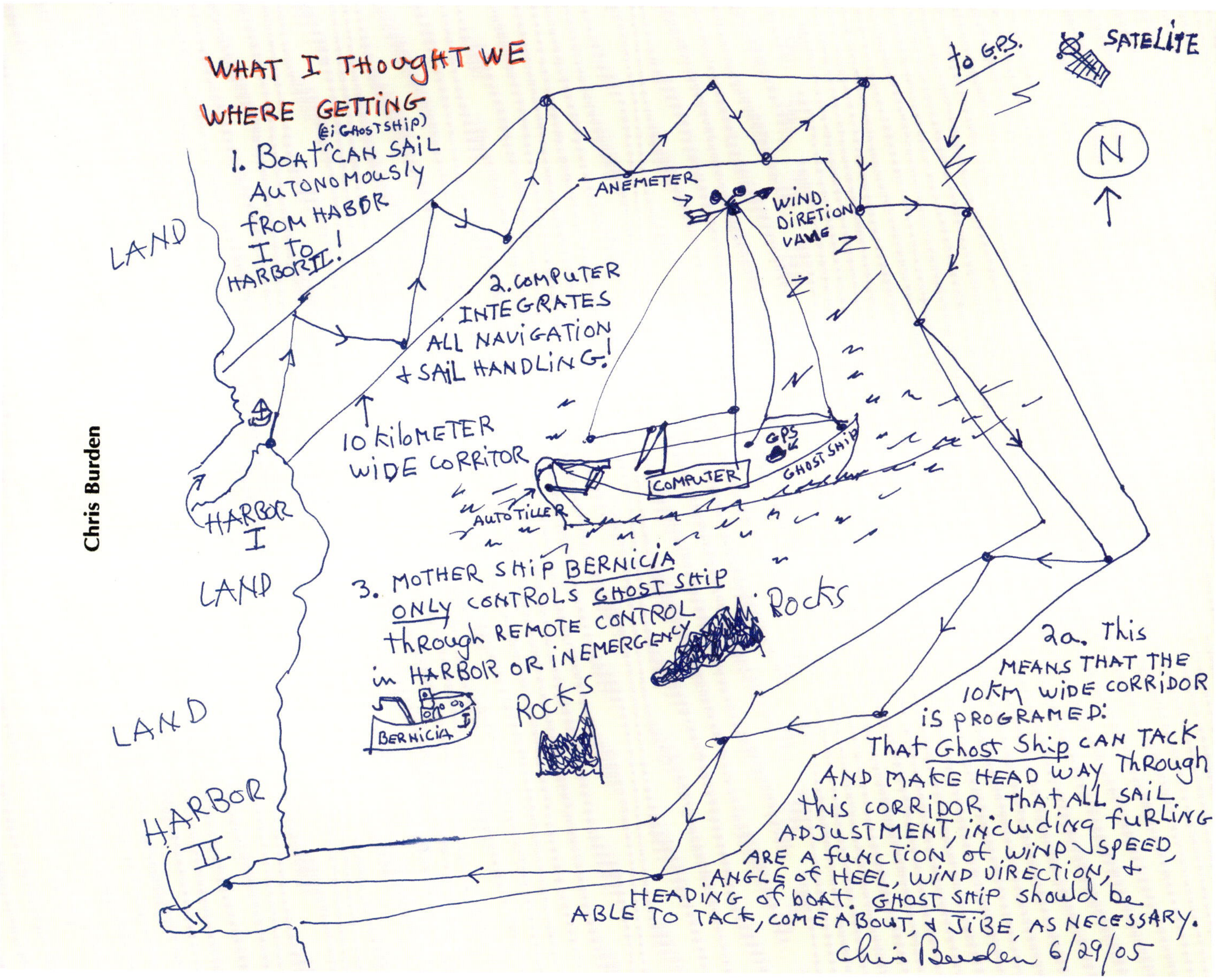

Ghost Ship: What I Thought We Were Getting 2005
Ink on paper, 8½ × 11 inches

often monumental sculptural practice, and they also exist as the culmination of his performance-based work when carefully paired with photographs and text. Works on paper have constituted either an end result of a project, as in the case of performances, or as almost schematic plans as in many projects from 1975 to the present. In fact, it can be argued that at the core of Burden's practice today are these propositions and/or studies for his monumental works. The documents and drawings have become a chief means of communicating a laundry list of propositions (and details of their execution) that his patrons or collaborators have the opportunity to consider simultaneously. It is perhaps too easy to become tangled up in the spectacle of Burden's performances, the sensation of his objects, the overwhelming ambition of his installations and architectural projects, and thus to overlook the often simple conceptual underpinnings from which his works develop.

Burden's most recent project, *Ghost Ship* (2005), is simultaneously simple in concept – a handcrafted, traditional single-masted ship sails from Fair Isle in Scotland to Newcastle upon Tyne in England – and complex in execution, because the ship is sailing unmanned. Burden's simple, often alarmingly precise diagrammatic drawings and the conceptual underpinnings on which they are based slice to the very core of the challenge of this massively complex project and represent perhaps his most significant contribution. After what amounted to thousands of hours of labor – both in the construction of the ship itself and the

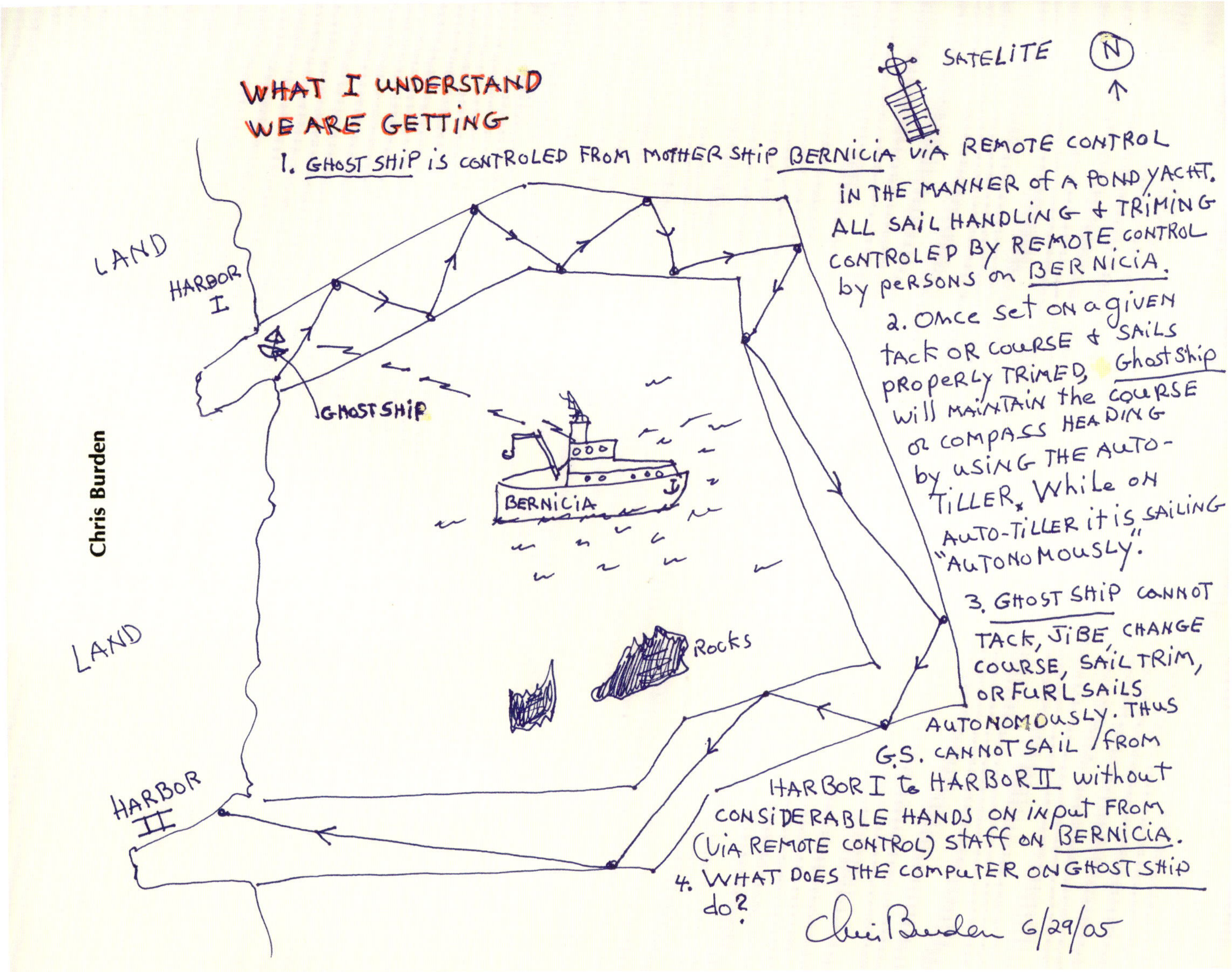

Ghost Ship: What I Understand We Are Getting 2005
Ink on paper, 8½ × 11 inches

design of the complex hydraulics and integration of off-the-shelf computer systems to control it on its voyage – over many months, the project was boiled down by Burden to a very basic question asked just weeks before the boat was to set sail: on June 29, 2005, in drawings he sent to his collaborators, Burden raised concerns about what, to him, was fundamentally the most important aspect of the work: would *Ghost Ship* truly be autonomous? How would the ship, following a preordained tack within a sailing corridor, know when it had reached the edge of the corridor and make the necessary adjustments? How would the computer utilize the measurements of the angle of the hull and wind speed and thereby know when to furl and unfurl the sails? Could the rudder and sail be adjusted autonomously, independent of human control?

The artist's decision to communicate through deceptively simple drawings at this final stage in the development of *Ghost Ship* allowed him to very clearly articulate – in a more effective way than through written words or conversation – the difference between his initial expectations and the final reality of the project. In two drawings, one entitled *What I Thought We Were Getting* and the other entitled *What I Understand We Are Getting*, Burden questions whether the boat will truly be able to navigate by itself and sail on its own. In *What I Thought We Were Getting*, *Ghost Ship* is drawn large and the accompanying sister (or mother) ship is quite tiny, revealing a craft able to sail largely independent of human intervention. In the second drawing, *Ghost Ship* is small and the mother ship dominates – *Ghost Ship* is, in effect, being navigated by remote control, as he puts it, 'in the manner of a pond yacht'. And Burden points out that although through the integration of software and hardware, *Ghost Ship* can maintain a course and sail autonomously, it appears not to be able to change course, trim, or furl its sails autonomously.

Burden has long been interested in creating autonomous, self-directed vessels and machines. He has investigated the concept of autonomy, with mixed results, in at least two previous projects. For a commission from the Spoleto Art Festival in 1991, Burden planned to sail three unmanned ships named the *U*, the *S*, and the *A* from Savannah, Georgia, to Europe. On a parallel track, Burden also created a partially completed but never satisfactorily independent model airplane factory *When Robots Rule: The Two-Minute Airplane Factory* (1999) for the Tate Gallery in London. *Ghost Ship* is the latest attempt to realize this conceptual ambition of autonomous machines of which drawing is an essential aspect of the conceptualization and conclusion of these projects.

Drawing has always been Burden's way to step outside of himself to comment on a subject. His first drawings/collages from 1975, titled *The Commentaries*, provided a way for the artist to respond to interpretations of his performance works in the popular press. As sensational as these performances were, both the mainstream and the art press were guilty of exploiting the reading public with misinformation even as they accused Burden of exploiting the art world. Works where he 'sacrificed' himself, such as *Shoot* (1971) and *Trans-fixed* (1974), became occasions for much derision and speculation. As a way of setting the record straight, Burden created collages from the original newspaper and magazine reviews of his performances. There are at least 16 of these works, in which he corrects misquotations, argues against faulty conclusions, points out plagiarism (both of his own words and between the journalists themselves) and questions the veracity and motivation of the individual newspapers and magazines and the entire journalistic profession. Burden's commentaries are not limited to the journalists who wrote the pieces: he also skewers the editorial process itself, taking particular pleasure in titling the collages in the same manner as did the publications, which often skewed or misrepresented the thrust of an article with misleading headlines. Some of Burden's titles include *King of the Avant-Garde* (1975), *Sane American with a Dream* (1975), *Serious Businessman* (1975) and – arguably the most important of *The Commentaries – Novitiate Franciscan* (1975). In this piece Burden critiques a *New York Times* article in which artist-critic Peter Plagens mocks what he sees as Burden's aspiration to become an avant-garde artist embraced by the art establishment. By having appeared in *Flash Art* and *Artforum*, Plagens writes that Burden 'is no freer than a Novitiate Franciscan

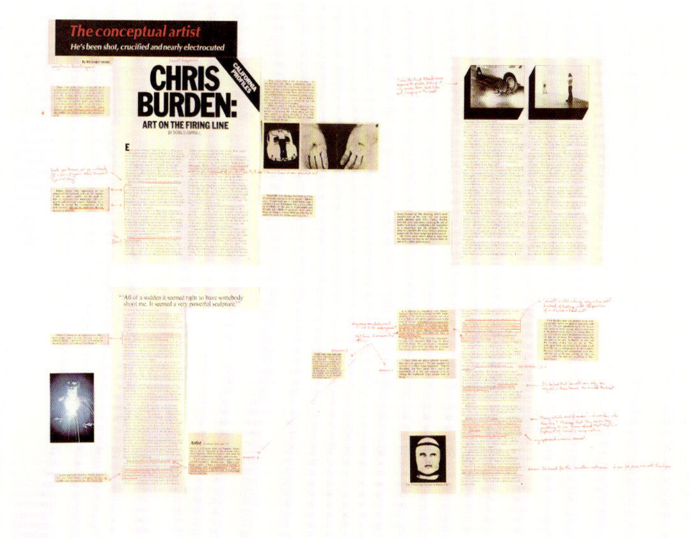

Sane American with a Dream 1975
Collage, 30 × 40 inches

conceding admittance into that order.[1] In *Novitiate Franciscan*, Burden admonishes Plagens and corrects him by stating, 'You've got it backwards. I dictate to *Avalanche*, *Flash Art* and *Artforum* what art is.'

The most significant body of Burden's drawings from the mid-1970s to the present is a group of working or preparatory drawings that communicate with collaborators, patrons and fabricators about various sculptures, installations and architectural projects. The use of drawing as a tool in the development of as yet unrealized work can be traced to a single drawing from 1971. This unique drawing is the only work on paper that specifically relates to the development of a performance. *You'll Never See My Face in Kansas City* was performed on November 7, 1971, only half a year after Burden's first graduate performance. In the drawing he thoughtfully and carefully considers all of the work's elements to ensure that his face will never be seen while he's in Kansas City (this included wearing a ski mask from the moment he drove into town). Using a combination of stick figures, cutaways, overviews and one-point perspective, Burden carefully diagrams the performance so as to achieve his objective. The drawing sketches out the three-foot-wide architectural scrim that extended flush from the gallery's ceiling down to between Burden's shoulders and chin, obscuring his face as he sat behind it. The performance was enacted exactly as conceived in the preparatory drawing. The rest of Burden's works on paper in the 1970s were dominated primarily by presentation drawings for exhibitions and a series of prints, including *If You Fly, If You Drive* (1973) and *Trans-fixed* (1974), which were directly related to his performance-based projects.

In the mid 1970s, Burden's work began to evolve from performances into projects based on large-scale construction and engineering. He realized that he needed to create collages, drawings, books and prints that could be acquired by a more traditional base of collectors to generate income that he could both live off of and use to create more art. As the artist came to consider financial concerns, he created two works in 1977 which directly address the intersection of art and currency and ironically undermine the value of financial transactions.

Part of a larger exhibition of Burden's work of the same title held at the Baum-Silverman Gallery in Los Angeles in September of 1977, *Full Financial Disclosure* consists of collages of every check written by Burden in 1976, organized by month. The checks' annotations provide a precise and accurate picture of every financial transaction he executed by check, from the payment of rent and phone bills to more specialized purchases at a hobby shop. The viewer thus notes that Burden purchased advertising time on television and bought a Thai stick. The checks are oddly revelatory with none of the sentiment normally

1 Peter Plagens, 'He got shot – for his art'. *New York Times*, September 2, 1973

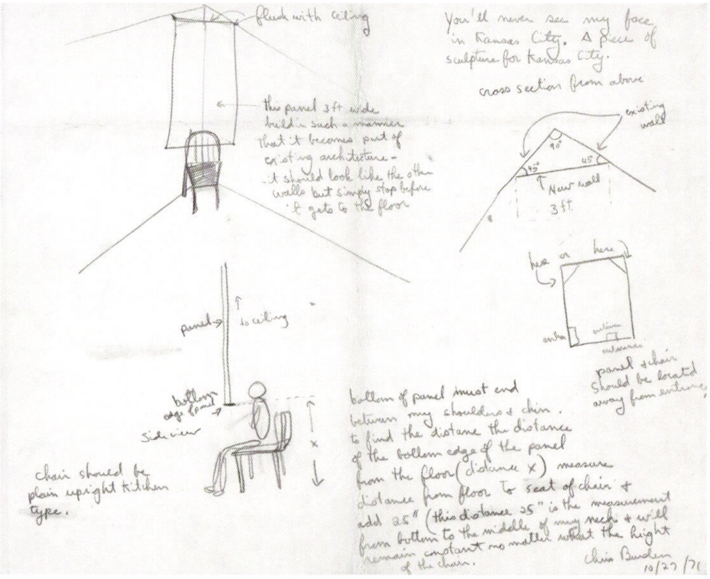

You'll Never See My Face in Kansas City 1971
Pencil on paper, 11 × 14 inches

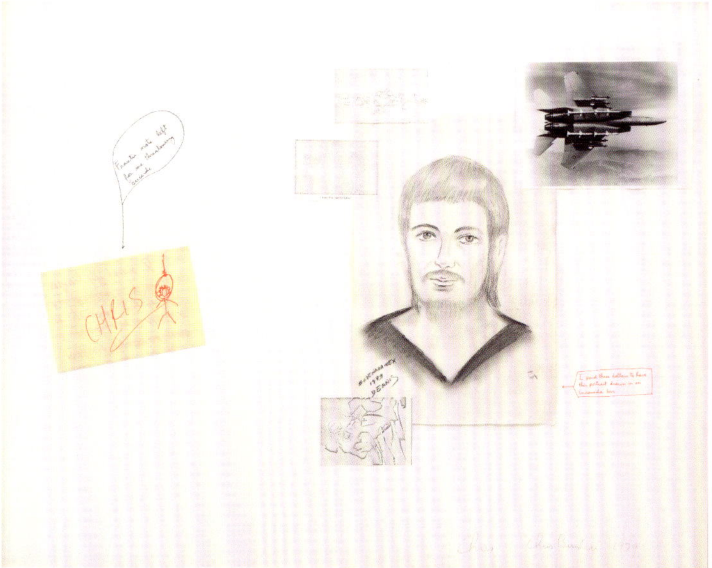

Chris 1979
Collage, 30 × 40 inches

associated with autobiography. Burden says, 'I thought about something as dry as somebody's checkbook, and all of a sudden that becomes revealing.' A significant part of the *Full Financial Disclosure* exhibition was the gallery's willingness to pay for TV advertising. In the commercial, Burden sat in front of the American Stars and Stripes and became the first artist to make a full financial disclosure on the air. The information provided in the TV commercial was substantiated through the collaged checks, which acted as documentary proof akin to photographs of a performance. The final collage of the series noted how much money Burden made during the year, as it consisted of his income tax return. *Full Financial Disclosure* was further documented in a small artist's book, which included a check for $3,000 from Chris Burden made out to his art dealer Ron Feldman. The irony of this gesture is the reversal of roles, as the dealer is supposed to pay the artist.

Also dating from 1977 is *Diecimila*, an exact copy – or exact as Crown Point Press was able to achieve – of a 10,000 Italian lire note, including the watermark and recto and verso printing. Among the most successful prints Burden was to make, *Diecimila* was simultaneously a great technical achievement and an egregiously illegal act, with both he and the publisher blatantly violating anti-forgery laws.

Burden's *Commentaries* and the collages using his financial documents mark an increasingly autobiographical turn in his work. This is evident in a 1979 work entitled *Chris*, one of the first the artist termed 'Devil Drawings'. *Chris* juxtaposed a portrait commissioned from a street artist in Tijuana depicting Burden with a photograph of a fully armed jet fighter. The drawing is annotated with the comment, 'Frantic note left for me threatening suicide'. At a time when he was experiencing a great deal of turmoil in his personal life, Burden chose increasingly harsh objects, some of which alluded to violence, to include in his collages. The autobiographical impulse continued with the inclusion of bloody relics from his own life, including handkerchiefs from a punk concert, a tuft of hair pulled from a drunk's head in Portland, Oregon, after the man had deliberately vandalized an installation piece by Burden, and a bloody tissue. The titles of the works from 1979 further indicate deep emotional trauma and strange violence, including *Poison Spear Ambush*, *Strangler Hunt Grows*, *American 180* and *N for Nigger, Z for Zorro*.

When Burden again returned to the format of collage drawings several years later, they were no longer based on personal mementos, but rather reflected his increasing interest in and exploration of economic and political subjects. Burden's ongoing interest in the emasculation of Japan's military machine in the postwar period was the subject of both a performance and a print,

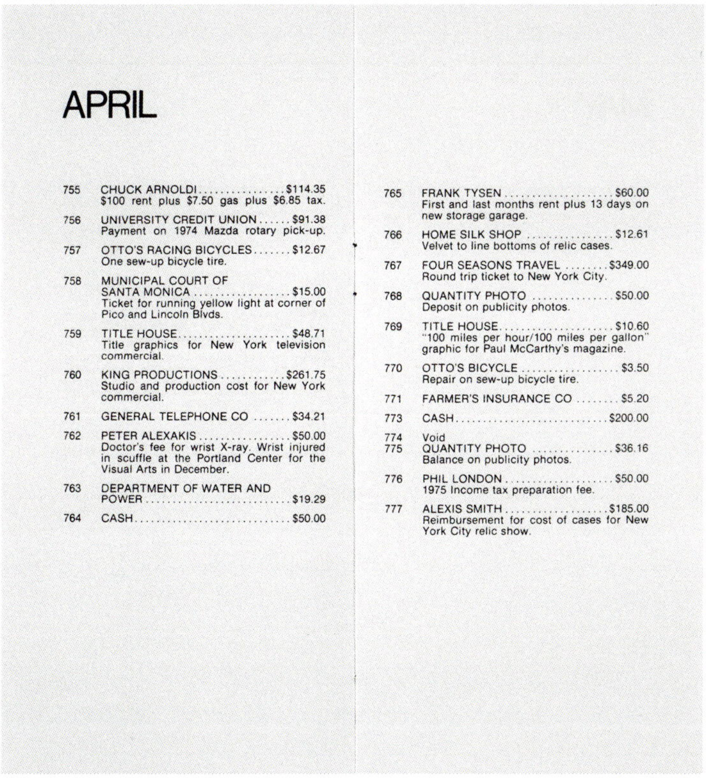

APRIL

755 CHUCK ARNOLDI $114.35
$100 rent plus $7.50 gas plus $6.85 tax.

756 UNIVERSITY CREDIT UNION $91.38
Payment on 1974 Mazda rotary pick-up.

757 OTTO'S RACING BICYCLES $12.67
One sew-up bicycle tire.

758 MUNICIPAL COURT OF SANTA MONICA $15.00
Ticket for running yellow light at corner of Pico and Lincoln Blvds.

759 TITLE HOUSE $48.71
Title graphics for New York television commercial.

760 KING PRODUCTIONS $261.75
Studio and production cost for New York commercial.

761 GENERAL TELEPHONE CO $34.21

762 PETER ALEXAKIS $50.00
Doctor's fee for wrist X-ray. Wrist injured in scuffle at the Portland Center for the Visual Arts in December.

763 DEPARTMENT OF WATER AND POWER $19.29

764 CASH $50.00

765 FRANK TYSEN $60.00
First and last months rent plus 13 days on new storage garage.

766 HOME SILK SHOP $12.61
Velvet to line bottoms of relic cases.

767 FOUR SEASONS TRAVEL $349.00
Round trip ticket to New York City.

768 QUANTITY PHOTO $50.00
Deposit on publicity photos.

769 TITLE HOUSE $10.60
"100 miles per hour/100 miles per gallon" graphic for Paul McCarthy's magazine.

770 OTTO'S BICYCLE $3.50
Repair on sew-up bicycle tire.

771 FARMER'S INSURANCE CO $5.20

773 CASH $200.00

774 Void

775 QUANTITY PHOTO $36.16
Balance on publicity photos.

776 PHIL LONDON $50.00
1975 Income tax preparation fee.

777 ALEXIS SMITH $185.00
Reimbursement for cost of cases for New York City relic show.

Full Financial Disclosure 1977
Spread from artist's book, 7⅝ × 3½ inches (closed)

both titled *The Atomic Alphabet* (1980). The print was based on a performance done in Japan. Because the majority of the audience didn't understand English, sheets of paper with corresponding English letters and Japanese characters were handed out. Burden kept one of these sheets and subsequently created a print much like a child's alphabet primer, in which he included Japanese characters, a word in English and a small illustration, reminiscent of a drawing in a child's book, all using the theme of wartime destruction: 'A' for 'atomic', 'B' for 'bomb', 'C' for 'combat', 'D' for 'dumb' and so forth.

Certainly, during the first half of the 1970s when he was still creating performance-based work, Burden thought of himself as belonging as much to the world of conceptual art as to that of 'performance art'. It was with the *B-Car* in 1975 that he began to move away from a more ephemeral word-, image-, and time-based mode into the increasingly object- or sculpture-oriented practice that continues today. During the early 1980s Burden began to create assemblages and small-scale sculptures, which could be displayed in a domestic setting (*Warship* [1981], *The Nina, The Pinta and The Santa Maria* [1982], *Ship-O-Corks* [1983], *Large Glass Ship* [1983], and *Small Glass Ship* [1984]). He simultaneously continued to explore the intersection between art and technology in such works as *C.B.T.V.* (1977), which – like the *B-Car* – was accompanied by a series of preparatory drawings. It was in 1984, at the end of this period of producing smaller and more easily collected assemblages, that Burden's focus on works on paper began to assume the significant role that it plays today, as he began to work on large-scale commissions for public display.

Beam Drop, executed in the Art Park in Lewiston, New York, on August 2nd 1984, was created by dropping approximately 60 large steel beams into a pit of wet cement from a crane 120 feet in height. In drawings Burden has proposed that such an example of 'plop art' would be appropriate in front of an office tower. In preparation for a 1985 exhibition at the Henry Art Gallery at the University of Washington in Seattle, Burden created a detailed drawing for *Samson*, a 100-ton jack connected to a gearbox on a turnstile. As each visitor to the museum entered through the turnstile, the jack would move, slowly pushing the walls of the institution down. In the drawing for this work Burden not only provides an overview of the specific placement of the jack within the space of the gallery, but also draws in detail the relationship of the worm gear box to the jack, the turnstile and the crank handle. Just as he had done 14 years earlier with *You'll Never See My Face in Kansas City*, Burden's preparatory drawing for *Samson* anticipates all the significant architectural and mechanical elements necessary to execute this work.

Burden next began work on *Sex Tower* with a series of drawings

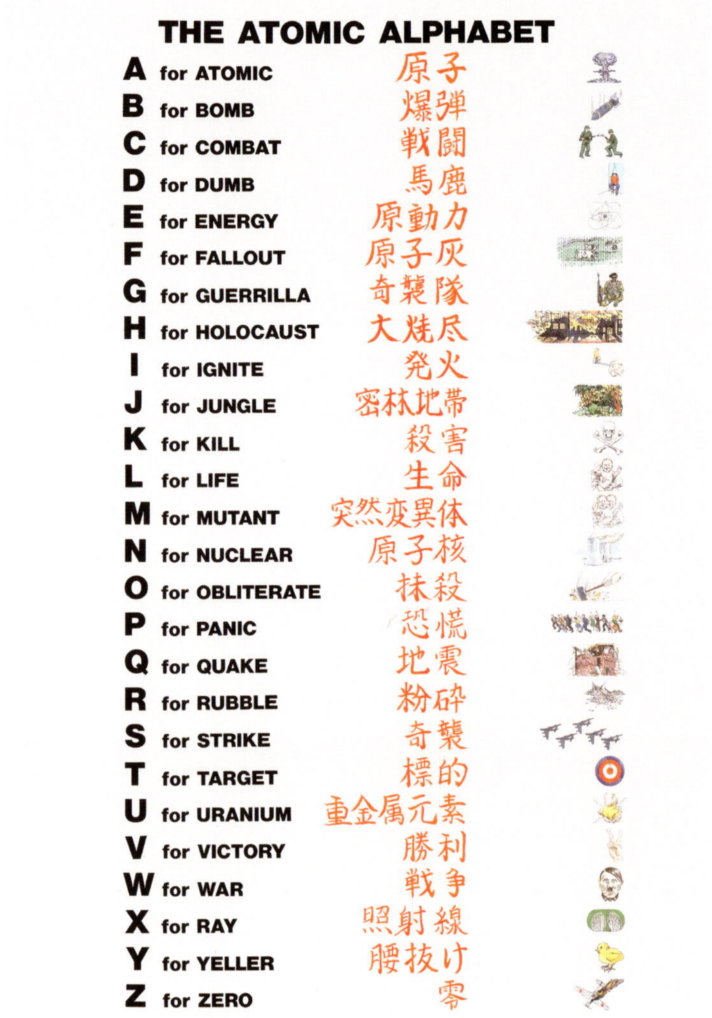

The Atomic Alphabet 1980
Photo etching with hand watercoloring,
57½ × 39 inches

and an architectural model (1:12 scale), made in 1986. Although this work has yet to be realized, it is a proposition to which Burden has returned subsequently on several occasions, including his proposal in 1994 for an exhibition at the MAK Center in Vienna. Also in 1986, Burden was commissioned by The Museum of Contemporary Art in Los Angeles to create a site-specific work for an exhibition celebrating the opening of the museum's new facility on Grand Avenue. The work on paper, entitled *Exposing the Foundation of the Museum*, consists of a photograph that has been drawn on to show how Burden would expose the concrete and steel I-beams supporting MOCA's Temporary Contemporary (now Geffen Contemporary) facility. When *Exposing the Foundation of the Museum* was executed in 1986, three staircases enabled viewers to descend into an open trench inside the museum down to below the foundation level.

Spinning Dervish (1986) is a kinetic steel sculpture first conceived in preparation for Burden's 1988 Newport Harbor Art Museum retrospective, but never executed. A pole mounted from floor to ceiling spins 42-inch-square pieces of one-inch-thick steel. As the pole spins, the plates rise upward and outward into a horizontal position. The drawing for this project depicts the dramatic dynamism of the metal elements set in motion. Increasingly, Burden began to conceive of works of fantasy such as *Another World* (1992), a drawing that depicts the Eiffel Tower being circumnavigated by two models of the *Titanic*. Similarly, *Wexner Castle* (1990), his plan to modify architect Peter Eisenman's Wexner Center for the Arts at Ohio State University, proposed using crenellations and merlons to turn the museum building into a postmodern medieval castle. In its final form, this work looked remarkably like the concept drawing.

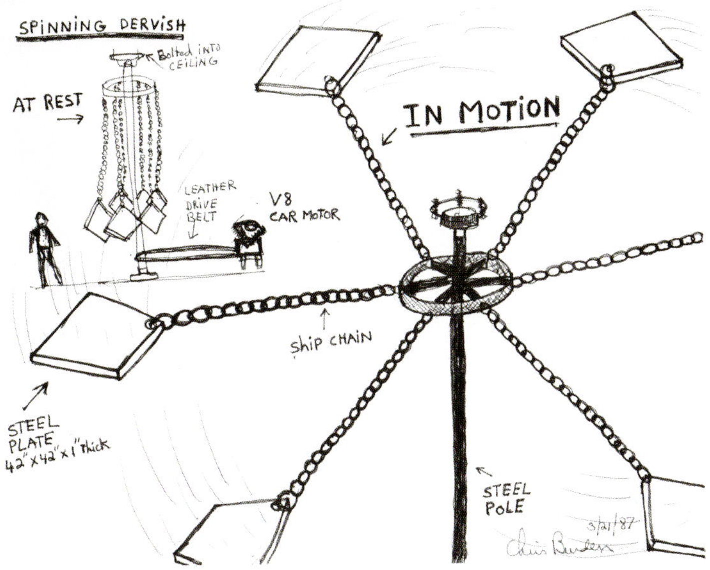

Spinning Dervish V 1987
Ink on paper, 8½ × 11 inches

While the Wexner Center embraced Burden's proposal, a year later the Seattle Art Museum rejected his idea of hanging a fishing boat on the side of the museum's new seafront location because it supposedly offended Robert Venturi, the building's architect. Burden saw this proposal as a way both to connect the new Seattle Art Museum with the city's harbor a few blocks away and to create an iconic image, so that when people asked for directions to the museum, one could say, 'Oh, it's the building with the fishing boat on its side' and it would therefore function like a signpost.

Not unlike the visionary architecture of Paolo Soleri or Frank Lloyd Wright, even Burden's most fantastic proposals feel achievable. Unlike most of Soleri's drawings, however, many of these projects have found a patron and an opportunity for realization, and this is in large measure due to the seductive persuasion of his drawings. One can, for example, imagine that some day Burden's olympian *Tower of Babel* (conceived in 1992 but unbuilt) might become reality. After all, *Small Skyscraper* was

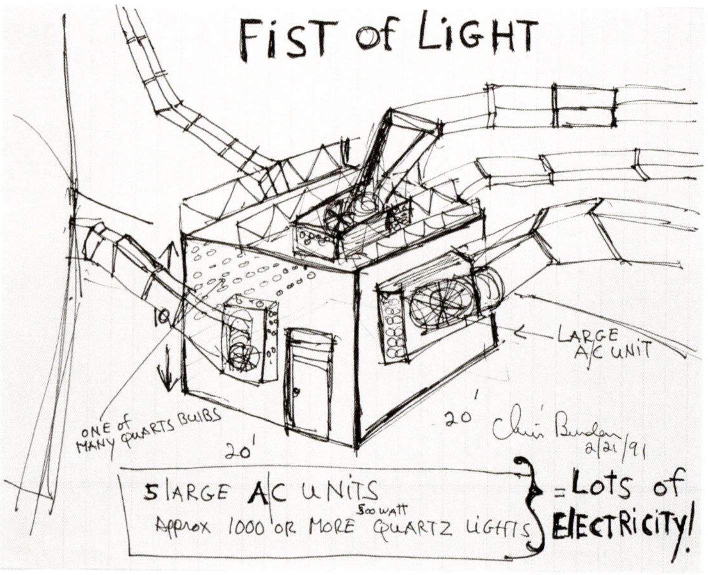

Fist of Light 1991
Ink on paper, 8½ × 11 inches

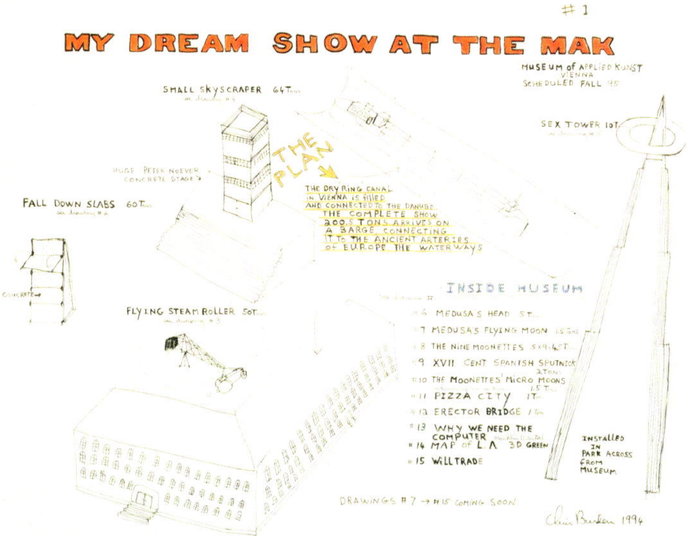

My Dream Show at the MAK 1994
Ink and colored pencil on paper, 17 × 22 inches

conceived in 1991 but not executed until 12 years later. As his diagrammatic drawing of that work illustrates, Burden's concept was for a 'quasi-legal' four-storey building, with basement, whose floors were each 10 × 10 feet. *Small Skyscraper* exploited a legal loophole in the Los Angeles County Building Code which allows small outbuildings under 400 square feet and no taller than 35 feet high to be built without a permit. The project was conceived when the artist was attempting to work with the County's arcane code to build a studio on his own residential property. In 2003, using Burden's drawings as a starting point and working with the architectural firm TK Architecture, a full-scale model of the building was constructed and installed horizontally at Los Angeles Contemporary Exhibitions (LACE).

Another work that seemed almost impossible to execute – *The Fist of Light* – was realized in 1993 at the Whitney Biennial in New York. Proposed and conceived originally for the New Museum in New York and subsequently for an exhibition at the Lannan Foundation, Los Angeles, in the late 1980s, the proposal was deemed unrealistic and unaffordable and was not fabricated at that time. *The Fist of Light* consisted of an enclosed 12 × 12-foot space saturated on its interior by halide light so intense that theoretically it could strip all color away. Generating massive amounts of heat, the monumental structure was cooled by a complex system of air-conditioning ducts. Much to the delight – and perhaps even surprise – of the artist, the final sculpture very closely resembled the concept drawing he had originally created. Similarly, the drawing of *Medusa's Head* (1987) for a proposed project to be included in an exhibition at Newport Harbor Art Museum in 1988, preceded the actual sculpture which was completed some three years later. The original drawing depicts a meteor-like sphere of rock encrusted with railroad tracks, bridges, underpasses and overpasses, with the entire piece suspended from a massive chain. The work on paper is remarkably similar to the finished project.

Another proposal for an as yet unrealized sculpture is entitled *The Sailing Destroyer* (1990). Burden is a life-long sailor with an interest in the intersection between modern technology and sailing vessels, proposed in a drawing for a project to convert the World War II destroyer, HMS *Cavalier,* from an obsolete warship into a stealth ship that could be sailed with the installation of two temporary sails and masts and with the use of large lee boards. As is often the case with the drawings, Burden was able to delineate the success of the proposition under very specific circumstances. Although this work has as yet only evolved to the next step of a three-dimensional model and naval architectural drawing, it has parallels with Burden's other vessels, including *Ghost Ship* (2005).

Burden's grandest visions can be seen in their most

unrestrained form in the drawings and proposals for complex multi-work exhibitions. This format allows him to lay out a series of investigations, some of which may have piqued his interest quite recently, while others may follow themes that Burden has explored for years. Following the somewhat traditional context of his 1988 retrospective at the Newport Harbor Art Museum, in 1996 Burden used the occasion of an exhibition at the Vienna Museum of Applied Arts (MAK) to create his 'dream show'. The artist conceived of the show as an opportunity to extend the creative process from the time the work left his studio to its transport, installation, exhibition and ultimate return from Vienna. Among the most significant aspects of the initial conception of the exhibition entitled 'Chris Burden: Beyond the Limits' was the drawing *My Dream Show at the MAK* (1994), which highlighted the outdoor pieces that Burden had conceived specifically for the exhibition, including *Ring Canal Project, Fall Down Slabs* and *The Flying Steamroller.* In addition to these exterior installations, Burden listed a group of works to be exhibited inside the museum. These included *Drawing No. 6* to *Drawing No. 15,* some of which had already been realized. *Drawing No. 2* and *Drawing No. 3* and *The Flying Steamroller* were works that the artist had never before presented, although they were ideas that he had been examining for quite some time.

The *Ring Canal Project* evokes the history of Europe when almost all goods moved on waterways and links the waters of the Pacific Ocean to the canals of Vienna. *Drawing No. 2: Fall Down Slabs* (1994) is based on the design of a simple child's toy consisting of pieces of wood connected by fabric that flip over in your hand as you rotate the object. In Burden's construction, the toy has grown to a gargantuan 70-foot-tall public monument in which 10 × 20-foot slabs of concrete reinforced with graphite fibers roll up a motorized armature. Of equally daunting proportions was the work depicted in *Drawing No. 3: The Flying Steamroller* (1994), in which a 12-ton steamroller suspended from a counterbalanced armature takes flight. This work illustrates Burden's ongoing interest in the use of mass to store energy, a theme of previous projects such as *The Big Wheel* (1979). Although the artist had already purchased the Navy surplus steamroller when he conceived of this piece, it seemed an unlikely challenge for MAK to undertake. However, MAK director Peter Noever did commission the work, and he and the artist were the first two to 'ride' this massive kinetic sculpture. In the case of *The Flying Steamroller*, as in many other works that seemed to be simply visionary or fantasy concepts, Burden found a patron equal to the ambition of the proposal.

Listed beside each one of the works represented in the group of drawings for the MAK exhibition is its estimated weight in gross tonnage, both for constructions that existed and for those that had yet to be executed: '*Small Skyscraper*, 64 tons; *Fall Down Slabs*, 60 tons; *The Flying Steamroller*, 50 tons.' The total weight of all the works combined to create a show that could be economically feasible in terms of shipping if one were to flood the canals that ring Vienna and float the works right up to the back door of the MAK, thereby saving enormously on transport costs. This weaving together of fantasy with a kind of empirically scientific act makes evident the artist's desire to see his conceptual drawings executed. Rather than artistic speculations, they are construction plans, however grandiose and visionary.

Burden's drawings frequently exhibit a deceptive simplicity, combining an almost childlike sensibility with significant problems of engineering and planning. Although it is certain that it was the artist's straightforward intention to create a fully functioning toy airplane factory for Tate Britain, in reality the project proved to be more vexing than either the artist or the fabricator had imagined, and it was, arguably, less than fully successful. Although the factory did produce planes, it did so with the aid of a technician.

The artist's drawing for *When Robots Rule: The Two-Minute Airplane Factory* (1998) is dominated by carefully considered diagrammatic sketches of the machine's elements and their assembly, and there are a number of wonderfully alluring descriptions: *Rubber band wound plane launched!; To top of Tate Gallery; One every minute!; 8 hours a day = 480 Airplanes each day × 6 months = 86,400 Airplanes; Flies to 60 feet altitude; Airplanes are retrieved by gallery attendants and sold (cheap) to public, who then litter London with crashed and stuck airplanes*. Indeed, Burden hoped the purchasers of the planes would attempt to fly their planes outside the gallery and during the course of the exhibition the grounds around the Tate would become littered with the debris from the model airplanes, thereby referencing the work of Barry Le Va. The plan seemed simple: without human intervention, an assembly line would be constructed that could produce rubber band driven balsawood and tissue model airplanes. (It should be noted that Burden might have had a premonition of the project's challenges, in particular the computer program needed to control the assembly mechanisms. In an early preparatory proposal with the title *As Proposed by Fabricator (Studio 5)*, he notes that problems might have less to do with the design and assembly of the airplanes themselves than with the computers set up to control the manufacturing functions.)

In a colorfully speculative drawing from 1999 entitled *How to Shrink L.A.*, Burden's salesmanship takes on the tone of a carnival barker. Above a banner reading 'How to Shrink L.A.', Burden has listed wildly impossible times for commutes: 'Woodland Hills to

Pasadena 15 minutes!; Santa Monica to Downtown 5 minutes!; Santa Monica to Pomona 28 minutes!; Santa Monica to Irvine 24 minutes!; Woodland Hills to Studio City 6 minutes!'. This fantasy – especially humorous to those living in Los Angeles – gives each car increasingly rapid lanes with speeds ranging from 40 miles per hour in lane one up to 250 miles an hour in lane seven, and a computer that links and controls every available space for a vehicle, each represented by a digital slot, in the greater Los Angeles freeway system. This implied reliance upon a complex computer system might be considered a bit perverse for an artist who has a profound distrust of computers. Burden has found electronic programming to be challenging to control, as in the project *When Robots Rule: The Two-Minute Airplane Factory*, and he has wondered about the role of the computer system in *Ghost Ship*.

Among the most exquisitely rendered, and certainly the most monumental, drawings in Burden's oeuvre are his 1998 studies for *Hell Gate Bridge* in New York and a bridge proposed to span a gorge in Mexico, entitled *Mexican Bridge*. Although executed on humble craft paper (one suspects without archival considerations), these monumental drawings have been exhibited on three occasions, at Crown Point Press in San Francisco in 2000, at the Arts Club of Chicago in 2001, and at the Baltic Centre for Contemporary Art, Gateshead, England in 2002. On two of these occasions, these drawings were shown along with the resulting large scale sculptures. These works are one-to-one scale representations of the Erector set sculptures to which they correspond, drawings in which every element, down to the screws that will hold the bridges together, is analyzed.

Burden's six drawings in 2000 for an as yet unrealized three-room exhibition at the Gagosian Gallery constitutes perhaps his most ambitious – and in some aspects fantastical – sculptural proposal based upon complex engineering. The monumental works presented in this proposal, including *Bigger Wheel*, *Here and There* and *Pneumatic Subway*, each relate to significant earlier achievements in Burden's oeuvre. *Bigger Wheel* is a version of a project from 1979, recreated at a scale three times larger than the original, or 40 feet in diameter, exceeding the ceiling height of the Gagosian Gallery by ten feet. As elegantly illustrated in Burden's drawing, the work pops ten feet above the building and also ten feet below it. Visible through large picture windows, the work would be lowered by a large electric motor both quiet and hidden from view. Because of the mass of the wheel itself, Burden anticipates a significant interval of five to six hours between periods of operation.

As challenging a concept as *Bigger Wheel* might represent, Burden's second and third proposals for the exhibition are even more speculative. *Here and There* combines aspects of *Another World* and *Spinning Dervish*. Three simple plywood boats, each 16 to 20 feet in length, would be suspended from a pole powered by an electric motor and, with centrifugal force, would cause the rotation of attached boats in a wide circle. Combining this engineering-based installation with his earlier performance works based in the experience of duration – such as *Five Day Locker Piece* and *White Light/White Heat* – three young sailors would 'sail' each vessel for the period of the exhibition, never leaving their boats, which would be equipped with food, water and a computer.

Pneumatic Subway continues Burden's longstanding exploration of the mechanics of transportation. *B-Car* (1975), *Flying Kayak* (1983) and *Frictionless Sled* (1983) all provide the conceptual foundations for this piece. In a nod to nostalgia, Burden's subway is entered through a cast-iron entryway arch reminiscent of a type of lamppost the artist has collected and reconditioned over the years. As indicated in the intricately detailed drawing of the work, viewers enter *Pneumatic Subway* by descending an elegant granite, marble, or terrazzo staircase into a station. They then enter a curved subway car that forms a circle circumference under the boundaries of the Gagosian Gallery. The subway carriage is driven by a huge fan and electric motor that create air pressure, thus pushing or pulling it within the airtight seal of a pneumatic tunnel. In a second detailed drawing for this project, Burden establishes that the richly appointed subway car is to be built to the highest standards possible. Although he conceived it as a 16–20 passenger carriage, in a nod to practicality, he notes within the drawing that 'For economical reasons a smaller version holding 8–12 people could be built.'

Since 1985 Chris Burden's large-scale commissioned installations and sculptures have involved drawings that investigate the boundaries between architecture, engineering, science and the visual arts. While many of the projects planned on paper remain unrealized, it is remarkable how many of these complex works have been completed over the past 20 years. Surely, what separates artists – sometimes considered visionaries and sometimes called crackpots – from scientists, engineers, or architects, is the artist's ability to freely propose that which is unimaginable and inconceivable in practical terms. With his works on paper, Chris Burden has found that first threshold of creativity where the inconceivable becomes visible. Throughout Burden's career, drawings have formed the conceptual origins for most of his works. They have provided a reservoir of ideas for sculptures and installations that have in some cases been achieved years later. Drawings have been used to realize Burden's work, but most importantly, they provide a vehicle through which projects can be conceived without restriction.

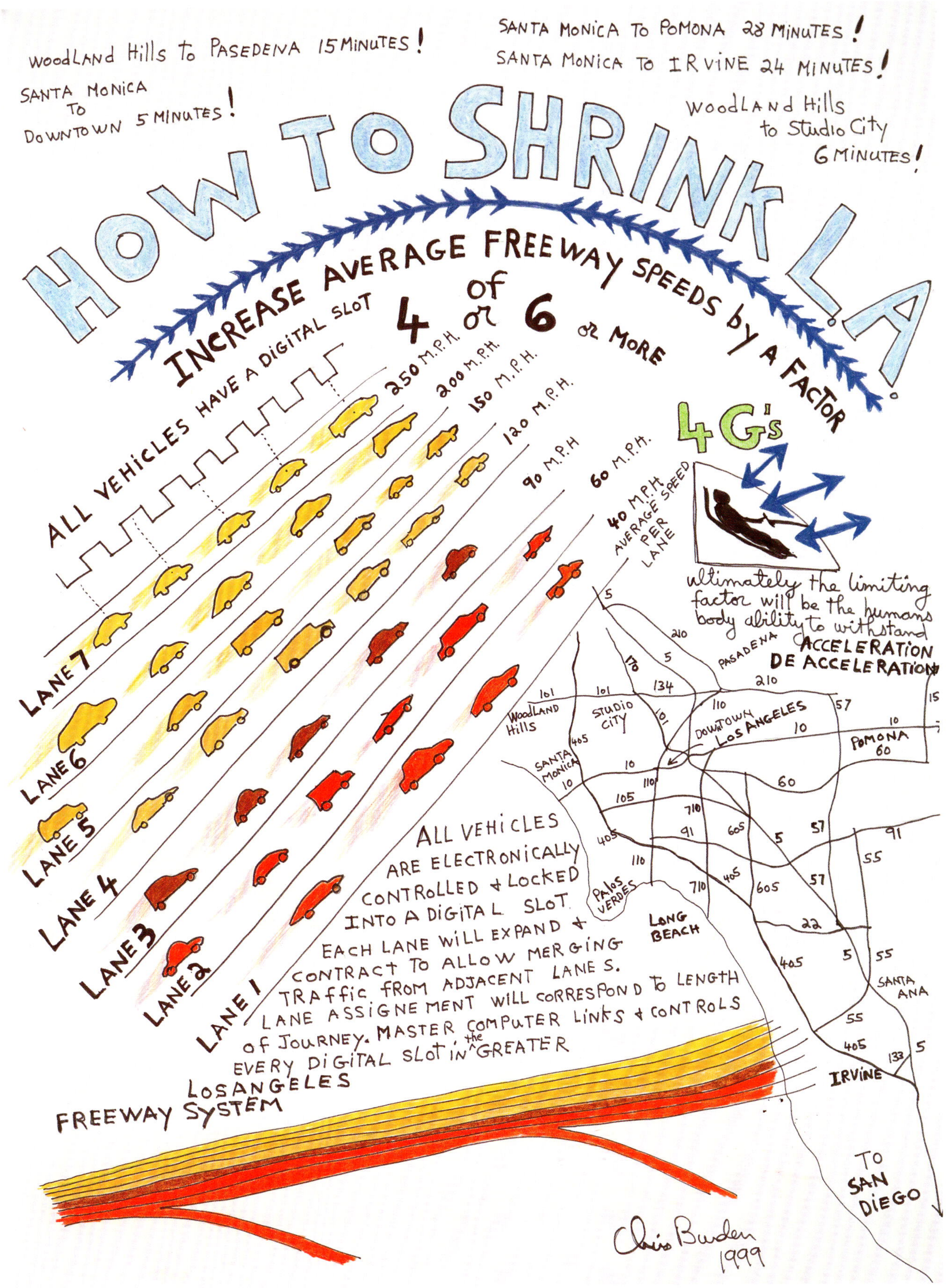

How to Shrink L.A. 1999
Ink on paper, 24 × 18 inches

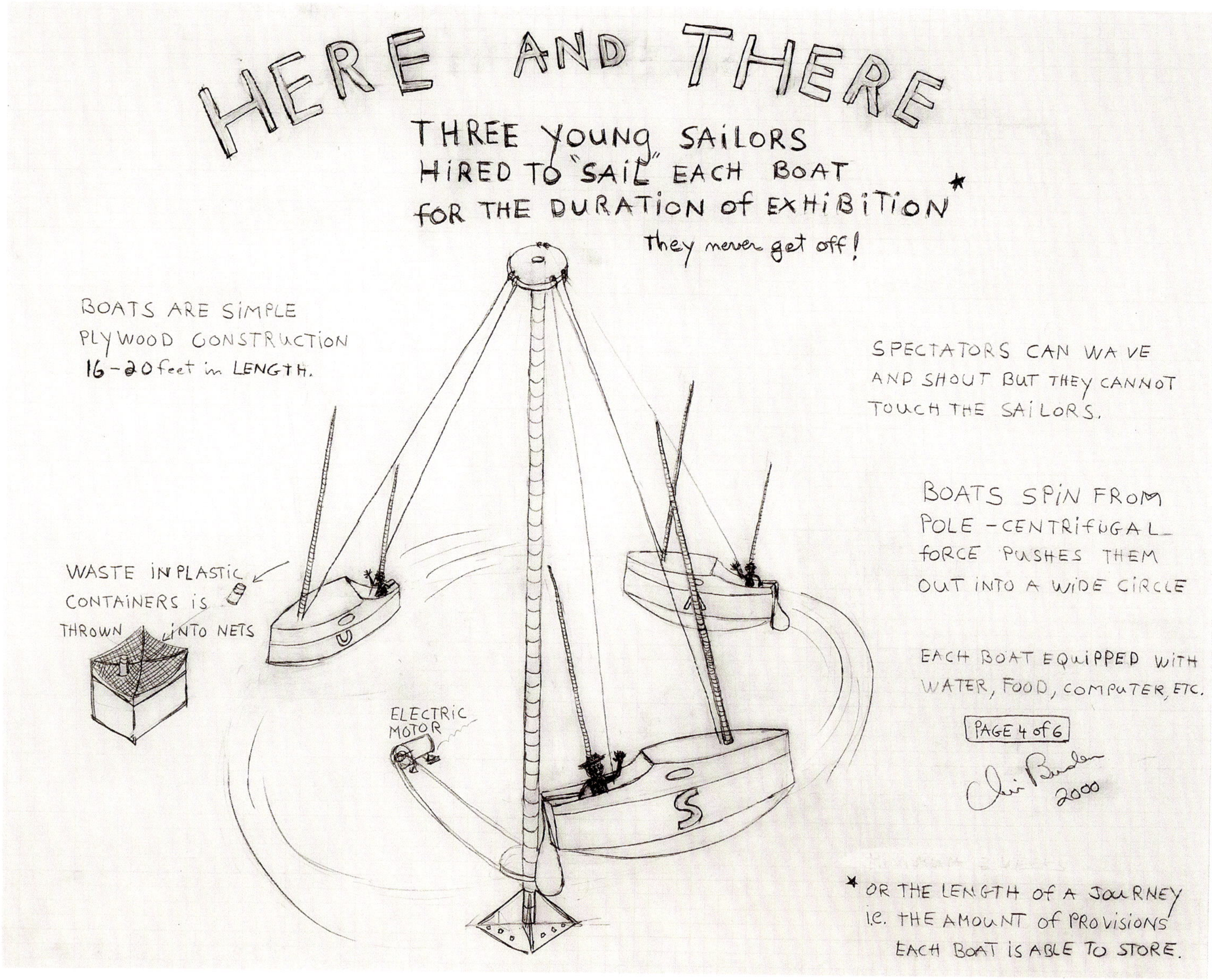

Here and There 2000
Ink on paper, 17 × 22 inches

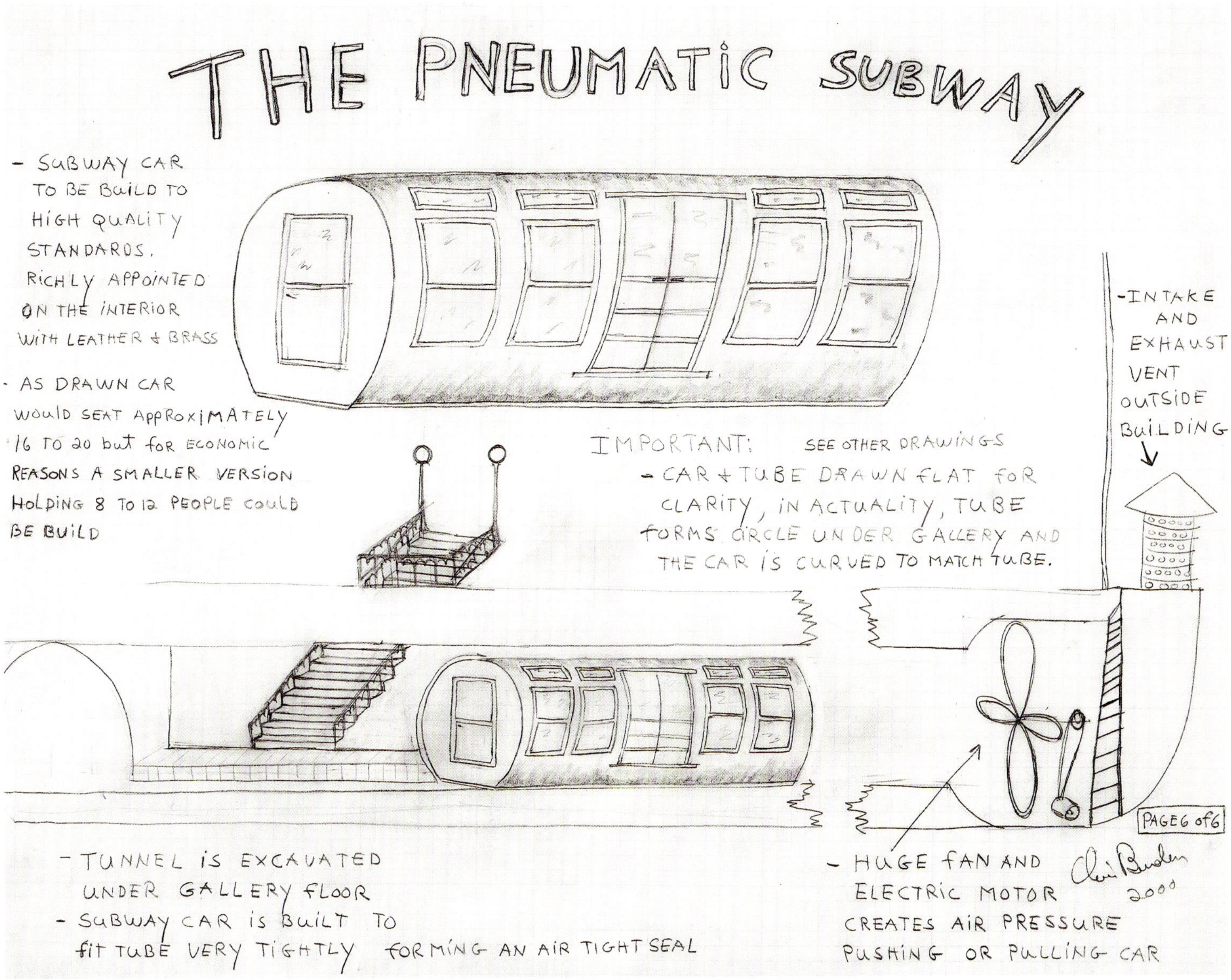

The Pneumatic Subway I 2000
Ink on paper, 17 × 22 inches

End

Selected Proposals

The Moon Piece 1986

Dear Edward Fry,
I am writing to give you some details on a sculpture project that I have discussed with you on the telephone (*The Moon Piece*) as a possible project for the upcoming Documenta.

The Moon Piece would consist of putting into orbit a very large (as large as possible) satellite whose only function and purpose would be to reflect sunlight back to earth. This special satellite would function much in the same manner that our present moon reflects sunlight. I foresee that this huge satellite could be manufactured out of fairly inexpensive, highly reflective Mylar film and be carried into outer space in a deflated state (like an uninflated balloon). Upon release the Mylar would be inflated with compressed gas and a huge, highly reflective sphere would be put into orbit. The whole apparatus would be relatively compact and lightweight making it feasible to actually carry it into orbit.

Considering the reflective property of the small communications satellites that can be presently observed in the night skies, *The Moon Piece*, a highly reflective Mylar balloon 30 to 100 times larger than present satellites, will be highly visible to the naked eye and appear, in relation to the pin points of starlight, as a bright automobile headlamp moving rapidly across the night sky, one-fifth to one-tenth the size of the moon. The most sophisticated and the most primitive of cultures will be aware that something has changed in the heavens.

This is not simply a conceptual project. This project is technically feasible and to function as a work of art it must be actualized. Until the recent shuttle disaster, this might have been a possible launch vehicle. Enclosed are a couple of Xeroxes of articles concerning possible launch vehicles and the cost of putting objects into orbit. All indications are that the costs are going to drop considerably soon, in fact, please note in the article 'Engineer gets a blast out of backyard rocket', Bob Truax, the engineer featured in this article, claims that he only needs two million dollars to get an object into space. It seems that in light of this preliminary information that other realistic and obtainable possibilities must exist for the successful completion of *The Moon Piece*. Perhaps the French Ariane Rocket program in conjunction with the West German government could be of help. Obviously, more research and information needs to be done on the specifics of the Mylar balloon such as size, thickness of Mylar, weight, etc., but I believe that *The Moon Piece* is physically and financially feasible given enough energy. If this idea, of putting into orbit a highly reflective satellite that would light up the heavens, could come to fruition I believe it would well be worth the effort. Please feel free to call me about any questions.

Sincerely,
Chris Burden

The Sex Tower 1986

The Sex Tower is a 125-foot tower to be built with bundles of 6 × 6-inch timbers joined by 900 bolts. The tip of the tower, the top 25 feet, is to be covered in gold leaf and is pierced by a 12 foot tubular ring, also covered in gold leaf. This sculpture refers to primitive fertility icons, steeples and contemporary minimal sculpture and architecture.

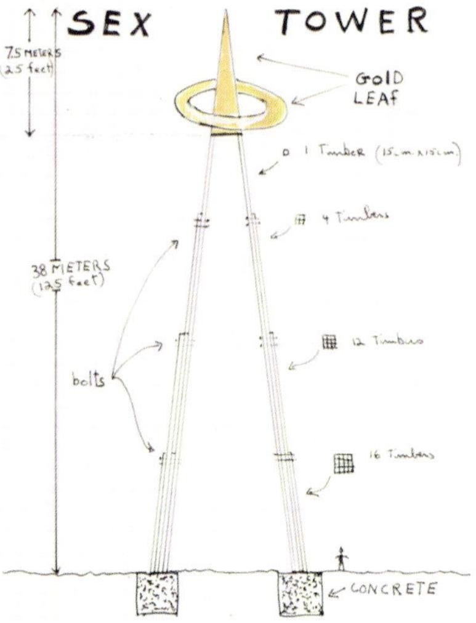

The Spinning Dervish 1987

The Spinning Dervish is a large kinetic steel sculpture similar to a maypole, but greatly enlarged. *The Spinning Dervish* will consist of a large steel pole mounted to the floor and ceiling. Six 42-inch square pieces of one-inch-thick steel plate will be suspended from the top of the pole by ship anchor chain. At rest, a small child can move and clank the plates together. Activated by a large belt connected to a running V-8 car motor, *The Spinning Dervish* will accelerate. Centrifugal force will cause the steel plates to move outwards and upwards to a horizontal position, thereby, taking control of the entire space. The viewer should be able to observe and experience the dual nature of the sculpture and the transformation from one state to the other. This sculpture is part of an ongoing investigation into the nature of space, kineticism, and the relationship between man and machine.

Proposal for Seattle Arts Commission, In Public 1991
June 1, 1990

I propose that a typical working fisherman's boat, 30 to 50 feet in length, be attached to the side of the new Seattle Art Museum building. The boat's bow would point skyward, its keel resting along one side of the building. A cable from the roof to the boat's bow, much like an anchor line, would hold the boat in place (see enclosed illustration).

A fisherman takes a fishing boat out to sea and catches fish (horizontal). An artist takes the same boat, attaches it to the side of the new museum building, and makes art (vertical). The same boat – different directions – equally real. A working fishing boat on the side of the Seattle Art Museum becomes a signpost to everyman as to what art is, and where art is. This project, by proposing to incorporate the new Venturi designed Seattle Art Museum building as its armature, also addresses the dichotomy of the museum building's function to serve both as an architectural masterpiece (Art) and as a mere shed to protect the contents (the Art stored inside). Ultimately, putting a fishing boat on the side of the museum's building becomes a testimony to the seriousness of art.

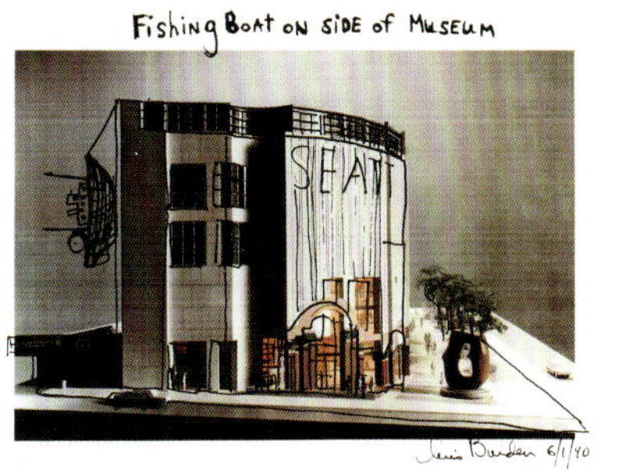

Placing this working fishing boat on the outside of the museum building in this radical configuration, is an attempt to make art that pays tribute to an important part of Seattle's heritage (fishing and the ocean), and integrates this heritage with the celebration of the opening of the new Seattle Art Museum building.

This project was never realized due to the vehement objections of the architect, Robert Venturi.

Proposal for *The Blacklisted Ten* at the School of Cinema-Television, at the University of Southern California
July, 1991

Following World War II, the United States experienced a heightened and irrational fear of Communism. This fear, in its ugliest form, took the name of McCarthyism, named after Senator Joseph McCarthy. McCarthy conducted an extensive series of Senate hearings and investigations into individuals suspected of being Communist, individuals associated with Communists and individuals who had Communist sympathies. One of the major groups targeted by Senator McCarthy was the film industry in Hollywood. Ten important and successful screenwriters were deemed by Senator McCarthy to have Communist affiliations and they were barred from working on any film scripts. Thus, the ten writers became collectively known as the Blacklisted Ten.

Two of these blacklisted writers are currently working at the School of Cinema-Television, at the University of Southern California, as faculty members. They decided to create a monument

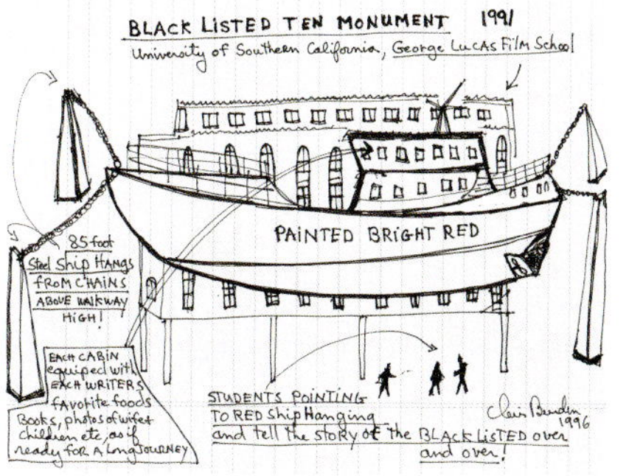

to these men whose lives were destroyed by the fanatical wave of anti-Communist sentiments that swept across the United States in the early 1950s.

My proposal for the Blacklisted Ten Monument at the University of Southern California was to suspend (using steel cables) a large, 85-foot fishing ship, so that the ship would hover over the walkway in front of the George Lucas building at the University of Southern California campus. The ship was to be fully operational and the ten individual staterooms were to be dedicated to the ten blacklisted film writers of the 1950s. Each stateroom would contain the favorite books, clothing and memorabilia of the particular film writers. And finally, the whole ship was to be painted red, symbolizing the Red Scare of the 1950s. This large red ship, hung in the air over the campus walkway, would be a bold and constant reminder to the students, resulting in the story of the Blacklisted Ten being told over and over.

The Tower of Babel *or* The Olympian Tower of Babel, if used for the 1992 Olympic Games in Barcelona
August, 1991

My idea would be that a standard-size piece of stone or marble would be cut to form a small curved building block, which would measure approximately 12 × 15½ inches (30 × 40 cm). Each block would have an arch cut into it. These standardized blocks would be used to build a huge physical model of the mythical Biblical Tower of Babel. The base of the spiraling tower

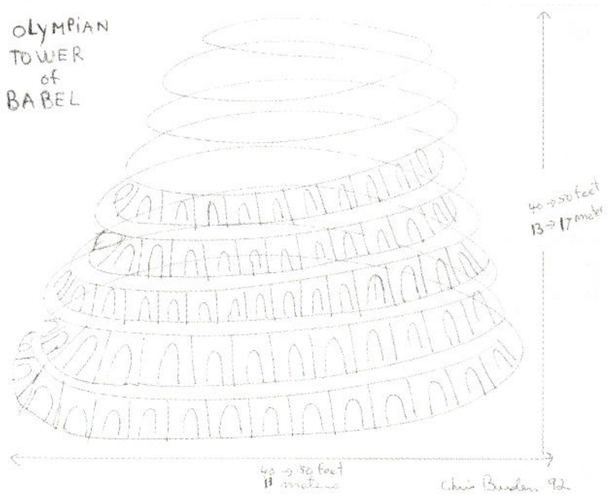

should be approximately 40 to 50 feet (13 to 17 m) in diameter. The set back on each spiral should be 4 to 5 inches (10 cm), thus making the tower very steep. The height of the tower should be equal to, or even a bit higher than the base. For example, if the base were 40 feet (13 m) wide, the height of the tower would be 40 to 50 feet (13 to 17 m) high. Like the Biblical Tower of Babel, this tower would be unfinished.

The Olympian Tower of Babel would be a colossal architectural model, physically bigger than an actual building. It would give the illusion of a truly massive tower that could actually reach the heavens. Looking at *The Olympian Tower of Babel*, the viewer could see the myth transformed into a larger than life concrete reality. Conceptually, for the Olympics, each of the arched building blocks would represent past Olympic Games. The unbuilt portion of the tower suggests future Olympic Games and mankind striving for a god-like physical perfection.

Capitalism and Communism
April 8, 1992

Dear Kim Levin,
It was good to talk to you several days ago and I will briefly describe the project that I am hoping to execute at the Center for Contemporary Art in Warsaw, Poland. It would consist of two similar flatbed trucks of one to two ton capacity. One truck would be displayed in its normal position, carrying a huge ship anchor on its bed. The second truck would be suspended in mid-air, hooked like a fish. The hook-anchor would hold the truck through the open cab windows. The anchor would be attached to a high point with a large chain. The sculpture could be installed either indoors or outdoors. If it were to be installed inside the castle, perhaps the trucks could be partially dismantled to get them through the doors.

For this project I will need:

1. Two old vintage flatbed trucks with a one to two ton capacity that are the same model, or very similar in appearance. It is not essential that the trucks be operational, but it must appear that they are in full working order. I will not destroy the trucks, but the one with the anchor hooked through the driver's compartment, could suffer from minor body damage.
2. I will also need two old, identical or very similar, large ship anchors.
3. A large length of heavy duty steel chain, also old and rusty. The length would be determined by distance of the attachment point.
4. Necessary technical assistance to install this piece.

Obviously, this work is a commentary on different economic systems. I hope my description is clear and look forward to hearing from you soon.

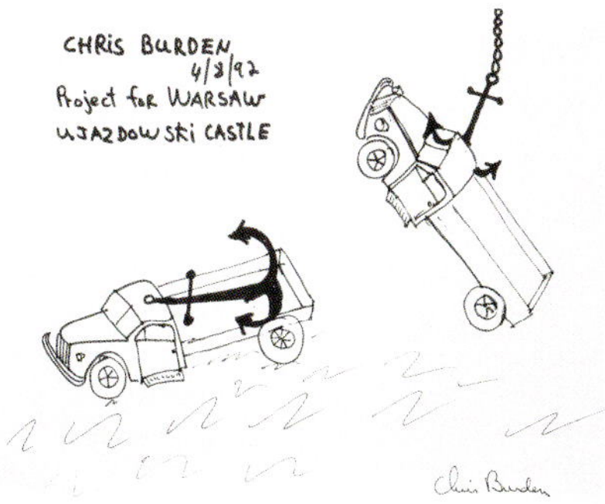

Sculpture for East Germany
Berlin, Germany
April 7, 1993

Dear Christoph Tannert,
I am in receipt of your fax of April 5 and I am flattered that you think my participation in the exhibition, 'Fontanelle', is so essential. I do have an idea for a site specific work based on the building plans that you sent January 4. I propose that a solid cement block be poured from the floor to the ceiling in the area that you have designated; in the 'square' formed by the first set of four columns directly after the entrance. The concrete cube should have the appropriate interior steel reinforcement. I do not know if your building can withstand the weight of the concrete cube. Perhaps the floor will have to be reinforced with vertical wooden beams all the way to the basement. The piece would entail pouring a cube of concrete that would be approximately 4 meters square by 3.4 meters high. The cement block must be clearly placed front and center of the exhibition hall. To me this cement block symbolizes the spiritual, social and material problems that the Germanies must overcome.

I do not think it is feasible, at this late date, to ship a second piece. To consider borrowing and shipping a second piece, in light of your limited finances, seems unrealistic.

I also received the letter of March 5 from Nike Batzner. He requested materials due by April 15 for the catalog. In order to fulfill this requirement, I need an answer as to whether you can produce the cement block, as described above. So I am not sending materials for the catalog until I hear back from you.

I would not be able to make a prior visit to Potsdam and Berlin in the next couple of weeks in order to see things for myself, as you suggested. If you think the cement block is something you could realize, I would be willing to come to Germany once, toward the end of May, middle of June, to supervise the construction of the project.

I have never received a definitive list of the other artists participating in this exhibition. Who are they? I look forward to hearing from you very soon, otherwise I will assume that you cannot execute this work.

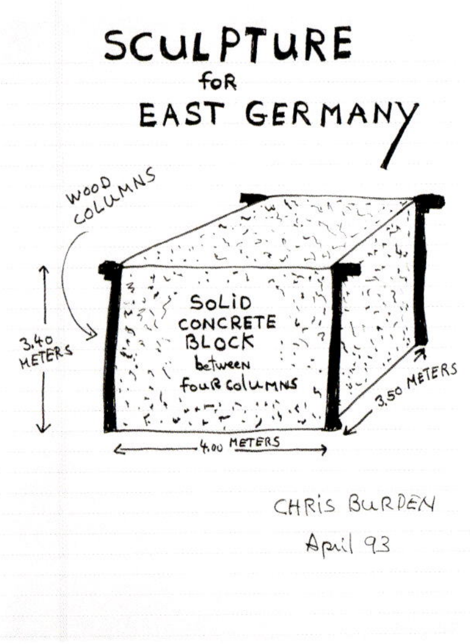

Proposal for the Chris Burden Exhibition at the Austrian Museum of Applied Arts (the MAK), Vienna, Austria
February 9, 1995

Dear Peter Noever,
In response to your fax of January 25 regarding scheduling my trip to Vienna, I teach classes at UCLA on Mondays and Wednesdays, but I will look into the possibility of leaving Los Angeles on Wednesday afternoon, March 1st and arriving in Vienna early Thursday afternoon. I would need to leave Vienna on Sunday morning, March 5th, in order to be back in Los Angeles for my Monday morning class. Alternately, I could come on the 19th or 20th of March and not be quite so rushed, as classes at the University end mid-March. Let me know soon what you think so I can schedule my time and buy my airplane ticket.

I have enclosed, as a separate document, a description of the *Ring Canal* Project. I hope it is what you need. I think it answers most of the major issues that you addressed and gives a good overall mechanical description and an artistic raison d'être.

On my trip to Vienna, I will bring all the material for the catalog that Danielle Zyman requested in her fax of February 1. I am happy you think my catalog should be most comprehensive and encompassing and I will do my best to gather all the photos, documentations and written texts that are needed to make it complete.

I have also enclosed a description of *Pizza City* and the accompanying *Three Dimensional Display of the Expanding/Contracting Cities*. After giving it much thought, I would like to take advantage of your invitation to create a special project at the MAK. I would like to complete and exhibit *Pizza City* in the main exhibition room, along with *Medusa's Head*, the five *Moonettes* and *Medusa's Flying Moon*. I think the addition of *Pizza City* to this never before shown assemblage, this gargantuan, bizarre 'solar system' (i.e. *Medusa's Head* and its six satellites) will generate contrast and help inform each about the other. The whole room will be energized by the interplay between the levels of detail, between the benign and ideal and the apocalyptic and captivating.

To finish *Pizza City* and the accompanying *Three Dimensional Display of the Expanding/Contracting Cities* will be a tremendous undertaking for myself and my staff for the next six or seven months that remain before the opening date of the exhibition. It will require my full attention. I will need to cancel some other projects that I have already committed to and I will need to hire more staff and, above all, start immediately. I would also like to budget $10,000 to produce the program, graphics and videotape for the *Three Dimensional Display of the Expanding/Contracting Cities*. I envision *Pizza City*, exclusive of the custom made crates and shipping costs, would cost approximately $60,000 (US dollars) to complete. Since 1989 to the present, I have personally invested approximately $60,000 into *Pizza City*. I ask the MAK to make an equal expenditure. I would need your immediate commitment and financial support for this amount so I can commence work. Some of the monies would have to be available immediately. If I must wait two to three months before I start to receive funding, it will be too late to realize this project.

I suggest that over a seven month period you send me $10,000 per month so that I can budget the money, get the project started and keep the project going smoothly. I would keep a complete accounting of all the money spent and would only use the money as I needed it. Of course, any unused funds would be returned to the MAK.

When we met in Santa Monica, you told me the budget for my exhibition is to be 600 million schillings, or approximately $550,000 (US dollars). You indicated that $100,000 would be used for the catalog, publicity, advertising and so on. This leaves $450,000 for the exhibition, the shipping costs to and from the exhibition, installation costs and the cost of a special project. Spending $70,000 on *Pizza City* and *Three Dimensional Display of the Expanding/Contracting Cities* leaves $380,000 for the exhibition, including the, as of yet, undecided *Ring Canal* Project. I am very excited about doing *Pizza City*, but I cannot emphasize enough how quickly I must begin to get started on it. Your suggestion in Santa Monica last month of doing a special project for the main exhibition room at the MAK captured my imagination. It is only in the last few days that I finally conceived the possibility of an all out effort to finish *Pizza City* for the November exhibition at the MAK.

I realize that finishing and installing *Pizza City* as the special project is a new idea and could conflict with the *Ring Canal* Project. Ideally, I would very much like to do both projects. I do not want either to be excluded at this stage. I hope you will continue to pursue the *Ring Canal* idea with full vigor. I think the *Ring Canal* Project helps illuminate some of my other ideas about time, travel, distance and power and would be a great addition to the exhibition.

Concerning the checklist that I discussed in my letter of January 19th, I called the fabricator in New York who was responsible for *The Fist of Light* at the Museum of Modern Art. Luckily, he is able and willing to reinstall *The Fist of Light* in Vienna for the November 1995 exhibition. He has begun preliminary investigations into the costs of replacing the transformers from 50Hv to 60Hv for all the special light bulbs. He envisions approximately five days to reconstruct it, as it is built out of modular aluminum panels. Many works, such as *Medusa's Head*, will require reconstruction and installation by several of my assistants. Even the *L.A.P.D. Uniforms* will need a special person from the Fabric Workshop, where they were produced, to install them. When I come to Vienna, we can start to discuss the specifics of each sculpture and what each would entail.

I hope I have not offended your staff as I

realized later that Jessica Beer is in charge of the catalog production and is not the curator of the exhibition. Is Danielle Zyman the curator?

I started this letter last week and had hoped to get it to you sooner, but my duties at the University have kept me busy from morning to evening. I also wanted to be clear and specific about the *Pizza City* and the *Ring Canal* projects. Please get back to me as quickly as possible about the suggested travel dates and let me know your thoughts on the two projects I have proposed.

Ring Canal Project for the Chris Burden Exhibition at the Austrian Museum of Applied Arts (the MAK)
Vienna, Austria
November, 1995

For my exhibition at the Museum of Applied Arts (the MAK) scheduled for November 1995, in Vienna, I have conceived a project which is both practical and poetic. This project would involve shipping all the artworks for my exhibition directly to the MAK, via the waterways of the world: the oceans, the seas, the canals and most importantly, the rivers of Europe, the ancient conduits of commerce and culture. Because my art materials are both heavy and bulky, the components of my exhibition will require approximately six to eight steel seagoing shipping containers. As well as being economical, shipping my exhibition by water will become an artwork in itself.

The six to eight, 20- and 40-foot long containers would either leave the port of Los Angeles and pass through the Panama Canal, or leave the port of New York. Both would travel by sea, across the Atlantic Ocean, through the Mediterranean Sea, the Aegean Sea and into the Black Sea. The containers would be unloaded off the ocean-going ships and onto barges to travel up the Danube River, through Romania and Bulgaria, Yugoslavia and Hungary, and finally arrive in Vienna, Austria. From the Danube, in Vienna, the shipping containers would be transferred to the partially flooded Ring Canal. Either the barges that brought the shipping containers up the Danube or a specially designed smaller barge would be used to transport the containers on the Ring Canal. The type of barge used on the Ring Canal would be determined by the level of the water allowed into the Ring Canal and the bridge specifications, i.e. the bridge clearance. The smaller, specially designed barge would be constructed so it could float in a very shallow level of water, perhaps as shallow as one meter. The barge would accommodate only one shipping container at a time. The small barge could be powered either by outboard motors, a small tugboat, or even pulled by an amphibious vehicle, possibly lent by the Austrian Army. The shipping containers would be transferred to the small barge somewhere on the Danube River and brought up, one by one, on the Ring Canal, next to the Museum. There, a crane would unload each container and bring each onto the Museum grounds. The crane, all the shipping containers and the special barge would be stacked on the Museum property during the length of the exhibition. These pieces and the story of their journey would be displayed and become an integral part of the exhibition. At the end of the exhibition, the return trip would be the same, only in reverse.

Using the waterways to move my entire exhibition to Vienna, right to the Museum's doorstep, is an important physical work that symbolically involves using the entire world. Water covers two-thirds of the world and the waterways are not only the lifeblood of our civilizations, but also the seminal fluid from which life itself and ultimately, humanity, has sprung. The oceans and the rivers are still a vital and essential part of our civilization, transporting not only goods, but also thoughts and ideas. Filling the Ring Canal with water and using it to bring my exhibition to the MAK would be a way to revitalize this unused, dry artery and give it new meaning in the context of the Museum, the gardens and the city of Vienna.

Proposal for The Three Dimensional Display of the Expanding/Contracting Cities
November, 1995

One of the most salient features of the 20th Century is that travel is no longer expressed in terms of actual physical distance, but in terms of time. In essence, distance and time have become synonymous. Now a person's concern is not how many miles or kilometers; it is, how long does it take to get there, 10 minutes, two hours, 18 hours, three light years? As the speed of travel accelerates, the distance between two points diminishes. For example, when the TGV train system is completed in France, in the year 2000, the size of France will literally shrink in half. Presently, it takes approximately six hours to fly across the Atlantic Ocean. Five hundred years ago, Columbus crossed the Atlantic Ocean in about 65 days. A six-hour airplane trip across the Atlantic is one two-hundred-sixtieth of the time it took Columbus to cross the Atlantic; thus, for all practical purposes, the Atlantic Ocean is 260 times smaller today than it was in Columbus's time.

To illustrate this concept of distance and time becoming one and the same, I would like to create two large video displays of constantly changing three dimensional maps of the cities of Los Angeles and New York. These maps would be created by using many different specific points in each of the cities and measuring the time it takes to travel from point A to point B. These time measurements would be taken during different moments in the city's daily life cycle. This information would be used to create a map of the ever changing three dimensional topography of these two cities. Thus, the screen displays would look like amoebas in constant motion, as parts of them expand and shrink. Occasionally, huge spikes or pimples would emerge from the surface as traffic congestion and weather changes translated into time delays. I envision these three dimensional displays to be shown on extremely large format monitors.

I think this active graphic display would enable a viewer to viscerally understand the concept of 'time = distance.'

C.B. World Transit
Proposal for De Appel, Amsterdam
June, 1996

Upon visiting the public-supported art institution, De Appel, in Amsterdam, in May 1995, one of the most interesting features was its present location in the inner city, nestled in an old antique and arts area and surrounded by the original ring canals of Amsterdam. The old ring canals were, at one time, obviously the center of a bustling port city with cargo being delivered literally to individual warehouses, stores and businesses. I was impressed with the idea that an object of commerce could move so efficiently from a boat cargo hold to a store shelf.

My idea for an exhibition at the Appel is to have a small cargo boat built in America. The boat I have in mind is designed by Phil Bolger, a noted boat designer, and is called the motor sailing cargo boat. It is 30 feet long and ten feet wide. It is presently in use in Alaska, under very arduous conditions. The boat is able to carry approximately three tons of cargo and is designed to service isolated fishing, hunting and scientific camps along the coastline of Alaska. The sailing rig and the engines are used together simultaneously. This enables the boat to have a small engine and a small fuel tank which allows for more cargo space. This hybrid propulsion system, which minimizes fuel consumption, could be the forerunner of a more environmentally friendly way of moving trans-oceanic cargo.

The boat would be built in South Carolina by Mark Bayne, a trustworthy and respected boat builder whom I have used in the past. This motor sailing cargo boat would sail up the eastern coast of the USA and Canada, stopping at various ports. It would sail in a Northeasterly direction, stopping at ports in Greenland, Iceland, the UK, with its final destination being the Appel in Amsterdam.

The boat would be built in the New World, in Charleston, South Carolina, and as it traveled up the eastern coast of the USA and Canada it would fill its cargo hold with goods and products from the New World, i.e. American tools, blue jeans, maple syrup, movie videocassettes, Coca-Cola, fur pelts, lumber, etc. These products are familiar objects and represent the Americas with both old exports (fur pelts, lumber) and new exports (blue jeans, movie cassettes, Coca-

Cola). The cargo would be unloaded in the canal next to De Appel and the goods would be put into the various exhibition spaces of De Appel. These goods would be for sale to the public. The motor sailing cargo boat would remain docked in the canal outside De Appel as a physical and visual reminder of how the goods were literally transported from the Americas to Amsterdam.

The voyage of the motor sailing cargo boat, bringing goods from the New World to the Old World, would have to start in the Spring and sail through the Spring and Summer, in hopefully favorable conditions, and dock in Amsterdam in the late Summer or early Fall. Because the trip would take four to six months, I would not be the captain of the boat, but rather the boat owner. Whenever possible, I would fly to a port to meet the ship and arrange for the purchase of goods and, perhaps, accompany the ship on certain sections of the journey.

Although my small personal international shipping effort is largely a symbolic gesture, I will have, in essence, subverted the present day corporate monopoly on shipping goods across the oceans. By sailing my boat and delivering my cargo to Amsterdam, I will feel that I have retaken control of the oceans and will have asserted my power as an American entrepreneur.

The Matterhorn
February 28, 1997

The Matterhorn would be a 25-foot-high sculpture, built from steel and cement, with an operating, large scale railroad train and tracks and a broadcasting system. The sculpture would be based on an actual mountain, the Trango Tower, which is located in North Pakistan. Trango Tower bears a strange resemblance to the Matterhorn, in Switzerland. However, Trango Tower appears to be stretched and pulled so that it gives the semblance of a tall, thin, elongated Matterhorn.

The model train track would start at the base of the mountain and spiral upwards to the peak. Most of the track would be hidden inside the mountain. Only occasionally would a section of the train track appear on the exterior, visible to the viewers below. One complete cycle of the sculpture would consist of the train starting at the base, winding up the spiral track, until it reached the peak. Very near the peak, the train would stop at a small junction, visible to the viewers below. A loudspeaker would broadcast, in German, a message which would be in a Führer-like cadence. The essence of the broadcast message would be, 'From these lofty peaks, the rightful destiny of the German people can be seen. From here you can see London, Rome, Moscow, Istanbul, Cairo. From here, my fellow Germans...' At the end of the short, loud speech, the train would resume its journey to the base of the mountain and the cycle would be complete. The total cycle would last five to ten minutes and the train would rest at the base of the mountain for approximately 15 to 20 minutes. A bell would ring and the cycle would begin again with the train spiraling upwards.

Although using the caricature of the conquering Germans, the phallic Matterhorn symbolizes, in a wry and humorous way, the aggressive and expansive impulses of all peoples and nations. And although *The Matterhorn* can initially be seen as humorous it is, in fact, like Picasso's *Guernica*, part of a long, historical tradition of socially critical art. *The Matterhorn* is a critique of the virulent nationalism that often leads to war.

My early art career was established in the 1970s, by a series of art actions, or performances, that became widely known and documented by art historians, critics and the general press. In the past 20 years, I have produced a series of large scale sculptures that, although they do not involve me directly, are performative in nature, such as *The Big Wheel* and *The Flying Steamroller*. Other international artists, such as Paul McCarthy and Vito Acconci, who began their art careers by doing art actions, have also turned to performative sculptures. This phenomenon of performing artists turning to performative sculpture will be documented in an upcoming major international art exhibition titled 'Out of Action'. This exhibition is being curated by Paul Schimmel, chief curator at the Museum of Contemporary Art in Los Angeles.

I would commence building *The Matterhorn* by making a full-scale cardboard outline of the mountain, Trango Tower, and attach it to a 25-foot-high tower of scaffolding. Based on the outline, I would begin the actual construction to the tower by making three-dimensional sections. Each section would be eight to nine feet tall and would be built with a steel frame armature, a steel mesh skin and a concrete stucco overlay. The three to four sections would stack upon each other to form the total mountain. All assembly would be done from the interior, via a built-in ladder.

It is my hope that this work, *The Matterhorn*, through its sheer size and subject matter, will be acknowledged as a major artwork and incorporated into the body of important late 20th Century art.

Water Cycle: Proposal for the City of San Diego's North City Water Reclamation Plant Public Art Project
December 10, 1997

For the City of San Diego's North City Water Reclamation Plant Public Art Project, I would like to propose a large, but extremely simple and elegant sculpture, titled *Water Cycle*.

The designated site for the sculpture consists of a large, elongated circle, measuring approximately 42 × 55 feet, and surrounded by an entry road and a series of parking spaces. The island site and the surrounding driveway slope down to the formal entrance of the administration building. The building's entrance extends out onto a large concrete walkway and shades the inlaid mosaic seal of the Metropolitan Water Department.

I propose to fill the entire site, the elongated circle, with water. A small wall would be built around the entire perimeter of the site, creating a reservoir. This wall would start at grade, at the higher end of the site and continue in a level line around the perimeter. At the low end of the site, the wall would be a couple of feet above grade. This shallow reservoir would be filled with reclaimed processed water. Incorporated into the wall, at the deep end of the reservoir, would be several flood gates. When the water reached a certain level in the reservoir, the flood gates would open and quickly release the entire stored reservoir. The water would surge out of the reservoir in a giant spreading sheet, covering the lower parking spaces, cresting over the driveway's curb and washing over the concrete entry walkway and finally wetting the mosaic seal of the Metropolitan Water Department. This thin, vast, glistening surface, several times larger than the reservoir itself, would exist for only a few moments before the water would recede and the wet surfaces would begin to dry off. The receding water would drain into existent curb drains and flow back to the reclamation plant. The flood gates would close and the reservoir would start to fill again with reclaimed water, repeating the cycle of storage, flow and ebb.

I anticipate this cycle would be repeated several times a week.

I see this sculpture as a poetic analogy of how water is used by both man and nature. Water is stored, used and then allowed to dissipate.

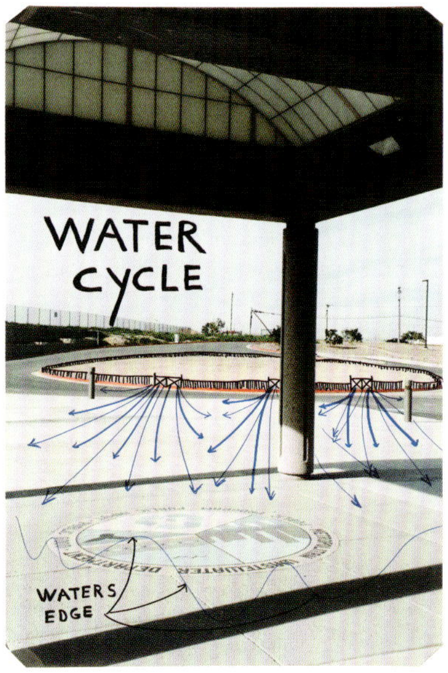

Proposal for the Exhibition at the 8th International Fukui Biennale, Japan
July 14, 1999

Dear Hisanori Gogota,
I am back from my Europe travels and except for a short trip to London, I plan on being in Los Angeles for most of July, August and September. I would be happy to receive you at my studio when it is convenient for you. I will know in the next few days if and when I must travel to London. I will let you know my travel plans as soon as possible.

Concerning your proposals:

1. I do have one specific idea for a new work that might be quite appropriate to your exhibition. I will briefly outline my idea, but I would like to discuss it further when you visit me. The idea is to build, out of Meccano parts (the same French metal construction parts that I used to build the bridges that were recently exhibited at the Magasin 3 Stockholm Konsthall in Sweden) two full scale replicas of the first Russian satellite, the Sputnik, which was approximately 600 cm in diameter. One of the replica Sputniks would actually be launched into orbit on a rocket and the other replica Sputnik would remain on exhibition. The orbiting Sputnik would be equipped with a radio transmitter in order that a rudimentary beep-beep signal could be broadcast back to the exhibition hall as the satellite passes overhead. Obviously, the most crucial and pressing problem would be to find space on a launch vehicle. Let's discuss these possibilities in person when you travel to LA. Perhaps you could commence to make inquiries into launch opportunities.

2. Regarding the exhibition of the five *Moonettes* and *Medusa's Flying Moon*, I do not think that this is a possibility. The five *Moonettes* are owned by individual collectors and are all in France. *Medusa's Flying Moon* is in a private collection here in LA and I know that they would absolutely refuse to lend it.

3. We can discuss my performance films and videos when you visit. However, I must tell you that except for my TV commercials, I do not consider the films or videos to fully represent my art.

I will keep you updated on my travel plans and look forward to hearing from you.

Sincerely,
Chris Burden

Future Bridge Projects
July, 2002

I have several different ideas for future Meccano/Erector bridge projects. One of the world's most magnificently engineered structures is the Forth Railway Bridge, which spans the Firth of Forth in Scotland. As I dreamed about building the Mexican Bridge for many years, I now find myself entertaining the possibility that, some day, I might be able to build the Forth Railway Bridge.

The key to being able to model this bridge in Meccano/Erector parts is to be able to duplicate the tubular members of the Forth Railway Bridge. Fortunately, a Meccano supplier in Argentina produces a series of parts that would enable several different sizes of tubes to be constructed. Using the two sizes of tubes displayed here, the resultant Meccano/Erector model of the Forth Railway Bridge would be approximately 120 feet (36.5 m) long by six feet (2 m) high. I anticipate that it would take several years to build the model. My hope would be to show it at the Baltic Centre, as a sequel to this exhibition.

Another direction that I have been exploring is to actually carry out physical stress tests on various Meccano/Erector parts to establish each part's structural limits. Using equipment employed to test mountain climbing gear, I would subject different Meccano/Erector parts and assemblies to physical forces until the point of failure, thus establishing empirical limits. I could then use these known limits to actually engineer Meccano/Erector bridges to support pedestrian traffic. Some of these bridges could be patterned after existing bridges, such as the two bridges illustrated (the Fink Through-Truss Bridge and the Lower Plymouth Rock Bridge). Others could be entirely of my design. In concept, these bridges would be similar to the *¼ Ton Bridge* in that they would be designed to carry an actual human load. Whereas the *¼ Ton Bridge* was built by trial and error, these new bridges would be fully engineered.

The Austrian Navy 2002

October 2, 2002

Ursula Krinzinger
Galerie Krinzinger

Dear Ursula,
Concerning a date for my exhibition at your gallery in Vienna, I think that late Spring, or early Summer of 2003 would be good. As we discussed, my idea for a solo exhibition at your gallery would be to create a navy which would consist of several hundred cardboard ships ranging in size from a half to one-and-a-half meters each. Like an architectural maquette, this model armada would represent my proposal for the construction of an actual Austrian navy. As part of the artwork, the day or night of the opening, I would have you plan a press conference and party at which approximately five handsome, capable young men would be dressed in custom-made uniforms. They would have studied naval history with me and would be able to carry forth on decisive naval battles in history to either the press or to the invited guests. The basic thrust of my exhibition would be to convince the Austrian nation that by maintaining a world class navy, Austria could again become a world power. The fact that Austria is landlocked is irrelevant. Perhaps it would make sense to videotape my officer's statements so that later, after the opening's 'live event', their individual presentations could be shown at the gallery. In addition, I will write a statement explaining my proposal.

Of course, I will have to ask for your production money in order to fabricate the ships, the uniforms, and to train my assistants to be able to recite naval history. I am not sure what the budget for these expenses would be. I will have to think more carefully on how to proceed and how much time and staff this project will entail.

I hope all is well with you. Please call me or write to me with your thoughts.

Sincerely,
Chris Burden

Two Stainless Steel Skyscrapers 2003
Trafalgar Square Fourth Plinth Project

Over the last six years, I have been using metal toy construction parts, namely Meccano (British and French) and Erector (American) to design and build a series of bridges. In the course of building my various bridges, I have used both new and used Erector and Meccano parts, and parts that I have designed to my own specifications. My bridges range in size from approximately one-and-a-half to ten meters in length. The most recent exhibition of these bridges was at the Baltic Centre for Contemporary Art's inaugural exhibition, in Gateshead, England, in the summer of 2002.

Legend has it that inventor A.C. Gilbert was leaving New York City in the early 1900s and was fascinated by the tall buildings being built with steel girders. He wanted to produce a toy that would enable children to build structures using prototypical miniature girders. He created the early 1913 Erector set, called Erector Mysto Type I, which uses a very rudimentary system that was based on a singular girder, complete with rivet detailing. A box beam can be formed using four girders, two nuts and two bolts. This strong, but light, box beam is the basis for the entire building system. With just a few basic parts it is much simpler, though less versatile than the later Erector and Meccano systems.

Because the Erector Mysto Type I parts are approaching 100 years old and are made of stamped steel that has been lacquered, they are extremely hard to obtain, expensive and subject to rust and corrosion. In conjunction with Fred Hoffman Fine Art, in Santa Monica, California, I have recently recreated the metal dies from the Erector Mysto Type I girders and am now reproducing this Erector system in stainless steel. These parts are electroplated to give them a very durable, highly polished nickel finish, which is resistant to rust, weather, sunlight and other environmental factors. Any construction built with these stainless steel parts can be exposed to the elements indefinitely.

For the Trafalgar Square Fourth Plinth project, I propose to build two prototypical skyscraper frameworks in model form using these reproduction stainless steel Erector girders. The primary decision to build two skyscrapers for the Trafalgar Square Fourth Plinth is in direct response to the dimensions of the plinth. The base of each skyscraper framework will measure 138 × 172 cm. Thus, the two skyscrapers will fit comfortably side by side on the plinth with approximately 30–35 cm separating them. These two skyscrapers represent the traditional skyscraper of stacking graduated blocks and a post and beam construction. In addition, viewers will undoubtedly reference the New York City World Trade Center Twin Towers that were destroyed. I see this association as positive, as it will spark a conversation about all the structural, economic, safety and aesthetic issues involved in building structures that push towards the heavens.

I have always wanted to build a model skyscraper using Erector parts. The proposed model skyscrapers, built from a toy and almost seven meters in height, takes on the dimensions of a full size two-story building. This circle of an actual building inspiring a toy, which is then used to build a model skyscraper the size of an actual building, is a beautiful metamorphosis.

Atomic Compass 2005

I live in a rural section of Los Angeles and several times a week, for the last 15 years, I hike with my dogs into the hills and along a dirt road that follows a ridgeline. There are no houses and, usually, no people on this one-hour walk. The road dead-ends at the top of a small mountain that has a 360-degree view stretching from the Los Angeles basin to the Pacific Ocean and the San Fernando Valley. At the end of the road there are approximately 11 derelict and abandoned cars and trucks. These automobiles date from the 1960s and represent the golden era of American automobile manufacturing. They are heavy and overbuilt. One is a Lincoln Continental, like the car J.F. Kennedy was assassinated in. The chrome plating is so thick on many of the parts, it has not yet started to rust. The cars have become filled with sticks and debris from animal nests and the cars are covered in graffiti, such as DOGTOWN and VALS SUCK, referring to local gang and surfer lingo. These decomposing carcasses are of a great curiosity to me and lend a somewhat ominous and spooky feeling to the area. People go to this area to be alone, take drugs, or to work out their hostilities on the derelict cars.

The *Atomic Compass* would consist of a large I-beam structure in the shape of a cross. The 11 or so DOGTOWN automobiles would be mounted on the large I-beam cross, like precious gemstones of a royal scepter. At the center of the cross, a pivot would be installed and the whole swinging cross would be laid flat, a few feet off the ground in the Museum garden. A Geiger counter would be installed at the apex of the cross and connected to an electric motor so that the cross would swing towards any detected radiation. I assume that most of the time the compass would point towards the harbor. But if a truck full of nuclear material passed close, the cross would swing in that direction. If Chernobyl happened, it would swing in that direction. If the Middle East degenerated into an all out nuclear war, the compass would swing south, towards the Middle East. In addition, numerous large flagpoles would be placed around the park, flying the US flag, the Stars and Stripes. The flags would not only be mounted upside down, an international sign of distress, they would also be flown at half-mast, a sign of mourning.

The project would involve retrieving the automobiles, shipping them to Rotterdam and building the steel cross and gearing mechanisms.

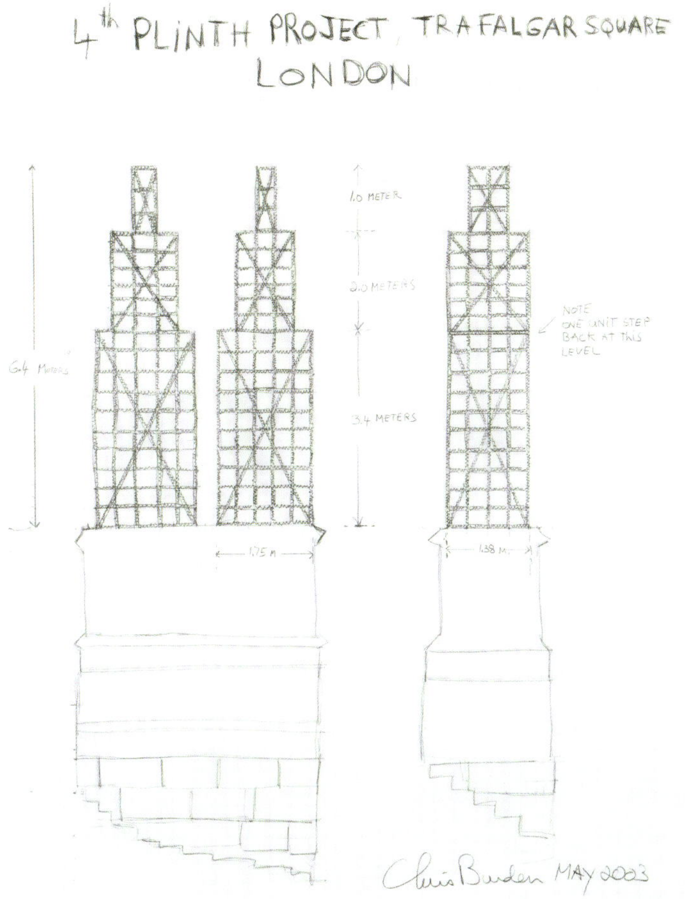

4th Plinth Project, Trafalgar Square, London, England 2003
Pencil and ink on paper
22 × 17 inches

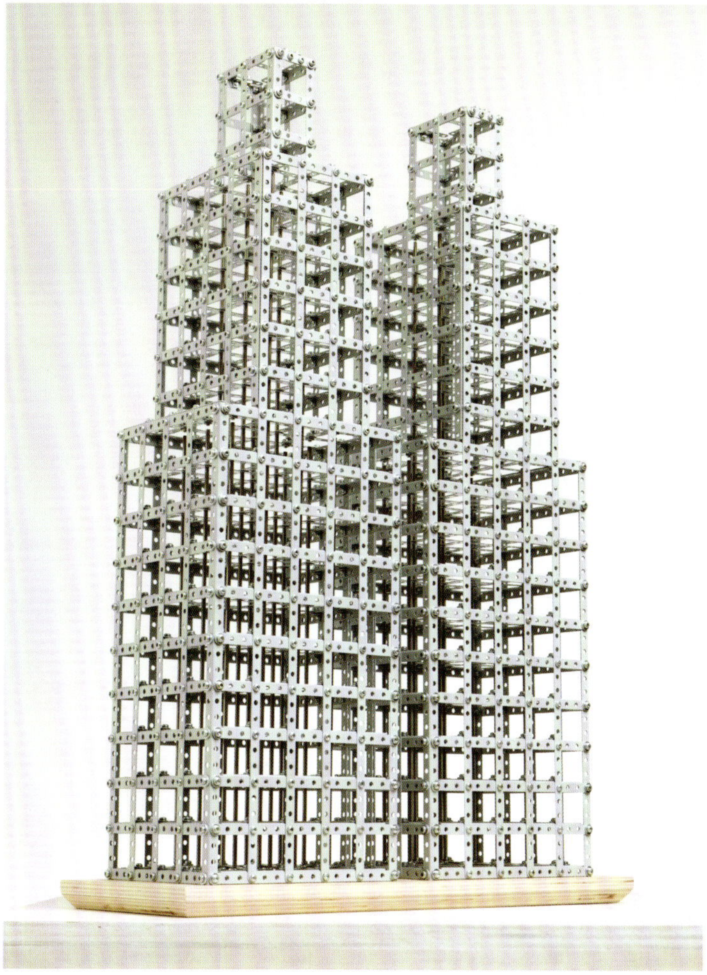

Skyscraper, 4th Plinth Project, Trafalgar Square, London, England 2003
Stainless steel reproduction Mysto Type I
Erector parts on wooden base
29¾ × 20 × 7¾ in.

Early Works

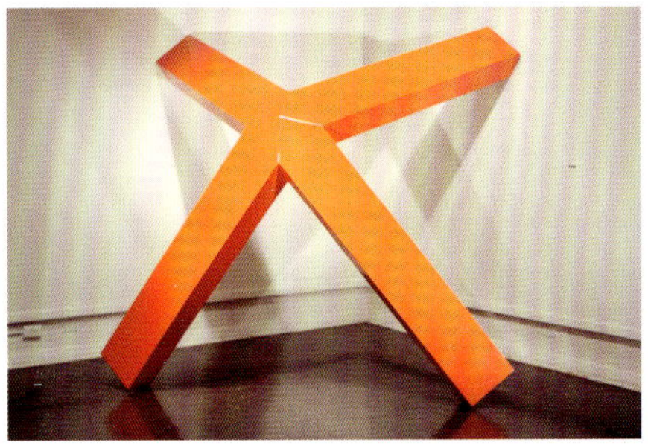
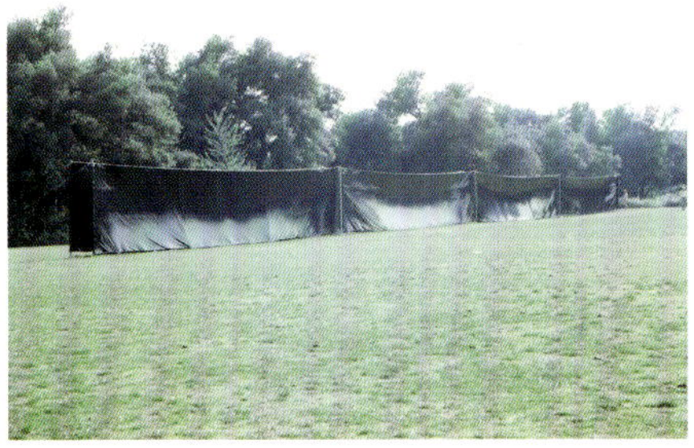
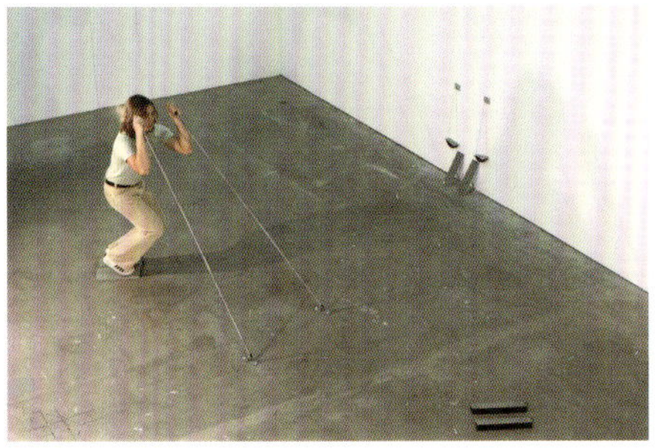
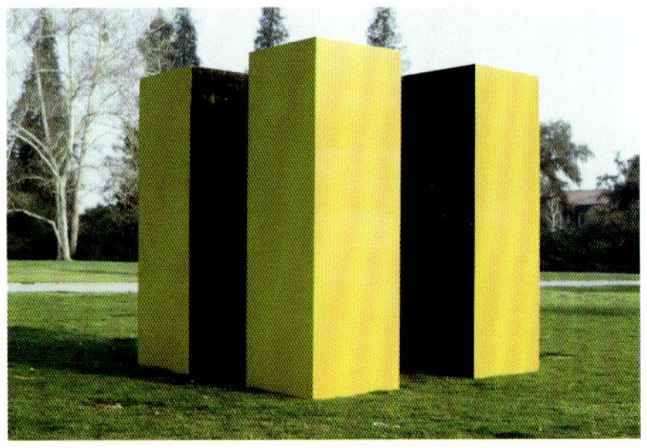
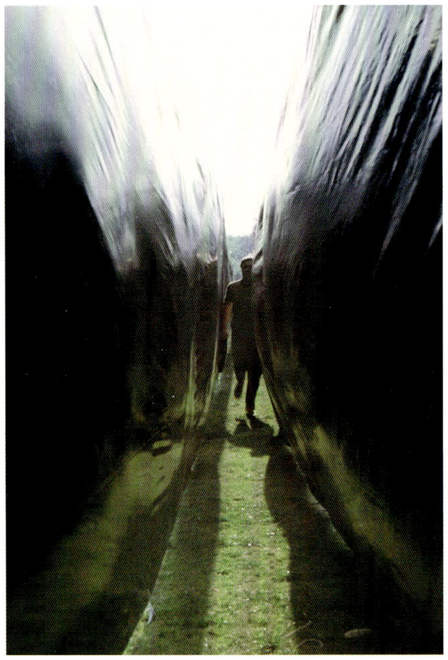
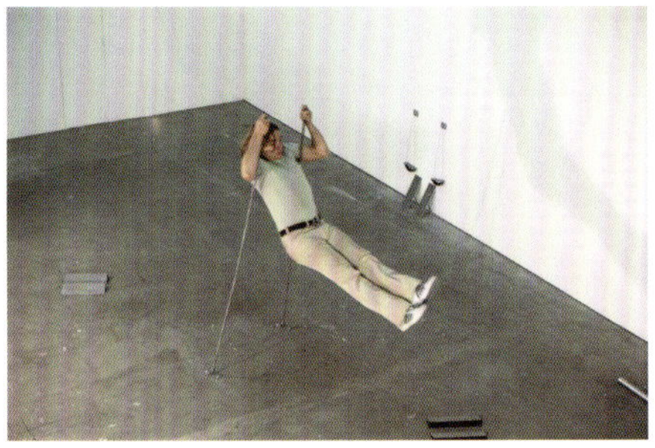
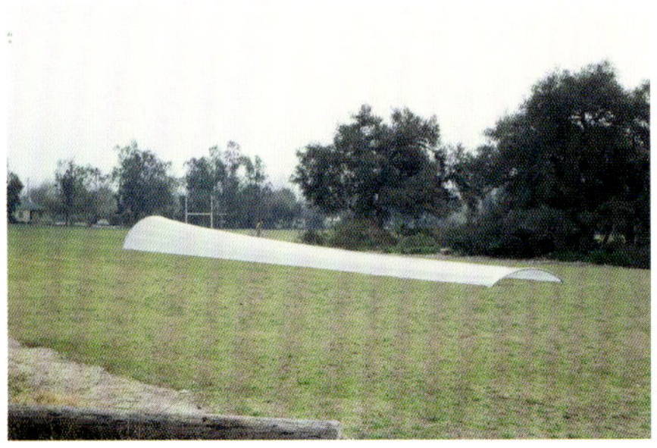
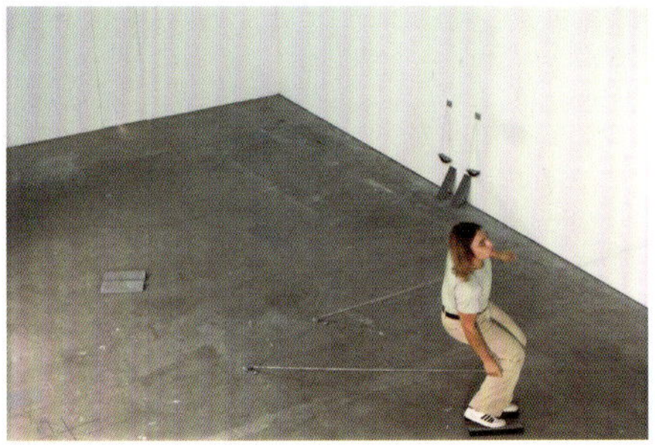
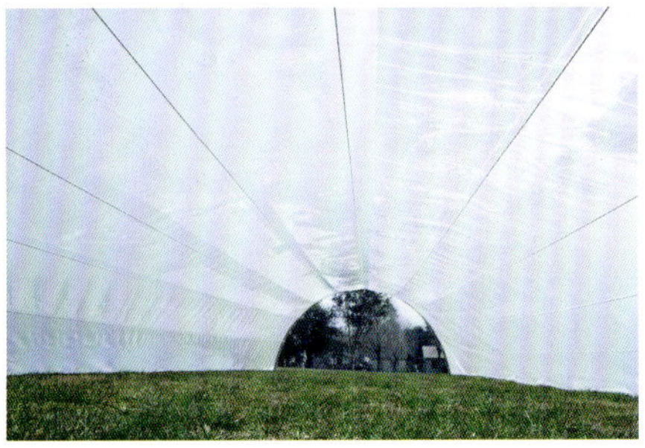
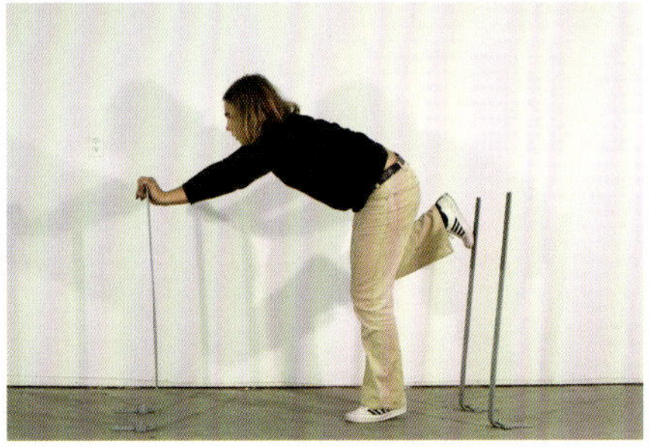
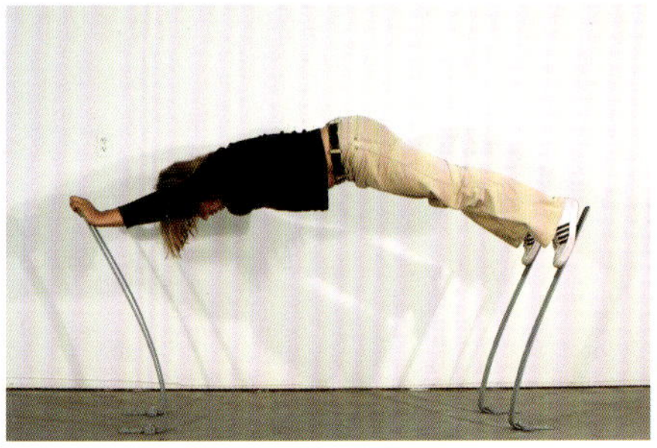

Extract from Robert Horvitz: 'Chris Burden', *Artforum*, Vol XIV, No 9 (May 1976)

'… Burden's present type of work derives genetically from environmental sculpture rather than from theater. As an undergraduate art major at Pomona College, he had been working in a highly competent, but still relatively conventional, Minimalist mode. Two large pieces built on the school soccer field as part of his senior project (1968–69) may have marked the high-point of this phase. The first consisted of a pair of arches made of hydraulically bent steel pipe set in concrete footings and connected by steel cables. The cables were canopied over with translucent plastic to form a tunnel 100 feet long and 20 feet wide, that diminished in height from nearly eight feet at the larger end to only two feet at the smaller end. The piece clearly invited one to enter, and as one moved into it, the flattening curve of the tunnel gradually forced one to stoop lower and lower, so that by the time one had reached the other end, one was crawling through a very wide, squat passageway. The other piece was similar in construction and probably was intended as a simple variation on the first. Steel pipes were set in the ground at three-foot intervals to form a narrow corridor 11 feet high and 200 feet long. The structure was stabilized with guy-wires and linked with black plastic sheeting. But two unplanned elements entered into this piece that in the long run proved crucial:

I thought of it as a corridor, but then things started happening that I didn't plan on. For one thing, it was getting vandalized, so I started having to live there to protect it. And the wind did a funny thing. It was such a big structure that the wind would hit one side of it and blow the plastic in, and this created some sort of vacuum that would suck in the plastic on the other side. So the whole thing was always pressed together. You couldn't see down it except on rare occasions. If you walked down it, it would engulf you, but if you started running, your body would make an air pocket that would push it open in front of you. It was like magic. The stuff would open in front of you and close behind you. That's when I realized that what I had made was not a piece of sculpture but something that had to be activated. These pieces were about physical activity, about how they manipulated my body. When I realized that, they stopped being sculptures and there was no reason to make them that big.

Following up this insight, his next series of works, done in the graduate program of the University of California at Irvine, were quite different in character, resembling isometric exercise equipment more than sculpture. One consisted of a metal T-bar that bolted to the floor, on which two people were supposed to stand, and a pair of metal rods connected to each other by short cords. Holding the rods in their hands, the two people leaned away from one another and attempted to strike a common balance. 'This balance point,' Burden comments, 'is very elusive and can only be maintained for a few seconds.' It is tantamount to trying to balance a top-heavy triangle on its point. A second piece consisted of four pairs of cables joined together at the end of another cable that attached to the ceiling. The free end of each pair had a stirrup for a person's hand or foot. The idea was to get into the stirrups and assume an arched position in order to hover somewhat precariously over the floor. The amount of effort required to sustain this position is inversely related to the degree of arching: the flatter the arch, the more difficult the task. A third piece was simply a large sheet of aluminum with two small footholds, supported in the center by a pivot that bolted to the floor. By lying down on the sheet and carefully adjusting one's position, one could balance on the pivot for an indefinite period of time.

All of these pieces attempt to establish a delicate sensual interplay between body and apparatus. They are extremely responsive to changes in position and muscle tension and seem to have been expressly designed to amplify these changes. They are not primarily to be looked at: they are to be donned and used. By drawing the viewer (viewer is obviously no longer the right word) into the work, giving him an active, literally constitutive role, Burden seemed to be trying to overcome the detachment and visual/intellectual distance usually entailed by object sculpture and replace it with an immediate kinesthetic involvement. Trading formal autonomy and stasis for dynamic equilibrium and engagement, his transition out of sculpture was well underway.

But not without problems. As these apparatuses were still one-of-a-kind, custom-made objects, and very elegant ones at that, most people continued to regard them as conventional sculpture, complete in themselves. While he had tried to make their intended use so self-evident that no further instructions or inducements were needed, it didn't quite work. People tended to read them as metaphors for activity rather than as literal opportunities. Eventually, Burden hit on a two-part strategy for dealing with this misunderstanding. The first was to use equipment that already existed so that it would not attract attention to itself as a specially invented form. The second was to further reduce the distance between himself, the experience he wished to convey, and the audience, by enacting the work himself.

The first definitive piece of this new kind was the *Five Day Locker Piece* (April 26–30, 1971, University of California at Irvine) …'

Catalogue of Works

[Collective titles in square brackets]

1971

PERFORMANCES

Being Photographed: Looking Out, Looking In
F Space, Santa Ana, California, USA; February 4–20
RELIC: 140 Polaroid photographs (each 4¼ × 3¼ in.), 11 date cards (each 4¼ × 3¼ in.)
Framed photographs and date cards: 25⅜ × 133 × 2 in. Drawing: 22½ × 30 in. (1971/2006)
Collection: Sender Collection, New York, USA

Five Day Locker Piece
University of California, Irvine, California, USA; April 26–30
RELIC: Padlock
Case: 6 × 9¼ × 7¼ in.
Collection: Gagosian Gallery, New York, USA

Bicycle Piece
University of California, Irvine, California, USA; May 6–20

Shout Piece
F Space, Santa Ana, California, USA; August 21

Prelude to 220, or 110
F Space, Santa Ana, California, USA; September 10–12
RELIC: Copper band
Case: 11 × 15 × 8½ in.
Collection: Ronald and Frayda Feldman, New York, USA

I Became a Secret Hippy
Museum of Conceptual Art, San Francisco, California, USA; October 3
RELIC: Tie, silver star
Case: 4½ × 6¼ × 18¼ in.
Collection: Andy Warhol Estate, New York, USA

220
F Space, Santa Ana, California, USA; October 9

You'll Never See My Face in Kansas City
Morgan Gallery, Kansas City, Missouri, USA; November 6
RELIC: Ski mask
Case: 5½ × 17 × 12 in.
Collection: Gilbert and Lila Silverman, Southfield, Michigan, USA

Shoot
F Space, Santa Ana, California, USA; November 19

Disappearing
December 22–24
RELIC: Void (empty case)
Collection: The artist

DRAWINGS

You'll Never See My Face in Kansas City
Pencil on paper. 11 × 14 in.

1972

PERFORMANCES

TV Hijack
Channel 3 Cablevision, Irvine, California, USA; February 9
RELIC: Knife, scabbard
Case: 7½ × 10 × 6 in.
Collection: Orange County Museum of Art, Newport Beach, California, USA

Bed Piece
Market Street, Venice, California, USA; February 18–March 10

Match Piece
Pomona College, Claremont, California, USA; March 20

Jaizu
Newport Harbor Art Museum, Newport Beach, California, USA; June 10–11
RELIC: Sunglasses, painted black on the back
Case: 6 × 10¼ × 8¼ in.
Collection: Gagosian Gallery, New York, USA

Dos Equis
Laguna Canyon Road, Laguna Beach, California, USA; October 16

Deadman
La Cienega Blvd, (Riko Mizuno Gallery), Los Angeles, California, USA; November 12
RELIC: Canvas tarpaulin
Folded: 1 × 10 × 15 in.
Open: ½ × 53 × 70 in.
Case: 9¾ × 19½ × 14½ in.
Collection: Sender Collection, New York, USA

1973

PERFORMANCES

747
Los Angeles, California, USA; January 5
RELIC: Revolver
Collection: The artist

Fire Roll
Museum of Conceptual Art, San Francisco, California, USA; February 28

Icarus
Venice, California, USA; April 13
RELIC: Glass wings
Case: 10 × 76 × 16 in.
Collection: Museum of Modern Art (MOMA), New York, USA

Movie on the Way Down
Oberlin College, Oberlin, Ohio, USA; May 1
RELIC: Kodak Super 8 movie camera
Case: 7½ × 10¼ × 8¼ in.
Collection: Gagosian Gallery, New York, USA

B.C. Mexico
Newspace, Newport Beach, California, USA; May 25–June 10
RELIC: Diary, seashell, stone
Case: 4¼ × 10¼ × 9¼ in.
Collection: Jasper Johns, New York, USA

Through the Night Softly
Main Street, Los Angeles, California, USA; September 12
RELIC: Broken glass
Case: 5¾ × 8¾ × 8¼ in.
Collection: Wexner Center for the Visual Arts, Ohio State University, Columbus, Ohio, USA

TV Ad
KHJ-Channel 9, Los Angeles, California, USA; November 5–December 2

Doorway to Heaven
Venice, California, USA; November 15
RELIC: Two wire coils
Case: 20 × 26 × 26 in.
Collection: Marilyn Oshman, Houston, Texas, USA

PRINTS

If You Drive
Edition of 50
Lithograph. 30 × 22 in.

If You Fly
Edition of 50
Lithograph. 30 × 22 in.

VIDEOS

Through the Night Softly
Black and white. 16mm. 10 seconds

1974

PERFORMANCES

Back to You
112 Greene St., New York, USA; January 16
RELIC: Push pins, stainless steel bowl
Case: 10 × 10 × 10 in.
Collection: The artist

Trans-fixed
Speedway Avenue, Venice, California, USA; April 23
RELIC: Two nails
Case: 6⅞ × 6¼ × 6¼ in.
Collection: Jasper Johns, New York, USA

Velvet Water
School of the Art Institute of Chicago, Chicago, Illinois, USA; May 7

Kunst Kick
Ronald Feldman Fine Arts, Basel Art Fair, Basel, Switzerland; June 19

Sculpture in Three Parts
Hansen Fuller Gallery, San Francisco, California, USA; September 10–21
RELIC: Stool (destroyed)

Oh, Dracula
Utah Museum of Art, Salt Lake City, Utah, USA; October 7

Dreamy Nights
Poolerie Gallery, Graz, Austria; October 15
RELIC: Corked bottle of Spiritus
Case: 10 × 8¼ × 8¼ in.
Collection: Jasper Johns, New York, USA

The Visitation
Hamilton College, Hamilton, New York, USA; November 9

The Confession
Contemporary Art Center, Cincinnati, Ohio, USA; December 12

PRINTS

Trans-fixed
Edition of 50
Hand colored lithograph. 16 × 20 in.
Collection: Museum of Contemporary Art (MOCA), Los Angeles, California, USA

Chris Burden Deluxe Photo Book 1971–73
Edition of 50 with ten Artist's Proofs (AP)
53 photographs (nine in color, 44 in black and white, each photograph signed on back) and text in loose-leaf binder with hand painted cover and cardboard storage box
12 × 12 × 3 in.

Four black and white photographs
Edition of five with one AP
Two photographs of *Prelude to 220 or 110*, 1971; one of *Bed Piece*, 1972; one of *747*, 1973
Each photograph: 13½ × 10½ in.

DRAWINGS

The Church of Human Energy, 1973–74
Pencil on paper. 7⅛ × 22½ in.
Private collection

1975

PERFORMANCES

White Light/White Heat
Ronald Feldman Fine Arts, New York, USA; February 8–March 1
RELIC: Section of board
Case: 7 × 15¼ × 10 in.
Collection: Noel Frackman, Scarsdale, New York, USA

Doomed
Museum of Contemporary Art, Chicago, Illinois, USA; April 11

La Chiaraficazione
Galleria Alessandra Castelli, Milan, Italy; May 5
RELIC: Hammer
Case: 5½ × 22¾ × 9¼ in.
Collection: Harvey La Tourette, Los Angeles, California, USA

Oracle
Schema Gallery, Florence, Italy; May 14

Poem for L.A.
KHJ-Channel 9 and KTLA-Channel 5, Los Angeles, California, USA; June 23–27

Art and Technology
De Appel, Amsterdam, Holland; October 18

Yankee Ingenuity
Galerie Stadler, Paris, France; October 23

Working Artist
University of Maryland, Baltimore, Maryland, USA; November 22–24

The Rise and Fall of Western Industrialism as Seen Through the Automobile
Hallwalls, Buffalo, New York, USA; December 5
RELIC: Chalk
Case: 6¼ × 7⅜ × 7¼ in.
Collection: The artist

1976

SCULPTURES

B-Car
200lb automobile
31 × 106 × 48 in.
First exhibited: De Appel, Amsterdam, Holland; October 18–November 13
Collection: Magasin 3 Stockholm Konsthall, Stockholm, Sweden

DRAWINGS

Oracle Text
10 × 18 in.
Collection: Galleria Schema, Florence, Italy

B-Car Drawings
121 pencil and/or ink on paper drawings and related documents
Dimensions variable
Collection: Magasin 3 Stockholm Konsthall, Stockholm, Sweden

[15 Commentaries]

#1. Attila the Hun
Collage. 30 × 40 in.
Collection: Riko Mizuno, Los Angeles, California, USA

#2. Donatello
Collage. 30 × 40 in.

#3. Electric Texas Conceptualist
Collage. 20 × 30 in.
Collection: Barbara Burden, Los Angeles, California, USA

#4. Harry Houdini
Collage. 20 × 30 in.
Collection: Laura Lee Woods, Malibu, California, USA

#5. Iconoclast
Collage. 30 × 48 in.
Collection: Museum of South Texas, Corpus Christi, Texas, USA

#6. Important Young California Conceptual Artist
Collage. 30 × 40 in.
Collection: Charles and Victoria Hill, Venice, California, USA

#7. King of the Avant-Garde
Collage. 30 × 40 in.
Collection: Whitney Museum of American Art, New York, USA

#8. Little Boy Lost
Collage. 20 × 30 in.
Private collection

#9. Man of the Seventies
Collage. 30 × 40 in.
Collection: Marcel Fleiss Gallery, Paris, France

#10. Michelangelo
Collage. 30 × 40 in.
Collection: Laura Lee Woods, Malibu, California, USA

#11. Novitiate Franciscan
Collage. 20 × 30 in.
Collection: Elyse and Stanley Grinstein, Los Angeles, California, USA

#12. Sadhu
Collage. 30 × 40 in.
Collection: Patricia Faure Gallery, Santa Monica, California, USA

#13. Sane American With a Dream
Collage. 30 × 40 in.
Collection: Kenny Schacter, London, England

#14. Serious Business Man
Collage. 30 × 40 in.
Collection: Gilbert and Lila Silverman, Southfield, Michigan, USA

#15. Unpredictable Genius
Collage. 30 × 40 in.
Collection: Riko Mizuno, Los Angeles, California, USA

VIDEOS

Selections 71–74
Black and white and color. 36 mins

Guru for Detroit
Black and white. 25 mins

Car Nut
Black and white. 25 mins

Art and Technology
Black and white. 25 mins

Poem for L.A.
Black and white. 10 seconds

PERFORMANCES

Natural Habitat
(with Alexis Smith)
Portland Center for the Visual Arts, Portland, Oregon, USA; January 8–15

Do You Believe in Television?
Alberta College of Art, Calgary, Canada; February 26

Shadow
Ohio State University, Columbus, Ohio, USA; April 26

Chris Burden Promo
Channels 4 and 9 New York, USA; May 1–21
Channels 5, 11 and 13, Los Angeles, California, USA; September 17–24

Garcon!
Hansen Fuller Gallery, San Francisco, California, USA; August 3–7
RELICS: Pitcher
Case: 9½ × 8 × 9 in.
Shirt

Death Valley Run
Death Valley, California, USA; October 14
RELIC: Customized bicycle
38 × 66 in.
Collection: Musées des Marseille, Marseille, France

Studio Tour
Venice, California, USA; October 24
RELIC: Roll of tickets

Merry Christmas from Chris Burden
US Mail; December 14
RELIC: Card, envelope, $10 bill

VIDEOS

Chris Burden Promo
Color. 30 seconds

1977

PERFORMANCES

Wiretap
Close Radio (KPFK-FM), Los Angeles, California, USA; January 17
RELIC: Telephone, tape recorder, audiotape

Full Financial Disclosure
Baum-Silverman Gallery, Los Angeles, California, USA; September 20

The Curse of BIG JOB
Venice, California, USA; December 14, 1977–June 22, 1978
RELIC: 24-inch pipe wrench
Case: 6¾ × 26 × 9 in.
Collection: Dallas Price-Van Breda, Los Angeles, California, USA

C.B.T.V. to Einstein
Air France Concorde flight between Paris, France and Washington, DC, USA; December 28
RELIC: Model airplane flown on Concorde
Case: 10 × 16 × 10 in.
Collection: Cliff and Mandy Einstein, Los Angeles, California, USA

SCULPTURES

C.B.T.V. (Chris Burden Television)
Motor, lens, photoelectric cell, two drums, two metal disks, 16 drawings in eight frames
Dimensions variable
First exhibited: Documenta 6, Kassel, Germany; June 21–26

COLLAGES

[15 Full Financial Disclosure Collages]

#1. Full Financial Disclosure – January, 1977
Collage – nine checks and labels mounted on paper
30 × 36 in.
Collection: Tom Patchett, Los Angeles, California, USA

#2. Full Financial Disclosure – February, 1977
Collage – 16 checks and labels mounted on paper
30 × 36 in.
Collection: Margo Leavin Gallery, Los Angeles, California, USA

#3. Full Financial Disclosure – March, 1977
Collage – 15 checks and labels mounted on paper
30 × 36 in.
Private collection

#4. Full Financial Disclosure – April, 1977
Collage – 18 checks and labels mounted on paper
30 × 36 in.
Collection: Jan and Richard Baum, Los Angeles, California, USA

#5. Full Financial Disclosure – May, 1977
Collage – four checks and labels mounted on paper
30 × 36 in.

#6. Full Financial Disclosure – June, 1977
Collage – 11 checks and labels mounted on paper
30 × 36 in.
Private collection

#7. Full Financial Disclosure – July, 1977
Collage – 18 checks and labels mounted on paper
30 × 36 in.
Collection: Chase Manhattan Bank, New York, USA

#8. Full Financial Disclosure – August, 1977
Collage – 16 checks and labels mounted on paper
30 × 36 in.
Private collection

#9. Full Financial Disclosure – September, 1977
Collage – 23 checks and labels mounted on paper
30 × 36 in.
Collection: Donald Young Gallery, Seattle, Washington, USA

#10. Full Financial Disclosure – October, 1977
Collage – 24 checks and labels mounted on paper
30 × 36 in.

#11. Full Financial Disclosure – November, 1977
Collage – 11 checks and labels mounted on paper
30 × 36 in.
Collection: Bruce Baltz, Jersey City, New Jersey, USA

#12. Full Financial Disclosure – December, 1977
Collage – 29 checks and labels mounted on paper
30 × 36 in.
Private collection

#13. Full Financial Disclosure – IRS Forms, 1977
Collage – four pages mounted on paper
19 × 40 ½ in.
Collection: Patrick Frey, Zurich, Switzerland

#14. Full Financial Disclosure – Bank Statements, 1977
Collage – 12 checks and labels mounted on paper
15 ¾ × 92 in.
Collection: Marvin and Alice Kosmin, New York, USA

#15. Full Financial Disclosure – Blank Check, 1977
Collage – one check and label mounted on paper
9½ × 13 in.

PRINTS

Diecimila
Edition of 35 with ten APs
Photo etchings of Italian 10,000 lire note on handmade paper
Image: 2⅝ × 5 ⅞ in. Paper: 10 × 14 in.
Printed at Crown Point Press, San Francisco, California, USA

VIDEOS

Full Financial Disclosure
Color. 39 seconds

AUDIO

Wiretap
14 minutes

1978

PERFORMANCES

The Citadel
Performance/installation, private studio, Los Angeles, California, USA; August 8–12

In Venice Money Grows on Trees
Venice, California, USA; October 6

Coals to Newcastle
Calexico, California, USA; December 17
RELIC: Two airplanes out of three
Case: 10 × 40 × 14 in.
Collection: Robert Shimshak, Berkeley, California, USA

DRAWINGS

Untitled – Big Job
Collage: Photograph, red marker
23½ × 19½ in.

AUDIO

The Citadel
9 minutes

1979

PERFORMANCES

Send Me Your Money
KPFK-FM Radio, Los Angeles, California, USA; March 21

Honest Labor
Vancouver, British Columbia, Canada; March 26–30

Big Wrench
KTSF-TV, San Francisco, California, USA; November 5

Atomic Alphabet
San Francisco Art Institute, San Francisco, California, USA; November 17
Manitoba Theatre Workshop, Winnipeg, Canada; November 20
Mudd Club, New York, USA; June 8, 1980
Artists Union, Osaka, Japan; September 9, 1980
RELIC: Leather jacket

Pearl Harbor
National Guard Armory, Santa Barbara, California, USA; December 8

SCULPTURES

The Reason for the Neutron Bomb
50,000 nickels, 50,000 matchsticks
368 × 210 in.
First exhibited: Ronald Feldman Fine Arts, New York, USA; February 28–May 28
Collection: MOCA, San Diego, California, USA

What the World Might Have Been
Wooden box, plastic airplanes, wire
12 × 19 × 21½ in.
First exhibited: Galerie Anne de Villepoix, Basel Art Fair, Basel, Switzerland; June 9–15

The Big Wheel
Three-ton, eight-foot diameter, cast iron flywheel powered by a motorcycle
112 × 175 × 143 in.
Collection: MOCA, Los Angeles, California, USA

[Ten Assemblages]

#1. Radio Sculpture
Radio speaker, miscellaneous objects, printed text, wood and glass case
28¼ × 15 × 14 in.
Collection: David and Lauren Greene, Santa Monica, California, USA

#2. New Improved Spaceport
Plastic toys, lead ships, slate, wood and glass case
12 × 12 × 18 in.
Collection: Marc Jancou, London, England

#3.Two .38 lb Slugs and One-Pound Weight
Two slugs, one-pound weight, printed text, wood and glass case
10¼ × 13 × 9 in.

#4. 16th Century Gunpowder
Mortar, pestle, charcoal, potassium nitrate, sulfur, printed text, wood and glass case
12¼ × 25 × 12 in.
Collection: MOCA, Chicago, Illinois, USA

#5. Airplane and Barbed Wire
Model airplane, barbed wire, printed text, wood and glass case
16¼ × 31 × 17 in.
Collection: Michael Keeley, Los Angeles, California, USA

#6. Spy Kit
Tin box, magnifying glass, razor, two way radio, cloth, printed text, wood and glass case
10¼ × 17 × 17 in.
Collection: MOCA, Chicago, Illinois, USA

#7. Pick, Bottle and Alcohol
Pick, bottle of alcohol, printed text, wood and glass case
12 × 23 × 19 in.
Collection: MOCA, Chicago, Illinois, USA

#8. T.V.s and Hat
Two TVs, hat, printed text, wood and glass case
16 × 21 × 16 in.
Collection: MOCA, Chicago, Illinois, USA

#9. Survival Kit
Tin box, red cloth, transistor radio, mirror, $100 bill, candle, matches, toothbrush, camping saw, fold out utensils, fishing hook and line, cigarette, printed text, wood and glass case
11¼ × 20 × 20 in.
Collection: Kunsthaus, Zurich, Switzerland

#10. Case of Street Weapons
Driftwood, car radio antenna, bungee cord, sardine can top rolled up with key, single edge razor blade, cardboard tube, sewing needles, printed text, wood and glass case
11¼ × 46 × 18 in.
Private collection

1980

DRAWINGS

[15 Devil Drawings]

#1. Chris
Collage. 30 × 40 in.
Collection: Rosamund Felsen Gallery, Santa Monica, California, USA

#2. American 180
Collage. 30 × 40 in.
Private collection

#3. Creatures Beyond Fathom of Science
Collage. 30 × 40 in.
Collection: Nicole Klagsbrun, New York, USA

#4. Gallant Gallic Warrior
Collage. 30 × 40 in.
Private collection

#5. Help Ma
Collage. 32 × 40 in.
Collection: MOCA, Chicago, Illinois, USA

#6. Here Comes Trouble
Collage. 30 × 40 in.
Private collection

#7. I Flew Back to L.A.X.
Collage. 20 × 40 in.
Collection: Emory University, Atlanta, Georgia, USA

#8. N for Nigger, Z for Zorro
Collage. 30 × 40 in.
Collection: MOCA, Los Angeles, California, USA

#9. Poison Spear Ambush
Collage. 30 × 40 in.
Collection: Praxis Group, Vancouver, Canada

#10. Some B-1's/Bombers That Weren't Built
Collage. 30 × 40 in.
Private collection

#11. Spook Planes
Collage. 30 × 40 in.
Collection: MOCA, Chicago, Illinois, USA

#12. Strangler Hunt Grows
Collage. 32¾ × 40¾ in.
Collection: MOCA, Chicago, Illinois, USA

#13. Thank You
Collage. 30 × 40 in.
Collection: Marcel Fleiss Gallery, Paris, France

#14. What Price Glory
Collage. 30 × 40 in.
Private collection

#15. Women in Ships
Collage. 30 × 40 in.
Private collection

Big Wheel Shop Drawing I,
(frame, wheel drawing)
Ink on paper. 11 × 8½ in.
Private collection

Big Wheel Shop Drawing II,
(bike against wheel)
Ink on paper. 11 × 8½ in.

First exhibited: 'The Big Wheel, Devil Drawings and Sculptures', Rosamund Felsen Gallery, Los Angeles, California, USA; October 19–November 13

AUDIO

Atomic Alphabet
30 seconds

Send Me Your Money
60 minutes

PERFORMANCES

Show the Hole
Italian Per/form/ance Festival, Florence, Italy; March 4

Cinque Cinque Cento (Five Five Hundreds)
Italian Per/form/ance Festival, Rome, Italy; March 9

Warning! Relax, Or You Will Be Nuked Again
Art House, Nishinomiya, Japan; September 13
RELICS: Three six inch diameter globes, each with one hemisphere colored red
Case: 10¾ × 10 × 10 in.
Collection:
#1. Ronny and Sam Heyman, Greenfarms, Connecticut, USA
#2. Donated to Art House, Nishinomiya, Japan
#3. The artist
World War II Japanese prayer flag and formed wire hanger
Collection: The artist

Solaris
Pacific Ocean, Santa Monica, California, USA; October 23, 1980
RELIC: Card table, walkie-talkie

SCULPTURES

C.B. Air Force
40 model airplanes of balsawood and paper, each equipped with a firecracker
Each plane 10 in. long × 10 in. wingspan
First exhibited: 'Tableau', Los Angeles Institute of Contemporary Art (LAICA), Los Angeles, California, USA; February–March
Collection: Arnold and Marie Ford, Laguna Beach, California, USA

DRAWING

Leading Edge of the Nuclear Fireball
Silkscreen with gouache and ink on paper
14¾ × 42¾ in.

PRINTS

The Atomic Alphabet
Edition of 20
Photo etching, soft ground etching and hand watercoloring
57½ × 39 in.
Printed at Crown Point Press, San Francisco, California, USA

VIDEOS

The Big Wheel
Color. 29:02 minutes

The Big Wrench
Color. 15:12 minutes

1981

PERFORMANCES

Napoleon d'Or
Musée National d'Art Moderne, Centre George Pompidou, Paris, France; April 6
RELIC: Gold figure on base
Case: 8 × 22 × 10 in.
Collection: Judy and Stuart Spence, Sunland, California, USA

Diamonds are Forever
Ikon Gallery, Birmingham, England; April 28–May 28
RELIC: Diamond, cubic zirconium
Case: 8 × 22 × 10 in.
Collection: Judy and Stuart Spence, Sunland, California, USA

There Have Been Some Pretty Wild Rumors About Me Lately and I Just Want to Set the Record Straight
San Francisco Video Festival, San Francisco, California, USA; October 28

SCULPTURES

Warship
Mixed media
10 × 33 × 6 in.
First exhibited: 'Chris Burden, A Twenty Year Survey', Newport Harbor Art Museum, Newport Beach, California, USA; May 17–June 12, 1988
Collection: Ruth and Jacob Bloom, Marina del Rey, California, USA

A Tale of Two Cities
Installation of two miniature cities with approximately 5,000 toys, sand, plants, boulders
Approximately 800 to 1,200 sq. ft.
First exhibited: 'The Museum As Site', Los Angeles County Museum of Art, Los Angeles, California, USA; July 21–October 4
Collection: Orange County Museum of Art, Newport Beach, California, USA

1982

PERFORMANCES

Hercules
Washington Project for the Arts, Washington, DC, USA; March 27

Fire by Friction
Satellite tele-conference between Los Angeles, Iowa and New York, USA; October 22

SCULPTURES

The Nina
Painted wood, motorcycle engine, toys, glass, plastic, wood, metal, electronic circuitry
20½ × 55 × 7 in.
Collection: The Oakland Museum, Oakland, California, USA

The Pinta
Painted wood, motorcycle engine, toys, glass, wood, metal, plastic, electronic circuitry
29¾ × 70¼ × 11¾ in.
Collection: MOCA, Los Angeles, California, USA

The Santa Maria
Painted wood, motorcycle engine, toys, glass, plastic, wood, metal, electronic circuitry
30 × 75½ × 15¼ in.
Collection: Marilyn Oshman, Houston, Texas, USA

First exhibited: 'Cost Effective Micro-Weaponry That Works', Ronald Feldman Fine Arts, New York, USA; October 15–November 12

The Flying Kayak
Canvas, wood, wooden set of stairs, fans, film, wire
46 × 156 × 120 in. wingspan
First exhibited: 'The Flying Kayak and Devil Drawings', Rosamund Felsen Gallery, Los Angeles, California, USA; March 6–May 3
Collection: Museum of Modern Art (MOMA), New York, USA

DRAWINGS

[15 Devil Drawings]

#1. Breakthrough
Paper collage with metal.
31½ × 39½ in.
Collection: Nicole Klagsbrun Gallery, New York, USA

#2. Cradle of Aviation
Paper collage. 31½ × 39½ in.
Collection: Chase Manhattan Bank, New York, USA

#3. Design Flaw
Paper collage. 31½ × 39½ in.
Private collection

#4. Devil Horns
Paper collage. 31½ × 39½ in.

#5. Foreign Lands
Paper collage with metal and plastic.
31½ × 39½ in.

#6. For or Against Marriage
Paper collage. 31½ × 39½ in.
Private collection

#7. Hell
Paper collage. 31½ × 39½ in.

#8. Honest John
Paper collage with firecracker.
31½ × 39½ in.

#9. Japanese Jesus
Paper collage with snakeskins.
31½ × 39½ in.
Collection: Chase Manhattan Bank, New York, USA

#10. Love Stick
Paper collage with wood.
31½ × 39½ in.

#11. Peace
Paper collage. 31½ × 39½ in.
Collection: MOCA, Los Angeles, California, USA

#12. Rush Human Blood
Paper collage with magnet
31½ × 39½ in.
Collection: Cincinnati Art Museum, Cincinnati, Ohio, USA

#13. Spare Parts
Paper collage with metal and cloth
31½ × 39½ in.

#14. Terrorist Alert
Paper collage with plastic
31½ × 39½ in.
Collection: Barry Sloane, Los Angeles, California, USA

#15. Who Pays For It
Paper collage. 31½ × 39½ in.
Collection: MOCA, Los Angeles, California, USA

VIDEOS

Fire by Friction
Black and white. 1 minute 45 seconds

1983

PERFORMANCES

From Neanderthal to the 20th Century
International Performance Festival, Rotterdam, Holland; April 6

The Hard Push
University of California, Los Angeles, California, USA; May 25
RELIC: Plywood wheel with attachment points for hands and feet
Dimensions: 114 diameter × 48 in.
Collection: The artist

SCULPTURES

Scale Model of the Solar System
Plastic, steel ball bearings, plexiglass
Dimensions variable
First exhibited: 'Deeds and Feats', Contemporary Art Center, New Orleans, Louisiana, USA; February 25–March 27

The Speed of Light Machine
Optical apparatus, lenses, mirrors
180 × 540 in.

The Frictionless Sled
Hollow aluminum bar, plastic, air compressor
37 × 256½ × 4½ in.

Flying Saucer
Lamp, brass rods, Cuisinart blades
9 × 21 × 30 in.
Collection: Tony Berlant, Santa Monica, California, USA

Exploding Subs
Cardboard, metal, wood, batteries, three model submarines
Each sub: 5 × 16 × 4 in.
Collection: Ariel Roger, Duesseldorf, Germany

Lucky Subs
Cardboard, Duco cement, wire, 17 model submarines
Each 2¾ × 8¼ × 1¾ in., one model submarine: 3¾ × 12 × 2½ in.
Collection: Marilyn Oshman, Houston, Texas, USA (5)
Orange County Museum of Art, Newport Beach, California, USA (4)
Robert Wilhite, Los Angeles, California , USA (1)

The Ship-O-Corks
2, 700 wine and champagne corks, copper wire, 12 dry cell batteries, wood, cardboard, child's 19th Century shotgun, eight paddle wheels, bamboo, nails, electric tape
12 × 54 × 12 in.
Collection: John Alexander, Amagansett, New York, USA

Large Glass Ship
¼ inch plate glass, lead toy soldiers, four *Lucky Subs*
2¾ × 51 × 39 in.
Collection: Orange County Museum of Art, Newport Beach, California, USA

Small Glass Ship
Glass, lead toy soldiers, five *Lucky Subs*
2½ × 33 × 36½ in.
Collection: Marilyn Oshman, Houston, Texas, USA

First exhibited: 'Cost Effective Micro-Weaponry That Works', Ronald Feldman Fine Arts, New York, USA; October 15–November 12

DRAWINGS

Beam Drop
Ink on paper. 11 × 8½ in.
Private collection

1984

SCULPTURES

Beam Drop
Approximately 60 steel I-beams, concrete
Approximately 35 square feet
Installation at Art Park, Lewiston, New York, USA; August 2
Dismantled May, 1987

DRAWINGS

Beam Drop
Black and white photograph with ink
16 × 20 in.
Private collection

Tower of Power I
Ink on paper. 11 × 8½ in.
Collection: Kenny Schacter, London, England

FILMS

Beam Drop
Black and white. 16mm. 6 min

1985

SCULPTURES

Tower of Power
100 32 oz (one kilo) pure gold bricks, matchsticks
Dimensions variable
First exhibited: Wadsworth Antheneum, Hartford, Connecticut, USA; January 12–20

Samson
Turnstile, winch, worm gear, leather strap, jack, timbers, steel, steel plates
Dimensions variable
First exhibited: 'NO! Contemporary American Dada', Henry Art Gallery, University of Washington, Seattle, Washington, USA;
November 6 1985–January 19, 1986
Collection: Inhotim-Centro de Arte Contemporânea, Minas Gerais, Brazil

DRAWINGS

Samson
Ink on paper. 11 × 8½ in.
Collection: Kenny Schacter, London, England

Tower of Power II
Ink on paper. 11 × 8½ in.
Collection: Kenny Schacter, London, England

Shoot Photomural
Photomural. Black and white.
48 × 68 in.
Collection: Gerard Beaufour, Paris, France

1986

SCULPTURES

Sprocket's Moon (with Nancy Rubins)
Airplane parts, water trough, bicycle wheels
Approximately 264 × 420 in.
New Langton Arts, San Francisco, California, USA; March 18–April 12

Sex Tower (Architectural Model)
Scale: 1 inch = 1 foot
Wood, concrete, metal, gold leaf
150 × 24 × 24 in.
First exhibited: 'Teaching Artists: The UCLA Faculty of Art and Design', Wight Gallery, University of California, Los Angeles, California, USA; October 7–November 9

Exposing the Foundation of the Museum
Excavation and removal of 52 × 16 ft. section of concrete floor. Three excavations of earth, each approximately 9 ft. deep × 16 ft. wide with three sets of wooden stairs
624 × 192 × 108 in.
Commissioned for the exhibition: 'Individuals: A Selected History of Contemporary Art, 1945–86', MOCA, Los Angeles, California, USA; December 10, 1986–June 19, 1988

DRAWINGS

Exposing the Foundation of the Museum
Black and white photograph with ink
11 × 14 in.
Collection: MOCA, Los Angeles, California, USA

Sex Tower I
Ink on paper. 11 × 8½ in.
Collection: Kenny Schacter, London, England

Sex Tower II
Pencil on paper. 40 × 8½ in.

Sex Tower III
Black and white photograph with marker pen
24 × 13½ in.

Spinning Dervish I
Ink on paper. 8½ × 11 in.
Private collection

Spinning Dervish II
Ink on paper. 8½ × 11 in.
Private collection

Spinning Dervish III
Ink on paper. 8½ × 11 in.
Private collection

1987

SCULPTURES

All the Submarines of the United States of America
625 miniature cardboard submarines
96 × 240 × 144 in. installed; each submarine 2¾ × 8¼ × 1½ in.
First exhibited: 'All the Submarines of the United States of America', Hoffman Borman Gallery, Santa Monica, California, USA; October 1–31
Collection: Dallas Museum of Art, Dallas, Texas, USA

Monument to Megalopolises Past and Future (with Nancy Rubins)
Airplane parts, halogen lights, bicycle wheels, bicycle generator, plastic cups, water
720 × 180 × 48 to 120 in.
Los Angeles Contemporary Exhibitions (LACE), Los Angeles, California, USA; November 13–December 12

DRAWINGS

Spinning Dervish IV
Ink on paper. 8½ × 11 in.
Private collection

Spinning Dervish V
Ink on paper. 8½ × 11 in.
Collection: Kenny Schacter, London, England

Medusa's Head
Ink on paper. 20 × 23½ in.
Collection: Cliff and Mandy Einstein, Los Angeles, California, USA

Tower of Babel/Medusa's Head
Ink on paper. 13 × 8½ in.

1988

DRAWINGS

Sailing Destroyer
Ink on paper. 8½ × 11 in.
Private collection

FOUND OBJECT

The Sailing Destroyer
Postcard. 5 × 7 in.

1990

SCULPTURES

Medusa's Head
Plywood, concrete, rocks, model railroad trains and tracks
Five ton sphere, 192 in. diameter
First exhibited: 'Seven Obsessions', Whitechapel Gallery, London, England; August 17–September 30
Collection: MOMA, New York, USA

The Sailing Destroyer
Model warship, metal table, framed drawings, blueprints, text
Model and table: 61 × 95 × 15 in.
First exhibited: 'TWSA: 4 Cities Project', HMS *Cavalier*, Gateshead, England; September 1–October 30

Wexner Castle
Addition of crenels and merlons to existing Peter Eisenman-designed museum building
Commissioned for exhibition: 'New Works for New Spaces: Into the Nineties', Wexner Center for the Visual Arts, Ohio State University, Columbus, Ohio, USA; October 6, 1990–January 6, 1991

The Front: A Forced Perspective
Steel cabinets, photographs, toys, dust
84 × 96¾ × 12¼ in.
First exhibited: 'Trains', Michael Klein Gallery, New York, USA;
December 15, 1990–January 26, 1991
Collection: Musées des Marseille, Marseille, France

DRAWINGS

Sailing Destroyer
Edition of four
Acetate overlay on technical photoprint
Framed: 89 × 42½ in.

Proposal for Wexner Castle I
Color photocopy with ink on acetate overlay. 11 × 17 in.
Private collection

Wexner Castle II
Ink on paper. 5½ × 8 in.
Private collection

Three Ghost Ships I
Ink on paper. 8½ × 13 in.

Three Ghost Ships II
Modified 1996
Ink on paper. 8½ × 14 in.
Collection: Dean Valentine, Los Angeles, California, USA

Fishing Boat on Side of Museum
Proposal for the Seattle Arts Commission
1. Text panel. Framed: 20 × 14 × 3 in.
2. Photograph of museum building
Framed: 13 × 16 × 3 in.
3. Landscape drawing of museum building with suspended gray toy boat. Framed: 13 × 16 × 3 in.
4. Portrait drawing of museum building with suspended multi-colored toy boat.
Framed: 16 × 13 × 3 in.
5. Series of 11, 4 × 6 in. color photographs of fishing boats.
Framed: 16 × 31 × 3 in.
Private collection

1991

SCULPTURES

Three Ghost Ships
Three Micro 16 sailboats, one equipped with navigational satellite system, robotic sail and rudder controls, concept drawing
Each boat: 276 × 192 × 72 in.
First exhibited: 'Places with a Past: Site Specific Art in Charleston', Spoleto Festival USA, Charleston, South Carolina, USA;
May 23–August 14

The Other Vietnam Memorial
Steel, aluminum, etched copper plates
164 × 119 in.
First exhibited: 'Dislocations', MOMA, New York, USA;
October 16, 1991–January 7, 1992
Collection: Museum of Contemporary Art, Chicago, Illinois, USA

DRAWINGS

The Flying Steamroller
Ink on paper. 8½ × 11 in.
Collection: Ed Ruscha, Los Angeles, California, USA

The Flying Steamroller with Man
Ink on photocopy. 8½ × 11 in.

Small Skyscraper Quasi Legal LA County
Ink on paper. 11 × 8½ in.
Collection: Arnold and Marie Ford, Laguna Beach, California, USA

Blacklisted Ten Monument
Ink on paper. 8½ × 11 in.

The Other Vietnam Memorial
Ink on paper. 11 × 8½ in.
Collection: Gilbert Silverman, Southfield, Michigan, USA

Fist of Light
Ink on paper. 8½ × 11 in.
Private collection

1992

SCULPTURES

Medusa's Flying Moon
Plywood, steel, tar, cement, rock, plaster, plastic, wood, model railroad trains and tracks, electric motor
72 in. diameter
Collection: Mandy and Cliff Einstein, Los Angeles, California, USA

[Five Ships]

#1. Noah's Arks
Mixed media. 58 × 63 × 42 in.
Collection: Marc Jancou, London, England

#2. U2 Boat
Mixed media. 12 × 30 × 10 in.
Collection: Ruth and Jacob Bloom, Marina del Rey, California, USA

#3. Grand Hotel
Mixed media. 12 × 28 × 8½ in.
Collection: Michael Klinger, Geneva, Switzerland

#4. Hospital Ship
Mixed media. 36 × 29 × 11 in.
Collection: Michael Klinger, Geneva, Switzerland

#5. Two Cannon, Three Sailor Battleship
Mixed media. 36 × 53 × 11 in.
Collection: Georges J. Guilband, Martinique

First exhibited: 'Chris Burden: 5 Ships', Miller Nordenhake Gallery, Cologne, Germany; November 13, 1992–January 15, 1993

Another World I
Wooden base, wooden block buildings, glass river, two Titanic model boats, metal Marklin model of Eiffel Tower, motor
96 × 60 × 60 in.
Model tower 72 in.
First exhibited: 'LAX', Galerie Krinzinger, Vienna, Austria;
November 14–December 22
Collection: FRAC Languedoc-Roussillon, Montpellier, France

1993

DRAWINGS

Project for Warsaw Ujazdowski Castle
Ink on paper. 8½ × 11 in.

Olympian Tower of Babel I
Ink on paper. 8½ × 11 in.

Olympian Tower of Babel II
Ink on paper. 8½ × 11 in.

Another World
Ink on paper. 11 × 8½ in.
Collection: Plains Art Museum, Fargo, North Dakota, USA

SCULPTURES

Father and Son, Iron Age
Mixed media, 22½ × 45 × 12½ in.
First exhibited: Brussels Art Fair, Miller Nordenhake Gallery, Brussels, Belgium; March
Collection: Nancy and Bob Magoon, Aspen, Colorado, USA

Another World II
Wooden base, wooden block buildings, glass river, two Titanic model boats, metal Meccano building parts, motor
66 × 60 × 60 in. Model tower 48 in.
First exhibited: 'Chris Burden', Centre d'Art Santa Monica, Barcelona, Spain; October 18, 1995–January 31, 1996
Collection: Gerard Beaufour, Paris, France

The Fist of Light
Aluminum, heating, ventilating and air conditioning equipment, halide lights
129 × 153 × 130 in.
First exhibited: 1993 Whitney Biennial, Whitney Museum of American Art, New York, USA; March 2–June 13

Chris Burden Publicity
Vinyl suitcase, newsprint
7¾ × 29½ × 19 in. (closed),
21 × 29½ × 19 in. (open at 135° angle)
First exhibited: 'Mr. Sterling's Neighborhood', Christopher Grimes Gallery, Santa Monica, California, USA; July 10–September 4

L.A.P.D. Uniforms
Edition of 30 with one AP
30 uniforms and 30 Beretta handguns
Wool serge, metal, leather, wood, plastic
Each uniform: 88 × 72 × 6 in.
First exhibited: 'Chris Burden: L.A.P.D. Uniforms, America's Darker Moments, Small Guns', Gagosian Gallery, New York, USA; February 26–March 26
Collection:
#1, 6, 8, 14. LACE, Los Angeles, California, USA
#10. Pedro Almeida, Portugal
#13. Steven Oakes, New York, USA
#17, 18, 19. Dr. Lothar Tirala, Innsbruck, Austria
#20, 21, 22, 24, 25, 26, 27, 31 (AP). Kippy Stroud, Philadelphia, Pennsylvania, USA
#23, 28, 30. The Fabric Workshop, Philadelphia, Pennsylvania, USA
#29. Gilbert Silverman, Southfield, Michigan, USA

DRAWINGS

Sculpture for East Germany
Ink on paper. 8½ × 11 in.

A New Plan for the Americas
Ink and colored pencil on paper
17 × 22 in.
Collection: Ron Ostrin, Santa Monica, California, USA

Trick Killer Gate
Ink and colored pencil on paper
24 × 30 in.
Collection: T. and L. Sebastian, San Francisco, California, USA

Drawing
Ink on paper. 24 × 78 in.
Collection: Albertina Museum, Vienna, Austria

The Hidden Force I
Ink on paper. 8½ × 11 in.

The Hidden Force II
Ink on paper. 8½ × 11 in.

1994

SCULPTURES

[Nine Small Guns]

#1. A Gentlemen's Duel
Two tin locomotives, two plastic figures (headless, one-armed Mr T and blond man), two metal cannons, plastic track (nine cross ties), fur
11 × 26 × 101 in.

#2. Men, Women and Children
Three blank shotgun shells, bird's nest, light bulb, ribbon, printed paper, saw blade, ceramic bowl, two metal figures.
Case: 3¾ × 12 × 15 in.

#3. On the Wings of an Angel
Toy bombs, dirt, wood
Case: 2½ × 9 × 26 in.

#4. One Small Complete Army
Plastic metal army figures and vehicles; one Commander in Chief on horseback, 40 officers, three commandos, one artillery commander with three horse-drawn cannons, 384 infantrymen, one naval destroyer, one attack helicopter, two biplanes, three medium tanks, one small tank with yellow turret, four one-man tanks (three winterized), two personnel carriers, two radio antennas (disguised as willow trees)
Case: 3¾ × 18 × 16 in.
Collection: Maguit Hahnloser-Ingold, Vienna, Austria

#5. Perfect, but Cruel
Chinese foot binding slippers, model battleships
Case: 8 × 19 × 20 in.

#6. The Right to Bear Arms
Straw and wood figure, metal model cannon, printed paper booklet, salt and pepper shakers
Case: 12½ × 29 × 11 in.
Collection: Norton Family Foundation, Santa Monica, California, USA

#7. A Young American's Arsenal
Toy guns, plastic hand grenade, socks
35 × 16¾× 14 in.
Collection: Armin Sadoff, Beverly Hills, California, USA

#8. The Father, the Son and the Holy Ghost
Wood, metal, three metal model cannons, light fixture, plastic figure, small cardboard tube, cardboard, plastic model horses
Case: 9¼ × 19 × 17 in.
Collection: Bruno Ribeyron-Monmartin, Paris, France

#9. Vons
Plastic gun, plastic children's sandals, nail row from nail gun
Dimensions variable

America's Darker Moments
Edition of three with one AP
Painted cast tin figures, wood, glass and plexiglass vitrine
Each case: 56½ × 36½ × 36½ in.
Collection:
#1. Yale University, New Haven, Connecticut, USA
#2. Whitney Museum of American Art, New York, USA
#3. Anders Palm, London, England
AP: Kippy Stroud, Philadelphia, Pennsylvania, USA

First exhibited: 'Chris Burden: L.A.P.D. Uniforms, America's Darker Moments, Small Guns', Gagosian Gallery, New York, USA; Feb 26–March 26

Stealth Flying Wings
Balsawood, tissue paper, CO2 motor, pendulum balance system
Six airplanes, each with 30-inch wingspan
Collection: Dallas Price-Van Breda, Santa Monica, California, USA

[Five Moonettes]

#1. The Coal Moon
Cement, steel, coal, model railroad trains and tracks
22 × 36 × 33 in.
Collection: Gerard Beaufour, Paris, France

#2. The Cubist
Cement, steel, model railroad trains and tracks
32 × 55 × 27 in.
Collection: Yves Mahe, Paris, France

#3. The Twist
Cement, steel, model railroad trains and tracks
42 × 112 × 42 in.
Collection: Musées des Marseilles, Marseilles, France

#4. The Deep Pit
Cement, steel, model railroad trains and tracks
32 × 40 × 34 in.
Collection: Gerard Beaufour, Paris, France

#5. The Logged Moon
Cement, steel, model railroad trains and tracks, wood
48 × 54 × 40 in.
Collection: Georges Guilbauld, Paris, France

First exhibited: 'Chris Burden: Five Moonettes', Galerie Anne de Villepoix, Paris, France; September 17–December 23

The Spirit of the Grape (L'esprit du vin)
Wood, foam, paint, toothpicks, thyme
86 × 531 × 120 in.
First exhibited: 'CLB, The Grape and Me and the Holy Trinity', FRAC Champagne-Ardenne, Reims, France; October 21, 1994–January 8, 1995

Tours des Trois Museaux
Wood, foam, paint, rocks
126 × 177 × 98 in.
First exhibited: 'CLB, The Grape and Me and the Holy Trinity', FRAC Champagne-Ardennes, Reims, France; October 21, 1994–January 8, 1995
Collection: FRAC Champagne-Ardennes, Reims, France

Mini Video Circus
Three Citroën 2CV vans, each equipped with canvas tent, six metal folding chairs, four video cassette decks, four TV monitors
Each van: 72 × 228 × 72 in.
First exhibited: Mini Video Circus, Le Consortium, Dijon, France; October 29, 1994–January 7, 1995

DRAWINGS

The Hidden Force III
Ink on paper. 8½ × 11 in.

The Hidden Force IV
Ink on paper. 4 × 7 in.

[Dream Show at the MAK]
(Museum of Applied Arts, Vienna, Austria)

[Six Drawings]

#1. My Dream Show at the MAK
Ink and colored pencil on paper
17 × 22 in.
Collection: Museum of Applied Arts, Vienna, Austria

#2. Fall Down Slabs
Ink and colored pencil on paper
17 × 22 in.
Collection: Museum of Applied Arts, Vienna, Austria

#3. The Flying Steamroller
Ink and colored pencil on paper
17 × 22 in.
Collection: Museum of Applied Arts, Vienna, Austria

#4. Small Skyscraper
Ink and colored pencil on paper
22 × 17 in.
Collection: Museum of Applied Arts, Vienna, Austria

#5. Sex Tower
Ink and colored pencil on paper
22 × 17 in.
Collection: Museum of Applied Arts, Vienna, Austria

#6. Medusa's Head
Ink and colored pencil on paper
17 × 22 in.
Collection: Museum of Applied Arts, Vienna, Austria

1995

SCULPTURES

The Hidden Force
Concrete, aluminum, water
Three pools with three floating elliptical shapes
Each pool: 108 × 36 in. deep, each elliptical shape: 18 in. high × 84 in. long
Collection: McNeil Island Correction Center, Seattle, Washington, USA

DRAWINGS

The Hidden Force V
Ink on paper. 8½ × 10½ in.

Stealth Flying Wing
Ink and collage on paper
24 × 30 in.
Collection: Dallas Price-Van Breda, Santa Monica, California, USA

PRINTS

The Blacklisted Ten
Proposal for University of Southern California, USA
Photomural. 124 × 366 in.

1996

SCULPTURES

The Flying Steamroller
Steel, concrete, 1968 Huber road grader
252 × 678 in. (diameter of circle)
First exhibited:
'Chris Burden, Beyond the Limits', Museum of Applied Arts, Vienna, Austria; February 28–August 4
Collection: Novartis, Basel, Switzerland

Pizza City
Toys, buildings (plastic, wood, metal and paper), foam, paint, mounted on 25 wooden and metal tables
Each table 36 × 84 × 48 in.
First exhibited:
'Chris Burden, Beyond the Limits', Museum of Applied Arts, Vienna, Austria; February 28–August 4
Collection: Novartis, Basel, Switzerland

1997

SCULPTURES

¼ Ton Bridge
Edition of three with one AP
Metal toy construction parts (Meccano and Erector)
Each bridge is accompanied by *Static Test* (2000), a signed and dated color photograph produced in an edition of 12
Bridge: 12¾ × 33 × 6¾ in.
Photograph: 20 × 16 in.
First exhibited: 'Chris Burden', Magasin 3 Stockholm Konsthall, Stockholm, Sweden;
February 6–May 16
Collection:
#1. Magasin 3 Stockholm Konsthall, Stockholm, Sweden, includes *Static Test*, 1 of 12
#2. Private collection, includes *Static Test*, 2 of 12

DRAWINGS

Water Cycle
Three photographic enlargements mounted on foam board with drawing on acetate overlay
Each 29¾ × 20 in.

Erector Set Bridge for Los Angeles County Museum of Art
Ink and pencil on paper
17 × 22 in.
Collection: Kenny Schacter, London, England

1998

SCULPTURES

Antique Bridge
Edition of two with one AP
Early 20th century (1913) metal toy construction parts (Mysto Type I Erector)
23¾ × 91 × 8½ in.
First exhibited: 'Chris Burden', Magasin 3 Stockholm Konsthall, Stockholm, Sweden;
February 6–May 16
Collection:
#1. Gerard Beaufour, Paris, France
#2. Private collection

Hell Gate
Metal toy construction parts (Meccano and Erector), wooden towers
88½ × 339 × 40 in.
First exhibited: 'Chris Burden', Magasin 3 Stockholm Konsthall, Stockholm, Sweden;
February 6–May 16
Collection: MOCA, Los Angeles, California, USA and Los Angeles County Museum of Art, Los Angeles, California, USA

Mexican Bridge
Metal toy construction parts (Meccano and Erector), wood
111¾ × 180 × 37 in.
First exhibited: 'Chris Burden', Magasin 3 Stockholm Konsthall, Stockholm, Sweden;
February 6–May 16
Collection: Magasin 3 Stockholm Konsthall, Stockholm, Sweden

DRAWINGS

[Airplane Factory Drawings]

#1. Airplane Factory
Pencil on paper. 19 × 24 in.

#2. Airplane Factory
Pencil on paper. 19 × 24 in.

#3. Airplane Factory
Pencil on paper. 19 × 24 in.

#4. Airplane Factory
Pencil on paper. 19 × 24 in.

#5a. Airplane Factory
Pencil on paper. 19 × 24 in.
Collection: Gilbert Silverman, Southfield, Michigan, USA

#5b. Airplane Factory
Ink and color pencil on photocopy
19 × 24 in.
Collection: Nancy and Bob Magoon, Aspen, Colorado, USA

Hell Gate Drawing
Pencil on brown craft paper
120 × 346 in.

Hell Gate Tower – Front View Drawing
Pencil on brown craft paper
87 × 60 in.

Hell Gate Tower – Side View Drawing
Pencil on brown craft paper
87½ × 60 in.

Small Mexican Bridge Drawing
Pencil on brown craft paper
115 × 119 in.

Large Mexican Bridge Drawing
Pencil on brown craft paper
135 × 209 in.

1999

SCULPTURES

When Robots Rule: The Two-Minute Airplane Factory
Dimensions variable
(requires minimum exhibition space of 60 × 25 ft)
First exhibited:
'When Robots Rule: The Two-Minute Airplane Factory', Tate Gallery (Britain), London, England;
March 18–June 18

DRAWINGS

How to Shrink L.A.
Ink on paper
24 × 18 in.
Collection: Bob and Linda Gersch, Los Angeles, California, USA

Cantilever Bridge
Photogravure print (trial proof for Master Edition)
10 × 16 in.
Printed by Crown Point Press, San Francisco, California, USA
Collection: Scott Solomon, Los Angeles, California, USA

2000

DRAWINGS

[6 Drawings for proposed show at Gagosian Gallery, New York, USA]

#1. The Bigger Wheel, Here and There and the Pneumatic Subway
Pencil on paper. 17 × 22 in.

#2. The Bigger Wheel
Pencil on paper. 17 × 22 in.

#3. The Bigger Wheel, View From Street
Pencil on paper. 17 × 22 in.

#4. Here and There
Pencil on paper. 17 × 22 in.

#5. The Pneumatic Subway I
Pencil on paper. 17 × 22 in.

#6. The Pneumatic Subway II
Pencil on paper. 17 × 22 in.

PRINTS

Arch Bridges
Edition of 25
Color photogravure with spit bite aquatint and aquatint
37½ × 44½ in.
Printed by Crown Point Press, San Francisco, California, USA

Draw Bridges
Edition of 25
Color photogravure with spit bite aquatint and aquatint
37½ × 44½ in.
Printed by Crown Point Press, San Francisco, California, USA

Cantilever Bridges
Edition of 25
Color photogravure with spit bite aquatint and aquatint
37½ × 44½ in.
Printed by Crown Point Press, San Francisco, California, USA

The Master Builder
Edition of 35
Boxed portfolio of 13 photogravure prints, one with aquatint
Each page: 8 × 12 in.
Printed by Crown Point Press, San Francisco, California, USA

What is a Family?
Edition of 60
Two color lithograph, nine color screenprint
26 × 36 in.
Printed by Gemini GEL, Los Angeles, California, USA

Static Test
Edition of 12 with four APs
Color photograph 20 × 16 in.
Numbers 1–4 accompany *¼ Ton Bridge* (1997)

VIDEOS

Four TV Commercials 1973–77/2000
Edition of four. DVD in hand crafted wooden box
Black and white
4 minutes 46 seconds.

Beam Drop 1984
Edition of four
Black and white
16 mm film on S-Star based loops to be continuously shown in 16mm looper box
6 minutes

2001

SCULPTURES

Bateau de Guerre
172 metal gasoline cans, three cannons on wooden swivels, eight plastic torpedoes, 18 plastic submarine bombers, four plastic rescue submarines, two metal lamps, five plastic castle towers (two on each side, one on top) with attached weaponry, one straw Chinese radar hat, four plastic crates, metal framework
71 × 174 × 41 in.
First exhibited: 'Un Art Populaire', Cartier Foundation, Paris, France;
June 20–November 4
Collection: The Broad Art Foundation, Santa Monica, California, USA

Nomadic Folly
Wooden platform, four cloth and metal umbrellas, woven carpets, braided ropes, pillows, silken fabrics, glass and metal lamps, CD player and speakers
138 × 240 × 240 in.
First exhibited: 7th International Istanbul Biennial, Istanbul, Turkey;
September 21–November 17

DRAWINGS

Hog Bucket
Pencil on paper
11 × 14 in.
Collection: Fred and Winter Hoffman, Santa Monica, California, USA

Bateau de Guerre
Ink on paper
8½ × 11 in.

Mini Scraper Deep in the Land
Black and white photograph with ink
10 × 8 in.

Mini Scraper on the Side of Cliff
Black and white photograph with ink
10 × 8 in.

Mini Scraper Floating as a House Boat or Anchored with Real Footing as a Castle with Moat
Black and white photograph with ink
10 × 8 in.

Mini Scraper on Little Mesa
Black and white photograph with ink sketches
10 × 8 in.
Collection: L.J. Cella, Kentfield, California, USA

Down Deep in the Land Mini Scraper
Black and white photograph with ink sketches
10 × 8 in.

New Dog and New Moon
Color photograph
14 × 11 in.

2002

SCULPTURES

Indo-China Bridge
Edition of 12 with four APs
Stainless steel reproduction Mysto Type I Erector parts
15¼ × 45¼ × 8¾ in.
First exhibited: Biennale of Sydney, Sydney, Australia; May 14–July 14

Tyne Bridge
Powder coated and made to order Meccano metal toy construction parts, wooden towers
111 × 372 × 60 in.
First exhibited: Baltic Centre for Contemporary Art, Gateshead, England; July 13–October 6
Private collection

Small–Small Skyscraper Model
(In collaboration with TK Architecture, Los Angeles, California, USA)
Aluminum extrusion, glass, wood, motorized elevator
99¼ × 27¼ × 27¼ in.
First exhibited: 'Trespassing: House × Artists', Bellevue Art Museum, Bellevue, Washington, USA; August 31, 2002–January 5, 2003

DRAWINGS

Erectus/Flacidus
Pencil on paper
11 × 14 in.
Collection: MOCA, Los Angeles, California, USA

2003

SCULPTURES

Small Skyscraper
(In collaboration with TK Architecture, Los Angeles, California, USA)
Structural aluminum framing, glass, wood 2 × 4s, steel hardware (stainless steel cable, turnbuckles, clips and angles, t-nuts, ½ inch bolts)
432 × 120 × 120 in.
First exhibited: LACE, Los Angeles, California, USA; May 1–July 27

Poured Concrete Bunker
Concrete, steel
158 × 138 × 138 in.
First exhibited: Cultural Capital of Europe 2003, Graz, Austria. May 26

Antique Bridge
Edition of six with three APs
Stainless steel reproduction Mysto Type I Erector parts
23½ × 91 × 8½ in.

Victoria Falls Bridge
Edition of six with four APs
Stainless steel reproduction Mysto Type I Erector parts, wooden base
Bridge: 24½ × 78 × 8¾ in.

Tower of London Bridge
Edition of six with three APs
Stainless steel reproduction Mysto Type I Erector parts, gearbox, wooden base
Bridge: 28¼ × 80¼ × 8½ in.

21 Foot Truss Bridge
Edition of three
Stainless steel reproduction Mysto Type I Erector parts
Bridge: 45¾ × 234 × 14¾ in.

Curved Bridge
Edition of three
Stainless steel reproduction Mysto Type I Erector parts, wood base
96 × 390 × 57 in.

Gold Bullets
Edition of ten with two APs
Ten 22 Karat gold bullets in two wooden and plexiglass display cases
Bullets: dimensions variable
Each case: 6¼ × 10¼ × 5¾ in.
First exhibited: 'Bridges and Bullets', Gagosian Gallery, Beverly Hills, California, USA; July 10–August 29

Trapezoid Bridge
Edition of 20
Stainless steel reproduction Mysto Type I Erector parts
17¼ × 23½ × 8½ in.
First exhibited: 'Chris Burden', Gagosian Gallery, New York, USA; January 20, 2003–February 28, 2004

Victorian Double Lamp
Fully restored Los Angeles street lamp from the 1920s (sand blasted, powder coated and electrified)
Approximately 240 × 30 × 60 in.
Collection: Dallas Price-Van Breda, Los Angeles, California, USA

Skyscraper, 4th Plinth Project, Trafalgar Square, London, England
Stainless steel reproduction Mysto Type I Erector parts on wooden base
Two towers on base 29¾ × 20 × 7¾ in.
First exhibited: '4th Plinth Project', National Gallery, London, England; December 11, 2003–February 28, 2004

DRAWINGS

4th Plinth Project, Trafalgar Square, London, England
Pencil and ink on paper
22 × 17 in.

PRINTS

Mini Scraper on Little Mesa
Edition of 100 with 30 APs
Three-color offset print on embossed metal
35 × 28 in.
Produced by Los Angeles Contemporary Exhibitions (LACE), Los Angeles, California, USA
Collection: L.J. Cella, Kentfield, California, USA

2004

SCULPTURES

Tyne Bridge Kit
Edition of two
Powder coated and made to order Meccano metal toy construction parts, wooden cabinet on casters
42½ × 65½ × 32¼ in.
First exhibited: 'Chris Burden', Gagosian Gallery, New York, USA; January 20–February 28
Collection: #2. Damien Hirst, England

Metropolis
Two one-twelfth-horsepower DC motors with motor controllers, four electric transformers, wood, plastic, steel, aluminum, magnets, cement, glue, Lego, Lincoln Logs, fired clay bricks, Hot Wheel cars and tracks, monorail trains and track
87 × 194 × 130 in.
First exhibited: Inaugural Exhibition, 21st Century Museum of Contemporary Art, Kanazawa, Japan; October 8
Collection: 21st Century Museum of Contemporary Art, Kanazawa, Japan

DRAWINGS

1,300 Foot Foot Bridge
Pencil on paper. 11 × 14 in.

Lost Forever
Colored pencil on paper
8½ × 11 in.
Collection: Stanley and Elyse Grinstein, Los Angeles, California, USA

Metropolis. Typical Track and Elevator Layout and Metropolis in Action
Pencil on paper and colored pencil on vellum overlay
17½ × 24 in.

Metropolis Sketch
Pink and blue colored pencil on vellum
8½ × 14 in.

Metropolis Sketch
Yellow pencil on vellum
8½ × 14 in.

Metropolis: Tower A – Tower B
Pencil and colored pencil on paper
8½ × 11 in.

Metropolis: Two Parts Shown From Above
Pencil and colored pencil on paper
8½ × 11 in.

2005

SCULPTURES

Ghost Ship
30 foot handmade sixareen, computers and software, hydraulics, Global Positioning System, auto-rudder, rigging
Dimensions: Infinite
First exhibited: Voyage from Fair Isle, Scotland to Newcastle upon Tyne, England, with arrival coinciding with the Tall Ships Race departing the Tyne for Norway; July 20 –28

Urban Light
150 fully restored Los Angeles street lamps from the 1920s (16 different styles that have been sandblasted, powder coated and electrified)
Dimensions variable

DRAWINGS

Small Skyscraper as Built at Basel
Pencil on paper. 14 × 11 in.
Collection: L.J. Cella, Kentfield, California, USA

Ghost Ship: What I Thought We Were Getting
Ink on paper. 8½ × 11 in.

Ghost Ship: What I Understand We Are Getting
Ink on paper. 8½ × 11 in.

The Atomic Compass I(a)
Ink on paper. 8½ × 11 in.

The Atomic Compass I(b)
Ink on paper. 11 × 8½ in.

Beehive Bunker
Ink on paper. 11 × 8½ in.

PRINTS

Curved Bridge I
Edition of ten with two APs
Color photograph
11 × 14 in.

Curved Bridge II
Edition of ten with two APs
Color photograph
11 × 14 in.

Coyote Stories
Edition of 18 with three APs
37 printed pages, 27 pages of text and ten pages of images
Each page: 15 × 12½ in.
Wooden box: 16½ × 14 × 2 in.
All pages signed and dated
Stored in a birchwood box with 'Coyote Stories' burnt into the box lid
Printed by Edition Jacob Samuel, Los Angeles, California, USA

2006

SCULPTURES

All the Submarines of the United States of America 1988–1992, 1988–2006
16 submarines in display case with labels
Cardboard over foam core, Ducco cement, wood toothpicks, steel wire
Case: maple wood, acrylic, glass, brass
60 × 51 × 22 in.
Each submarine 2¾ × 8¼ × 1½ in.
Collection: Dallas Price-Van Breda, Santa Monica, California, USA

Beehive Bunker
An edition of three and one single artwork consisting of three bunkers in a triangular configuration
Concrete, steel rebar, steel wire, cast iron manhole cover, plastic hoses
120 in. high × 112 in. wide
Single bunker first exhibited: Basel Art Fair, Basel Switzerland; June 14–18

14 Magnolia Doubles
14 fully restored Los Angeles street lamps from the 1920s (sand blasted, powder coated and electrified)
Each lamp: 242½ × 47 × 22 in.
First exhibited: South London Gallery, London, England; September 15–November 5

DRAWINGS

Being Photographed: Looking Out, Looking In (1971/2006)
Ink, pencil and colored pencil on paper
22½ × 30 in.
Collection: Sender Collection, New York, USA

Beehive Bunker Poetic Architecture
Ink on paper. 14 × 17 in.

Axis of Power: Three Beehive Bunkers
Ink on paper. 14 × 17 in.

Never Feed Gravel to a Coyote
Pencil and colored pencil on paper
22 × 30 in.
Collection: Tony Berlant, Santa Monica, California, USA

The Atomic Compass II
Ink on paper. 8¼ × 11⅝ in.

PHOTOGRAPHS

Big Pointy
Color Polaroid. 24 × 20 in.
Private collection

Big Pointy #1
Color Polaroid. 24 × 20 in.

Big Pointy #2
Color Polaroid. 24 × 20 in.

Big Pointy #3
Color Polaroid. 24 × 20 in.

Big Pointy #4
Color Polaroid. 24 × 20 in.

1973 Lotus, 2006
Color Polaroid. 24 × 20 in.

[CB and Lotus]

Set of six photographs

1973 Lotus Europa #1 of six
1973 Lotus Europa #2 of six
1973 Lotus Europa #3 of six
1973 Lotus Europa #4 of six
1973 Lotus Europa #5 of six
1973 Lotus Europa #6 of six

Color Polaroids
Each 24 × 20 in.

VIDEO

The Rant
Edition of 10
DVD. Color.
2 minutes 10 seconds
Monologue in French
First shown: Galleria Massimo De Carlo, Milan, Italy; September 22

Publications

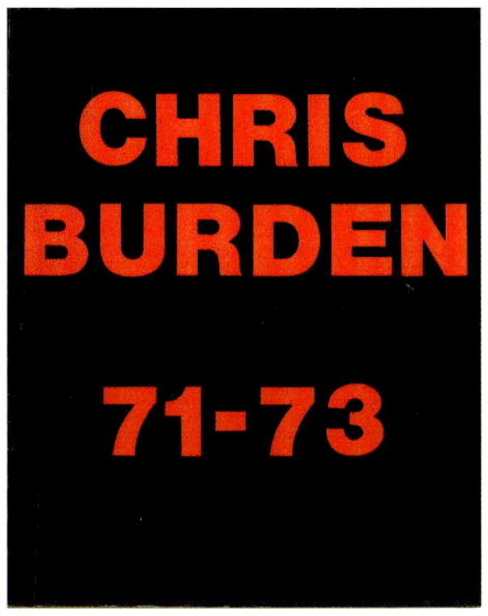

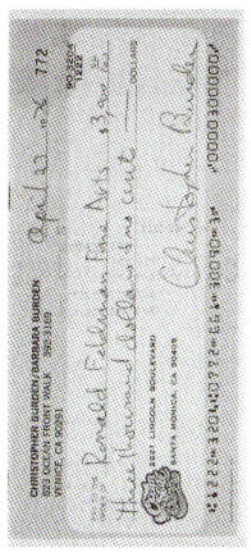

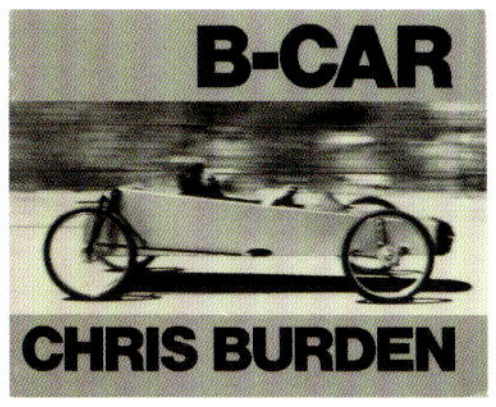

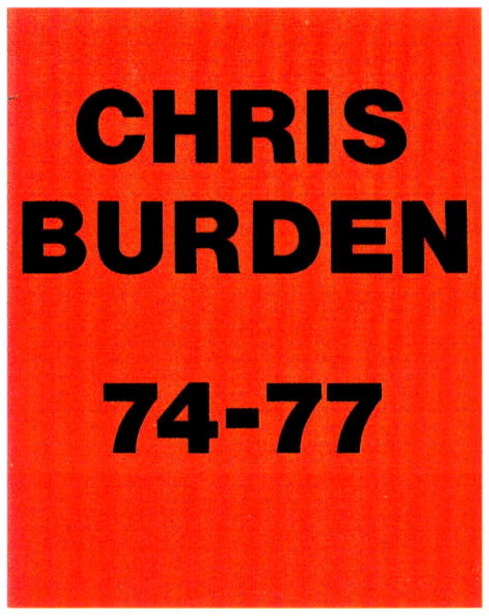

BOOKS BY THE ARTIST

Chris Burden 71–73
Chris Burden, 1974 (edition of 1,000)
10½ × 8½ in.

Full Financial Disclosure
Jan Baum–Iris Silverman Gallery,
Los Angeles, USA, 1977
7⅝ × 3½ in.

B-Car, The Story of Chris Burden's Bicycle Car
Text by Chris Burden and Alexis Smith
Choke Publications, 1977
5½ × 6½ in.

Chris Burden 74–77
Chris Burden, 1978 (edition of 2,000)
10½ × 8½ in.

SOLO EXHIBITION CATALOGUES AND BOOKS

1986
Chris Burden, The Artist and His Models
Lowe Art Museum, Miami, Florida, USA

1988
Chris Burden: A Twenty Year Survey
Newport Harbor Art Museum,
Newport Beach, California, USA

1992
Chris Burden: LAX
Galerie Krinzinger, Vienna, Austria

1994
Chris Burden, France 1994–1995
Galerie Anne de Villepoix, Paris;
FRAC Champagne-Ardenne, Reims;
Le Consortium, Dijon;
FRAC Languedoc-Roussillon,
Montpellier

1995
Chris Burden
Centre d'Art Santa Monica,
Barcelona, Spain

Chris Burden
Blocnotes, Paris, France

1996
Chris Burden: Beyond the Limits
Museum of Applied Arts, Vienna,
Austria

1999
When Robots Rule: The Two-Minute Airplane Factory
Tate Gallery Publishing, London,
England

Chris Burden
Magasin 3 Stockholm Konsthall,
Stockholm, Sweden

2001
Chris Burden
The Arts Club of Chicago, Chicago,
Illinois, USA

2004
Chris Burden: Early Work
Zwirner and Wirth, New York, USA

Index

Author biographies

FRED HOFFMAN is a private dealer, curator, and lecturer. From 1986 to 1997, his gallery presented over 300 exhibitions by national and international artists. He was the curator of 'Basquiat' (Brooklyn Museum; Museum of Contemporary Art (MOCA), Los Angeles; Houston Museum of Fine Arts) and is a lecturer in the Department of Art, University of California, Los Angeles.

LISA LE FEUVRE is a writer, curator of contemporary art at the National Maritime Museum, London, and teacher on the Curatorial Programme at Goldsmiths' College. Her recent curatorial projects include 'Avalanche 1970–1976'; 'Dennis Oppenheim: Recall'; 'Simon Faithfull: Ice Blink'; and 'Dan Holdsworth: At the Edge of Space, Parts 1–3'.

PAUL SCHIMMEL has been chief curator of the Museum of Contemporary Art (MOCA), Los Angeles, since 1990, prior to which he was chief curator at the Newport Harbor Art Museum, Newport Beach, California, from 1981 to 1989. He has organized major exhibitions such as 'Chris Burden: A Twenty Year Survey'; 'Hand-Painted Pop: American Art in Transition'; 'Helter Skelter: Los Angeles Art in the 1990s'; 'Sigmar Polke Photoworks: When Pictures Vanish'; 'Charles Ray'; 'Out of Actions: Between Performance and the Object, 1949–1979'; 'Ecstasy: In and About Altered States'; and 'Robert Rauschenberg: Combines'. In 2001, he received the Bard College Center for Curatorial Studies Award for Curatorial Excellence. His exhibitions and accompanying catalogues have received prestigious awards from AICA and AAMC.

KRISTINE STILES is professor of Art and Art History at Duke University, North Carolina. She is internationally recognized for her writing on performance and experimental art. Her publications include *Theories and Documents of Contemporary Art*, co-edited with Peter Selz (University of California Press, 1996) and the forthcoming *Concerning Consequences of Trauma in Art and Culture* (University of Chicago Press, 2007).

ROBERT STORR is the Dean of the Yale School of Art, consulting curator of modern and contemporary art at the Philadelphia Museum of Art, and director of the 2007 Venice Biennale. From 1990 to 2002 he was curator in the Department of Painting and Sculpture at the Museum of Modern Art, New York, before becoming Rosalie Solow Professor of Modern Art at the Institute of Fine Arts, New York University. He has written many monographs and catalogues, including *Gerhard Richter: Forty Years of Painting* (MOMA, 2002), *Philip Guston* (Abbeville, 1986), *Chuck Close* (with Lisa Lyons, Rizzoli, 1987), and the forthcoming *Intimate Geometries: The Work and Life of Louise Bourgeois*.

Colophon

First published in 2007 by Locus+ Publishing Ltd

Coordinated by Fred Hoffman
Edited by Jon Bewley and Jonty Tarbuck
Designed by Mark Thomson

Assistant Editor: Rachel Leah Baum
The typeface is Adobe Chaparral Pro, designed by Carol Twombly
Produced by International Design UK
Production managed by David Grover
Printed and bound in Italy by Conti Tipocolor

Jon Bewley, Jonty Tarbuck,
Matt Hearn and Hannah Kirkham
Locus+,
Wards Building, 31–39 High Bridge
Newcastle upon Tyne NE1 1EW, UK
t: +44[0]191 233 1450
f: +44[0]191 233 1451
e: locusplus@newart.demon.co.uk
www.locusplus.org.uk

Locus + is a company limited by guarantee no. 293 9638
Registered office as above
Locus+ Publishing is a company limited by guarantee no. 485 8278
Registered office as above

Reproductions of artworks courtesy of Chris Burden

ISBN: 978–1–899377–18–3

Available through DAP/Distributed Art Publishers
155 Sixth Avenue, 2nd Floor, New York, NY 10013
t: (212) 627–1999
f: (212) 627–9484

Locus+ acknowledges the support of Gagosian Gallery

The Trustees and staff of Locus+ would like to express a very warm thank you to Chris Burden, Fred Hoffman and Katy Lucas, without whom this book would not have been possible.

This publication would also not have been possible without the help and kind support of: Jeannie Adams, Carolyn and Allen Atherfold, Simon Bolton, Helen Cadwallader, Sid Clarke, Mike and Liz Collier, Peter Davies, Richard Grayson and Suzie Treister, Cat Newton Groves, Simon and Ellen Herbert, Helen Kippin, Anne Vibeke Mou, Rob Payne, Enid Rogers, Annabel Rooker, Nancy Rubins, Norbert Schoerner, Michael Smithson, Sharon and Alex Summers, Amynta, Grace and Digby Warde Aldham, Lynn Watson, Mark Waugh, Miss Yorke.

For Alwyn and Ian; the reason.
In memory of Maggie.
For Sophie and Phoebe.

Photography credits:
Billy Adler, Stephen Agetstein, S. Anzai, Peggy Barnett, Gary Beydler, Robert Boss, Michael Brewster, Will Brown, Barbara Burden, Chris Burden, Linda Burnham, Courtesy of Crown Point Press, D. James Dee, Chris Eden, Susan Einstein, Charles Erikson, Tom van Eynde, M. Lee Fatherree, Ronald Feldman, Courtesy Ronald Feldman Fine Art, Courtesy of Rosamund Felsen Gallery, Marc Feidus, Brian Forrest, Courtesy Gagosian Gallery, Paula Goldman, Neil Goldstein, Jeffrey Gubbins, Marc Gulezian, Anthony Gunna, Judy Herzog, Charles Hill, Eeva Inkeri, Bill Jacobson, Jan Kempengers, Barry Klinger, Alan Koch, Erich Koyama, Courtesy of La Jolla Museum of Contemporary Art, Erik Landsberg, Alan Leder, Alfred Lutjeans, Terry McDonnell, John McWilliams, Joshua Nefsky, Gene Ogami, Alistair Overbruck, Douglas M. Parker Studio, Paul Pasquarelle, Hajo Piebenga, Tom Power, Linda Purdey, David Regen, Bill Roughen, J.A. Rutkowski, Norbert Schoerner, David Sine, Alexis Smith, Barbara Smith, Athene Spear, Squidds and Nunns, Jonty Tarbuck, Grant Taylor, Hans Trapper, Courtesy Galerie Anne de Villepoix, Joshua White, Ziebell Zhotography, Daniel Zimhaldi, Diana Zlotnick, Gerald Zugmann

Locus+ have made every effort to fully attribute the photographic credits to the images in this publication. If there are any omissions please contact Locus+ so that the record can be corrected.

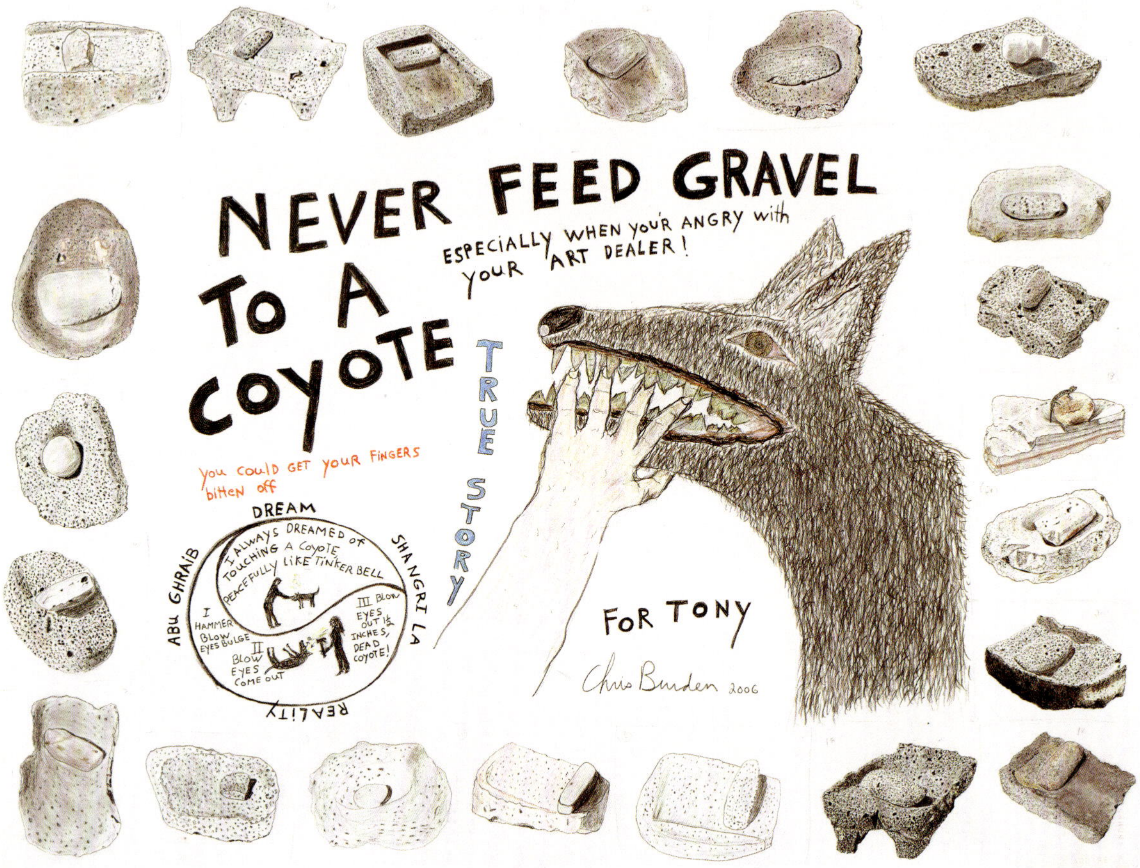

Never Feed Gravel to a Coyote 2006
Pencil and colored pencil on paper, 22 × 30 inches